THE BOOK OF DOW

GENEALOGICAL
MEMOIRS

of the descendants of Henry Dow 1637, Thomas Dow 1639 and others
of the name, immigrants to America during Colonial Times

Also the allied family of Nudd

———

Written, compiled, edited by

ROBERT PIERCY DOW

of Laguna Beach, California,
and Claremont, N. H.

———

Published by

ROBERT P. DOW, JOHN W. DOW and SUSAN F. DOW
of Claremont, N. H.

———

Offered to all who are Dow by birth or ancestry or marriage; all imbued
with the honest pride of Dow; all interested in Massachusetts
Bay genealogy, in the study of heredity, or the
personal side of American History

1929

Another Quality Reprint of a Classic Book
by

The Apple Manor Press

Markham, Virginia

2016

Thousands of titles available at:
www.AppleManorPress.com

ISBN 13: 978-1-5421-0001-4 Part 1
ISBN 13: 978-1-5421-0002-1 Part 2

THE BOOK OF DOW

GENEALOGICAL
MEMOIRS

of the descendants of Henry Dow 1637, Thomas Dow 1639 and others
of the name, immigrants to America during Colonial Times

Also the allied family of Nudd

Written, compiled, edited by

ROBERT PIERCY DOW

of Laguna Beach, California,
and Claremont, N. H.

Published by

ROBERT P. Dow, JOHN W. Dow and SUSAN F. Dow
of Claremont, N. H.

Offered to all who are Dow by birth or ancestry or marriage; all imbued
with the honest pride of Dow; all interested in Massachusetts
Bay genealogy, in the study of heredity, or the
personal side of American History

1929

THE TUTTLE COMPANY
Publishers
RUTLAND, VERMONT

Copyright 1929 by
ROBERT P. DOW

Printed in U. S. A.

The BOOK *of* DOW

"Of all the queer families I ever see, the Dows is the durndest queer," Harvey Nourse, descendant of Rebecca Nourse, adjudged and burned as a witch, Salem, Mass.

"Any sane man claiming to be a Dow is an impostor," Major Joseph Dow, U. S. A. to President James Monroe, 1818.

On board S. S. Carmania 1912:

Head Steward: "Whom shall I seat at your table, Captain?"

Capt. Daniel Dow (absently): "Oh, anyone."

H. S.: "Might I venture to say that there is a large family aboard named Dow?"

Capt. Daniel (impatiently): "Go ahead, bring on the whole d—— family."

The Author obediently now brings on the whole d—— family.

Dedication

To

Edgar Randolph Dow

who died Portland, Me., 1909, the Pioneer of Dow Genealogy, whose letters of inquiry, from 1881 to 1908, amounted high into the thousands, whose life ambition was to publish this volume, who died without knowing that such was possible.

And to

Herbert Beeman Dow

of Woburn, Mass., who gave freely every item collected painstakingly in nearly forty years, a great Genealogical collection.

The Author, who has built upon their foundation, offers a grateful dedication.

WHILE many genealogical writers have keys of their own for ready identification of each individual named in their work, there is an orthodox (say, rather, time-honored) system in general use, alone meeting the approval of librarians and cataloguers. If space is of little importance and if a family be not very large, it works well; but in an unhomogeneous collection of over 30,000 names, derived from at least a dozen unrelated ancestors, it is cumbersome, even ambiguous. It fails to show the degree of relationship between any two individuals. If each person is numbered, the task must be done while the Book is a closed document (else any addition would require renumbering every subsequent person). If each traced individual is designated as (say) Robert 11, John 10, James 9, etc., the unnecessary repetition alone would consume over 75 pages of this Book. Moreover, an index is needed every moment by the author as his work progresses year after year. Such index must be a catalogue of full data needful to identify any new name. It must be used in abbreviated form for the published Book. To type and check an index of 30,000 names is a half year's labor.

Therefore we have adopted a key, just beginning to be used in published works, which, so far as we know, was invented for his own convenience by Herbert B. Dow and which is the simplest, clearest ever devised. This key must be learned, each reader giving almost sixty seconds to it, else this Book will be unreadable. To each immigrant Dow is given a letter, in order of date of arrival. We omit Matthew Doue of Amesbury in 1650 and Francis Doue of Salisbury in 1639, for they are properly Doves. Our work covers such Dow as arrived prior to Aug. 1775. The order will be:

a   Henry Dow, from Ormsby to Watertown 1637
b   Thomas Dow, grantee of Newbury 1639
c   Samuel Dow, mariner, of Hartford 1660
d   John Dow, of Piscataway by 1692
e   ——, father of Lieuts John and James Dow, Philadelphia 1757 or before
f   ——, father of John, Moses and William Dow, arrived N Y about 1768
g   ——, father of James Dow, presumably pioneer of Acadia after its conquest
     from the French

Order of primogeniture must be rigidly kept throughout. A second letter is added for the second generation. Thus the 1stborn of Henry Dow immigrant is aa. The 3rd letter denotes 3rd generation. The 1stborn grandson of Thomas Dow immigrant is baa. And so on. The 12th generation has arrived. At worst the individual identification mark will be 12 letters. The combination of letters is inexhaustible, accommodating every descendant, the actual total of whom is over 250,000. Moreover, the combination of letters sticks in one's mind, as digits would not. They show relationship at a glance. bcdebac and bcdebbd must be own cousins. To the Author adggdccab is as familiar as his baptismal name. Besides, all of us are easily grouped. All Quaker Dow must begin with an ad. All beginning with bcde are descendants of four brothers who met at Lexington 1775. All Connecticut Dows (c line excepted) are from ahc, ahd or ahg. The abbe line is peculiarly of Hampton, N. H. And so on.

As primogeniture is strictly followed, the key fills every requirement which consecutive pagination does. If the order of birth is not known, any person becomes x, y, z, symbols of unknown. adgx figures much in this Book. The only exception is Thomas Nudd, *quasi* adopted son of Henry Dow; he skips a letter to become (for convenience, he being older than the true sons) ak.

Unnecessary punctuation is omitted, saving many pages. Abbreviations are numerous as possible, but all are the usual and recognized ones. The word "untraced" appears on almost every page, attached in table of children to each male whose subsequent career is unknown to the Author. It is seldom attached to female names, for over half of them would be untraced. If no comment follows a male name in a birth table, he is to be followed up under his individual letter key. *Per contra*, in tables of births many appear with death, marriage, etc. This does not preclude a subsequent item. The genealogist does not follow with great keenness females. They are hard to discover; vital statistics ignore them shamefully. Moreover, in a next generation they belong to some other family, the married name. Our space forbids, except in rare instances, the inclusion of a third female generation. It is our (and should be of all) duty to carry as far as possible every female child through a second generation. Thus, and only thus, can a genealogy be a document of historical and public usefulness.

No American genealogy is complete or anything like complete. Except for a very few small families, no single span of life, no succession of lives has sufficed to dig out the pedigree of every one of the name, even if records of them had ever existed. Over one-half of the vital statistics of colonial times have been lost by fire or time or carelessness of officials appointed to keep them. Perhaps a fourth never were recorded. It was not thought worth while in early inland settlements to bother with records. Even at this, the average town clerk thought he did his whole duty if he wrote: wid Dow d May 1, 1729. A record: wid Mary Dow m John Fox, for example. Whose wid? What her name? It is rare that an entry is clear as John Dow m Mary Smith, wid of James Davis. The parish clerk was no better. He wrote the baptismal record of John Dow, son of John; who the mother and what John did not seem necessary. Five John Dow were born about 1712 in a radius of 25 miles. How do we know which is which? They all married about the same time. Have we identified each aright? There is no proving record. It becomes a matter of partial proof, of inference, of other evidence, of wills, deeds, family tradition, finally of *reductio ad absurdum*.   People do not stay put.   They move even in the 17th century.   How can we identify John Dow of Seabrook by birth with John Dow of unknown origin who settles in young manhood in Maine?   One needs his wits even to connect John of 1900 born in Maine and married in Montana.

All of our genealogically inclined Dow have been steadily of the opinion that a published Dow Book is out of the question on account of the enormous total of errors, as well as omissions.   Our best early collector admitted himself that it would take a year to check up dates alone and still be laughed at by other genealogists for palpable errors.   Besides, there are too many untraced, too many disconnected Dow.   The Author deems otherwise and shoulders the responsibility for every wrong date, wrong name, wrong identity, often occurring from his own clerical error. He has eliminated thousands of errors, but also added new ones.   This volume is the mine of low grade ore, from which future workers may discard slag and expose the fine gold.   No good Dow Genealogy can ever be printed, if some Dow Genealogy is not printed now.   In another generation it would be too unwieldy.   Moreover, the work is going on constantly.   Every owner of this Book will make his own additions from time to time..   The actuarial expectation of life of the Author is still 16 years and in that time he hopes to make sundry thousand additions and corrections.   That a Dow genealogy is needed by all students of Massachusetts Bay families is a prominent fact, for the name interlinks with every one in the colony, and the obscurity of Dow has hitherto been a great stumbling block.

An ideal genealogy should give in every case the authority for a date, place or circumstance.   It is impossible in a work of this size. Thousands of the dates differ, State, township, family Bible disagreeing. In vast numbers of instances our manuscript has been crowded with pencil corrections, with no space or time to note the authority.   Spellings differ; must we load up page after page with authority for each?   Official rec give a man two very distinct wives; we have no space for each authority.   On the whole, town vital records are the most reliable; Quaker records very reliable as far as they go, but they go little.   Church records are often careless.   Family Bibles are notorious liars, never complete liars, only inclined to add some absolutely wrong item to throw confusion into the Book, as deadly as a monkey wrench in an engine.   The author has drawn from many sources. In addition to the genealogical material collected by H. B. Dow and Edgar R. Dow, he has obtained the complete lists of all births, marriages and deaths to 1920 or so from each New England State, Massachusetts as far as published.   He has added the information obtained from the 1790 census, neglected by his predecessors. He has also the 1850 census of all New England, the 1860 and 1870 in spots.   He has collated every reference in every well known genealogical periodical.   He has read every genealogical page of Transcript or other

authority for over 25 years back.   He looked through every local history
in the New York Public Library; read every genealogy or other reference
book in Los Angeles.   He has corresponded with every other genealogist
willing to compare notes with him.   He cannot print his "authority."
Life is not long enough, printing too expensive.

We have remarked that the greatest of genealogical difficulties is
individual mobility.   If a family remained century after century in its
original town, all would be easy.   But the younger son of 1750 had to
emigrate then as now.   From the coast there came to Gilmanton at its
settlement a dozen Dow families.   Not a record in Gilmanton indicates
whence they came, what their origin, place or parentage.   Among them
were 3 Jonathans, 3 Johns, 2 Nathaniels, 2 Benjamins.   In Maine the
early settlers all came over the border.   No vital statistics were collected until 1892.   Prior to 1830 a record, "went to Maine" was equivalent
to being lost, settlers seldom writing home or keeping any knowledge of
absent brothers.   About 1790 to 1812 Ohio is as bad.   All settlers to the
Western Reserve are "lost" so far as the East is concerned.   California
looms as a trouble-maker.   Most of its early permanent settlers had little
to say about family.   New England town histories end their genealogies
about 1850, as a rule.   From 1850 onward for a single generation is a
terrible source of "untraceds."   To get data after 1850 one must depend
on personal correspondence.   To search church records, town by town,
would cost a fortune.   Now, replies from individuals are generally un-
satisfactory, few bothering to write more than a dozen sentences of vague
pedigree.   If they have any curiosity, they can wait and get it out of the
printed Dow Genealogy.   Why put it in themselves? That 3,000 living
Dow are not included in this Book is because they were too lazy, too
indifferent, too something, to reply at all to a clearly worded letter asking
genealogical information and promising to give freely the line of ancestors
back to the earliest possible date.   Indifference is not the only reason.
There is lurking in many minds a suspicion of sinister motive in seeking
names of one's parents, grandparents, etc.   There is the miserly instinct,
too.   A worthy farmer wrote that if information of his grandfather was
so valuable, he had better keep it to himself.   The Author caused to be
compiled a complete list of Dows from over 2,100 directories published
in America and wrote to most of them.   Not 5 per cent ever replied.   Fifty
interviewed Dows admitted (or claimed) they did not know their grandparents' names.   There are over 600 families of Dow immigrated since
1830, mostly from Scotland, next from Ireland, none from England.

It is difficult to get genealogical data by letter.   No matter how carefully the wants are specified, only one reply in 20,000 has been complete
and concise.   A Massachusetts judge wrote such a letter, 2 pages, but not
omitting a name, date or important circumstance and not containing a
superfluous word.   No other letter has said as much in 20 pages.   On the
average it takes five letters to get what should have been contained in

the first reply. The first mentions a few names; the second adds some dates requested, and takes them mainly from memory. The third, if at all, is inclined to argue on the uselessness of adding a mother's maiden name. The Author has written over 20,000 letters to make this Book. Edgar Dow used to send out great numbers of his printed form, to be filled in. The form had space for mention of each child, including his marriage, with date, and his children, grandchildren of the addressee. Most of these forms which came back specified under marriage "husband" or "wife," it not occurring to the answerer to insert the names. Grandchildren, yes, 3, or as the case might be. Seldom were they named or dated.

Collections of data for a Dow Genealogy were begun within the year of each other by three men. Edgar R. Dow of Portland, Me., was the pioneer, his letters beginning 1881. His interest in the subject began with tracing the descendants of his own great grandfather, who was a Revolutionary captain. Following this, with great patience, he gained the data of the two immigrants, Henry and Thomas, with most of their descendants of the third generation, several to the fifth. He had to work without the great libraries existing today and there were omissions in his 3rd generation. As soon as his idea broadened to include a general Dow genealogy, he collected every name and address of a Dow throughout the country, every newspaper mention of the name. Excepting two years lost by ill health, he kept up this practice for 25 years and sent out thousands of blank forms. Such genealogies as he was able to connect with the main line, he kept on special printed page forms, the whole bound in loose leaf ledgers. After his death, the work was very occasionally kept up by his brother, Dr. George E. Dow. That gentleman, finally realizing that the ledgers were useless at home and that the Author meant business, sent them on. They contained somewhat over 6,000 names, of which over 2,000 were new to the Author and to other Dow collectors. James J. Dow of Faribault, Minn., had conceived the idea of a genealogy and had started on one, with similar method of sending out blanks. The two men found each other. The James J. Dow work was a hopeless failure, wrong in his own line, which he was never able to straighten out. His collections were finally thrown away. He also met D. Webster Dow of Epping, devotee of his own line. Correspondence with the Author's father began in 1888. One great value of Edgar's work was its exact birth dates, which replaced great numbers of approximated dates, as will later be explained.

When Edgar died, his widow was inclined to destroy the manuscripts, which did not seem useful to any one and which had been a contributing cause to his ill health and death. They were rescued by his brother, who in turn died in 1921. It finally dawned upon the Author's mind that all he had received from Edgar was in finished form, with no disconnected Dow, no unformulated, scattered leftovers. He wrote for

such in 1923 and received two more ledgers. One was halfway formulated,—lines to date, occasionally back to the 5th generation, but left
unconnected with the main tree. This was of fully 3,000 names. Lapse
of time and added knowledge enabled the Author to identify 95 per cent
of these names, and in almost every instance, family records interpolated
one or more children between those found in public vital statistics. This
necessitated changing the letter keys to date in most of the lines. The
second ledger was of wholly unconnected material, letters and the original blanks filled in. Their comparative illegibility entailed vast work, but
they finally added over 5,000 names. Even of this, 95 per cent had become connectible through lapse of time. This necessitated re-typing this
entire Book for the fourth time.

Herbert Beeman Dow began about the same time and had the first
three or four generations properly identified. Then a school principal,
he liked to spend the long vacations perusing wills, deeds, etc. He thus
got many names rightly connected. Of course, a name found in a will
has no birth date. To aid his search, he was accustomed to approximate
such birthdate. When his work was copied for the Author, the copyist
did not specify what dates were approximated. Some were 20 years out
of the way. Almost all of these have been eliminated, either from actual
vital data or from Edgar's letters. Herbert was a past master in rightly
conjecturing the right father for the right son. His hypotheses, when put
to proof by subsequent knowledge, were singularly good. About 6,000
names were his contribution. His good nature impelled him for thirty
years to answer every letter of inquiry. In recent years an arduous
daily occupation has compelled him to halt. The Author has stored in
Herbert's safe a duplicate of every record collected by himself, so that,
in case of fire, death or calamity, a complete Dow collection would exist.

Richard Sylvester Dow of Boston became interested at Herbert's
instance and spent much money on professional genealogists to find, in
time to insert into the history of Essex County, the antecedents of Thomas
Dow b. In this he failed utterly. His work was in 1916 stored hopelessly in a summer home, but all its useful data had been copied by Herbert and thus came to the Author. The work is marred badly by the
methods of professional genealogists who sacrificed all truth to happy and
easy guessing.

Mrs. Sarah B. Carrow of Methuen, professionally a searcher to
establish lines for membership in D. A. R., has become a very dear friend
and great helper. Her kinsman, Judge Harry Robinson Dow of No.
Andover, Mass., wrote his own family faultlessly.

The late Joseph Dow of Hampton, N. H., President of the New
Hampshire Historical Society, held genealogy as a constant tracemate
of the History of Hampton, his life monument, the two being identical
to no small extent. He could not do much outside Hampton or outside
the abbe line, but his Dow fundamentals are the final and unimpeach-

able authority.   So is Hist. Hampton, consulted by every historian and genealogist, with many errors, all minor ones, an authority behind which few have been able to go.

Dr. Frank F. Dow of Rochester, N. Y., prepared a wellnigh perfect account of the posterity of adgge.   Joy Wheeler Dow is the best authority on ahc, ahd and ahg, but neither work has been available for this Book.

Miss Flora Dow of Centerville, N. Y., took up the genealogy of adacea to entertain an invalid father, but became an enthusiast, although with very limited opportunities.   Her narrative started that line rightly for its completer form herein.   Her kinswoman, Mrs. Eudalia J. More, was a great help, elucidating the adacf and adacg lines, most of her details never having been gained elsewhere.   She and Flora came by accident on the bcdec line, thitherto unknown.   She has been a faithful friend, full of zeal to add something useful.

Miss Grace A. Price of Cleveland began by tracing her own quarterings when the ahbc line was to us unknown.   Since 1915 she has contributed several thousand hours to this work.   As she was a Dow only two generations back, only two motives are possible for her aid,—an innate spirit of helpfulness and a fondness for a corner of the big and quiet library where genealogical books were ample.   No Dow item ever reaching her keen eye remained uncopied.   As Mrs. Rawson, she no doubt continues still more useful.

Sterling Tucker Dow of Kennebunkport, Me., entered late, but made up for lost time by getting every member of the then unknown bbbfaa line, its identity established by the Author.

Mrs. Eva (Dow) Connor of Pittsfield, Me., has helped much in the adbab line, the Maine Quakers, not one of whom remains today in the Friends.   She and the Author were aided much by Mrs. Cynthia Jones of Haddon Heights, N. J., who has retained to great age the sweet simplicity of character characteristic of the Quaker matron of long ago. Mrs. Laura (Dow) Wilson of Raton, N. M., helped clear up her own line, adbabf.

Miss Mary J. Greene of Hampton Falls, the authority on Judge Henry (1) Green, identified much with Henry Dow a in the most illustrious days of Hampton's history, received some unimportant help from the Author, magnified its consequence and sought ways to reciprocate. The Dow of Seabrook were an unarranged mass of thousands, so unknown to vital statistics, that all previous collectors deemed a Dow Book impossible on account of them.   The Author had made almost no headway. She plunged into the task of rescue.   Her discovery of the adaim line was followed up until it was cleared thoroughly, as complete as any in this Book.   They constituted nearly a third of lost Seabrook.   She then found the record of adai, the next most important of the seemingly lost lines.   This was followed by complete conquest of adgx, by the only light

obtained on adaii.   Four-fifths of Seabrook was genealogically arranged
by her, a work of brains and patience never excelled in American genealogy.   She has been the only helper in the still hopeless-looking Dow
family of Kensington.

John Mark Moses of Northwood, secretary of the Piscataway Pioneers, sought, among many other tasks, to perfect a history of Northwood.
He got back to its founder, Beniah Dow, but was then confused, there being a Beniah adgfcd.   His appeal to the Transcript was answered by the
Author, setting him right about Beniah 5 of Epping. He then discovered
the lost Epping records and copied every Dow name.   He started to
copy the records of the Second church and did so to 1772, when one morning he was found dead in bed from an old heart trouble.   He was un-
married and left a mother of 83.

Other acknowledgments might be made up to the hundreds.

When the present Author undertook to publish a Book about Dow,
nothing was farther from his mind than to undertake the family genealogy and he had no knowledge of the subject.   His brother John W.
Dow had prepared a 20-page manuscript tracing our own line only.   Joy
W. Dow had prepared, during twenty years or so, work on the so-called
Connecticut Dows, ahc, ahd and ahg, but he never expected to be able
to publish.   The Author suggested putting the two works together,
copying what Herbert B. Dow had, devoting a few months to the editing,
and then publishing materials to start a Dow Genealogy.   This will-o'-
the-wisp was pursued for a while, in spite of Herbert's warning of its
futility.   The job of copying Herbert's work took Joy over 6 weeks, not
including the Conn. lines, which Joy had already.   As the mass was inspected, enlightenment came surely but slowly.   A little later Joy Dow
withdrew from a difference of opinion over editorial policy.

The matter of Dow Genealogy had by this time progressed until its
fascination became engrossing.   The original idea of six months devoted
to editing existing materia was lengthened to two years; and in six months
more was lengthened into a minimum of five years.

Since then we have realized constantly that a lifetime is too short.

We have always hoped against hope of succeeding where all predecessors have failed and always been conscious of the great need by all
students of a Dow genealogy, its family obscurity blocking all search
in all other lines from Mass. Bay.   As time went on, the work ahead
kept increasing.   The mass of unconnected statistics, obtained almost
daily from new searches, rose table high.   When the original collections
were made, libraries were few and small.   The original collectors did
not know what a big modern library is.   This quest the Author began
and pursued through 10,000 volumes.   An unindexed book is a menace
to public health.   Over fifty volumes in the New York Public Library
have genealogical tables of 10,000 names upward, absolutely unindexed.
One has to scan each page.   For several years, the daily search swelled

the disconnected list. At one time the Author had 20,000 names disconnected. Only since 1921 was the peak passed. Each search now, each new material of solidity, lessens the disconnected mass, the total under 5,000.

In addition, correspondence increased so that each day's mail entailed work. A majority of letters necessitated some addition or alteration, often of a single word or date. Such pencil interlineations before long made the manuscript illegible to a printer. It has been re-typed from start to finish no less than five times. Each name and date has been each time checked as well as we could, to prevent copying errors. An index had to be kept alongside. It had to be a card affair, with data on each card to establish any disconnected new name. The letter keys changed every day. Often a line from fifth generation must be altered to make it correct. We find that he whom we had supposed to be adadh is really adadi. This alone means altering 500 cards. Five times our carelessness in keeping index to date, unsatisfactoriness of the system, or other cause, has compelled us to re-index. To correct each card would take five times the effort to begin *de novo*. We have done it five times.

Let us not forget that the Author is the sole publisher and bearer of expense, and realizes full well that works of this kind are disastrous financial failures, that under the best of conditions he can scarcely get back the bare cost of printing. D. B. Hoyt's Old Families of Salisbury and Amesbury is a classic, yet has not returned to its author the printing cost. The total cost of this Book is a fortune, the Author does not expect, does not want, a penny back for 5,000 hours of his own labor. No money has ever been asked for or expected. The price of the published Book, luxury as it is, necessary to no one, may seem a little high. It is below half the actual cost, even if every volume is sold. Let this be remembered. Many who have written some single letter to aid expect the gift of the Book. The average public librarian, even of the largest libraries, expects such books to come as gifts, published to satisfy the Author's vanity. In this case, it will not be done. Endowed libraries should buy what books they need, otherwise go without.

A propos of expense account, a few anecdotes: A sample Dow is a Scot by birth, of Syracuse, N. Y., traveling salesman. To a letter of genealogical inquiry, he replies that he knows quite a lot of Dows and will look them up, but wishes first to know "what there is in it for me." One commercial traveler fixed the price of information, it being a side line, at $5.00 for each Dow interviewed. Happily, this ilk is always of recent immigration, devoid of pride, perhaps of parentage. No professional genealogist of Dow blood has ever suggested that the Author pay anything. Some of them gave material abundantly. Cash outlay is for stationery and return postage, largely, with an occasional dollar to a town clerk. The latter, especially in New England, are a fine race of men, generally past middle age, almost always identified with their home community, with long memories and a zeal to aid anything which might contribute to the history of their towns. The professional genealogists—bless 'em—have a living to make, but they seldom see that their contributions to a Book like this would cost more in time to collate that they would add. One of the best genealogists in the land wrote one day that in a certain account book in a certain town in Maine was an excellent autograph of one Joseph Dow of 1783. For this information he charged 50 cents, which, he added, the Author was under no obligations, moral, legal or equitable, to pay. At this rate, the Author replied, the whole Dow Book would cost over $575,000, a sum which he did not possess.

Given equal birth and environment, or given most unequal conditions, families average up pretty much the same in the long run. The line from a degenerate generally becomes extinct. Some are for several generations a little more prosperous, more distinguished, more honest than others, often more warlike, with more soldiers, but not enough so to justify vanity in the matter. No pride so liable to take a fall as pride genealogical. The richest Dow in this Book sprang from an ancestor who died from poverty and gradual starvation. The slacker who went to jail for a term of years had for ancestors throughout the bravest male line in this book. The adage holds fairly well of three generations from shirtsleeves to shirtsleeves, in spite of the tendency to make a practical entail of many swollen fortunes. It is also true that the family having most wealth in individual cases will also have its balance in complete failures. The family having conspicuous genius has more than its usual compensating number of idiots. A family replete with nonogenarians will have a high infant mortality rate. Caste, entail, pride cannot overthrow the superhuman law of evening-up in the long run. The posterity of Alfred the Great averages just equal to the posterity of Piers, plowman.

Yet:—we are a pretty good lot, we Dow. We are generally queer. Some of us are horrible cads, but we believe with good ground that for each cad we have more than the average of generous impulse-bearers and lovable natures. We have had shameless slackers in high places, but in low places we have had men who led a forlorn hope from Fort this or that. The number of millionaires, of profiteers in war time, of captains of industry, is average; the number of paupers equally average. Illegitimate births seem below the average, and this statement is made after careful comparisons. Owing to the Quaker stock of a third of us (perhaps this is true), our reputation for honesty is better than average, as well as our prison record. Remarkably few of us have seen prisons from the inside. We have three *sus per coll*; one a wronged man, two notorious brigands, not vulgar murderers. Every king in Europe sprang

from a notorious brigand who succeeded. We have had only one conspicuous failure through crime and he fell not from a criminal instinct,
but from too dizzy height in high finance, climbing too eagerly toward
a captaincy of industry. Perhaps the Quaker leaven has increased the
proportion of humble farmers and millhands. The workers in shoe-
factories are far above the average. The number of men who will cheat
the conductor of a nickel is below the average. No case of bigamy has
been found, only one of wife desertion. Suicides are fully the average.
In martial spirit, the Quaker line has not lessened the average. This
is due to the law of compensation. The proportion of Dow in the Revolution is second to no family. Nine of us were at Bunker Hill. In
the towns around Haverhill not a single Dow stayed at home, if he were
of military age. The proportion of volunteers in 1861 is above the
average.

In counting profit and loss in his enterprise, the Author must not
omit mention of the richest reward of his labors. He has made from
coast to coast firm and lifelong friends of the best of men and women,
unknown to him until they aided this Book. He has united a score of
brothers and sisters who had for years lost sight of each other. He has
found a dozen Dow who, orphaned early, never knew a relative. He
has been able to re-unite parted couples, to heal quarrels of twenty years
standing, to rescue a cast-off. There is an *esprit du corps*, a meaning
to the phrase:—

THE PRIDE OF DOW

Robert Piercy Dow

Laguna Beach, Calif., May 25, 1926

THE acquisition of surnames by the people of Great Britain was gradual, the process covering about five centuries following the Norman conquest. The Cromwellian wars meant a wide change of surnames. In France and Germany and all western Europe the process was almost synchronous and equally gradual. Surnames were not reduced to a fixed spelling until about 1700, and even after that they varied, altho mostly through ignorance of spelling. There were in England no laws governing the taking of a permanent family name, as there were in Germany and Austria, where all Jews were compelled to take binomial names. In England it was merely for convenience, as the population increased and the names John, William, Richard, Henry increased with each king of that name until they were not separable by the tax collector. It was to prevent confusion that each man became known to his neighbors by a qualifying epithet. John the little man became permanently John Little. John who lived on a hill became John Hill and left the fixed name to his children. So did John the smith and John the strong. A member of a noble family got a fixed name from his land. For the yeomanry and peasantry some personal characteristic had to be found. In a majority of instances a patronymic was employed. We have a John Williamson, son of William Johnson, son of John. A son of Alexander may become Sanders, Saunders, Sandys, even Elshioner. A son of David may be Davis, David, Davison, Davidson, Dawson, Daw, etc. A John who was in trade was generally dubbed by it—Baker, Tyler, Weaver, etc. The son of some undersized Peter became Peterkins, then Perkins. Many persons, however, without trade, without place, had some mental or physical characteristic seized upon by the neighbors, generally in rough jest, and were dubbed willy nilly with a surname which became permanent. Thus, a dull-eyed became Fish; another man Lyon (unless he came from Lyons, France); another Fox, Marten, Sparkes (sparrow hawk), etc. The first man named Hogg had habits justifying his neighbors' choice of a name for him. Cowards might have been brave men, they were cowherds. The surnames Cuckold, Trull, Trollop, Harridan, etc., have not entirely disappeared.

In many counties of England there were men of mild manner, whose personalities called for a gentle name. One easily imagines newlyweds so given to billing and cooing that they found themselves forever dubbed the "doves." This name is not peculiar to England. It was applied for the same reason in Italy. Christopher Columbus (Colombo) is a dove. In England we find the name close to 1200 in a Parliamentary writ directed to a Nicholas le Duv and a Richard le Duv. As time went on, the method of spelling tended to crystallize differently in different countries. In Norfolk the whole tendency was toward Dowe and probably all Norfolk Dow have a common Dow ancestor. In Hants the tendency was toward Doue. In another country the spelling Dove is wholly now used. There were not fewer than twenty original families of Dow. The name is not indigenous to Wales or Ireland, the Dow of those places being migrants from England or Scotland. In Norfolk it is a very common name; Smith is less common here. In England the pronunciation is never as we pronounce it in America (as in cow and now); it is long, and half way between the pronunciation of doe and dove. Our present pronunciation is yankee twang, and began not before 1650. The earliest spelling Dow that we find is in Oct. 1505, when Eleanore Dow of Rekynhale received a legacy from Edmund Sparhawke of Laxfield. Henry Dow of Runham spells his name in 1613 indifferently Dowe and Dove. In Massachusetts Bay Colony Henry Dow in 1653 spelled it Dowe, Dow and Dove. About 1725 the final e became lost, but has been resumed recently by a few individuals. Several branches of the Connecticut Dows have been Dowe for three generations. It is a matter of choice; it confuses the genealogist only a little. A member of the Doe family thought it more dignified to call himself Dowe (pronounced long as in doe). This was a little confusing, but we discovered him and banished him from our Book.

The name Doe is confused with Dow only in ignorance, but this ignorance extended to a San Francisco amateur of pretension who aided the making of the Doe Genealogy. To get an origin to the name the travel was absurdly afield. A Norman chevalier D'O was quoted; there was a family Deaux. A George Do of Jesus College, Cambridge, was quoted, who had arms—3 dogs rampant. This member of the Dogge family did not like his name but he could not get rid of his arms. The deer tribe has furnished many surnames,—Stagg, Buck, Roe, Hart, etc. This is the origin of the several original families of Doe.

The name Dow is even more common in Scotland than in England, and from Scotland the Dows invaded Ireland in vast hordes. In Dublin in one year twelve Thomas Dow died. No Scotch Dow is entitled to arms. One is pictured in Fairbanks, but it is a dove, either stolen or belonging to an emigrant from England. The Scotch name is Dhu, meaning dark, swarthy, any such man being conspicuous among those of the blonde or red race. As in England, there was never a single Dow family of Scotland. They were never a clan or a sept, and most of them took the name comparatively recently.

Alexander Dow of Detroit explains how the sept Appin, Clan Stewart, proscribed five generations ago, scattered and took refuge under the name of Dow. This name in Aberdeen is today pronounced as the Dhu. We know well the word daw, best known as jackdaw, a black bird. There is in England a family formerly Daw but now Black. It is absurdly far-fetched to assume, as has Joel N. Eno, A. M., in "Fiery Cross," that the Dow of Clan Davidson are daws, or that the Dow of Clan Buchanan are doves. For dove he gives from Colman (columba, dove), a hero of the Clan Buchanan. In the Weekly Scotsman, March 2, 1918, there appears a note:—"Dow, Dowe, Dove—Anglicized forms of Calum, dove from St. Columba. The ancestor of the Dows was Colman, third son of the seventh chief of the Buchanans. The Dows are therefore a sept of the clan Buchanan. This is rank absurdity. Col means crafty, sly, and was in early Scotland a complimentary adjective. It shows in Colfax, Colburn, etc., sly fox and sly bear. To transpose Columba into Colman does not accord with any law of philology.

One must not confuse Scotch Daw with Welsh Daw, the latter merely son of David, Dawes, Dawey, Dawson being variants. Scott's hero, Sir Rhoderick Dhu, was not of a clan, but outlaw, making his own ancestry or posterity, his own clan. The border Dhu were dark with robbery and rapine aplenty. The main point to be made, so far as this Book is concerned, is that there is no connection between English and Scotch Dow. An etymological cousin of Dhu is Duirche, surviving as a surname in Durgin, possibly as Dowkin.

The Dutch Douw have no connection, but are best known from Gerard Douw, famous painter, whose kin came to New Amsterdam about 1630, settling near Albany, and are today far from weak numerically. A German family of Dau (pronounced as our own) has even less kinship. It is well known in New York City.

There is no connection between Dow and Dows. The latter, a family well represented in early Boston, is Norman and originally Douce from *dulcis*. One English branch of this family has become Sweet, and some sweet Isabella was the mother of families of Dowsabell, Dussabell, Duzzabel. The Dowsons are sons of Dows, not of Dow. The names Dowie, Dowrie, Dowing are of uncertain connection with Dow.

We must not confuse the word Dowgate. This is never the gate of the doves. It is the water-gate, old Anglo Saxon. The best known was the watergate of London, described by Samuel Pepys. It was an exit from London, crossing a ford and going straight on to Dover. Dover is the water town, and this was a famous Roman road. A family of Dowser exists. They were originally searchers for springs, with rod of witch hazel in hand, as it is still done. To douse the glim is thieves' cant of great antiquity. While it means to extinguish a light, it is by throwing water on a torch. The family of Dowrst, neighbors of Dow in New Hampshire at an early date, are water-men.

There are well known Dow in Boston and Montreal, Chinese. Many occurrences of the syllable compounded are of Continental, or even of Oriental origin, Dowkout faintly suggests Holland, Dowhovych Russia, Dowiak Finnish or Tartar, Dowjiboom Armenia or Persia. All of these are in the New York directory. Chann Dow of Louisville is very black, but a faithful porter.

With heraldic devices this Book has little concern, altho the vanity of Dow is constantly appealing to his sympathy. No Dow in America has any right whatever to any arms and the whole idea is repugnant to our sturdy original yeomanry. We are yeomen, neither nobles or peasants, never Saxon serfs. To say, as was said in a genealogical weekly newspaper, that the Dow arms are: Sable a fesse dancette ermine between three doves argent, is a lie, i. e., deliberately intended to deceive. A number of families of Dow have received arms from the College of Heraldry, and the basis of all is the dove crest, the three doves, generally in a sable star, and the ribbon, generally with the word *"patiens."* A Scotch crest, figured in Fairbanks, is a pegasus rampant. Those who have received Dow arms are of three classes,—have paid cash, had some mayoralty or petty preferment, or been polite to the King's mistress. There was no grant of arms to a Norfolk Dow, altho some of them did enter the gentry by marriage to some heiress.

There can be no Dow plaid. A quarter-century ago a tourist in Edinburgh brought home a piece of plaid guaranteed by the merchant who sold it to be genuine Dow plaid. This was cut up and small pieces were given to several Dows. Twenty years later the tale connected with it grew to include the statement that it was the plaid of Thomas Dow, immigrant of 1639. Now, poor Thomas, who practically starved to death, never knew a plaid. When the tale finally reached the Author, he submitted a sample to as many experts as he could reach. A few made guarded replies, but one was honest enough to say that it was not a genuine tartan at all, that it came nearest to the plaid of Clan Davidson. Business is business and one can readily buy in Edinburgh a plaid guaranteed to have been worn for centuries by Ipstein or Flaherty.

One immigrant Dow we will dispose of in passing. ffrancis Dow was a pioneer of Salisbury, Mass., in the first division of land. He came from Wilts and returned there after 1655. In 1650 he was an influential citizen of Salisbury, and was addressed as Mr., the title reserved then for the few best. Aug. 4, 1655, John Sanders sells to Andrew Greele a "lot for a saw mill ate the hither end of ye great meadows encompassed with ye grwat neck of Mr. Dow's Rie Lott—in Salsberry." The Greeley tide mill was run by a Dow in 1729.

Francis Dow had been mayor and justice of the peace in New Sarum, England, and came to Massachusetts, tempted, perhaps, by tales of great richness, of gold, etc. It may be noted that many noblemen and gentry were among the immigrants prior to 1650 and most of them returned to England. They found no riches here, but they found hardships such as they did not wish to stand. They found also a democratic atmosphere not easy to endure. While British caste ideas prevailed a little and the gentry was looked up to, even in Boston, the illiterate peasant, if he had the ability, was equal in politics and readily asserted his equality, soon getting the upper hand, if there was suffrage. Francis Dow was a Dove, rather than a true Dow.　He had a son Peter, who never came to this country, but was a gentleman of New Sarum, high sheriff of Wilts in 1673.　Peter thought little of his American inheritance, and did not dispose of it for fifteen years.

Francis Dow was one of the first to bring rye to Massachusetts. Two documents bear on this rye lot.　Sept. 5, 1674, Peter Dow of New Sarum in ye county of Wiltes, esquire, appointed his friend Timothy Lindall of Boston merchant his attorney to collect rents, etc., in New England.　Nov. 5, 1674, Peter Dow of ye citti of New Sarum in the county of Wilts, England, deeded to Timothy Lindall of Boston land in Salisbury, New England, which land ffrancis Dow owned, and which descended and came of right to Peter Dow, ye only son and heire of Francis Dow. Feb. 1, 1683, land is deeded to Joseph Dow of Salisbury, a piece of ground of 20 acres, as it was laid out to Mr. ffrancis Dowe.

Timothy Lindall, gent, carried on an extensive merchandizing business from Boston, and was agent for a number of English land holders.

Joseph Dow was our ad, the first Quaker Dow.　This twenty acres was one of nine purchases made by him when the Hampton Quakers were secretly planning to come to Seabrook, an uninhabited region and a semi-isolated refuge.

IN the History of Hampton, N. H., by the late Joseph Dow, by far the richest treasury of information about the beginnings of the Dow family in America, it is stated that Henry Dow, immigrant, was descended from John Dow of Tylner, Norfolk Co., whose will was probated July 23, 1561. In making this erroneous statement (which has been copied far and widely) he was grossly imposed upon by a professional English genealogist, who later confessed that he "took a chance." He took the money and kept it, out of the slender means of Joseph Dow. This will was inspected afterwards and found to be that of a John Downet.

Perhaps (and the author thinks probably) there was only one original family of Dow in Norfolk. The name occurs in the yeomanry in the 13th century in Norfolk. By 1500 the name was common throughout Norfolk. Some of them were land-owners by 1450; others had leaseholds in practically permanent form. Some had become of the gentry.

A Parliamentary writ of about 1200 cites one Richard le Duv and one Nicholas le Duv, apparently father and son, land-holders of Great Yarmouth. It is quite possible that the elder of these was the first to bear the name. It is certain that such surname could not have been in existence, as Norfolk County was slow in adopting surnames. Beyond much doubt here is the origin of the family. As a whole their position from the first was high in the yeomanry but not in the gentry. Individual members entered the gentry through marriages with heiresses and one member was created a knight banneret. Beyond a doubt, too, every Dow of Norfolk County is descended from one ancestor, a Saxon, and Norman inter-marriages occurred from 1400 onward.

The first definitely known, except as a name, is one John Dow of East Herling, 1487. His son and heir John Dow of Diss, gave to the guilds their house in Heyton St. This sounds like a man of property who had risen from a trade.

In Hapham May 8, 1498, John Dow succeeded an incumbent priest. Such instances are mostly younger sons of gentry.

Mr. Dowe of Brisingham married the daughter and heiress of Thomas Howard of Burston. The Howards were noble, even connected with royalty. She in her widowhood passed the priory manor on to the Bungloes.

After this, there are some interesting mentions of Dow, of lines which can be no more than collateral to ours.

John Dowe of Alltburgh, who died 1620, a character and large landholder, married Anne Cockett, daughter of Thomas of Brownsthorp. She outlived him until 1626, very charitable to the poor, a benefactress t o the church. This John Dowe composed his epitaph:

Vpon old John Dowe an Unprofitable townsman of great estate in land and yet not worth a mortuary at his Death in Goods.

John Dowe an antient townsman was buried in divers years past before
And lyeth buried within the Church South Door.
De quo hoc verum Epitaphium hebaeri posset.

Here lyeth the Dowe who ne'er in life did good
Nor would have done though longer he had stood
A wife he had both Beautifull and wise
But he ne'er would such goodness exercise
Death was his Freind to bring him to his grave
For he in life commendam none could have.

We now come back to the yeomanry. The Society of Antiquaries of London, Archaeologia vol 25, p 421, gives extracts from the household and privy purse accounts of the Lestranges of Hunstanton, Norfolk, from 1519 to 1578:

This booke make mencyon of all payments for the hows & receyts from the xxvth day of September in the xjth yere of ye leigue of Kyng Henry the VIIIth on to ye next accompts
The ljd Weke
Item pd to John Dowe for making of a Cowle for the Hennys at Anan ljd.

A cowl is the wooden cross piece to be worn on the shoulders, from which a pail or other load may be suspended at each end. It is possible, even rather probable, that this John Dow is father of our earliest known ancestor, but no evidence of it exists.

From C C Norwich: Baynes 127, comes the first mention found of our own line.

WILL of **John Dow** of Great Yarmouth, Norfolk, joiner, dated 1 July, 1544.
High Altar, Reparation of Church, the lazars at Yarmouth gates, Sisters of the Hospital in Yarmouth,
Sons—Thomas and Christopher, 40s apiece at their ages, etc.
Wife Johan my "Place" in Yarmouth.
Residuary legatee and sole executrix—wife Johan.
Supervisor uncle Christopher Coop.

From this we make out that John Dow was thrifty and had a home; that his bequests to charity were not inconsiderable for his time, that the name of his wife was Johan Coop.
The will of the widow adds another name:

WILL of Johan Dewe (sic) of Great Yarmouth, widow, dated 22 August, 1549.

Sole legatees—children, Thomas, Christopher and Katherine.

At this time the Dow family of Yarmouth, notably of Runham parish, was not so numerous to make it improbable that they were all closely akin. It seems probable that John Dow had a brother Thomas of Runham. This Thomas had at least three sons:

  a William bur Dec 29, 1567   b John bur Feb 13, 1572
  c Thomas bur Good Friday Apr 6, 1599

This 3rd born Thomas had a wife Elizabeth and a son Thomas b Oct 28, 1640. We cannot differentiate between Thomas Dow bur Apr 23, 1642, and Thomas Dow bur Oct 2, 1666.

Of this line seems Henry Dow with wife Ann and a son Thomas b June 2, 1673; d Sept 28, 1673. Also Elizabeth Dowe m Mch 13, 1614, Gregorie Davie (also spelled Davye). Also Ellen Dowe m Runham Jan 15, 1643, John Holmes.

Thomas Dow xa, whose children repeat the names of the previous generation, may have seen service in his youth, for he possessed and bequeathed a piece of land, not owned by his father, held of the King for military service. He was 16 when his father died. He m Oct 5, 1549, Margaret England. For many years he kept an inn in Runham Parish, Yarmouth, and probably farmed his arable lands. It is on record that Thomas Dow, an honest man and good housekeeper, was bur: the xth day of May, 1591. Again: Margaret Dowe, wid: bur: Sept 5, 1616. Little doubt that the list of children is complete:

  a Henry b 1550. Oddly, the Parish rec, which gives many names prior as well as later, does not contain his birth or baptism
  b Thomas bap Mch 20, 1551-2. Thomas, son of Thomas, a single man, m Runham May 24, 1596, Lucie Church, widowe. She d Dec 4, 1612. He m 2nd July 18, 1614, Sarah Manchepp of Hempsbye, who was bur May 7, 1615. Albeit of full years he m 3rd at Runham by special license Apr 7, 1617, Grace Smith and had by her a dau Elinor b July 9, 1618
  c Katherine m May 7, 1576, John Sowter. She had only dau; therefore the Sowter family of Seabrook, N H, who came originally from Norfolk Co, was only collaterally related
  d Christopher bap Mch 25, 1569-70; m Runham Aug 11, 1606, Elizabeth ffranklin
  e John bap Sept 7, 1572; bur Feb 13, 1572-3
  f Edmond, mentioned in father's will with children Robert and Margaret. Edmunde Dove, almost surely identical, gentleman of Filby (Filby, Thrigsby, Ormsby, Runham are all parishes of Great Yarmouth), had a dau Sarah bap Mch 16, 1603

C C Norwich, Andrews 85: WILL of Thomas Dowe of Runham, Norfolk, yeoman, dated 2 May, 1591

Poor of Runham, a cowe worth twentie shillings, and 20s for penny dole.

Wife Margaret, messuages and lands in Runham, Mautbye, etc, for her life.

Son Henry m the said messuages after the death of my wife.

Son Christopher Dowe, Daughter Katherine and Susan Sowter, "daughters of said Katherine Sowter."

Son Edmond all debts owing to me by Thomas Clere esqr. and Richard Ryper of Yarmouth.

Robert and Margaret Dowe, children of my son Edmond.

Edmond Church my godchild, all the rest of my godchildren unnamed in epitome.

WILL of Margaret Dowe, of Runham, Norfolk, wid: dated 19 August, 1615.

To be buried in Runham Church.

Mary, Francis, Thomas, Harrys, Edward and William Dowe,—the syx children that my sonne Henry Dowe did leave behind him."

Elizabeth Ann. Ezekell, Rewth, Ellen, Judith, Sarah, Thomas, and Nathaniel Dowe, children of my sonne Christopher Dowe.

Sole Executor Christopher Dowe.

Proved at Yarmouth, 10 September, 1616, by executor named.

Henry Dow xaa, oldest child, b 1550, m May 12, 1594, Elizabeth March. In spite of his late marriage, he did much toward a posterity. He d three years before his mother, Apr 21, 1613. He was the parish clerk at Runham and for four years signed the register as church warden. The fourth year he signed as Dove. Children:

a   Mary bap Mch 16, 1594-5   b   Lucy bap Oct 28, 1596; d Jan 11, 1600
c   Thomas bap Apr 1, 1599; bur Apr 6, 1599   d   Frances bap Apr 6, 1600
e   Thomas bap Jan 16, 1601-2. It was once assumed that he was the 1639 emigrant to Newbury, Mass, which is absurd, as the Newbury man was only about 35 in 1654. Thomas inherited the land, lived, died and had a family in England, where his posterity still lives
f   Henry bap Oct 6, 1605; first Dow of America
g   Edward bap Feb 21, 1607; lived Ormsby; m Elizabeth Robbins
h   William bap Jan 20, 1610

This generation married into the families of March and Farrar and continues to this day of Norfolk Co. The mother of Elizabeth March was a Farrar.

In Chancery Inquisitions Post Mortem vol 344, no 94:

Inquisition taken at Walton, co Norfolk, 19th April, 12 James I, after the death of Henry Dowe, yeoman,

The said Henry was seized of a close of arable land called le Wonge close in Runham, containing about 14 acres; in reversion after the death of his mother Margaret Dowe, late the wife of Thomas Dowe, a messuage of land in Runham, Thrigby, and Maultby, still in the occupation of the said Margaret. By his will he bequeathed the said messuages to his wife for life, remainder of his son Thomas.

He died 21 April 11 James I (1614), Thomas his said son and heir being then aged 11 years three months. He is now in the custody of his mother Elizabeth.

The said close called le Wonge is held of the King by military service, and is worth 13s 3d yearly.

The Messuage, etc., is held of Sir Thomas Birney, Knight, as of his manor of Strumpsall by fealty and a rent of 16d yearly.

From these records it appears that this particular Dow family were fairly well-to-do and of good standing. Both generations possessed some education and the family came from Catholicism through the Reformation into the Church of England. Henry of the next generation was probably the only dissenter, surely the only Puritan.

Henry Dow, xaaf, to be known as a progenitor of the largest American family, was at 25 a farmer in Ormsby. He had a little inheritance from his mother, more than enough to equip his holding of land. Ormsby is not far from Runham. Its parish register was copied in 1880 by Rev R S Blofield, rector. In it occur three important items, which prove that Henry b 1606 of Runham is Henry of Ormsby and America:

Edward Dow and Elizabeth Robbins were married ye xxvij of January, anno Dom 1628.

Henry Dow and Jane Nud was married ye 11 of February 1630
oe   Anno Domini 1631
Thomas doue filius Thomas Doue et Joane uxoris ejus vicesimo Septi mo die December baptirjatus fuit.

The mention of the father as Thomas is an obvious pen slip. We follow the youngster to America, where he died at 10.

It is clear that the brothers Edward and Henry were together as husbandmen in Ormsby, that each found a wife there, that the ties of Runham gradually were loosed as Ormsby ties grew strong. What happened to Edward we have not traced. Of Henry's path, the account is fairly ample. Of Joan Nudd we know but little: not her maiden name. She was 23 at her marriage and had a baby boy. Her husband was Roger Nudd, son of John, who died in Ormsby 1629. Probably Henry and Roger were fellow farmers. The Nudds were numerous in Norfolk, mostly in the seaward parish. Vital rec. of that parish are not extant prior to 1671. The Nudd affairs are fully discussed under the chapter of Thomas Nudd, immigrant of 1637.

Under what circumstances Henry and Joan became dissenters is not known. They were of the established church in 1630. There arose in Ormsby a great deal of dissatisfaction, religious and otherwise. This crystallized into a determination of seven families to try the New World. It was an arrangement planned long in advance and was consummated on the same boat. Hotten's Original Lists give all the families, who afterwards appear together in Hampton, N H, the Page, Moulton, Marston families intermarried with Dow with especial frequency. It has often been asserted, with more or less cynicism, that a desire to better one's material condition was the paramount reason for going to America, desire for religious freedom being very secondary. It may be that these people were at no time dissenters in England. They had to be, in Massachusetts Bay, for there were no others. That all of them were of strong religious feeling is sure. No others could stand the intensely religious atmosphere of New England, a situation in which one must travel a very narrow path of rectitude, almost all ordinary pleasures being outside the pale. If the percentage of immigrants whose motive was improvement of material conditions and not intense religiousness had been at all large, the stern puritan life could not have maintained its iron grip, but would have degenerated into the free and easy morals of Virginia during the same period. In Massachusetts Bay all were of the persuasion which became Congregationalism, in contrast to that of the Plymouth colony whose notion of Government became Presbyterianism.

In the Rolls Office, Chancery Lane, London, is a small parchment-bound volume labelled on the cover:

T C 27.   979 A   A. D. 1637
13 Car. 1

This is filled with entries of persons "desirous to pass beyond seas" and consists of 16 pp, most of which are taken up by names of Puritans on the way to Holland. The contents has been copied into Hotten's Original Lists, Drake's Founders of New England, etc.

The entry vital to us is:

"These people went to New England: with William: Andrewes: of Ipswich M'r of the: John: and Dorethy: of Ipswich and with William Andrewes his son M'r of the Rose: of Yarmouth Aprill the 11th 1637. The examination of Henerey Dowe of Ormsby in Norff Husband man, aged 29 yeares and Joane: his wife ageed 30 yeares with four children, and one Saruant Ann Maning aged 17 yeares, are desirous to passe into New England to inhabitt."

This is all clear. Henry Dow of Ormsby married the widow of his friend, a year older than himself, took her baby boy; had three children of his own and was able to start with a servant. This latter does not indicate affluence. Passage to America was very costly. Young men and women of good family gladly indentured themselves for a long term if the employer would pay the passage. It was in this way that Margaret Cole, who became Henry Dow's second wife, came to Dedham with the family of Mitchill Metcalfe. But, it does show that Henry was decidedly thrifty or charitable to bring the maid. Of Ann Manning, saruant ageed 17 nothing further appears; no doubt she found a husband as soon as her term of service was up. The Andrewes, father and son, were in the regular business of carrying emigrants across, so they do not appear again in these pages.

From Henry Dow are descended nearly three-fifths of all the Dows of America.   The party landed in Boston after a long voyage, no details of which have appeared.   One child either died on voyage or on land before Watertown statistics were begun.   How and why Henry parted from his companions we do not know.   All but he turned up 1640 in Hampton and asked him to join them there.   Henry proceeded almost at once to Watertown, just being settled about ten miles west of Boston.   Presumably the selection of the place was influenced by the opportunity to become a grantee on equal terms, with allotment of land free.   No settler in those days had to buy land unless it was thought desirable to pay the Indians for a title.   He remained seven years in Watertown, a very inconspicuous citizen.   He was admitted a freeman May 2, 1638, but held no office in his town.   In fact, the only mentions of him in Watertown are in the land records and vital statistics.   He could have had free land in Hampton in 1640, but decided not to accept it.   There is reason to think that he stayed in Watertown until the land boomed. In a few years the settled place commanded a price at which the original settlers took profits and moved on to begin anew and clear forest land.   We know that Henry Dow left Watertown a moderate capitalist.

In Lands, Grants & Possessions, first Inventory, we find:
Henry Dow
1. An Homestall of Eight acres more or less bounded on the Eaft with Hill ftreet and weft with William Rix the North with Thomas Haftings & the South with Robert Veazey.
2. A farm of Ninety seven acres of Vpland in the 5 divifion

In the third Inventory is entered:

Henry Dow.
1. An Homestall of Eight Acres by eftimation bounded on the Eaft w'th the highway the West with Thomas Smith and Eliz Barron the North w'th Thomas Boyson & the South w'th William Godfree in his possession.

Clearly, between the two inventories an almost complete change of adjacent land ownership had taken place, the original settlers selling out to new comers.   Henry's farm has not been placed, no effort having been made.   The home was on the west side of School St.

An entry of April 9, 1638: A Divifion of Land at y'e Townplott,
Henry Dow   Six acres
In 1642: Ordered that all the Townes Men that had no farms laid out formerly fhall take them by ten in a Divifion, and to caft Lotts for the severall Divifions allowing 13 acres of Vpland to every head of Persons and cattle.

	Lott:	No of lot
Henry Dow	Ninety seven acres	102

The little book of Watertown vital records is extant:

The Records of the
Births, Deathes and
Marriages in Watertown

Keppt according to
the order of Court
Made in the yeare
1638.

p 6. 1638 Jofeth Dow of Henry and Jone Dow borne the 20'd—11 mo
p 9 of the book is blank, the clerk having neglected his duty, but what belongs there is in the records of the Clerk of the Court of Middlesex Co:

1640 Joan the wife of Henry Dow buried 20 (4)
1641   Daniell the son of Henry & Margaret Dow borne 22 (7)
Thomas the son of Henry & Jone Dow buried 10 (5)
1643 Mary the daughter of Henry & Margaret Dow borne 14 (7)

In the transcript of Don Gleason Hill of the First Church (of Dedham): Margarette Cole our sister by p'dence being maried to a brother of Watertown named Dow was dismissed to y't Church 1643.   The wedding was not at Watertown.

Thus is recorded the birth of Joseph Dow, first Dow ever born in America, whose posterity is the most numerous; also the death of his older brother; the death of his mother at 33, twice a wife, five times a mother; the birth of two new children, following his father's speedy remarriage.   We must not accuse Henry of indelicacy.   In primitive New England life for a man without a wife's help was hard indeed; for a woman without help from a husband harder yet; for children without both parents almost unsupportable.   Margaret Cole had known Henry Dow in Ormsby, had come to America in 1639 with the Metcalfe family and had settled in Dedham.   She was indentured, just as Ann Manning had been, and was younger than Henry Dow.   In First Church Dedham: Margaret Coole, a maid servant, giving good satisfaction to ye church was received in ye 3rd month of this yeare, 1639.   Others from Ormsby were admitted about the same time.   Margaret survived her husband by 16 years; m 2nd (Martgrit Dow) Aug 23, 1661, Richard Kimball of Ipswich.   He was of Watertown 1641 to 1644 and came then to know the Dows.

In 1644 the time was ripe to move.   Henry sold out all his lands and started overland for Hampton.   In that town is an entry: June 16, 1640, grant of a house lot to Henry Dow, if he come.   Evidently he had thought then of moving. But, he had become an astute land speculator. In 1644 he got enough for his Watertown property to buy treble the property offered as a gift. In 1644 he bought his house lot from John Sanders, freeman, of Ipswich in 1634, who came early to Hampton, but sold out, went to Newbury, returning finally to Hampton. In 1649 Henry bought the homestead of William Wakefield, freeman of 1638, who moved to Newbury in 1646. It was from this latter plot that Henry set off 10 acres for Thomas Nudd as his home. He bought a house already built from John Sanborn (where the store of J J Leavitt stood in 1890). The original Sanders purchase was on the road from Hampton village to Hampton Beach, about 1½ miles from the ocean. In the part of the town now known as Boar's Head was the Oxe Common, land where the share holders pastured. The Cow Common was divided in 1645 into 147 shares and allotted to proprietors of house lots, Hen: Dow receiving 3 shares by virtue of proportionate lot owning. The homestead remained long in the family, sold by Olive Dow, unm, of the 6th generation.

The fates were much kinder in Hampton than in Watertown. Henry was there a man of influence, his merits known. Of course, currency was scarce to all alike and it was wholly in the usual conduct of business that Henry in 1650 binds himself to pay a debt in good merchantable wheat. He was selectman in 1651, Deputy to the General Court of Massachusetts 1655-6. He traded briskly in real estate at all times. In 1650 he sells to Manuel Hiliard a 10 acre house lot and 3 acres of salt marsh for money. He signs his name this year as Doue. Feb 16, 1659, he made provision for his oldest son: a house and barn bought from Thomas Sleeper, 100 rods of adjoining land, a share of the oxe common, the share of the cow common bought from Thomas Sleeper, also 6 acres of planting ground in the east field. He was appointed with two others to examine the land grants and highways, but died before this was completed, Apr 21, 1659. He was one of the dozen men of Hampton always styled "gentleman" and as "Mr." His children:

a Thomas b Eng; bap Dec 27, 1631; d July 10, 1642   b Henry b Eng 1634
c —— b Eng. Appears on manifest 1637 but never later; probably d on voyage
d Joseph b Watertown Mch 20, 1639
e Daniel b Sept 2 or 22, 1641   f Mary b Sept 14, 1643
g Hannah b Hampton, Hampton rec gives 1649, and d Hampton Aug 6, 1704
h Thomas b Apr 28, 1653. If this were right he would have m at 15. Somehow
    the rec of Hampton are mixed. Hannah was b about 4 years earlier and
    Thomas about 7 years than the dates of record
i Jeremiah b Sept 6, 1657; also should be earlier

All men and women of early Hampton attended strictly to their religious observances. In the meeting house every detail was arranged: All the men to sett at the west end and all the women to sett at the east end and the devotion to be at the greet poest that is betwin the two windos. Second seat: hen grene hene dou steu Sanborn tho louit wi fifield jo merian.

Margaret Cole Dow sat by ould mistris husse her dafter husse goody swaine goody pebody goody brown mistris stanyen Mary Perkinges. Bro Page and Bro: Dow were the committee to negotiate for the services of Rev Seaborn Cotton after the resignation of Rev. Wheelwright.

Ten years prior to making his last will and testament, Henry Dow filed the following, now in Probate Court at Exeter: Upon a promise made unto my former wife that if I were the longer liver I would make him as my own sonne, he now being grown to man's estate, I doe now and freely give and grant unto Thomas Nudd, my sonne in law to him and his heirs a parcell of lande out of my house lott, containing 10 acres be it more or lesse, etc.

Thus God, who tempers the wind to the shorn lamb, proved kind to little Tommy Nudd, to whom was given a stepfather before he was 2 and a stepmother at 12. His name occurs with that of his half-brother Henry many times as witness, etc. In 1648 he was official keeper of the calves at a princely salary of 11 £ a year. The job was no sinecure; he drove all calves to the common at sunrise and separated each to its home at sunset. In the list of the first selectmen of Hampton his name appears among five. This was error, perhaps arising from his position keeping calves. He had a share in the Common, the gift of Henry Dow. In 1663 the shares were Henry Dow ab 1, Daniel Dow 1, bought from Nicholas Boulter, Henry's widow 1.

The original of Henry's will is on file in Salem, Mass. It reads:

The last Will and testament of Henry Dowe of Hampton, being sick and weake of body but sound of understanding and memorie:

Item: I give and bequethe to Margerite my loveing wyfe my house lott being by estimation tenn acres more or lesse and six acres of fresh meadow at the springs, and one share of the cowes Common, three of my cowe and the dwelling house uppon the aforesaid, and my household stuff, excepting what shall be otherways disposed of:

Item: I give and bequethe unto my Sonne Henry Dowe all the planting ground that is in my hands in the East Field, and my seventeen acres of Salt marsh, and one share of the Cowe commons, and one share of the Oxe Common and all my cattell excepting the three Coess abovesaid.

Item: to my Sonne Henry one feather bed wch hee useth to lie uppon and all the bed clothes thereunto belonging and the middlemost iron pott, and I do by these presents make and appoint my Sonne Henry my sole executor to this my last will and testament.

Item: I do give and bequeath unto my Sonne Joseph the sum of thirty pounds to be paid when he shall arrive to the age of twenty and one years.

Item: I doe give and bequeath unto my Sonne Daniell and to my daughters Mary and Hannah five pounds apiece to be paid to them when they arrive to their ages of twenty and one years.

Item: I give unto my Sonne Thomas and to my Sonne Jeremei five pounds apeece to be paid to them att the age of one and twenty years, and after my wyfes decease, the house and house lott and six acres of meadow to returne into the hands of my executor. In case that he please to resigne up the house and fifty rods of ground which was sometimes possessed by Thomas Sleeper into the hands of my Sonne Joseph, and to pay unto my five youngest children abovesaid five and twenty pounds, that is to say, five pounds apeece to be payd, five pounds to the Eldest the yeare after my wyfes decease, and so five pounds a yeare to the younger untill the summe of five pounds be payd to the youngest; and still with this proviso, that in case my Sonne Henry bee not willing to leave the place where Thomas Sleeper lived and take the land aforesaid after my wyfes decease upon the condicons above named, then the said house and house lott with the six acres of meadow are to return to my Sonne Joseph, who upon the taking possession is to undertake for the paying of the twenty five pounds above s'd to my five youngest children according to the terms mentioned.

Item: I give unto my wyfe two of the best of my swine, and so much of the corne in the house as may maintaine hir and my Children untill harvest, and the corn till harvest to bee twenty bushells.

To this my last will and testament I set my hand and Seale ye 16th 2nd mo 1659.

Henry Dowe
with seale to it

Witness
Robert × Page
 his mark
Sam: Dalton

This is the only appearance of Samuel Dalton, substantial citizen of Hampton. Robert Page was shipmate from Ormsby. Henry Dow ab m his dau and then his dau in law.

The estate was carefully administered, as was customary in those days, and the appraisal made by three disinterested experts. Some of the valuations now seem very high, some very low. Salt marsh, for its hay very easy to cut, was the most valuable land and its abundance was the primary cause of choosing Hampton for settlement. On the invention of the mowing machine, salt marsh fell in a year from very high prices to almost nothing

A true inventory of ye lands & goods of Henry Dow gent. of Hampton late deceased uppon ye 25th day of Aprill 1659

	£	s	d
Invt.Ye house and house lot	40	00	00
It: Six acres of fresh meadow	10	00	00

		£	d	s
It:	8 acres of other planting ground in ye East field	14	00	00
It:	17 acres of salt marsh	40	00	00
It:	two oxen	12	00	00
It:	4 cows two 3 year old heifers	23	00	00
It:	two 2 year old steers & a young calf	05	16	00
It:	4 swine att	03	00	00
It:	30 bu of Indian corn & 4 bu of wheat att	05	08	00
It:	a feather bed, a rug and clothes on ye bed	07	00	00
It:	an other feather bed & clothes belonging thereto	02	00	00
It:	a flock bed & clothes belonging thereto	02	00	00
It:	two old hogsheads & a butt & other old tubbs	00	10	00
It:	20 lbs of hemp & a bag of old bedclothes	01	13	00
It:	all his wearing clothes and a hatt att	03	11	00
It:	a musket pike and ammunicon	01	00	00
It:	2 brass kettles att	01	15	00
It:	Iron potts & earthen potts	01	11	00
It:	A cherne, 8 trays, 4 cheese fatts, 3 bowles & dary things	00	15	00
It:	½ firkin of soape, old tubs and pailes	01	15	00
It:	an iron skillet a brafs skillet, a possit & a warming pan	00	13	00
It:	3 pewter platters & other pewter att	01	00	00
It:	2 earthen panns, a latlin pan & other things	00	10	00
It:	4 cushings, chayres & stooles	01	03	06
It:	a cupboard and a chayre att	00	03	06
It:	a parcell, a tow comb, a clenser and 2 seives	00	05	06
It:	4 iron hoops, a chaine, plough irons, 2 axes, 4 wedges, a payer of Bitle rings & other odd irons	04	00	00
It:	a payer of sheets, 2 pillow bars, a napkin att	04	00	00
It:	One thousand hosghead staves att	02	00	00
It:	An old Bible, Mr Dod & other books	01	00	00
It:	2 basketts, a lamp, & other trifling things	00	05	00
It:	2 chestes, 2 boxes, 3 baggs, a spinning wheel and other lumber	03	05	00
		193	04	06

These goods were pused uppon ye 19th of May 1659

Robert X Page his mark
William M Godfrey ➡his mark
Henry Roby

Of the posterity of Henry Dow a, there is no aa line, as Thomas Dow aa d ae 10. All right of primogeniture, then, belongs to:

Henry Dow ab. Nature qualified him richly for headship of the family, the responsibilities of which were shared before his father's death. He was in many ways a remarkable man and had the makings of a national figure, had his lot fallen in times of greater political freedom or in an environment where the government was shared by a people instead of under the iron fist of some thoroughly venal, conscienceless, grafting, British political appointee, and an almost equally dictatorial local minister, church and town being one. As it was, he was for his whole mature life the most powerful, the most prominent figure in Hampton, with a career not wholly local, but often touching the whole province, especially during the brief period when New Hampshire was distinct from Massachusetts. Without education, be became on the whole a scholarly man. Without training, he was a diplomat and courtier, altho never giving up the independence of his own soul, his sense of right, and the rights of his fellow citizens. He was a gentleman in all senses of the word, and was so classed in the system of caste where the gentry and yeomen were as far apart as in England.

His duties under the will of his father were fully, liberally carried out. Two months after his father's death he m Hannah Page dau of Robert and Lucy, American-born in 1641, whose father was first deacon of Hampton church. There seems no likelihood that this family was related to the Page of Hingham. Hannah d Aug 6, 1704. Her husband, then town clerk, wrote "one just in her generation."

After her death Capt Henry, then 70, selected within three months a second wife, a friend of 47 years standing. She was Mary Hussey, dau of Capt Christopher, wid of Thomas Page, Henry's brother in law. Of her when she d ae 95, Jan 21, 1732-3, the Boston newspaper said, "a gracious gentlewoman." She was indeed a lady of great charm. Capt Christopher Hussey m Theodate Bachiler and thus she was of a truth the grand dau of Hampton's first citizen. Her 2nd husband was Judge and Councillor Henry Green, who d Aug 5, 1700, Esqr, aged above 80 years, for seuerall years a member of the Counsill until by age he layd downe that place but a justice till he died. Of Christopher Hussey it may be said that John Greenleaf Whittier was fond of recalling descent from him.

For a brief time his wife accompanied her 3rd husband to public functions, in which he had to take always a prominent part. The whole life of Henry Dow was political and social; he was trusted all his life with public and private interests; yet he was never accused of lack of piety or neglect of duty. He understood the art of avoiding making enemies.

Almost from the first he was as financially prosperous as one's ambition could require. After first marriage, the cost of living was met with much versatility of labor. He continued to operate the family farm, and until his stepmother remarried maintained the homestead for the entire family. He acquired an interest in a home-made vessel and in a boat-building business. He kept a general store, albeit a clerk was always necessary for an over-busy man. An account book of this store is extant, giving purchases of stock, which he always made in person, and the credit granted very generally to all Hampton. Almost all farm products were listed at fixed prices and passed as currency. It was Henry Dow's business to take these products, and transport them to Boston or other wide market, taking pay in merchandise or credit. This naturally could be best done on vessels of his own. As timber was a vital constituent of the trade, he became part-owner of a saw mill, making frequent entries in his diary of the number of feet sawn and the kinds of timber. He did some land-surveying, altho his brother Joseph was the expert at that. In 1686 he was admitted and sworn as an attorney and paid his fee. Thereafter he invariably acted for the town in all litigation. His military connection from 1689 brought probably no revenue; his town offices a trifle. When he had completed ten years as town clerk, he was voted 40s as compensation for the whole time. His service as selectman was six years in all from 1661 to 1698.

His court service was long and varied. He began as an assistant clerk. During the administrations of Andros and Dudley he was one of the justices of the court for New Hampshire; in 1695 justice of the inferior court of Common Pleas, re-appointed two years later. He was senior justice from 1699 until his death in 1707, and from 1702 a mandamus councillor. In addition to all this, he remained town clerk until two years before his death.

His military career began as a private under Capt Joseph Gardiner for the Narragansett campaign Feb 29, 1675-6. He does not appear to have fought. He received 1 £ 16s for service, probably in transportation of troops. He was not in the Swamp fight. He was ensign of Hampton militia from 1689, captain in 1692, commissioned by Sir William Phipps, on whose staff he was; he was chosen for a naval attack on Quebec. Fighting Indians was a constant affair for years and most troublesome. He was in command of the system of block houses around the town. Sept 29, 1691, he wrote to Major Robert Pike:

Sir: We have received intelligence from Sandybeach (now Rye) that since 12 o'clock this day the enemy have killed or carried away 16 persons of whom old goodman Brackett's and goodman Rand's families have the greatest blow. The messengers that brought this news, on returning home about the time the moon did rise this night, at a place called Raggyneck, about half a mile this side of Sandybeach garrison, they do affirm to me they saw, as they adjudged, about 40 enemies coming toward Hampton with five or six canoes on their heads, which caused them to come back to Hampton again, and brought us word of it; lest they should come along with their canoes in the night and do damage to houses near the sea. We are in a sad condition, the enemy is so violent. The Lord give us all wisdom to teach us what we ought to do.

So with respects presented to you, I remain your loving friend and servant,

Henry Dow

A diary which he kept for many years has become famous, altho the little leather-covered book which he kept in his pocket contains much of petty personal items of no public interest. It was kept in a cipher invented by himself, a sort of short hand, the key to which has been worked out only recently, and there are many arbitrary signs, not letters, not yet understood. Some entries contain much secret political history of the time. Two pages are torn out, probably by himself, for their date is at the time of Mr. Weare's mission to England. The administration of Gov Cranfield had become too wicked for endurance. There had been trouble from the first and the Governor's deputy had been escorted out of town with a rope around his neck. The prominence and probity of Mr. Weare made him the best envoy to the King and he carried a long list of complaints charging specific dishonesties, cruelties and malfeasances. Henry Dow did his full share in drawing up these complaints. Discovery by a spy of Cranfield might have laid him liable to any degree of punishment on a charge of treason, and the high judges were appointees of Cranfield.

Sometimes the entries are the simplest: "1687:—millions of streaked worms this year." There are details about his farm work, an account of a huge tree struck by lightning, launching of a vessel in which he was part owner, the number of cedar logs sawn at his mill during some month, items of labor on public works, details of tax rates which he had to make up and afterwards collect, the day's doings at the Assembly, consultations with high officials, hasty political or business trips to Haverhill, Ipswich, Newbury or Boston. During the Indian fights he kept track of those who were faithful and those who skimped garrison-watching duty, those who were derelict in other ways. He records drilling his company and teaching them tactics. He is at the head of his company in the field. It is a marvel how the restless man found time to eat or sleep. He was Vice-Marshal of Norfolk Co, deputy to the General Assembly, Clerk of the House, Speaker *pro tem*, and more besides. From his diary or public records fifty errands are mentioned,—on committee to sue Nath Boulter for trespass on the rights of the Commons, committee to keep dry cattle off the Commons, attorney for the town in the Huggins land suit and then on committee to secure to Huggins his rights won at law from Boulter, who had foolishly bought land from Mason, the claimant whose title, if good at all, covered the whole province of New Hampshire. In 1685 he made a census of the town,—707 humans including 5 slaves, 202 living on the south, or Seabrook side. In 1682 he was the scapegoat to resist a tax illegally levied by the Colonial Council. A warrant was issued given to the notorious Constable Barefoote to arrest Capt Henry Dow and keep him in jail until the tax was paid. What actually happened is not recorded, but a receipt for the tax is dated four months later. At this time the Government was rebuked from England. He was chairman of committees in 1689 and 1690 to consult with similar committees of other towns to fix upon common plans of government during the uncertainty whether the region should become a separate province of New Hampshire or remain part of Mass. Capt Henry favored re-union with Mass. It was voted to uphold the common law of England and the King's statutes until final decision was made in favor of the colonial statutes of one or the other.

The will of William Moulton of Hampton, dated Mch 8, 1663, says: "I do make, Costitute and appoint my louing father in law Robert Page, yeoman and my louing Brother in law henery Dow to bee my lawful Exequetors, etc." It was he who had charge of paying the minister's salary, and he noted very carefully when that reverend gentleman overdrew by three months. It was his duty to tabulate the increased cost of living due to the depreciation of the currency. The minister asked for a raise and submitted a long list of simple necessities once costing 3d but risen to as many shillings. The minister got the raise. Capt Henry was on the committee to build a parsonage and was messenger of the church to assist in the ordination of a new minister in Exeter. On the side were missions to conduct the litigation over the Salisbury border, to define the boundaries of Hampton, to re-survey the Exeter-Hampton line, to fight against the encroachments of the newly organized town of Kingston, to litigate against the claims of Newcastle for a strip of Hampton land, attempting to levy taxes twice over, to serve on a committee to investigate the feasibility of a straighter, better road to Portsmouth.

Forty days before his death he sat in Council for the last time. He d at home May 6, 1707, three score, ten and 3, in times when men wore out but never had a chance to rust out. The stone over his grave in Hampton churchyard is gone long since, but the spot is known, quite close to the longest lived stone in Hampton, lasting until the present century, inscribed to Susanna, wife of Robert Smith, Slaine by ye thunder, June 12, 1680

The children of Henry and Hannah Page:

a   Joseph b Mch 30, 1660; d Aug 17, 1680, unm
b   Samuel b Nov 4 (Sept, State rec), 1662; d June 20, 1714
c   Simon b Mch 4 (Jan 1, State rec), 1667; d Jan 14, 1752
d   Jabez b Feb 8, 1672

Samuel Dow abb, while not the equal of his father in any way, unless in devotion to the church, was a man of great activity and as prominent as any in Hampton. He, too, learned land surveying and assisted his uncle Joseph in the survey to fix the Mass-N H line. He succeeded his father as town clerk, holding the office until his death; was once representative to the General Court; selectman six years in all. He carried on the home farm, owned shares in vessels, notably the 40-ton home-built brigantine. Most prized of all was his diaconate, which came in 1711. A subscription of 32£ 1s was raised for additional communion silver, and Dea Dow was chosen to go to Boston by ship and select it. He was voted 20s for the expenses of the trip. He bought eight silver beakers or cups for 29£, and these are still in possession of the successor church, a bone of contention when it split a century later into a Congregational and a Presbyterian. The meeting house being constricted, he was on a committee "for to give Liberty to those men that wil Apeare for to build Puese in the Hinder Seates in the meeting house." In 1711 he layd off twelve acres for a parsonage for the Quakers, not a pleasant task for the orthodox deacon, altho his cousins were all leading Quakers. The church arrangements were that Deacon Samuel Dow was to tune the psalm in the forenoon, Dea John Tuck and Dea Dow to read the psalms in the afternoon. Now, Dea Tuck was a small man, with high-pitched voice, Dea Dow burly and deep of tone: One may imagine the rendition of the then used version of 102nd Psalm,—Dea Tuck bordering on falsetto:

"I'm like unto a pelican."

Dea Dow in basso profundo:

"And like an owl am I."

It was at a later date that the attempt was first made to sing the hymn without lining it but by the congregation all together. The first results were painful. One aged man arose and addressed the minister: "Reverend sir, do you allow all this?" Another shrieked: "Toll the bell, ye devils, toll the bell." The most aged of the vociferous protestors against the innovation felt so badly at his own temerity that, after a night's reflection, he went voluntarily before a magistrate, complained of himself for a breach of the peace and was fined 1s.

To compete with the junior deacon was no easy task, for Dea Tuck was greatly devoted to the scriptures. He was a carpenter, later a miller, and cultivated a farm at the same time. Yet, he found time to read the Bible from cover to cover twelve times during his diaconate. In his diary, still preserved, is an entry: "The 13th day of February, 1677, I began to read ye Bible through and I read it all through from ye 1st chapter of Gennesis to ye last chapter of Revelations: by ye 18th day of December, John Tuck."

The one appearance of Dea Samuel in law was as deputy to contest the claim of one Allen, inherited from Mason on an old royal grant of all the land in Hampton (for that matter, all of New Hampshire). It was in the line of his surveying that he was on the committee to divide up the

west common into lots, and to ascertain to date the rightful owners of the
much confused Cow Commons. For fifty years that pasture was the
most troublesome land in the province, never free from litigated claim.

He d June 20, 1714; m Dec 12, 1683, Abigail Hobbs b July 29, 1664,
d May 12, 1700, dau of Morris and Sarah (Easton); m 2nd Feb 13, 1703,
Sarah, wid of Peter Garland, and dau of John and Deborah (Godfrey)
Taylor. He left a bequest to her son John Garland. Children:

    a Hannah b Nov 12, 1684; d July 22, 1687
    b Joseph b Dec 13, 1686; d Aug 2, 1707, unm
    c Abigail b Apr 17, 1689; d Aug 23, 1707, unm
    d Sarah b May 22, 1691   e   Samuel b May 25, 1693
    f Rachel b Sept 20, 1695   g   Mehitable b Apr 10, 1698; d Feb 27, 1704
    h and i twins still born May 12, 1700
    j Hannah b Jan 10, 1709, bap Jan 20, 1709

Sarah Dow abbd m. Feb 28, 1712, Samuel Clifford b. Mch. 28,
1689, son of Israel and Ann (Smith). Children:

    a Abigail b Apr 2, 1713. Hist Hampton errs in giving m Abraham Sanborn.
       She is mentioned in her father's will Feb 8, 1760, as Abigail Carr, surely she
       who d Epping June 4, 1797, ae 84. Abraham Sanborn m Abigail Dow, dau
       of Joseph. If this rec be right, it must be a dau of adaj, the only known
       reference to her existence
    b Samuel b Nov 9, 1716; m Jan 17, 1738, Elizabeth Gove, dau of Edward and
       Bethia (Clark)
    c Sarah b about 1721; m Mch 20, 1746, Moses Cass; her posterity re-married
       into Dow several times
    d Rachel b 1723   e   Benjamin b 1727   f   Hannah b 1730
    g Joseph b 1732. These dates seem conjecture, names from father's will

Samuel Dow abbe d Hampton Mch 29, 1755, of an "awfull fever."
He succeeded his father as deacon, was generally known as Dea Samuel
Jr; also succeeded as town clerk, holding the position until his death.
He served four years in all as selectman and was the first town treasurer, the office being created for him in 1747. Hist Hampton says nothing about his business. He m Sept 12, 1717, Mary Page b Dec 13, 1695,
d Mch 6, 1760, dau of Christopher and Abigail (Tilton). Children:

    a Samuel b Oct 10, 1718   b   Abigail b Feb 25, 1721
    c Mary b Sept 12, 1724   d   Hannah b Sept 20, 1727
    e Joseph b Dec 21, 1729   f   Tabitha b Aug 24, 1731
    g Jonathan b Mch 10, 1734   h   Sarah b Feb 21, 1736
    i Comfort b Aug 20, 1738; d Nov 4, 1756

Samuel Dow abbea succeeded as deacon but failed of re-election
in 1792; signed the Association Test; selectman 1 year, for a brief time
town clerk; m Oct 20, 1748, Mary Batchelder b May 20, 1719, d Dec
24, 1808, dau of Thomas and Sarah (Tuck). Children:

    a Abigail b Mch 16, 1750   b   Mary b Nov 5, 1751
    c John b Sept 19, 1753   d   Sarah b Dec 31, 1756; d Feb 22, 1760
    e Comfort b Mch 16, 1759; d Feb 15, 1760
    f Samuel b Mch 5, 1761; d May 13, 1779

Abigail Dow abbeaa d Nov 13, 1794; m Amos Towle; always lived
Hampton. Children:

a Amos b Apr 1776; d 1855; m Hannah Drake
b Sarah b June 22, 1778; d 1852; m Moses Leavitt
c Comfort b June 1781; d 1832; m David Marston; 2nd Cotton Marston
d Oliver b Mch 1783; blacksmith, m Betty Leavitt; d 1855
e Dolly b Feb 1785; m Jonathan Robinson; 2nd Simon Leavitt
f Hannah b Nov 1789; d 1866; m——Leavitt; 2nd Theodate Sanborn
g Abigail b Dec 3, 1791; d 1857; m Thomas Nudd akecaab

Mary Dow abbeab d Feb 13, 1828; m Jan 8, 1777, William Lane of
Hampton b Nov 23, 1753, d Oct 24, 1837, son of Dea William and Rachel
(Ward). Children:

a William b Oct 30, 1777; d Mch 6, 1793
b Samuel Dow b Oct 9, 1779; m May 19, 1805, Susanna James, dau of Joshua
    and Huldah (Fogg); settled in Exeter
c Joshua b Jan 22, 1782; d Sept 27, 1825, unm   d John b May 18, 1784
e Mary b Oct 24, 1786; d Apr 21, 1788
f Meshech b Apr 15, 1789; d June 15, 1862, unm
g Joel b Aug 25, 1791   h William b Apr 29, 1794

John Dow abbeac always lived in Hampton, d Feb 1, 1829; signed
the Association Test; served five days at defense of Portsmouth; always
active in town affairs; selectman 1812-3; in 1797 on important church
committee; in 1803 on committee to disentangle the town finances; in
1809 to arrange the town treatment of paupers; m Aug 1, 1781, Elizabeth Mace b June 6, 1763, d Feb 26, 1848, dau of Samuel and Sarah (May).
Children:

a Olive b Dec 19, 1782; d unm Apr 14, 1854; her son Oliver Dow b June 9, 1806,
    d unm Aug 24, 1848. A girl of 13 cannot be severely censured, and she was
    her father's heir. A notable laxity of morals is seen during this generation
    in Hampton, illegitimate children appearing in a number of the oldest
    families. Olive Dow sold the homestead, there being no one in her line to
    take it over
b Samuel b Aug 8, 1784
c Sarah b June 16, 1786; d Sept 2, 1865; m Nov 25, 1806, John Lane of No.
    Hampton; 4 children
d John b Apr 24, 1788; d May 6, 1788
e Elizabeth b July 10, 1789   f Nancy b May 26, 1796

Samuel Dow abbeacb, Lieut in 3rd N H 1814, later in Col Lovering's reg, received a grant of land and settled in Enosburg, Vt; m Nov
15, 1814, Louisa L Smith of Chester b 1789, d Enosburg after long widowhood July 27, 1863.   Children:

a Elizabeth Ladd b Sept 15, 1815; d Mch 5, 1879; m Sept 8, 1842, Levi Nichols;
    children,—George, Garrise, Helen, Lucy
b Martha Smith b Feb 18, 1817; m Jan 6, 1841, Lorin C Leach, farmer of Troy,
    Vt; children,—Isabella, Chloe, Martha Jane
c George Hamilton b Mch 11, 1819; d unm   d Samuel Henry b Dec 6, 1821
e Louisa Jane b Mch 1824; d Dec 20, 1825
f Horace Smith b May 4, 1831; d May 16, 1863; m and left a dau d young

Samuel H Dow abbeacbd succeeded to the 160 acre homestead
and was deacon of Congregational church. Census of 1850 gives him
as Daniel, his mother Louisa living with him, farm assessed $1300. Wife
Joanna is mentioned, also a Samuel Dow, probably a son d young. Samuel H d Mch 27, 1907; m Mch 31, 1847, Joanna K Adams of New
Ipswich, N H b Vt Apr 12, 1827, d Dec 27, 1891, dau of Ephraim and Sally

(Boutelle). Adams Gen gives them 6 children, but this is error. Two relatives named Adams lived with them but were never legally adopted; there were no other young people in the home, the line dying out. The Adams children:

a Addie b 1849   b James Henry b 1851

Sarah Dow abbeacc d Sept 2, 1865; m Nov 25, 1806, John Lane bap Jan 14, 1776, d June 14, 1868, son of Ebenezer and Huldah (Fogg); settled in Little River, N H. Children:

a John Dow d May 28, 1892, contractor and builder of Boston; m Margaret Dow aeeaeb of No Hampton; left 2 children
b Samuel Dow m May 11, 1853, Nancy Leavitt Lane, dau of Thomas; 2 children
c Nancy m John Knowles of Rye   d Ebenezer d June 5, 1875, ae 53

Elizabeth Dow abbeace d Jan 21, 1873; m May 16, 1810, Jabez Towle of Hampton b Apr 19, 1785, d June 6, 1847, son of Jabez and Sarah (Garland). A seaman at Newburyport, he became a carpenter after marriage; finally returning to Hampton, buying the Gen Jonathan Moulton mansion. Children, all in Newburyport:

a Charles Lewis d in infancy   b Charles d young
c Samuel m Pamelia Jones   d John Dow d Newburyport ae about 20
e Anthony m Hannah Jones, sister of Pamelia; moved to Greenfield, Mass.
f Elizabeth Frances b Feb 19, 1831; m Josiah D Mace of Hampton

Nancy Dow abbeacf d Mch 13, 1877; m June 25, 1815, Moses Brown b Oct 25, 1794, d Aug 3, 1866, son of Elisha and Annie L (Brown). Children:

a Jeremiah b Dec 8, 1816; d July 10, 1862; m Martha A Lane
b Oliver Albert b Oct 11, 1819; m Maria Clark
c Elizabeth Ann b Sept 1, 1829; d Apr 20, 1881; m Thomas J Towle

Abigail Dow abbeb d Jan 10, 1815; m Apr 4, 1745, Winthrop Sanborn, grandson of Josiah. He d Hampton Nov 17, 1796. Children:

a Abner b May 14, 1746; m 2nd Sarah Johnson
b Samuel b July 1, 1748; d Oct 4, 1748
c Molly b Nov 16, 1749; m 1st——Hall; 2nd Nathan Blake, son of Nathan abbee; d without issue Dec 23, 1820

Mary Dow abbec d Oct 16, 1819; m Dec 28, 1749, Benjamin Batchelder, son of Thomas and Sarah (Tuck) of Hampton. Children:

a John b Jan 23, 1751; d June 14, 1821; m Abigail Marston
b Comfort b Nov 8, 1756; m Joseph Keniston
c Mary b Jan 26, 1760; m David Moulton of Newmarket
d Benjamin b June 27, 1762; m Apr 7, 1789, Mary Brown, dau of Nathan
e Sarah b Oct 11, 1763; d Oct 15, 1840; m 1st Daniel Marston; 2nd Nathaniel Johnson
f Hannah b July 15, 1766; m Jan 18, 1789, John Sanborn of Newmarket and Parsonsfield

Hannah Batchelder abbecf m John Sanborn. Their dau Mary Sanborn m Col Bartlett Doe b 1785, d 1872; a child,——Charles Franklin Doe b 1833, d 1904, who gave the great library to the Univ of Calif.

Hannah Dow abbed d Sept 19, 1775; m Dec 28, 1749, Maj John Lane b Feb 14, 1726, d Mch 21, 1811, son of Dea Joshua and Bathsheba (Robie); they lived Kensington; he m 2nd Hannah Tuck, dau of Edward. Children:

  a Samuel b Dec 17, 1750; d 1811; m Judith Clifford; lived Sanbornton; 9 children
  b John b Feb 23, 1753; m Elizabeth Batchelder; lived Sanbornton; 8 children
  c Hannah b Nov 12, 1755; d July 26, 1778, unm
  d Comfort b Mch 23, 1758; d July 20, 1758
  e Mary b Oct 15, 1759; d 1806; m William Harper of Deerfield
  f Joshua b Aug 28, 1762; d 1829; m Huldah Hilliard
  g David b Feb 27, 1765; d 1810; m Judith Philbrick; lived Sanbornton
  h Joseph b Feb 26, 1769; m Elizabeth Lang; d 1813; lived Kensington; 9 children

Joseph Dow abbee, squire Dow, was town clerk for 35 years, succeeding his father and grandfather. Without being a politician, he was all his life in positions of town trust; selectman 1760 and 1775; signed Association Test; on committee to arrange money allowances to those who enlisted. In 1797 the church property was divided between the Congregationalists and Presbyterians, and he was chairman of the committee to make the division. All Hampton Dow remained Congregational. He was member of the Legislatures of 1782, 1787, 1788 and 1792; d Dec 16, 1806; m Dec 26, 1759, Dorothy Blake b May 30, 1734, d Nov 4, 1815, dau of Nathan abbebc and Judith (Batchelder). Children:

  a Dorothy b Dec 15, 1760 (Dolle in rec)
  b Josiah b Dec 25, 1764   c Isaiah b Sept 14, 1767; d Feb 1, 1808, unm
  d Reuben b Apr 17, 1770   e Simeon b Apr 17, 1770; d May 17, 1770

Dorothy Dow abbeea d Jan 18, 1849; m Jan 13, 1785, Simon Philbrick b Jan 12, 1757, d Aug 15, 1819, son of James and Tabitha (Dow) abbef; they settled in Effingham. Children:

  a Simeon   b Dorothy   c Joseph   d Ara   e Isaiah

Josiah Dow abbeeb, fourth generation of town clerks of Hampton, held that office 20 years; d Hampton Oct 11, 1840; m Oct 1, 1801, Hannah Moulton b May 6, 1766, d Aug 4, 1839, wid of John and dau of John (Josiah in State rec error) and Mary (Marston). Children:

  a Hannah b and d July 10, 1802   b Josiah b Nov 2, 1803
  c Joseph b Apr 12, 1807

Josiah Dow (Col) abbeebb was prominent in Hampton until he moved May 1870 to Charlton, Mass; d Aug 23, 1883. In 1827 he was made captain of the local rifle company and went to Boston to buy rifles. They were considered very handsome and cost $11 each. The company became the crack one of the regiment and Josiah became Colonel in 1832, always keeping the title. An organizer of the first fire company in Hampton and in 1833 prosecutor of illegal liquor sellers: m 1st Sept 23, 1828, Almira Nudd akecafd d May 10, 1834; 2nd Apr 29, 1835, Eunice Young b 1800, d Feb 6, 1858, dau of Daniel of Hollis, Me, and wid of Jeremiah

Moulton; 3rd Aug 19, 1858, Mary Ann Lamprey, dau of Reuben and
Polly (Marston).   Children:

    a John Moulton b July 9, 1829   b Joseph Warren b Dec 3, 1830
    c Jonathan Nudd b Jan 1, 1833
    d Charles Edwin b July 11, 1860; d Aug 3, 1880

John M Dow abbeebba m Nov 7, 1860, Mary E Crouse of Lawrence, Mass.   Child:

    a Eva May b July 22, 1866; d Sept 18, 1890

Joseph W Dow abbeebbb moved to Boston 1883; was 1st sgt of
Winnacunnett Guards, disabled after year of service; thereafter re-
cruiting officer for New Hampshire; postmaster about 1860.   His house
and barn burned in 1867; rebuilt, to burn again 1874. Selectman 1872;
d Hampton Apr 18, 1912; m 1st Sept 15, 1856, Hannah Ann Perkins
b Rye, d Hampton Nov 1, 1858, ae 23-7-26, dau of James and Sarah
(Rand); 2nd Nov 24, 1859, Victoria A. Knowles, dau of Jesse and
Miriam (Leavitt).   Children:

    a Henry Warren b Mch 2, 1858; d Sept 9, 1858
    b Amy Warren b June 15, 1861
    c Almira Burton b July 12, 1863; m Jan 21, 1892, Thomas Otis Ward
    d Ralph Percy b Apr 4, 1867; d Apr 23, 1890
    e Electa Wilder b May 5, 1869; d Jan 28, 1888

Amy W Dow abbeebbbb m Aug 17, 1882, Edward O Gilman of Boston.   Children:

    a Leroy Sutherland b Jan 10, 1885
    b Ralph Edward b May 19, 1891; d Jan 16, 1892

Jonathan N Dow abbeebbc, first man of Hampton to die in Civil
War, corporal, promoted to color sgt for gallantry.   Eleven Hampton
men in Guards, attached to brigade of Gen Neal Dow adhccbb, division
of W T Sherman.   Jonathan contracted typhoid and d Hilton Head,
S C, Feb 20, 1862.   His brother brought the body back to Hampton.
He m Apr 10, 1858, Mirabah A Lane, dau of James and Mary Ann
(Blake); she m 2nd Nov 20, 1864, Freeman Brown; 3rd Horace O Mace.
Child by Jonathan:

    a Luella Almira b Sept 9, 1858

Luella A Dow abbeebbca m Henry Warren Emery b May 24, 1852,
son of Isaac and Susan (Pitts); lived Rand's Hill, Hampton.   Children:

    a Annie Lawrie b July 23, 1880
    b Ella May b Nov 19, 1882; d Apr 18, 1883

Joseph Dow abbeebc, illustrious author of Hist Hampton, was well
qualified for the work, his five ancestors in direct line having been town
clerks for 100 consecutive years.   He grad Dartmouth 1833; A M in
1836; salutatorian of his class, which included Judge Asa Fowler of Con-

cord, Dr Edward Spaulding of Nashua, Hon James F Joy of Detroit, John Ford LL D, and others of distinction. He became principal of Pembroke Academy for 4 years; then in charge of the Gardiner, Me, Lyceum. The panic of 1837 came and next year this school went down in the general crash. He then taught in academies at West Machias, Pompey, N Y, and elsewhere until in 1862 he retired to his native Hampton. He was commissioned Maj of militia in 1867 by Gov Isaac Hill; was justice of the peace and quorum throughout the State. One of his first duties on return to Hampton was to make a new survey of the town. In 1860 he was elected president of the N H Historical Society. He engaged in probate and other legal business, which brought him in contact with the old wills and deeds of Hampton. From 1852 to his death he devoted himself to writing the History of Hampton, which was almost finished. His daughter completed it within a year and published it. Little sale was anticipated for the two-volume work and the edition was small. It was not "pushed." After several years Miss Dow sold the "remainder" for a trifle to a dealer. For years it was obtainable at about original price, $7.00. It is now worth about treble that. That the book is the finest example of a New England town history is everywhere conceded. No equal genealogical effort has ever been accomplished.

Joseph d Dec 16, 1889; M Apr 14, 1835, m Abigail French b Aug. 4, 1810, d Jan 28, 1870, dau of Rev Jonathan D D of No Hampton. Children:

   a Joseph Henry b Apr 22, 1836
   b Hannah Maria b Gardiner Mch 1, 1838; d unm Saginaw, Mich, Jan 3, 1919; a devoted Methodist; lived with a niece in Saginaw; completed the abbeeb line for this Book
   c Lucy Ellen b Oct 4, 1840; d Cleveland, Ohio, Jan 1896, unm. Her father's companion and amanuensis, the history was always almost as familiar to her as to him
   d Abby Frances b Dec 25, 1842; d Dec 29, 1869, unm
   e Eunice Appleton b June 14, 1846; d Sept 17, 1847
   f Elizabeth French b and d May 19, 1848
   g Lemira Farrar b and d May 19, 1848

Joseph H Dow abbeebca lived Cleveland, master mechanic of Chisholm Steel Shovel Works; m Nov 24, 1863, Sarah Jane Bunnell, dau of Capt Alva. Children:

   a Herbert Henry b Canada Feb 26, 1866
   b Mary Edith b Derby, Conn, Aug 19, 1868
   c Abby French b Derby June 20, 1870
   d Helen Josephine b May 30, 1876

Herbert H Dow abbeebcaa of Midland, Mich, is manager of the Dow Chemical Co, a distinguished chemist. Mch 16, 1917: Herbert H Dow is making synthetic indigo at the rate of 400 lbs daily. This is the first made in the United States. The Government dyestuff expert reports the American consumption as about 35,000 lbs a day, all of which has been imported. (News clipping.) He m Nov 16, 1892, Grace A Ball, dau of George William.   Children:

  a Helen b Midland Mch 16, 1894
  b Ruth Alden b Nov 16, 1895; m Apr 7, 1917, Leland I Doan of Detroit
  c Willard Henry b Jan 4, 1897; grad Univ of Mich; m Sept 3, 1921, Martha L
     Pratt, dau of L E
  d Osborn Curtis b Nov 20, 1899; d young
  e Alden Ball b Apr 10, 1904   f Margaret Grace b Jan 3, 1906
  g Dorothy Darling b Jan 2, 1908

Helen J Dow abbeebcad m Thomas Griswold Jr of Midland. Children:

  a Josephine b Dec 11, 1899   b Nelson Dow b June 1901
  c Leila Ruth b Aug 1913

Mary Edith Dow abbeebcab has been since 1912 head of the Saginaw Public Library, resigning 1923.

Reuben Dow abbeed was in the militia 1814; d Nov 12, 1848; m Jan 26, 1797, Mary Clark bap July 1, 1770, d Mch 3, 1850, dau of John and Mary (Mace) of Portsmouth.   Children:

  a Dorothy b about 1798; d Dec 30, 1835, unm
  b Polly b Nov 27, 1800; d Nov 20, 1879
  c Hannah b about 1802; d May 7, 1837

Hannah Dow abbeedc m John D Lamprey of Hampton b Nov 1801, d May 10, 1874, son of Dudley and Miriam (Locke).   After her d he m 2nd her sister Polly.   Children, by Hannah:

  a Mary Abby b July 26, 1831; m 1st Levi A Brown, son of Levi; 2nd Daniel
     Palmer
  b Joseph A b July 1835; d May 10, 1836

Tabitha Dow abbef d May 6, 1812; m Sept 3, 1754, James Philbrick b Feb 10, 1727, d Feb 28, 1809, son of Dea Joseph and Ann (Dearborn).   Children:

  a Joseph b June 7, 1755; d Dec 21, 1814; m Jemima Blake
  b Simon b Jan 12, 1757
  c James b Oct 3, 1761; d Aug 8, 1836; m Mary Towle
  d Samuel b Nov 10, 1763; d May 20, 1851; m Priscilla Towle
  e David b June 30, 1767; d Feb 15, 1831; m 1st Jane Marston; dau of Simon;
     2nd Hannah Graves; settled in Ossipee

Jonathan Dow abbeg m July 31, 1761, Comfort Brown of Hampton b Sept 14, 1738, d ae 99; moved to Brentwood in 1769, where he enlisted July 1775, under Capt Henry Dearborn, Col John Stark; receipted Sept for 3 mos, 3 days pay; settlers of New Hampton by 1784, perhaps earlier.   Children:

  a Samuel b Apr 16, 1762; d Apr 23, 1762   b Levi b Mch 31, 1763
  c Comfort bap Jan 27, 1765; d July 24, 1766
  d Hannah b June 9, 1767; m 1787 Jacob Brown
  e Ruth b May 20, 1769   f Jonathan b July 31, 1771
  g Comfort b Dec 25, 1773
  h Mary b Sept 7, 1776; d Oct 14, 1810; m Nathaniel Sanborn
  i Joseph b 1778; d unm

Levi Dow abbegb, farmer of New Hampton, d of small pox Dec 17, 1849; m Jan 1785 Abigail Godfrey b Oct 10, 1756, d Dec 17, 1822, dau of Joseph and Susannah (Morrill) of Poplin. Children:

  a Susanna b Sept 19, 1784
  b Sarah b Mch 19, 1786; d 1825; m Nov 15, 1804; Thomas Dolloff of Meredith
  c Comfort b Nov 20, 1787; d Aug 30, 1790
  d Joseph Godfrey b Aug 30, 1789   e Jonathan b Oct 5, 1791
  f Nancy b Sept 6, 1796; m John Gordon. State rec gives Mary m Apr 17, 1825, John Gordon, both of New Hampton
  g Abigail b Nov 25, 1799; d Apr 21, 1884; m June 29, 1826, Robert W Moore of Bristol
  h Eliza b Dec 5, 1801; d Sept 12, 1803   i Levi b Dec 15, 1803

Susanna Dow abbegba m Josiah Robinson of Pembroke d Sept 1864, ae 84, farmer and shoemaker, son of Benjamin and Elizabeth (Colby). Children:

  a Leavitt b Sept 1804; d Feb 2, 1882; m Nov 1853 Nancy Cawley of Sanbornton
  b Eliza Dow b Oct 1806; m June 1827 James Blake of Sanbornton
  c Abigail Dow b Aug 1808; m Jan 1831 William Moore of Bristol
  d Sally Tilton b July 1810; m May 1830 John Calvin Gordon of New Hampton
  e Isaac Leavitt b June 22, 1812; m 1st Jan 1836 Tirzah G Gordon; 2nd 1845 Sarah A Adams of Methuen, Mass
  f Nancy Dow b June 1814; d Dec 1857; m June 1836 Payne Blake of Sanbornton
  g Joseph Dow b May 1816; m Apr 19, 1851, Jerusha Mason of Bristol
  h Mary Ann b Apr 13, 1819; m Dec 1837 Samuel John Dearborn
  i Susannah b June 1821; m Martin Luther Fowler of Haverhill and New Hampton
  j Harriet Dow b July 4, 1823; d Aug 1826
  k Angeline b Mch 1825; m John Knox Robinson of Pembroke, her cousin
  l Rufus Lewis b Apr 1827; m Pauline Lowell of Frankfort, N Y; a teacher of penmanship, he lost his right hand in Civil War; learned to write expertly with left hand

Sarah Dow abbegbb m Thomas Dolloff; moved to Sutton, Vt. He d; she m 2nd—Allen, by whom a son Nathaniel lived to old age. A son by 1st m married Melissa Thompson b Coventry, Vt; their dau Melissa Sally m—Stevens and had a son Charles Dolloff Stevens, in 1926 clerk and treasurer of Lyndon, Vt.

Joseph G Dow abbegbd of Bridgewater d Dec 3, 1831; m Dec 8, 1811, Polly Boynton b Mch 22, 1791, d July 31, 1863, m 2nd Robert Heath. Children:

  a Mary Jane Boynton b Feb 8, 1813
  b William Boynton b Apr 2, 1815; d July 17, 1893
  c George Washington b May 6, 1817   d Eliza Ann b Dec 2, 1819
  e John Mooney b Mch 10, 1822; d Bristol Dec 20, 1845
  f Joseph Godfrey b Mch 22, 1825; d Larene, Wash, June 9, 1885
  g Martha Custis b Dec 20, 1827

Mary J B Dow abbegbda d Mch 10, 1894; m (int pub Mch 3, 1834) John C Downing, carpenter of New Hampton. They moved 1853 to Healdsburg, Calif, where he established a furniture store and was an undertaker. Both became enthusiastic in the Christian Adventist denomination, but in later years not one of the children continued in it. Mrs Downing never lost track of the kinsfolk who remained behind in N H and kept a sort of family record, in which she noted 31 1st cousins of her children.   This document has been a great genealogical help.   Her own children:

a   Ellen Antoinette b Bristol Dec 22, 1838; m Nov 14, 1858, John Washington Bagley; 7 children; her youngest Alice has been for many years traveling nurse for the Metropolitan Life Insurance Co
b   Joseph Henry b Bristol Nov 28, 1840; photographer, m Healdsburg Dec 3, 1873, Mrs Matilda (Prince) Burlinghame; 1 child
c   Clarence Victor Blossom b Lowell, Mass, May 22, 1850; m May 22, 1878, Mary Ann Frances Smith; lived San Francisco

William B Dow abbegbdb lived some years in Lowell, Mass, where his brother in law came and found jobs from time to time.   The two families remained closely together all their lives.   William m Barnstead, N H Oct 31, 1838, Rooxbe George Tuttle b 1821.   Several years later they bought a farm in Thornton, where the 1850 census gives him as farmer assessed $1,000.   In 1853 he drops from tax list, for many years genealogically untraced.   A letter from his brother, who discovered Calif while a soldier in the Mexican War, changed the whole current of the lives of two families.   William Dow and John Downing sold out completely and crossed the continent with wives and eleven small children.   They landed at Healdsburg.   William took up a ranch and, as population came, building up quite a town, he subdivided most of his ranch, the tract still known as Dow's Addition.   Rooxbe Dow died nine years after coming to Calif: he m 2nd 1864 Mrs Fannie Tamar (White) Love b Kane Co, Ill, 1833, d Los Gatos Oct 8, 1895.   In 1883 he was living San Francisco on a competence; d Los Gatos June 17, 1893.

Thornton 1850 census gives Mary Dow b 1816 and Eliza Dow b 1843, presumably wid mother and dau, but apparently not of abbegb line.   Children of William B and Rooxbe:

a   Francis Orett b Sept 21, 1840; d Oct 27, 1854
b   Lorenzo b Apr 5, 1842; d Calif Dec 12, 1905; unt
c   George Powers b Feb 27, 1844; unt
d   Mary Hannah b Jan 16, 1846; m Healdsburg Jan 1, 1863, Allan H Kirkpatrick; d Mch 27, 1864, with infant dau
e   Frank Tuttle b Jan 16, 1848.   The Downing family rec says he m Hattie A Sprey, but makes no subsequent mention, nothing of the two other brothers except as above
f   Abigail Moore b Thornton Jan 16, 1850
g   William Robert b July 16, 1852
h   John Mooney b Feb 12, 1858; d Dec 8, 1859
i   Julia Elizabeth b June 13, d Sept 1860

Abigail M Dow abbegbdbf d Boulder Creek; m Nov 7, 1869, Washington Irving Robinson b Galveston, Tex, Oct 29, 1846; lived Healdsburg and Cloverdale, ranchers.   No member of this whole family went into gold mining.   Children:

a   Cornelius Irving b Dec 24, 1871; d Jan 1, 1872
b   Frederick William b Dec 31, 1872   c   Ruel Ambrose b Jan 4, 1875
d   Irving Henry b Feb 1, 1876   e   Harriet Ellen b Apr 25, 1878
f   Chester Garfield b Sept 7, 1880; d Jan 1, 1882
g   Gertrude Lavinia b Oct 28, 1885   h   Alice Emily b Nov 27, 1887

William R Dow abbegbdbg lived several places in Calif; d Mch 26, 1907; m Santa Rosa Nov 12, 1877, Laura Christina MacReynolds b Sonoma Co Jan 31, 1859. Children:

a   Edna Orett b Sept 1, 1878
b   Jessie Lee b Aug 20, 1880; d July 8, 1886

George Washington Dow abbegbdc, farmer, d Bristol May 9, 1891; owned considerable interest in some strawboard mills; m Oct 14, 1841, Adeline Center Gurdy b Bristol Dec 8, 1816, d Bristol Sept 10, 1865, dau of Elisha; m 2nd Worcester, Mass, Nov 26, 1869, Amanda Jane Rollins b Bristol June 11, 1826, d 1921, dau of Gilman and Sally (Roberts), wid of Joseph F. Children:

a   Charles Boynton b Lowell, Mass, Dec 22, 1842
b   John Mooney b Bristol Apr 16, 1846; d Strafford Bow Lake Sept 14, 1909

Charles B Dow abbegbdca m Bristol Sept 26, 1863, Eliza Adeline Blake b Haverhill, N H Mch 22, 1846. He was fairly prominent in Bristol, secy of K of P; but for some unstated reason he changed his name rather late in life to Charles Dow Stone and went to California. His children remained. Children:

a   Cora Moore b Feb 13, 1864; m Sept 7, 1899, Frank C Heald of Manchester
b   Mary Ethel b Sept 14, 1867; m Sanbornton Mch 11, 1893, Josiah R Dearborn of Sanbornton
c   James Leon b Aug 15, 1868

James L Dow abbegbdcac, druggist of Lancaster, m Aug 25, 1891, Jennie A Porter b Lancaster. At least one child:

a   Dorothea Porter b Mch 31, 1897; d Lancaster Feb 2, 1898

John M Dow abbegbdcb, in 1880 peddler of Bristol, later hotel keeper of Strafford, d Strafford Sept 14, 1909; m Meredith Dec 21, 1881, Elizabeth Randolph b Eng Oct 29, 1855; d July 14, 1910, dau of William F and Lucy (Sharp). In State transcript of rec this name has wrongly become Flude. No children.

Eliza A Dow abbegbdd m Jan 2, 1840, John Blake Marston of New Hampton b Bridgewater Jan 17, 1812, son of Jeremiah and Polly (Blake). In 1885 they visited the kinsfolk in Healdsburg, the first meeting in 32 years. Children:

a   Mary Ellen b Dec 21, 1840; m Elbridge Frank Lowe; 2nd John Elliott Wright of Redding, Calif
b   Louisa Webster b Feb 10, 1843; d Dec 10, 1880; m Dec 10, 1868, George W Armstrong, founder of Armstrong Transfer Co
c   George Dow b Feb 27, 1845; d Apr 6, 1855
d   Emma Frances b Jan 30, 1847; m David Mitchell Brown
e   Jennette Eliza b Apr 22, 1849; m Dec 12, 1878, James Daws Woodruff of Everett, Mass
f   Albert Jeremiah b Mch 19, 1852; physician of Philadelphia; m Ella May Green

Joseph G Dow abbegbdf volunteered 1846 for the Mexican war, his regiment stationed N Y City and taking 6 mos around the Horn to San Francisco. While stationed at Sonoma he met Mary Ann Crouch, whom he m Apr 20, 1850. This energetic young woman b near Crawfordsville, Ind, not satisfied with her step mother ran away, joined a family of neighbors and drove an ox cart all the way to Sonoma, a journey of over 6 mos. She was a grand dau of James Crouch, Rev veteran, and was living Spokane 1923 ae 92. Mustered out of the army, Joseph became a pioneer temperance lecturer, traveling all over the Pacific slope. For three-quarters of a century the American use of the word temperance seems confined to total abstinence from alcohol. It is rather notable that the pioneers in this line in Maine and California were both Dows. Lecturing on temperance, however, could not furnish a livelihood, but Joseph was an able worker between times. In 1878 the Northern Pacific R R was approaching Spokane and Joseph took a contract for constructing a division. This was done quite profitably for both parties and Joseph took up land at Larene, where he d June 19, 1885.

Children:

a Martha Matilda b Apr 20, 1851; d about 1900, unm
b George William b Sept 10, 1852   c Andrew Jackson b June 18, 1854
d Charles Henry b Apr 17, 1856   e Joseph Boynton b 1858; d May 24, 1875
f Mary Elizabeth b July 24, 1868; all b Healdsburg

George W Dow abbegbdfb d Spokane Jan 26, 1919; of Healdsburg, m Nov 2, 1879, Lucinda Jane Dutton b Pike County, Ill. They moved to Crescent City, later to Spokane. Children:

a George Harold b Oct 31, 1880   b Elsie b and d Sept 13, 1882
c Alma b Apr 15, 1885; d Apr 19, 1892   d Ina

Harold George Dow abbegbdfba m Spokane May 5, 1919, Mrs Anna Henghan. Only child:

a Robert Harold b La Grande June 12, 1921

Ina Dow abbegbdfbc m Spokane Sept 27, 1908, Paul E Weatherhead; div Oct 1920; m 2nd Colville, Wash, Mch 11, 1922, Benjamin Lockrem Johnson; took a college course, returned west in 1925. Children:

a Paul Elton (Weatherhead) b Spokane Mch 9, 1913
b Lockrem Harold b Davenport Mch 15, 1924

Andrew J Dow abbegbdfc m Healdsburg Apr 22, 1875, Fidelia Rosella Catlin b May 25, 1860; moved to Crescent City, thence about 1920 to Spokane, where he d Nov 17, 1925, survived by wid and 8 children:

a Alice Estella b May 10, 1876; m——Apr 15, 1895
b Andrew Elmer b Oct 30, 1878; d Sept 14, 1893
c Bertha Ula b Dec 14, 1884   d Ralph Elom b Apr 22, 1887; of Spokane
e Marcia Cecil b May 16, 1890   f Frieda Grace b Mch 10, 1892
g Hugh Arnold b May 20, 1894; now of Santa Rosa, Calif
h Orrin Ernest b Aug 12, 1897; in 1925 of Davenport, Wash
i ——dau. His obituary names the dau, Mrs D Gilmore, Mrs W W Blagden, Mrs W Morrill of Harbor, Mrs W S Pollock of Seattle, Mrs G E Huffman of Davenport

Charles H Dow abbegbdfd m Oct 12, 1873, Anjenet Ella Augusta May Tubbs of Healdsburg b Utica, Wis, Apr 29, 1855; moved to Spokane about 1880; div; he now lives Roundup, Mont.   Children:

    a Charles Arthur b Aug 12, 1874; of Tacoma
    b Allan Clare b Aug 23, 1876
    c Eva Alice b Mch 5, 1879   d Nettie May b July 4, 1882
    e Joseph Ross b Apr 10, 1885   f Ruis Elnora b Oct 3, 1887

Mary E Dow abbegbdff m Oct 23, 1887, Albert Wyman Maltbie; now live Wenatchie, Wash. She sent to the Author a copy of the Downing family rec, which established the connection of the family with its N H forebears.   Children, both grad Univ Washington: .

    a Achsah Adelia b Larene Oct 9, 1888; m Oct 9, 1911, Milton Rawlings; of Athol, Idaho; 3 children. A keen genealogist, quite successful in tracing lines of Rev ancestry
    b Edna Alice Theodora b Waterville, Wash, Sept 12, 1890; m June 8, 1913, James Collins; live La Grange, Ill; 3 children

Martha C Dow abbegbdg m Apr 6, 1843, Charles B Heath of Bristol; later joined the family in Healdsburg. Children:

    a Henry Ayers b Apr 16, 1844; m Feb 16, 1874, Barbara McEachern; 1 child
    b Hannah May b Apr 1847; d New Hampton, unm
    c William Augustus b Mch 7, 1849; m Mary Caroline Dame; 7 children
    d Olive Jane b July 1852; d unm   e Josephine b Oct 1854; d unm

Jonathan Dow abbegbe, farmer and school master, moved from New Hampton to Salem; d 1833; m Aug 10, 1817, Harriet Sanborn b Rumney Jan 20, 1797, d New Hampton Nov 19, 1865.   Children:

    a Stephen Bean b Plymouth about 1818
    b David Moore Russell b Oct 1820

Stephen B Dow abbegbea made Salem, Mass, his home port; followed the sea 38 years, 9 as mate, 13 as master; normal weight about 240; was known to hoist unaided an anchor weighing 1,000 lbs. He d New Hampton Mch 17, 1871, from inflammation of tongue after 36 hours; m July 30, 1854, Frances Maria Harris b Lowell, Mass, Mch 28, 1834, d New Hampton July 11, 1917, dau of Rufus and Lucy (Sanborn). Children, all b New Hampton:

    a Charles Warren b Jan 22, 1855   b William Henry, his twin
    c Hattie Simpson b June 23, 1860   d Stephen Webster b June 24, 1864
    e Walter Raleigh b Nov 11, 1868   f Edward Everett b Dec 4, 1871

Charles W Dow abbegbeaa located in Chicago; at 17 went to Zanzibar as clerk for a N Y importing house; stayed 3 years; went to Bombay for same house, then to New Zealand; returned to La Crosse, Wis; in 1921 manager for R G Dun & Co, Minneapolis, Minn; m 1st May 1, 1882, Pauline Avery Whidden; 2nd June 6, 1900, Louise Caldwell. Children:

    a Arthur Stephen b Oct 14, 1882; murdered Newberry Mts, Nev, about 1911 ' unm
    b Helen Louise b Jan 22, 1884; m and lives Santa Monica, Calif
    c Alice Azuza b Dec 25, 1887; m and lives Los Angeles

William H Dow abbegbeab went to Cedarvale, Kan; returned to New Hampton; 1921 of Enfield, N H; m Mch 1, 1893, Mrs Ellen (Hall) Ellis, ae 27. No children.

Stephen W Dow abbegbead was killed on railroad July 31, 1889; m Apr 1, 1888, Carrie F Fletcher, dau of Samuel and Mary. No children.

Walter R Dow abbegbeae lives New Hampton; was postmaster; m Dec 25, 1893, Sarah M Curtis, ae 18, dau of John and Caroline (Bailey). No children.

Edward Everett Dow abbegbeaf, *repairer of pipe organs in La Crosse, Wis,* m Oct 19, 1900, Amy M Tappan.

David M R Dow abbegbeb, carpenter of Charlestown, Mass, was for 20 years Constable in the Superior Court, Boston; d Sept 16, 1879; m Aug 27, 1844, Mary Elvira Bullock b Boston May 24, 1824.   Children:

  a   Mary Florietta b Mch 1845   b   Jabez Stephen b Nov 15, 1846
  c   Harriet   d   Elizabeth   e   ——, a son

Jabez S Dow abbegbebb, machinist of Dorchester, m Nov 16, 1868, Sarah Mitchell Ricker b Avon, Me, Jan 29, 1847.   Children:

  a   David Elwyn b May 8, 1870; in 1915 manager in Bangor, Me; letter in 1922
        returned, not found.   Untraced
  b   Stephen Ricker b Feb 18, 1872; m July 20, 1892, Marie Elizabeth Weale; m
        2nd Feb 18, 1905; Amy E. Gaskell, ae 37, dau of Tyler 13 and Eliza H (Daniel)
        Member Boston Stock Exchange and president of a chain of copper com-
        panies, having exhausted all his own recourses to sustain the stocks of them
        on the Exchange, used treasury funds for the purpose.   Was expelled and
        served in State's prison, paroled 1917
  c   Sadie May b July 25, 1876
  d   Nina Celeste b July 15, 1881; d Sept 3, 1881
  e   Martha Louise b Feb 19, 1888

Levi Dow abbegbi, farmer of New Hampton, assessed 1850 at $1,500, moved to Canterbury; d Nov 23, 1889; m Dec 27, 1831, Hannah Goss Drake d Dec 8, 1878, ae 67, dau of Dea Nathaniel and Deborah. His family became considerable land owners and figure frequently in Hist Canterbury.   Children, all b New Hampton:

  a   Hosea b Feb 4, 1833; d Aug 13, 1834
  b   Sumner Adams b Apr 24, 1834   c   Olwyn Warland b Apr 10, 1836
  d   Mary Amanda b Mch 19, 1839   e   Tirzah Ann Robinson b July 11, 1843
  f   Nathaniel Harland b Feb 8, 1845

Sumner A Dow abbegbib d Concord July 27, 1903; m May 30, 1856, Ann Maria Gordon of New Hampton, d Northfield Apr 22, 1882, dau of Daniel S and Belinda (Cass); moved 1858 to Canterbury, thence to Northfield, where he had a meat business; postmaster of Northfield Depot 11 years; moved 1885 to Concord.   Children:

  a   Electa M b New Hampton Apr 8, 1857
  b   Lellen M (Lillian Maria) b Canterbury Nov 25, 1862
  c   Charles S b Jan 29, 1865
  d   Lura Amanda b Sanbornton Bridge Aug 28, 1868
  e   Guy b Northfield Oct 11, 1872   f   Levi Smith b Sept 8, 1876

Electa M Dow abbegbiba d Concord Feb 1, 1895; m Apr 10, 1875, Whitten Ludlow, railroad employe of Northfield.   Children:

a   Bertha H   b   Carroll H m 1898
c   Effie L m 1899 Edward D Paige   d   Maria P   e   Roy E
f   Emilie E

Lellen M Dow abbegbibb m July 22, 1880, Laurien Davis of Northfield.   Children:

a   Allen T   b   Mary Lake

Charles S Dow abebgbibc, stationary engineer, d July 28, 1904; m July 1, 1886, Lizzie Hoyt of Canaan.   Children:

a   Anna   b   John b Mch 26, 1889: d Mch 27, 1889
c   Robert William b Canaan May 29, 1892; d Oct 30, 1892

Lura A Dow abbegbibd m Oct 22, 1886, Elmer Young, railroad employe of Concord.   Children:

a   Elizabeth J   b   William D   c   Electa M   d   Ernest E
e   Helen S

Guy Dow abbgebibe of Pembroke and Concord, railroad employe, was killed in collision Mch 20, 1908; m Dec 16, 1893, Ida Eldean Colby, ae 19, of Bow, dau of Dicy and Eldora.   Children:

a   Robert Guy b Oct 5, 1895
b   Sumner Adams b Concord July 5, 1897; d Pembroke Oct 7, 1906
c   Ethel May b May 19, 1899; d Concord May 28, 1899
d   Ruth Evelyn b May 19, 1899
e   Lura Maude d Concord Oct 2, 1901, ae 9 days

Robert G Dow abbegbibea, car inspector of Concord, m Rockland, Me, Aug 11, 1919, Ethel E Kalloch, ae 22, dau of Adam B and Caroline T (Staples)

Levi Smith Dow abbegbibf, veteran of 1898, railroad engineer of Haverhill, N H, m Sept 25, 1903, Arabella Peck Bailey, ae 23, dau of Thomas and Mary (Corey).   Children:

a   Allein (dau) b June 1, 1908
b   Levi Paul b Dec 26, 1909   c —, son b June 18, 1915

Olwyn W Dow abbegbic, shoemaker of Belmont, m Sophia Ingalls Clifford, dau of Solomon M and Matilda (Ingalls); went to Calif 1858 and 1863; returned 1865 to Canterbury, a farmer.   Children:

a   —d Dec 30, 1863; ae 2 days
b   Leonora Mary b June 15, 1866; d Canterbury Mch 1, 1898; m Jan 1, 1890,
        John Peverley; child, George Dow b Canterbury Jan 19, 1895
c   Lizzie Adella b May 27, 1868; d Dec 8, 1876
d   Edwin Weston b Jan 22, 1871
e   Mary Amanda b June 17, 1873; d Apr 1, 1899

Edwin W Dow abbegbicd of East Canterbury m May 27, 1906, Annie May Pickard b 1876.   Child:

a   Pauline b Dec 22, 1908

Mary Amanda Dow abbegbid d 1868; m George W Dearborn of Canterbury; left a son,—Elmer W m Northfield 1893.

Tirzah A R Dow abbegbie, teacher, m Dec 13, 1876, Jonathan Smith, son of John and Susan (Stearns) of Peterborough, grad Dartmouth 1871, veteran of Civil War, editor, member of Legislature and for many years a judge. She d Clinton, Mass, Aug 28, 1881. Children:

a　Theodore b Sept 25, 1877
b　Susan Dow b May 24, 1879; grad Smith College 1902; asst principal Clinton
　　High School

Nathaniel H Dow abbegbif moved 1864 to Methuen, Mass, and 1869 to Calif; settled 1871 in Wakefield, Mass, stone mason and contractor; was road commissioner; m 1st Margaret Campbell b Boston, d Wakefield, dau of Philip and Mary Ann of Scotland; 2nd 1894 Ida M Stinson (State rec gives Harlon and his age 47). Another rec gives m 2nd Aug 15, 1893, Louisa Frances Smith, ae 35, dau of Rufus and Elizabeth. Children:

a　Agnes M b Wakefield Mch 3, 1874; m J W Murphy, leather merchant of Boston; children,—Norman, William, Arthur, Agnes, Pearl
b　Bertha b 1876; d 1878　　c　Nathan Drake b Canterbury Oct 26, 1895

Nathan D Dow abbegbifc lives Belmont; m July 23, 1917, Eliza M Smith, ae 17, dau of Elmer H and Hattie (Weymouth).

Hannah Dow abbegd m Jacob Brown; moved 1819 from New Hampton to Sutton, Vt. At least 2 dau:

a　——m——Gordon. A son Lewis was alive in Lyndon, ae 84, in 1923
b　——m——Chapman. A son David, ae 91, was vigorous in Lyndon 1923

Ruth Dow abbege m Sanbornton Mch 15, 1800, Dudley Kelley b 1761, of New Durham, d 1836, son of Darby and Sarah (Dudley); they lived New Hampton; she d May 21, 1830. Children:

a　Jonathan Dow m Polly Gordon　　b　Polly Nichols m Eliphalet Gordon
c　Nancy b July 30, 1807; m Otto W Perkins; a dau Sarah Dudley m Harvey
　　A Jones of Sycamore, Ill
d　Sarah Dudley m Nathan W Dearborn

Jonathan Dow abbegf of Brentwood was a pioneer of New Hampton by 1782; d Jan 31, 1850; m 1790 Sally Hanniford (also Hunnaford) b Sept 17, 1771, d Nov 24, 1832, dau of Capt Peter, who lived New Hampton by 1790. At that time he took into his household his father David of Northwood and stepmother, both being old and liable to become public charges. Children:

a　Abigail b Feb 26, 1791　　b　Comfort b Mch 5, 1793
c　Peter b May 2, 1795　　　d　Jonathan b Mch 27, 1797
e　Dana b July 16, 1799　　　f　Joseph b Sept 29, 1801; d Mch 8, 1822, unm
g　Jacob b Nov 7, 1803
h　Sally b Apr 3, 1806; m Nov 4, 1827, David Gordon, both of New Hampton
i　Polly b June 1808; d Apr 7, 1817
j　Mark b Jan 24, 1812　　　k　Levi b Mch 15, 1814
l　John H b Apr 13, 1816; d Feb 21, 1844; presumably unm

Abigail Dow abbegfa d Sept 29, 1872; m Sept 17, 1807, Daniel Huckins, son of Dea James and Dorcas (Bickford) of New Hampton. Children:

- a Nathan b Apr 5, 1808   b David b Feb 12, 1810
- c Jonathan Dolloff b Mch 24, 1812; m Abigail Smith, wid of Stephen Dolloff
- d Daniel b May 21, 1814; d June 19, 1818   e Calvin b Nov 5, 1816
- f Sarah b Aug 25, 1819; d Aug 2, 1894; m Jan 10, 1841, Ezekiel Pike, son of Daniel and Sarah (French) of New Hampton
- g Abigail b Sept 25, 1824; d May 6, 1849; m Daniel C Kelley, son of Daniel and Sarah of Manchester
- h Daniel B b 1826   i Joseph D b Aug 4, 1828
- j Dana D b New Hampton May 22, 1830; d Bay City, Mich, May 1, 1865; lived Lowell, Mass; left a son Albert D b Mch 23, 1859
- k Hosea Q b 1832; of Saugus, Mass; m Helen Davis Nickerson

Comfort Dow abbegfb m Apr 2, 1818, Rufus Prescott. A dau:

- a Mary Dow b New Hampton Nov 20, 1818; d Mch 31, 1893; m John H Harper, farmer of New Hampton, b Sept 5, 1914, d Dec 1906.

Peter Dow abbegfc d Dec 16, 1863; farm assessed $2,000 in 1850; m Apr 7, 1817, Mary Ann Prescott b 1798, both of New Hampton. Children, all b New Hampton, perhaps more than here appear:

- a Perrin B   b Oct 17, 1820   b Sarah H b Oct 19, 1824
- c Oren Frank b May 25, 1830   d John b 1835; untraced

Perrin B Dow abbegfca, drayman, d Calif about 1853; m Dec 8, 1841, Ruth B Huckins b July 4, 1812, d Feb 5, 1907. Children:

- a George L b Aug 1842; d Jan 5, 1892, farmer of Gilmanton; m Aug 18, 1866, Emma F Bryant of Laconia, ae 19; dau of Charles D and Meribah Taylor (Cotton); she m 2nd Reuben G Hoyt; presumably no children
- b John M b New Hampton Sept 1844; d Washington of war disabilities July 7, 1864
- c Elizabeth A b Oct 2, 1846; living 1910; m 2nd Nov 30, 1877, Samuel Hodgdon of Meredith
- d Rufus P b Jan 1, 1849; m May 23, 1871, Abigail O Sawyer b Nov 28, 1852, dau of Smith and Susanna C (Woodbury); in 1910 machinist of Laconia, 1915 of Lakeport
- e Charles H b Feb 28, 1851; farmer of Ashland, unm in 1910

Sarah H Dow abbegfcb d Feb 14, 1875; m Oct 19, 1843, Martin Luther Huckins, farmer, b Dec 22, 1820, d July 28, 1908, son of James; he m 2nd Nov 1876 Mary Mudgett. Children of Sarah H:

- a Aurelia b Plymouth Nov 15, 1845; d Apr 28, 1863; m Oct 26, 1862, Frank True Russell Colby; a son d unm
- b Fred Peter b Plymouth Nov 15, 1845; d Jan 28, 1901; plumber of Reading, Mass; m Ella B Hileman

Oren Frank Dow abbegfcc, called Frank, farmer, preacher, then for many years overseer in hosiery mill, fearing tuberculosis, built a hut in the woods just out of town and lived the rest of his life as a sociable hermit, declining to the last a home offered by his sons. He kept a visitors' book, in which there were over 2,000 names. He d Meredith Oct 18, 1907; m 1st Martha C Smith of Holderness; div; m 2nd May 28, 1878, Lizzie M Pike, ae 19, dau of E and S. Apparently 4 children:

- a ——, son b Dec 19, 1858   b ——, son b New Hampton July 1863
- c ——, perhaps a 1st born d young

d   Harvey b New Hampton 1865 (by own m rec)
e   Harman b New Hampton 1870; of Laconia; m Dec 25, 1895, Minnie Josephine Smith, ae 28, b Liverpool, Que, dau of James and Mary (Sinjohn).   No rec of children

Harry Dow abbegfccd (sic in all later rec) m Dec 25, 1889, Mary Nellie Howland b Lyme 1868, dau of Harrison C and Mary J; in 1890 knitter of Laconia, 1896 farmer of Meredith, 1908 painter of Meredith. Children:

a   Mildred L b Lake Village Nov 23, 1890
b   Frank Howland b Meredith July 1, 1896

Jonathan Dow abbegfd b 1797 is either untraced or confused elsewhere.

Dana Dow abbegfe m July 4, 1822, Melinda Gordon, both of New Hampton.   Neither in 1850 census; not traced.

Jacob Dow abbegfg m New Hampton Mch 6, 1825, Mary Atwell, both of Holderness.   Inferentially, their son:

a   Jeremiah (or Jeremiah A) b Holderness Jan 1, 1826

Jeremiah Dow abbegfga d Mch 23, 1895; m Mch 22, 1847, Lucretia Ann Glines b Northfield June 22, 1833, d Feb 18, 1913; employed over half his life by Jeremiah Smith of Northfield, he was a man of considerable ability and influence in the community.   Rec of children suffer much from garbling:

a   Alexander Clark b Nov 25, 1848
b   Joseph Morse b Aug 6, 1849 (also 1857); no further mention and may be garbled for Johanna Morse Dow
c   Frank Hayes b Apr 3, 1851 (1852 by m rec, Jan 9, 1854 by town rec)
d   Herbert Gerry b Jan 9, 1854 (Herbert Gerrish, 4th child, by State rec; b 1857 by m rec)
e   Albert G b Jan 3, 1857 (no further mention)
f   Byron Kendrick b Apr 23, 1857 (Jan 5, 1861, State rec)
g   Jeremiah Smith b Nov 6, 1859 (State, 1867)
h   Joanna Morse b Aug 23, 1867; d ae 10   i   Elizabeth Ann b Nov 20, 1871
j   Myrtil Estelle b May 22, 1872; d ae 5 (State calls her 3rd child b Jan 25, 1854, also b June 16, 1872)

Alexander C Dow abbegfgaa holds the record for marriages, 6 times before he was 41.   A kindly and respected man, he was no Blue Beard, merely unlucky in matrimony.   Farmer of Bean Hill, Northfield, he d Aug 26, 1896 (Dec by State rec); m 1st Feb 20, 1865, Joanna M Dearborn, ae 17, dau of James; 2nd Sanbornton Bridge Apr 21, 1868, Rhoda J Arlin b 1845, d Oct 11, 1869, dau of John and Lovina (Minot) of Northfield; 3rd Tilton Jan 15, 1870, Sarah Abby Smith, ae 19, d on her wedding day; 4th Sept 3, 1871, Susan F Brocklebank, ae 18, b Plainfield, dau of Napoleon and Aurilla; 5th Josephine (Harris) Clark b Ashland 1844, d Apr 3, 1889, dau of Noah and Mary J (Bowen); 6th Northfield Dec 12, 1889, Amarette Kimball (her 2nd) b Belmont 1847, dau of James F and Caroline P.   She survived.   Two children, both d in infancy:

a   ——by Rhoda Arlin   b   (by Susan Brocklebank) son b Apr 30, 1872

Frank H Dow abbegfgac, farmer of Northfield, m Feb 26, 1898, Hannah (or Anna) Bruce, div, b Northfield, Vt, dau of Jesse S and Nancy Anna of Montpelier.

Herbert J Dow abbegfgad, farmer of Northfield, m 1st 1880 Lizzie Herbert of Franklin; 2nd (her 2nd) Dec 1, 1886, Orianna E Herbert, ae 28, b Sanbornton, dau of Josiah. Child:

    a Ernest Gerry b Nov 4, 1881; laborer of Northfield, m Jan 24, 1905, Mildred Prescott of Laconia, ae 19, dau of Herbert L and Eliza (Durgin)

Byron K Dow abbegfgaf d Northfield Oct 12, 1909; m 1st Lulu Belle Reed, dau of Roswell C and Emma Ann (Shaw); she got div; m 2nd Oct 15, 1888, George A Glines, 3rd Julian Morse; he m 2nd Mary Monahan. One child:

    a Ethel Vara b June 26, 1881; d in infancy

Jeremiah S Dow abbegfgag lived Dowtown, Northfield; d Dec 22, 1912; m Sept 27, 1883, Nellie V Maynard, ae 19, b Vt, dau of Frank T and Mary F Ridgeley, Vt; div. Only child:

    a Mertie May b July 2, 1884; m 1903 Frank A Brace of Tilton; twins: Leonard Francis and Marion Estelle b Mch 8, 1904

Elizabeth A Dow abbegfgai m Northfield Mch 25, 1893, Charles H Folger of Lowell, Mass. Children:

    a Wilfred b Mch 20, 1896; d in infancy   b Archie Leonard b Aug 22, 1898

Mark Dow abbegfj went early to Boston; m Boston July 3, 1834, Charlotte Parsons b Gloucester Oct 29, 1811. He d June 14, 1846, leaving 4 children, oldest 11:

    a Charles H b June 3, 1835; m Boston Oct 12, 1859, Sarah Elizabeth Moulton b Ossipee, N H, Mch 23, 1835; in 1881 bookkeeper of Boston; no children. She, dau of Dr Alvah and Mary (Dalton), wid m 2nd, ae 66 (his 2nd) Pittsfield, Mass, Oct 22, 1910, George F Marsh, ae 56, son of George and Louise C (Close)
    b Howard Malcolm b Mch 11, 1837   c Albert W   d Charlotte

Howard Malcolm Dow abbegfjb d 1913; lived later years in Calif. Organist and composer, author of masonic ritual music of high excellence. With touches of genius, he deserved better recognition; his writings brought him lamentably little. He m 1865 Mary Agnes Rice b Feb 16, 1839. Children:

    a Arthur Malcolm b Dec 12, 1865
    b Lillian E b Oct 14, 1867; m Albert W Dow abbegfjca; in 1922 of Glendale, Calif
    c Hattie Long b Dec 28, 1869   d James Rice b Dec 23, 1873
    e Marion Howard b Oct 13, 1876; d Oct 7, 1877

Arthur M Dow abbegfjba d Pelham Manor, N Y, June 22, 1916; m June 1908 Nella May Hallenback, ae 34, dau of Augustus and Electa (Church). No children. Mrs Dow engaged 1918 in war work in France.

Hattie L Dow abbegfjbc d Nov 1902; m Apr 1894 Rufus Bates. Children:

    a Herman M b Feb 8, 1895; m Mch 29, 1916, Olive Marion Studley; lives Boston; children: Charlotte Reed, Olive Winslow
    b Rufus Edward b June 11, 1897

James R Dow abbegfjbd, business man of Brooklyn, N Y, m Nettie Lambert. Children:

    a Eleanor Lambert b Jan 11, 1897   b Philip Rice b Sept 1, 1900

Albert W Dow abbegfjc m Harriet M—, who survived in 1921; settled in Glendale, Calif. Children:

    a Albert W   b Walter, d Glendale, unm

Albert W Dow abbegfjca d about 1912; m Lillian E Dow abbegfjab. Only child:

    a Dorothy Howard b Oct 1895; m Mch 18, 1919, V E Phipp of Chicago

Charlotte Dow abbegfjd m William Batterson of Boston. Child:

    a Howard m Hortense Batterson; has Harold b about 1892 and Mabel m William Litchfield

Levi Dow abbegfk. Some Levi Dow, not identified, m June 3, 1823, Elizabeth Swan, both of New Hampton. Our Levi appears in 1850 census as carpenter of Holderness, with wife Susan b Mass 1814. Two children, a third is in census, but not necessarily theirs:

    a Isaac b Mass 1839   b Levi b Mass 1839, twins, both untraced
    c Abraham b 1848; d 1849

John H Dow abbegfl, ordained Free Will Baptist Clergyman Thornton Oct 1838, d Feb 21, 1844; m 1842 Polly K Shaw. No rec of child.

Comfort Dow abbegg m Samuel Ladd b Apr 7, 1765, d Jan 17, 1817, son of Stephen and Abigail (Webster); she d Feb 6, 1842. Children:

    a Ruth b Sept 21, 1794; m Eben C Gordon
    b Abigail b Oct 10, 1796; m Daniel Morrison
    c Stephen b July 4, 1798; m Amanda Austin
    d Nancy b 1800; d 1844; m Eben Morrison
    e Samuel b Dec 12, 1802; m Nancy Young
    f Lewis b June 1806; d Nov 8, 1865
    g Jonathan b May 8, 1808; m Susan Young
    h Levi Dow b Mch 10, 1811; m Hannah Young
    i Gordon b Aug 3, 1813; m Dolly Young

Mary Dow abbegh m Nathaniel Sanborn. Child:

    a Comfort Dow b New Hampton Aug 3, 1802; d 1872; m Mch 15, 1834, Thomas Huckins b Nov 16, 1805, d Apr 1, 1888, son of Robert

Sarah Dow abbeh m May 13, 1755, Sgt Jonathan Moulton b Apr 1, 1730, d Apr 22, 1821, son of John and Elizabeth (Lamprey); in 1795 moved to Scarborough, Me. Children, all b Hampton:

    a Mehetabel b Oct 16, 1755; d 1825; m Simeon Marston
    b Sarah b Feb 25, 1757; d 1846; m Daniel Emery

c Joseph b Apr 13, 1759; d 1844; m Catherine Jameson
d Mary b Aug 25, 1761; d 1815; m Benjamin Emery
e Lucy b Jan 3, 1764; d 1819; m Francis Libbey
f Jonathan bap May 21, 1766; d 1845; m Rebecca Burnham who m 2nd Samuel Meserve (?)
i Daniel bap Aug 28, 1774; d 1862; m Mary Libbey

Rachel Dow abbf d June 22, 1755; m Jonathan Garland, shoe-maker, b Oct 28, 1689, d May 11, 1760, son of Peter and Elizabeth. Children:

a Samuel b Nov 21, 1716; d Jan 28, 1772; m Lydia Moulton
b Jonathan b July 16, 1719; d May 1, 1756; m Bethia Taylor
c Abigail b Mch 6, 1722; d No Hampton Oct 1813; m David Marston
d Mary b Jan 20, 1724; d young
e Sarah b May 12, 1725; m Benjamin Tuck
f James b Nov 13, 1726; d July 13, 1750
g Rachel b May 25, 1729; m Benjamin Johnson, son of John
h Anne b July 1, 1731; d Dec 27, 1735
i Joseph b May 11, 1734; m Hannah Marston, dau of Obadiah
j Simon b Jan 18, 1736; d Mch 3, 1738
k Simon b Oct 7, 1738; d Dec 2, 1759
l Mary b Apr 6, 1741; d Mch 13, 1815; m Samuel Blake

Hannah Dow abbj d Nov 13, 1796; m Jan 21, 1731, Shubael Page b Feb 15, 1707, d May 16, 1791, son of Christopher and Abigail (Tilton); continued to live Hampton. Children:

a Abigail b Nov 27, 1731; d Dec 28, 1790; m Joseph Hobbs
b Sarah b Apr 1, 1734; d July 19, 1831; m Benjamin Philbrick, son of Nathan
c Reuben b May 24, 1736; lost at sea 1789
d Mary b Apr 6, 1738; d Mch 28, 1778; m Dea Christopher Smith
e ——b and d Nov 30, 1740
f Samuel b Dec 1, 1741; d Dec 8, 1821; m Sarah Sherburne
g ——b and d Jan 15, 1745
h Nathaniel b Jan 26, 1746; d Sept 1806; m Betty Leavitt; moved to Parsonsfield, Me
i Abner b Nov 1748; d Apr 28, 1832; m Abigail Moulton
j ——b and d Sept 1752   k Josiah b Oct 17, 1753; d Nov 14, 1754

Of these three senior lines from Capt Henry Dow ab, the eldest long identified with Hampton, the second going to Vermont, the third penetrating upstate as pioneers, one notices a common tendency,—1st to marry for several generations among a small number of old families, new blood being uncommon; second, to approach, if not reach extinction of the male line; a rejuvenescence seen when some branch goes west. Hampton has not been a Dow home for many years; a few are left, but are the elderly ones.

ROM the second son of Capt. Henry Dow ab, the line divides once, the senior branch identified for a little time with Hampton, then going upstate into new territory, the junior going a brief distance to Rye and becoming almost extinct. That is to say,—the male lines; for the female lines we have no data.

Simon Dow abc lived where Moses Swett Lamprey was living 1890. He served only two years as selectman, but, in compensation, as it were, was chairman of the committee appointed to build a barn on the parsonage lot. As constable he was rigorous; he is on record as never skimping garrison duty and rendered a good account of himself in the Indian fights. He m 1st Nov 5, 1685, Sarah Marston b Nov 20, 1665, d Mch 8, 1698, dau of Thomas and Mary (Easton), and cousin of the wife of his older brother. He m May 29, 1700, Mehitable Green, dau of Isaac and Mary (Cass). He made a will Sept 11, 1707, making his brother Jabez executor, leaving to his wife Mehitable land between that of his brothers Samuel and Jabez "toward Hampton Beach, commonly known as the Capt Dow pasture, a marsh given to me by my Honor'd father." His will mentions all the children except Henry, who was posthumous. A marriage intention is between O Page and Mahittabill Dow and a subsequent entry Henry Dow, son of Solomon and Mehetable, now wife of Onesiphorus Page, d Dec 30, 1727. Solomon is pen slip for Simon and his wid duly married O Page. An O Page Jr m a cousin, a dau of Jeremiah Dow adg. This Page family, some of whom became Quakers at an early date, was the one of Hingham, Mass, and all Hampton annals tend to indicate that there was no blood relationship with the family of Robert Page of Ormsby and Hampton. Onesiphorus (3) Page b Feb 10, 1678-9, son of Onesiphorus and Mary (Hauxworth), had five children by his first wife; by Mehitable he had a dau Mary b Aug 18, 1713. Children of Simon:

a	Mary b Nov 19, 1686	b	Hannah b Nov 7, 1688
c	Simon b Dec 5, 1690	d	Sarah b May 23, 1693
e	Isaac b Oct 19, 1701	f	Jonathan b Oct 1, 1703
g	Mehitable b Jan 13, 1706	h	Henry b Mch 28, 1708; d 1727

Mary Dow abca was the Dow pioneer of Rye; d Rye 1755 or 1765; m Feb 9, 1710, Capt Richard Jenness b June 8, 1686, son of Francis and Hannah (Swain). He was bap Apr 24, 1715, when he and his wife joined the church; d 1769; was representative to Legislature half of his life. Children:

a Sarah b Mch 6, 1711; m——Marston of No Hampton
b Mary b Dec 27, 1711; m Joshua Weeks of Greenland
c Hannah b July 4, 1714; m Joseph Locke, son of Joseph
d Francis b Dec 1, 1715; m Sarah Garland, dau of John
e Richard b Dec 1, 1715; m Abigail Sleeper

f Simon b Mch 1, 1720; was imbecile   g Jonathan b Oct 1, 1721; d young
h Samuel b May 9, 1724; m 1st Nov 15, 1748, Abigail Garland, dau of John; 2nd
   wid Elizabeth Shipley
i Joseph b Feb 28, 1727; d 1815; m 1st at Rye Mary Dow abceb; 2nd Anna
   Parker

Hannah Dow abcb d Feb 10, 1717; m Oct 28, 1708, Henry Dearborn b Oct 28, 1688, d Apr 26, 1756, son of Henry and Elizabeth (Marrian); m 2nd Jan 12, 1721, Mary Robie, dau of Samuel, by whom a dau Mary m Ebenezer Lovering; m 3rd Esther—. Children of Hannah:

a Sarah b Feb 20, 1709; d Dec 8, 1789; m John Taylor
b Hannah b Dec 19, 1710; d Nov 20, 1724
c Elizabeth b Apr 29, 1713; d Dec 21, 1781; m William Sanborn
d Henry b about 1715; d June 13, 1741   e Simon b Jan 21, 1717

Simon Dow abcc m Jan 8, 1713, Mary Lancaster; served 2 weeks, 2 days at 6s a week in the 1712 Indian campaign under Capt James Davis. His farm was near Black Swamp and he held from time to time various town offices; selectman one year; on committee to divide the plantation tract into lots for individual ownership. Children:

a Sarah b Feb 15, 1714
b Simon b Sept 1716; m Oct 3, 1748, Phoebe Marston, dau of Ephraim and Abigail (Knowles); signed Association Test 1775; d without children Dec 29, 1785
c Richard b Aug 2, 1722; bap Aug 22, d young
d Jeremiah b Dec 10, 1723   e Hannah b May 23, 1726
f Mary b July 4, 1731   g Noah b May 1, 1736

Sarah Dow abcca m Apr 19, 1737, Peter Johnson b July 11, 1714, son of Peter and Esther (Hobbs); miller of Rye, owned the covenant and was bap with his oldest child. Children:

a Esther bap May 13, 1739; m Samuel Towle, son of Jonathan
b Ruth bap Oct 7, 1739
c Peter bap Feb 28, 1742; m Sept 18, 1767, Mary Yeaton
d Sarah bap Apr 29, 1744   e Simon bap Dec 22, 1745
f Mary bap July 24, 1748; all in Hampton church

Jeremiah Dow abccd, yeoman of Hampton, bought July 6, 1770, land next east of the parade of Northwood Center, then Nottingham, and lived on it until Jan 11, 1773, when he sold it to Valentine Keniston. Probably then moved to Kensington. He was 52 at the outbreak of the war, but, like many others of similar age, enlisted promptly for the defense of the coast towns; impossible to determine positively the identities of the four or five Jeremiahs who fought, but it was surely he who, with John Dow and Richard Dow, was in Capt Elkins' company for defense of Portsmouth, unable to write, signing "his mark." Only possibly was he the Jeremiah who enlisted July 1775 under Capt Henry Dearborn, Col John Stark, or who was in Capt Abraham Drake's militia, receipting Dec 1, 1777, for 3£ 10s 8d. He m Sept 25, 1746, by Rev Jos. Adams, Abiah Brown b Dec 25, 1721, dau of Thomas and Dorcas (Farming). Children:

a Jeremiah b Dec 26, 1747
b Elizabeth Allen b Feb 12, 1749; d Oct 2, 1754   c Ruth b June 9, 1752
d Richard b June 14, 1753; d Oct 3, 1754   e Elizabeth Allen bap Aug 31, 1755
f Benjamin Brown b Hampton; bap May 13, 1759
g Simon b Dec 31, 1761

Jeremiah Dow abccda m Aug 23, 1768, Elizabeth Stanyan; that fall went to the Grand Banks, cod fishing; vessel and crew lost. Mrs. Elizabeth Stanyan Dow m 2nd Philip Burns; 3rd Daniel Sanborn. His posthumous dau:

a Anna b Feb 28, 1769

Anna Dow abccdaa d Jan 13, 1860; m Mch 11, 1800, Daniel Lamprey b Oct 10, 1781, son of Lieut Daniel and Sarah (Lane); lived Hampton. Children:

a Ruth b 1800; d May 10, 1863; m Jonathan Godfrey
b Eli b May 27, 1802; d Nov 17, 1770; m Hannah Sanborn
c Jeremiah Dow b 1804 or later; enlisted in navy; one of the few able to swim ashore when the Cumberland was sunk by the Merrimack; d in the service Newport, R I
d Anna b 1806 or later; d Boston Aug 24, 1845; m Simon Godfrey, son of Simon
e Elizabeth m Mark Safford of Boston and Washington, N H
f Sally m William Hunting of Boston; moved to Gilmore City, Iowa; large family, 6 sons in Civil War
g Samuel b Jan 5, 1816; m Melissa J Barnes

Benjamin B Dow abccdf, whose youth was spent in Kensington, was apprenticed Feb 13, 1774, for 6 years, 7 days, to Asahel Blake of Northwood. His middle name seldom appears. His apprenticeship ended abruptly at the beginning of the war, he making his subsequent home with Walter Bryant of Newmarket. He received 4£ 10s bounty for first enlistment and re-enlisted at least twice. July 1, 1777, marched 5 days toward Ticonderoga, Capt Duncan, Lieut Col Moses Kelly. In 1781 received $182.60 allowance for depreciation of currency, the Continental paper falling to about 1¼ per cent of its face, later becoming worthless. Feb 14, 1781, he was under Capt Sartwell.

After the war, Benjamin became the subject of considerable litigation between the towns claiming credit for his services. In his last muster roll he is entered as of Northwood. Kensington and Newmarket claimed him. Simon, his brother, deposed that Benjamin had been apprenticed by their father to one Blake of Northwood, whence he went to Cambridge and "'listed for one year"; that when he was not in service he always stayed with Walter Bryant, for whom Simon worked, and that he never went to Northwood except for one night to settle with his master [for his broken apprenticeship] and one short visit to Hampton, where he had been born. The deposition of Walter Bryant, of lawfull age, testifieth & Saith that Benjamin Dow, a soldier in the army, having a brother a Sarvent with the Deponant, soposed that he made his house his home and accordingly always looked for him to come to his the Deponant's house as he hath from time to time and staid about six weeks at a time. About four years ago the Deponant and said Benjamin hath conversed about his belonging to Newmarket; said he expected Newmarket would do something for him, as he was returned for Newmarket; and he had Cloaths made in my house & washed there & Cloths Left there and there now: Walter Bryant sworn July 18, 1781.

It seems easy to read between the lines that Benjamin was a simple-hearted, likable youth who failed to inherit his share of the abilities of his grandsires.   He was entitled to, and presumably received 160 acres of land under the act of 1783; he may still be found among disconnected Dow of some interior town, but so far no record known can be attributed safely to him.

Simon Dow abccdg was paid for 3 mos military service in 1781; m Newmarket July 23, 1786, Agibail Murray (Murry in rec) of Stratham b Newmarket 1765, d Barnstead Jan 1820.   He must be the Simon m Northwood Sept 27, 1823, Ruth Johnson of Northwood.   He eluded all Dow genealogists until a letter from his grandson was found 1923 in the miscellaneous memoranda of Edgar R Dow.   A farmer and influential citizen of Barnstead, he d July 1840, ancestor of the principal Dow family of Barnstead, a town whose vital rec are in very poor shape.   He had 4 sons, 3 dau, of whom:

   a Jeremiah; representative to Legislature 1819, but not found otherwise
   b (no attempt at correct order) Margarett of Barnstead m New Durham Feb 21,
       1822, James Murray of Farmington
   c Timothy b 1797   d John Osborn b Barnstead Nov 15, 1805

Timothy Dow abccdgc d Barnstead 1861;   known as General, but origin of title not found; selectman 1828-30;   representative 1837-8; m Mary P Hodgdon; of children, two proved:

   a Charles H b July 9, 1822   b John b July 11, 1825
   c (guess) Permelia b Barnstead (no parents mentioned) Dec 1, 1818

Charles H Dow abccdgca, farmer of Barnstead, d Mch 29, 1903; m Feb 2, 1845, Susan M Drew, both of Barnstead; 2nd Aug 13, 1854, Lydia A Shackford of Barnstead.   No rec of children by 1st m; by 2nd:

   a George W b Barnstead after 1854
   b Addie A of Barnstead m May 7, 1892, Charles F Leighton of Farmington

George W Dow abccdgcaa, farmer of Barnstead, m Edith M Shackford.   Children:

   a William H b Sept 20, 1892; d Feb 13, 1895
   b Mary Edith b Mch 10, 1896   c Mildred b Oct 26, 1897

John Dow abccdgcb, farmer of Barnstead, 4 years selectman, 1853-68 justice of the peace, d Mch 1, 1911; m Dec 30, 1849, Mary Jane Lang b Alton 1829.   Children b Barnstead, possibly others:

   a Charles J b Roxbury, Mass, 1850
   b John C b 1855   c Frederick b Aug 12, 1859

Charles J. Dow abccdgcba, jeweler of Concord and Lebanon, m Franklin Mch 18, 1879, Eliza A Houston, ae 19, dau of Frank K

John C Dow abccdgcbb, wholesale feed dealer of Boston in 1923, has never replied to letters of genealogical inquiry; of Berlin, Mass, m

Dec 25, 1878, Ida S Elliott b Gilmanton, ae 23, dau of John W. A son
by own m rec:

    a   Fred Harold b Cambridge 1882

Fred H Dow abccdgcbba, confectionery manufacturer of Cambridge,
m Feb 21, 1906, Lucia Morse Parcher b Saco, Me, 1884, dau of Sumner
C and Ida May (Stockman) (rec also as Stickman). Child:

    a   Harold Parcher b Cambridge Aug 7, 1907

John O Dow abccdgd, farmer of Barnstead, lived a while in Gilmanton (perhaps missing sons of abccdg were of Gilmanton, a melting
pot of many families). He d at son's home, Cambridge, Mass, Apr 5,
1895; m Dec 19, 1830, Mary Clough Natter b July 18, 1812, d Barnstead
Jan 22, 1893, dau of Joseph and Mary (Clough). Married life lasted 63
years. Three sons, 2 dau, of whom:

    c   William Henry b Gilmanton Aug 19, 1836

William H Dow abccdgdc, soap manufacturer of Cambridge, m
Oct 1, 1861, Mary Phylura Heald b Ludlow, Vt, Apr 12, 1841, living 1881.
Children, all b Roxbury:

    a   William b Aug 16, 1863, d same day
    b   George W b Dec 6, 1867; d Aug 22, 1868
    c   Harland E b Nov 30, 1869; d Sept 21, 1870

Hannah Dow abcce m Dec 27, 1749, Nathaniel Jenness b Aug 22,
1725, son of John and Mary (Mason); m 2nd wid Mary Tarlton; of 19
children about 9 belong to Hannah:

    a   Simon; wrote on fireplace "you shall see my face no more"; went to Eng; never
          came back
    b   Mary m Nathaniel Foss of Barrington
    c   Jonathan d unm in army, Boston
    d   John   e   Noah   f   Hannah d young   g   Nathaniel
    h   Polly   i   Hannah m Sept 1799 Theodore Fuller
    j   James drowned, ae 24, unm

Mary Dow abccf m Oct 11, 1769, Nathan Moulton, son of William
and Abigail (Page). No children.

Noah Dow abccg m Greenland May 21, 1761, Elizabeth Palmer
(Phoebe in Hist Rye). Hist Rye has little to say about him. He was
diminutive, the shortest man in Rye. A grandson writes he was a farmer,
but tax book gives him only ¼ acre. Hist Rye dismisses the family,
saying son Nathan moved into the country. Children, all b Rye:

    a   Simon b Sept 1762   b   Daniel b May 10 (bap May 20), 1764
    c   Nathan b Feb 3, 1773   d   Jonathan, twin, both bap Feb 21

Simon Dow abccga m Mary Blake d Sept 14, 1834, dau of Thomas
[and probably Hannah (Dearborn)]; moved to Hampton, thence 1800
to Gilmanton; heir to Uncle Simon. Children, all b Hampton:

    a   Phoebe b 1784; d Apr 1, 1784
    b   Simon b July 11, 1786; m Nov 3, 1813, Patty Lang Rand b Oct 1792, dau of
          Dowrst and Hannah (Lang). She m 2nd George Bragg; lived Gilmanton;
          probably no children

c John Taylor b May 18, 1788
d Phoebe b Feb 2, 1790; d Hampton Feb 3, 1865; m Reuben Page
e Taylor b May 29, 1792

John T Dow abccgac located on Little Boar Isle, Hampton, a fisherman; moved to Isles of Shoals; finally to No. Hampton; m 1st Belmont Dec 18, 1807, Deborah Page, dau of Noah and Betty (Locke); 2nd June 16, 1822, wid Betsey Newman, born Knowles, adopting her 2 children, who took his name.

If any romance be built out of genealogical memoirs, it might be of those who lived on the New Hampshire coast and followed the sea. No man knew when he embarked on glassy water, whether he would come back or figure among the missing; storms were bad, fogs worse. Hundreds of dories put out from schooner for cod and drifted in the fog until engulfed by swell or perished from thirst, hunger or cold, while the parent schooner cruised for days in vain search. In every town along the coast some spot on the dunes was a cemetery with half its stones over empty graves,—commemorating "lost at sea." Every schooner load of fishermen left behind a score of wives and babies, some unborn, as in the case of Jeremiah Dow, half expectant of being widowed or orphaned. It was custom that those who survived should care for the families of those who did not.

So with John Taylor Dow. His oldest son lost at sea; having a whole brood of his own, he m a widow of the sea, adopting her children and adding more of his own until the total was 11. In old age he went back a little from the shore, but still within easy walk of the water. No matter how many fish in the sea, no matter how plentifully potatoes grew in the sandy soil, it was no easy task to fill a dozen hungry young mouths. Let us hope he was kind to all his younkers:

a Elizabeth L b Oct 25, 1808; d 1890; m 1st Joseph Branscombe of Newcastle; 2nd——Simonds; 3rd Chandler Spinney of Epping
b Daniel Weymouth b Apr 14, 1810; lost at sea, unm
c John Taylor b Mch 31, 1812
d Mary Ann b Feb 7, 1814; m Asa Palmer of Lynn; 2 sons, 1 dau
e Sally G b Apr 27, 1816; d about 1890; m Joseph Purington, a Civil War veteran
f Martha Brown b July 13, 1818; m Joseph Stone; moved to Peabody, Mass
g Betty Locke b Belmont Oct 26, 1818. Rec is clear but must be error
h Simon B b July 8, 1824
i Rosilla b Oct 13, 1827; m Dec 23, 1852, Daniel B Bagley of Raymond; d June 1891; 9 children
j Winthrop Y b Mch 21, 1830; m Mary J Ackerman, half-sister of Meshech S; no children. She d Boston Nov 3, 1902, ae 73-8-21
k Eveline Adelaide b Jan 18, 1832; d Nov 14, 1833
l ——dau d in infancy
m (adopted) Mary Ann b Feb 6, 1814; d Hampton July 27, 1883, m 1837 Meshech S Ackerman d Oct 8, 1886
n Samuel K (adopted) b Apr 7, 1815; untraced

John T Dow abccgacc moved a little farther inland; d Newington Apr 12, 1874; wife Martha A—. At least one child:

a John H or John T H b 1841 or 1844 (rec differ)

John T H Dow abccgacca suffers from clerical errors; ae 25, farmer of Newington, m July 29, 1866, Mary Ann Leavitt, ae 24, b Quebec. Also, ae 31, b Newington, farmer, m Dec 25, 1875, Annie A Floid, ae 32, of Portsmouth. These probably identical, altho 3 years discrepancy in dates. A man always lies about his age on 2nd m. At least one child, by 1st wife:

    a John T b Portsmouth 1870, son of John and Mary

John T Dow abccgaccaa, shoemaker of Portsmouth, m Sept 14, 1889, Dottie (Dorothy) Yeaton, ae 20, dau of Nathaniel and Louisa. Census of 1906 gives him teamster, 1917 foreman. A Margaret B Dow at same address in 1917 directory. In b rec of son Mother's name Dolly Maloon Yeaton. Children:

    a ——, son b Nov 13, 1890   b Frances E b July 8, 1892
    c Harold T b Newcastle June 3, 1894
    d Lawrence Taylor b July 8, 1896; Portsmouth helper in 1915

Harold T Dow abccgaccaac, teamster, in 1917 pipe fitter of Portsmouth, m June 5, 1917, Lora M Cole, ae 28, b Eliot, Me, dau of Henry C and Eliza A (Fernald)

Simon B Dow abccgach of Little River, N H, returned to Hampton Apr 1886; farmer d Hampton Jan 16, 1894; m Oct 3, 1852, Elizabeth C Fogg, ae 18, dau of Ebenezer and Mina (Philbrick); she living Hampton 1907. Children:

    a Mary O b Dec 5, 1855
    b John J b Dec 26, 1857; m Hattie Maria Blodgett; teamster of No Hampton,
        d accident Hampton Apr 22, 1903
    c Vira b Oct 28, 1863; d Apr 1864

Mary O Dow abccgacha m Nov 11, 1879, Fred More of No Hampton; moved to Amesbury, son of Christopher. Children:

    a George I   b Fannie J   c Mabel L

Mary Ann Dow abccgacl m Meshech S Ackerman, for 30 years at Hampton railroad station. Children b Kensington and Hampton Falls:

    a Charlotte A d Dec 31, 1858, ae 19, 9 mos
    b J Warren m Mary E Martin of Rumford, Me; d Haverhill July 4, 1892
    c Charles P m Apr 1865 Elizabeth F Blake, dau of Joseph L; station master at
        Hampton Falls
    d John M m Nellie E Elkins; 8 years postmaster and town clerk of Hampton
    e George H d Jan 5, 1851, ae 5
    f Augustus D, asst postmaster, Hampton
    g James O b Hampton May 1848; d Aug 1848

Phoebe Dow abccgad m Dec 25, 1811, Reuben Page b Feb 29, 1784 d Jan 13, 1850, son of Samuel and Sarah (Sherburne) of Gilmanton and Hampton. Children:

    a Mary Sherburne b Nov 1812; d Jan, 2 1880; m David Brown
    b Phoebe   c Eliza d in infancy   d Eliza Ann m George N Young
    e Sarah Sherburne m Samuel C Haskell of Boston
    f (adopted) James A d Ayer, Mass, Sept 1891; twice m

Phoebe Page abccgadb m Amos Wheeler; their son, Rev Benjamin Wheeler, m Mary E Ide.   A son, Benjamin Ide Wheeler, long president of Univ of Calif.

Taylor Dow abccgae m 1st 1817 Abigail Foss of Dover; 2nd Mary Emerson; d Gilmanton 1839; probably the Taylor Dow joined Baptist church Exeter about 1833.   Newspaper obituary in Gilmanton spoke highly of him, tailor, prominent mason.   At least two children:

  a George W b Epsom Mch 2, 1832; d widower Gilmanton Oct 30, 1912
  b Mary A m Oct 1858 Charles E Flower, both of Epsom.   This must be the same as a garbled Epsom rec—Susan M Dow m Nov 13, 1849, Charles Flower, both of Epsom

George W Dow abccgaea, veteran of Civil War, retired farmer of Gilmanton, m Mary L Sawyer b Gilmanton Aug 30, 1829, d Gilmanton Jan 30, 1910, dau of William and Betsey H (Currier).   At least 2 children:

  a George H, married laborer, d Windsor Oct 29, 1892, ae 37-7-21
  b Willie T, painter; untraced

George H Dow abccgaeaa moved to Canterbury, later to Windsor; m Lucy A Hoyt b Gilmanton.   Children, b Loudon:

  a Clara J b July 30, 1880 b Oscar W b Jan 4, 1882; d Windsor Dec 17, 1897

Clara (H in rec) **J Dow** abccgaeaaa m Loudon Feb 25, 1897, William H Lake b Apr 23, 1873, son of William R and Susan Lydia (Worrald).   A child:

  a Susan Viola b Canterbury Aug 15, 1908

Daniel Dow abccgb m Oct 29, 1794, Elizabeth Moulton of Northfield, ae 24; moved to Tamworth, place whose vital data are few.   Children:

  a Jonathan b July 28, 1795
  b Fannie b Tamworth Jan 6, 1802.   One suspects intervening children
  c Beriah B b Tamworth Sept 6, 1804   d Anna b Tamworth Nov 24, 1806

Jonathan Dow abccgba m Tamworth Dec 4, 1818, Lucinda (also Lavinia and Lavina) Cushing; in 1850 farmer of Tamworth, realty assessed $300.   Children, by census, oldest probably married and gone:

  a Eliza J b 1825   b Daniel b 1826 or 1829   c Mary b 1828
  d John C b Tamworth May 28, 1838   e George Frank (Franklin G in d rec)

Daniel Dow abccgbab, farmer of Tamworth, m Apr 8, 1860, Ruth Brown b Tamworth Sept 18, 1838, d Aug 18, 1902, dau of Stephen, farmer, and Nancy (Bean).   Children:

  a Charles E
  b Mary Eliza b May 8, 1863; m Lakeport Jan 4, 1893, Charles O Banfill
  c Nellie J m Tamworth Dec 22, 1892, Henry M Darling of Sandwich
  d Addie B m Dec 28, 1897, Edwin G Clark of Tamworth

Charles E Dow abccgbaba, knitter of Laconia, m Apr 29, 1905, wid Abbie M Vittum, ae 39, b Tamworth, dau of John (Dow?) and Augusta Smith; 1908 both of Tamworth.

John C Dow abccgbad, farmer of Tamworth, d widower Dec 17, 1916; m Apr 30, 1859, Augusta A Smith, ae 15, dau of Jacob B and Abigail.   At least one child:

  a   Charles L b Tamworth Apr 4, 1864   b   Abbie M b 1866 (?)

Charles L Dow abccgbada, farmer of Tamworth, in 1913 laborer of Sandwich; d Concord Mch 7, 1915 (Mother's name given as Gertrude Wallace); m 1st—; div; 2nd about 1908 Nettie M Tewksbury, div, ae 23, dau of Samuel W and Emma (Bean) Barnes; div; m 3rd Mch 17, 1913, wid Etta Palmer, ae 48, dau of Alpheus and Almira Vittum. She had dau Sadie M m —Tilton.   Child of Nettie:

  a   ——, son b Tamworth Feb 27, 1909; d Mch 2, 1909

George Frank Dow abccgbae d Tamworth Oct 7, 1914; m June 1863 Phoebe M Brown, ae 24, both of Tamworth.   Child:

  a   Jane b Sept 10, 1863; d July 1864

Beriah B Dow abccgbc of Sandwich m Dec 15, 1827, Wyatt Moulton of Tamworth. We cannot explain this confusion. Marie E Dow of Sandwich m Wyatt Moulton b Sandwich, d 1840, drayman of Bangor and Portland, Me. Moulton Children:

  a   Lewis B b Portland May 22, 1831; d Apr 4, 1885
  b   Sarah B b Portland 1833; m Phineas Harrington

Nathan Dow abccgc was a tailor and with his twin brother Jonathan came to Prospect, Me, before he was 21. The two brothers had a strong resemblance in looks and thoughts. Nathan d Prospect June 6, 1820, clearly recalled by his son, who wrote a genealogical letter in 1881. He m Jan 21, 1793, Betsey Prible, both then of Pownalsborough. She b Manchester, N H, d Prospect Jan 9, 1840. They had 5 sons, 3 dau, but these were not named in the 1881 letter:

  a   Jefferson, known to be 1st born; untraced
  b   Nathan b about 1797
  d   ——, b 1801, possibly Ephraim, unknown, untraced
  f   Orchard C b Nov 12, 1806   h   Noah E G b Monroe Feb 15, 1810.

Nathan Dow abccgcb located m Swanville; wife not found. Some Nathan m Harriet———.   Children:

  a   Susan m Alfred Curtis; a large family
  b   Caroline m Wilson Dickey b Monroe Nov 2, 1825, m 2nd Lucinda Burgess. Probably no children

Orchard C Dow abccgcf, farmer, joiner, school teacher of Prospect and Monroe, d widower June 16, 1894; his genealogical letter written ae 75 was firm and in old-fashioned copper plate style, legible as print. A local history says that the father of Orchard Dow took his whole family for a short trip to Philadelphia and suddenly d there. We cannot reconcile this story. He m Dec 20, 1830, Jane Crocker, b Prospect Dec 20,

1910. His letter gives 10 children, but there were 3 others; apparently he omitted those not living in 1886; all b Prospect:

a Wealthy J b Feb 3, 1831; d Boston July 28, 1879, unm
b Mary A b Sept 9, 1832   c George Washington b Jan 9, 1834
d Orchard C b Aug 11, 1835   e Enoch C b——; killed at Gettysburg
f Richard C b Apr 9, 1837
g Sarah H b May 11, 1838; m May 2, 1859, ——; moved to Boston; 3 children
h Ellen b Jan 13, 1840; m Marion Harriman of Prospect; moved to Bucksport.
    Children,—Heslyn, not living; Charles of Belfast; Annie m Jeremiah Emerson.
i Emma L b Mch 15, 1842; m Jan 5, 1867, Amos Moulton of Dedham, Me.
    Children,—Leonard, Harry, a dau
j Leonard E b Apr 19, 1845   k William C b Mch 29, 1850
l Charles   m Justine O; both d young

Mary A Dow abccgcfb m Dec 11, 1851, Capt Samuel Ginn of Prospect (3 children); m 2nd Capt Evander Harriman, 6 children:

a Percival M b Mch 5, 1852; d Dec 1917;
b Justina b 1853; living 1923; m Frank Harding
c Frances b 1855; d Nov 1910; m Willard Harding
d Washington D b Sept 5, 1857 e Wealthy b Sept 5, d Sept 26, 1857
f William H b Oct 30, 1859   g Adelaide T b June 17, 1862; d May 23, 1867
h Lester H b Nov 28, 1870   i Rufus A b Oct 19, 1872

George W Dow abccgcfc, deep sea captain, retired and returned to Prospect; m Jan 9, 1855, Sarah A Blanchard; 2nd Sarah M Harding, wid of George Heagan, d Prospect Oct 8, 1914, ae 76, 5 mos, dau of Nathan and Sarah (Crocker). Children, by 1st wife:

a Millard G b Prospect May 3, 1859; d Bucksport Nov 17, 1919
b Minnie B m W A Remick of Bucksport; no children

Millard G Dow abccgcfca, for many years captain between Hamburg and Rio de Janeiro, m Jeannette Parker of Bucksport, who survived. Children:

a George Millard   b Norman R   c Laura B
d Jeannette Parker b Aug 26, 1894   e Mary Eleanor b Aug 28, 1897

George M Dow abccgcfcaa, electrician of Old Town, m June 28, 1911, Lura M Stairs ae 20, dau of Nathan Y and Hester J (Smith). Children:

a Millard George b Old Town June 10, 1912
b Vivian Jennie b Oct 30, 1914   c Leslie Alexander b May 20, 1919

Norman R Dow abccgcfcab, machinist of Bucksport and Ellsworth, m July 16, 1913, Augusta Whitmore ae 22, dau of Richard A and Jennie (Danforth). Children:

a Norman R b Apr 29, 1914   b Richard Whitmore b Nov 14, 1916

Orchard C Dow abccgcfd, carpenter of Monroe, d June 5, 1905; m Aug 5, 1860, Caroline P Ridley b Prospect, living 1923, ae 81, with her son Oscar B in the homestead. Five children:

a Elmer E b Jan 26, 1863   b Enoch C b Prospect May 13, 1864
c Cora M b Nov 5, 1865; m Alfred F Beverage of Camden; a son Henry S
d Herman L b June 26, 1869   e Oscar B b Monroe Aug 15, 1877

Elmer E Dow abccgcfda m Alice Doe (2 children); 2nd Cora Walton of Danvers; for many years builder of Worcester, Mass; now Pres of Worcester Ornamental Iron Co. Children:

a Harry b Percival c Elmer E b Worcester Apr 13, 1904

Enoch C Dow abccgcfdb, farmer of Monroe, m Dec 3, 1900, Eva May Ward teacher ae 28, dau of George P and Flora (Maxim). Moved to Belfast on another farm. His buildings burned 1922 and he went to join his brothers in Worcester. Child:

a Neil Ward b Belfast Mch 30, 1906

Herman L Dow abccgcfdd is treas and manager of Worcester Ornamental Iron Co; m Nellie M Jewett, both b Me. Children:

a Alma b Evelyn c Norman E b Worcester Jan 3, 1901

Oscar B Dow abccgcfde, farmer of Monroe, was 1923 serving seventh term as 1st selectman; m Brooks Nov 28, 1907, Maud M Webb ae 21, dau of William and Annabel (Pease). Children:

a Ormand Clair b Nov 5, 1909 b Vivien Arline b Dec 11, 1916
c Hilda Margaret b Feb 2, 1918

Richard C Dow abccgcff, mariner, is apparently not the Richard C Dow who enlisted 1861 from Stockport. He m Belfast Sept 14, 1863, Annie M Snow of Northport; moved to N H; spent later years in Sailors' Snug Harbor. Only child d in infancy.

Sarah H Dow abccgcfg m Leonard Bowden, by whom Fred and Jane (neither living 1923); 2nd James Richards, 1 dau,—Evelyn.

Leonard E Dow abccgcfi, carpenter of Norway, m Lizzie Bennett b Westbrook; in 1881 living Waterville. Improbably other sons:

a Leon Kelsey b July 27, 1876

Leon K Dow abccgcfia, electrician of Norway, d Andover Oct 16, 1918; m Apr 9, 1911, Lucy Viola Frost ae 21, dau of Arthur W and Fannie (Holden). Of children:

b ——son b Norway Jan 14, 1915

William C Dow abccgcfk moved to Saxonville; m Aug 5, 1870, —, Only child:

a William drowned in boyhood

Noah E G Dow abccgch, farmer of Bradford, d Nov 12, 1896, ae 86-8-27; m Lucy Coy. Five children, of whom 3 matured:

a Fred d 1877, leaving wife and 4 children. All grew up and m, all but one living 1923
b Olive b 1851; m Alphonse Rand of Thorndike and Stetson, Me; 6 children, she and 3 surviving 1923
c Eliab Coy of Bradford d Jan 24, 1914, ae 57-11-15; m Feb 8, 1881, Lovisa A Marshall. No children. He established a considerable business in growing and shipping potatoes from Bradford, East Corinth and Milo. In 1923 his wid living in Bradford

Fred C Dow abccgcha d Bradford; m Angie Drew b Charleston.
Of children, 2 found by own rec:

    b William H b Bradford 1868   d Thomas Jefferson b Bradford 1871

William H Dow abccgchab, farmer of Island Falls, delirious from
grippe, hung himself June 6, 1915, ae 47-8-7; m Oct 20, 1898, Lucinda
A Edwards b Searsport 1878, dau of Joseph and Lizzie (Fields).   Children:

    a Bernice b May 29, 1900   b Fred Hudson b Apr 3, 1902
    c ——dau b June 5, 1903   d ——son b Dec 7, 1905
    e Vinal Williams b Jan 14, 1908

Thomas J Dow abccgchad, farmer of Island Falls, m Nov 20, 1894,
Luella Mary Small b Smyrna 1877, dau of George and Isadore (Drew)
Children:

    a Freda L b July 29, 1896   b Mary d Sept 3, 1899, ae 6 mos
    c Hazel b June 5, 1901 (father now merchant of Smyrna)

Jonathan Dow abccgd came to Prospect about 1792; d Prospect
Mch 13, 1834; m Sept 13, 1796, Mary (always Polly in rec) Black, b
Mch 23, 1778. An influential man, appears 1827 as justice of the peace.
Ten children:

    a Noah b Jan 19, 1797; d Aug 24, 1818
    b Jonathan b Oct 9, 1799; d Jan 7, 1832
    c Alexander b Dec 31, 1801; d Nov 2, 1850
    d Eliza b June 17, 1804; d Oct 10, 1849
    e Josiah b Feb 22, 1806; d Mch 6, 1806
    f David b Feb 6, 1807   g Mary J b Jan 3, 1813
    h Sarah A b Jan 10, 1815   i Daniel b Jan 10, 1819; d Jan 19, 1846
    j Ruby B b Sept 2, 1823; d July 22, 1857. This branch is the Dow family of
       No Searsport

Jonathan Dow abccgdb m Prospect Dec 13, 1821, Charlotte S
True of Belfast.   This family from Salisbury, Mass, is often intermarried
with Dow.   Jonathan d soon after reaching No Searsport, leaving only
child:

    a Amos b 1826 or 1827

Amos Dow abccgdba drowned at sea; m Searsport Nov 14, 1848,
Milicent Turg b Eng, d Jan 1, 1905, ae 72-7-19, dau of Bennet and Elizabeth (Tinney).   Older children b Tremont, younger Searsport:

    a Iona b Apr 1, 1851; d in girlhood
    b James b 1852-3; d young
    c Melicent; now Mrs Charles Nichols of Searsport
    d Nellie, her twin, b May 6, 1855; m George Patterson; not living
    e James Wallace b Apr 25, 1859; d ae about 14
    f Mabel True; now Mrs Putnam of Baltimore, Md
    g Myra McKeen b July 9, 1867; dressmaker, d June 1907
    h Amos Alfred b June 1, 1870; now captain between Baltimore and South Amer-
       ica; m Aug 24, 1911, Marion Elesa Robinson of Thomaston, dau of George
       W and Abbie Helen (Huyler)

Alexander Dow abccgdc abandoned the sea to become farmer of
No Searsport; d Nov 2, 1850; m May 22, 1823, Sarah Mason b Feb 9,

1803, d Aug 6, 1863.   Two brothers m 2 sisters.   One child d in infancy,
the survivors:

    a   Katherine b Aug 29, 1824; d Oct 25, 1887
    b   Eliza b Sept 10, 1825   c   George Freeman b Feb 17, 1828; untraced
    d   Henry Sewell b May 17, 1829; d May 20, 1880; untraced
    e   James L b Oct 25, 1830   f   Jonathan Mch 5, 1832
    g   Sarah Ann b June 16, 1833   h   Amanda b Apr 13, 1835
    i   Celia Maria b Dec 2, 1838; d May 2, 1871
    j   Mary b Apr 1, 1841   k   Leroy b Jan 21, 1842
    l   Harriet b Aug 23, 1844   m   Clara b June 28, 1848

James L Dow abccgdce, farmer of Searsport, d Oct 11, 1899; m
Caroline Littlefield b Winterport, d Belfast Mch 20, 1911, ae 74-2-25,
dau of Daniel H and Rebecca H (Eldridge). Searsport directory 1907
gives children:

    a   Frank, sea captain of N Y City; untraced
    b   Lucy m——Colcord of Belfast   c   John L b 1880

John L Dow abccgdcec, machinist of Belfast, m Sept 13, 1906,
Georgie A Triggs, ae 23, of Belfast, dau of William and Augusta (Emerton). Child:

    a   Laurance Everett b Belfast May 19, 1913

Jonathan Dow abccgdcf, deep sea captain, d San Francisco Mch
19, 1879; m May 25, 1858, Annie E Black b Searsport May 1, 1840.
Children:

    a   Kate b Dec 19, 1859; married   b   Sarah b Nov 16, 1863; married
    c   Fred Alexander b Dec 6, 1865; in 1889 bookkeeper of Franklin Grove, Ill, unm
    d   Clytie b Nov 11, 1867; married
    e   Scott J b Sept 21, 1869; in 1921 dept mgr of Chicago; letter of genealogical
        inquiry unanswered

David Dow abccgdf is not found in 1850 census; m Louisa Mason.
Probably more children:

    a   John B b Jan 1, 1845   b   Wilson N b 1848
    c   Freeman J b Aug 10, 1853

John B Dow abccgdfa, sailor of Searsport, later clerk of Cambridgeport, Mass, d Searsport Oct 5, 1900; m Aug 27, 1864, Ellen E Carter, ae 19, dau of James and Catherine (George). Children:

    a   La Forrest b Searsport 1867; m 2nd Mass June 28, 1904, Mary Margaret Dunn,
        ae 24, dau of John H and Louise (Ward)
    b   Catherine May b 1873; m Somerville, Mass, July 8, 1907, James Anthony Mc-
        Cue b Eng, ae 42, son of Thomas and Honora (Houlihan)

Wilson N Dow abccgdfb, farmer of Frankfort, returned to Searsport; d Aug 8, 1911, ae 62-10-25; m Elizabeth Eaton (Nancy E) d Searsport Mch 1, 1920, ae 70-7-15, dau of Hiram and Nancy (Staples).   Children, by Frankfort 1893 directory:

    a   Lester C b 1882   b   Mabel m ——Kingsbury of Frankfort
    c   Chester E, farmer   d   Ellen M b Searsport Aug 15, 1892

Lester C Dow abccgdfba, grocer of Frankfort, bought a farm in Prospect; m May 29, 1904, Hannah M Clark, ae 21, dau of Thomas and D M (Dunlap). In 1923 town clerk of Prospect. Children, b Prospect:

 a Earl C b Feb 28, 1905   b Ruth Mildred b Dec 23, 1916

Freeman J Dow abccgdfc, stone cutter, in 1905 boarding house keeper, d Camden Nov 20, 1915; m Julia A Waterhouse, who survived. Children:

 a Bertha C d Camden June 12, 1905; ae 20-8-5
 b Louise M d Searsport Dec 8, 1892, ae 16, 6 mos
 c Raymond F b Mch 2, 1893; untraced
 d Bessie Lola b Searsport May 15, 1897

Leroy Dow abccgdck, master mariner of Searsport, d Mch 7, 1902; m Cora E Eaton of Searsport. Children, both with mother in recent directory:

 a Sallie E b Sept 26, 1892   b Kate M b May 14, 1895

Sarah Dow abcd m Feb 7, 1711, Benjamin Lamprey b Oct 9, 1688, son of Benjamin and Jane (Batchelder); settled in No Hampton. Children:

 a Sarah b Mch 8, 1713; m Nov 11, 1738, Israel Dolbear of Rye
 b Hannah b Apr 7, 1717   c Jane b Apr 9, 1719
 d Mary b Jan 7, 1722
 e Benjamin b Jan 11, 1728; m Abigail Dearborn; 2nd Comfort Shepard
 f Simon m Patience Hobbs
 g Elizabeth bap Aug 28, 1733; d Mch 30, 1811; m Jonathan Godfrey

F ROM No Hampton, a village which has never grown up, but remains about what it was two centuries ago, to Rye is a short
step. For a century and a half the Dow family of Rye was
large and influential, among the local aristocracy. Characteristically,
just as in Hampton, it has absolutely disappeared, the male lines almost
extinct.

Isaac Dow abce bought a farm of 76 acres in Rye, but stocked it
well. Hist Hampton makes one of its few errors in giving him m 1726
Charity Philbrick b Apr 29, 1702, d June 22, 1772. She is Charity
Berry, dau of Nathaniel, who m 1691 Elizabeth Philbrick of Hampton.
Charity d wid June 22, 1772; m by Rev William Allen, Greenland, Oct
12, 1727. Isaac d 1735. Children:

    a Henry b Dec 29, 1727
    b Mary b Sept 6, 1730; m Dec 25, 1750, Capt Joseph Jenness b Feb 28, 1727,
       d 1815
    c Eleanor b Dec 8, 1733; m 1st Samuel Brackett; 2nd Sept 8, 1771, Jesse Berry

Henry Dow abcea, selectman of Rye 5 years 1757 to 1768; d Oct
4, 1772, ae given as 40. Hist Hampton gives d Hampton 1779. This
5 years discrepancy is not serious. He m Martha Perkins of Hampton
bap Apr 23, 1732, dau of James and Huldah (Robie); m 2nd July 31, 1781,
Simon Lamprey of No Hampton. Children:

    a Hannah b Oct 15, 1752   b Isaac b Dec 13, 1754
    c Martha b Oct 6, 1758; d Jan 31, 1792; m June 25, 1778, Joseph Locke
    d Mary b Dec 25, 1761   e James b Jan 8, 1765

Hannah Dow abceaa m Aug 28, 1777, Isaac Jenness b 1751, son of
Joseph and Mary (Dow) abceb; d Apr 20, 1840. Children:

    a Mary b Feb 20, 1780; m Nathan Brown
    b Hannah b Dec 27, 1782; d 1862
    c Henry b Apr 7, 1785; m 1813 Charlotte Lamprey

Isaac Dow abceab m Aug 21, 1777, Elizabeth Seavey b June 19,
1753, d Dec 7, 1823, dau of William and Mary (Langdon); served 1775
under Capt Jacob Webster; selectman 1783-4. When the church was
enlarged in 1781, he paid at auction $5,425 for one of the five new pews.
This was in Continental currency, then at 75 for each gold dollar. Children:

    a Patty b Oct 28, 1779; d July 17, 1819   b Amos b 1781   c Isaac b 1782
    d Henry b Apr 6, 1783   e James b June 3, 1785
    f Betsey b 1791; d Mch 18, 1834; m John T Rand

Patty Dow abceaba m Col Amos Seavey Parsons b Oct 9, 1768,
son of Dr Joseph and Mary (Seavey); Lieut Col with fine record in 1812.
He d Nov 7, 1850. Children:

    a Polly Dow b Jan 29, 1797; m Jan 9, 1825, Joseph Dalton
    b Isaac Dow b May 7, 1799

    c   Eliza b Dec 27, 1800; m Apr 4, 1822, Lyman Seavey
    d   Martha b Nov 24, 1802; m Apr 4, 1822, Cotton W Drake
    e   Samuel b Feb 27, 1804
    f   Anna Seavey b Dec 24, 1806; m July 14, 1822, John Drake
    g   Almira b Jan 20, 1809; m Jan 3, 1822, Jonathan Brown
    h   Joseph b Feb 11, 1811; unm
    i   Lovina b June 11, 1813; m May 11, 1839, Lewis L Perkins
    j   James Monroe b Aug 7, 1816; m Nov 15, 1844, wid Minerva Cox

Amos Dow abceabb, farmer of Newington, assessed 1850 at $3,000,
d Newington Oct 1, 1855, ae 73; m Lydia Fabens d Newington July 14,
1873, ae 83, 9 mos. This family is properly Fabyan and gave its name
to a White Mts place. Hist Rye is painfully inaccurate regarding all
Dow genealogy, due, doubtless, to the fact that the Dows soon moved
to Newington. Order of children, combined from Hist Rye and State
rec:

    a   Eliza Ann (2nd child, Hist Rye) d Newington Apr 20, 1853; m July 13, 1842,
        Rev William Padman of Portsmouth
    b   Amos (not in Hist Rye) d Concord Insane Asylum Feb 1, 1859, ae 50
    c   Samuel (not in Hist Rye), son of Amos, d Newington Feb 2, 1846, ae 35, pre-
        sumably unm
    d   Emeline (3rd, Hist Rye) d Newington Dec 15, 1853, ae 40
    e   Lydia P (4th, Hist Rye). L Priscilla Dow m Newington Oct 18, 1835, Levi
        Carkin
    f   Priscilla (5th, Hist Rye) not found elsewhere. Some Clarissa J Dow m New-
        ington July 9, 1844, Joseph C Huckins of Dover. The known Huckins inter-
        marriages are with abbegf line
    g   Langdon (1st born, Hist Rye) b 1826 by census, farmer of Newington, d Jan
        6, 1856, ae 33; his wid Margaret M m 2nd Nov 25, 1856, Richard P Hoyt
        of Portsmouth

Isaac Dow abceabc moved to Newington; d Feb 25, 1869, his neck
broken by a fall from a shed which he was building for his son; m Rye
Feb 25, 1809, Lydia Pickering (Fabens is error of Hist Rye) b 1789. Hist
Rockingham Co has a contributed sketch of his family, slightly differing
from vital statistics:

    a   Lydia (5th, Hist Rye) m Portsmouth June 26, 1838, John M Furber
    b   Valentine P b Feb 4, 1808 by Hist Rye, 1813 by census, 1814 by d rec
    c   Eliza Ann b 1815 by census; not in Hist Rock; perhaps error for abceabba
    d   Frances T m Nov 10, 1847, Isaac Brackett of Boston
    e   Martha McClaren b 1827 (census); Martha A of Hist Rye; d Dec 5, 1855, ae
        25, unm
    f   Mclauren (not in Hist Rye) d at sea Sept 16, 1843, ae 25, presumably unm
    g   Isaac b Apr 29, 1826

Valentine P Dow abceabcb d June 27, 1865; carpenter of Newington, m July 18, 1837, wid Sarah Folsom of Portsmouth; 2nd Dec 5,
1849, Mary Jane Cotton of Holderness.

Isaac Dow abceabcg, in 1898 only living member of his family, carpenter, several times selectman and representative from Rye; retiring,
bought a farm in Newington; d May 7, 1914; m Jan 12, 1862, Abbie
Whidden Beane, ae 24, d July 15, 1910, dau of Ruel J and Sarah of Milton, Mass. Children:

    a   Herbert Beane b Newington Mch 10, 1865; Episcopalian, unm in 1910
    b   Greenleaf Clough b Mch 9, 1870; d Jan 14, 1875

Henry Dow abceabd, carpenter of Rye, moved to Portsmouth; m 1st Jan 22, 1811, Elizabeth Fabyan (Flynn, by erroneous m rec) b June 8, 1787, d Apr 20, 1826; 2nd m June 1, 1828, Elizabeth (Lowd) Briggs b Portsmouth May 17, 1790, d Portsmouth Dec 23, 1884, dau of Daniel and Mary (Tucker).   Henry d Portsmouth Oct 22, 1865.   Seven children by 1st wife:

a   Elizabeth Seavey b Oct 11, 1811; d Oct 20, 1881; m Newington May 7, 1837, Thomas G Furber
b   Isaac b Mch 28, 1813
c   George Washington b Dec 16, 1814; d Portsmouth Sept 4, 1847, unm
d   Henry b Apr 15, 1817; went south early in life; lost sight of by rest of family
e   Thomas Jefferson b May 25, 1819; d Baltimore Feb 28, 1842, unm
f   Joseph Fabyan b Feb 13, 1822; drowned Charles River, Boston, Oct 24, 1876, unm
g   Martha Parsons b June 28, 1824; d Oct 13, 1824
h   Martha Parsons b Mch 25, 1829; d from carriage accident Sept 20, 1881, unm
i   Hannah Pickering b July 4, 1830; d Portsmouth Apr 24, 1903, unm
j   William Wallace b Portsmouth Nov 27, 1832

Isaac Dow abceabdb, tinsmith and well known citizen of Portsmouth, d from a fall Aug 28, 1880; m Mch 9, 1837, Mary E Briggs of Portsmouth d Nov 22, 1890, ae 77-8-15, dau of William and Elizabeth (Lowd).   Children:

a   Mary E D b June 4, 1837; d Gorham, Me, Sept 21, 1902, unm
b   James H b 1840, by rec of 3rd m
c   Emily F b 1844; m Portsmouth June 18, 1881, Joseph B Fletcher

James H Dow abceabdbb, trader, salesman, clerk, m June 9, 1868, Emma F Ackerman, ae 19; m 3rd Sept 12, 1892, Susetta (Zettie, Hist Rock) M Bond, ae 35, b Kittery.

William W Dow abceabdj, grad Dartmouth, clergyman with pastorates Farmington Falls, No Chesterville, army of Shenandoah in 1865, West Brockville, Waterford, Kittery, Lebanon Center; m May 14, 1868, Elizabeth Ham French, ae 36, dau of Thomas and Sarah (Griffin).   D rec July 23, 1901, gives her b June 16, 1827.

James Dow abceabe, farmer of Rye, assessed 1850 at $3,000; d Rye May 19, 1853; private 1813 under Capt Jonathan Wedgewood; m Feb 6, 1812, Data Drake b Apr 15, 1792, d Apr 24, 1848, dau of Jonathan and Sarah (Ward).   Children:

a   Jonathan Drake b 1814; d Bloomington, Ill, Oct 5, 1850. An Eli S Dow d Rye May 24, 1860, ae 2 years, 9 mos, if dates are right, cannot belong here
b   Elizabeth S d Oct 9, 1848; m May 30, 1837, Langdon Brown
c   Albert b Feb 28, 1819
d   Sarah Ann d Nov 2, 1850; m Jan 1, 1845, Dr Warren Parsons
e   Martha Ann b Aug 1823; d Apr 11, 1845   f   James Henry b Oct 23, 1825
g   Eli Sawtelle b Dec 25, 1827; bought farm of his own; d Aug 30, 1858, unm
h   Cazacana (Casendary, family rec; Cassandra?) b Jan 20, 1830; d Apr 15, 1847
i   Harriet A b Aug 20, 1832; d Sept 1, 1858; m Sept 5, 1855, Levi T Walker

Elizabeth S Dow abceabeb m Langdon Brown b June 2, 1814, son of Simon and Polly (Seavey).   Children:

a   Ann Eliza b Nov 1845; d June 11, 1877; m May 24, 1870, Charles Austin Jenness
b   Otis Simon b Mch 31, 1848; d Dec 25, 1848

Albert Dow abceabec d Rye Apr 9, 1886; m Nov 21, 1847, Ann Elizabeth Seavey b Dec 20, 1825-6, d 1854, dau of John Langdon and Sidney (Seavey). Children:

  a John H b 1848; d accident July 29, 1865
  b Mary b 1850; m Charles Wendell; children,—Auburn, Olive
  c James W d Nov 13, 1861, ae 10

Sarah Ann Dow abceabed m Warren Parsons b May 28, 1818, m 2nd Julia A Gove. Children:

  a William Irving b June 27, 1848; d Mch 30, 1851
  b Joseph Warren b June 1, 1850; m Annie Emerson

James Henry Dow abceabef d Rye Jan 20, 1864; selectman 1862-3: m June 3, 1849, Angelina Brown b Jan 3, 1826, dau of Nathan and Mary (Locke). Children:

  a Clara Maria b Apr 5, 1850; m Nov 4, 1869, James Alba Rand
  b ——, dau b and d July 22, 1852
  c Charles H b July 31, 1854; d Mch 18, 1869
  d Flora b Jan 15, 1860; inherited the homestead; m Oct 21, 1896, Arthur H Ballard of Worcester, Mass; she sold the home, the last of the Dow of Rye
  e Ella F b Sept 12, 1863; d Feb 28, 1864

Betsey Dow abceabf m John Tuck Rand b July 7, 1791, son of Thomas and Mary (Tuck). Children:

  a Elizabeth Martha b Jan 26, 1821; d unm
  b Isaac Dow b Dec 14, 1828; unm   c Mary Tuck b Jan 31, 1831; unm

Martha Dow abceac m Joseph Locke, son of Jeremiah and Mary (Elkins). Children:

  a Jeremiah b Dec 9, 1778   b Henry b Aug 25, 1780; d in infancy
  c Mary b Apr 30, 1782; m Jonathan Perkins
  d Mercy b Jan 11, 1784; m Samuel Mason   e Joseph b May 4, 1787

Mary Dow abcead m 1st John Dowrst b Feb 22, 1762, son of Ozem J and Elizabeth (Jenness) moved to Deerfield. Children:

  a Martha J b Mch 5, 1782; d Nov 22, 1782   b Isaac   c Henry

James Dow abceae of Rye, selectman 1800, m Greenland Jan 19, 1790, Mary Parsons b 1770, d Dec 7, 1842, dau of Dr Joseph and Mary (Seavey). Child:

  a Martha Locke b May 12, 1799

Martha L Dow abceaea d Sept 18, 1885; m Aug 10, 1820, Nathaniel Graves Foye b Sept 10, 1798, son of John and Elizabeth (Seavey). Children:

  a Mary Elizabeth b Feb 25, 1821; m Dec 9, 1841, Joseph Disco Jenness
  b Ann Cecilia b Apr 22, 1822; m June 7, 1843, Samuel Marden
  c Orion Leavitt b Aug 9, 1824
  d Elizabeth b Jan 25, 1827; d June 22, 1843
  e Martha Abby b Mch 10, 1829; d July 15, 1844
  f Fidelia E b Oct 13, 1830; d May 6, 1861
  g James Nathaniel b Apr 27, 1833
  h Ellen Ruthdian b Mch 6, 1835; m (his 2nd) Joseph Disco Jenness
  i Sarah Ann b Mch 25, 1837; d Aug 26, 1838
  j Sophia Jenness b Mch 8, 1839
  k John Harrison b Mch 6, 1841; killed in 13th N H vols

Mary Dow abceb m Capt Joseph Jenness, son of Richard and Mary (Dow) abca; selectman of Rye 1776; m 2nd Anna Parker. Children:

a Mary bap Jan 9, 1752   b Isaac bap Mch 26, 1754; d in infancy
c Isaac bap Oct 1755; m Hannah Dow abceaa
d Richard bap Jan 1, 1758; m Mary Paige; killed by lightning
e Jonathan bap July 27, 1760   f Sarah bap May 13, 1764
g Joseph bap Feb 24, 1771   h Hannah bap Mch 19, 1773

Eleanor Dow abcec, 1st—, son of Anthony Brackett, immigrant from Wales. Only child:

a Love b Aug 9, 1758; m Nov 10, 1774, William Berry

Jonathan Dow abcf of Hampton m Nov 20, 1729, Sarah Weare b July 5, 1709, dau of Nathaniel and Mary (Waite). Their farm was in Hampton Falls, where all but two children were born. About 1754 they moved to a farm in Kensington, close to or possibly across the Kingston line. Here he served as deacon. He does not appear in Association Test; in 1790 census 3a, 3c, the rest of the family married and gone. He d 1796; will dated 1787 and mentions wife Sarah; children Mehitable, Abigail, Elizabeth, Nathaniel; grandson Samuel Barnard. Sarah Weare Dow d about 1798. Son Nathaniel was executor of both wills. The list of children seems complete from Hampton Falls rec. We cannot place a Reuben Dow of Kensington who appears in 1790 census, and in a few scattering mentions as a prominent citizen. The early Kensington rec are in deplorable condition, would be hopeless were it not that Rev Jeremiah Fogg, Kensington incumbent for many years, kept his own rec of births, baptisms, marriages and deaths at which he officiated. Kensington rec gives 3 children of Nathaniel but without giving name or sex— d 1739, d 1749 ae 12, d 1749 ae 4:

a Nathaniel b Nov 14, 1730; a genealogical stumbling block; does not appear in Rev rosters, nor in Association Test, nor in 1790 census. He was executor for both parents 1796 and 1798. One would presume he had posterity
b Mary b Jan 27, 1733; m John Tuck b July 28, 1736, son of Edward and Sarah (Dearborn) of Kensington. He m 2nd Susan Smith and had 7 children in all. Will of Jonathan Dow mentions only Nathan Tuck, but Mary and John were possibly children of Mary Dow
c Mehitable b Sept 9, 1735; m June 13, 1769, Samuel Prescot
d Sarah b Aug 26, 1738; prob d 1749   e Hannah b Sept 8, 1740
f Abigail b Apr 11, 1743; presumably m Feb 7, 1792, Capt Andrew Greeley of East Kingston
g Elizabeth d in infancy   h Simon b July 21, 1748; prob d young
i Elizabeth   j Nathan b Feb 7, 1753; d June 6, 1758, ae 3
k Esther m Aug 14, 1769, Samuel Locke of Brentwood
l Asabel; Abihal in Association Test; Asahel in son's rec

Hannah Dow abcfe. We do not understand why Asahel Dow fails to figure in his father's will made 1787, Asahel living in 1790; nor do we understand why Esther (Dow) Locke is missing. Hannah also fails to appear. Various Dow of abbeg and abcc lines appear later in Brentwood, but among them there does not seem to be any place for a Hannah or Susannah. Ladd Gen gives a Susannah Dow of Brentwood m (his 2nd) Daniel Ladd b Kingston Jan 25, 1726, veteran of Louisburg campaign, son of Daniel. He m 3rd Ruth Bradley and he made the first survey of Unity, N H. The birthdates of Susannah's older children seem approximated and not from any actual rec. It is possible that Susannah is error for Hannah and the marriage 4 or 5 years later than indicated by the stated birthdate of 1st born. These children:

a Peter b 1756; m Abigail Martin of Deerfield
b Joseph b 1758; m Rachel Fifield
c Joannah b 1760; m Theodore Marston
d Samuel b 1762; m Dolly Brown
e Susannah b 1764; m Benjamin Bartlett
f Jedediah b 1767; m Nancy Brown
g Jeremiah b 1769; lost at sea, unm
h Mehitable b July 10, 1771; m Dec 15, 1796, Eleazer Robbins
i Polly b 1773; m Sawyer Brown
j Miriam b 1773; m——Proctor; 2nd Nathaniel Ladd

Asahel Dow abcfl appears in Kensington 1790 census 1a, 2b, 3c. His wife (family rec) was a Miss Bradish. If Asahel is the youngest, surely not b before 1770, he surely had to speed up to be a father of 4 in 1790. Presumably he was not the youngest born. We guess his 4 children, the 1st born a sure guess:

a Jonathan Bradish b 1787; drowned Newburyport Sept 22, 1830, unm
b Dida Dow m Feb 23, 1812, Benjamin Palmer, both of Kensington
c Ephraim of Kensington m Newburyport Dec 17, 1812, Mrs Rachel Currill; further unt
d Sally of Kensington int pub Aug 31, 1811, to Joseph Stickney of Newburyport

JABEZ DOW abd, weaver of Hampton, a by no means unimportant trade in those days, was thrifty and bought the Hampton estate of his cousin, who had gone to Ipswich. His homestead was where Jacob D Godfrey lived in 1890. He served 9 years in all as selectman, generally alternating years; between times he was almost invariably moderator of town meeting. As a fighter he appears well in Indian scrimmages and was captain of militia in King William's War. Altogether, he maintained the family standing in Hampton. In 1715 he was elected deputy to the General Court, but after election it was remembered that he was already constable. So another deputy was chosen. Each sheep owner had his distinguishing mark. That of Jabez: a crop on the left eare and a slit on the Right eare not at the end but a littell slanting downward. He m Mch 24, 1693, Esther Shaw b Nov 17, 1666, d Apr 26, 1756, dau of Benjamin and Esther (Richardson). Children:

a Benjamin b Dec 4, 1693; served 3 weeks at 6s in the Indian campaign of 1712 under Capt James Davis; prominent citizen, moderator in 1751, on many committees; d suddenly Dec 19, 1762, unm. A Hampton rec: Mary Dow dau of Benjamin and Franfis, b Mch 30, 1705, is error, not Dow at all
b Lucy b Oct 26, 1695   c Ezekiel b Jan 5, 1698
d Lydia b Nov 5, 1700; d Apr 17, 1766
e Esther (Hester) b Oct 31, 1702; d Jan 7, 1731
f Patience b Nov 15, 1705; d Dec 10, 1762; m July 25, 1749, Lieut William Stanford, clothier with mill on Nilus Creek, widower with 3 children. First wife wid Frances (Sherburne) Dole; no children by Patience
g Comfort b Oct 28, 1708   h Mary d July 10, 1751; m Eben Knowlton
i Elizabeth d, ae 24, Sept 21, 1755; m Nathan Green of Kensington; no children

Lucy Dow abdb d Dec 27, 1755; m Jan 1, 1720, James Hobbs, son of Morris and Sarah (Swett); lived Little River, Hampton, in a house torn down after the deaths of their great grandchildren, who occupied it. Children:

a Esther b Oct 9, 1720; m Reuben Dearborn
b Jonathan b Apr 7, 1722; d Jan 3, 1756; m Mary Berry
c Sarah b Apr 11, 1724; d Aug 17, 1749, unm
d James b June 6, 1726; grad Harvard 1748; first pastor of Pelham; d June 20, 1765
e Benjamin b Apr 18, 1728; m Deborah Batchelder; 2nd Elizabeth Fogg; d Apr 22, 1804
f Morris b June 27, 1730; d June 20, 1810; m Theodate Page
g Lucy b Dec 14, 1732; d Sanbornton July 15, 1813; m Daniel Sanborn, son of Dea Daniel
h Patience b Mch 10, 1734; m Simon Lamprey, son of Benjamin
i Comfort b Mch 28, 1736; d Apr 8, 1830; m John Shepard; 2nd Benjamin Lamprey

Ezekiel Dow abdc d Kensington July 31, 1767; m 1st Mch 3, 1726 Abigail Robie b Apr 6, 1703, d 1734, dau of Samuel and Mary (Page); m 2nd Sept 25, 1735, Elizabeth Cram, dau of Thomas and Elizabeth (Weare). She and Sarah Dow (probably abcf) were dismissed from Hampton Falls church in 1737 to form a new church in Kensington. Mch

3, 1736, Elizabeth, wife of Ezekiel Dow, made a public confession of adultery, which was formally accepted and she was restored to communion. This church rec is among those published long ago. At first it seems rather serious, considering the times; but an examination of the church rec show that almost every young married woman had made a similar confession; that all were thereupon restored to communion. Genealogical writers pass rather completely over published data of this sort, genealogy being generally a sop to family vanity. Writers, instead, are inclined to fill in with paragraphs about the remarkable purity and sweetness of each individual. Now, if genealogy is of value at all, it is because it permits a study of heredity. If manners and customs are distorted or omitted, the value of the work becomes little.

Century in and century out, the proportion of births of 1st born within nine months of marriage is large and not very varying. The proportion was not smaller in 1730 than 1830. A few authors mention "bundling," but this practice had no hold in New England, altho beds were scarce and distances so long that a fiance was almost compelled to stay over night. The fact is that in 1730 social pleasures were scarce. Engaged couples could not keep in large groups.

From Ezekiel has come the only male line of abd:

a Abigail b Dec 3, 1727; d Feb 27, 1771; m Mch 1, 1753, Jonathan Rowe
b Comfort b Dec 28, 1729; m Oct 13, 1751, Josiah Batchelder
c Benjamin b Feb 19, 1732   d Esther b Apr 5, 1734
e Nathan b Dec 5, 1735   f Lydia b June 3, 1737; d Sept 8, 1746
g Patience b Feb 5, 1740; d Nov 3, 1828; m July 11, 1781, Stephen Brown b Nov 19, 1724, d Feb 24, 1786, son of William and Ann (Heath). His 1st wife was Mary Weare
h Lucy b Oct 1, 1741; d Jan 9, 1831; m May 1, 1760, John Weare
i Jabez b Aug 25, 1747

Benjamin Dow abdcc of Hampton d Dec 27, 1762; m June 17, 1756, Mary Marston of Kensington b Jan 28, 1734, d July 19, 1766, dau of Ephraim and Abigail (Knowles). Children:

a Mary b May 13, 1759   b Esther b Feb 11, 1761

Mary Dow abdcca m Mch 18, 1781, Nathaniel Shannon d 1826. She d July 27, 1834. He was member of N H constitutional convention of 1798, presidential elector 1820. Children:

a Abigail b Dec 4, 1781; d Apr 14, 1866; m John Wiggin; 2nd E Hoyt
b Thomas b Dec 25, 1783; d July 5, 1864; m July 8, 1808, Margaret V Moses
c Nathaniel Vaughan b July 9, 1790; d June 26, 1859; m 1813 Betsey Brown

Esther Dow abdccb m Mch 5, 1780, Jonathan Philbrick b Jan 28, 1756, d May 9, 1822, son of Daniel and Margaret (Ayres). Children:

a Polly b June 18, 1780; d Sept 19, 1860; m John Lamprey
b John d Oct 16, 1864; m Hannah Godfrey   c Cynthia d 1831 unm
d David b June 7, 1793; d Sept 19, 1875; m Nancy Coffin
e Jonathan b Nov 9, 1796; d Nov 12, 1856; m Abigail Marston; 2nd Mary A Brewster

Esther Dow abdcd.   Barely possible that she, and not abcfk m Samuel Locke b July 28, 1740, d 1770, son of Samuel and Jerusha (Shaw). She left children:

a and b, Benjamin and Betsey, necessarily twins

Nathan Dow abdce d Dec 2, 1810; m Aug 14, 1760, Elizabeth Batchelder b Aug 14, 1736.   Influential citizen of Kensington, he has been found only in vital statistics.   Children:

a Betsey b Apr 9, 1761; d Feb 15, 1830, unm
b Benjamin b Dec 22, 1762
c Nathan b Feb 6, 1768; d married farmer of Kensington, Dec 29, 1841. Census of 1790 gives him 1a, 1b, 3c. So far, one may only guess at the missing children.

Benjamin Dow abdceb, lifelong resident of Kensington, m May 12, 1789, Tabitha Blake d Kensington Dec 25, 1833.   Children:

a Sewall b Nov 28, 1790; d 1873, unm; lived on homestead, caring for two sisters; farm assessed $3,000 in 1850
b Polly b July 11, 1792; d 1873, unm   c Nathan b Nov 18, 1793
d Myra b May 29, 1795; m Apr 10, 1837, John Moulton of So Hampton; no children
e John b Aug 23, 1796
f Tabitha b June 21, 1798; m Samuel P Tilton; lived Kensington
g Eliza b Jan 1, 1800; d unm on homestead
h Sarah b Apr 22, 1801
i Lydia b Oct 28, 1803; m Edward C Stevens; a dau Anna
j Lucy b Apr 22, 1805; m Jan 30, 1840, Weare D Tilton, brother of Samuel P, son of Joseph and Nancy (Healey) of Hampton Falls. He lived always in the Tilton homestead; d Jan 14, 1869, ae 62; no children. He built on his own land a house for Polly Dow abkdbd and her cousin, Sally Healey, taking tender care of them. Both Tiltons were outlived many years by their wives
k Abigail b Apr 18, 1807   l Benjamin b Feb 11, 1810

Nathan Dow abdcebc d Kensington Apr 11, 1862, ae given as 64,— five years too young; farmer assessed at $2,000 in 1850; m Kensington Nov 4, 1816, Mary Prescott d Feb 21, 1863, ae 67, 8 mo. Children:

a Charles b Kensington Sept 5, 1818
b Mary Elizabeth b July 21, 1822. Census gives Betsey b 1830; she m June 23, 1852, Joseph F Piper of Kensington
c Tabitha Blake b June 10, 1824; m Samuel Tilton of Kensington; a son Eldridge
d Henry b Oct 19, 1826

Charles Dow abdcebca m Kensington Jan 17, 1844, Eliza A Peacock. In 1850 he appears as a boat builder of Kensington; moved 1863 to Newburyport to accommodate an increasing business. A son was born 1850 in Manchester. Charles is said to have died in the army, albeit of quite mature years. Children:

a Ellen b 1848; in 1921 was Mrs Rideout of Lynn, Mass
b George Edwin b 1850   c Herbert d ae 7   d Henry Alvah

George E Dow abdcebcab d after 1915; came to California 1868; m 1873 Cora Jane Leach of Maine.   Brought up in the boat building

business, he organized a large pump manufacturing business in San
Francisco, now carried on by his son. Children:

a George Alvah b Apr 17, 1874   b Wallace Hanscom b June 25, 1875
c Edwin Tyson b Oct 21, 1876; d 1909
d Mabel Lillian b July 24, 1880; m 1906 James Wheeler Davidson of Austin,
  Minn

George A Dow abdcebcaba succeeded as president of the business;
m Feb 22, 1905, Lillian J Wilson.

Wallace H Dow abdcebcabb is a civil engineer of San Francisco.

Henry A Dow abdcebcad is connected with the pump works in Ala-
meda. Directory 1915 gives at same address (presumably his children):

a Chester E, foreman   b Hazel, art goods   c Melvin, driver

Henry Dow abdcebcd, shoe dealer of Exeter, d Sept 7, 1899; m
Kensington May 30 1850, Mary K Bowles, ae 25, b Eng; div; no children.

John Dow abdcebe received his medical education from his uncle
Dr Jabez Dow abdced of Dover; began practice 1837 in Pittston, Me;
m Sept 23, 1824, Mary Morrill b Wells Mch 19, 1796, dau of Hon Nahum
and Sarah (Littlefield). Nahum Morrill was merchant and vessel owner,
for many years in Legislature. Dr Dow was an unusually successful
practitioner in Boston for many years; d Chelsea Mch 19, 1871.
Children:

a John Edwin b Sanford Oct 14, 1825   b Nahum Morrill b Feb 11, 1827
c Benjamin b Jan 19, 1829   d Mary Morrill b Feb 23, 1832
e Sarah b July 6, 1834; m Dec 14, 1855, George W Chase
f Martha Williamson b May 6, 1836; m William N Snow
g James Jewett b Dec 13, 1838; d Aug 16, 1864
h William Lovett Walker b Feb 3, 1841; d Aug 16, 1864

John Edwin Dow abdcebea of Cambridge m Jan 1, 1855, Mary
Elizabeth Trott b Bath, Me, Apr 25, 1839. Children:

a Sarah Lizzie b Sept 14, 1859   b Ellen Augusta b Mch 13, 1864
c Annie Marion b Sept 30, 1866
d William Snow b Nov 12, 1868; d July 18, 1871
e Lena Ellsworth b Dec 1, 1870
f Frances Mabel b Nov 26, 1873; m Ernest Snow
g Mary Florence b Nov 26, 1873
h David Crocker b Apr 6, 1875; Cambridge physician by recent directory
i James Arthur b Apr 6, 1875; d May 24, 1875
j William Snow b July 23, 1878   k Edith Morrill b Feb 10, 1881

Annie M Dow abdcebeac of Cambridge m June 19, 1900, Albert
Green Gardiner, son of Benjamin and Caroline (Green). Children:

a Elizabeth Trott b Apr 23, 1901   b Caroline Green b Sept 21, 1904

David Crocker Dow abdcebeah, physician of Cambridge, Mass, is
among the thousand Dows who never answered letters of genealogical
inquiry; m Cambridge Oct 2, 1902, Edith Leslie Atwood, ae 26, dau of
David and Maria (Graham). Child, Cambridge rec:

a David C b Nov 13, 1905   b Margaret b Jan 25, 1908

William S Dow abdcebeaj, dentist of Warner, N H, did not answer letter of genealogical inquiry; m Cambridge Sept 16, 1907, Mary E Lathrop, ae 24, b Providence, R I, dau of Eugene R and Susan (Case). Child:

   a Virginia Lathrop b Warner Dec 6, 1815

Nahum Morrill Dow abdcebeb m Martha Russell; untraced.

Benjamin Dow abdcebec b Sanford, Me, d Chelsea Feb 27, 1882; traveling salesman of Cambridge, m Dec 25, 1861, Mary Ann Leys b Peacham, Vt. Children:

   a Jennie Lincoln b May 22, 1866; m Fred Barbour
   b Mary Alice b Feb 12, 1868

Mary M Dow abdcebed m June 4, 1866, Joseph Henry Flitner b Nov 28, 1840, son of Zachariah and Elizabeth (Cutts). Children:

   a Mary Elizabeth b Jan 14, 1870   b Arthur Dow b Oct 2, 1872

Sarah Dow abdcebh m Exeter Mch 14, 1831, Lewis F Shepard; moved June 7, 1833, to Belfast, Me. Son John F m his cousin Elizabeth Knight abdcebk.

Abigail Dow abdcebk d Oct 17, 1890; m June 6, 1833, Stephen Tilton Knight of Hampton Falls. Children:

   a Elizabeth Ann b Oct 14, 1838; d Sept 16, 1909; m Apr 20, 1856, John F Shepard. Children:
      a Lewis Frederick b May 15, 1857; d Dec 1857
      b Sarah Lizzie b Oshkosh, Wis, Apr. 1858; d Apr 4, 1886; m Jack Sanborn of Hampton Falls; son Thomas Lowell m Oct 1917 Sarah Gookin
      c Abbie Eliza b June 11, 1861; m Richard Cunningham; 2nd James B Goodrich. Children: Arthur Leslie (Cunningham) m Alice W Gambrell; Doris Elinor (Goodrich) b Aug 1907
      d Florence Louisa b Apr 1863; m Fred Tourtillot
      e Frederick Knight b Mch 1868; d Jan 1905; m Emma McLaughlin; child,—Helen Beatrice b 1898
      f Helen Patterson b Sept 15, 1870; d Nov 1904; m Herbert C Crowell; child,—Doris Elizabeth d young

   b Henry Harrison b July 20, 1841; d May 8, 1907; m Dec 20, 1879, Ruth J Green of Kensington. Children:
      a Grace Green b May 30, 1881
      b Agnes Ruth b Dec 19, 1882
      c Mildred Frances b Jan 29, 1885; m June 30, 1917, Harry Raybold of Exeter

Benjamin Dow abdcebl d Gilford June 13, 1860; m Sept 19, 1833, Mary Ann Evans (Evarts seems error), dau of Josiah. Lived Gilmanton until after 1850, then Laconia; a successful teacher. In middle life he was afflicted with religious mania never recovering sufficiently to resume teaching. A place was made for him as watchman on the Meredith bridge, and this he held many years. Children:

   a ——b 1833; d young   b ——b 1835; d young
   c George W b 1837; for many years a steamship engineer on the Pacific coast; untraced

d Sarah F b 1839; m F F French of Lynn, Mass
e Helen B b 1841   f John H b May 3, 1843
g Charles G b 1846; lived Laconia; untraced
h Georgianna b 1849; m Joseph Ayer   i Leander b 1853
j ——b 1855; d young   k ——b 1857; d young

Helen B Dow abdceble m Winthrop Hilton Smith b Feb 3, 1832; enlisted thrice in inf and artillery; later a prominent temperance advocate. Children:

a Bertha Eldora b Lake Village Feb 10, 1861
b Edwin Hilton b June 16, 1867   c Charles Horace b May 1, 1870
d Frank French T b Dec 8, 1877

John Henry Dow abdceblf of Gilford, veteran of Civil War, d Dec 5, 1916; m Feb 20, 1871, Alice L Sanborn, ae 18, dau of Levi and Frances. Child:

a Charles Henry b Nov 4, 1872

Charles H Dow abdceblfa, coal dealer of Laconia, m Mch 4, 1903, Lillian Hannah Page, ae 22, dau of Ezra A and Emma (McGlouchlin). Children:

a Sheldon Page b Feb 8, 1906   b John Henry b Apr 9, 1907
c Lillian Louisa b Nov 8, 1913

Leander Dow abdcebli of Concord, later spinner of Laconia, m Aug 31, 1871, Carrie M Hicks, ae 21, dau of Charles. At least one child:

a George H b 1873

George H Dow abdceblia, teamster of Franklin, m Feb 18, 1893, Minnie M Wells, ae 18, dau of Andrew and Sarah F of Salisbury, N H. Child:

a ——dau b Salisbury Sept 2, 1895

Jabez Dow abdced located 1793 in Dover, N H; practiced medicine until he d Jan 9, 1839; became quite well to do; m July 30, 1801, Hannah Waitt of Malden, Mass, b 1781, older half-sister of Rev Thaddeus Mason Harris of Harvard, secy to Jared Sparks and author of Natural History of the Bible. His grandson Edward Doubleday Harris was an amateur genealogist of high rank. Children of Jabez:

a Samuel Waite b Sept 26, 1802   b Henry b 1806
c Nathan Thompson b Dec 27, 1807
d Thaddeus Mason d Mch 26, 1814, ae 1 year, 2 weeks

Samuel W Dow abdceda m Oct 8, 1829, Elizabeth Wallingford b Dec 2, 1806, d May 6, 1830, dau of George W and Abigail (Chadbourne). He practiced medicine in Dover; d without children Somerville, Mass, May 15, 1837.

Henry Dow abdcedb d Aug 18, 1889; m ae 76, Mary Edna Hull, wid of George Gray; dau of Nathaniel and Esther. No children; she inherited the Dover homestead and headship of the street railway.

Nathan T Dow abdcedc grad Dartmouth, taking A M; taught a year in Haverhill; practiced law 2 years in Dover; then to Boston. After practice in Grafton and Worcester, returned 1839 to Boston; d 1870; unm.

Jabez Dow abdci d Deerfield Sept 19, 1808; m So Hampton Feb 13, 1777, Anna Jewell b Hampton Apr 16, 1755, d Laconia May 22, 1840. Farmer of Kingston, moved to Deerfield after the war; served 4 years as private; taking part in Battles of White Plains, Ticonderoga, Stillwater and many minor engagements. As usual, the State rolls are incomplete. He enlisted June 8, 1775, Capt William Hudson Ballard, Col James Frye; receipted for pay Dec 13, 1775. An entry of Oct 6, 1775, reports him as gone to Quebec; next appears enlisting for 3 years, Capt Robinson, Col Nathan Hale, 1777; reported as deserter N Y City, back soon in good order. Most of the country boys were named as deserters in N Y, wanting to see the town. In service 1780, 5th company, Col George Reid; allowed $182.60 for depreciation of currency. Children:

  a Lydia b Dec 1, 1777; d Laconia unm May 17, 1870; many years a teacher in Deerfield and Meredith
  b Sarah b Mch 22, 1781   c Ezekiel b June 21, 1785

Sarah Dow abdcib m Apr 14, 1801, Sewell Dearborn b Feb 26, 1773, son of Edward and Susanna (Brown). She d Oct 31, 1878. Children:

  a Melinda b Feb 26, 1802   b Samuel b 1805   c Mary b May 4, 1807
  d Joseph Jewell b Mch 8, 1818; m 1st Sarah Jenness; 2nd Hannah G Chadwick; 3rd Phebe L McIntire
  e Edward Harris b Oct 21, 1823

Ezekiel Dow abdcic, farmer of Meredith, moved to Laconia; d Nov 20, 1849; m Feb 27, 1814, Sally Hill b Northwood Nov 2, 1785, d Laconia Mch 7, 1880, dau of Jonathan and Abigail (Tilton). Children:

  a Lorenzo Ware b June 27, 1815   b Jonathan G b Dec 4, 1818

Lorenzo W Dow abdcica, familiarly known in political and social life as Honest Ware Dow, of Meredith, d Somerville, Mass, Jan 5, 1912, ae 97; m Feb 8, 1842, Susan Evans Morrison b Sanbornton June 27, 1821. Children:

  a Sarah Frances b Sept 1, 1843
  b Henry Ware b Apr 26, 1850; m Oct 5, 1880, Elizabeth Nichols; lives West Somerville, Mass
  c Susan Emma b Aug 3, 1854   d Walter Amsden b Apr 29, 1858
  e William Morrison b Apr 29, 1858; d Mch 29, 1863

Susan E Dow abdcicac m July 15, 1880, Windsor L Snow; d Dec 2, 1899. Children:

  a Ethel   b Gertrude

Walter Amsden Dow abdcicad of Somerville, member of Sons of Rev; m Nov 26, 1885, Stella Jackson Griffin. Child:

  a Walter Ware b Jan 1888; now of Somerville

Jonathan G Dow abdcicb, farmer of Laconia, assessed 1850 **at** $3,700; d July 9, 1885; mother and unm sister with him in 1850. He m Aug 20, 1854, Mary M Tilton b Deerfield Oct 1, 1830, dau of Elbridge and Melinda (Dearborn) abdciba. She d Laconia Oct 15, 1909. Children:

  a Myra E b Laconia Sept 10, 1855; d Jan 23, 1893, unm
  b Charles E b Aug 7, 1864; d Oct 29, 1866

Lydia Dow abdd m Mch 4, 1723, Philip Towle b Aug 18, 1698, d Feb 15, 1785, son of Caleb and Zipporah (Brackett). Philip was one of nine brothers whose names were often strung together, as in counting-out verses:

<blockquote>
"Philly, Caley, Anthy, Zach,
'Thias, Jerry, Frank and Nat,
And long legged Sam."
</blockquote>

Children:

  a Jabez b Nov 24, 1724; d Dec 25, 1745, at siege of Louisburg
  b Philip b Mch 30, 1727; d June 11, 1736, of throat distemper, the diphtheria plague which more than decimated the children that year
  c Jeremiah b Aug 17, 1729
  d Ezekiel b Jan 16, 1731; d June 13, 1736, throat distemper
  e Esther b Jan 16, 1734; d June 17, 1815; m Benjamin Leavitt
  f Benjamin b Jan 5, 1735; d Jan 8, 1736, throat distemper
  g Philip b Oct 20, 1737; d Mch 19, 1792; m Anna Page, dau of Stephen
  h Patience b Oct 14, 1740; d July 28, 1788, unm

Comfort Dow abdg d June 30, 1736; m Nov 12, 1730, Dr Abraham Green (John 3, Abraham 2, Henry 1) b 1707, son of John and Abial (Marston). Such was the grasp of Hist Hampton that seven generations appear in that book. Comfort and two children d of throat distemper. Dr Green d 1751; m 2nd Sarah Treadwell. Children:

  a Esther b Aug 22, 1731; d June 3, 1736
  b Asahel b Sept 9, 1733; d June 8, 1736   c Comfort b 1735

Comfort Green abdgc d 1757; m 1752 John Marston b 1731, d 1785, son of Capt Ephraim and Mary (Nudd) akea. Child:

  a Samuel b 1754; d Nov 18, 1797

Samuel Marston abdgca m Rhoda Melcher b 1765, d Ossipee 1854, dau of Samuel of Hampton Falls. Children:

  a Betty bap 1785; d Feb 23, 1796
  b Nancy bap Nov 20, 1787; m 1st John Shaw; 2nd Simeon Philbrick
  c John Melcher bap Apr. 25, 1790; m——Thayer; was consul at Palermo; a grandson is partner in Monroe & Cie, bankers, Paris
  d Jonathan bap Jan 21, 1795; d Nov 1795
  e Jonathan bap Jan 26, 1797; d May 24, 1798
  f Eliza Hilliard b Feb 1798; d 1899, over the century

Eliza H Marston abdgcaf, b Boston, lived with her uncle Hon Levi Melcher; m Jan 4, 1824, Henry Bruce, U S N, b 1798 d Boston 1895, son of Phineas and Jane (Savage). Children:

  a Eliza Marston b Oct 30, 1825; d May 10, 1857
  b James b 1834; d 1863   c William d about 1870

   d Jane Savage d Feb 3, 1886   e Mary d Jan 17, 1917
   f Sarah Marston b 1838; living 1917 Lakewood, N J; m 1st William W Tuttle;
      2nd Philip Voorhees, son of Admiral Voorhees U S N

Eliza M Bruce abdgcafa m Jabez Spicer Ryan of Boston b Oct 21, 1814, d June 9, 1894, son of Isaac and Mehitabel (Bradbury) of Plymouth, N H. Children:

   a Henry Bruce b 1848; d 1917   b Eliza Bruce b 1850; lives Boston
   c William Spicer b 1854; d 1907

William S Ryan abdgcafac m 1883 Sarah Moody Bond b 1855, now of Berkeley, Calif, dau of Norman J and Jane of Niantic, Conn. Children:

   a Norman William b 1884; vol 1917, 26th U S ca   b Eliza Marston b 1886
   c Elizabeth Bond b 1888; m William H Vogel of Union, Ore
   d Esther Bradbury b 1890; of Berkeley

Eliza M Ryan abdgcafacb m George M Post, son of Owen and Maria of Deep River, Conn; live Salem, Ore. Child:

   a Hanford Palmer b 1908

The posterity of Capt Henry Dow ab is probably not a fifth as large as that of his brother Joseph or his brother Thomas. One notes that, of the male lines, not more are living today than in 1723 and much fewer than in 1800. Under present conditions it takes an average of about 3¼ children to each family to perpetuate the race, provided that that number reaches 21 years.

FOLLOWING the death of Henry Dow a, his wid m 2nd Oct 23, 1661, Richard Kimball of Ipswich, whose large family had grown into homes of their own. Richard, a wealthy man for his times, was a bit of a "tightwad," making a prenuptial contract that his wife should have 50 £ and the "stuff she brought with her." He d 1675, his will probated Sept 28, inventorying about 4,000 £. Margaret Cole Dow Kimball d Mch 1, 1675. She took to Ipswich all but the oldest of her own children, leaving three Dows to make the Hampton family.

Josehp Dow ad, first Dow b in America, then 22, had been self-supporting some years, his property interests already considerable and growing. He continued an important factor in Hampton life until in 1683 he voluntarily withdrew, a Quaker, from public life and, with associates, moved to the southerly part of Hampton, then almost without a population. The new home extended into what is now fixed as Salisbury, Mass, and into what is now Hampton Falls. Most of the new Quaker colony lay within the present boundaries of Seabrook. The Dow family sprung from Seabrook is the largest of any. Nearly one-fifth of all Dow in America are of Quaker Stock.

While Joseph was at all times less influential in public affairs than his older brother, he was a man of much force of character, of natural leadership, whose influence upon the destinies of the Province can be distinctly traced. His persecution in 1683 had more to do than any other single cause with the removal of the notorious Governor Cranfield and the inauguration of a somewhat more liberal government, altho he was but one of a dozen who appealed successfully to the English King. He was sergeant of militia and saw much fighting against the Indians. He held this position May 31, 1671, when, with all the officers of Norfolk Co., he petitioned the General Court for the retention of their former major (Mass Archives, vol 67, pp 56-7, provincial series)'.

A farmer, as were all, he turned to many lines. There is preserved in the N H Historical Society a steel trap, belonging to him, the first ever imported into America. Muskrat and mink fur was abundant in Hampton. Ability to survey land was not a common accomplishment before 1800, and Joseph bought in England the best compass and other equipment that the time knew. This was inherited by his son Samuel. His town offices were few. He appears on the grand jury 1676; Feb 12, 1669, appointed to survey the Exeter-Hampton line, a source of trouble; in 1671 to make additional survey of that line; in 1680 to lay out the marshes. This also was highly important, as the salt hay was the largest single source of individual income. Appointed Dec 16, 1680, to rebuild the municipal saw mill. In vol 17, Rev Rolls, p 632, is: "At a Councill held 20th October 1693, Ordered that the Bounds of this Province from three miles Northward of Merrimack River be run off on the 14th of November next according to the order of Council made last March & that notice be given to the Govern'r & that Mr Joseph Dow & Capt Joseph Smith be Com'rs for the same and that they be payd by the Treasurer out of the Public Revenue & that they make a returne thereof to this board." This was an important step in the history of the Province, altho it was litigated for the next half century. New Hampshire boundary was a line three miles north of the river, but its bed was tortuous and sometimes shifting. For many years Mass had claimed much more than its possible maximum and had levied taxes. The survey of 1693 added a long tier of farms to Hampton and extended about 20 miles. West of this, subsequent surveys until 1741 were made by many authorities. Curiously, the surveyor who laid off the straight line west to N Y State did not allow properly for the variation of his compass, so that at the west extremity a wedge seven miles thick was put into Mass, belonging properly to Vt. This includes the whole township of Williamstown. The final survey of 1741 made the greatest change. From Haverhill was taken land constituting two new townships, Salem and Plaistow. This is important to anyone who traces the Haverhill Dow. In many cases a man b in Haverhill, d in Plaistow, altho he never left his house. Eight Dow families were so shifted from one Province to the other.

Aug 25, 1701, not quite two years before his death, Joseph Dow was chosen one of the trustees for the land ordered set off for a meeting house for "those Christian people called 'Quakers.' " The events leading up to this are by far the most important in the history of over 10,000 Dows.

The first Quakers to reach America were two female preachers coming to Boston July 1656. A woman preacher was more than the orthodox puritan could endure, they holding in law and fact that woman should be seen and not heard. Apart from sex, the propaganda threatened to interfere with the iron rule of the local ministers, whose control had been unquestioned, more absolute than the papacy had ever been. Other Quaker preachers followed so rapidly that in less than ten years the Government yielded to clamor and took extreme measures, combatting the heresy with as much vehemence as they had witchcraft. Laws were enacted rendering Quakers liable to have their ears cut off, their tongues bored with hot irons, and many other inflictions according to prevailing ideas of Christian charity. The people were with the government. The good old lady who, when they told her a Quaker was being hanged, remarked, "and serve him right", and went on reading her Bible, was typical.

The act which brought the new idea into Hampton occurred 1662. The constables of each town from Dover to Dedham were ordered to "take these vagabond Quakers (Alice Ambrose, Anna Colman, Mary

Tompkins, young women) and make them fast to the cart's tail, and drawing the cart through your several towns, to whip them upon their naked backs not exceeding ten stripes on each of them in each town, and so convey them out of this jurisdiction."

This order was carried out in Dover, Hampton and Salisbury, to the everlasting shame of its citizens. In Salisbury, one Walter Barefoote, later a constable, as precious a scoundrel as ever remained unhanged, performed his almost praiseworthy act; took the women from the constable under pretense of delivering them to the next and secretly got them out of the Province. This proceeding entailed some risk. A jailer one day allowed a Quaker prisoner to go home, on his promise to return the next day. Emboldened by the man's keeping his word, he gave a similar parole to a non-Quaker, imprisoned for debt. This man fled the Province. The jailer lost his position, was mulcted of all his property until he and his family were absolutely destitute. He went insane under the strain and was for 25 years a wanderer dependent on public charity.

Half of the men of Hampton had come from England to escape from persecution on account of their religious beliefs by those who adhered to the Established Church, many fleeing to Holland to save their own lives and limbs. Yet, in less than a full generation, these very men (all the ruling class of them) had become persecutors of those who differed in faith, much more relentless, much more barbarous than their own persecutors had been. It must be imagined that there were a few in Hampton who looked upon this infamous whipping with horror, who in an uncharitable age held some vague notion of the milk of human kindness. Nothing makes religious converts like persecution. No one dared open his mouth in remonstrance, much less express sympathy with a new, strange faith which carried humility and forgiveness to an incomprehensible extent. But:—many thought it over. It was 30 years before it was legally safe to become a Quaker, and even after that it was suicidal for any ambitious man. It precluded service in army or militia, it was a bar to all political life, depending on popular election or not. It was social ostracism. Town and church were a unit, the minister the central figure. He above all fought the man or woman who did not yield blind subservience to him. Against the Quaker, also, was discrimination in everyday business; the non-Quaker would not trade if he could find another market. Yet, the very night of that whipping there were waverers; in a dozen years a dozen citizens had more or less secretly embraced the faith. The leading spirits were Joseph Dow, sturdy and ever unafraid, and Abraham Perkins, son of Abraham, styled the Father of Hampton. Tradition says that Joseph joined in 1675, when he was 34. His wife was equally an enthusiast. In 1683 came trouble. Joseph and other jurymen, all Quakers, were passing the Governor's house (the notorious Cranfield), were invited in and friendly received, but on asking the question whether they might not when sworn (as before they had done) hold up their hands instead of kissing the Book, the Governor fell into a rage and asked them how they came there, to whom Dow replied "at your honor's invitation." Mr Cranfield complained of this matter to the next court as a riot. Dow was forced to give 100 £ bónds for his appearance next session. When Dow appeared nothing was alleged against him, he was discharged and his arms restored; but at another session, after Dow was called again on the same bond, and the penalty was enforced against him, he was forced to flee out of the province with his wife and nine children, leaving his house and goods, with the corn in the ground, to the Governor,

This paragraph is in the words embodied in the complaint against the Governor. It is only one in a hundred. Capt Henry Dow framed it and many others, taking up cudgels for his brother with diplomatic caution. It may be remembered that the two pages torn out of his secret diary are just of the dates to cover these matters. The two Dows and Mr Weare held many conferences, and Mr Weare undertook the journey to London, where he was at least half successful. Cranfield was at once transferred to a West Indian post, but the colony ran much risk of having as his successor the notorious Walter Barefoote.

Some amends for loss of crop were made to Joseph Dow, who returned in the fall of 1683, but this was not by Cranfield. The Friends met and quickly evolved a plan to sell out in Hampton village and move southward. Another small circle had come into existence in Amesbury, and a move in their direction might be advantageous. The new site had been *carefully surveyed by Joseph Dow.* As farm land it was as good as that in Hampton, barring the salt hay crop. It could be bought for a small fraction the cost of similar acreage near Hampton village. About this time Joseph was at the height of his material prosperity, so he bought as freely as his means afforded. He took 20 acres in Salisbury once owned by ffrancis Dow and about nine pieces in all, from 20 to 50 acres each. At a point just over the Seabrook border the first meeting house was put up, following plans made, no doubt, years previously. Here the community began as wholly Quaker. It made once and for all an impassable gulf between Hampton and Seabrook. Capt Henry Dow, astute political leader, tactful diplomat, could not be expected to show sympathy with the outcast faith; his son Dea Samuel Dow was orthodox of the orthodox. Between Henry and Joseph Dow, however, there was a lifelong brotherly love. No appeal from one to the other was ever disregarded. Thereafter, however, the two great genealogical lines never met. Quaker sought Quaker in marriage and dismissed such as married outside the Society. On the other hand, church people were seldom inclined to risk the social consequences of marrying into a Quaker family.

The record books of Hampton meeting begin 8 mo: 15: 1701, at Hampton. The meetings then alternated with Amesbury. For the house the town set off a piece from common land, Dea Samuel Dow abb surveying the plot. Thomas Chase was the first keeper of the minutes. He, Abraham Green and Joseph Dow were the committee to oversee the building. The cost was defrayed by subscriptions, Aug 23, 1701, by Benjamin Brown, Joseph Chase, Thomas Chase, Joseph Dow, Josiah Dow, Abraham Green, Edmund Johnson, James Stanyan, John Stanyan, Moses Swett, Christian Williams. For several years trouble was had with the town authorities over the minister's tax. The Books record seizures by force of property to pay the salary "of the priest of the hireling ministry,"—John Collins 1703, Henry Dow 1703 and 1705, Joseph Dow Jr 1703, Jacob Morel (Morrill) 1701, James Purington 1705, Richard Smith 1701, Ezeakel Wathen (Worthen) of Amesbury 1702 and 1703. These seizures were serious matters, the property taken generally much in excess of the tax. Once the seizure was sold for more than double the tax. The balance was proffered to the victim, who refused to touch it. It lay on his mantel and next year was seized for the new tax. The first marriage in the Society was that of John Peasley of Haverhill and Mary Martin of Amesbury, 1: 5mo: 1705. It took place in Thomas Barnard's house after, at the previous monthly meeting, Thomas Nickolls and Joshua Purington had been appointed a committee to inquire if they were free to marry. The register was signed by 47 guests as witnesses, including Mary, Hannah, Charety, Josias, Jeremiah, Joseph, Henery, and John Dow. In 1705 the Society meeting sent 3 delegates to the Rhode Island Yearly Meeting, Joseph Chase, Joshua Purington and Moses Swett. In 1705 a second meeting house was resolved upon, to be in Salisbury, and Henry Dow and Thomas Chalis were appointed to look for the land.

Record books up to 1758 are extant; all now preserved in the Brown School at Providence; about 1739 Philip Rowell kept them. Births, marriages and deaths at Berwick, Me, are often entered but there is a dearth of such records from home. Occasional dismissals for cause were made. In 1706 Samuel Cass was declared not to be in the true faith. Action signed by 14 men, including Henry and Jeremiah Dow. In 1707 John Colins was similarly disciplined, altho he was restored and even sent delegate to the Salem 1715 Quarterly Meeting. This action was signed by 18, including Henry, Jeremiah, Charety, Mary and Thomas Dow. This was the first time women voted in such matters.

By the time the second generation of Quakers had grown old, the membership in Seabrook had become very small. Lack of religion of any kind was one cause. Another was that the more ambitious men of Seabrook moved away. In the decay of about 1840 nearly all abandoned the meetings. Of the ada line, those who remained in Seabrook had no taste for religious meetings, the others had moved away. The adb line was consistent, but all moved away to become the Quaker Dow of Maine, a large number of them, but after 1840 they all drifted out, generally into the churches. The adf line was steadfast, but moved away in 1737. All the adg line abandoned the faith, any faith. The adh line was most stead-

fast of all, but all except one junior line became pioneers of the new
Quaker colony in Weare. The children of adk were all baptized into
the church at the demand of their mother. Today there is not a single
Friend in the adb line; of the adh line there is a single family in Bolton,
Mass, consistent from 1675. Another reason was that the young people
found the meeting house dull and preferred the slender social opportunities of the church circles. Those who moved away often found themselves in communities far from meeting house and soon drifted into
churches. The colony from Weare who went to Lincoln, Vt, all drifted
out for this reason.

The denominational preferences of the whole Dow family embrace
the whole field. Only two cases are found of reversion to the older Roman Catholic. The Protestant Episcopalians are many and it is the rule
that once in that denomination, the later generations continue. It drew
considerably from the Quakers. The Methodists were at first very exceptional; embraced by some single individual, the rest of the family
strongly dissenting. The plurality are Congregationalists, because in
rural New England that is often the only church in a whole township.
The Presbyterians are mainly those who came in contact with the only
village churches in Connecticut. Various controversies made big changes.
About 1800 there was a world-wide controversy over free will vs predestination. The free will Baptists gained enormously through it. During
the last century the Unitarians and Universalists have gained many
earnest, thoughtful Dows. Until well into the 19th century almost no one,
even the irreligious, failed to attend weekly church, for the Sunday meeting was the one social opportunity of the week, and even the chance to
transact important business between sermons. Farmers were too hard-
working, too separated to swap cattle except on the day of rest.

A community isolated as was Seabrook is sure to degenerate. The
Quakers came there first for the sake of that isolation. Later, inhabitants came for the same result but from a wholly different cause. Those
who were intolerable in town found freedom in the neck of Seabrook, on
three sides being the ocean. For a few years the high Quaker standards
prevailed, ethical, moral, business and private. No courts were needed,
no hasty marriages to legitimatize an unborn child, no debts incurred.
But that could not endure. The isolated community is unavoidably poor.
As the next generation of Quakers felt all the more the sting of poverty,
they lost the keen edge of supporting faith. The Seabrook farm, originally supporting, say, four, now had to keep eight. Either one must go
outside for employment or do with almost nothing. In either case the
handiest remedy is drink. Soon the inner side of Seabrook degenerated
into about the toughest place in America. On the Hampton Falls border,
the place kept fair, people with averagely high principles, average
standards of education, with pride in themselves and their ancestry.

Within it was all too different. The land was poor, mixed with sand.

By fishing and by driftwood one satisfied hunger and need for warmth. Miserable huts became the rule. Here compulsory education could never come, religious observance nil. marriages mostly by the justice of the peace. Hard cider cost only the labor of pressing it from half wild apples; rum was cheap. But, no matter how primitively one lives, a little money is needed each year for the tax collector. The "red necked" Seabrook men soon found how to get it. They became, and are today, the most expert slipper makers in the world. They worked wholly by the piece, going weekly to Newburyport to deliver finished goods and receive raw material, buy a little food and much liquor. Amid squalid surroundings these people produced slippers, the kinds used only by millionaires and demi-mondaines, jeweled, of gold cloth, seed pearls, often costing several hundred dollars a pair. Between slippers, the people fished or played. Clearly, this was no place for an ambitious man. As soon as the French and Indian War was ended and the interior made safe, all the best moved from Seabrook to pioneer towns.

About sixty years ago William Rand, living in 1920, studied to become a foreign missionary; proposing as a matter of course, to take whatever foreign assignment might be offered. After a final survey of the whole field, Rand decided that no place was more benighted than South Seabrook. He married a Miss Eaton, a native, and entered upon a ministry to last over sixty years. Little by little he worked for cleaner homes, for less whiskey, a little more school, and, at last, a little more Sunday observance.

The greatest regeneration, however, came from economic cause. Two young men of Newburyport, of the agdx line were heirs to the old homestead in Seabrook. They wished to start a shoe factory and decided to use the homestead for this purpose. The result was very satisfactory. Labor was plenty at hand and good. Soon, the business grew greatly. The Seabrookites went less and less to Newburyport; they became little by little more interested in their homes. Gardens started; schools began. The factory burned, but had to be rebuilt at once, and several big Haverhill manufacturers located branches in Seabrook. In 1921 the town looked quite attractive, quite neat. Homes were generally unassuming. Folks still marry young, younger than at most places now. There are lots of children, no where more.

Joseph Dow m Dec 17, 1662, Mary Sanborn, dau of William and Mary (Moulton). These three families are intimately associated since Hampton's foundation. No other Sanborn or any Moulton was among the early Quakers. Mary d of old age Jan 21, 1732-3, a consistent Quaker, living on the homestead and caring for the grandchildren. Joseph d when his youngest child was 16. Hampton rec gives: Sergeant Joseph Dow aged 64 years dyed the 4 April 1703. No doubt his brother, who was town clerk, made the entry. His military title, long scorned by himself, covers the uncertainty of his position in the caste system of the

time. His father was Henry Dow, gent; his brother Henry Dow, gent.
Joseph was still too powerful to be termed yeoman, altho all the next generation were so styled. His children:

a Joseph b Oct 20, 1663   b   John b Dec 12, 1665
c Mary b Jan 15, 1668; m by Rev John Pike Aug 23, 1694, William Richards.
   At this date such marriage does not necessarily mean that she left the Friends;
   they had no meetings as yet. Richards is genealogically undiscovered. An
   impression remains that he came from Portsmouth and left no children
d James b Sept 17, 1670; never grew up
e Hannah b Aug 25, 1672   f   Henry b Nov 7, 1674
g Jeremiah b May 24, 1677   h   Josiah b July 22, 1679
i Thomas b Apr 26, 1782; living 1721; d unm
j Charitye b Dec 7, 1684; d Mch 26, 1768, unm
k Samuel b Apr (or June) 4, 1687
l Aaron b Apr 4, 1692; d before 1703

All these are recorded in Hampton. Joseph's will mentions all surviving; it was probated Apr 19, 1703, and appointed Josiah his executor,
he being the best business man. Josiah is enjoined to teach Samuel
weaving and to provide for him until of age. He also mentions "grandson Philip who lived with me."

Joseph Dow ada was in young manhood sgt of militia and saw considerable Indian fighting. He made a rather brilliant marriage,—to Mary
Challis b Aug 27, 1668, d May 14, 1697 (one of 12 children), dau of Lieut
Philip and Mary (Sargent) of Amesbury. Philip Challis came from England to Ipswich 1637; received allotment of land in Salisbury 1640;
representative to General Court 1662; d Amesbury about 1681. His wid
b about 1652, dau of William Sargent, pioneer of Salisbury, d Alesbury
Sept 27, 1716. Mary Challis readily joined the Friends and one of her
brothers had preceded her. Joseph continued Quaker after his 2nd m,
altho laxly. Children, by Mary:

a Joseph b Feb 6, 1688   b   John b Dec 16, 1689
c James b Oct 8, 1693   d   Philip b Apr 26, 1695
e Mary b May 11, 1697, whose coming cost her mother's life. Hist Hampton errs
   in saying she died May 11, 1697; she joined her consent with her four brothers to a deed given in 1715 by her father to William Davis and John Cottle.
   In 1703 Mary was probably living with her father, while Philip was with his
   grandfather. Not known if Mary married

Left a widower, Joseph Dow could not expect to make a second marriage as brilliantly as his first, for the Quaker colony was then holding very
much aloof. Nevertheless, he was in the prime of manhood, of promise,
and, as times went, of considerable property. That he sank into
obscurity is partly due to the surrender of his own ambition, partly to
the Seabrook environment. Seabrook had few records of its own and was
becoming forgotten by the rest of the world. Joseph's 2nd m and 2nd
family were unknown until 1918, altho a number of Dow were known,
unplaced but near to him. A recent search of court rec in Salem cleared
up a mystery which has been the despair of Dow genealogists for forty
years. It is now known that Joseph lived in his own home until his death

in 1734. His farm was near those of his brothers Jeremiah and Henry, the three being parts of a single property owned by their father. It was he who first spied the Indians in the great raid of Aug 17, 1703, and ran giving the alarm to the nearest blockhouse. While this raid was engineered by the French government of Canada, it is worthy of note that Joseph's family did not suffer from it. Perhaps this was due to Joseph's Indian wife.

The second marriage took place between 1698 and 1703. It is a vague tradition that Joseph Dow had disapproved and would not recognize the bride. However, Joseph Jr soon received his full share of inheritance. The bride was Hannah, a child taken from her Indian parents with full permission by a Seabrook Quaker family to be brought up and educated as a Christian. Such were becoming quite customary, and as a rule the girls became valuable members of the community. This, however, is the only recorded mixed marriage in Seabrook. Hannah proved a good wife and mother; as wid Hannah Dow she appears on the Hampton Falls tax books, paying on a small piece of real estate until 1751. This date probably marks her death. Vague tradition has it that she had two dau, besides the known four sons, and that a dau was 1st born. It appears under abbd that Abraham Sanborn m Abigail Dow, dau of Joseph. This may be error, and not Dow at all. If correct, she can only be dau of Joseph ada. The matter is too uncertain to appear in our letter key.

The four sons, known always as individuals, altho unplaced, are proved by Salem court rec, birthdates conjectured from various sources:

f   Eliphaz b 1705 (Annals of Portsmouth)
g   Noah b about 1710 (Annals of Portsmouth and fact that he was of age in 1734-5)
h   Bildad b before 1714, being of age 1734-5
i   Judah b 1719; date proven by an odd coincidence. It was long known that Joseph had a son Judah by an Indian mother, but he was supposed to be illegitimate and b 1700 or before. In the tax book of Salisbury Beach there is a list of settlers and among them is Jadah Dow 1719. If a tax payer or settler by 1719, he must be b before 1700. The spelling is, of course, a penslip. The entry is in a different hand than the others. As a matter of fact, the town clerk, deep in hard cider, tried to record Judah's birth and pulled down the wrong book. Judah was the baby of the family, an object of tender solicitude of his brothers

Joseph managed to keep his full share of his inheritance, his estate, 787 £ 8 s being about its equal. To him belongs the Seabrook rec: d Feb 6, 1734-5, but earlier genealogists stumbled because no d rec had appeared for Joseph Dow adaa, whose estate was administered in 1738, it being guessed that three years might have intervened. Salem court rec set the matter right. Joseph ada d intestate and his son John applied promptly for letters of administration. By this time the children by 1st m all had homes of their own. Administration was granted Feb 21, 1734-5, and the administrator had trouble in making an inventory of the property, so complaining to the court alleging that Noah, Eliphaz and Bildad were withholding oxen and other personal property from the estate. This was followed by a citation Mch 4, 1734-5, to Eliphaz, Noah and Bildad. Judah was not cited because he was not of age. The matter was speedily adjusted.

Joseph Dow adaa. Already we find that the ad line is far less known than the ab, the latter so well kept in hand by Hist Hampton. Joseph bought in 1725 a half interest in the historic tidewater grist mill built before 1660 by Andrew Greeley in Salisbury, but this he sold in 1728-9. He was fairly thrifty, his wife was Mary, and he d some time in 1738. This covers all we know of him. Mary was living 1730 and probably d before 1738, as she is not named in administration papers. That he and his oldest son continued Quakers seems sure. His son John administered his estate July 3, 1738, in Salisbury; it inventoried 768 £. He seems to have had but two children:

    a Samuel b about 1710   **b** John b about 1712

Samuel Dow adaaaa outlived his father many years and no reason appears why he should not have been his father's administrator. He lived on or near the homestead. Some error in dates occurs in connection with his estate. His will dated Dec 17, 1762, probated Aug 30, 1773; apparently unsettled or re-opened 1778. The will mentions three children as being still minors. A petition by his heirs mentions Joanna as wife of Josiah Shove, a marriage made in 1778, and mentions Reuben as father of Reuben and Nabby. Now, Reuben Jr was born 1790. Samuel's wife was Marcia Heath. Rec reads: Samuel Dow, s Joseph and Mary, and Marcy Heath int 5 mo: 16: 1730. Her parents not stated. List of children apparently complete and none wrongly attributed:

  a Nehimiah b Oct 22, 1731   **b** Ruth b Oct 28, 1733
  c Mary b June 30, 1735; m Salisbury Nov 15, 1755, Edward Beacham
  d Johannah b Nov 15, 1737; d young
  e Sarah b June 26, 1739; int to Jonathan Marvel, son of David and Esther, pub 15: 10: 1761, rec in Newbury and elsewhere, Danvers his home; also spelled Marbel and Marble
  f Henry b May 1, 1741   **g** Elizabeth b Aug 28, 1744
  h Elijah b Feb 22, 1746   **i** Reuben b Jan 24, 1749
  j Judah b Oct 24, 1751; signed Association Test Hampton Falls; taxed Hampton Falls 1787 (Judah adai drops from tax list before 1777); in 1790 census with 3 sons, 2 dau. Absolutely no trace of this posterity
  k Johannah b Nov 14 1754; m Sept 23 (int 20: 8), 1778, Josiah Shove of Mendon, blacksmith, son of Nathaniel and Hannah dec of Dighton

Nehimiah Dow adaaaaa m Feb 4, 1756, Patience Brown, dau of John dec and Abigail of Hampton. As children b Newbury, it is inferred he moved thither:

  a Elijah b Dec 23, 1756   **b** ——, d in infancy
  c Nehimiah b Sept 13, 1761   **d** Patience b Feb 21, 1763

Elijah Dow adaaaaaa. Either he or adaaah was drowned 1781. This Elijah was surely he who m (int pub June 17, 1780) Elesebeth Bartlett of Amesbury bap July 27, 1755, dau of Gershom and Elizabeth (Wingate). For mixup between the two Elijahs, cf adaaah. There seem to have been two children:

a ——, dau b 1780 b Jacob b Salisbury Nov 18, 1780 (1781?)

Jacob Dow adaaaaab cannot be identified with any certainty

Nehimiah Dow adaaaac. Mass Rev rolls give him of Salisbury, 5 feet, 8, ae 18, deserted Sept 25, 1781, also on pay roll Oct 1781. There are very many such desertions, lasting a few days. He was back in Salisbury in good odor and gets into 1790 census 1a, 1b, 2c. Might have been more children later. No m or other rec found. Posterity unknown, except that one son is almost sure:

c Benaiah S probably b after 1790

Benaiah S Dow adaaaacc of Salisbury m (int pub Jan 16, 1824) Maria Bartlett Shores of Amesbury b June 30, 1807, dau of Matthew and Rhoda (Barnard). A child:

a Jacob Flanders b (by m rec) 1824

Jacob F Dow adaaaacca, carpenter, m May 14, 1848, Sarah Ann Bartlett of Salisbury, ae 24, dau of Stephen and Rebecca (Walton) of Seabrook. A child:

a Frank B b Jan 23, 1849 (at ferry house, Amesbury rec); untraced

Mass vital statistics of recent date show two more sons:

b Charles W b 1852 c Wallace E b 1856

Charles W Dow adaaaaccab of Newburyport, div, m 2nd Dec 7, 1908, Mary A (Banker) Morse, div ae 50, dau of John and Elizabeth (Nichols) Banker

Wallace E Dow adaaaaccac of Amesbury m (his 1st) Nov 17, 1908, Carrie J Gurney, ae 38, div, dau of James K and Lucy F Mitchell

Ruth Dow adaaab m David Challis, son of Thomas and Sarah. This is Quaker; the whole family seem to have been more or less consistent Friends

Henry Dow adaaaf d Nantucket Nov 5, 1802; m 1st Abigail Chase, wid of Jethro Gardiner of Nantucket, b Apr 15, 1737, d Mch 4, 1786; m 2nd Jan 1, 1787, Huldah Coleman Pitts d Sept 25, 1789; m 3rd July 27, 1790, Mary Wharton. All these names are Quaker. Children:

a Samuel b Aug 25, 1768   b Elizabeth b Aug 9, 1770
c Ruth b Apr 25, 1772   d Reuben b Jan 26, 1774
e ——dau b 1777   f ——dau b 1780   g Sally b Apr 25, 1789

Samuel Dow adaaafa. We have to guess here, there being no proof. He fits and probably is the Samuel who d Billingsbridge, Ont, 1805, ae 36 or 37. This Samuel lived and d a Quaker and is barely possibly adfcc. We think not; age of adaaafa fits too perfectly. He m in R I

Joanna Harkness; the young couple moved to Vt, thence to Ontario. He is probably the Samuel who set up a trip hammer Danby, Vt, for making steel tools; also probably the Quaker Dow who entertained and helped Lorenzo Dow ahgge, the preacher, as described in latter's journal. One dau is known:

a ——m——Billings. A son Charles Billings was an elderly Quaker of Billingsbridge, Ont, in 1881

Reuben Dow adaaafd m Nantucket 1800 Elizabeth Bunker; further untraced. A dateless rec of So Hampton,—Reuben Dow m Elizabeth James, dau of Josiah, probably has no connection. Nothing to show that any member of this family ever returned to Mass.

Elijah Dow adaaah is vaguely called Capt. Of Salisbury, he, 5 feet, 7, served 5 mos in 1780 in Capt Frothingham's artillery. Some Elijah, probably he, enlisted July 14, 1780, under Lieut Piper for defense of Portsmouth. In enlistment he is given of Strafford Co, quite likely an error. Some Elijah Dow is in 1790 census of Northern Liberties, Pa, 1a, 1b, 2c, but identity is unlikely. Our Elijah is surely he who m Second Church, Salisbury May 20, 1781, Hannah Blazedell b Salisbury Plain July 25, 1757, dau of Jacob and Mary.

Reuben Dow adaaai. We find confusion here. Some Reuben Dow was of Kensington 1790 with 5 sons, 3 dau. If really Dow, we cannot even guess his identity. Reuben adaaai d So Hampton 1823, ae 59. This makes him b 1764. Now, adaaafd b 1774 could not have child by 1787. Reuben adaaai was b 1749. we having the actual rec. We are forced to think that age is understated in d rec. At all events Reuben m 1st Kensington Dec 12, 1785, Betsey (Elizabeth) Fitts (Fitz in rec) b 1765, d Apr 28, 1803; m 2nd Dec 13, 1803, Betsey Leavitt, both of So Hampton. She m 2nd Nov 26, 1840, Jacob Eaton of So Kingston, survived, known several years as wid Eaton. By 1st wife 2 children. Betsey Leavitt was sister of Dudley, originator of the Farmer's Almanac, famous for a century.

Reuben was always known as Reuben Smith Dow, but the middle name was assumed by himself. His will dated Jan 25, 1823, probated Apr 10, is signed Reuben Dow. A tailor by trade he worked almost to the day of his death. His first entry in So Hampton tax books is 1803, probably coming then from Kensington. Was tax collector 1803 to 1820. He was reputed by the young people to be a wizard. Thrifty, he invested largely in land. Will mentions 6 children, a son by 1st wife dying young:

b Nabby b Jan 24, 1787; called Nabby Stuart in will; m John Stuart. Abigail
   Dow of So Hampton m Kingston Feb 3, 1805, John Stewart of Newtown
c Reuben b May 2, 1790; d 1861; in 1850 census alone as farmer of East Kingston, realty $1,000
d Ploomy, called Basset in will; Kensington gives Ploomy Dow m Dec 22, 1811,
   William Bursiel, both of So Hampton
e Gilman b 1807; d 1847   f Rufus b 1809; d 1871

g Betsey Fitts b 1811; d 1884
x Betty Low. This name appears in old ms, probably wholly error; probably
   no such person existed

Reuben Dow adaaaic. A So Hampton rec: Dorothy, dau of Reuben Dow, bap Nov 9, 1743, cannot be correct, no such Reuben known. Our Reuben had but 2 children; name of wife not appearing:

a Mary m Cyrus Smith; posterity now in So Hampton
b Elizabeth m Philip Currier; no children

Gilman Dow adaaaie of So Hampton m Newton Jan 7, 1830, Sarah E Currier of Rochester and Newton; she m 2nd June 28, 1848 George W Goodwin, by him Agnes D and Ada.   Children:

a Octavia m in Lawrence, Mass; d without children May 25, 1901. In 1866
   the heirs of Gilman Dow sold to Jacob Eaton a piece of 20 acres, all signing
   the deed. She signed Sarah O Evans, wife of William H
b Gilman L b So Hampton Nov 26, 1836
c Julia O d Feb 28, 1897, without children; m John M Fleming of Lawrence
d George Newell   e Rufus F E

Gilman L Dow adaaaieb, laborer of East Kingston, d widower Haverhill Sept 8, 1894. He sold his share of the 20 acres to Jacob Eaton before the rest of the family. The 1850 census shows him of Newton, ae 14, with mother Betsey, latter having $1,000 realty. Gilman m 1st May 14, 1855, Marie J Kennard of East Kingston; m 2nd Helen B Ring of Amesbury. She d Haverhill Sept 10, 1903, ae 65-6-6, dau of Page and Betsey (Flanders). More children than here appear, some still in Haverhill:

a Mary S S b E Kingston Dec 1862; d scarlet fever May 18, 1865
b Octavia J b Dec 1863 (d rec gives Feb 14, 1864, and mother as Betsey H); d
   scarlet fever June 10, 1865
c Alice O b July 7, 1867; So Hampton; presumably m and lived Haverhill; name
   seems to be Alice Severance; perhaps married name

George Newell Dow adaaaied went early in life to Lawrence, Mass, thence to Salt Lake City, Utah, where he became warden of State's prison; m Alice J ——, now of Los Angeles.   Children:

a George R S, of Los Angeles d 1923
b Florence m George Ames of Los Angeles

Rufus F E Dow adaaaiee went west; m Lizzie M ——.   No grandchildren. The children:

a Agnes D m——Ireland of Salt Lake City
b Ada m——Richardson of New Bedford, Mass
c Fred L d Ocean Park, Calif 1914; his wife d 1920, childless
d Burrith Newell, well known physician of San Francisco; his wife, well known
   club member, d 1920 without children

Rufus Dow adaaaif appears 1850 census as farmer of So Hampton, realty $2,000. He must be the Rufus Dow warden 1850-3 of State's prison, Concord. He m Mch 11, 1829, Sally Fitts b 1808. Two children:

a Rufus Franklin b 1831   b Charles H b 1843

Rufus F Dow adaaaifa, farmer of So Hampton, m Mary M Merrill b Amesbury Dec 21, 1834, d So Hampton Jan 24, 1914, dau of Joseph and Dolly (Morrill).   Children:

- a Rufus Frank b So Hampton 1862, shoe cutter of So Hampton, d May 9, 1897; m Oct 20, 1892, Carrie M Chase, ae 39, wid, dau of Charles H and Almira C (Bartlett) Mowatt; no children
- b Mary d without children
- c Carrie Lillian m E W Wyman; living 1923
- d Fannie A m So Hampton Sept 26, 1883, Josiah Bartlett Greeley of East Kingston; living 1923

Charles H Dow adaaaifb (Mother was a Morse), Civil War veteran, shoemaker of So Hampton, d East Kingston June 29, 1869; m Francena A Gale b Newton.   Children:

- a Alice E b E Kingston Apr 12, 1866; m |Mch 15,|1888, Francis E French; d recently without children
- b Charles W b E Kingston June 22, 1869; an excellent musician; has a music store in Newburyport

Betsey F Dow adaaaig m So Hampton Feb 1, 1832, George W Pillsbury of Kingston; d without children

---

John Dow adaab appeared in Salisbury 1738, yeoman of Amesbury, to administer the estate of his father.   From that time he disappears absolutely; his wife or wives never found.   Only in 1923 were family rec found which prove him.   When Benjamin Dow ahba reached Epping in 1748, he found already there a substantial citizen and family, named John Dow.   This is adaab.   Epping rec are very fragmentary, in spite of a transcript made by Gov Plumer and preserved in N H Historical Society, Concord.   Beniah Dow adada was of Epping, but his children are all proved, so he makes no confusion.   From 1748 the families of John and Benjamin lived in close harmony, both intermarrying with the Gilman family, founders of Gilmanton.   John Dow adaab was an early share owner of Gilmanton, was a man comparatively well to do, and lived long.   Some John Dow m in Rhode Island 1742, name or place not in pub rec; improbably our John.   The 1790 census gives John Dow of Epping 3a, 3c.   This is adaab.   The Epping 1790 census also gives Samuel Dow 1a, 2b, 3c, and Josiah Dow 2a, 1b, 5c.   No other mention of these is found in Epping.   Hence, it is improbable that they were sons of adaab.   They fit somewhat the missing members of the adf line (q v).   Epping rec gives: Elizabeth Dow, dau of James, bap May 28, 1758.   A deed signed 1760 by Benjamin Dow ahba is witnessed by Benjamin A Dow, necessarily b by 1739.   A John Dow father by 1759 is probably adaab himself and not a son b 1730 or so.   Benjamin Dow, a father by 1761, seems to be a son of adaab.   With such lapse of time between children, it is probable that adaab had two wives.   No d rec of any are found in Epping.   To reconstruct as best we can, the children:

- a Benjamin A b 1735 onward
- b Elizabeth bap (dau of James) May 28, 1758

c Nathaniel b 1758; d 1843 in Walden, Vt
d Benjamin bap Nov 4, 1759; unless he is son of Benj A, the former must be thrown out as error, probably so. But, he had children.
e John (son of John Dow Jr) bap Nov 4, 1759

We dare not guess further; the situation is too much involved as it is.

Benjamin Dow adaaba. A Benjamin Dow of Gilmanton in 1790 is 2a, 2b, 3c. We cannot distinguish between three Benjamins known to exist. In Epping we find four children bap, all specified as of Benjamin. Epping bap rec never give a mother's name. These are:

a John bap June 14, 1761. There are five Johns of Epping
b Elizabeth bap Oct 24, 1762
c Benjamin bap June 10, 1764
d Molly bap (dau of Benjamin Dow Jr) June 14, 1766

Some Benjamin Dow signed the Association Test Gilmanton 1775; in 1778 built an iron foundry and mill; a few years later built another a little further down the stream. In this mill Stephen P Dow, unplaced, was killed by accident June 2, 1831

For study let us put here some unplaced Gilmanton rec:

Benjamin Dow Jr 1a in 1790 census; possibly adaabac

Rebecca Dow m Belmont Dec 8, 1796, Abel Glidden, both of Gilmanton

Jonathan Dow b Epping about 1777; of Gilmanton

Samuel Otis Dow b Gilmanton 1779-83

Lydia Dow of Gilmanton m Belmont Feb 5, 1789, John Boynton

Susanna Dow m Belmont Apr 25, 1799, Dudley Marsh

Susanna Dow m Belmont Oct 15, 1795, Joshua Gilman Jr

Hannah Dow m Belmont June 20, 1791, William Mitchell, both of Gilmanton

Benjamin Dow adaabac. In some way we must account for Benjamin who m May 16, 1784, Dorothy Connor, both of Gilmanton. They are found no more in Gilmanton rec which are hopelessly fragmentary. The church rec might fill many gaps but the author of Hist Gilmanton never looked at them. To account for a Benjamin b Me 1789, we guess that adaabac and bride moved over the Maine border. The identity is pure guess:

a Benjamin b Me 1789

Benjamin Dow adaabaca appears in 1850 census of Enosburg, Vt; farmer, realty $400; wife Deborah b Vt 1797. We doubt place of her birth, such error easily made by careless census taker. From a grandson we find that she was Deborah Gilman. There were near Gilmanton at this time two Deborah Gilmans. The marriage with a Gilman argues coming from Gilmanton. We find that at first Benjamin had a wood working shop in Buffalo, Me, a town not now extant. He presumably came to Vermont to be nearer a supply of birch wood, the material most used in his son's large plant. In spite of small real estate holding, Benjamin was a progressive man. Census of 1850 gives 6 children. The grandson gives 8, authoritatively:

a Amherst W b Vt 1822 (Census gives Albert, chair maker)
b Charles   c Dennis (neither in census)
d Susan b 1833 (census gives Betsey); m Fernando Stevens; children,—Schuyler and Lovicie
e Charlotte b 1841; m Wallace Tracy; dau,—Etta
f Abbie (not in census) m George Heath; dau,—Gannie and Emma
g Julette (census, Jabette b 1835) m——Andrus
h Rossanah (Roxana b 1838, census); doubtless the Rosina W Dow of Enosburg m Oct 8, 1867, George W Doyle of Richford

Amherst W Dow adaabacaa had by 1850 census wife Sarah b Vt 1831. In 1883 gazetteer he is woodware manufacturer of Montgomery. Thirteen children, none traced, spelling of names surely a little careless:

a Amherst   b Clarck   c Bell   d Neal   e Benjamin
f Oscar   g Loren   h Sheridan i Charles j Cynthia
k Nettie   l Cajaolia   m Deborah

Charles Dow adaabacab lived Vt. Only two children:

a David   b Mysan; both untraced

Dennis Dow adaabacac appears in 1883 gazetteer as owning 10 acres in Enosburg. A son:

a John E, in 1919 a lumber dealer of Enosburg; gave the children of adaabaca, but gave no further particulars

Nathaniel Dow adaabc d 1846; his wife Esther 1842; was for many years pensioner of Walden, Vt, with his brother, ancestor of the entire Dow family of Walden, giver of the name Dow's, still a hamlet of Walden.

Gilmanton civic rec are detached. Nathaniel appears in 1775 to sign the Association Test. In 1793 Nathaniel Dow appears as a new name on the tax list. Perhaps he did not live in town 1782 to 1793. His military experience begins 1775, Capt Moody, Col Badger, for N Y State service. He is almost always in same company with Benjamin Dow, his brother, and Jonathan Dow (tentatively adgfc). Nathaniel receipts for 10£-5-6 in the Crown Point campaign. Again he receipts for 36£-8-0 and a half pint of rum. The other Dows got the same. July 6, 1780, finds him serving in Worcester Co, Mass. Coming home at the end of the war, he m Belmont Aug 8, 1782, Esther Gilman. It must have been some years later that they bought a farm in what soon became Walden, Vt. The family moved there not earlier than 1794, not later than 1801. His nephew arrived 1797 and that was probably the date for all. Here he was a farmer, active to old age. A grandson living in 1922 recalls him clearly. He had 12 children. Census of 1790 shows 2 sons, 2 dau in Gilmanton. Our earlier informant named 9:

    a Polly m Aug 4, 1800, Samuel Carr of Walden
    b John Gilman b June 15, 1785
    c Betsey b 1788; m Cabot Sept 26, 1811, Ebenezer Chamberlain
    d Nathaniel B b 1790; rec in Gilmanton
    e Zebulon b 1793   f Hazen b 1794
    g, h and i presumably the three missing occur here. It is not wise to guess names
       too much
    j Porter b Walden 1801
    k Sally b 1803; m Sept 4, 1827, Nathaniel G Knight of Walden
    l James Bell b 1810

John G Dow adaabcb. While there are not a few sketches of this distinguished Methodist preacher, none mentions his parentage. Denominational feeling ran strong in those days; early conversions to Methodism were almost always of individuals and caused hostility on the part of the rest of the family. The Walden Dow and the locality were strongly Congregational. John G was a farmer and militia captain when "converted" 1822, ae 37. He m 1st (John G E Dow of Walden) Oct 6, 1811, Sally Lance of Cabot; 2nd Mch 24, 1816, Betsey Lance of Cabot b Chester, N H, 1796, d Worcester, Mass, 1860. Sketches of his life mention but one marriage. From 1822 he was 36 years in the active ministry, 12 years presiding elder of Vermont. Several of his pastorates were in New Hampshire and in 1831 he was chaplain of the Concord State's prison. In 1837 he became pastor at Newbury, Vt, soon returning to N H. In 1844 he rejoined the Vt conference and in 1854 was again assigned to Newbury. Here he interested himself in what he considered his most important work,—the Newbury Seminary, of which he was trustee. He did not live long after its firm establishment, dying suddenly May 18, 1858, while on a visit to a dau in Chelsea, Mass. Children:

    a Sarah (Maria, State rec) b Walden 1814; d Claremont, N H, Mch 21, 1897;
       m (his 2nd) Apr 1844 Albert Haller Danforth of Montpelier; lived Barnard,
       Vt; no children
    b Betsey b Cabot 1818; teacher of French, etc, in Rochester, N H; later precept-
       ress of Newbury Seminary; d Newtonville, Mass, Feb 3, 1900; m Nov 26,
       1844, Rev John Hanson Twombly of Wilbraham, well known Methodist
       clergyman, b Rochester July 19, 1814, son of Tobias and Lois (Wentworth)
    c Lorenzo b Cabot 1821
    d Frances Ann b Dover, N H, 1835; d Chicago 1887; m 1860 Lorin F Kitler

Lorenzo Dow adaabcbc d Iowa City, Iowa, 1898; car conductor of Concord, N H, m 1844, Mary Mills b Concord. Probably more children than:

    a John G b Montpelier Oct 22, 1844; d Concord Jan 19, 1914. No rec of m or
       children

Nathaniel B Dow adaabcd, carpenter of Walden, m Dorcas G——— b N H. (presumably Gilman); both of Walden 1870; realty in 1850 $300. Children by census:

    a James H (Harvey James, family rec) b Vt 1823, farmer of So Walden; living
       1916; untraced
    b Jane b 1831; at home 1870, unm

Zebulon Dow adaabce, farmer of Walden, m Irene Flint b Gilmanton 1801; years subsequently seem to have visited the old home; both living 1860, dropping out before 1870.   Children:

a Jason F b Sept 11, 1820   b   Martha b 1824
c John Calen b 1836; m Ellen F——; moved to Northwood, N H; shoemaker;
      child,—Etta A b Northwood Nov 4, 1866
d Henry b 1844; untraced
e Almena b 1847 (called Alton in 1870 census)
f Aden b 1849
g Juliet Philene b 1850; d before 1860

Jason F Dow adaabcea, 1850 farmer, 1870 stage driver, m May 14, 1845, Martha E Bean of Salisbury, Mass, b Jan 12, 1824, d Salisbury Aug 23, 1901, dau of John, farmer, and Nancy (Hill).   After the father's death, the children went to Boston.   Children:

a Henry b 1855; untraced   b   Alton F b 1857; of Winthrop, Mass, 1922
c Ada b 1860   d   Fred b 1868; untraced

Aden W Dow adaabcef.   As the name Aden has no other appearance in Dow annals, we feel sure of identity, altho known only from b and m rec of a dau.   His wife was Gertrude Peabody.   Quite possibly other children:

a Florence Gertrude b Revere, Mass 1890

Gertrude Dow adaabcefa of Dorchester m Boston Oct 12, 1910, Samuel Herman Sawyer ae 21, son of Samuel Rufus and Ellen Susan (Stone).   Children:

a Thelma Allen b Oct 11, 1911   b   Myrtle Gertrude b Apr 5, 1914

Hazen Dow adaabcf, in 1850 carpenter of Walden, 1860 cooper, 1870 farmer, realty in 1850 $1,800; d 1872; m 1st Oct 11, 1818, Sary G Buck of Walden, by whom 1 child; 2nd Mary A Johnson b 1814, d 1898 (census gives b 1795).   Children:

a Joel L b 1826; farmer, moved to Clinton, Wis; d 1911; left a son
b Florantha b 1835; d 1860, unm
c Ellen J b 1839; d 1913; m Peterboro, N H, July 27, 1873, Joseph Lewis of
      East Hardwick
d Rosina b 1842; d 1864.   Census gives all these dates 10 years older
e Edwin J b 1854 (his own statement; census giving 1844), farmer of East Hard-
      wick; m 1879 Ida L Low
f Irwin J, his twin, m Abbie Ingram; not living 1916

Porter Dow adaabcj is listed as Peter in census; m Laurinda Reed b Mch 17, 1818, d Northwood Oct 1873, dau of Chauncey and Nancy. Her sisters rejoiced in the names Laurilla and Philansa.   Porter was a carpenter in Canada; returned to Walden 1850; moved in old age to a son's home; d Apr 3, 1874.   Children:

a Esther C b Mch 10, 1836; m Orrison Twombly; son Charles; m 2nd Fred D
      Chandler. A dau Mary Laurinda m Laconia, N H, 1895 Louis Buffum Martin
b Mary C b June 26, 1837; m John C Frye of Danville; children,—George M,
      Fred J
c Sarah A b May 16, 1839; m William Buzzell of Laconia; son,—Elmer E

d   Martha E b June 4, 1841; d in infancy
e   Peasley B b Apr 22, 1843   f   Clinton John b Apr 10, 1845
g   Roswell G b Dec 2, 1847; carpenter of Weirs, N H, m May 4, 1912, Elizabeth
     Adelaide Hughes, wid, dau of John C and Almira S Shepard.   No children
h   Alma B b June 30, 1850; m Charles Buzzell of Concord; child Jennie m Charles
     Danforth of Danbury; m 2nd Stillman Walker of Concord; no children
i   Julia B b Feb 7, 1853; m Thaddeus Griffin of Gloucester, Mass; no children
j   Charles B b Apr 19, 1856; m June 18, 1903 Minnie E Cook, dau of William
     and Esther (McAllister); lives Lynn, Mass; no children

Peasley B Dow adaabcje, Civil War veteran, settled at Northwood Center; in 1920 postmaster and justice of the peace; m Sarah E Sherburne b Oct 25, 1843, d May 15, 1909, dau of William B and Sarah A (Davis) of Northwood.   No children

Clinton John Dow adaabcjf, veteran of Civil War, m Mch 25, 1865, Helen Frances Piper b Northfield Sept 1846, d Laconia Feb 8, 1908, dau of Arthur Bennett and Dorothy A (Piper) of Northwood.   For about 20 years they had a large Montana ranch.   Children:

a   Ettie Agnes b Nov 4, 1866; d young
b   De Witt Clinton b July 29, 1871

De Witt C Dow adaabcjfb was in 1922 shoe cutter of Lynn; m 1st —— who d leaving 1 dau; m 2nd Lynn Aug 26, 1907, Mary E Gallagher, ae 47, dau of Patrick and Nora (McKenna).

James B Dow adaabcl, farmer of Walden, taxed 1870 on $3,620, m Amy D Hodgden b 1823.   Children:

a   Mary b 1847; d in infancy
b   Abby M b 1857; m George H Burbank; a son Arthur J
c   William E b 1859

William E Dow adaabclc, farmer of East Hardwick, m Carrie Dutton.   Children:

a   Gladys E b 1900; at home 1923, teacher
b   Glen H b 1902; d 1916

Benjamin Dow adaabd was a pensioner in Walden, dying after 1840. Rec at hand give nothing of him after his military experience from Gilmanton.   The natural supposition is that he bought 160 acres in 1783 and came with his brother Nathaniel.   We know that Jonathan Dow, b 1776, came to Walden with his bride in 1797; his children (like those of Nathaniel) are known.   William Gilman Dow, writing in 1887, gives his own grandfather as Samuel Dow, Walden farmer, captain of militia, m —— Gilman; d Oct 1831, leaving an only child, Samuel.   If this is right, Samuel Sr must have been b before 1780.   This matter must be left for later solution, when more facts are known.   We know that a Gilman Dow was elected deacon of the Walden church 1805.   He must date from Revolutionary time.   We have guessed him to be the missing James Gilman Dow ahbaai.   The Author believes that Samuel Sr is error (as

Wm G Dow lost his father at age of 10) for Jonathan who m Joanna Gilman.   All the Dows of Coventry descend from the Walden colony.   The
only reasonable hypothesis is to assume that the disconnected Dow of
Walden of right age are children of Benjamin adaabd, who presumably
added to his family until, say, 1810, as did Nathaniel.

To facilitate matters, let us collect here the disconnected Walden
records:

Isa (or Ira) **Dow** b Mass 1804 (census); m 1832

Samuel Dow m May 4, 1831, Sophronia Gould of Walden

Alice Dow m Oct 11, 1827, James Smith of Walden

Dolly Dow m Oct 11, 1827, Levi Levermore of Walden

Jeremiah W Dow b Vt 1807; m 1831

Merrill F Dow b Walden about 1820

Betsey Dow b 1831 and **Roxana Dow** b 1832, employed in
Walden 1850

Edwin Dow b 1834; farm worker of Walden 1870

Abby Dow b 1857, in family of N Z Cameron of Walden 1860, perhaps a grandchild

A family Bible recently unearthed gives definitely a son of Benjamin,
to wit,—Greeley. As said before, it seems hopeless to try to unravel the
defective rec of Gilmanton. The Bible in question does not mention
Greeley's mother. Possible that he was 2nd born son of Benjamin and
Dorothy (Connor) and that Benjamin now provisionally adaabaca was
3rd born. Gravestone extant in Albany, Vt, gives:

  a   Greeley b Gilmanton Dec 26, 1786; d Albany Nov 18, 1843

Greeley Dow adaabda must have come to Walden with his parents;
was of Peacham when he m Jan 3, 1815, Nancy Glines ahbcaaa d Albany
Nov 23, 1863. They bought a farm in Craftsbury, near the Albany line.
Children:

  a   James Glines b Jan 6, 1816; d Aug 17, 1863; apparently unm
  b   John Chipman b Walden Jan 6, 1818; d Albany Oct 28, 1887
  c   Lawson Sedgwick b Oct 6, 1819; d Apr 3, 1820
  d   Emeline b May 5, 1821; d May 23, 1843
  e   Luther Calvin b Walden Aug 31, 1823; d Hardwick Sept 11, 1902
  f   Louisa A b Jan 12, 1827; d Nov 30, 1845
  g   Samantha b Jan 11, 1829; d Apr 3, 1888; m June 5, 1847, Orville Comstock of
     Craftsbury
  h   Nancy b Feb 20, 1832; d Brattleboro Mch 25, 1881; m Apr 23, 1854, Sias B
     George of Craftsbury

John C Dow adaabdab, hotel keeper, cattle buyer, appears in 1883
gazetteer as owning 400 acres in Albany; m May 9, 1843, Azubah J Hay-

den b May 6, 1826, d Lowell, Mass, Apr 5, 1890, dau of William V and Azubah (Culver). Children:

- a Alvina Hayden b Jan 15, 1844; d Sept 26, 1909
- b Albert John b Sept 29, 1845; d Tewksbury, Mass, Jan 1, 1914
- c Alfred Perry b Nov 13, 1847; d Lowell, Mass, July 18, 1901
- d Lilla Azubah b Feb 15, 1854; d Albany Oct 1, 1875
- e James Buchanan b July 13, 1857
- f Henry Eugene b Aug 12, 1859; d Feb 16, 1864
- g George b July 18, 1863   h Gertrude b July 1, 1865

Alvina H Dow adaabdaba m Jan 1, 1862, Thomas McLellan b June 8, 1837, d Dec 15, 1916. Children:

- a Jessie Alvina b June 17, 1862; d Feb 24, 1864
- b Jessie Lydia b July 24, 1864; m Wallace J Eldridge
- c Ida Lilla b Aug 25, 1866; m Orra S Rowell
- d Alvina Azubah b Jan 16, 1868; m——Pollard
- e John C Dow b Jan 17, 1869; m Bertha Atkinson; no children
- f Don Thomas b Feb 1, 1886; m Angie (Kelley) Fenn; no children

John Albert Dow (as he preferred to be known) adaabdabb m Dora Rowell b Albany Nov 8, 1846, d Sept 27, 1907, dau of Joshua and Mary (Bill). She div him and m 2nd —— Burchardt. He veterinary surgeon of Malden, Mass, m 2nd Sept 16, 1897, Ada Frances Bond (her 2nd) music teacher from Randolph, Me, dau of Emery F and Harriet (Mew). Presumably no children

Alfred P Dow adaabdabc appears in 1883 gazetteer as cattle dealer of Albany; m Ella M Conerty. Children:

- a John Chipman b Oct 18, 1878; of Lowell 1923; 1924 real estate broker of Woburn; m Chelmsford Oct 18, 1905, Mary A Converse ae 26, dau of Robert and Isabelle (Ballou) (Ballue, rec)
- b Herbert C b Feb 28, 1881; in 1923 clerk of Winthrop, Mass
- c Hazel Alice b Mch 29, d Aug 5, 1887   d Wilsie b Jan 10, 1890

Lilla A Dow adaabdabd m Robert Rogers Beede of Albany d Hardwick July 6, 1913, son of Nathan and Mary R (Rogers). Children:

- a Rolla b Aug 13, 1873; d Aug 29, 1875
- b Will b Albany; m Gertrude F Rowell; 2 sons

James B Dow adaabdabe appears in 1883 gazetteer as owning 170 acres in Albany; m May 3, 1881, Ellen Metcalf b Aug 29, 1861, dau of Eli and Diana (Clough). Children:

- a William Dwight b Oct 24, 1881
- b Henry Eugene b Oct 10, 1882; d Waterbury, Vt, May 31, 1919, unm
- c Maude b Oct 10, 1884   d Constance b Jan 4, 1890
- e Mahlon Chipman b July 22, 1894; d Camp Devens, Ayer, Mass, Jan 23, 1918, unm
- f Lloyd Luther b Feb 1, 1896; d Feb 25, 1897
- g Dorothy May b June 30, 1904; m June 17, 1922, Harold Ray Chaffee

William D Dow adaabdabea m Katherine Dana. Children:
- a Mildred Arline b Jan 7, 1914   b Sybil Ellen b Apr 15, 1918

Maude Dow adaabdabec m Feb 15, 1904, Arthur Harlow b Apr 16, 1876. Children, b Irasburg:

- a Helen b July 31, 1905   b Kenneth b Oct 29, 1908
- c Gerald b Mch 7, 1912   d Margaret b Dec 21, 1916

Constance Dow adaabdabed m June 30, 1908, Elmer Wallace, son of Thomas J and Fannie (Rogers).   Child:

a   Iola b June 22, 1909

George Dow adaabdabg, harness maker, m Belle McCaffrey and moved a few years later to Skowhegan, Me.   Child:

a   Foster Seymore b Albany Feb 16, 1886; now m

Gertrude Dow adaabdabh m Dec 23, 1881, John C Burke, son of Walter.   Moved from Albany to Malden, Mass, lawyer, member of Legislature.   She d suicide from nervous prostration Apr 7, 19—(year not given in newspaper clipping).   Children:

a   Walter Scott b June 26, 1885; d Newport, Vt, July 27, 1886
b   George W   c   Julia Lillian

Luther C Dow adaabdae appears in 1883 gazetteer as owning 140 acres in Irasburg; m Lowell, Mass, Apr 5, 1847, Lovina (Louisa, rec) Dewey b Irasburg June 3, 1825, d Jan 6, 1902, dau of Chandler and Lucinda (Buck).   He d East Hardwick Sept 11, 1902.   Children, all b Albany:

a   Emma Lovina b Dec 23, 1847; d Waterbury Jan 18, 1919
b   Wallace Luther b Apr 16, 1850
c   Clara Jane b June 3, 1852; d Apr 30, 1876; m George Sanders of Albany
d   Ellen Maria b May 2, 1854   e   Ida May b Oct 18, 1857
f   Flora Ann b June 22, 1859; d Sept 16, 1882
g   Nelson Lucius b June 8, 1861; d Glover, Vt, Nov 26, 1914
h   Lizzie b June 20, 1863; d Aug 22, 1864
i   Avis M b May 26, 1866; d Nov 30, 1869
j   Charlotte Mabel b June 8, 1868

Emma L Dow adaabdaea m Oct 10, 1870, Grenville Edgar Barstow MD d Feb 5, 1885; lived Springfield, Mass; no children

Wallace L Dow adaabdaeb of Albany m Jan 1, 1874, Lillian Fairman, dau of Dr Erastus Philo and Louisa (Porter); in 1924 real estate broker of Woburn, Mass.   Children:

a   Ernest Fairman b Nov 29, 1875
b   Cleo Veronica b Feb 9, 1887; m Oct 6, 1909, Murry McFarland; 1 dau

Ernest F Dow adaabdaeba, for years letter carrier of West Newton, now owns a printing and publishing plant; m Euphemia Coffrin Pevear, dau of Frank W and Marie Emma (Parfitt).   Only child:

a   Earle Pevear b 1900; d 1917

Clara J Dow adaabdaec m Mch 24, 1870, George Sanders d Orleans, Vt, May 28, 1921, son of Isaac L and Lovisa (Wilder).   No children

Ellen Maria Dow adaabdaed m Sept 28, 1872, Hon Willard W Miles b Albany Feb 6, 1845, son of Orin and Eunice (Clark); many years chief superior judge, 7 years associate justice of the Supreme Court, retiring 1923.   Children:

  a Ida Maude b Dec 9, 1873; m Henry R Cutler bank pres of Barton, Vt
  b Mabel Augusta b Sept 8, 1875; m Hon Frank D Thompson; no children
  c Orin Luther b Apr 5, 1879; d 1888   d Dorothy d in infancy

Ida M Dow adaabdaee m June 14, 1882, T Frank Smith, son of Thomas and Lydia (Knight).   Children:

  a Luther Thomas b Jan 22, 1887   b Orin b Aug 28, d Oct 5, 1891

Nelson L Dow adaabdaeg physician m Dec 31, 1889, Lillian B Pierce b Jan 18, 1868, dau of Ira T and Mary (Kelley).   Child:

  a Grace b Apr 4, 1897; m Dr Percy Buck, son,—Ralph A

Charlotte M Dow adaabdaej m Jan 1, 1898, Charles Willis.   Children:

  a Glenn Charles b May 23, 1908; d Mch 20, 1909
  b Jack Edgar b Sept 26, 1909

Samantha Dow adaabdag m Orville Comstock. Children:

  a Elva. Her dau m Charles Holbrook   b Lucius O b and d 1849

Nancy Dow adaabdah m Sias B George b Worcester, Vt, Oct 14, 1828, d Albany Sept 22, 1916, son of Stephen and Eliza (Brown).   Children:

  a Mina Minerva b Craftsbury Feb 8, 1855; m Apr 22, 1875, Willard Samuel Eldridge
  b Cora Estelle b Oct 8, 1857   c ——son b and d 1859

As we have already stated, no list of children of Benjamin Dow adaabd has appeared.   The disconnected Dows of Walden, Coventry and Craftsbury presumably are all of his direct line or closely akin.   One more son is highly probable:

Hollis Dow adaabdc. Of Craftsbury he m Jan 16, 1816, Louisa Gardner of Coventry.   If children, they certainly do not appear in vital statistics.   The rest of the Dows considerable here follow with letter keys attached for convenience.

A **George Dow** who witnessed the will of Joseph Day, Coventry Nov 6, 1815, was probably a Day

Ira Dow adaabdd m Nov 25, 1832, Polly Farnsworth of Walden, census giving Mary b N H 1800.   The Farnsworth marriages were mostly with the bcfif Dow line, but there seems no vacancy in that line, altho a member of bcfif lived only a short distance away.   In 1850 Ira was a farmer with $1,000 realty.   Children, by census:

  a Lucy A b 1835; m Nov 5, 1856, Charles Shepard of Springvale, Mo
  b Lydia b 1836   c Mary J b 1838   d Alma b 1841

  Charles Dow working for them 1850, not necessarily related

Jeremiah W Dow adaabde, farmer of Walden, taxed on $2,400, m Oct 12, 1831, Sophia Durant b Vt 1811.   Children, by census:

  a   David B b 1833   b   Roswell b 1840; untraced

David B Dow adaabdea, by 1860 census shoemaker of Lyndon, had wife Charlotte.   Child:

  a   Isabella b 1850

Merrill F Dow adaabdf, b Walden, Vt, stage driver, m Georgetown, Mass, Anna Green, dau of Jonathan and Abigail (Locke).   Haverhill rec says both b Ire, surely error.   Jonathan Green descended from the pioneer Henry Green of Hampton; d at sea July 10, 1822, leaving two small children.   Merrill and wife soon moved to Boston.   Child, Haverhill rec:

  a   Charles M b Georgetown Oct 28, 1848 or 1849; untraced

Jonathan Dow adaabf (wholly for convenience).   Said to be b Epping 1776, will probably be proved as soon as someone searches rec of Epping second church.   The late John Mark Moses began this search and had transcribed to 1772 before his untimely death.   He cannot be son of a Benjamin b 1759.   Perhaps he was one of the missing sons of Noah Dow of Gilmanton ahbac; if so, what was he doing in Walden?   Kinship with Nathaniel is much more likely.   At all events Jonathan m Jan 7, 1796, Joanna Gilman b Dec 17, 1777, dau of Samuel and Alice (Gilman) of Newmarket.   This Gilman family intermarried with ahba line.   The young couple settled in Walden 1797.   The children appear first in Coventry and by the time they matured were as much at home in Gilmanton as in Vt.

  a   Samuel (middle name Gilman?) b about 1797
  b   Joanna b about 1800   c   Mary C (somewhat doubtful identity)
  d   Harrison (his d rec gives William H b Gilmanton Dec 8, 1819: we never forget that a twice married man invariably lies about his age)
  e   Winslow; living 1889 in West Danville, Vt
  f   Darius Jerome b Gilmanton (his d rec) Feb 14, 1811.   It is clearly stated on family authority that he was youngest
  h   Elsie

Samuel Dow adaabfa, farmer of Walden, d tuberculosis Oct 1831; m Sept 6, 1820, Lucy Smith b Walden, d tuberculosis Jan 1831.   Samuel was a deacon in Walden church.   One child known:

  a   William Gilman b Walden Nov 20, 1820
  b   (guess) Lydia Ann m Feb 22, 1848, Ebenezer Chamberlain of Groton, presumably adaabccx
  c   (guess) George W b Vt 1829; working 1850 in Walden; otherwise unknown. Neither is mentioned in 1889 letter of Wm Gilman Dow

Samuel Dow adaabfx.   We must in some way separate a distinct Samuel Dow of Walden, whose wife was a Blanchard, presumably Susan.   They m before 1827.   He also is called Deacon.   Known children:

a   Abial Blanchard b Vt 1827 (census)
b   Susan Celia (dau of Dea Samuel and——Blanchard; from sketch of husband)
c   Ellen S; living 1860 with her brother; otherwise unknown

Abial B Dow adaabxa, by 1860 census farmer of Walden, realty $1,000; m May 8, 1850, Sallie Robinson Durant of Walden. In his home 1860 were Susan Dow, presumably his mother, and Ellen S Dow, assumed to be his sister. No children in 1860 census

Susan C Dow adaabxb d Burlington July 18, 1856; m 1849 Moses Harman Bixby b Warren, N H, Aug 21, 1827, son of Benjamin and Mary Bruce (Cleasby), clergyman, grad Baptist College, Montreal, pastor at Johnson, missionary to Burmah 1853-6. He made a 2nd marriage; no children mentioned

William G Dow adaabfaa, orphaned before 11, moved to Coventry; m Dec 12, 1841, Emma Knight of Coventry, b June 5, 1823. Living 1889; in 1860 Coventry farmer assessed $300; in 1883 cooper of Coventry, owning 75 acres. Children:

a   Alice Maria b Sept 29, 1842; d Apr 25, 1910; m Apr 9, 1864, Charles Bergoine of Coventry. Only child is 1923 Mrs Lida Niles of Newport. She wrote as fully as she could of her own line
b   Mary b Jan 8, 1844; d Apr 25, 1910; m June 1, 1875, Osias Boynton of Coventry; only surviving child,—Mrs Charles Young of Newport Center
c   William Wilder b Apr 19, 1845; d Jan 26, 1919
d   Emma Farnsworth b Sept 1, 1847; m Sept 25, 1868, Stephen Gilbert of Newport. Children,—Arthur, Wallace, Helen, all of Inglewood, Calif
e   Clara Adella b Mch 26, 1850; d Nov 7, 1869, unm
f   George Washington b Dec 3, 1852; of Newport 1922, unm
g   Marion Mayfield b Sept 8, 1855; d Feb 8, 1903; m Apr 4, 1875, Osman Smith of Brighton; left 4 children
h   Jennie Cutler b Apr 14, 1858; m Feb 20, 1883, Moody Kimball of West Derby; 2 dau in 1923 of Boston
i   ——baby Budd b Aug 27, d Oct 10, 1860
j   Samuel Gilman b Feb 8, 1862; d Dec 1, 1912; m Alice Boynton; 1922 of Newport; no children
k   Carroll Lincoln b Oct 27, 1864; m Sarah Scott; only child,—Mrs Ralph West of Woodstock
l   Etta Bernice b June 4, 1867; m ¦Braintree, Mass, Oct 29, 1907 (his 2nd), Frank A Smith, ae 43, son of Clark and Betsey A (Niles). No children
m   Carrie Bell b Nov 16, 1869; m Henry Barnard; 1922 of Manchester, N H; 3 children

William W Dow adaabfaac d Jan 26, 1919; m Feb 26, 1870 Addie M Hinckley, b Georgia Nov 23, 1848. Gazetteer of 1883 gives him of Newport, owning 280 acres. Five children:

a   Forrest F b Mch 25, 1873; of N Y City; untraced
b   Josie A b June 17, 1876; m Clinton Ward of Newport
c   Sumner W b June 28, 1881; of N Y City, untraced
d   Harold W b Dec 17, 1888; 1922 of Newport Center
e   Hazel b after 1889; 1922 of Newport, unm

Joanna Dow adaabfb m Belmont, N H, Jan 1, 1825, John Gunnison b Gilmanton Apr 5, 1798, son of Henry and Experience (Wilson); ordained 1830; had Congregational pastorates, Lyman, Me, Salisbury-Amesbury, Mass, Newmarket, Brentwood, N H, Falmouth and Westbrook, Me.

Joanna d early without children: he d New Gloucester, Me, 18-6; m 2nd Saco 1831, Nancy Murray Starbird of Gorham d Sept 18, 1853.

Mary C Dow adaabfc d Feb 21, 1871; m Belmont June 25, 1838, William C Osgood b Nov 14, 1812, d July 23, 1869, town clerk of Pittsfield, son of Capt David and Betsey (Osgood). Children:

  a Martha A b Mch 8, 1840; d Sept 28, 1865
  b Henry W b Oct 9, 1842
  c Edwin S b Aug 26, 1844; m Martha E Allen   d J Frank b 1850

Harrison Dow adaabfd may have been youngest child; census of 1850 gives him cooper of Craftsbury, b Vt 1820; assessment $300; of Walden 1857-8; of Coventry 1860, a Civil War Veteran, of Manchester, N H, several years; finally farmer of Tuftonborough, N H, d Dec 22, 1901. He m 1st Mch 14, 1844, Fannie F Ransom b Walden, d Tuftonborough Sept 19, 1897, ae 75, 5 mos, dau of Ammi C and Betsey (Carson); m 2nd (her 2nd) Jane Jackson Bran b Madison Jan 1, 1826, d Dover Mch 10, 1914, dau of George Quint, farmer, and Mary J. Census of 1850 gives some children, rest from widely scattered rec:

  a Emma K (obviously named for adaabfaa) b 1845; of Londonderry, N H, m
      Jan 4, 1864, Nathan C Hazelton of Manchester
  b (presumably twin) Ruanna b Jan 4, 1845
  c Helen E (stated, dau of Harrison, must be identical with Ruanna) d Manchester
      May 5, 1858, ae 13-11-1
  d Fanny F b 1846   e Ephraim b 1848; untraced; both in census
 ·f Alvah E b Grafton, N H, 1850 (from m rec)
  g Julia b Mch 28, 1852
  h Lucy b Walden; d Manchester May 2, 1867, ae 10, 10 mos
  i William Edwin b Walden 1858

Alvah E Dow adaabfdf of Sandwich, N H, m Jan 29, 1882, Mary Jane (Caverly) Foss, dau of Benjamin and Mary; 2nd Tuftonborough Dec 19, 1885, Anna Natter (Nutter in dau's rec error), ae 31, dau of Jacob and Nancy. Children:

  a Fannie Ethel b Sandwich Apr 13, 1882; of Laconia m June 30, 1897, Willis Free-
      man Merrill of Laconia
  b Albert H b Tuftonborough 1887
  c Edith d Tuftonborough Sept 27, 1892, ae 3
  d ——, son b Tuftonborough May 14, 1891

Albert H Dow adaabfdfb, draftsman of Boston, m Oct 22, 1910, Bessie Pearson, ae 26, dau of Jacob and Emma C (Lanning)

William E Dow adaabfdi, laborer of Dover, m Nov 24, 1881, Della J Applebee, ae 19, d Bath, Me, Feb 24, 1905, dau of Samuel and Harriet (Kelly) of Sanford, Me; m 2nd, carpenter of Biddeford, Oct 21, 1917, Lurie May Dow, ae 25, operative, dau of Simon B adgfdaaa and Lucinda Day (Gordon).

Winslow Dow adaabf appears in 1850 census b Vt 1809, it being doubtless correct that his brother Darwin J was youngest of the family. A cooper of Cabot, he lived long; m Adeline —— b Vt 1820. No knowledge of children except from 1850 census:

| a George b 1838 | b Betsey b 1841 | c Polly b 1844 |
| d Eveline b 1847 | e Edward b 1849 | |

William G Dow adaabfy is perhaps of this family; b Vt 1821, farmer of Cabot, m Mch 20, 1843, Mehitable Martin b Vt 1822 of Peacham. Census 1870 gives him teamster of St Johnsbury and children:

a Lucinda b 1844	b Ethan A b 1846	c Ellen J b 1848
d Mehitable L b 1850	e Flora b 1852	f Comi b 1854
g Lizzie b 1859	h Josephine b 1862	

Perhaps Wm G Dow is of the bcfif line.

Darius J Dow adaabff d Tuftonborough Nov 3, 1893, rec giving names of both parents. A grandson is authority for statement that he was youngest of family, perhaps not accurate. Teacher, cabinet maker and farmer, most of his life was in Tuftonborough; m 1st Mary Ann Osgood b Apr 17, 1817, d Mch 1, 1840, dau of Dudley and Martha (Moore) of London. This, correct in Osgood Gen, badly garbled in Hist Canterbury. Of Newmarket, he m 2nd Dec 8, 1842, Lydia D Lucy of Pittsfield. A 3rd m is surely his: Darwin J b Gilmanton, ae 56, farmer of Tuftonborough, son of Jonathan and Joanna, m Apr 25, 1882, wid Lizzie R Graves, ae 52. If correct, Darwin would come 33 years after marriage. A man invariably lies about his age at 2nd m, but it is, nevertheless, astounding that a man of 71 should say he was 56 and get away with it. Children:

a Martha m Foss A Burnham of No Berwick, Me
b Christiania m Webster Wells of Wells, Me
c Alice d unm   d Sidney Jerome b Newmarket July 2, 1846

Sidney J Dow adaabffd, traveling salesman of Boston, d Bridgewater Apr 3, 1908; m Great Falls, N H, June 6, 1868, Elmira Abigail Perkins b Wells, Me, Sept 30, 1853. Children:

a Fred d in infancy
b Grace Lillian, now Mrs Forgate of Medford, Mass; letter returned "not found"
c Charles Pike b Peabody, Mass, June 13, 1877
d Arthur Francis; now bond broker of Boston and Somerville

Charles P Dow adaabffdc became an orange broker and dealer in mortgages in Orlando, Fla, returned to Boston about 1920 and organized the firm of C P Dow & Co, investment bonds. The failure of this firm in 1925 with liabilities well into the millions produced no small sensation, its assets small. Indicted on many counts in the Federal Court, he finally pleaded guilty on a charge of using the mails to defraud and was punished by a fine of $2,000. That the firm was very recklessly conducted was freely admitted. The penalty indicates that the Court did not find a degree of criminality charged by the sensational press. A little later he pleaded guilty to a charge of bucket-shopping and was fined $2,500. His unsecured creditors got 10 per cent on $6,000,000 liabilities.

He m Boston Jan 1, 1901, Carolyn Barker Heal b Westport, Me, Feb 23, 1878, dau of William and Harriet G (Cunningham).   Children:

   a   Carolyn Eva b Boston Oct 15, 1902
   b   Marion Heal b Orlando Nov 29, 1906
   c   Eleanor Pike b Medford, Mass, July 31, 1908

Arthur F Dow adaabffdd m Grace Iva Godfrey.   Children:

   a   Constance b Somerville Feb 9, 1902
   b   Richard Godfrey b Medford Apr 6, 1909

O UR next line remained Quaker for only a generation, except the youngest son: the parents figure always with the Friends.

John Dow adab appears as buying a Salisbury farm 1731, but he did not live with his father for years previously. There is a clearly defined family tradition that the children of Joseph Dow ada by his 1st wife, all more or less austere Quakers, regarded with horror what seemed to them the wild life of the family by 2nd wife. No love was lost between them when John came to administer the estate in 1734. He m 1st Jan 6, 1713-4, Dinah Severance (always Severans in rec) b Sept 3, 1692; dau of Ephraim and Lydia (Morrill); 2nd about 1719-20 Mary Challis a 2nd cousin: 3rd Feb 13, 1739, wid Elizabeth Simonds. She had m 1st Oct 8, 1705, John Simonds of Haverhill and had a grown family, one son being of Goffstown. Presumably she individually joined the Friends at marriage. John was living in So Hampton later than 1758. Children, all by Salisbury rec:

a   Jemima b Apr 16, 1714; d Oct 6, 1725
b   Nathan b Aug 6, 1716   c   Abigail b Apr 17, 1718
d   Challis (by 2nd wife) b Dec 22, 1721 (rec gives Chall—a dau)
e   Lydia b Apr 24, 1724   f   Jemima b Mch 30, 1727; d July 13, 1730
g   Mercy b Apr 5, 1730; d July 30, 1730
h   Mary b Apr 5, 1735; d Aug 3, 1736, of throat distemper. A neighbor lost all six children in this great epidemic
i   Jonathan b Oct 25, 1737   j   Johanna b Aug 6, 1740

Nathan Dow adabb got at outs with the Friends, when he m, 2nd church Salisbury Oct 25, 1739-40, Mary (Sarah in rec) Flanders, dau of John and Sarah. For 20 years they lived somewhere around Salisbury or Haverhill; all children by Salisbury rec. About 1760 he took his entire family to Maine and presumably the home folks never heard of them again. Presumably he went by water, for there was no overland route, but perhaps not with the original settlers of Deer Island, led from Haverhill in 1762 by Major William Eaton. Nathan was not in the original division of Deer Island, but came there from the mainland in 1767. Here he d almost at once, his will dated Deer Isl May 13, 1767, probated in Brunswick the same year. In 1764 Nathan was living not far from Bath. Children:

a   Jemima b Sept 22, 1740; bap Dec 11, 1743; possibly the father delayed a little, hoping his wife would become a Friend, with reconciliation with the family
b   Nathan b before 1746. Rec not found but he was of age 1767 and here is the only available gap
c   Sarah b Aug 5, 1744; bap Sept 9, 1744 (no delay this time)
d   Dinah b June 14, 1747; bap July 17, 1747
e   Mary bap July 1, 1750   f   Judith b Oct 15, 1752
g   John bap Nov 10, 1754

A generation ago William Dow, sailor of Tremont, Me, too advanced in years for aught save short fishing trips, used to take his grandchildren on his knee and tell them tales of his own grandsire, of old times, of wars, Indian fights, privation, massacres, scalping, bravery. He enjoined upon the open mouthed youngsters that they should remember these tales, these names, and repeat all to their own grandchildren, to pass down to many generations yet unborn.   Youth is careless.   These grandchildren, now past middle age, wish to recall the tales, but only scraps come to mind.   It was only by coincidence of names that the connection of Deer Island appeared and only by comparison of records that the first Dow of Deer Isl was found to be the Quaker born from old Salisbury.

In 1762 the place was settled by a party from Haverhill.   That town had grown until the individual farm was too small to support a family. One must emigrate or starve.   The end of the French War made Maine a safe place and most of it was uninhabited.   It is not hard to understand why Deer Island was chosen.   No one tried to forsee a city to come a century later, to see real estate increasing greatly in value.   All they asked was a safe place with plenty of food.   Here the abundance of deer named the island. The rock bound coast forbade any landing of an enemy. Timber was abundant, the soil, when cleared, not unfertile, fish in great plenty.   Nothing seemed lacking; the land was theirs from the bare fact of occupancy.   So, here settled about 30 families, mostly from Haverhill or around Gloucester; a few from the Salisbury region.

Jemima Dow adabba came to Me with her parents; m 1764 Lieut Stephen Coombs of Bath, son of Joshua, grandson of Anthony; they lived near Foster's Point, New River Meadow; she d Bath Apr 16, 1811. Children:

a   Stephen   b   David
c   Sarah b Dec 11, 1766; m 1st —— Lyon d by 1790; 2nd July 26, 1792, Luke
      Ryerson of New Gloucester, later of Paris and Buckfield, 4th generation
      from Marten Ryerson, immigrant. He d Aug 28, 1808, leaving 12 children
      by Sarah,—Sarah, Joseph, Howell, Nancy, Nehimiah, Esther, Reading,
      Nathaniel, Osgood, Christina, Simeon and Ebenezer. Sarah m 3rd Benjamin
      Cox of Sumner, evidently a very brave man
d   Jemima   e   Daniel   f   Mary   g   Nathaniel   h   Judith
j   Jonathan

Nathan Dow adabbb, executor of his father's estate, lived on the farm still known as Dow's Point.   This was presumably inherited.   His nearest neighbor was Jonathan Eaton, who came from the mainland in 1767 with Nathan Dow Sr. A phrase in Hosmer, Hist Deer Isl, suggests that Nathan Jr got himself a grant of land.   Possibly this was under the 1783 bounty law.   It is doubtless this Nathan who enlisted Mch 4, 1777, Capt Brooks, Col Marshall Battle.   It is possible that there was another Nathan Dow in Hancock Co, whose identity is as yet undiscovered. Some Nathan Dow of Castine took a contract in 1778 to carry mails between Belfast and Bangor.   This does not seem like the same man.   The

1790 census gives in Hancock Co Nathan Dow and Nathan Dow Jr, each la, lb, 3c. As we well know, the term Jr is employed to distinguish wholly unrelated men. Neither can be Nathan Dow abccgc. About 1885 a grandson wrote to Edgar R Dow saying clearly that our Nathan had 7 children, but did not give the name of wife. Beyond this we have had to depend on the data of the 1850 census and on the vital statistics collected by the State subsequent to 1892. In 1924 the town clerk of Deer Island collected and sent to the Author the complete list of vital statistics from 1785. Of course, the early records are more or less defective, but the kindly act enables us to reconstruct the history of the entire Deer Island family. The children appear as of Nathan and Jemimah. His d rec does not appear, nor hers, altho Judith Dow, wife of Nathan, d Aug 6, 1825. Children:

a	Abigail b Sept 8, 1785	b	David b June 11, 1787
c	Jeremiah b Aug 27, 1789	d	Nathan b Sept 5, 1792
e	John b Jan 15, 1795	f	Hannah b Nov 15, 1796; d Feb 20, 1848
g	Ephraim b Dec 19, 1798	h	Joshua b Aug 10, 1801

Here are 8 children as against 7 by family rec. From Hist Deer Island we get impression that 3 dau belong here, but this is incorrect; they are children of Nathan adabb

David Dow adabbbb is untraced; probably is the David d Deer Isl Oct 11, 1826. It is a notable coincidence that four David Dow were born 1787. The 1850 census has a Jemima Dow b Me 1787 living with Joshua Dow adabbbh. This might be wid of David or his brother Jeremiah. Deer Isl rec gives to David and Bettsey Dow a dau:

a   Susan W b Nov 28, 1825; untraced

Jeremiah Dow adabbbc does not reappear in Deer Isl rec and cannot be associated with any known Jeremiah.

Nathan Dow adabbbd m June 9, 1820, Mary (Polly in rec) Weed. Census 1850 shows him farmer of Deer Isl, realty assessed $300. This is relatively high. The highest assessment of any Deer Isl Dow was $400 and lowest $25.

Census gives his wife Hannah b Me 1803; if correct, this would be 2nd wife. Census gives 3 children:

a   Martha b 1822   b   John b July 19, 1823   c   David b Apr 23, 1827
d   Louis b 1829; census, otherwise unknown
e   Nathan b Dec 19, 18—, to Nathan and Dolly; not in census
f   Polly b Dec 3, 1832 (to Nathan and wife). No rec attributable to either of these younger

John Dow adabbbdb. Some John Dow d Deer Isl Nov 1835. No other Deer Isl rec possibly attributable and this probably applies to John adabbg

David Dow adabbbdc, farmer of Deer Isl, d Oct 17, 1910, ae 83-7-15;

m presumably on mainland Sophia Pickering d Nov 11, 1904, **dau of** Thomas S and Lucy (Bray), ae 76-10-23.   Children:

a   David William b Aug 31, 1855; **d Dec 1875**
b   Lucy H b May 17, 1857; **d Dec 1875**
c   Eliza A b Sept 15, 1861   d   Mary E b Dec 14, 1863
e   Crockett E b 1868   f   Augustus A b Apr 14, 1871; unt
g   Willie M b Mch 12, 1876
      Four children found by d rec but not by b rec
w   William W d Dec 28, 1875   x   Henry d Jan 13, 1876
y   Benjamin drowned Oct 20, 1877 (parents not specified, but entry occurs be-
      tween two children of David and Sophia)   z   John H d Jan 1876

Crockett E Dow adabbbdce yachtsman of Deer Isl, m Dec 15, 1890, Georgie E Haskell d Deer Isl Oct 16, 1895, ae 29, dau of Eben and Dorothy (Haskell); 2nd Dec 25, 1902, Susie B Morey ae 22, d Apr 23, 1915; dau of William and Izora (Eaton).   Children, all b Deer Isl:

a   Laurance A b Oct 21, 1891   b   Augustus b Jan 6, 1893
c   Sybil Marian b June 3, 1903   d   Doris Crocker b July 11, 1904
e   William V b July 18, 1910   f   ——dau b Aug 1, d Aug 4, 1913

John Dow adabbbe.   No rec safely attributable to him

Ephraim Dow adabbbg, sailor of Deer Isl, appears in 1850 census, assessed $200; wife Harriet b 1825.   No further rec attributable

Joshua Dow adabbbh appears in 1850 census sailor of Deer Isl, assessed $300; wife Dorothy b Me 1818.   No children in census.   Next name is Jemima Dow b Me 1787, not placeable.   Town rec gives children:

a   Lois E b Sept 26, 1852   b   Sylvanus P b Oct 29, 1854; unt

Sarah Dow adabbc.   One dau of Nathan Dow m Josiah Crockett of Deer Isl

Dinah Dow adabbd appears in Hist Deer Isl as Diana; m (his 2nd) Jonathan Eaton, her nearest neighbor

Mary Dow adabbe and **Judith Dow** adabbf appear correctly named in Hist Deer Isl; not stated if m.   Judith Dow d Mch 30, 1832, probably identical

John Dow adabbg.   Hist Deer Isl has little to say about him. Local rec, however, give all (presumably) his children, and their families were identified with Deer Isl.   There cannot be much doubt that he is the John Dow who at an early date settled on an inland in Penobscot Bay and some years later induced six other families to join him.   Census 1790 calls this Shamm Island and finds John 1a, 4b, 3c.   The new colonists petitioned the Legislature again and again that this island being owner-less, not even included in the limits of any county, should be granted to them.   Such is red tape that not until 1802 was this done and the place received the name Holt's Island.   Children are credited in rec to John and Betty, but no further rec of her is found except the d of John and Betsey in 1835.   Hist Deer Isl calls her dau of Thomas Saunders, correct as is shown by name of 1st born:

a   Thomas Saunders b Apr 2, 1779   b   Ephraim b Feb 12, 1782
c   Stephen b Aug 14, 1784   d   Samuel b May 11, 1787
e   Molly b Oct 20, 1789   f   Anna b Apr 13, 1792; m July 12, 1810,
      John Staples.   Hist Deer Isl says some dau m William Staples
g   Hannah b Aug 11, 1795
h   Elisebeth b Nov 23, 1798; m Sept 3, 1816, Capt Jacob Carlton
i   Susannah b May 9, 1799; this date is impossible.   Hist Deer Isl says a dau m
      Joseph C Stinson and another Capt John Kempton.   These do not appear
      in town rec

Thomas S Dow adabbga appears in 1850 census as farmer of Deer Isl, assessed $300; wife Elizabeth b Me 1785.   She was Betsey E Haskell b Deer Isl, one rec giving 1791.   In death they were not divided; she d Dec 13, he Dec 16, 1866.   In d rec of son Thomas, mother appears as Aletha Joyce, probably copyist's error.   A grandson in 1888 gave the names of 11 children.   Local rec contain only 7 of these, 2 oldest credited to Thomas and Betty:

a   Betsey b June 8, 1803; m——Green, rec not extant
b   Thomas b Nov 27, 1804
c   Julia b Feb 11, 1810.   Family rec does not give her, but does give Judith m
      ——Low, Jane m——Scott, Dorothy d unm, Mary m——Small and living
      in 1888.   Three of these are confirmed by local rec: Jane Dow m Dec 1,
      1834, Leonard Scott; Judith Dow m Oct 15, 1831, Thomas Lowe; Mary C
      Dow m Jan 8, 1844, Lemuel Small
d   Sarah H b Mch 31, 1813; d unm
g   Jonathan, living 1888   h   Benjamin d by 1888
i   Amos Angell b Dec 4, 1822   j   Moses Angell b Apr 4, 1825
      A son William b Jan 19, 1831, to Thomas and Betsey must be a grandchild

Thomas Dow adabbgab.   Local rec give Thomas Dow d Apr 4, 1879, and Mary E, wife of Thomas, d Aug 21, 1875.   She was Mary Green, dau of Asa and wid of Thomas Haskell.   Census 1850 gives him sailor, realty $300.   Children:

a   Mary E b Nov 29, 1829   b   Martha G b Oct 27, 1831; d before 1850
c   Eliza F b May 7, 1835   d   Dudley H b Oct 30, 1838

Dudley H Dow adabbgabd d May 15, 1907, ae 68-5-15; m Nov 22, 1868, Helen E Haskell d Dec 28, 1870; m 2nd Rose Creole b Boston, Mass.   Children, Deer Isl rec:

a   George C b Oct 30, 1869
b   Isaac C b June 13, 1874; d Apr 18, 1896, unm
c   Clarence T b Oct 31, 1875   d   Theodore E b Jan 28, 1877
e   Warren H b Sept 18, 1878; d Oct 31, 1879
f   Winfield Scott b Sept 14, 1880   g   Charles W b Aug 11, 1882
h   Elmer S b Apr 1, 1886
      No rec of four of these appear and no names in the disconnected lists are at-
      tributable

Winfield Scott Dow adabbgabdf, yachtsman of Deer Isl, m Nov 7, 1916, Alice Smith.   Only child:

a   Henry Keith b May 22, 1917

Elmer S Dow adabbgabdh m May 8, 1922, Bessie Bray.   Child:

a   Mabel V b Aug 3, 1922

Jonathan Haskell Dow adabbgag, b 1809, sailor later farmer of
Deer Isl, d Sept 4, 1896; assessed 1850 at $400; m May 28, 1835, Sarah
Haskell b 1812, d Mch 24, 1897 ae 84-4-24, dau of Jonathan and Nabby
(Hardy).   All Haskells of Deer Isl descend from Jonathan Haskell, Revolutionary veteran of Gloucester, Mass.   One of his sons ran away from
home and located permanently on Deer Isl.   Another son is progenitor
of the Haskells of central and western Me.   Deer Isl rec give all children:

a   Nelson H b Oct 27, 1836; unt   b   Charlotte B b June 21, 1839
c   George W b Dec 20, 1844   d   Charles Hallet b Dec 2, 1846
e   Laura A b Nov 8, 1851

Charlotte B Dow adabbgagb m Jan 28, 1858, William H Haskell,
master mariner.   Several children, of whom:

a   Nelson, killed by fall from mast head   b   Warren, sea capt

George W Dow adabbgagc d seaman of Deer Isl widower Nov 14,
1916.   No m rec found, but children are credited to George and Sarah
E.   She must be Sarah E, wid of —— Dow (wife, it should be), d Deer
Isl May 28, 1899, ae 56-0-23, dau of Washington and Susan (Bray) Haskell:

a   Laura E b Sept 17, d Sept 20, 1871
b   Sarah G b Dec 14, d Dec 18, 1872
c   Lottie M b Dec 1, d Dec 14, 1873   d   Laura A b Dec 6, 1875
e   William D b May 1, 1878; unt
f   George B b Oct 20, 1881; d June 25, 1882

Charles H Dow adabbgagd d Dec 5, 1888, aboard his own ship in
Delaware Bay; m Deer Isl Oct 15, 1872, Alice Smith, who d childless;
2nd Isabella Florence Clark b Oct 4, 1854, dau of Capt Mansfield and
Betsey (Coombs), great grand dau of Lieut Anthony Coombs adabba.
They soon moved to Camden; she living 1924 with two dau in Glendale,
Calif.   Children:

a   Charles Lee b Islesboro Sept 21, 1876
b   Nellie Richardson b Sept 2, 1878; d Jan 14, 1900; m Henry A Howard of Rock-
      land
c   Elizabeth Drury b 1881; now secretary in Portland
d   Geneva Florence b June 1, 1885; m——Lamoreaux; no children
e   Madeline Adella b Feb 7, 1888; m Edgar J Gowen; now of Glendale; dau Ruth
      Elizabeth b May 12, 1923

Charles L Dow adabbgagda.   Rec garbled says: Clarence Lee
Dow, son of late Clarence H, mill hand of Camden m Dec 24, 1902, Catherine Frances Bowen ae 20, dau of John b Ire and Anna (Keenan).   She
d Lynn Dec 1, 1909, childless; he m 2nd Mary Magdalene Shea; lives
Van Nuys, Calif.   Children:

a   Marion Anastasia b Oct 8, 1911   b   Charles Hallet b Apr 19, 1917
c   Geneva Isabelle b July 25, 1923

Benjamin Dow adabbgah appears in census b 1823, sailor of Deer Isl, wife Eliza b Me 1823. She d Feb 13, 1865; in son's rec called Eliza Dow, but this is probably not her maiden name. Children:

  a Asa H b Oct 15, 1844; hostler of Rockland, d exposure (found dead in stable)
       June 7, 1917, unm
  b Francis H b Nov 22, 1848   c Eliza E b Nov 12, 1849
  d Benjamin D b Dec 29, 1856   e Eben S b Nov 5, 1859

Francis H Dow adabbgahb. There is a little confusion here. Deer Isl rec gives Frank Dow, son of Benjamin and Eliza, d Mch 9, 1889. Also Caroline wife of Frank Dow d Sept 17, 1887. Anna Dow, dau of Frank and Caroline, d Jan 19, 1890. Deer Isl rec also give to Francis H Dow and wife Caroline: (He m Caroline Gray Aug 31, 1870)

  a Ada F b June 16, 1871
  b Eliza E b Sept 25, 1873; d (Emma) Jan 11, 1892
  c Carrie E b Dec 13, 1875   d Elizabeth B b Nov 20, 1878
  e Lillian b Nov 9, 1885   f Annie B b Sept 11, 1891
  g Alice B b Sept 11, 1891

Benjamin D Dow adabbgahd is untraced

Eben S Dow adabbgahe m Mch 17, 1889, Mamie Norton. In rec of children he appears as fisherman of Deer Isl and she as Mary F Norton. Children:

  a Lena F b Mch 4, 1892   c Edward E b Apr 23, 1895
  d Maurice R b May 10, 1910

Amos Angell Dow adabbgai appears in 1850 census as sailor of Deer Isl, assessed $100; wife Caroline b Me 1828. In later life he was a caulker; d married Deer Isl May 23, 1906. She was Eunice Caroline Snowman b Castine, d Deer Isl July 4, 1881. His son gave in 1888 a list of 11 children, 10 found in Deer Isl rec:

  a Esther E b Nov 26, 1846; d Nov 5, 1876
  b Frances Eleanor b Nov 16, 1849; m——Scott of Deer Isl
  c Amos Fulton b Jan 15, 1853
  d Judith L b Mch 10, 1856; m Aug 17, 1875, Melvill Thompson of Deer Isl
  e Edward Y H b June 6, 1857
  f William W b Nov 11, 1859; d Jan 29, 1877
  g Moses Angell b Oct 11, 1861   h John Snowman b May 6, 1864
  i Simeon Low b June 10, 1867   j Joshua H b July 11, 1869
  k Daisy D b June 3, 1873; m——Powers

Amos F Dow adabbgaic, sea captain, d Stonington July 1, 1906. At 2nd m was a stone mason; m Sept 14, 1873, Lydia A Hardy b Deer Isl; m 2nd Anna M Sellers b Deer Isl. Twelve children; all Deer Isl rec:

  a Charles L b Oct 9, 1875; untraced
  b Billings Putnam (B T in rec) b Apr 12, 1877
  c Edward b Dec 31, 1878; d Nov 27, 1895
  d Nellie F b Oct 16, 1880; d Jan 13, 1895   e Albert Dean b Sept 26, 1882
  f Margrett b Aug 17, 1884; d (Margaret F) Nov 12, 1902
  g Callie B b Feb 4, 1887   h Lillian A b June 29, 1888
  i Bertie L b July 18, 1890
  j Ernest L b Nov 27, 1891   k Emma H b Dec 16, 1893
  l Lester C b Dec 24, 1894

Billings P Dow adabbgaicb, master mariner of Stonington, m Jan 5, 1910, Alta H Greenlaw, ae 29, b Deer Isl, dau of Clara E Greenlaw and Theodore H Bray.   Children:

a   Vera Madeline b Stonington Aug 18, 1912
b   Edward Amos b Portland June 4, d June 6, 1919

Albert D Dow adabbgaice, quarryman of Stonington, m May 2, 1903, Ada Maud Gross, ae 19, dau of Augustus H and Mary O (Trundy). Child:

a   Margaret Olive b Stonington Sept 29, 1903

Edward Y Dow adabbgaie, b Deer Isl, mariner, m Carrie E Pierce b Mt Desert; moved to Rockland.   Five children:

a   Albert L b Rockland 1889; m Boston Nov 7, 1910, Daisy Lindburg, ae 20, dau
    of Magnus and Lulu (Austin)
c   Rodney b Rockland May 24, d July 4, 1895
    Rockland directory of 1923 has Dows, possibly belonging here: Elmer P, Edwin
    O, Geraldine, Harry L

Moses A Dow adabbgaig, in 1893 carpenter of Rockport, 1895 quarryman of Deer Isl, from 1912 carpenter of Rockland; m Aug 11, 1881, Mary Frances Webster d Stonington Dec 14, 1904, dau of John and Hannah (Robbins); 2nd (carpenter of Belfast) Dec 28, 1909, Gertrude Day, wid, dau of Charles and Susan (Gray) Gray of Belfast.   Children:

a   Horace b May 18, 1882; d Stonington Nov 7, 1900
b   William Wallace b Sept 14, 1884
c   Caroline E b Dec 7, 1885; d Stonington Sept 3, 1901
d   Minnie b Oct 7, 1888; living 1893
e   Arthur b 1891; living 1893   f ——dau b Sept 16, 1893
g   ——her twin   h   Eva b Mch 27, d Apr 8, 1895
i   Sumner E b Deer Isl; d Sept 6, 1896, ae 2 mos, 4 days
j   Eva d Mch 27, 1897, ae 6 mos, 10 days
k   Carlton b Stonington Mch 22, d Sept 15, 1900
l   ——son b Belfast Aug 31, 1910   m ——son b Aug 13, 1912
n   ——son b July 25, 1914

Wallace W Dow adabbgaigb, laborer of Rockland, teamster of Stonington, m Mch 15, 1905, Ella F Ingersoll, ae 29 div, dau of Charles F and Josephine (Dushane) of Vinal Haven. She d Feb 7, 1907; he m 2nd Apr 18, 1908, Hattie Witham, ae 21, dau of Clifford and Annie (Dow) unplaced; div, m 3rd (her 2nd, div) Aug 9, 1913, Lena M Freeman, ae 36, dau of Nathaniel and Addie (Barber) Thomas of Aroostook Co.   One child found:

a   Wallace T b July 9, 1905; d Dec 14, 1908

Arthur Dow adabbgaige, steamboater of Rockland, later laborer, m Oct 8, 1914, Eva M Shea (Spear in one rec is error), ae 21, dau of Charles and Ida E (Andrews).   Children:

a   ——dau b Jan 24, 1915   b   ——son b Sept 3, 1916

John S Dow adabbgaih, mason and cooper of Deer Isl, d Stonington

Feb 25, 1898; m Nov 11, 1888, Ada Maude Lane b Deer Isl Mch 21, 1871.
Children:

    a   Alton Dennis b July 10, 1890; d Nov 24, 1915, unm
    b   Maurice L b Aug 8, 1898

Maurice L Dow adabbgaihb, machinist of Portland, m July 5, 1919,
Julia Alice Stinson, ae 20, dau of Herbert W and Addie E.   Child:

    a   Chester Newman b Portland June 25, 1920

Simeon L Dow adabbgaii, caulker of Deer Isl, later quarryman of
Stonington, d Jan 19, 1913; m Mch 3, 1889, Julia B Stinson b Deer Isl,
of Sunset.   Children:

    a   Elmer Pearl b Sept 8, 1898   b ——son b May 20, 1900
    c   Edward Francis b Mch 24, d Dec 25, 1903
    d   Warren Roland b Dec 1, 1904; d Sept 23, 1905
    e   Lawrence Amos b Dec 5, 1906
    f   Henry Cecil b May 3, 1909; d Apr 10, 1910
    g   Cecile Caroline b Aug 8, 1910; d Dec 10, 1918

Elmer P Dow adabbgaiia, brakeman of Rockland, m Nov 27, 1918,
Gladys A Hurd, div ae 18, dau of Joseph E and Virgie F (Jameson) Smith
of N Y

Joshua H Dow adabbgaij, fisherman, m July 28, 1887, Mary J
Scott, both of Deer Isl.   She d Rockland Feb 22, 1919, ae 48-6-22, dau
of Samuel A and Mary J (Howard).   Fifth child missing:

    a   Warren O b May 30, 1888; d Aug 14, 1901
    b   Jasper b Feb 7, 1892, ae 2 mos, 12 days
    c   Myron H b Aug 8, 1893; d Mch 8, 1912
    d   Priscilla E b Oct 20, 1889; d Apr 23, 1895
    e   Philip G b Apr 15, 1897; d Jan 27, 1918
    g   Elsie M b Oct 15, 1902   h ——son b and d Mch 17, 1908

Moses A Dow adabbgaj appears in 1850 census as farmer with his
parents, later caulker of Deer Isl; m Hipsabeth Dow, dau of Nathan
adabbbd.   She d Rockland May 1, 1904, ae 74-1-14.   Children, all but
youngest, by Deer Isl rec:

    a   Lemuel S (Samuel, census) b Nov 25, 1845
    b   Nathan b Jan 12, 1849; probably the Nathan d Feb 1885
    c   Lucy M b Apr 17, 1853; surely d young
    d   Alonzo G b Apr 12, 1855; d in infancy (rec gives Apr 5, 1855)
    e   Victor W T b Dec 28, 1857; untraced
    f   Lucy Maria b Jan 18, 1860   g Anna H b Dec 7, 1863
    h   Armenia b Feb 5, 1865   i Freeman H (by own rec only)
    j   Martha Flavilla d Rockland, nurse, Sept 1, 1900, ae 31, unm

Lemuel S Dow adabbgaja, laborer of Rockland, m Hattie E Weed.
He d Oct 5, 1918.   Two children found:

    a   Gracie E, telegrapher of Rockland, d Apr 21, 1913, ae 21-10-2
    b   Harrison L b Rockland 1889; untraced

Freeman H Dow adabbgaji, laborer of Rockland, widower, m 2nd
June 11, 1894, Eliza Johnson, ae 22, dau of William and Eliza (Curtis)
of Bowdoinham.   Some Freeman Dow in 1915 driver of Bath.

Ephraim Dow adabbgb is not found in 1850 census, is said to have lived Mt Desert. He was of Deer Isl at least from 1814 to 1821; his children settled in Tremont and Brooklyn. A nephew reports 5 children, of whom 4 appear in Deer Isl rec: His wife (m 1807) was Rebecca M Mullen.

  a Lydia J b July 5, 1814; m George Galley; 2nd John Norwood
  b Maria m Jonathan Robbins
  c William H b Aug 3, 1813 (family Bible; 1814 rec)
  d Emeline b Dec 24, 1817; m James Madison Butler
  e Thurlough (many spellings) b June 21, 1821

William H Dow adabbgbc, sailor of Tremont, d June 19, 1907. Realty assessed 1850 at $458. He m Isabelle Billings b Me 1818. It was he who in old age used to tell to his grandchildren the tales told to him by his own grandsire. As these tales contained much about Indian fighting and old Haverhill, one wonders how much had to do with direct experience of any grandsire. His grandfather b 1754 does not appear anywhere in rosters. Possibly Nathan Dow adabb during the twenty years he spent somewhere near Salisbury and Haverhill had a military experience of which the record has not been found. The history of the family from 1767 onward is one of complete peace. His posterity is proven by two descendants, discrepancies being negligible. Children:

  a Isaac Carlton b 1838 (census)
  b Reuben Billings b 1841; Civil War vet; d unm
  c Willard Sawyer b 1843; all dates from census
  d Harriet Ann b 1846; m Charles Spinney of Lynn, Mass; several children, 1 named Charles
  e Elnora T b 1848; d unm   f Charlotte Adell
  g Arthur Henry d unm   h Zelinda Josephine

Isaac C Dow adabbgbca served throughout the war; d May 23, 1919, ae 81-5-1; m Rebecca H Smith of Trenton d Nov 18, 1912, ae 67-0-24, dau of John and Abigail (Babbidge). Children:

  a Henry Alfred   b Reuben Ernest d in childhood
  c Abbie Belle m Henry J McKeown of Boston, Mass
  d John William d Aug 20, 1898, ae 19-1-10
  e Nellie Blanche m Harold W Chatto of Blue Hill
  f Elsie Estella unm in 1920
  g Robert Carlton, now of Seal Cove, unm; a good informant on his line

Henry A Dow adabbgbcaa, fisherman of Vinal Haven, m Aug 30, 1898, Annie M Farley, ae 27, div wife of George Marshall, dau of Thomas and Rebecca (Kelley). Children:

  a Bert B, fisherman of Tremont, m Nov 20, 1915, Viola S Higgins, ae 24, dau of Eugene P and Carrie B (Richarsdon)
  c Pearl H b Apr 19, 1900

Willard S Dow adabbgbcc, veteran of Civil War, m Edwina C Hodgson. Children, b probably Tremont:

  a Josephine Z b Oct 14, 1866; m Newell J Kane; children,—George, Elmer, Willard, Rudolph, Doris, son d in infancy
  b Dora d unm   c Isaac William b Jan 18, 1871   d Ruby d unm
  e Bessie   f Mattie; both grew up and m

Isaac W Dow adabbgbccc of Ft Kent confirmed list of children; m Jan 1, 1894, Etta M Conary.   Child:

a   Robert Byron b Mch 14, 1898

Charlotte Adell Dow adabbgbcf m M Mark Worth of Lynn. Child:

a   Margaret grew up and m

Zelinda J Dow adabbgbch m Charles Cook.   Children:

a   Charles   b and c——daughters

Thurlough Dow adabbgbe appears in Tremont 1850 census; assessment $75; wife Harriet b Me 1827.   In rec of dau she is given as H Milliken. Story contributed by nephews calls his wife Maria Candage; if correct must be 2nd m.   Probably more children after 1850:

a   Cornelius b 1847; untraced   b   Shubal b 1849
c   Mary A d Tremont Jan 19, 1905, ae 48-4-11, unm

S Morton Dow adabbgbeb is wholly an arbitrary identification for Shubal of the census; master mariner, later motorman, m Clara A Robbins.   Sons found by own rec, presumably other children:

a   Ernest E b Mt Desert 1868-70   b   Clarence E b 1875
c   Albert b Center 1882; m Arlington, Mass, Apr 19, 1906, Minnie May McKensie, ae 28, b N B, dau of Edward and Annie M (Anderson)

Ernest E Dow adabbgbeba, mechanic of Calais, m Dec 8, 1893, Mary B Hickey, ae 21, dau of James and Mary (Chandler); moved to Mass after 1896.   Children:

a   Clarence Eugene b Oct 21, 1894   b   Josie M b Feb 16, 1896
c   Clara Viola b Revere Oct 3, 1902
d   Albert W b Somerville Mch 18, 1904
e   Evelyn L b Revere June 2, 1906

Clarence E Dow adabbgbebb, gardener and bookkeeper of Tremont, m Sept 1, 1900, Mabel Moore Leighton, ae 21, dau of Daniel W and Louise M (Tabbutt).   Children:

a   Ronald b Eden July 29, 1902; d in infancy
b   Ronald Morton b Eden Nov 2, 1903; d Bar Harbor Mch 4, 1911
c   ——son b Bar Harbor June 16, 1908

Stephen Dow adabbgc m 1808 Sally Sellers; drowned while fishing Nov 1833.   Both rec Deer Isl, which gives children:

a   Martha b Jan 19, 1810; m Jan 23, 1829, Otis Stinson
b   Elizabeth b July 18, 1816   c   Mary b Jan 2, 1819
d   Ebenezer b Apr 27, 1822   e   Stephen b Aug 30, 1825
f   Deborah W b Oct 14, 1828.
    Of Ebenezer no trace

Stephen Dow adabbgce.   One rec may be attributable; **wife** Elizabeth; child:

a   Eveline b Deer Isl July 18, 1866

Samuel Dow adabbgd in 1850 was sailor of Tremont, assessed $485; m Mary Stewart b Me 1794. Census gives 7 children, some may have m and gone:

a Samuel T b 1816   b William H b 1820   c Jonathan b 1825
d Willis O b 1833   e Sarah b 1834   f Hannah b 1837
g Otis b 1844

Samuel T Dow adabbgda, mariner until after 1864, then farmer of Hancock, m Lucetta C Brown d Hancock Feb 11, 1894, ae 47-11-11, dau of James and Louise (Leighton). Children, by own rec; probably others, and probably many disconnected Dow of Hancock belong here:

a Horace Lincoln b Hancock Aug 2, 1864   b Adelbert F b 1874

Horace L Dow adabbgdaa, farmer of Hancock, m Icy, Isy, Isey (all spellings in rec) Day of Rockland. Two older children not found:

c Samuel A b Mch 27, 1893   d Charlotte B b July 17, 1894
e George William b Dec 16, 1896   f Florence S b May 12, 1899

Samuel A Dow adabbgdaac, road house tender, d Ellsworth Oct 11, 1918, ae 26-6-14; m Conilla (or Corilla) E Cole of Harrington, d Ellsworth May 23, 1916, ae 28, dau of William and Effie (Willey). Child:

a Lorance E d Hancock Sept 12, 1917, ae 3-9-16

Adelbert F Dow adabbgdab of Ellsworth d Gardiner June 30, 1919, ae 47-1-22, m Mch 3, 1907, Berdelia Moore, ae 28, div dau of John W and Susanna (Cole) Taylor of N B

William H Dow adabbgdb, sea captain d Gouldsboro Sept 25, 1894; m Naomi —— b Me 1821; in 1850 farmer of Tremont assessed $225. Children by census, others possible later:

a Martha b 1841   b Mary V b 1843   c George b 1847
Mary Dow b 1850 appears in this family, possibly a cousin

George W Dow adabbgdbc may belong here, but letter of genealogical inquiry to his son remains unanswered. This man came from Hancock, b about 1847, and was skipper of the famous four-masted schooner Thomas W Lawson, surviving its wreck in 1907. A newspaper account at the time gave his residence Melrose and his wife Jennie W Bush an invalid. Two sons mentioned:

a Orville Howard b No Hancock 1871
b Richard E, chemist of Boston, not found in recent directory

Orville H Dow adabbgdbca was in 1902 druggist of Boston, but appears in directory as clerk of East Boston; m Mch 26, 1902, Hazel Anita Lorde ae 20, dau of Edward S and Josephine J (Howe). Children, Mass rec:

a George Orville b Boston Feb 10, 1903. Name suggests kinship with George O Dow adabbgo, mature in Rockland 1861
b Josephine Hazel b Sept 17, 1907

Jonathan Dow adabbgdc, ship carpenter, d married Surry Aug 2, 1899, ae 73-9-10. In census wife Sarah b Me 1816. Orphia E Dow b 1834, wid of Jonathan Dow, dau of Andrew and Miranda Flood of Surry, d Surry Mch 24, 1904. Perhaps children after 1850:

a Alvenett b 1848; untraced

Willis O Dow adabbgdd, laborer, widower, d Tremont Sept 11, 1901, ae 67-11-3; in 1861 farmer; m Rhoda A Murphy d July 24, 1894, ae 54-0-20, dau of Joshua and Lois (Butters). Perhaps other children:

a Willis E b 1861
g Stephen B d Eden Mch 15, 1903, ae 23-6-10, farmer unm

Willis E Dow adabbgdda (Edd in son's rec), seaman of Tremont, m Jan 31, 1902, Agnes M Trundy, ae 21, dau of Henry E and Ella M (Carter). Of children:

b ——son b Aug 6, 1905   d ——dau b Aug 15, 1909

William T Dow adabbgh quoted in Hist Deer Isl as son of John, proved by rec. Hist Deer Isl says he moved to Tinker's Isl, but census 1850 gives him farmer of Brooklyn, assessed $200, and his children appear in Deer Isl rec. He m Apr 3, 1823, Abigail T Davis (Dawse in rec) b Nov 18, 1803, d Deer Isl Nov 25, 1882. William T Dow b May 31, 1801, d Apr 26, 1868, by family Bible. Ten children, 9 appearing in census, 8 in Deer Isl rec:

a Abigail b June 25, 1824   b Jonathan b Mch 29, 1826
c Hosea b Jan 6, 1829; sailor, untraced
e Eliza A b July 16, 1831; m Feb 5, 1878, William I Jarvis
f Thornton b Mch 18, 1835; farmer, untraced. Rec resembles Thurston
g Carleton b July 9, 1837; untraced   h Reuben A b Feb 8, 1840
i Phebe b 1844   j Frances b 1845; both from census only

Jonathan Dow adabbghb d Blue Hill Mch 22, 1905, ae 78-11-24, sailor, widower; census shows him of Brooklyn, assessed $27. Wife Lavinia b Me 1823. Probably more children:

a Sygnoria b 1849

Reuben A Dow adabbghh, sailor, served from July 24, 1862, to July 6, 1865; d No Brooklin Dec 14, 1891; m Feb 11, 1871, Georgia C Hale b Brooklin (Gale in son's rec). Children:

a Forest N d Brooklin Feb 2, 1893, ae 19-2-22
b Hawley D b June 4, 1876   c Laura M d Sept 4, 1895, ae 17-1-20

Hawley D Dow adabbghhb, laborer then carpenter of Brooklin, m by Rev E S Dow of Sedgwick Jan 9, 1899, Josie May Bowden b Blue Hill May 24, 1880, dau of Oscar and Emma (Friend). Children:

a Howard B b Oct 6, 1901   b Kenneth Brooks b Oct 19, 1908

Altho the vital statistics of Deer Isl eliminated very many of those previously unplaced, it added some and there are left a number of disconnected individuals certainly belonging to the adabb line. These are collected here for convenience of indexing and reference.

Israel Dow adabbgi had wife Lydia; apparently b by 1780, as child:

a   Reuben b Deer Isl Sept 6, 1802; untraced
b   Hannah, dau of Israel and Lydia, d Sept 1833
    Reuben was b 1832, as is proved by 1850 census of Buckport. It shows Israel b Me 1798, seaman, and Lydia b Me 1796. Realty $250

Minah Dow adabbgj d Jan 1866; possibly is Jemima sub adabbbh

Sarah Dow adabbgk b 1836, in family of Gilman and Harriet Fly 1850

Sarah Dow adabbgl m Mch 2, 1835, Stephen Babbidge who m 2nd Apr 3, 1850, Mary Thompson. This was copied from Hist Deer Isl as **Jane Dow**. Clueless

Mary D Dow adabbgm m Apr 13, 1842, Asa G Haskell. Deer Isl rec

Mary Dow adabbgn of Deer Isl m Aug 5, 1851, Eben Saunders

George O Dow adabbgo, mariner, b Mt Desert presumably 1832-40, m Rebecca Hall b Brooklin. Presumably other children and adabbg line indicated:

a   James Everett b 1861, lime burner of Rockland, m Nov 11, 1894, Annie E Taylor, div, ae 35, dau of Charles and Roxana (Lawrence) Butman of Lowell, Mass; appeared in 1915 Rockland directory, but "not found" by letter 1924. One associates this with a Rockland rec: James E Dow of Rockland m Nellie Dow (last name?). A child:
d   —— dau b Rockland Apr 24, 1897

Charles Dow adabbgp appearing only in son's rec as b (surely before 1816) Mt Desert, sea captain, had a son:

a   Samuel L b Mt Desert Dec 2, 1836

Samuel L Dow adabbgpa, sea captain, was after 1899 farmer of Hancock; m Evelyn F Grant b Hancock Nov 26, 1848, d Aug 24, 1919, dau of Daniel and Mary E (Moon). One child found, but presumably more children:

a   Charles Hardy b Hancock 1876

Charles H Dow adabbgpaa, railroad employe of Hancock, m Oct 25, 1894, Della M De Witt, ae 18 b N B, dau of Jeremiah and Adelaide (Mason). She d Feb 27, 1898; he m 2nd July 5, 1899, Eliza Freelove Wheeldon (also Whidden), ae 19, dau of Levi and Mary S (Moon). Children:

a   Lyman De Witt b Feb 4, 1898; d Sept 17, 1898
b   Ruth M b Hancock Oct 16, 1899

Charles Dow adabbgq (cf Charles Dow immediately preceding), for many years a sea captain, finally ran the ferry from Hancock to the mainland; was twice m, with children by each wife. One rec of son gives Charles b Deer Isl and wife Roxana Blanchard b Franklin, rec of other son gives Charles b Duxbury, Mass, and wife Melinda Blanchard of Franklin. Presumably he m sisters. Line filled out by his son's wife. Children:

    a Hattie M, in 1923 Mrs Seavey of So Harlow
    b Lydia, in 1923 Mrs Chittick of Hall's Quarry
    c Forest b Hancock 1871 (date?); d Aug 2, 1894, unm
    d William Henry b Hancock 1871 (date from m rec)

William H Dow adabbgqd, fisherman, later stone cutter of Millbridge, living there 1923; m June 20, 1895, Jennie May Norton, ae 18, dau of Elverde and Sarah (Sprague). Children:

    a Forest Edward b Dec 13, 1895; served 14 months in France, much at the front;
        now in shoe factory Augusta
    b Charles Henry b Jan 15, 1898
    c Gordon A d Aug 11, 1906, ae 6 yrs, 9 mos
    d Emery L b Aug 11, 1902   e Neil K b May 7, 1905
    f Harold L b Dec 14, 1908   g Frank Milton b Jan 2, 1911
    h William Henry b Feb 7, 1913   i Evelyn G b May 10, 1916
    j Clarence A b Mch 10, 1918
    k Margaret Nona d June 7, 1920, ae 9 mos, 7 days
    l Beatrice E d Oct 7, 1921, ae 1 yr, 4 mos

Charles H Dow adabbgqdb, truck driver of Millbridge, m Sept 24, 1918, Olive Merchant, ae 20, dau of Clifford and Alice (Dorr). Child:

    a Phillis May b Feb 9, 1921

Neal F Dow adabbgr b Hancock or Brooklin (both in rec), m Lizzie B Babson b Brooklin; in 1907 farmer of Brookville. Children:

    a Harold E b 1889   b Charles B; untraced
    c James C b Aug 26, d Aug 27, 1893   d Neal Francis b Dec 28, 1894
    e Fidelia Merle b July 4, 1898; d Nov 2, 1918
    f Faith b and d Oct 5, 1903

Harold Leslie Dow adabbgra (no evidence of identity), laborer of Hancock, m Apr 30, 1917, Mattie Mildred Phippen, ae 30, wid, dau of Walden and Nellie (Davis) Pierce of Mt Desert.

Samuel Dow adabbgs b Me 1818, seaman, realty $300; wife Edith b Me 1821, appears in 1850 census, with children. There is no evidence that Hancock Dows need be of adabb line, but the place is not enormous and there are big gaps in the line.

    a Abigail b 1841   b Alonzo b 1843   c Charity b 1844
    d Samuel b 1845   e Catherine b 1847
    f William b 1849; all untraced

William Dow adabbgt cannot be the immediately preceding; appears only as a father:

    a Llewellyn H b Hancock or Somerville (both in rec)

Llewellyn H Dow adabbgta d married Silver Ridge Mch 30, 1896; m Ida L Crabtree. Three children, found by own rec:

a Amos Leroy b Franklin 1885
b Hallie Calvin b 1893, cook of Hancock, m Feb 13, 1915, Madge Hazel Moon, ae 25, teacher, dau of Eugne and Flavilla (Webster)
c William Allen b Hancock Apr 3, 1895

Amos L Dow adabbgtaa, laborer of Hancock, m Dec 21, 1916, Gertrude Thelma Dow (see just below). Children:

a Amos L b Jan 25, 1918   b Merle Monroe b Feb 5, 1920

William A Dow adabbgtac, laborer of Hancock, moved to Hermon, gate-tender and car-checker; m Oct 17, 1914, Adaline K Grass, ae 17, dau of Whitfield H and Abigail H (De Witt). Children b Hermon:

a Virginia Grace b Dec 16, 1914   b ——son b May 20, 1916
c William (Jr) b Feb 13, 1919

Galen M Dow adabbgu, surely kin of above, car inspector, m ae 21 Jan 1, 1894, Lizzie O Moon, ae 16, dau of Stillman and Lucy W (Smith); 2nd Margaret J Townsend b Hancock. Children:

a Harold Leslie b Nov 28, 1894; is now adabbgra above
b Jesse Elmer b Oct 12, d Nov 2, 1896
c Gertrude Thelma b July 6, 1898; m adabbgtaa

William A Dow adabbgv (cf adabbgqdb), laborer of Hancock, m Marian A Merchant. A child:

a Robert Edward Merchant b Hancock Jan 20, 1915

Flossie S Dow adabbgw b Hancock had:

a ——son b Mch 7, 1915

Winfield M Dow adabbgx is unknown to family of Winfield S Dow adabbgabdf. Of Deer Isl, he m Alta S Robbins b Tremont. Of children:

c Sophia S b Mt Desert 1890; m Everett, Mass, Mch 20, 1909, William P Hutchinson, ae 26, son of William E and Mary A (Brudy; spelling?)
d ——dau b July 11, 1892   e ——son b June 18, 1895
f ——son b Feb 19, 1897   g ——child b June 24, 1898

Solomon G Dow adabbgy, sailor, b Tremont, m Mary Gott Webster. Recurrence of name Thurston and repetition of Mary G suggest rec is garbled and is Thornton Dow adabbghe. Rec is only from rec of son at m:

a Thurston Willis b Tremont 1867, sailor of Tremont, m May 27, 1895, Hattie M Garman, music teacher ae 21, b Bangor dau of George and Mary G. Further untraced

Daniel M Dow adabbgz b Tremont, seaman and stone-cutter, m Jennie M Farrell (also as Jane Farwell) b Tremont. Two children found:

d Raymond W b 1885   g ——son b Apr 4, 1892

Raymond W Dow adabbgza, laborer, m Nov 5, 1906, Sylvia N Higgins ae 16, dau of Robert B and Isabella (Robbins). Children:

a ——son b Mch 24, 1907   b   Raymond W b Apr 19, 1908
c ——son b July 5, 1909

Nathan H Dow adabbha m Nov 6, 1871, Florence H Spofford. One imagines adabbb line.

Ellen E Dow adabbhb m July 10, 1872, Melvin Pressey. Both items Deer Isl.

Amos I Dow adabbhc b June 1889 to Amos and Anna. This Deer Isl item adjoins the list of children of Amos adabbgai and Caroline.

Thomas Dow adabbhd m Deer Isl Jan 15, 1878, Helen M Walton. Date surely wrong, for to Thomas and Helen M, children:
a   Millie E b June 11, 1870   b   Eliza A b June 11, 1872

David H Dow adabbhe, stone-cutter, m Feb 5, 1879, Mary H Haskell, both of Deer Isl.   Five children:
b   Bertran L b Dec 4, 1884   c   Gertrude d Aug 27, 1886
d   Samuel P d Oct 17, 1888   e   Frank R b Deer Isl Feb 24, 1897

Eliza M (Moers) **Dow** adabbhg, d Rockland Apr 21, 1893, dau of Levi B and Mary Ann (Barbour), both b Deer Isl

Eugene T Dow adabbhh, carpenter, b Tremont, m Maud Burns b Eden.   A child:
a   Harold Eugene b Jan 6, 1900; d Bar Harbor Nov 29, 1918

Ina L Dow adabbhi b Tremont had:
a   Beatrice L d Tremont July 30, 1897, ae 2 mos, 13 days

Lester Dow adabbhj, b Carmel laborer of Tremont, m Maude M Candage b Blue Hill.   Child:
a   Dexter De Witt b Tremont Oct 19, 1907

Hannah adabbhk wife of Nathan Dow d Deer Isl Feb 20, 1881; presumably Nathan Dow adabbbde d Feb 1885

Augustus Dow adabbhl d July 17, 1888; probably adabbbdcf

Elizabeth B Dow adabbhm m Feb 1, 1910, Whitney B Lowe

Willette Dow adabbhn m Aug 16, 1899, William Ellis

Carrie E Dow adabbho m Aug 3, 1902, Benjamin T Sole

Grace E Dow adabbhp m July 14, 1912, John A Douglass.   These last seven items of Deer Isl

---

Abigail Dow adabc m Nov 10, 1738, Ephraim Collins, son of Ephraim and Esther (Shortbridge).   She dau of Richard and Alice (Asher). adabc had,—Richard, Levi b Jan 1, 1760, John, Esther, perhaps others.

Ephraim with sons Richard and Levi were with Gen Benedict Arnold in Canada. Levi m Sept 13, 1787, Abigail Stanton of Preston, Conn; moved to Romeo, Mich, where he d Apr 10, 1837. Of 11 children, one was Abigail Dow.

Challis Dow adabd of Kingston m Dec 30, 1746, Sarah Colman (Ipswich rec); lived So Hampton. Perhaps more children:

a Lydia b Feb 4, 1747; bap So Hampton July 15, 1750
b Mary bap Kingston July 6, 1752   c Rebecca bap Oct 19, 1755

Lydia Dow adabe m Kingston Nov 8, 1739, Michael Brooks of Biddeford, Me. Apparently this was outside the Friends.

Jonathan Dow adabi. We have seen that the three older sons of John Dow, Quaker, married outside the Society. Probably as an act of disinheritance of them he deeded Apr 14, 1763, in consideration of filial love his house and barn in So Hampton to his youngest son, Jonathan adabi. Jonathan seems to have been always a consistent Friend. He m Hannah Shaw, whose identity is not cleared in Shaw Gen. A Hannah bap 1733, dau of Benjamin of Kingston by 2nd wife Mary, is rather mature and not a birthright Friend. Their children appear for the most part in So Hampton rec, altho several b Gilmanton. Jonathan appears in Gilmanton 1775, refusing to sign the Association Test, offering the usual Quaker substitute granting all but exercise of physical force. As Jonathan was in So Hampton 1779 and again in Gilmanton 1781, it is possible that, as war spirit ran unusually high in Gilmanton, Quakers were unpopular and Jonathan retired temporarily. He was of Gilmanton 1781 to his death. In 1790 census he is either 2a, 2b, 3c or 3a, 3b, 3c, it being not easy to distinguish between the several Jonathan Dow of Gilmanton. The eight known children are probably all:

a Richard b Apr 20, 1768
b Ephraim (probably a twin)   c Jemima b Feb 24, 1770
d Hannah b June 16, 1772; she who m June 20, 1791, William Mitchel, both of Gilmanton
e Mina m——Merrill (identical with Jemima above?)
f Dolly b Feb 20, 1779   g John b Feb 20, 1779
h Jonathan b July 17, 1781

Richard Dow adabia had by family rec 1 son, 1 dau; is genealogically a little obscure; in Sanbornton a householder 1798; in Newburyport, Mass, by 1802; d there of old age; wife Lucinda b 1770, d Newburyport Nov 21, 1843. A child:

a ——, sex not stated, nor age, d Newburyport June 4, 1802

Ephraim Dow adabib m 1790 Elizabeth French, apparently both then of So Hampton. She had brother Elihu, sisters —— who m —— Mudgett, went upstate; —— m —— Fitts, moved away; —— m —— Brigham, went down east.

A grandson of Elihu is Fred B French of So Hampton, active in 1923, ae 85, keen genealogist of the French family and local historian; a great help to the Author. Elizabeth d Gilmanton ae 93 June 24, 1863. Twelve children. They located in Gilmanton at once after marriage:

a Hannah b Sept 20, 1791; some Hannah m Belmont Jan 23, 1826, Debonair
    Farrar, both of Gilmanton, son of Josiah and Mary (Dow)
b Betsey b Dec 17, 1792; of Gilmanton m Sanbornton Mch 14, 1813, William
    Bell of So Hampton
c Chellis b Gilmanton Nov 13, 1794; m Eliza Dow adabigc
d Elihu F b Aug 4, 1797
e Clarissa b Feb 26, 1799; m Nathaniel B Osgood
f Mahala b Oct 25, 1800; of Gilmanton m Gilford June 12, 1828, Dudley Hayes
    of Somersworth
g Mary b Sept 4, 1802; m of Gilmanton Belmont July 27, 1824, Prescott V Ken-
    dall of Pembroke; at least 2 children,—Mary J m Bristol 1870 Clark K
    Lewis; William H m Bristol 1870
h Sally b June 11, 1804; of Gilmanton m Gilford June 4, 1829, John A Leonard
    of Allenstown
i Benjamin Randall b Gilmanton Dec 1, 1806
j Ephraim b Sept 26, 1808   k   Daniel b Nov 18, 1810
l Samuel b Jan 30, 1815

Chellis Dow adabibc (Chalice, Challis, Charles, etc, in rec), farmer and shoemaker, as was his father, d Gilmanton Apr 10, 1882; not found in 1850 census. Six children; m 1830 Eliza Dow adabigc. She d at advanced age

a Charles F b Mch 29, 1832   b   George W d in infancy
c Daniel b Dec 2, 1836
d Eliza b 1840; d Laconia May 17, 1916, unm
e George William b Nov 26, 1844
f Mary A b Feb 5, 1850; m July 4, 1885, Hamilton P Perkins b Concord Oct 15,
    1849, farmer of Laconia; no children. A Gilmanton rec is probably a 1st m,
    followed by div; not mentioned in family rec:
    Mary A Dow, dau of Chelice and Eliza, m Gilmanton May 7, 1865, John K
    Fifield of Upper Gilmanton

Charles F Dow adabibca, shoemaker of Gilmanton, appears with various middle initials and perhaps is the Charles W Dow, Gilmanton Civil War veteran. A farmer of Upper Gilmanton, he moved before 1877 to Thornton; d after 1887; m Nov 27, 1862, Hannah L Buswell (Busswell, Buzzell in rec) b Andover Mch 27, 1843, d Thornton July 16, 1899, dau of John, stone cutter, and Hepzibah (Edwards) (in d rec mother given as Louisa Sawyer, error). He was an able man; his letter of 1887 doing much to establish the whole adabib line. Six children: older b Belmont:

a Charles H b Apr 6, 1865   b   Daniel B b Feb 1868
c Jennie B b Gilmanton Sept 1871; m May 7, 1888, John W Morse of Campton
d Walter E b Thornton Jan 31, 1876
e Orren John b Jan 31, 1876
f Fred D b Sept 1882; living 1887; untraced

Charles H Dow adabibcaa, farmer of Bridgewater, and New Hampton, m 1st Sept 10, 1889, Jennie S (Harriman) Page, ae 29, dau of William and Betsey E (Heath); div; m 2nd Nov 17, 1914, Eva E Johnson

ae 26 div, dau of Norman B and Clara B (Wiser) Tobins of Bridgewater.
Children, by 2nd wife:

a   Raymond J b Mch 27, 1915   b ——dau b Mch 22, d Mch 23, 1916

Daniel B Dow adabibcab, expressman and job teamster of Concord,
m May 28, 1897, Flora J (Richardson) Smith, ae 24, b Mt Desert, Me,
1871, dau of B M and Fannie (Wade).   Children:

a   Edward Daniel b Aug 30, 1897; d young
b   Everett Richardson, twin, d Nov 4, 1897
c   ——dau b Nov 8, 1899; there were others

Walter J Dow adabibcad, farmer of Andover, m May 21, 1898,
Rosa Desfosses, ae 19, of Sanbornton, dau of Frank and Leah (Shepard)
b Canada.   Children:

a   Henry d Andover Sept 7, 1899, ae 1 day
b   Eva May b Andover Sept 14, 1900   c——dau b July 25, 1902
f   Dorothy Genevieve Marie b Franklin Jan 12, 1912

John O Dow adabibcae, farmer of Andover, m Campton Jan 6,
1901, Alice M Elliott, ae 22, dau of John and Laura (Ham).   Children:

a   —— b and d May 19, 1902   b   Conrad W b Ashland Apr 28, 1914

Daniel Dow adabibcc, farmer of Gilmanton, m Dec 3, 1866, Olive
A Chase b Gilmanton Mch 22, 1848.   He d Jan 1, 1920, resident for 55
years.   Children:

a   Addie C b Nov 3, 1867   b   Esther A b Mch 25, 1869; d Mch 13, 1889
c   Arthur L b July 2, 1870   d   Oscar Chase b Mch 11, 1882

Addie C Dow adabibcca of Loudon d Sept 9, 1895; m Oct 2, 1889
(his 2nd) John Ham Lyford of Canterbury.   Children b Belmont:

a   Paul John b May 9, d Sept 15, 1890
b   Ruby Elizabeth b Apr 17, 1891
c   John Pearl b Aug 9, 1892; d Sept 3, 1893
d   Addie Grace b Aug 2, 1893

Arthur L Dow adabibccc, carpenter of Belmont, m Nellie A Rowe.
Children:

a   Westley b Apr 4, d May 15, 1900   b   Mildred
c   Pauline Isabel b Jan 9, 1903   d   ——dau b July 3, 1908

Oscar C Dow adabibccd, teacher of Gilmanton, d Dec 12, 1903,
m July 2, 1903, Zilla N Pease, ae 16, dau of Fred V and Annie L (Pierce).
Posthumous child:

a   Oscar Everett b Apr 15, 1904

George W Dow adabibce was 1889 carpenter of Gilmanton, unm

Elihu F Dow adabibd, farmer of Gilmanton, assessed 1850 at $1,000.
No wife in census, but Betsey Dow b 1790 living with him.   One child
in census:

a   Lydia M b 1831; m May 19, 1861, Joseph Flanders Jr of Sanbornton

Clarissa Dow adabibe of Gilmanton, m Jan 4, 1829, Nathan B Osgood, postmaster of Pembroke, b Aug 18, 1799, d Oct 15, 1854. Children, from Osgood Gen:

    a Julia A b Feb 24, 1830; m E C Spiller of Ellwood, Minn
    b Mary E b Jan 12, 1832; d May 3, 1838
    c Frances Ann b June 29, 1835; m E B Clark of Manchester
    d Celestia b Dec 4, 1837; d May 4, 1839

Benjamin R Dow adabibi, in 1850 brick maker of Pembroke; came from Suncook; later moved to Boscawen; d Aug 19, 1886; m Pembroke June 27, 1836, Frances Ann Moulton b Pittsfield Oct 8, 1817, dau of Enoch b Pittsfield and Dolly (Robinson) b Bath, Me. Children:

    a Ann Elizabeth b Gilmanton 1837-8; d Washington, D C; m Joseph Clifford, d Washington, son of Clarence. Children,—Arthur E now of N Y, Clarence
    b Georgianna b Suncook 1840; d unm
    c Frederick Charles b Dec 19, 1843
    d Gertrude Moulton b Pembroke 1845; m Dec 27, 1871, George H Blake of Wolfboro and N Y City; children,—Hortense D b Mch 28, 1875; ——d in infancy
    e Frank M b after 1850; lived Brooklyn m and had children, untraced
    f Benjamin Randall b Sept 1854
    g Hortense Robinson m Nov 24, 1887, Oscar V Pitman of Concord, later of Milford, Conn
    h Charles d in infancy

Frederick C Dow adabibic, dealer in boots and shoes Manchester, m Boston Apr 27, 1868, Hattie E Millis. Children:

    a Frederick Irving b Apr 2, 1871; m Haverhill Aug 2, 1897; no children
    b Lansing Millis b Mch 13, 1875

Lansing M Dow adabibicb of Washington, D C, m N Y City Aug 9, 1898, Janet Crawford McGowan. Children:

    a Irving Millis b Washington Feb 2, 1903
    b Adine Crawford b Vienna, Va, May 29, 1915

Benjamin R Dow adabibif, Baptist clergyman with pastorates at Fulton, N Y, and West Medway, Mass, m Manchester July 28, 1888, Florence Morton of Fulton, one son, name not found

Ephraim Dow adabibj m Feb 20, 1838, Mrs Sophia Weaver; untraced

Daniel Dow adabibk has appeared so far only in rec of wife and dau. Mary J Pushard, ae 87-7-13, dau of Charles and Mary and wife of Daniel Dow, d Boston July 28, 1902. The dau:

    a Mary Jane of Dover, dau of Daniel and Mary, m Moultonborough Sept 3, 1864, Alonzo G Blaisdell of Moultonborough. A son Herbert G m Moultonborough 1893

Samuel Dow adabibl is uncertain. It is possible that he was one of the Samuels now in Chichester disconnected, and may be the Samuel b New Hampton, widower, laborer of Raymond, d Brentwood County farm Nov 21, 1903, ae 87

Jemima Dow adabic seems identical with sister appearing as Mina; she m Belmont Mch 25, 1790, Wiggins Merrill

Hannah Dow adabid m William Mitchill and they evidently moved soon to Carmel, Me, farmers. One child found:

a   Meriba H b Jan 26, 1807; m Sept 4, 1833, Dr Paul Ruggles b June 20, 1801, grad Bowdoin; 4 children

Dolly Dow adabif m Belmont Nov 13, 1796, Josiah Farrar, both of Gilmanton. This is the correct statement, many garbled forms appearing in print. He b July 5, 1767, so d Apr 16, 1845, son of Israel who came to Gilmanton from Epping. He has appeared as John Farrah and she as Mary Dow and Hannah Dow, thus making much genealogical trouble. Children:

a Sally   b Israel   c Perley
d Debonair, m Belmont Jan 23, 1826, Hannah Dow, presumably adabiba his 1st cousin
e Julia   f Ira   g Hiram

John Dow adabig m Sept 22, 1803, Elizabeth Chapman, dau of Edward of Sanbornton, b Apr 4, 1778, d Gilmanton Dec 1842. Some John Dow of Gilmanton, suddenly deranged, ran from the meeting house, threw himself into the pond and was drowned May 28, 1819. One son, 7 dau:

a Nancy b Jan 4, 1804; living 1887; m Smith Glidden of Meredith Center; 1 dau
b Sarah b June 16, 1805; d Fitchburg, Mass; m John McCarthy; 2 dau
c Eliza b Gilmanton Aug 30, 1807; m Chellis Dow adabibc
d Arvilla b Feb 17, 1809; m David Sanborn; 2 sons
e Hannah b May 13, 1813
f Abbie b Mch 14, 1814; living 1887; m John Clement; 4 children
g John b Sept 30, 1815
h Mary J b Apr 12, d Dec 7, 1817

Hannah Dow adabige living 1887; m Nov 26, 1835, Nathaniel Sanborn, carpenter, of Lake Village. Children:

a Julia Ann b Dec 8, 1837; m Jan 13, 1858, George B Randall of Lake Village; no children
b Hannah M b Aug 30, 1841; d Nov 23, 1880; m Feb 16, 1861, William D Sargent of Lake Village; 4 children

John Dow adabigg m Betsey Dow (unplaced; living 1887 in Wentworth). He is hard to trace; his 6th child b Gilmanton 1861. He often in rec has initial John A. He moved about 1848 to Vershire, Vt; back before 1860. He seems to be the John A d Campton June 20, 1894, and the John A leasing 160 acres in Rumney 1883. By safe family rec he had 2 dau, 4 sons:

a Nancy b 1840   b Elizabeth A b 1841
Fannie H Dow of Vershire m Rumney Nov 15, 1874, E G Putney of Wentworth, is either one of these, or does not belong to this family
c Artemas b Gilmanton 1843; enlisted from Gilmanton; d tuberculosis Alexandria, Va, Jan 12, 1863
d John A b 1843   e Nathaniel S b Vershire 1849
f Clarence H b Gilmanton Nov 25, 1861

John A Dow adabiggd, blacksmith of Gilmanton, Plymouth and Campton, m Sept 4, 1870, Helen M Simonds b Lawrence, Mass, 1852. Children, by local directory:

a De Witt C b Northwood 1870
b Jennie M m Lucius D Estes, teamster; 4 children in Campton
c Lola Bessie b Wentworth July 8, 1873; m Nov 21, 1891, Leon L Adams
d Emma F b Apr 19, 1877; m——Hadley of Campton
e Albert J b 1878   f Muriel H R
g ——dau b Campton Feb 26, 1896

De Witt C Dow adabiggda, shoemaker of Northwood and Manchester, m Manchester Dec 14, 1893, Nellie J Turcotte d phthisis Apr 13, 1900, ae 29-1-12, dau of Joseph and Pauline (Leary) of Canada.   Children:

a ——son b Northwood Nov 20, 1894
c Robert Elmer b Apr 3, 1897; d phthisis May 14, 1900
d Hellen Etta b Manchester May 27, 1899

Albert J Dow adabiggde, blacksmith of Campton, m Oct 27, 1898, Ada L Morse, ae 17; 2nd Mch 21, 1908, Marion E Clark, ae 35, div, dau of John F Mullen

Nathaniel S Dow adabigge, farmer of Dorchester, N H, m 1st Jan 3, 1871, Anna D Hardy, ae 17, dau of Abrah; farmer of New Hampton, m 2nd Aug 10, 1879, Louisa J Batchelder, dau of J and M, wid of —— Pippin.   Children:

a Lucy Josephine b Concord Sept 3, 1873; d Manchester Mch 7, 1883
b Lottie A b Dorchester June 5, 1876; d Bristol Dec 10, 1881

Clarence H Dow adabiggf, farmer of Ellsworth and Campton, m 1st Nov 18, 1882, Hattie A Kelley; 2nd Rumney Nov 14, 1886, Lizzie Bailey, dau of William and Jane; 3rd Lake Village July 4, 1890, Eznona (Emma B) Comstock b Hill, ae 19, d Campton Aug 3, 1891, ae 20-1-8, dau of Willard H and Mary L.   Children:

a ——dau b and d Ellsworth May 8, 1884
b Loretta May b No Groton Sept 15, 1887; d in infancy
c ——son b Campton July 21, 1891

Jonathan Dow adabih appears in 1850 census as laborer of Upper Gilmanton.   No other name with his.   We know from indisputable family rec that he had 1 son, 3 dau

---

Joanna Dow adabj m (int pub So Hampton Nov 17, 1764) Elliott Carr b Salisbury July 5, 1742, son of Robert and Hannah (Elliott). Children:

a Hannah b Nov 3, 1765   b Betty b Nov 27, 1767
c Jemima b Dec 4, 1769   d Rhoda b July 18, 1772
e Sarah b Feb 20, 1775   f John b Mch 11, 1778
g Nathan b June 5, 1781   h Nanne b Nov 28, 1787

OUR next line remained Quaker until in western Mass their community had no meeting house, no other Friends. Over half the data herein were originally dug up by Flora Dow and Mrs E J More, the connection at point adac established many years later.

James Dow adac m May 24, 1721, Mary Nichols b Oct 19, 1702, dau of John and Abigail (Sargent). They soon left Salisbury, in 1726 settled in west parish, Amesbury, paying the minister's tax; 1741 they were in east parish, freed from the tax as being Quakers. They were old when they went to New Braintree, where their children had located. James d Dec 11, 1773, the town clerk thinking he did his whole duty when he entered "Mr Dow." Seventeen years later, with equal clarity, he recorded the death of "widow Dow." With such things does the genealogist battle. The entries defied identification for years. Children, Salisbury-Amesbury rec:

a Abigail b July 1, 1724
b Mary b June 28, 1728; m Billerica Oct 22, 1745, Joseph Foster, Quaker
c Anna b Mch 15, 1730-1   d Lydia b Oct 24, 1733
e James b June 28, 1736   f Isaiah b Feb 4, 1738
   Joseph b June 11, 1741

Abigail Dow adaca m Aug 8, 1745, William Whittier of Amesbury. Children, Amesbury rec:

a Anna b Jan 16, 1746; d young   b Mitchel b Dec 27, 1747
c Anna b Oct 30, 1750
d William b Feb 18, 1753; a well known physician of Danville, Vt, and Stanstead, P Q
e Moses b Feb 22, 1760   f John b June 8, 1763

Lydia Dow adacd. While it seems improbable that she was the Lydia m Kensington June 1, 1757, Timothy Blake Locke, no other eligible Lydia is known. He b Oct 30, 1735, son of Edward and Hannah (Blake), m 2nd Patience Perkins. Lydia's children:

a Josiah b Nov 10, 1757; drowned Sept 23, 1816; m Bethia——
b Simon b Aug 13, 1759
c Edward b Dec 15, 1760; m Nov 27, 1781, Betty Perkins
d James b Nov 14, 1762; lived Andover, Mass   e John b Feb 29, 1764

James Dow adace of Amesbury m Dec 7, 1758, Rebecca Pepper, known in her time as Becca, a woman of much energy and character. They went to Ware, Mass, but altho children's rec are not in Amesbury, it is unlikely they went by 1759. About 1789 they joined their 1st born in Leicester, Vt. Children:

a Moses b 1759   b James b 1762
c Lydia b 1765; m 1780 Theophilus Sweat of Brandon, Vt
d Joel b 1767   e Sybil b 1770; d ae 18
f Isaac b Apr 18, 1775 (family Bible)

Moses Dow adacea enlisted from Ware for 5 mos from Oct 1776, re-enlisting for 2 mos in 1777. Returning home, a well set up, slender youth who rode a horse to perfection and had a good one, he had the added glory of being a veteran. Going to Boston to buy supplies, he hitched his horse in front of the store kept by one Molyneux, a French merchant. The merchant's daughter Fannie happened to be sitting in the window. How quickly things happened we do not know, but a fortnight later he and Fannie mounted his horse and were out of sight before father saw them. They stopped at Deering and were married by Rev Jeremiah Bannard of Amherst. In that gentleman's diary is entered: "Mr Moses Dow and Miss Fanny Mollineaux, both of Deering." Both evidently told a little fib. Town rec gives Moses Dow 2nd and Phany, June 25, 1780. The feelings of Pere Molyneux are not chronicled, but the marriage was not a failure, as both in good health had 10 children at the golden wedding. They took the veterans' 160 acres somewhere but swapped for a farm at Leicester, Vt, going in old age to Hinesburg, where both are buried. He was a pensioner in 1840. Children not appearing in public rec, collected by Flora Dow:

- a Jacob b Jan 12, 1781. Accuracy of order of rest is doubtful
- b Rebecca m 1803 Joseph Atwood of Chittenden, Vt
- c Fannie m 1805 Royal Briggs of Hinesburg
- d Sallie d ae 22   e Moses, perhaps 1790   f Michael
- g John b Nov 24, 1787   h Monroe   i Frederick d ae 5
- j Augustus d ae 22   k Margaret m 1850 Rufus Beebe
- l Robert Myron
- m Lewis m 1835 Laura Allen; both d soon after, leaving dau Helen

Jacob Dow adaceaa of Hinesburg m 1808 Elizabeth Conger d May 10, 1869; built a home of white marble, famed for miles around. They moved to Centerville, N Y, selling the home. The buyer sold the best stones and built a new house with the remainder. Jacob d Mch 22, 1866. Children, b Vt:

- a Sallie b 1809; d ae 6   b Louisa b Jan 8, 1811
- c Caroline b 1814; m 1835 Cook Waite. Children,—Mary, Louisa Amelinette
- d Asher b 1815   e Samuel b May 6, 1817   f Fannie b 1820
- g Mariette b May 4, 1823   h Orin Moses b May 14, 1825
- i Marshall L b 1827   j Sarah M b Aug 29, 1829

Louisa Dow adaceaab d Centerville Sept 1901; m Jan 7, 1838, Asa Robbins. Children,—Emma, Wilson, Wilmot, Roana, Loraine, Vernice, Wilbur

Asher Dow adaceaad d Cresco, Iowa, Dec 1893; m 1840 Alice Rudd d 1910. All children b Centerville:

- a Newton Calvin   b Warren b 1841; d ae 16
- c William b 1844; moved to Calif; had 12 children; lived to old age, but paid no attention to many letters of genealogical inquiry
- d Dwight b 1847; moved to Washington State; 4 children, equally uncommunicative
- e Lura b 1850; of Cresco, m Dorr Norton

Newton C Dow adaceaada of Cresco moved to Janesville, Wis; m Feb 24, 1863, Martha Stoughton Spalding b Feb 5, 1840, dau of Joseph and Lydia Stoughton (Ellsworth). Untraced.

Samuel Dow adaceaae d Centerville Mch 24, 1853; m 1847 Eliza Vanduzen of Fillmore, N Y.   Children:

   a Delia b July 20, 1848; m 1870 William Duncan
   b Jennie b Sept 24, 1851; m 1873 Adelbert Brockway
   c Samuel b Nov 12, 1853; d May 16, 1888; m July 3, 1884, Myrtle McLaughlin.
      Children,—Niles, Milly, both d in infancy

Fannie Dow adeaceaaf of Brandon m June 10, 1845, Richard Ede of Norfolk Co, Eng; in 1916 living Whitewater, Wis.   Children:

   a Leland   b Clayton   c Antoinette   d Elizabeth

Mariette Dow adaceaag m 1845 John Clark of Canada; lived Centerville; a dau:

   a Louise b 1846; d Apr 6, 18-5; m George Fox

Orin M Dow adaceaah, veteran of Civil War, d Oct 19, 1907; m 1st Sept 8, 1849, Josephine Hewitt of Chittenden, Vt, b 1829, d Mch 25, 1855; m 2nd Jan 21, 1869, Abbie L Robbins d 1917.   Only child:

   a Flora.   Went to N Y City, developed business ability, had an excellent position, but abandoned it to go back and care for her parents, both partly invalided. To amuse the father, she dabbled in her own family genealogy. When the parents died, too long time had lapsed to get back into business; the farm was of 180 acres, but not near town. For a few years she ran it, but later took a teaching position. She has now married. Her work is excellent, considering that she could search only by correspondence

Marshall L Dow adaceaai d Feb 19, 1883; m 1865 Betsey A Peak d Dec 27, 1901.   Children:

   a Varis b Oct 31, 1867   b Adelbert b May 18, 1870
   c Blanche b Feb 3, 1879; m Dec 4, 1904, Millard Chapman; son Leon b Dec 4, 1910

Varis Dow adaceaaia m 1st Nov 25, 1892, Katie E Sartor d Dec 17, 1904; 2nd July 1907 Blanche Moon of Cumberland Springs, Tenn. Child:

   a Harold b Mch 1914

Adelbert Dow (Rev) adaceaaib m Mch 17, 1893, Mary Gardiner. Children:

   a Pearl d June 4, 1905   b Doris   c——a son

Sarah M Dow adaceaaj d 1904; m 1849 Daniel Lee Bangs b Nov 30, 1829, d 1903; moved 1850 to Idaho.   Children:

   a Medora b June 20, 1850   b Daniel Eugene b Nov 25, 1852
   c Henry Heman b Oct 14, 1857   d Charles Edwin b Feb 25, 1859
   e Burr H b May 31, 1862   f Ella b July 8, 1866
   g Hattie Lee b Aug 29, 1867

Fannie Dow adaceac m Royal Briggs of Hinesburg; a large family, of them:

   a Amelia Ann m——Kenyon   b Lotica   c Calphurnia
   d Murray   e Frank
   A number of Dow-Kenyon marriages occurred around Hinesburg

Moses Dow adaceae m July 29, 1804, Hannah Phillips of Danby; moved after 1835 from Leicester to Hinesburg, where both are buried. He d 1860, an ardent Free Will Baptist. Of 12 children, vital statistics fail to mention one. Only 5 are proved, others guesses:

    a Frederick b 1811
    b Lorenzo m Clarissa Hibbard of Hinesburg; no children
    c Cummings
    d Porter Two sons of Moses went to Boston, one a policeman, the other a
        wholesale grocer
    e Moses m July 23, 1848, Lydia Sears
    f James b 1817; d Leicester Oct 13, 1897
    g Laura m Leicester Oct 2, 1836, Alden Spooner of Salisbury

Frederick Dow adaceaea, carpenter, d Nashua, N H, July 25, 1885, ae 74-1-29; m 1st Calista Bullock, by whom one or more; 2nd Nashua Jan 1, 1848, Elvira H Moar b Peterboro Feb 17, 1820, d wid Nashua Feb 1 1906, dau of Timothy, farmer, and Betsey (Hopkins), both b Mitford. Children:

    a Ellen A b Mass 1841; m July 29, 1861, George A Gould, both of Nashua
    b Isabella J of Nashua m Apr 3, 1864, Clinton J Farley of Londonderry

Lorenzo Dow adaceaeb. The rec which gives him m Clarissa Hibbard is wrong unless she was a 1st wife. Census 1850 gives him blacksmith of Hinesburg, wife Betsey A b Vt 1819. She was Betsey Kenyon and she was many years later wid living in Burlington. Children, by census:

    a William F b 1838; untraced   b Loren S b Williston 1840
    c Marilla b 1842
    d Louisa A b 1847; m Mch 17, 1867, Allen S Wright of Williston

William F Dow adaceaeba. Some one of this name m Anna McCarty. Son, by own rec:

    a William F b 1886; of Worcester m Feb 16, 1907, Eva J Meade of West Acton,
        ae 19, dau of Lyman W and Julia A (Littlefield)

Loren S Dow adaceaebb d Cottage City, Mass, Nov 1, 1905 (rec: Louis S); was a carpenter of Nashua, N H; m May 11, 1869 (her 2nd) Harriet B Marble, ae 25, d Effingham May 12, 1916, ae 73, dau of Daniel and Harriet (Bray) Downs of Poland, Me. State rec specifies a 9th child:

    a Leon O b Vt 1871   b ——dau b June 26, d July 15, 1877
    e Harry d Nashua July 26, 1879, ae 7 mos
    f ——dau b June 19, 1881   g ——son b Oct 13, 1882
    i ——son b Dec 7, 1887

Leon O Dow adaceaebba, card shop employe, m Nashua Nov 29, 1890, Lillian Josephine Lincoln, ae 19, dau of Edward and Martha Josephine (Forester). Lincoln Gen gives them of Malden, Mass, and says no children. This is error; at least one dau

Michael Dow adaceaf b about 1791 suffered in the original ms from a duplication; he m Sophia Greene, a son m Sophia White. There was but one Sophia,—Sophia Greene b Highgate. Both are buried in Leicester. Children by family rec, order hopelessly mixed:

a   Fannie (Frances M) m July 3, 1828, John Emerson of Rochester
b   Isaac moved to Scroon, N Y; untraced; must be he who m Sept 12, 1837,
      Marietta Dodge of Brandon
c   Dimmick moved to Oregon; untraced
d   William, a sailor, never heard from after embarking
e   Lafayette d Chittenden, Vt, leaving 3 untraced children
f   Moses Roy m in 1852
g   John Emerson b Goshen Sept 12, 1827
h   Lewis; a wood chopper in Gilsum, N H, 1872-5; d unm
i   Sarah M m Leicester Jan 1, 1845, Thaddeus (F C S) Cudworth of Shoreham.
      Extra initials not understood
j   Mary m 1850 Ebenezer Sawyer
k   George O b Brandon Jan 4, 1831

Frances M Dow adaceafa, by Emerson Gen b 1808.   John Emerson b 1802, d Minnesota 1892, son of John and Dorothy (Martin).   Children:

a   Daniel b June 9, 1829; m Charlotte Lamkin; went to Nevada
b   William Philander b Oct 10, 1831; d 1882; m Jane Cassidy
c   Adaline Martin b May 2, 1834; m Rue Perrins; Eaton Rapids, Mich
d   Frances Martin b Mch 3, 1836; m Oct 30, 1856, Hiram Hopkins; Ames, Iowa

Moses Roy Dow adaceaff m 1st Mch 1, 1852, Harriet Spencer; 2nd 1858 a Miss Harriet Bump; always lived Leicester, she wid in Leicester 1881.   Child:

a   Joanna b 1858; unm, in 1916 last Dow in Leicester

John E Dow adaceafg moved to Gilsum.   Keene gives him d Dec 16, 1877, probably error for 1897; directory 1884 gives him laborer.   He m Feb 5, 1857, Almira Barret b Washington, N H, Apr 1, 1839, living Keene 1815, dau of Alonzo and Elizabeth (Peacock).   Children:

a   Walter John b Sullivan May 22, 1859; d Nelson Apr 26, 1861
b   Florence Adelaide b May 9, 1861; m Dec 24, 1878, Edward Wilson Abbot b
      Nelson Jan 22, 1858; son of James W and Nellie Rebecca (Blodget).   Dau
      Maria Florence b Keene Mch 5, 1880
c   George Elmer b Apr 28, d Dec 16, 1864
d   Ida May b Feb 18, 1866   e   Elmer Ulysses b Nov 23, 1868
f   Guy Linwood b Jan 26, 1874; untraced
g   Ray Elson b Feb 7, 1879

Elmer U Dow adaceafge, painter of Keene, m Nov 29, 1888, Elizabeth R Cameron, ae 20, wid in Keene 1915.   Children:

a   Lee Burton b Oct 28, 1889; box maker of Keene, m June 1, 1916, Bessie Bertha
      Lancey, ae 16, dau of William and Emily (Collins)
b   Paul L (Pearl Elinor) b Keene Jan 24, d Aug 20, 1891
c   Ruth E b Nov 15, 1892   d   Verne Elmer b Apr 3, 1895
e   Don Cameron b Nov 13, 1896   f   ——dau b Nov 13, 1898
g   Henry Edward b May 5, 1901   h and i ——, no rec
j   Virginia Seaton b Dec 27, 1911

Ray E Dow adaceafgg, painter of Sullivan, m Mary A Stock ae 28, dau of Thomas and Cecelia (Keenaghan).   Children:

a   Walter Emerson b Aug 19, 1908   b   Mary Almira b Apr 4, 1915

George O Dow adaceafk was in 5th Vt 1861; moved to Sullivan;

d Keene Sept 7, 1904; m Emma G Banker b Ticonderoga, N **Y; wid** Keene 1921. Children:

 a Nellie M b Gilsum July 21, 1869
 b Addie V b Aug 27, 1871; d Oct 11, 1881
 c Eldridge N b Apr 1, 1874   d   Myrtle May b Dec 5, 1877
 e Eva Susie b Nov 12, 1884; unm in 1915
 f Agnes Jane d Nov 3, 1899, ae 11-2-12
 g Fred O d Keene Dec 29, 1890, ae 4 mos, 23 days

Eldridge N Dow adaceafkc d Troy, N H; m July 16, 1895, by Rev Ernest W Dow, Susie C Hale, ae 22, m 2nd —— Addy. Child:

 a ——son b Troy Apr 21, 1900

John Dow adaceag, veteran of 1812, d Dec 25, 1880; m 1817 **Anna** Huntley of Williston b 1790, d Oct 18, 1834; moved to Centerville. Children not in State rec, data mostly furnished by Jay Adelbert Dow:

 a Henry S b June 15, 1818
 b Rhoda A b June 27, 1820; m Sept 27, 1843, David Wetmore
 c Richardson Olin b Mch 21, 1822
 d John Draper b Mch 3, 1824
 e Orpha L b Mch 15, 1829; m July 1851 Somersette Hoyte Bean
 f Lucy A b Oct 1832; m Charles Tilton

Henry S Dow adaceaga came in boyhood to Yorkshire Center, now Delavan, N Y; d there Feb 11, 1914. He is described as a man of medium height, rather light complexion, very much dried up looking in extreme old age; he d quietly in his bed without medical attention, of the general dissolution of old age; m Otsego Mch 1841 Dorcas Bishop b June 25, 1825, d Delavan July 25, 1902, dau of Ira and Margaret. Children, all b Delavan:

 a Emma b Sept 8, 1842; d Aug 22, 1913; m Nelson Smith of Delavan d 1910; son,—Herbert of Mayville
 b Lorenzo b Mch 11, 1846; d July 1, 1848
 c Anna b Aug 1850; living 1920; m Charles Jenkins of Delavan; dau,—Pearl
 d Margaret b 1859; d Delavan Feb 19, 1896; m and child,—Bertha E b Nov 15, 1875

Rhoda Annie Dow adaceagb m David Wetmore. At least one child:

 a Ellen Jeannette b Chittenden Aug 29, 1858; 1st——Walton; 2nd **Wilber** Bucklin Avery, postmaster of Brandon

Richardson O Dow adaceagc d Nov 20, 1908; m Mch 24, 1850, Mercy Maria Stanley b Nov 26, 1830, d Oct 12, 1910; settled 1851 in Chittenden; town official for 30, justice of the peace for 50 consecutive years,—longest tenure in history of Vermont. Children:

 a Jennie Eugenia b Feb 25, 1851
 b Jeannette Lucy b May 7, 1855
 c Wallace Eugene b Jan 10, 1856
 d William Stanley b Apr 3, 1858; untraced
 e Annie Maria b Dec 19, 1860; d Apr 4, 1874
 f Olin Heney b Feb 18, 1864; untraced
 g Marion Addie b Nov 29, 1866; d Feb 16, 1868
 h May Electa b Mch 21, 1869; d Apr 5, 1874
 i Jay Adelbert b 1870

Jennie E Dow adaceagca m Feb 17, 1878, Albert Woods. Children:

a Elroy Russel b Nov 27, 1879; m Jan 3, 1903, Eva Stone
b Carter Richardson b Nov 5, 1880; m Oct 16, 1912, Mabel Root
c Alberta Eugenia b Dec 25, 1882   d Adeline Mercy b June 3, 1885
e Eve Jennette b Aug 20, 1893

Jeannette L Dow adaceagcb m Mch 15, 1885, William Hunter. Children:

a Mercy Jeannette b Feb 3, 1885   b Daisy Annie b Sept 16, 1888

Wallace E Dow adaceagcc m July 4, 1883, Nellie Lockwood. Children:

a	Maud Annie b Aug 18, 1884	b	May Charity b Mch 16, 1886
c	Helen Jeannette b Mch 31, 1888	d	Mildred Mercy b Jan 7, 1890
e	Albert Jay b May 29, 1892	f	Richardson Wallace b Apr 29, 1894
g	Frederick Edward b Sept 6, 1897	h	Marian Jewel b Apr 19, 1900
i	Margariete Augusta b Aug 7, 1904		

Jay A Dow adaceagci of Rutland m Sept 20, 1900, Mabel (Cobb) Andrews.

John Draper Dow adaceagd m Sept 27, 1843, Ellen Hewitt; lived Centerville; took a trip in 1860 with Orin Moses Dow to revisit the old Vt home. Altho he settled a few miles away, was lost sight of by Orin. He d old age, about 95. Children:

a Clarence, now of Salamanca
b Charles H, a clergyman of Moore Haven, Fla
c Anna, now of Cattaraugus

Monroe Dow adaceah m 1817 Nabby Briggs; apparently moved away. Children:

a	Roxy m 1840——Burlinghame	b	Mary m 1842 Wesley Rogers
c	Horace, a sea captain, untraced	d	Lucius moved to Ellicottville, N Y
e	Miranda moved to Ellicottville	f	Edwin

Edwin Dow adaceahf m Roselette Van Ocker. Children:

a William; untraced   b Vernie   c Miranda

Robert M Dow adaceal of Leicester m Oct 16, 1817, Mary Irish, of Brandon. Children:

a Moses b 1822; d in infancy   b Moses b 1823; d in infancy
c Mary Jane b 1824; m 1846 Richard Ellis
d Montreville b 1826; m 1850 Jane Baird; son Daniel b Plainfield, Vt, 1851; untraced
e Charlotte b 1828   f Francis b 1830; d in infancy
g Margaret b 1832; d in infancy
h Harriet b July 1, 1834; m 1855 Charles Trall
i Rosaltha Addie b 1837; m 1858 George Smith; 2nd 1870 ——Kilbourne
j Ruth Ella b 1840; d 1877
k Lewis Frederick b Apr 16, 1845; m 1880 Margaret Styring; untraced

Lewis L Dow adaceam. The original family compilation giving him d young is incorrect. He appears in 1850 census blacksmith of Hinesburg, wife Alvina b Vt 1820. He may be the Lewis L Dow appearing in 1882 gazetteer as owning 45 and leasing 300 acres in Highgate; with him in 1882 was Theodore H Dow, presumably his son.

James Dow adaceb d Oct 13, 1847; m Nov 15, 1792, Sarah Joy of Leicester b Feb 17, 1758; continued in Leicester. Children:

a	James b July 29, 1793	b	Silas b May 19, 1795
c	Sarah b May 2, 1798	d	Sybil b Apr 28, 1801
e	Stephen b Dec 2, 1803; d Dec 4, 1809		
f	Stephen b Dec 3, 1804	g	Clarissa b Apr 1, 1808

James Dow adaceba m Leicester Sept 15, 1816, Susanna Burnap of Salisbury; moved to Potsdam, N Y. Untraced; had Harrison, Edison, James, perhaps others.

Silas Dow adacebb m Polly ——. One child known:

a   Sarah Helen m Leicester Feb 13, 1848, Amos S Tracy

Sarah Dow adacebc m Leicester Nov 27, 1836, Lewis Bump of Chittenden.

Sybil Dow adacebd (entered by clerk as Pibie) m Leicester Nov 18, 1821, Cyrus Bump of Salisbury.

Stephen Dow adacebf m Dec 7, 1826, Candace Church of Brandon. At least 3 children:

a   Francis J   b   Orator
c   Melinda M b 1838; m Leicester Feb 9, 1857, Albert Morse; dau—Blanche V
    now of Brandon

Francis J Dow adacebfa m Sarah ——; moved to Alamota, Kan; killed by lightning; wife d shortly afterwards; dau,—Gertrude Nellie now dead, Grace

Orator Dow adacebfb had in 1881 fine 115 acre farm in Brandon. At least 1 child:

a   Cora, now Mrs Guy Williams of Sudbury. A cousin is Mrs Charles Farmer of
    Brandon

Clarissa Dow adacebg m Leicester Oct 22, 1829, Ichabod Paine of Leicester

---

Joel Dow adaced m Nov 20, 1794, his cousin Elizabeth Dow adacgc; lived Leicester until after 1808; then moved to Malone, N Y, where he d 1837. It is notable that prior to 1800 marriages of first cousins do not result in deterioration either in quantity or quality of posterity. A century later, with a denser population, the ill effects were generally patent. Eight children:

a	Joseph b 1798, untraced	b	Elizabeth b 1800
c	Joel b 1802, untraced	d	Warren b July 1804
e	Eloisa b 1806	f	William b Leicester Mch 21, 1808
g	Hiram b 1810, untraced	h	Leonard C b Malone Nov 20, 1812

Warren Dow adacedd in some way reached Malden, Mass, probably apprenticed; m Malden Apr 21, 1827, Rachel Richardson of Malden d Danvers Aug 5, 1837, ae 32.   Warren then moved to Vt; m 2nd Roxana —— d Roxbury, Vt.   Was no longer young when he settled in No Lawrence, N Y.   List of children furnished by a great grand dau

    a   George b Aug 12, 1827; d No Lawrence about 1870; no wife mentioned
    b   Warren L b Malden Aug 12, 1827   c   Joseph L
    d   Ellen b 1829; m Elijah B Hedding of Port Henry, N Y; son,—Frank S of Port
        Henry
    e   Jonas Richardson   f   Rachel m Orrin Flint of Roxbury, Vt

Warren L Dow adaceddb after his mother's death was bound out to a Mr Allen, printer of Salem, Mass; moved to Plattsburg, N Y, after 1850;   m Salem Dec 6, 1849, Martha J Collyer b Lynn, Mass, June 8, 1832, dau of Samuel B.   Warren L was a printer, d Plattsburg Oct 16, 1901.   Children:

    a   Mary Jane b Salem Sept 18, 1850; d Plattsburg July 2, 1866
    b   Nellie Maria b Apr 14, 1863; m Dec 21, 1887, Levi J Needham of Plattsburg
    c   Nettie b Mch 5, 1868

Nettie Dow adaceddbc m Port Henry May 11, 1891, J Mitchell Studholme of Plattsburg.   Children:

    a   Jeannette Dow b Dec 12, 1892; d Dec 15, 1892
    b   Donald Mitchell b July 29, 1896; grad Dartmouth
    c   Raymond Collyer b Oct 14, 1898; d Feb 17, 1899
    d   Janet May b Jan 4, 1905

Joseph L Dow adaceddc, farmer of Brockville, Ont., after the war; enlisted in 92nd N Y vols Jan 3, 1862; disch Feb 6, 1866; was in 21 battles;   3 years a sharpshooter.   Retired, he d Arlington Heights, Mass, after 1901;   m Mch 24, 1858, Rose Ann De Rose b Massena, N Y, Sept 15, 1838;   living 1903.   Children:

    a   Ellen M b Malone Sept 25, 1859
    b   Warren C b Canton, N Y, Nov 9, 1861
    c   Edwin C b Lawrence Feb 9, 1870; of N Y City, untraced
    d   Mabel M A b Stockholme Sept 4, 1881

Ellen M Dow adaceddca m Dec 26, 1882, J Udell Batchelder b Peru, Vt, Aug 22, 1859.   A large contractor and machinist of Hartford, Conn, he turned farmer for his health.   Children:

    a   E Geneva M b Standish, Mich, Oct 7, 1883
    b   Ethel M b Wilmington, Vt, Feb 25, 1885
    c   Mildred T b Feb 12, 1887

Warren C Dow adaceddcb m Oct 18, 1885, Minnie MacLennan b Hyde Park, N Y, July 29, 1864; learned telegraphy and entered journalism by that route; edited many publications and was for ten years news editor of the Boston Globe.   Attacked by tuberculosis, he went to Trinidad, Colo, fighting the disease for 3 years, dying Nov 19, 1907.   Child:

    a   Warren MacLennan b Nov 27, 1885; in 1907 with 1st Nat Bank, Trinidad

Mabelle A Dow adaceddcd of Arlington m Aug 1, 1907, Frank A Higgins, ae 23, son of William M and Lena (Owens)

Jonas Richardson Dow adacedde d No Lawrence about 1873; m Lurinda Polina Avery b Aug 21, 1841. Children, by Avery Gen, untraced:

   a Polina b Mch 17, 1867; m——Ostrum
   b Grant b Mch 29, 1869; m Lulu Banister
   c Sherman b June 9, 1872; m Olive Huntington
   d Bertha b Aug 29, 1875; m Lewis Barlow

William Dow adacedf, farmer of Parishville, N Y, m June 11, 1835, Caroline Foster b Barnard, Vt, 1806, d July 30, 1850; m 2nd Julia E Foster b Pierpont, N Y, 1823. Seven children by 1st wife; 6 b Potsdam, rest Pierpont (some dates inaccurate):

   a Caroline Louise b June 10, 1836; d Aug 30, 1862, unm
   b Foster W b Aug 25, 1838; killed Cold Harbor June 2, 1864
   c Lucia E b Nov 21, 1841; m Andrew Yates; went to Illinois; 6 children
   d Borsha Ann b Mch 17, 1845; m Jan 3, 1870, Julius B Strobeck b Nov 10, 1846, farmer of Parishville
   e Willard C b May 12, 1848
   f Julia Amy b Oct 30, 1851; m 1876 Henry Stone of Colton; 3 children
   g Sarah J b May 22, 1853; d Nov 24, 1882; m 1875 E D Crockett; 2 children
   h Orrin A b Mch 22, 1857
   i Seymour G b Nov 9, 1858; d Nov 8, 1896; m 1883 A Simpson
   j Lucy Josephine b Apr 22, 1859; m Nov 10, 1876, William W Webber
   k Austin A b Dec 12, 1860; of Parishville m 1884 Clara Harford; 2 children
   l Ida E b Dec 17, 1862; d Mch 4, 1863

Willard C Dow adacedfe of Colton m Oct 4, 1875, Mary E Beach; b Mishawaka, Ind, Oct 7, 1856. Children:

   a Mabelle E b May 26, 1883   b John M b July 21, 1887 (1877?)

Borsha A Dow adacedfd and Julius B Strobeck had:

   a Byron K b Sept 11, 1871   b Oland H b Apr 18, 1873
   c Laura L b Sept 21, 1876   d Arthur W b Oct 19, 1878
   e Amy L b Mch 11, 1880   f Charlie C b Mch 22, 1883

Josephine L Dow adacedfj m W W Webber of Dover, N H. After serving in navy, he became a physician. Children:

   a William Greenleaf b Newfield, Me, Nov 20, 1878
   b Annie Peters b Rochester, N H, Aug 23, 1880; d Aug 6, 1881
   c Mavis Eloise b Stockholm, N Y, Nov 20, 1882; d Nov 13, 1884
   d Raymond Sullivan b Dover Feb 9, 1885

Leonard C Dow adacedh, hop raiser of No Bangor, living 1887, m Dec 6, 1836, Mary A Davis b Quebec June 10, 1817. Ten children:

   a Addie E m Charles Eldred; living 1919
   b Edgar A; untraced   c Worthford L b Mch 26, 1851
   d Frank B   e Alfred C   f Alexander; all untraced
   g Esther Ann b Potsdam Apr 3, 1841   h Ida May
   i Freddie L; untraced   j ——not found

Worthford L Dow adacedhc, portrait artist of Providence, R I, m Apr 20, 1876, Mary P Sherman b Fletcher, Vt, Nov 20, 1857. Children:

a   Clifford L b Bangor Dec 24, 1876
b   Arthur G b Springfield, Mass, May 4, 1878
c   Maud M b Springfield Dec 30, 1881

Clifford S Dow adacedhca m Longmeadow, Mass, July 15, 1903, Minnie G Dean, ae 28, dau of Maurice and Mary (Cornell).

Esther A Dow adacedhg m Sept 5, 1859, George W French b No Bangor, June 6, 1838, carpenter and machinist of Holyoke, Mass, d June 18, 1884. Children:

a   Edna M b June 8, 1860
b   Addie May b Sept 21, 1861; m Dec 31, 1879, Joel Allen
c   Freddie L b Mch 2, 1863; d Holyoke May 23, 1885
d   Alpha E b Dec 8, 1864; m Sept 9, 1886, William T Gibson
e   Charles H b Jan 16, 1868; d Aug 30, 1883
f   Erwin B b Dec 8, 1874   g   Burdette E b Apr 13, 1878

Isaac Dow adacef d Mch 11, 1849; m 1803 Deborah Griffith b Dec 19, 1789, d Sept 21, 1863. Children:

a   Walter b May 30, 1804; d June 10, 1834
b   Deborah b Apr 4, 1805; m 1826 Alfred Ames; d Mch 11, 1882; 3 sons, 1 dau
c   Clementine b July 5, 1807; d Aug 7, 1857; m 1829 Jacob—

Isaiah Dow adacf who m Sarah was for 20 years a man of mystery, altho Mrs E J More had found him and Sarah and assumed correctly that he came from Amesbury. But there was no Amesbury Isaiah to fit. A new search of original rec proved that a copyist, writing from sound, had written Sarah among the b rec. Search of Hampstead demonstrated he m 1758 Sarah Kimball, not in Kimball Gen. They lived about 4 years in Hampstead, moving from Amesbury to New Braintree between 1770 and 1776. Three youngest children by family rec:

a   Mary b Hampstead Apr 4, 1760. Family rec giving her 4th child and m Isaiah
      Pepper is error. New Braintree church rec gives Mary Dow, young woman,
      bap Jan 12, 1779, m Apr 14, 1780, John Pepper of New Braintree. She was b
      Quaker
b   Martha b Hampstead Jan 4, 1762
c   Sarah b Apr 5, 1766; m Samuel Merritt
d   Isaiah b Amesbury Apr 1, 1768   e   John b Sept 18, 1770
f   Jonathan b Worcester Co 1776
g   Pattie   h   Miriam m Daniel Russel; 2nd Joseph Fairbanks

Isaiah Dow adacfd. Family Bible gives names of his 4 children but no other data. He must have gone to Vt, as did most of his relatives. Children:

a   James; presumably of Middlesex m Nov 20, 1820, Betsey Siloway of Mont-
      pelier; untraced
b   Isaiah m Orwell, Vt, Jan 2, 1819, Loving Cutting of Bristol; untraced
c   Amarilla   d   Polly

John Dow adacfe is wholly unknown. A large family of New Braintree are entered on town rec as Dow, but are Dorr, coming from Boston. Lest one or more be actually Dow, the list is:

Moses Dow m Aug 28, 1781, wid Abigail Wilson; m Brookfield June 24, 1788, Hannah White. Priscilla Dow m Sept 9, 1787, Samuel Marcy. George Dow m Aug 26, 1790, Lydia Cutler. Asel Dow int pub New Braintree Aug 14, 1796, to Juley Goulden of Western. Mary Dow (proven Dorr) m Jan 24, 1804, Capt Oliver Fox of Fitchburg.

Catherine Dow m Feb 22, 1807, Solomon Ingalls. Sarah Dow wid m Sept 18, 1811, Lieut Joseph Newell of New Braintree. Thomas Sheperd Dow m Nov 7, 1813, Melinda Persons

Jonathan Dow adacff of Western m (int pub Dec 22, 1799) Polly Wolcott of Western, whose father had been killed in Battle of Trenton. This family rec is surely correct, but inspection of rolls has failed to locate him. The young couple located in Bridport, Vt; lived long; had 10 children, all maturing:

a Nancy b Aug 29, 1800   b Polly b Dec 8, 1801
c Eliza b Sept 5, 1803   d Caroline b Jan 12, 1804
e John b Feb 26, 1807   f Mariol b Aug 24, 1808
g Sophronia b Oct 31, 1809 h Miriam b July 17, 1811
i Kimball b Aug 19, 1813   j Lavias, not in town rec

Nancy Dow adacffa m Isaac Johnson. Children:

a Mary   b Elizabeth   c Isaac W
d and e Lucas, Lucius, twins   f James

Polly Dow adacffb m David Russell. Children:

a Gideon   b Joseph   c Eliza   d Helen   e Jeannette
f Amanda   g Miriam   h Amy   i Ruthven
j and k Gustavus, Adolphus, twins   l Alphonso

Eliza Dow adacffc m Newell Hemingway. Children:

a Antoinette Jane   b Eliza   c Sarah

Caroline Dow adacffd m Hugh Harsha; 2nd —— Artlip. Youngest child by her 2nd husband:

a Mortimer   b Marion   c Mary   d George   e Eugene
f Catherine   g Homer

John Dow adacffe left home at 7, cared for by a N Y State family; gained a scholarship in Poughkeepsie business college, another in Hillsdale, Mich, where his children were subsequently educated. He m Alden, N Y, Nov 30, 1834, Sallie L Horton; moved 1850 to Illinois, by steamer from Buffalo to Chicago. Their goods drawn by ox team driven by oldest son; much trouble encountered when the oxen ran away in the woods, now heart of Chicago. They located a farm in De Kalb Co, now Courtland. He prospered for 17 years, then endorsed a note to oblige a kinsman, with result that he lost his farm. He went to Olathe, Kan, to his son's home. Children:

a Jonathan Horton b Holland, N Y, Oct 22, 1835
b Newell H b Mch 9, 1838; d Jan 22, 1839
c Philena b Mch 1, 1840

    d Ellen H b Jan 8, 1843; m Rev George H Linderman of Grand Rapids, Mich ;
        d June 1885; no children
    e Finando E b June 10, 1845
    f Theresa b Dec 25, 1847   g Mary E b Apr 28, 1850
    h Herman Furness b Nov 22, 1852   i—b June 22, d July 4, 1855

Jonathan H Dow adacffea was in Walla Walla, Wash, at the outbreak of war; started at once for Chicago, a trip of months. On arrival, he organized a company, being its captain, of 133rd, later 147th. This company achieved notable service. Jonathan was offered a Colonelcy in regulars but preferred to enter business. He m Sycamore, Ill, Feb 13, 1866, Mary Ann Judd b Mohawk, N Y, of English parents. Three of her brothers were killed in Union army. He established a department store and aided similar business by two brothers. In Olathe, Kan, he built a fine home, surrounded by 20 acres, with a brook. Here he spent his later years, somewhat invalided, but able to take keen enjoyment in his environment. His wife d Oct 20, 1866; m 2nd Luvina Mahaffie. He d July 30, 1901; his wife sold the place, moved to Lawrence, Kan, and devoted herself to the support and education of the children:

    a Nelly b Dec 29, 1867; m Nov 16, 1893, William Alexander Burden, merchant
        of Joliet, Ill; no children
    b Floyd b July 14, 1872; d unm   c Zada b Mch 4, 1881; d unm
    d Horton b Feb 21, 1885; lived Chicago, now Kansas City, unm
    e Marian b July 4, 1889; d Jan 8, 1912, unm
    f Lillian, twin, d Dec 31, 1911, unm
    g Herman b Jan 1, 1891; d 1896
    h Jonathan Mahaffie b June 6, 1893; Grad N Y Univ with highest honors and
        European scholarship; now teaching Junior College, Kansas City, unm

Philena Andalusia Dow adacffec m S L Linderman, her brother in law; lives Chico, Calif. Children:

    a George m Ada Haffine   b Eva m Scott Wolff
    c Montie m Alice Cosgrove   d Hubert m Zilpha Clark

Finando E Dow adacffee, merchant, at one time mayor of Colorado Springs, d Apr 23, 1912; m Sycamore, Ill, Apr 30, 1867, Helen Hayden b Courtland Sept 2, 1848. Children:

    a Lottie May b Courtland May 27, 1868; d Olathe Sept 28, 1869
    b Netta Helen b De Soto, Kan, Apr 1, 1871; d Colo Springs Apr 20, 1892
    c Gertrude b Gardner, Kan, Dec 10, 1872; m Colo Springs June 8, 1904, Arthur
        Newcomb Cruff b Boston, Mass, June 11, 1871, of Roxbury. No children
    d Florence b Oct 29, 1879   e Frank Hayden b July 3, 1886

Florence Dow adacffeed m Colo Springs Sept 2, 1903, Julius Tefft Kirby b Muncie, Ind, May 10, 1881. Children:

    a John Dow b Aug 21, 1904
    b Julius Tefft b Nov 14, 1912; d Feb 2, 1918

Frank H Dow adacffeee m Colo Springs Oct 28, 1911, Jessie Idaline Fuller b Oklahoma City Oct 16, 1891. Children:

    a Frank Hayden b Colo Springs July 12, 1912
    b Randall Fuller b Dawson, N M, June 11, 1915
    c Helen Laura b Colo Springs Nov 19, 1919

Mary E Dow adacffeg m George Mordhoff; lives Medford, Ore; 6 children

Herman F Dow adacffeh was a successful clothing merchant of Sioux City; later of Kansas City; m Colo Springs Aug 10, 1881, Mary McMorris b Le Mars, Iowa; 2nd Chicago July 27, 1902, Mame Wall Magner, well known singer and teacher. He d Medford, Ore, Mch 21, 1922. Children, by 1st wife:

  a McMorris Marshall b Le Mars June 23, 1882
  b Ruth V b Jan 7, 1884; m Sioux City Sept 10, 1902, Roland O Smith; 2nd Kansas City 1912 Charles H Pierson; moved to Los Angeles. Children, by 2nd husband,—Charles Dow, Herman Dow

McMorris M Dow adacffeha, physician and surgeon, Medford, Ore, pres of Medford Hospital Society, m 1st Los Angeles Sept 18, 1907, Lydia M Spengler, osteopathic physician; 2nd Medford Jan 27, 1920, Fernn R Beebe. Child by 2nd wife:

  a McMorris Marshall

Mariol Dow adacfff m Ezra Croft. Children:

a Dwight	b Byron	c Ezra	d Nancy	e Sophronia
f James	g Cyrus			

Sophronia Dow adacffg m Herman Furness. Children:

a Orlando	b Margaret	c Jane	d George	e Herman
f Lavinia	g Nettie	h ——d in infancy		

Miriam Dow adacffh m Chauncey Luce. Child:

  a Catherine

Kimball Dow adacffi, merchant of Sycamore, later De Soto, Kan, m Euphrasia Hiscox, dau of John. Children:

  a Polly b 1839; d 1899   b Harriet b 1845
  c Clement Kimball b 1852; d 1919

Polly Dow adacffia m Frank Hildebrand of Chicago. Children, all b Chicago:

  a Lewis K, editor of Breeder's Gazette
  b Lizzie m A H Sanders   c Robert

Harriet Dow adacffib m —— Taylor; lives Paola, Kan. Children:

  a Lizzie m Jeff Cummings   b Susan m——Scothern

Clement K Dow adacffic, member Sons of Revolution, m Alice Smith; lived Lawrence, Kan. Children:

  a Burton S b 1873; of Kansas City; has son,—Burton S
  b Lewis C b 1875, banker of Oxnard, Calif; has 2 dau
  c E Ross b 1878; lives Chicago; has son,—E Ross
  d Mabel m W B Hess; sons,—Vernon, Alvin
  e Leslie W b 1891; lives Pratt, Kan; sons,—Allison, Clement, William Leslie

Lavias Dow adacffj m Aristeen Joslyn. Children:

  a Augusta   b Fillmore L   c Mary

Patty Dow adacfg (Hattie in family rec) of Wendell, Mass, m Dea Samuel Osgood, son of Capt Joseph, d Hamilton, N Y, 1829. Children:

a Samuel W b Apr 25, 1787; d Apr 1841
b Josiah d Hamilton 1839; m Diana Hoyt
c Martha d 1845; m Jonathan O Pierce

Joseph Dow adacg d New Braintree Apr 2, 1814; corporal under Capt Thomas Whipple, Col James Converse, 3 days in 1777, starting for Ticonderoga, turned back in a few days, not needed; m 1st Elizabeth Cummings d Aug 27, 1781; 2nd Apr 30, 1782, Sarah Pepper b Dec 24, 1748, d Feb 10, 1818.   His gravestone still stands in New Braintree churchyard.   Children:

a Mary b May 29, 1768; m Sept 15, 1785, Oliver Stone
b Anna b Sept 26, 1770; d Oct 7, 1782
c Elizabeth b Mch 18, 1773; m Joel Dow adaced
d Levina b Feb 5, 1775   e Lydia b Mch 12, 1777; d Dec 14, 1778
f Joseph b Dec 12, 1779   g Josiah b Mch 22, 1783; d May 31, 1786
h Sallie b Sept 4, 1784; m (int pub Sept 26, 1803) James Nelson; left only
     adopted child
i Daniel b Apr 11, 1787   j Sewell b Mch 8, 1789
k Zenas b Apr 3, 1791; m Feb 3, 1833, Elvira Dudley, both of Bakersfield, Vt;
     untraced
l Pliny b Jan 9, 1794

Joseph Dow adacgf lost his mother at age of 3, brought up by her family.   A blue-eyed youth of mild manners, he acquired a taste for reading and music; at 20 teaching school in West Brookfield, adding a little income by an evening singing school.   Olive Cobb b May 12, 1777, dau of Perez and Abiah (Richmond), was black-eyed, tall, handsome, and, like her father, very "sot in her ways."   Singing school and teacher, 2 years younger than herself, were much to her liking.   So, they went hand in hand to ask the consent of the old folks.   No fault could be found with Joseph except his youth and lack of money.   Perez said no emphatically.   Next, the dry entry in vital statistics,—m Nov 3, 1799. A few days later they returned to seek forgiveness and a temporary home on the Cobb farm.   Perez crossed Olive's name out of the family Bible and made a new will.   He'd show her, by heck, what filial obedience meant.   He never relented; 41 years later his son Joseph died a bachelor and intestate.   A son of Olive drove with his bride from Pennsylvania to Brookfield and collected Olive's share of the inheritance, several hundred dollars, then much needed by the old folks.

West Brookfield was thenceforth a closed book; the young couple packed their entire earthly possessions in a carpet bag, mounted the horse which Joseph had bought with every penny saved from singing school, and started for Pennsylvania, where they imagined teaching prospects were better.   Preston offered them a haven; Joseph captured the school.   It paid poor wages, but Joseph was useful in many ways.   He played the fiddle and could pitch the tune, so he led the choir.   He had a small library of English classics, out of which he found euphonious names,—Joseph Addison, Charles Grandison, etc., applied freely to his own and to others' grandchildren.   He knew about fairies, Jack of Bean stock fame, and Red Riding Hood, and wove them into his school primer. Everybody liked him, but the glass factory at Bethany was needed to supply a living, for himself and later his children.   Education of them cost every penny that Joseph could save and he gave the best he could. All of them taught school at some time, the oldest also a preacher.   Joseph d June 22, 1852; Olive Oct 5, 1858.   Of 10 children, 7 grew up, all inheriting musical, mathematical or artistic talents.   Three were dark, stern, arbitrary,—the Cobb inheritance.   Four blue-eyed, gentle, lovable,—next editions of Joseph Dow.

a   Joseph b 1800; d June 3, 1876   b   Enos b 1803
c   Sallie b Apr 15, 1806; d Mch 27, 1893
d   Melita b May 9, 1812; d Jan 7, 1899
e   Lorenzo b Aug 31, 1814; d Jan 28, 1878
f   Philena b May 5, 1817; d Apr 8, 1900
g   George Peck b Mch 14, 1820; d Oct 14, 1907

Joseph Dow adacgfa, teacher and preacher of Mt Pleasant, Pa; m Oct 28, 1824, Abbie King b Aug 30, 1800, d Sept 29, 1894.   Children:

a   Surilla b Jan 10, 1825; d Oct 7, 1826
b   Joseph Addison b May 6, 1829   c   Saphroneus b July 25, 1831
d   Elom King b May 23, 1834; d Jan 5, 1837
e   Edwin Elom b Aug 12, 1836

Joseph A Dow adacgfab d Aug 18, 1906; m Aug 25, 1850, Mary Homans b June 20, 1826; d Oct 11, 1893.   Children:

a   Josephine b June 16, 1851; m June 15, 1876, Abraham Dingham
b   Frank b Nov 6, 1853; d Apr 8, 1856
c   Annie b Aug 5, 1856; m Nov 27, 1877, Alfred Decker
d   Frank b Nov 16, 1859; d Sept 3, 1862
e   Fannie b Nov 16, 1859; d Sept 3, 1862

Josephine Dow adacgfaba m Abraham Dingham; dau Nellie b Aug 13, 1879, m —— Ammerman

Saphroneus Dow adacgfac lived Carbondale; d Nov 15, 1881; m Jan 9, 1860, Alpha A Belcher d 1880; 2nd Helen M Harrison d Jan 5, 1882.   Children:

a   Carrie Estella b Nov 22, 1860; m Frederick R Hotaling
b   Charles Ambrose b Jan 28, 1864; m May 4, 1896, Geraldine Vroman
c   Frank Howard b Aug 9, 1865; m 1891 Ida J Cox; d Dec 24, 1908; dau,—Gertrude b 1897
d   Jennie Evelyn b June 2, 1866; m Apr 4, 1887, C T Lingfelter; d 1901; children,—Helen M b 1889, Mildred Isabel b 1895
e   Cora Ella b Mch 11, 1869   f   George Saphroneus b Dec 13, 1872
g   Florence Elgiva b May 25, 1874   h   Nina Adelaide b Sept 2, 1875
i   Robert b June 13, 1877; untraced

Cora E Dow adacgface m Oct 16, 1888, Wallace Copeland.   Children:

a   Grace Mildred b May 27, 1895   b   Raymond Wallace b July 31, 1897

George S Dow adacgfacf m June 1899 Maud Odell.   Child:

a   George Saphroneus b May 21, 1901

Nina A Dow adacgfach m Dec 26, 1893, Charles R Munn.   Child:

a   Marion Margaretta b 1895

Edwin E Dow adacgfae, blacksmith of Los Gatos, Calif, d May 5, 1920; m May 11, 1856, Caroline Lydia Salisbury b Dec 31, 1837.   Children:

a   Ella V b Mch 16, 1857   b   Edwin Joseph b May 29, 1862

Ella V Dow adacgfaea m Oct 10, 1876, Judson L Gelatt b Nov 9, 1852. Children:

a   Vivian b Jan 16, 1878; m Mch 26, 1901, John D Crummey
b   Harry B b Aug 3, 1881; m Oct 18, 1911, Dora V Hook
c   David Clifford b Mch 20, 1897; d Sept 12, 1910

Edwin J Dow adacgfaeb m Sept 30, 1882, Florence Johnson b Dec 22, 1865.   Children:

a   Harry Raymond b May 12, 1884   b   Hazel Aileen b June 28, 1886
c   Daphne b Sept 16, 1900   d   Neal L b Feb 10, 1904

Harry R Dow adacgfaeba m 1907 Alfhild Johnson.   Child:

a   Florence b Aug 16, 1908

Hazel A Dow adacgfaebb m Sept 1910 Hugh Kness.   Children:

a   Hugh Salisbury b Apr 1913   b   Ellsworth b July 25, 1917

Enos Dow adacgfb of Mt Pleasant m 1825 Miranda Baldwin of Bethany; had a disagreement with rest of family; went west about 1836 with 3 surviving children, never meeting again.   Children:

a   George W b 1826; d Red Cloud, Neb 1907, leaving wid Fannie
b   Charles b 1828   c   Francis b 1830; both untraced
d   Olive b 1832; d Bethany ae 3

Sally Dow adacgfc of Mt Pleasant d Mch 27, 1893; m Sept 30, 1824, David Cramer b Mch 24, 1800, d Nov 12, 1874.   Children:

a   Ezra b Sept 25, 1825; d Oct 1, 1855
b   Olive b Aug 24, 1827; d May 11, 1878; m John H More; 2nd Frederick Smith
c   Edward O b May 27, 1829; d Kansas 1859
d   Adon W b Mch 3, 1831; d July 15, 1903; m Lora Roberts; 2nd Eliza Brooks;
      3rd Ellen Woods
e   Belinda b July 18, 1833; d Apr 6, 1903; m F B Eddy
f   Julia b Mch 31, 1835; d June 22, 1842
g   Ara B b Dec 12, 1837; d July 10, 1870   h   David Amer b Sept 6, 1840
i   George Dow b May 28, 1842; d Sept 21, 1915; m Josie L Smith; 2nd Amanda
      Lavo
j   Henry Abner b July 2, 1844; d June 24, 1901; m Sept 19, 1871, Henrietta E
      Borchers
k   Philena b May 13, 1846; d Nov 10, 1908; m Burgess Spencer
l   Mary b June 13, 1849; d Aug 21, 1851

Melita Dow adacgfd m May 7, 1834, Elom Treadwell Case b May 12, 1807, d June 18, 1884.   Children:

a   Olive Abigail b Feb 9, 1835; d May 17, 1867; m Feb 9, 1853, William Roberts
      Baker

b Sophia Dimmock b Dec 19, 1836; d Mch 24, 1904; m July 2, 1859, Ellis Tyler;
    2nd Aug 15, 1868, Jasper J Savory
c Philena Melita b Feb 18, 1839; d Dec 25, 1866; m Luther Carpenter
d George William b Mch 19, 1841; d Dec 17, 1872; m Mch 19, 1862, Anna R
    Moore
e Julia Sallie b May 4, 1843; d Nov 28, 1862
f Charles Joseph b Nov 8, 1845; m Aug 12, 1867, Olive J Carpenter
g Robert Bruce b Feb 28, 1848; m Oct 18, 1880, Content Ferris
h Virgil Tallman b July 6, 1850; m Adele——; 3 children
i Horace Riley b Nov 1, 1853; m Mch 24, 1880, Kenia Arvilla Bryant
j Ella Louise b Apr 6, 1855; d Sept 27, 1912; m Aug 22, 1875, Edson A Barrett
k Eva Eloise b Apr 6, 1855; m Sept 27, 1877, Charles D Corey

Lorenzo Dow adacgfe d Jan 28, 1878; m 1842 Polly Cole; 2nd 1859
Cornelia Ogden. Children:

a Alice L b May 6, 1843   b Lorenzo Nelson b Nov 1853
c Hannah Ann b 1855; m Charles Kingsbury; children,—Thomas, Burt, Mabel
d Lydia A b 1860; m Edward Tucker; children,—Blanche, Ida F
e Phoebe E b 1862; m Philander Dopp rc

Alice L Dow adacgfea m William R Baker. Children:

a Sidney Ernest b 1874; m Carrie Shaffer
b Alice Mary b Jan 30, 1876; m Frank Whitehill

Lorenzo N Dow adacgfeb lived Starucca, Pa; m Mary Gritman.
Child:

a Nelson

Nelson Dow adacgfeba m Bertha Lee. Children:

a Wanda   b Reba

Philena Dow adacgff d Apr 8, 1900; m Mch 10, 1836, Christopher
Palmer Tallman b Apr 22, 1806. Children:

a Edwin Ephraim b Jan 5, 1838; d Apr 1, 1908; m Oct 9, 1860, M J Van Horne
b Alanson Benjamin b Mch 4, 1840; d Dec 25, 1912 m Jan 1 1861, S Melvina
    Dix
c Philena Jane b Oct 23, 1843; m Jan 1, 1869 T A D Campbell
d Darwin Washington b Oct 26, 1846; d Feb 6, 1905; m 1868 Julia A Stanton
e Eudalia Josephine b Mch 29, 1851
f Olive Lucretia b Apr 5, 1857; m Dec 19, 1876, F D Benedict

Eudalia J Tallman adacgffe m Mch 19, 1878, Addis E More;
survives him; lived many places Kansas and eastward. With 3 children,
she has long made her home with a dau. 1919-22 in Univ of Ill, where
her dau took degree in music, a teacher and superintendent of music in
many schools. With her, genealogy has been 20 years a method of em-
ploying what spare hours she had. The adacgf line is all her work, its
detail requiring unlimited patience. She has for years aided the Author in
every possible way.

George P Dow adacgfg had his physical inheritance from Joseph;
was the mainstay of his parents in their old age; m 1850 Luania Prentice.
Children:

a Elvira Philena b 1851   b Elmira Luania, twin
c Olive Cobb b 1853   d Mary Belinda b Feb 5, 1853

e Sophia Janet b 1857   f Annie Melita b 1858
g Joseph Perry b Aug 13, 1860
h Emma Luania b May 19, 1863; m A E Kingsbury

Mary B Dow adacgfgd m Edgar Joseph Sanford b Sept 28, 1848. Children:

a Lynn Edgar b Jan 27, 1894; d Mch 24, 1895
b Greta Marie b Aug 17, 1897

Joseph P Dow adacgfgg m Lillian Truax; 2nd Melinda Burch. Children:

a Deforest George b 1885; untraced   b Arthur A b 1887; m Inya Warner
c Clara Emma b 1889; m 1911 James Cargill   d Mary Jane b 1891

Daniel Dow adacgi m Brookfield Nov 25, 1815, Sally Sanford. Altho list of children probably complete, no further rec of him found, presumably lived Vermont. Children:

a Susan White b Sept 17, 1816   b Mary Ann b Sept 15, 1818
c Elizabeth b Feb 18, 1821   d Henry Austin b Jan 17, 1823; untraced

Sewell Dow adacgj m Brookfield Dec 13, 1813, Hannah Pepper; moved to Ware; d there 1823, survived by wid and very young children:

a Charles Henry b New Braintree May 2, 1814
b Harriet b May 5, 1816
c Lawson Myrick b May 21, 1818; d Ware 1823
d Harvey Warren b June 14, 1820; d Sept 7, 1834
e Sewell Lawson bap Dec 22, 1822; untraced

Charles H Dow adacgja m Sarah A —— of New Braintree. Census 1850 finds him apparently widower. With him Harriet E Dow b Mass 1792 may be Hannah Pepper. Children:

a Sarah A b 1837   b Sewell b 1839; untraced
c Henry F b 1841; untraced   d Charles H b 1845; untraced
e Austin V b 1847

Austin V Dow adacgjae m Jan 15, 1878, Hattie V Kelley, both of Canaan, N H. Child:

a ——dau b and d Apr 30, 1879

Zenas Dow adacgk conveyed land in Malone, N Y, in 1857; evident, then, that he and his wife settled there, not far from the 50 acre farm of Joel Dow adacedd in what was known as the Gleason district.

Pliny Dow adacgl m Brookfield Apr 1, 1824, Zena Sanford. Hist Hardwick gives Viah and knows little of them. They probably lived Hardwick only a few years; perhaps went west. Children:

a Pliny Augustus b Nov 7, 1826; untraced
b Martha Sophia b May 17, 1829
c George b Oct 31, 1831   d Emily b Jan 2, d Jan 17, 1834
e William B b July 31, 1837; m 1857 Abbie Root of Enfield. He d Hardwick,
   Mass, Feb 16, 1905, ae 67, 7 mos; otherwise untraced

Martha S Dow adacglb apparently remained in Hardwick; m Apr 8, 1853, Lysander B Wesson.   Children:

a Edwin A b 1852
b George McClellan b 1861; m Elizabeth Abbott
c Almon Frank b 1864; m Cora Wiley
d William Pliny b 1868; m Mary A Johnson
e Ellen M b 1870; m Harry E Brown
f Elizabeth (twin) m Harry Harper

George Dow adacglc.   This untraced member of a Vt family agrees in age with George Dow, farmer of Alton, N H, in 1850 census; wife Lavina. A child:

a —— (sex?) (rec defective) b Alton Mch 7, 1855

PHILIP Dow adad may be recalled as the child living with his Quaker grandfather following his father's second marriage. Presumably he left the Friends on account of his marriage. A gap of three years between birth of oldest child and baptism might indicate that a long debate was held over the matter of denomination. Philip might have been the one who favored baptism. His wife joined Kingston church July 14, 1728, seven months after her child was baptized. Philip was a yeoman of Kingston 1728, of Hampton 1731, Kensington 1736, later until his death in Kingston. He m 1st June 2, 1723-4, Hannah Griffin b Salisbury Mch 25, 1702, dau of John and Susanna (Brown). She d suicide July 23, 1753. He m 2nd Sarah, wid of Jonathan Freeze. Only one child was a Quaker, and he by his own choice made at mature age. The posterity has been large as the average and very local, mostly in New Hampshire until this day. Children:

a Benaiah b Oct 4, 1724; bap Kingston Nov 27, 1727
b ——, child d Sept 19, 1728
c Ezekiel b May 1, 1731; d June 21, 1736
d Ephraim b Aug 25, 1732; d June 22, 1736   e Jemima b Jan 30, 1734
f Hannah b Aug 13, 1736; d Apr 30, 1738
g Phineas b Jan 22, 1738; d June 12, 1749
h Ebenezer b Nov 9, 1739   i Jonathan b Mch 29, 1741
j Hannah b June 20, 1743; d June 22, 1749
   State has a rec: Jeremiah, dau of Philip, b Jan 30, 1739, obvious error, probably garbled adade

Benaiah Dow adada, ancestor of the Dows of Northwood, m So Hampton Sept 24, 1751, Miriam French b Jan 11, 1727-8, dau of Samuel and Mary (Collins).

Miriam French was dau of Samuel of So Hampton. She m 1st Ebenezer Gove b 1724, d in army before Louisburg 1745-6. His will, written in the field, left his property elsewhere unless she had a child. A child was born posthumously. Benaiah and Miriam moved 1753 to Epping, there a member of the Congregational church. Epping rec: April 9, 1803, ae 77, Benaiah Dow, a peaceable, quiet, honest man, a member of the Congregational Society. His inheritance came during his father's life, for: June 15, 1747-8, Philip Dow of Kensington deeds to Benaiah Dow for fatherly love 20 acres in Exeter (the part now Epping). Epping rec: 1811, ae 79, the widow of the late Benaiah Dow. As Miriam was b 1727-8, this is 5 years out. Epping rec are very apt to err in this way. Town rec of children inaccurate, corrected by gravestone rec:

a Phineas b Feb 28, 1752; an idiot; d (Epping rec) 1782, ae 22
b Winthrop b 1754
c Hannah b 1758. Epping bap register, apparently a transcript from the original, condenses: 1756-7-8: Bap Phinehas, Wintrep, and Hannah, children of Beniare Dow
d Jemima b after 1758
e Mary. Northwood d rec says b Dec 26, 1758
f Sarah bap Apr 26, 1761; Plumer ms gives her d 1791, ae 27; unm

g   Samuel b 1766 by gravestone rec
h   Minah bap May 4, 1766; presumably twin of Samuel
i   Miriam b 1772 by gravestone rec

Winthrop Dow adadab signed the Association Test and was one of
the prominent citizens of Epping; m Nov 18, 1779, Sarah Cass, dau of
Moses abbdc. Epping rec: Dec 26, 1818, ae 64, Winthrop Dow, son of
the late Benaiah, a peaceable, honest, industrious man, a Congregationalist. He joined the army promptly, first in Capt Stephen Clark's Epping
company 1775, Zebulon Dow ahbaa in same company; re-enlisted 1776
for N Y State service, Capt Daniel Gordon, Col Tash, receipted Sept 20,
1776, for £8-10-0. In this company were also Zebulon and Ebenezer
Dow adadh. He enlisted a third time for the Rhode Island campaign,
Capt Nathan Brown, Col Jacob Gale, mustered out after serving 28
days to Aug 1778.   Children:

a   Mary b Nov 22, 1780   b   Phineas b May 6, 1782
c   Moses b Jan 27, 1784   d   Sarah b Oct 3, 1785; d Jan 31, 1870
e   Abigail b June 6, 1787
f   Delila b July 22, 1789; d Jan 26, 1861. This d rec wholly error; Delila m Ep-
        ping Oct 1, 1811, Mead Folsom. One wonders if Epping rec is not also wrong
        above; Abigail Dow m Feb 10, 1784, True Rundlett (date?)
g   Samuel b Feb 13, 1792

Mary Dow adadaba d Mch 13, 1846; m Mch 14, 1806, Nathaniel
Durgin b June 16, 1782, son of Samuel of Lee, grandson of Jonathan and
Judith (Edgerly) of Lee. They lived Sunset Hill, Northwood. Children:

a   Sarah b Oct 19, 1807; d Feb 8, 1878; m Oct 1829, Daniel Bean
b   Gardner b July 1810; d Oct 8, 1877; m Lucinda Folsom of Epping; dau m——
        Holt of Epping
c   Olive J b June 1812; m Sept 8, 1831, Edson Hill of Northwood and Manchester
d   Mary A b June 1814; d Apr 27, 1875; m John Nealley of Northwood; daus,—
        Loanna, Rouetta
e   Samuel b Sept 30, 1816; d 1837
f   Harriett T b July 1817; m Smith Knowles of Northwood; son Henry in 1922
        merchant of Epsom

Phineas Dow adadabb d Apr 14, 1845; farmer and tanner of the
turnpike south of the Narrows, where the brook was dammed for power;
m Nov 26, 1807, Elizabeth Hoyt (Hoitt, rec) b Sept 5, 1790, d May 14,
1879, dau of Joshua and Betsey (Gerrish) (Smith, State rec) of Northwood Narrows. Children:

a   Elizabeth b Dec 1, 1808; m Benaiah Dow adadagd; 2nd Apr 2, 1843, Benjamin
        Cram of Pittsfield; d Apr 29, 1898; son,—Melvin D Cram
b   Lucinda J b Dec 23, 1811; d Oct 23, 1830
c   Miriam F b Mch 8, 1814; d Feb 9, 1895; m Jan 1, 1835, Asa Bickford Jr of
        Northwood; 2nd Benjamin Coffin of Concord. Children, by 1st husband,—
        Charles H, Anna, Clara
d   Eben Coe b Apr 2, 1818
e   Sarah C b Feb 13, 1822; m May 11, 1843, Samuel B Cilley d 1874
f   Emily M b Mch 1, 1827; m June 21, 1845, John B Hill of Northwood; chil-
        dren,—Laura, Frank, Jennie, Fred

Eben Coe Dow adadabbd inherited the homestead and carried on
the business begun by his father; realty assessed 1850 at $1,500; m June

19, 1845, Naomi Maxfield b Feb 7, 1819, d Apr 30, 1898, dau of James and Rachel (Blake) of Chichester.   Children:

a   Irving b Oct 20, 1846
b   James Everett b June 25, 1850; census names these Phineas E and Eben
c   Sarah E b June 26, 1852; d Dec 22, 1857

Irving Dow adadabbda of Northwood Narrows, active in business and local politics; owns a shoe factory and other industries; m July 3, 1876, Lizetta Emerson, dau of Henry and Maria (Carter) of Northwood. Children:

a   Fred Everett b Apr 15, 1879
b   Frank Irving b June 16, 1881; d July 5, 1900

Fred E Dow adadabbdaa, shoe cutter, moved to Manchester; **m** Georgetown, Mass, Oct 27, 1896, Jennie A Harris, ae 18, b Brewer, Me, dau of Abner M and Carrie A (Greenleaf); 2nd Sept 21, 1907, Sadie Agnes Gillan, ae 29, dau of John L and Annie (Jameson).   Three children by 1st wife:

a   Abner Harris b Apr 1, 1897; of Northwood 1915
b   Irving b Aug 12, 1898; vol 9th Mass, in France 1917
c   ——b and d Laconia June 18, 1903   d   Lizetta
e   ——b and d Manchester May 20, 1921

James E Dow adadabbdb lives Ardmore, Pa, salesman of Furniture, m July 3, 1882, Genevieve Wheeler b Sheboygan Falls, Wis, Apr 25, 1859; div; m 2nd Hattie Merry. Two children by 1st wife:

a   Robert Irving b Pittsburgh Apr 25, 1885; not living
b   Hoyt Eben b Phila Jan 3, 1889; went with mother
c   Theodosia N b Dec 21, 1898

Hoyt E Dow adadabbdbb, teacher of Denver, Colo, m Apr 10, 1915, Ollie Kate Winner of Durango.   Children:

a   David Hoyt b Feb 28, 1916   b   ——b June 1918

Moses Dow adadabc d Epping Mch 12, 1862, well known citizen all his life; farmer, m June 23, 1813, Nancy (Anna, census) Sanborn of Brentwood b Apr 11, 1786, d Jan 30, 1875.   Children:

a   Theodore Moses b 1814; d Epping Sept 30, 1835, unm; will named father executor
b   Sarah Ann b Oct 10, 1816; d Oct 25, 1836
c   Eliza Jane b Apr 17, 1819; d 1892; m Capt A Chaser Barber of Epping
d   Emily Greenleaf b Aug 17, 1821; d Sept 13, 1826
e   Winthrop Sanborn b Mch 9, 1824; d May 28, 1825
f   Winthrop Norris b Apr 9, 1828

Winthrop N Dow adadabcf, educated at Pembroke Academy, roommate of B F Prescott, afterwards Governor; for several years merchant, drifted into the lumber business, incidentally owning great tracts of standing timber; became one of the best known and wealthiest men in the State, always prominent in political and social life; mason of high degree; many positions of honor, many years treasurer of Rockingham Co, colonel on Gov Head's staff, trustee of Robinson's Female Seminary, special railroad commissioner 1888-92, director of Five Cents Savings Bank of Exeter, vice pres of Exeter Banking Co, etc; lived Exeter; d suddenly Sept 12, 1903; m June 18, 1859, Judith Ellen Robinson of Brentwood, dau of Jonathan and Nancy (Lane). Children:

   a   Albert Nelson b May 30, 1860
   b   Annie Marietta b Sept 8, 1863; 1919 artist of Exeter, mother with her; unm
   c   Florence b Mch 24, 1867; unm

Albert N Dow adadabcfa, prominent citizen and business man of Exeter, bank officer, carrying on timber business, m Aug 8, 1898, Florence E Griffin of New London b 1870, dau of Leroy and Ruth A (Fitts).   Children:

   a   Ruth Ellen b May 8, 1899; Wellesley College 1920
   b   Winthrop Griffin b June 4, 1901; Harvard 1922
   c   Emily Robinson b May 26, 1904; Robinson Female Seminary 1922
   d   Albert Neal b Apr 23, 1906; Exeter High School 1923
   e   Richard Lane b Mch 13, 1914   f   Norris Fitz b Apr 17, 1916

Delia Dow adadabf m Mead Folsom b July 1, 1885, of Epping, son of Benjamin and Abigail (Peaslee). Children:

   a   Lucinda b Dec 8, 1811; m May 19, 1840; Gardner D Durgin; dau,—**Mary D**
   b   Abigail E b Nov 15, 1813; d May 29, 1834; m Theophilus Norris

Samuel Dow adadabg lived West Epping; d Jan 26, 1861; m Mary Folsom b 1801, d Jan 22, 1870. Children:

   a   Folsom b 1827   b   ——twin dau

Folsom Dow adadabga located in Wahpeton, S D, about 1870; d about 1915; m Josephine Losinger of Chicago. Children:

   a   Clarence Samuel d 1917 on a Montana ranch, unm
   b   Mary m——Richter

—— **Dow** adadabgb m L M Blake of West Epping. Children:

   a   Abbie m George Bean of Springvale, Mo; d without children
   b   Sarah m Frank Prescott; no children
   c   A Trask of Manchester; m twice; 1 child by 1st wife

Mary Dow adadae m Jonathan Blake of Northwood b Nov 25, 1754 d Nov 4, 1825. She d Nov 30, 1825. Children:

   a   Jonathan d Jan 19, 1825
   b   Marcy Morris m Nov 27, 1806 John Foss, son of Jonathan of Northwood
   c   John Lauris b Dec 21, 1788; d July 6, 1857
   d   Dudley Dow b 1792; d Mch 6, 1862

Samuel Dow adadag b Nottingham May 5, 1840; m 1791 Dolly Sanborn b Jan 9, 1872, d Jan 4, 1841, dau of Henry and Anna of Kensington. Anna was dau of Jedediah Blake of Epping. Moved to Northwood 1793. Hist Northwood calls him an excellent pioneer and worthy citizen; aided in cutting the first road to the narrows; of great physical strength, not easily discouraged by obstacles. Children:

a Henry b Apr 3, 1792   b Sally b June 21, 1794
c Nancy Sanborn b 1796   d Beniah d Mch 11, 1830
e Samuel b Nov 10, 1809   f John R b Nov 6, 1813

Henry Dow adadaga, selectman of Northwood, for many years justice of the peace, d July 25, 1873; cooper, house joiner, man of much general aptitude, m Dec 29, 1813, Betsey Watson b June 1789, d Sept 17, 1878, dau of William and Elsie (Cilley) of Northwood and Nottingham. They settled near the Narrows. Children:

a Sewell Watson b July 14, 1814   b Joseph T b Jan 6, 1816
c George E b Jan 22, 1819   d Sarah E b Mch 27, 1824

Sewell W Dow adadagaa of Newmarket, where children were born, moved to Hampton, d Jan 16, 1890, selectman 1878 and 1882, presidential elector 1876, leading citizen, taking active part in preparations for Civil War; thoroughly imbued with pride of Hampton, earnest student of its history. He shared historical material with Joseph Dow abbeebbc for incorporation into Hist Hampton. He m Apr 12, 1836, Nancy L Towle b 1813, d Mch 2, 1881; m 2nd, ae 70, Oct 23, 1884, Lydia A Watson, ae 35, dau of Sewell and Lydia; she survived many years, one of the last Dows of Hampton. Children:

a Philene A b Sept 9, 1839; d Newmarket June 15, 1862, unm
b Albon A b Oct 22, 1842; d Feb 24, 1865

Joseph T Dowe adadagab adopted, as did his children, the longer spelling; learned tailoring in Newmarket; pursued it until 1885; in 1850 of Chicopee, Mass, realty assessed $1,800; m Wealthea Ann Higgins b So Hadley, Mass, d Sept 26, 1871; m 2nd (late in life) Mary Van Name of Newark, N J, b Mch 16, 1830. Ten children, of whom:

a Helen Maria b Oct 30, 1840; d Apr 20, 1858
b Francis E b Sept 5, 1842   c Adelaide L b June 18, 1844
d Ella Francilea b Mch 12, 1846   e Henry Sylvester b June 16, 1855
f Shelton Edward b Oct 27, 1857

Francis E Dowe adadagabb, merchant of Philadelphia, moved about 1900 to Norwich, Conn, merchant; m Jan 31, 1872, Emma Frances Haslam b Christiania, Pa, Feb 24, 1844, d Oct 1917, member of Society of Friends, descended from the Steelman and Godfrey families, member of D A R, active always in philanthropic work. During reconstruction Francis was clerk of the court in Va. Children:

a Warren Kinsman b July 23, 1873; Detroit 1922; m 2nd Oct 29, 1918, Margaret Thompson
b Amy Haslam, teacher of Philadelphia and Norwich; unm

Adelaide E Dowe adadagabc d Dec 3, 1891; m Feb 16, 1865, Warren Downe Kinsman, merchant of Springfield, Mass, son of Timothy W and Johanna (Downe). Children:

a ——dau d young   b Helen I of Springfield, unm
c Rose A m Arthur F Bassett   d Howard L of Springfield

Ella F Dowe adadagabd m Nov 14, 1871, S F Littlefield of Milton, Mass; d Jan 13, 1882; 2 children

Henry S Dowe adadagabe d July 29, 1882, unm. Some Henry S Dowe d Brookline, Mass, Feb 10, 1918

Shelton E Dowe adadagabf m Feb 21, 1889, Jessie McDowall Cochran b Madison, Ind; moved to Denver, Colo; 1 child, untraced

George E Dow adadagac, whip maker and salesman of Westfield, Mass, worked 1863-4 in Govt armory in Springfield; d Oct 13, 1902; m Feb 1, 1841, Julia E Sackett.   Children:

  a Maria b Sept 12, 1842; m May 26, 1869, A G Taylor of Springfield.   3 dau, 1 son, latter d ae 4
  b Henry B b Apr 26, 1846; d Jan 8, 1847
  c Charles E b Nov 24, 1847; m Sept 20, 1871, Mary M De Witt of Springfield; 3 dau (2 d young), 1 son

Charles E Dow adadagacc and Mary De Witt had:

  a George F b Springfield 1873; m June 22, 1903, Etta N Wells, ae 24, dau of John and Sarah F (Root)

Sarah E Dow adadagad m Mch 1, 1854, Israel Buzzell of Barrington d in army, son of David and Lois (Leighton).   Child:

  a Henry Dow b Mch 18, 1858; d Feb 25, 1916; m Mrs Addie I Worthen of Concord, dau of John and Polly Carter; dau,—Blanche

Sally Dow adadagb m Jan 25, 1815, Joseph M Trickey, saddler of Portsmouth, genealogy untraced; went 1827 to Gilmanton; she m 2nd very late in life Eliphalet Emerson of Northwood.   All buried in old south meeting house ground in Gilmanton.   Children, by 1st husband:

  a Henry D b June 15, 1816; d Aug 31, 1865
  b Charles T b Dec 28, 1818; d Dec 18, 1829
  c Dorothy A b Nov 21, 1822; m H A Jackson; went to Chicago
  d Joseph S b Dec 12, 1827; merchant at Northwood Narrows; d Mch 10, 1901; m Mary J Russell b Franconia Dec 5, 1834, d Northwood Mch 15, 1906, dau of Joseph S and Abigail S (Pinkham). Children,—Frank E, Fred, Abigail, Nellie A, Mary Ann
  e George B b Mch 25, 1834; lived Lawrence, Mass; 2 children

Nancy S Dow adadagc m Dec 9, 1817, George James of Northwood. Children:

  a Winthrop Dow b May 18, 1819; d July 24, 1847
  b Beniah M b Dec 2, 1824; m Mary D Haynes
  c Frances A b Nov 8, 1840; m Henry A Willard of Westminster, Vt

Benaiah Dow adadagd m Eliza Dow adadaab; lived but a short time afterwards; no children

Samuel Dow adadage, whip manufacturer of Westfield, d Sept 25, 1885; m June 1, 1835, Belinda Rose Robinson b Nov 16, 1812, dau of

Jonathan and Lucy (Dunton) of Pembroke; m 2nd Aug 31, 1870, E Maria Herrick.   Children, by 1st wife:

  a Ellen b Apr 2, 1840; m July 1867 Rev Thomas B Woods, missionary of Rosario, S A
  b Agnes b Feb 6, 1842; d Feb 17, 1845
  c Edwin b Sept 7, 1847; d May 31, 1854

John R Dow adadagf lived on the homestead, d Mch 24, 1890; m Nov 17, 1836, Rhoda Swain b Northfield Aug 30, 1818, d Nov 19, 1893, dau of William and Betsey (Durgin), grand dau of Phineas Swain, Rev soldier of Northwood.   Children:

  a Charles E b Jan 7, 1838   b Samuel T b Apr 26, 1840
  c William A b Sept 2, 1843; corporal, d in army Feb 2, 1864, unm
  d Nancy S b Jan 12, 1845; d Aug 20, 1847
  e John Plumer b July 20, 1847; d Sept 15, 1880; m Eva Morrison, dau of John of Northwood, survived him. No children
  f Frank B b Feb 17, 1851; d Aug 10, 1882; m May 31, 1878, Hattie M Webster, ae 19, d July 16, 1910. No children
  g George H b May 26, 1858; d Sept 5, 1859

Charles E Dow adadagfa m Mch 2, 1859, Susan C Hoitt, dau of John and Judith (Hoitt) of Northwood; both living East Northwood 1917.   Children:

  a Annie Belle b May 5, 1866; d 1879
  b Susie Ethel b Mch 20, 1876; m Aug 19, 1897, William B Noyes, teacher in Conn; son Russell Dow b 1898, grad Worcester Polytechnic

Samuel T Dow adadagfb, veteran of Civil War, d Northwood Aug 1, 1915; m Oct 1, 1859, Laury A Yeaton, ae 22, dau of John Jr and Lucretia (McDaniels); m 2nd Mch 29, 1873, wid Lizzie L Kelley b Mch 8, 1848, d Apr 15, 1900, dau of Pierce L and Mary A (Smith) Burt of Bath, Me.   Children, by 1st wife:

  a Nellie b Nov 1864; for several years Christian Adventist missionary in China; unm
  b Nettie J b Aug 29, 1866; m Mch 31, 1888, Walter L Chesley of Framington, N H; no children
  c Grace L b 1867; m Dec 25, 1888, Lemuel C Tasker b 1866, d Sept 3, 1917, son of Nathaniel and Susan (Richardson) of Northwood; no children
  d George Albert b Aug 6, 1871; d Aug 25, 1895; m Mch 5, 1892, Angie M Palmer, ae 23, dau of Orrin A and Rebecca (Towle) of Northwood. No children; she m 2nd Rev Edwin Joy

Miriam Dow adadai d Sept 15, 1833, ae 61 (gravestone rec); m Oct 23, 1799, Benjamin Bickford b Aug 24, 1769, d Northwood Apr 28, 1849, son of Solomon and Susan (Fox).   They settled in Northwood, next home to her brother Samuel.   Children:

  a Dudley d Apr 7, 1824, ae 24
  b Samuel b July 14, 1802; moved to Belmont; m Belinda Towle of Gilmanton, dau of Simon. Children,—Martha, Dudley D, Belinda Jane
  c James b Dec 3, 1807   d George b Dec 2, 1809; d Aug 1833

Ebenezer Dow adadh has been always a genealogical trouble maker, not content to stay in any one place, but moving frequently where vital statistics were ill kept. He himself disappears 1784. He m So Hampton May 19, 1761, Sarah French, whose sister Miriam m Benaiah, his brother. No evidence of association with the Friends. He bought Mch 19, 1767, 33 acres in Nottingham, now East Northwood. Nothing more appears here and 30 years later this land was owned by Daniel Hoitt. He enlisted Epping, Capt John Norris, Col Poor, drawing pay for 2 mos 15 days from June 15, 1775, with $4 allowance for overcoat. Next year he, Winthrop and Zebulon Dow in same company, was in company of Capt Samuel Gordon, Col Tash, for N Y State service. The three drew the same pay Sept 20, 1776, 8£-10-0. The sgt Ebenezer Dow at Saratoga Sept 1777 is ahbg. Ebenezer appears next Feb 7, 1780, buying a homestead farm from Henry Dearborn. This he sold Nov 8, 1784. All subsequent references to him point to Meredith, N H. Several legal papers have been quoted to prove his children, but the Author only knows these at second hand. Land was passed by Ebenezer to Philip, Jonathan and Jenny Dow. Next:—Philip had a brother Sewell b 1780. Finally, a great grandson asserts that Jenny was not a Dow but an unm sister of Jonathan's wife. As she does not appear further, this is of no consequence. No b rec appear for any of them, but they may be in the unsearched rec of Epping 2nd church. There may have been children who d young, but we can safely record only the three:

    a Philip probably 1st born. No other line has the name Philip in it
    b Jonathan; identity far from certain
    c Sewell b 1780

    Leon C Dow, a great grandson, writes 1927 that Philip was b Epping; d Meredith ae 77-7-7 (date not given); that his brothers and sisters were,—Ebenezer b Dec 5, 1798; Jonathan b Apr 28, 1801; Gilman; Susan; Polly; Lucy b May 12, 1804

Philip Dow adadha was known only in fragments until a letter from a descendant was found 1923 in Edgar Dow's unedited papers. He d before 1850; census gives his wid Lydia b 1775, living in Meredith. She was Lydia Swain, said b and d Meredith, but probably from New Hampton. Philip was a cooper of Meredith and had 7 sons, 5 dau. As official proof has been found of only one, some guessing must ensue:

    a Ebenezer b Jan 5, 1799, possibly in New Hampton (identity certain)
    b Jonathan   c Abram S b Nov 10, 1816 (identity certain)

Let us repeat here the Meredith disconnected Dows for comparison: Gustavus m Mch 11, 1844, Sarah F Evans of Meredith; untraced
—— Dow (female) b Meredith Sept 10, 1855
Hannah of Meredith m New Hampton Apr 22, 1821, Greenleaf Fogg of Thornton.
Jane b Meredith, d Meredith 1859; no other data.
Sabrina b Meredith m George Hilliard; dau Catherine m Laconia 1861 Henry Moulton.
Mary of Meredith int pub Apr 1, 1833, to Nathan Clay

Ebenezer Dow adadhaa is said in 1850 census b 1793; d Moulton-borough Mch 6, 1881; of Meredith m Dec 12, 1826, Nancy Wiggin of Meredith d Aug 27, 1882, ae 77, dau of Chase and Mary (Eaton). Known children tally with 1850 census:

    a Ebenezer Lawrence b Sept 6, 1827   b Smith b 1830 (census, 1832 by d rec)
    c Lucien b Moultonborough Sept 28, 1834
    d Mary A b 1844; m July 3, 1861, James E Bickford of Meredith

Ebenezer L Dow adadhaaa, 1848 of Gilford, 1894 merchant of Laconia and very substantial citizen, m Mary Octavia Libbey b San-bornton, d Lakeport Jan 31, 1912, ae 77-1-13, dau of George W, carpenter, and Martha (Graves). Libby Gen gives Geo W and Sally M (Sanborn) of Belmont. Perhaps more children than here appear:

    a ——son b Laconia July 21, 1856; unknown
    b George W b Oct 17, 1862; d Laconia Feb 1, 1912, unm
    c Herbert Edgar b Laconia July 9, 1868   d Albert E b Laconia 1869

Herbert E Dow adadhaaac, meat dealer of Laconia, m Waverly, Mass, Nov 27, 1887, Grace Madeline Shepard, ae 25, dau of James and Elizabeth (Douglass) of Laconia. No rec of children. He d Concord Oct 17, 1906, of "poisoning from D Mile's Restorative Nervine."

Albert E Dow adadhaaad of Laconia m June 26, 1894, Verdie V Vesey, ae 17, dau of E and Alice V (Moulton). In 1908 carpenter of Belmont with wife and 2 children:

    a Ruth Evelyn b Laconia Jan 25, 1896; 1915 bookkeeper of Laconia
    b Alice V

Smith Dow adadhaab, farmer of Meredith, d tuberculosis Jan 30, 1865, ae 33; m Jan 1853 Louisa Boardman Clark b Aug 20, 183-, dau of Stephen and Ezza (Muller). Children, perhaps others:

    a —son b Meredith Aug 31, 1856; unknown
    b —Louisa m 2nd B F Wentworth

Lucien Dow adadhaac, wood and grain dealer of Laconia, d Mch 15, 1903; m 1st Harriet A —— (Chase?) b Meredith Aug 18, 1834, d Laconia Mch 20, 1901, dau of Daniel R and Belinda C (Chase), farmers of New Hampton; m 2nd May 7, 1902, Vittie M Chase, ae 65, dau of Madison and Nancy (Roberts). Meredith 1908 directory gives her wid. Child:

    a Emma E b Meredith Sept 2, 1860; m Jan 1, 1881, James L Chace of Mere-dith

Jonathan Dow adadhab has been thought the missing son of adabig, the only basis being the recurrence of name Smith Glidden. This error arose from the popularity of Smith Glidden, for whom several children were named. Jonathan of Meredith d Jan 5, 1846; m Eliza Glidden b Sutton, Vt, July 12, 1812, living 1883. Indisputable family rec says 3 sons:

    a   John M b Meredith Aug 23, 1836
    b   Smith Glidden b Meredith Jan 28, 1840   c   (guess) Joseph S

John M Dow adadhaba, in 1883 laborer of Boston replied to a genealogical inquiry by Edgar R Dow; m Mch 29, 1860, Elvira Kimball. Kimball Gen wrongly calls him John Mooney Dow (abbegbde); she b Nov 3, 1836 (Nov 4, 1835, Kimball Gen), dau of Thomas Jefferson and Betsey Burnham (Dolloff). Only child:

    a   Minnie E b Boston Feb 15, 1871; about 1915 artist in Laconia, unm with father

Smith G Dow adadhabb, Meredith shoemaker 1860, stable keeper of Newton, Mass, 1898, restaurant keeper Weymouth 1910, d Meredith Aug 3, 1913; m Dec 22, 1860, Anna C Bickford; 2nd Oct 8, 1898, Anna (Currier) Dow, div, b Dover, dau of Samuel and Sarah (Hayes). Child:

    a   Frank Clifton b Weymouth 1883, shoemaker of Manchester, m Jan 1, 1910,
        Ora Janet Sanborn, ae 19, dau of Edward J and Oressa J (Barker)

Joseph S Dow adadhabc is found in two rec, presumably identical. Joseph, laborer of Meredith, had:

    a   ——dau b Dec 13, 1862

Joseph S b Meredith, shoemaker of Natick, Mass, had:

    b   ——son b Meredith Aug 3, 1864. This son is Herbert S Dow, in 1896 connected
        with an entertainment bureau of Boston

Abram S Dow adadhac is the ancestor of the Bristol, N H, Dows; farmer of Meredith, Alexandria and Bristol, d Bristol Mch 15, 1881; m Jan 8, 1849, Mary Jane Moore (Morse, State rec) b New Hampton Jan 8, 1822, d Bristol Apr 18, 1877, dau of Joseph. Children:

    a   Charles G b Meredith July 22, 1850
    b   Anna M b Sept 10, 1852; d July 26, 1871
    c   John G b June 2, 1854   d   George H b May 7, 1859
    e   Ellie M b Aug 2, 1865; m Edwin Smith

Charles G Dow adadhaca inherited the homestead, d Bristol July 1, 1906; m 1st New Hampton Sept 2, 1877, Maria B (Clifford Gen) or Martha H (State rec) Clifford b Alexandria 1861, dau of Sylvester and Hannah (Gordon); div; she m 2nd May 27, 1900, Henry L Cranton of Haverhill. He m 2nd July 5, 1900, Katie A Keyser, ae 47, dau of Allen and Sarah (Barrett) of Hardwick, Vt. Children:

    a   Lewis Sylvester b Bristol Aug 18, 1880
    b   Leon Chester b Nov 23, 1882   c   Alfred b Dec 3, 1884
    d   von Carl b Jan 16, 1887   e   Richard b Apr 12, 1890
    f   ——dau b Bristol Feb 22, 1893

Lewis S Dow adadhacaa, laborer of New Hampton, m Aug 13, 1902,

Ethel Maud Wells b 1877, dau of Lyman B and Ellen J (Gordon).   Children:

    a   Ethel Gordon Wells b May 30, 1904
    b   Daniel Sherman b Dec 28, 1906
    c   George E b Franklin Sept 27, 1908
    d   ——son b Bristol July 8, d July 9, 1909
    e   Dorothy E b Laconia Apr 16, 1912
    f   Raymond C b Belmont Nov 24, 1913
    g   Frank Harrison b Gilford July 30, 1915

Leon C Dow adadhacab, farmer and school teacher of New Hampton, m 1st Dec 13, 1905, Ethel Jennie Morrill (Merrill, State rec) d Concord Mch 29, 1910, dau of Henry H and Mary D (Smith); m 2nd Dec 30, 1912, Hazel G Blake, ae 18, dau of Simeon W and Amy R (Smith) of New Hampton.   Children:

    a   Arthur Sanborn b Aug 2, 1907
    b   Pauline Morrill b Mch 14, d May 10, 1910
    c   (By 2nd wife) Rachel   d   Frances

Alfred Dow adadhacac, farmer of Bristol, m Dec 14, 1909, Edna May Bean, ae 18, dau of Warren M and Helen J (Cameron) of Laconia

V Carl Dow adadgacad, farmer, m Concord Apr 24, 1914, Melva Green, ae 21, b Atlanta, Ga, dau of James A, merchant, and Emma (Thomas)

Richard Dow adadhacae, farmer of Gilford, m Berwick, Me, Aug 31, 1913, Susie H Willard b Bristol 1894, dau of Daniel M and Amorilla (Thompson).   Children:

    a   ——son b Dec 31, 1913   b   Grace Ruth b Oct 30, 1914

John G Dow adadhacc, farmer of Bristol, d Sept 24, 1884; m 1877 Laura A Fellows, ae 19, of Plymouth

George H Dow adadhacd, farmer of Bristol, m New Hampton July 4, 1877, Zoa Olive (Lora A, Hist Bristol) Wiggin, ae 19, dau of Stephen. He d Apr 22, 1880; she m 2nd Sept 28, 1881, Joseph Nelson b Nov 19, 1856, son of Stephen

Sewell Dow adadhc d tuberculosis Lynn, Mass, Oct 12, 1835, ae 55; m June 12, 1804 Eleanor Whitcher of New Hampton.   His father's homestead was in Meredith Bridge, part now Laconia.   They bought a farm in Thornton, where he appears in the 1821 tax list, having lived there over 15 years.   His sons having gone to Lynn, he presumably followed with his wife.   Children:

    a   Luke Whitcher b about 1803   b   Perkins Hewes b about 1808
    c   Thomas Wooster b about 1812
    d   John b about 1816; d unm in young manhood
    e   Ebenezer b Meredith 1822   f   Eleanor b about 1825

A grandson says that Eleanor Whitcher m 2nd late in life.   **This is**

to be doubted; she was living 1850 with her son Ebenezer in Methuen, Mass.

Luke W Dow adadhca d Lynn Apr 10, 1885; m Lynn Oct 27, 1831, Eliza Guilford b 1812, dau of Rufus of Lynn and Susan (Pitman). Children, 7 older mentioned in Lynn published rec:

a   ——b and d Feb 7, 1833   b   Marietta b Jan 1, 1834
c   Elbridge b Nov 28, 1835; d Dec 27, 1843
d   Caroline Augusta b Nov 12, 1837
e   Joseph b Nov 10, 1839; living 1850. Some son of Luke W d Dec 25, 1846
f   Charles Warren b Nov 18, 1843   g   George Elbridge b Feb 25, 1845
h   Elwin Pitman b Feb 25, 1850   i   Edwin Guilford, his twin
j   Annie Eliza b June 15, 1853
k   Charles, son of Luke W, d Aug 20, 1852; not in any family rec

Marietta Dow adadhcab m Benjamin F Hall of Marshfield, Mass. children:

a   Irvin, unm   b   Walter   c   Charles Warren
d   Solon Alexander   e   Etta Maria

Charles W Dow adadhcaf m May 11, 1867, Sarah Jane Graham; in 1922 writes an interesting genealogical letter with firm, clear hand. Children:

a   John Charles b Dec 17, 1867   b   Francis William b Sept 27, 1872
c   Frederick Warren b May 29, 1876; manufacturer of Swampscott and Boston, returned 1922 to Lynn; member Sons of Revolution

John C Dow adadhcafa of Lynn m Dec 1895 Ellen Light b Eng. Children:

a   Charles Warren b 1896   b   Alice Denise b Dec 10, 1902

Frederick W Dow adadhcafc m Harriet Grant b Me.   Children:

a——b and d Apr 10, 1901   b   Dorothy Louise b Lynn Aug 28, 1905

Elwin Pitman Dow adadhcah of Lynn m Ida M Allen.   At least 4 children:

a   Harry A b 1879   b   Clarence E b 1881   c   Edwin P
d   Helena C b Lynn 1888; m July 27, 1910, William S Thomas, ae 24, son of Thomas and Isabella D (Maxwell)

Harry A Dow adadhcaha of Lynn m Feb 24, 1903, Mabel May Healey, ae 26, dau of William and Elvira

Clarence E Dow adadhcahb m Lynn Dec 29, 1901, Melvina Cook, ae 20, dau of Richard and Mary (Duff)

Edwin P Dow adadhcahc m Almira Pond Kenney.   Children, b Lynn:

a   Elizabeth P b Feb 23, 1906   b   Wallace Edwin b May 5, 1909

Edwin G Dow adadhcai, shoemaker of Lynn, writes 1903 particulars of his own line, thinking Sewell Dow to be son of Jonathan; evidently a

man of education and ability; m July 3, 1879, Annie A Harris b 1854 of
Danvers.   Children, all b Lynn:

   a Ernest G b Sept 14, 1881; unm in 1903   b Howard F b Apr 28, 1883
   c Edith I b July 6, 1885   d Mary b Dec 13, 1889

Ernest G Dow adadhcaia m Leonie M Gautro.   Children, b Lynn:

   a Ruth Estella b Aug 31, 1903; d Apr 7, 1904
   b Helen Frances b Aug 17, 1906

Howard F Dow adadhcaib, electrician of Portsmouth, N H, m Nov
27, 1907, Blanche M Wholley, dau of Dennis and Annie (Herbert).   Children:

   a Frances G b Everett July 31, 1908   b Richard Herbert b Lynn May 7, 1910

Edith Isabelle Dow adadhcaic m Feb 18, 1905, Cyrus Howard
Hapgood, ae 26, of Lynn, son of Cyrus S and Clara A (Connor)

Perkins H Dow adadhcb (name Hughes in one rec), in 1850 census
laborer, mason, realty $1,500;   later farmer, m Lynn June 15, 1834,
Catherine Tuttle b N H 1810.   Lynn pub rec give oldest 3, census all,
family rec completes the list:

   a Almira L b 1835; living Lynn 1923, unm and "pretty smart for my age."
   b Martha A b 1837; m William Warren Emerton son of John and Eliza Brewer
      (Mudge) of Lynn. He d about 1913; children,— Emma, Katie, and William
   c Frances E b 1839; m Henry Lindsay of Lynn, now of Boston; children,— Edmond and Ella
   d Charles Sewall b 1841; left 4 children, of whom,—Bertha, Elizabeth, Fred
   e Amanda Alvina b Oct 23, 1843; m Frank Chase
   f James Otis b Nov 3, 1845; left 1 child
   g Andrew; in 1923 living Beverly; married but no children
   h Nathan T N b Oct 4, 1847; d scarlet fever Jan 1, 1849
   i Henry living Lynn 1923; m but no children

Charles S Dow adadhcbd of Beverly, m Lois A Bray.   A dau:

   a Bertha Louise b 1874, of Beverly, m July 4, 1902, Frank Sidney Cleaves, ae 32,
      son of Joseph F and Julia E (Thompson)

Andrew Jackson Dow adadhcbg of Lynn m 3rd (giving ae 56)
Peabody June 5, 1907, Lola Montey Cate, ae 43, dau of William and
Susan F (Hanson)

Thomas W Dow adadhcc m Haverhill, Mass, Nov 29, 1838, Melinda
Haynes, dau of Warren and Polly (Nichols).   Only child:

   a John Chase b 1839; killed at Antietam

Ebenezer Dow adadhce d tuberculosis Woburn, Mass, Jan 5, 1857
(rec gives parents Jesse and Eleanor);   shoemaker, worked in Maine,
coming to Woburn after 1848;   m Lynn July 15, 1845, Mary E Wentworth (in census Nancy E b Me 1824).   Census gives 2 children b Me;
perhaps others later:

   a Evelyn b 1846   b Sarah E b 1848

Eleanor Dow adadhcf m May 18, 1851, Ephraim Wentworth, both of Woburn; his sister m her brother

Jonathan Dow adadi. Whatever may have been the feelings of Philip Dow adad regarding the Society of Friends, which he had left at the time of his marriage, none of the children continued in it. There have been four instances of return to the Friends, a notable one being at least two sons of adgf. The return of Jonathan Dow adadi must be attributed to his individual choice, probably at his marriage. We know that Jonathan and Elijah Peaslee were close and lifelong friends; that Elijah, whose ancestors and posterity have always been in the Society, was a pioneer of Pittsfield, N H, about 1760, coming from So Hampton or nearby. Jonathan Dow m Lydia —— of Merrimac. The presumption is that she was a birthright Friend, altho there seems no place for her in the Peaslee family. At all events Jonathan was a Friend until his death Aug 5, 1812. His wid d Pittsfield Mch 28, 1834. Three of his descendants bore the name Elijah Peaslee Dow.

While Pittsfield had its meeting house, it never was an independent meeting, but a branch of the Amesbury monthly meeting, not having its own pastor, when that functionary came into existence. Cyrus Dow, last Quaker Dow of Pittsfield, died 1917. Later Charles E Peaslee, great grandson of Elijah, long pastor of the Gonic meeting and the Peaslee family were the only ones in Pittsfield actively in the Society. The spirit has not died out and there was a plan on foot in 1923 for a resumption of regular meetings. Charles E Peaslee has now retired to Dowborough, Pittsfield. In the summer of 1927 the Author visited the place, on the hill top southeast of Pittsfield village. The meeting house is now spick and span and well attended each first day.

In the 1790 census Pittsfield people are generally listed as of Pembroke; here Jonathan appears 1a, 3b, 2c, according with our knowledge of his children. One child was born after 1790. That only one was born prior to 1774 indicates that Jonathan married at a little more than the usual age for that time. He was a farmer. His will names wife and four children, the son Jeremiah being disinherited. In Quakerdom there is only one reason for such act. Children in order of mention in will:

a   Jonathan b about 1799   b   David b by 1787
c   Moses, probably 1st born d   Lydia
e   Jeremiah b 1792 (census)

Jonathan Dow adadia, farmer of Pittsfield, d Aug 28, 1833 (Friends rec); m Amesbury meeting June 2, 1814, Abigail Gove of Epsom b 5: 2: 1791; d 11: 5: 1830, dau of Moses and Abigail (Brown). Rochester and Epsom Friends rec have not been searched. Throughout, there is always genealogical difficulty from the Friends practice of avoiding mention of a maiden name. All children in Amesbury minutes:

a   Sarah G b 24: 4 mo: 1815   b   Lewis b 6: 3 mo: 1817

c   Anna b 1: 12 mo: 1818; m James T Higgins
d   Arland b 27: 8 mo: 1822; d unm ae about 21, Oct 15, 1841
e   Gardner b 2: 1 mo: 1830; in 1850 unm laborer of Colebrook, N H; d unm in
    Conn

Sarah G Dow (Sarah Gove) adadiaa m Rochester meeting Dec 28, 1854, Elijah Peaslee of Rochester, son of Samuel and Mary. A son is today member of the Friends

An error occurs in Rochester rec, giving him as Abijah Gove b Dec 17, 1801. Date is right. The son:

a   Henry Wheeler b Rochester Nov 11, 1855; in 1923 of Rochester

Lewis Dow adadiab, shoemaker of Pittsfield, d July 4, 1880; m Northwood Sept 15, 1844, Mary Dow adadice. While the place was unusual, the marriage was according to Friends customs. Mary d Dec 24, 1901. Children:

a   Mary Elizabeth b 1845; d Mch 9, 1864   b   Abigail G b 1847
c   Silas Wright b Dec 4, 1848; last of the Pittsfield Quaker Dow, d Nov 7, 1917,
    unm
d   ——dau b and d Oct 23, 18—
e   Lewis Leroy b Aug 13, 1853; d Mch 23, 1858
f   Almys Laforest b July 14, 1857; d Dec 22, 1917, without issue
g   Florence A b Aug 25, 1861; d Aug 13, 1906, unm

Abigail G Dow adadiabb living Pittsfield 1922, member of the Friends, m Nov 12, 1873, Josiah Prentice Staniels d Oct 10, 1888. Mrs Staniels corrected or furnished the data of every descendant of adadi. Children:

a   Lizzie T b Dec 16, 1874; d May 25, 1913, unm
b   Martha A b Sept 23, 1877; m Pittsfield Sept 15, 1900, Mayland P Ames of
    Epsom; div. Martha Ames lives hardby the meeting house, a cheery soul,
    bed ridden many years and busying herself making hooked rugs

Annie Dow adadiac, employed in So Danvers, Mass, m Dover Oct 29, 1862, James T Higgins of Rochester

Arland Dow adadiad. Some unknown Arland makes confusion, for Amesbury gives:

a   Arland, son of Arnol and Phebe A of Amesbury, b 15: 10 mo: 1841. He is un-
    found

David Dow adadib, generally known as deacon, a colloquial title, as he was always a Friend.

He was for many years an elder in the Friends meeting; farmer, then saddler, next harness maker, and finally clock maker. His specialty was large 8 day clocks, of brass and large size, of excellent quality. Some of these clocks are still dependence for time keeping in Pittsfield households. He m Sept 28, 1807, Elinor (Ellanor in rec) Gove of Weare, youngest child of John and Martha (Dow) adaha. She d Oct 2, 1821. He m 2nd Berwick, Me, 13: 11 mo: 1825, Esther Morrill, dau of David and Sarah of

Berwick, 4th in descent from Jacob Morrill, Quaker of Hampton 1701.
Children; none by Esther:

a   James Gove b June 25, 1810   b   Moses b July 4, 1812
c   Squiers b May 26, 1821, d young
d   David Greeley b Aug 4, 1820. Rec gave 1824, Gove Gen correctly gives 1820
    and David Gove

James G Dow adadiba m Bolton Oct 18, 1835 Sarah Houghton of
Bolton, Mass; lived in later life in Milton. He was major of militia.
Children:

a   Herbert b 1834; killed at July 4 celebration, ae about 21
b   James Edwin (Ebenezer, census) b 1838
c   David b Pittsfield 1839
d   Sarah E b Pittsfield 1842; of Milton m Nov 4, 1861, Sewall S Ingraham

James E Dow adadibab of Milton m Jan 15, 1860, Abbie L Warren
b 1841, dau of Oren O and Abby, all of Pittsfield; enlisted, she d while
he was at the front; he m 2nd Olivia Towne; moved to Mass; d in a
soldier's home.   Children:

a   Oren d ae 2 mos   b   Walter, untraced   c   William d young
d   Herbert, untraced   e   Nellie

David Dow adadibac of Milton m Dec 16, 1862, Lucy A Hayward of
Concord, dau of Reuben and Sarah (Houghton); moved to Boston; only
child:

a   Etta

Moses Dow adadibb, in 1850 shoemaker of Pittsfield, assessed $600;
d June 11, 1854; m June 1, 1836, Betsey B Jones of Pittsfield b 1815, d
Aug 24, 1854.   Only child:

a   Moses Emery b Sept 23, 1836; m Lydia Remmond (Raymond?) of Lynn, Mass;
    d Moultonborough, laborer, married, Oct 4, 1899. A number of children.
    Moultonborough town clerk does not recall any, so they must have left town
    long ago. One child was,—Annie

David G Dow adadibd, shoemaker, lived at times in the Pittsfield
homestead but worked mostly in Seabrook; frozen to death Pittsfield
Dec 1, 1871, ae mis-stated as 49.   In 1850 census he is of No Hampton;
m Abigail Munsey of Barnstead.   After his death, she returned to Pittsfield, surviving 37 years, with 3 children remaining with her.

Durham has her d rec garbled,—Abigail Munsey of Durham, wid of
William Dow, b July 25, 1819, d Pittsfield June 23, 1908, dau of **Henry**
and (Simpson). Twelve in all. Only one name lacking (no posterity
except as given below):

a   Abbie   b   Hannah   c   Anna G b 1849
d   Melvin d in Civil War, unm   e   Addison, unm   f   Miriam
g   Melvina   h   Ida   i   Ada d Pittsfield unm
j   Cinderilla (Cinda E of rec)   k   Lettie J b Pittsfield

Melvina Dow adadibdg m Allen Peabody b Meredith; **moved to**
Woodstock. Two children appear in Lisbon, N H:

a   Frank   m 1894   b   Louise m 1886 James A Hart

Ida Dow adadibdh m —— Sykes; both dead, leaving son,—Harry

Cinda E Dow adadibdj living Pittsfield 1921; m Sept 7, 1887, Benjamin T Blaisdell of Pittsfield

Lettie J Dow adadibdk m Jan 17, 1881, Frank L Moses, both of Pittsfield; 2nd Henry Doningal; living Pittsfield 1921

Moses Dow adadic, farmer of Pittsfield, b Oct 26, 1785, d after 1851; m Mch 27, 1811, Mary Peaslee b Pittsfield Feb 18, 1786; m 2nd May 1, 1826, Hannah Jones b 1790, living 1850, both of Pittsfield. Second m outside Society, hence youngest child not in Friends rec:

a   Lydia b 1: 22: 1812; d Mch 6, 1838
b   Elijah Peaslee b 8: 12 mo: 1813; d Pittsfield Jan 23, 1893, unm
c   Cyrus B b 9: 2: 1817   d   Abraham b 12: 16: 1818
e   Mary b 30: 7 mo: 1823; d 24: 12 mo: 1901; m Lewis Dow adadiab
f   Jonathan b July 30, 1826

Lydia Dow adadica m Loudon June 3, 1854, Amos Peaslee of Rochester; d leaving 2 children. He m 2nd Rhoda Varney; dismissed on that account, but restored when she joined the Society. Lydia's children:

a   Sarah b Apr 3, 1835   b   Lydia Ann b Oct 8, 1836

Cyrus B Dow adadicc m 4: 6 mo: 1846, Sarah S Gove b 16: 9 mo: 1825, dau of Elijah and Anstriss (Southwick) of Epsom
He d Feb 18, 1858; she d Sept 18, 1863. Children:

a   Sarah Abigail b Mch 23, 1847   b   Cyrus F b Dec 11, 1850; d Apr 5, 1851
c   Cyrus F b Apr 24, 1854; d Epping Sept 23, 1883, unm

Sarah Abby Dow adadicca, not living 1921, m Warren E Hilliard b Chichester. Children:

a   Harland m Epsom 1891   b   Frank R m Epsom 1897

Abraham Dow adadicd left the Society; m Pittsfield Oct 14, 1840, Malinda Hilliard b 1823; 2nd Oct 24, 1854, Mary L B Drake, ae 24. Late in life he took his family to Calif. Children, by 1st wife:

a   Cyrus d San Francisco, untraced   b   Lydia A; married, living 1921 in Calif

Jonathan Dow adadicf appears in 1850 census shoemaker, realty $400; m outside the Society Louisa Brown b 1829. Louisa A (Brown) Dow m 2nd Mch 31, 1873, Charles H Osgood, both of Pittsfield. Children:

a   Moses Addison b 1849; d 1850   b   Elijah Peaslee b May 10, 1851

Elijah P Dow adadicfb, farmer of Loudon road, Pittsfield, d Mch 20, 1922; a kindly, well informed gentleman: maintained warm feeling for Friends, but lived far from old meeting house; m Hattie A Lane. Children:

a   Everett A b Pittsfield Feb 17, 1877
b   J Louise b Northwood July 28, 1880; m Arthur Berganson; in 1922 wid with
     2 children

Everett A Dow adadicfba, farmer of Pittsfield, m Jan 2, 1901, Elbra A Babb, ae 23, dau of William S and Jane (Heath).   Child:

a   Marguerite Ethel b Nov 24, 1903

Lydia Dow adadid b Rochester Apr 15, 1789; d China, Me, Mch 10, 1822; m John Jepson b Berwick Aug 24, 1782, d Sept 23, 1822. An epidemic, presumably typhoid, carried off half this family.   Children:

a   Jedediah b Sept 8, 1807   b   Benjamin b July 24, 1809
c   Daniel b Dec 27, 1811; d Nov 12, 1822   d   Isaac b Feb 24, 1814
e   Elijah Dow b Aug 15, 1816; d Sept 5, 1822
f   William b Aug 31, 1818; d Oct 14, 1822   g   John b Mch 4, 1820

Jeremiah Dow adadie appears in 1850 census with no land and no occupation given.   He m Jan 18, 1816, Nancy Dow, both of Pittsfield. She appears in census as Anna b N H 1794.   They separated, she going to Ripton, Vt, with her son.   Her identity not yet found.   A considerable list of Pittsfield Dow in the disconnected chapter may be of adai, bcdbaa, or other lines, but are certainly not of adad.   Jeremiah d 1864.   Children:

a   Newell   b   Asa d Vineland, N J, unm
c   Lucy A   d   Rhoda d Portsmouth June 25, 1896, ae 88, unm

Newell Dow adadiea, farmer of Ripton, Vt, revisited Pittsfield occasionally for many years, recalled by kinsfolk.   His data not found in Vt pub rec, preserved in Hendricks Gen.   He m Almira Folsom.   Children, possibly more:

a   George Newell b Dec 7, 1852   b   Almira

George N Dow adadieaa, farmer of Ripton, moved to Brockport, N Y, where family now live; m Jan 19, 1870, Jessie Edwina Hendricks b Nov 30, 1855, dau of Samuel Henry and Miranda (Payne).   Children:

a   Ira Luther b Ripton Apr 2, 1872; m Apr 9, 1895, Nellie Curran
b   ——b Salisbury, Vt, July 19, 1877

Almira Dow adadieab.   Gove Gen gives Abram Alson Gove b Lincoln, Vt, about 1852, farmer of Ripton, son of Edward S and Mary A (Folsom), m 1st Sept 20, 1874, Elsie A Green b Ripton about 1859, dau of Newell and Almira (Dow).   This seems a penslip.   Almira is dau of Newell and Almira (Folsom).   She d; he m 2nd Kate (Geary) (Stringham) Green, who became a wid the second time.   Almira's children:

a   George Mark b Dec 9, 1874
b   Clara Adaline b Feb 17, 1877; m Melvin Stone
c   Bennie Guy b Mch 2, 1883; of Hinsdale, m Pearl King
d   Henry Garfield b July 30, 1888   e   Charles Alson b Sept 28, 1889

Lucy A Dow adadiec m May 9, 1849, Simon G Jones, both of Pittsfield.   Children:

a   Viola   b   Leonora   c   Otis d young
d   Otis W m Pittsfield 1889; went to Lynn   e   Rhena   f   Helen

FROM 1683 vital statistics were neglected in that part of Hampton now Seabrook. In 1711 this region was set off as a separate township, Hampton Falls, but little improvement is noted. Half a century later it became Seabrook, but the town books were kept no better. Some years ago an effort was made to inspect them, and it was found that they had from time to time been given to children as playthings. More than half the pages had been torn out. Much was unintelligible. Moreover, from 1702 the Friends were not at all careful to keep their vital statistics in the regular minute books. Probably the town clerk paid no attention to Friends' doings, so neither made entries. The snarl thus created was the despair of every genealogist for many years. The Dows of Seabrook were more numerous than anywhere else and seemed irredeemably untraceable. Little by little order has been restored. The discovery of the second family of Joseph Dow ada cleared the situation wonderfully.

Eliphaz Dow adaf grew up on his father's farm and learned the shoemaker's trade; m Newbury Sept 2, 1729, Elizabeth Flood. Undoubtedly no children. Henry Dow, administrator of his estate, was abcea of Portsmouth and was appointed by the court.

May 8, 1755, the inhabitants of Portsmouth and far and near gathered to witness the edifying show of the hanging of Eliphaz Dow, who for the purpose had been taken from the county jail to the cross roads near the foot of the hill where a gallows had been erected. It was the first hanging in the county and the people were anxious for it, the authorities wishing to carry out good old English precedent. About 1850 the road at this point was being repaired and the workmen uncovered his restless bones. A hanging seems always to exert a fascination upon people. Albert Gallatin Dow in his autobiography describes the first boat on the Erie canal and notes that fewer than a score rose in the chill early morning to witness the consummation of this vast work. Almost on the same page he speaks of the vast crowds gathered to make holiday and witness the hanging of the three Thayer brothers, more than trebly more attractive than a single hanging. And so, people gathered to watch Fliphaz Dow choke to death from a rope around his neck.

The accounts of all which led up to this event are clear, and unbiased, and make us feel sorry that Eliphaz lived a century too soon. Today, any district attorney would have accepted his plea of manslaughter in minor degree and, if he had any money or influence, he would be acquitted at once. If a Quaker, albeit a degenerate one, he would now go free, but then it was all the more reason for hanging him.

There had been ill feeling for some time between Eliphaz, who traveled from door to door making or mending shoes, and Peter Clough of

Hampton Falls, burly blacksmith.   He b Oct 25, 1707, son of Samuel and
Mary (Blaisdell), m July 24, 1735, Sarah Hunt.   The two met one day at
the house of Noah Dow, Eliphaz' brother.   It was the social set of Seabrook in which hard cider figured as the invariable entertainer.   Presumably Eliphaz and Peter poured out liberal amounts into the tin
dipper.   At all events, there were high words and Peter dared Dow to
come out and fight.   Now Eliphaz was slight and no fighter, Peter a blacksmith.   So, when Peter heeded his host's request to make himself scarcer
and went out, Eliphaz waited for the storm to blow over.   When he
finally left, he picked up Noah's hoe as a precaution.   Clough started
for him and Eliphaz struck him on the side of the head, killing him instantly.   Dow was promptly arrested, examined before magistrate
Meshech Weare and committed to the county jail.   This was Dec 12,
1754.   In Feb he was tried and convicted, sentenced to die Mch 20.   He
was reprieved twice by the Governor, but the people demanded his hanging.

People's opinions differ about a hanging.   They should regret that
too many who need hanging get away.   One good hanging should occur
about once a century in each family.   It is a cure for family degeneracy,
keeps down undeserved pride, and tones up morale.   Two more Dow
have been hanged, one an honest privateersman; the other a splendid
brigand on a large scale.   Philip Dow, said in the newspapers to be an
American, was a successful man in South America.   His organized band
was strong, well armed and well drilled.   They never molested the country folks, their neighbors or the poor.   In raiding a town, they were
inclined to take away everything portable. Whether Philip left heirs is
not recorded; it is said that he lived somewhat on the caveman plan,
carrying off wives by force of arms.   He was especially successful in
politics.   When Chile could stand his doings no longer, he gained amnesty
by conducting an expedition against Peru.   Before laying on the last
straw, he placated the Peruvians by proceeding to rob their hereditary
enemies, the Bolivians.   The patience of all finally gave out and they
hanged the gentleman in the early eighties, much mourned by hundreds
to whom he gave steady, lucrative employment, and by a country side
accustomed to feed from his largess.

Noah Dow adag was of age in 1735, when cited to court with his
brothers; our guess that he was b 1710 must be pretty close.   May 16,
1744, he sold some So Hampton land to his brother Bildad; he is on the
Hampton Falls tax list each year from 1740 to 1768 inclusive.   His will
dated 1770 does not indicate wife or children, but names his nephew
Zebulon as his heir.   His tax bills were about the average size, he was
an inconspicuous farmer and probably never married.

Bildad Dow adah, also of age by 1735, is almost as little known as

Noah, his civic life confined to the tax lists.   From 1744 to 1747 he lived So Hampton, from 1747 to 1767 he is regularly on the Hampton Falls tax books.   He was alive 1770.   He was not a signer of the Association Test, but none of the Quaker Dow was.   He m (int pub Mch 20, 1735-6) Eleanor (Getchell) Selley, dau of Benoni of Seabrook and Salisbury.   His cousin Elihu had m her sister Mehitable.   Their own rec are not found in Friends minutes, but Amesbury has preserved the rec of 2 dau:

a   Martha, dau of Bildad of Seabrook and Eleanor
b   Hildah of Weare, dau Bildad and Elinor, both dec, m 22: 4: 1795, Amos Chase adhaab of Deering, son of Thomas of Seabrook and Mary (Dow); no children
c   Asa b probably later than the 2 sisters (identity unproved)
d   Aaron m 1787; must not be confused with adaif or adkfbd.   While there is no proof of identity of these two sons, their position among the Friends, their being of Weare, coupled with the fact that there is no vacancy for them in any other Quaker line, is satisfactory evidence.   We remember that almost no birth rec from So Hampton are extant

Martha Dow adaha m (presumably at Amesbury meeting) Jan 31, 1770, John Gove, son of Edward and Judith (Hoag).   Judith is also by 2nd m adhad.   John Gove was a Quaker of much force of character, settled in Weare 1768, d Aug 25, 1826; m 2nd wid Abigail (Knox) Leighton of Farmingdale, dau of James and Anne.   Martha's children:

a   James b Sept 20, 1770; m Sarah Austin; 2 children
b   John b Apr 26, 1772; m Hannah Chase; saddler, moved to Vt, thence to Mass; 4 children
c   Jonathan b May 27, 1774; m Hannah Gould; moved to Lincoln, Vt.   A very considerable settlement of Quakers from Weare was made at Lincoln shortly after 1800.   The second generation of them seem to have drifted out of the Society
d   Aaron b Sept 7, 1775; m Mary Dow adhaff; moved to Lincoln
e   Judith b Jan 7, 1781
f   Moses b Mch 2, 1783; m Sally Chase; 6 children
g   Elinor b Jan 7, 1787; m David Dow adadib of Pittsfield

Asa Dow adahc.   Hist Weare mention individuals of three Dow families but gives no ancestry.   One of these was Asa Dow, a traveling tailor, who went from house to house following his trade.   He was a Quaker and there appears no possible ancestry for him other than Bildad. Perhaps Bildad himself appeared in Weare.   Asa m Deering Apr 4, 1805, Mary Gove adgxbba.   Many years later he m Huldah Brackenbury b Sept 11, 1790, dau of David and Sarah (Brown).   An only child:

a   Sally W G b crippled.   She was brought up by a Gove family and was able to do ordinary housework.   She d unm Feb 7, 1876, ae 67.   Her appearance was so much older that a newspaper note of her death spoke of her as almost 90

Aaron Dow adahd gets brief mention in Hist Weare, which names 5 children.   Hist Sanbornton gets us into trouble by identifying with him an Aaron Dow of the adkf line.   Our Aaron m Mch 17, 1787, Adalia Gove, dau of John and Lydia (Purington).   Both these are Quaker families who came to Weare from Seabrook.   Like other Weare Quakers, Aaron's family moved to Henniker, where the 1790 census gives him 1a, 1b, 2c.   The existence of a dau argues that the death rec of his dau Phebe gives her age incorrectly. From Henniker the family moved to Hinesburg, Vt, perhaps by way of the Lincoln Quaker settlement. Some of the children and most of the grandchildren eventually returned to Weare. Children:

a Zacchaeus b 1788; d Vt unm   b John Gove b 1789
c Samuel S   d Sweet G; Vt rec gives Swett (G probably for Gove)
e Phoebe d Deering, Quaker, May 1, 1872, ae 83

John G Dow adahdb, shoemaker, d Mch 1858; m Jan 29, 1823, Mehitable Green b Weare Mch 3, 1798, dau of Isaiah and Mehitable (Gove), Quakers. She d Weare Jan 22, 1852. Children:

a Hannah b 1823; living Weare 1850   b Obed H b Hinesburg Mch 25, 1832
c Mary Ann b Dec 1837; m Sidney Taft of Huntington, Vt

Obed H Dow adahdbb, cordwainer, returned to Weare; d Henniker June 22, 1885; m Jan 18, 1862, Sarah R Coggswell, ae 28, dau of George H and Mary L of Henniker. No rec of children

Samuel S Dow adahdc apostatized, joining the Concord Congregational church 1836; settled 1823 in Francestown: m May 15, 1822, Anna Palmer of Deering; moved to Deering about 1850. She d Feb 13, 1849, ae 55; he d June 10, 1862, ae about 68; m 2nd Bridget McCoy of Deering, dau of Daniel. She m 2nd Cyrus Barrett. Children:

a Lorenzo b Aug 29, 1823   b Lydia b Jan 16, 1825; lived Medford, unm

Lorenzo Dow adahdca returned to Weare; d 1868; m June 20, 1849, Laura M Philbrick of Weare, dau of Andrew and Ruth (Perkins). She m 2nd James M Grant and d 1886. Apparently no children.

Sweet G Dow adahdd appears in 1850 census as laborer of Bristol, Vt, with wife Lydia b Vt 1800. Two of their children are buried in Lee cemetery, indicating that the family were among the Lincoln Quakers. They moved away sometime after 1856. Children:

a Phebe Ann d Aug 5, 1855, ae 29   b Lorenzo b 1830; living 1850
c Alonzo d June 7, 1856, ae 19. In various rec father is called Swet, Swett, Sweat
d Malissa b 1840; living 1850

Lorenzo Dow adahddb is untraced. The 1883 gazetteer gives two Lorenzos in Lincoln, both blacksmiths. One may be adahddb

Jeremiah Dow adahdx. There are no data, only inferences concerning this Quaker of Lincoln b Oct 31, 1816, d Dec 7, 1871. We merely guess him to be a grandson of Bildad Dow, no other origin seeming plausible. He m —— Barnard; 2nd Phebe Martell. He was commonly known as Jed and lived inconspicuously. He had an only son:

a Lorenzo m Mary Clark and had a son John. Inquiry in Lincoln recalls them all clearly but fails to ascertain where they moved

There is in the Lincoln Friends cemetery a stone to Margaret M (Percival) Dow b 1812, d Jan 27, 1857. We guess her wife or wid of some Dow of adah line

Judah Dow adai. For many years the genealogists knew of his existence because of a curious entry in the tax book and that he was related to Noah Dow adag was known. This very relationship made his identity uncertain, for he was entered as a tax payer of Salisbury Beach in 1719. From that entry, it seemed certain that he was b by 1698. What really happened was this: The Salisbury clerk, probably deep in hard cider at the time, wished to record Judah's birth in 1719. He reached and took down the wrong book, entering the name as Jadah.

Judah was the baby of the family, the especial pet of his father and later the object of especial solicitude of his older brothers. He developed into a man of much gentleness, and likeable qualities. He married outside the Friends, Sept 25 (int Sept 5), 1740, by Rev Jeremiah Fogg of Kensington, Mary Wilber. In published works she is given of Hampton; this is error, there were no Wilbers of Hampton; her family were all of Kingston. He was all his life closely intimate with Elihu Dow adgx, whose parentage is not proven. From 1741 to 1768 inclusive Judah appears always on the Hampton Falls tax books. He seems to have d just before 1777, his wife probably d earlier. His posterity may be the largest of any Dow of 4th generation. This posterity, a hopeless muddle apparently, was disconnected until Edward A Brown, librarian of Amesbury, discovered in possession of a great grandson of Elihu Dow adgx Judah's family Bible, the entries all in his own clearly legible hand. Children:

a	Jesse b Dec 22, 1741	b	Elizabeth b Aug 12, 1743
c	John b May 2, 1745	d	Isaiah b Mch 17, 1747
e	Moses b Mch 23, 1749	f	Aaron b Nov 28, 1750
g	Phineas b Jan 7, 1753	h	Lois b Jan 29, 1755
i	Levi b July 10, 1756	j	Zebulon b Jan 23, 1758
k	Zelpha b May 17, 1762	l	Zopher b June 8, 1764
m	Zachaeus b May 25, 1769		

With this huge family, all of whom grew up, Judah and wife were desperately poor. Each child added a burden. One imagines that when the 10th arrived, both parents chose the last letter of the alphabet as a token of desire. Alas, of no avail. Then followed Zelpha, Zopher, Zachaeus before nature was exhausted

Jesse Dow adaia. The practice by Rev Sam Perley of noting in a little pocket book the weddings at which he officiated has preserved much information of a time when town rec were at their worst. This shows that Jesse m May 25, 1768, Deborah Fellows, both of Seabrook. Jesse paid Hampton Falls taxes 1763-7. The latter date is approximately when some of his brothers moved to Pittsfield, settling toward the north end. Probably Jesse went to Pittsfield 1768. The Pembroke 1790 census gives him 1a, 1b, 3c, and all the Pittsfield Dow are censused as of Pembroke. Here are three lost children. It is not safe to pick out candidates from the Pittsfield disconnected list.

John Dow adaic m by Rev Sam Perley Seabrook Sept 21, 1772, Abigail Purington. She also broke away from the Friends. John Dow, cooper of Pittsfield, bought land 1778 from Phineas Dow adaig. John Dow in 1790 Pembroke census 1a, 4b, 6c. Here is a family of 9 children genealogically lost.

Isaiah Dow adaid does not reappear after birth. Only the existence of Isaiah Dow Jr places him. He must have gone to Pittsfield with his brothers. That he had more children than 3 is probable:

  a Isaiah b Pittsfield Oct 10, 1773   b John b Aug 31, 1776
  c Sallie b presumably about 1780

Isaiah Dow adaida d Pittsfield Feb 5, 1818; m Betsey Burns b Aug 7, 1775, d Feb 11, 1841. It is patent that this family lived in Topsham, Vt, in 1806 and returned by 1812 to Pittsfield. That there were eight children is attested by a reliable family rec. Only 2 are proven:

  a (wild guess) Hannah b Mch 22, 1794
  b Benjamin b about 1797 (Merely certainly of adai line)
  e (order guessed) Jeremiah Burns b Topsham Jan 4, 1806
  g (order guessed) Jonathan S b Pittsfield June 3, 1812

Hannah Dow adaidaa d Strafford, N H, June 16, 1889; m Samuel Hill b Jan 17, 1787, son of William and Lucy (Leighton) of Lee; settled in Barnstead, moving about 1830 to Strafford. Children:

  a Harriet b 1812; d 1864; m Seth Shackford of Barnstead
  b Betsey b 1813; d 1896; m Samuel Fernald of Strafford
  c William lived Bowdenham (Bowdoinham?), Me ·
  d Daniel b 1819; d 1862; m Mary Blake; lived Boston
  e Joseph b 1821; d 1904; lived Strafford; m Mary Bond, by whom son George
      and grandson Ernest; m 2nd Florence I Sherman
  f Abbie b 1824; d 1832
  g Mary b 1826; living 1911; m William H Pearl; 2nd George Bennett
  h Samuel living 1911; m Sarah Tuttle i Emily b 1833; d 1909

Benjamin Dow adaidab, merchant of Rowley, Mass, m Rowley Aug 12, 1821, Elizabeth Tenney b Rowley July 20, 1788, d Oct 1, 1852, dau of Thomas and Elizabeth (Jewett). Only child:

  a Justin Edwards b Pittsfield about 1830

Justin E Dow adaidaba, grad Dartmouth 1854, studied law but preferred teaching; m Dec 21, 1854, Grace Fletcher White, his former teacher, b Pittsfield May 1, 1819, grad Pittsfield Academy, teacher in N H and Mass. She continued to teach with her husband in Peoria, Ill, d Aurora Dec 21, 1878. He m 2nd Theresa Spando of Peoria; d Houston, Tex, 1897, presumably without children.

Jeremiah B Dow adaidæ, teacher for over 50 years in Wilkes-Barre, Pa, d there; m Jan 17, 1847, Hannah Welding Fell b Wilkes-Barre Aug 18, 1825, dau of Samuel and Mary Dingman (Kyte). Children:

  a Mary Elizabeth b Oct 7, 1847   b William Burns b Jan 12, 1850
  c Alphonso Burns b Apr 7, 1852; d Aug 11, 1854

d Ruth Ella b Jan 25, 1856   e John Dorrance b June 13, 1858
f Sarah Leah b Oct 10, 1861; d 1891, unm
g Daisy b June 15, 1864
h Stella Willetts b July 10, 1869; d Jan 14, 1872

Mary E Dow adaidaea m Sept 7, 1880, Simeon Decker Goff, son of William R and Annie (Decker).   Children:

a Ruth b June 28, 1881   b Elton Mills b Sept 26, 1882
c Burns b July 25, 1884   d Katherine Welding b Dec 22, 1889

William B Dow adaidaeb m Sept 2, 1874, Mary Emma Fell of Pittston, Pa, dau of George W and Margaret (Baird).   Children:

a Helen b Feb 13, 1876   b Baird b Oct 28, 1879; untraced
c Marjorie b Aug 16, 1881

Ruth E Dow adaidaed m Mch 16, 1879, Henry Newton Young, dentist, son of Jacob Suydam and Martha (Vorhis).   Children:

a Nathalie May b Nov 27, 1880   b Henry Newton b Feb 16, 1885

John D Dow adaidaee, dentist of St Paul, Minn, m Sept 15, 1880, Melissa J Denman of Chicago.   Children:

a Earl b July 1881; d Nov 13, 1882   b Edna b May 1884; d young

Jonathan S Dow adaidag named his 1st born for his mother, who seems to have been a woman of much character; went as a lad to work for Enoch French, early settler of Canterbury, m his dau and in time succeeded to the homestead, lot 13, school district 5 of the original grant, section known as Hackleborough.   This farm was assessed $400 in 1850. Jonathan d Feb 11, 1880, ae 67; m Henrietta S French b Loudon Dec 19, 1807, d Canterbury Aug 13, 1885.   Children, b Canterbury:

a Betsey Burns b Aug 9, 1836; d Feb 1891; m May 26, 1859, Cyrus T Lane of
      Candia; son,—John T
b Enoch French b Mch 30, 1839; d Sept 1, 1842
c Abbie A b Aug 5, 1841; d May 1873; m George A Lane of Danvers, Mass
d Harriet A b Mch 30, 1844; m N A Pitts of Lynn, Mass
e Amanda M b Mch 3, 1847; d Aug 1871; m Apr 10, 1869, Byron Hobert
      (Byram Hobart, Hist Canterbury) of Loudon
f Frank Pierce b Jan 30, 1850

Abbie A Dow adaidagc m Feb 18, 1868, Geo A Lane who d Nov 25, 1876, ae 33.   Children:

a Frank T   b Nellie

Frank P Dow adaidagf m Chichester Sept 27, 1875, Adeline W West b Chichester Dec 19, 1855, dau of George W and Mary P (Seavey). Children:

a Nellie Addie b Canterbury July 25, 1876; asst principal 1894-5, later steno-
      grapher
b George West b Oct 6, 1880; killed mill accident Fitchburg Apr 4, 1911, unm

John Dow adaidb appears in 1850 census as farmer of Topsham, b Stowe, Vt.   This last probably careless error.   At least 4 oldest children b Topsham. The family returned to Moultonborough shortly after 1850. He d Moultonborough June 10, 1852, ae 76-9-11; m Mary Mc-Crillis b Milton, N H (or Rochester), d Moultonborough July 28, 1877, ae 96-3-29, dau of Robert and Mary. Children, by census mostly:

<blockquote>
a Theodate b Feb 9, 1802; m Moultonborough Aug 13, 1864, Daniel A Hall of Sandwich
b Charles Granderson b Dec 3, 1803   c Nabby McCrillis b Dec 5, 1806
d Eli Stedman b Aug 13, 1808; surely grew up; untraced
f (specified 6th child) John B b 1817
g Philena M b 1821; living 1850. Family seems to have been in N H 1817 to 1821
</blockquote>

Charles G Dow adaidbb m Jan 21 (Moultonborough rec; Feb 27, Meredith rec), 1827, Lydia Hawkins, both of Moultonborough; 2nd, Dec 21, 1831, Comfort Hawkins of Moultonborough b 1807. Children, by 1850 census:

<blockquote>
a Eli S b 1833   b Levi H b 1835; both untraced
c Lydia A b 1841; m June 16, 1862, Daniel Kelley, both of Moultonborough
</blockquote>

John B Dow adaidbf, shoemaker of Center Harbor, d widower Moultonborough Jan 5, 1908; m Nov 26, 1840, Clarissa D Richardson of Dover; 2nd Rochester July 7, 1858, Ruth A Sanborn. Children:

<blockquote>
a Betsey A b 1848   b Nellie F m Nov 2, 1873, Henry R Gould of Moultonborough; son Everett H m Moultonborough 1899
</blockquote>

Sallie Dow adaide, dau of Isaiah Dow of Bow, cannot be anyone else. All the adai Dows of Pittsfield appear in 1790 census as of Bow. Sallie's aunt Lois married a Greene of Pittsfield. Sallie m about 1801 Jacob Greene b Bow Apr 3, 1779, son of Jacob and Anna (Hazeltine). They moved to Gilmanton. Children:

<blockquote>
a Asenath b Nov 21, 1802; m——Perkins of Belmont
b Calvin b Dec 31, 1804
c Nathaniel b June 14, 1806; became a Colonel in Confederate army; planter of Richmond, Va
d Mary A b Jan 3, 1809; m——Sawyer
e Samuel Sanders b Oct 11, 1810; m Margaret Cary
f Gardner b Dec 11, 1813   g Emma b Apr 3, 1816; m——Kidder
</blockquote>

Moses Dow adaie. His very existence was unknown until the discovery of his father's family Bible. A Moses figuring in Hist Hampton was he but was dated 14 years wrongly. Some Moses Dow, we know not whom, enlisted Capt Nathan Brown, Col Jacob Gale, for R I service, mustered out Aug 1778, service 23 days. Some Moses, no longer liable for military service, paid the bounty for another soldier in Epping. This could hardly be adaie; possibly is ahbb. The Author communicated his theories about Moses to Miss Mary J Greene of Hampton Falls, at which that indefatigable lady set to work, soon encountering a very old gentleman of Seabrook whose memories and hearsay were decisive. "Down on an island at Farm Dock lived Moses Dow and a sister Polly, called an old witch." (This can only be Elizabeth Dow adaib.) That Moses had a wife Elizabeth appears from d rec of son. In 1790 census he is la

3b, 6c.   As a matter of fact, he had 4 sons, but did not have 5 dau.   One or more sisters or grand dau must make up this number.   One informant says there was but one dau.   Children:

a   Aaron b 1775 (by 1850 census)
b   Moses (Seabrook informant recalled he had children). Hist Hampton gives him
    son of Moses b 1763, 14 years wrong
c   Samuel, husbandman, son of Moses and Elizabeth, d Seabrook 1862, ae 80.
    Town rec in error says bachelor; he was widower
d   John (old bachelor, says our informant).   Rec gives: unm, son of Moses and
    Elizabeth, laborer, d Apr 4, 1858
e   Miriam m Sept 19, 1825, Edward Cilley; d at county farm

Aaron Dow adaiea.   This line suffers from the ill kept rec of inner Seabrook.   Mentioned only in d rec of son, which gives his wife Mary b Me 1780.   Our excellent informant says an only child:

a   Moses b Seabrook 1807

Moses Dow adaieaa had wife Hannah, who survived him; shoemaker, d Dec 10, 1869.   Town rec gives children c and f:

a   Rhoda Ann b 1831.   Original informant does not give her.   Another says he
    m——Bragg; perhaps confused for adaija
b   George S b 1832; d Seabrook Sept 2, 1879; "left no sons."
c   Lewis W b Feb 26, 1835; private 1861 in Winnacunnett Guards; m but "left
    no sons." He d June 12, 1906
d   Vienna b 1836; m Elijah McQuillen.   Kensington rec bears this: Estella Mc-
    Quillen, ae 23, dau of Elijah and Vienna, m Seabrook Nov 18, 1882, Charles
    A Dow adkddgda
e   Hannah E b 1842   f   Franklin b 1843; m and "left sons."

Vienna Dow adaieaad in m rec is Lavina; m Oct 4, 1852, Elijah P McQuillen b Newburyport, of Seabrook.   Children:

a   Estella b 1859; m Chas A Dow adkddgda
b   Mary E m——Shepard; 2nd Hampton 1897 Everett L Godfrey

Moses Franklin Dow adaieaaf.   The husband of Jane Maria Ramsdell of Kensington appears as Moses, Moses F, Frank, Frank B, etc.   We can only suppose that our identification is right.   He moved from Seabrook to Kensington after 1870, from Kensington to Exeter after 1880.   Unless there is an absolutely unknown Moses, this man had 20 children, the largest family in this Book.   He was a mason and a shoemaker.   Children, so far as found:

a   Franklin H, son of Moses F, b Oct 4, 1866; d Apr 19, 1874
c   George S, son of Moses F, b Seabrook June 10, 1870
f   Charles A (son of J M Ramsdell) b Kensington 1877
g   Emily J b Kensington Nov 28, 1880
l   ——(to Moses F and Jane M Ramsdell) b Exeter June 20, 1886
r   ——dau b Exeter Sept 27, 1888
t   (to Moses Dow and——Currier)——dau b Exeter Sept 23, 1892

George S Dow adaieaafc, shoemaker of Exeter, m Oct 18, 1889, Mary O Kelley b Stratham, ae 21, dau of Josiah B and Corinne A.   Children:

a   ——dau b Jan 4, 1890   b   Laura M b July 7, 1894; d Nov 14, 1895

Alice J Dow adaieaafca b Exeter, m Newburyport Jan 19, 1910, Hallett J Rogers, ae 32, son of Leonard M and Jessie L (Jackman)

Charles A Dow adaieaaff, farmer of Greenland, m Mch 14, 1902, Lillian Gertrude Chauncey, ae 23, dau of Henry Israel and Ellen (Perkins) of Newburyport.

Martha Dow adaieaafl (tentative, for she is given as dau of Frank and Jane M and b Seabrook) m Newburyport Apr 13, 1904, John S Rowe, ae 19, son of Jerry and Mary (Walton)

Moses Dow adaieb was private, Col Lovering, in 1814; d May 14, 1851; m Sept 12, 1812, Margaret Downs of Gosport d Feb 23, 1866.   He sold out in Seabrook and bought a farm in Hampton.   Only child:

   a   Moses Abner b Feb 11, 1813

Moses A Dow adaieba inherited the farm, enjoyed some prominence in Hampton, capt of the artillery company, on the fire company and many town committees; d July 12, 1888; m Sophronia McCann b Stratham Nov 2, 1829.   Children:

   a   Lizzie Ellen b July 26, 1852   b   Abby Ann b July 13, 1855
   c   Mary Akerman b Sept 27, 1859   d   Sarah Frances b June 11, 1865
   e   William Ward b Nov 21, 1868; d Sept 8, 1884

Lizzie Ellen Dow adaiebaa m Nov 28, 1874, Thomas E Stoodley of Portsmouth; went to Elliot, Me; returned to Hampton.   No children.

Abby A Dow adaiebab d May 9, 1888; m 1876 David Amos Towle b Apr 10, 1845, son of David and Mary (Garland); lived Newmarket returning to Hampton.   Children:

   a   Maud A b June 27, 1877; d Jan 16, 1890
   b   Anna B b Oct 29, 1880   c   Alice R b Apr 27, 1887

Mary A Dow adaiebac m Feb 18, 1880, George Ballard Brown b Mch 29, 1857, d Jan 1891, son of Jeremiah W and Sarah A (Page) of Haverhill.   Child:

   a   Walter Edward b Mch 12, 1880

Sarah Frances Dow adaiebad m Dec 22, 1884, Wesley Howard Mitchell of Concord, Mass, later of So Boston.   Children b Hampton:

   a   William Dow b June 22, 1885   b   Guy Melvin b May 27, 1888

Samuel Dow adaiec lived on Rocks Road, north part of Seabrook; 1850 census gives him b 1784; wife Nancy b 1805.   Children, by census:

   a   Robert R b 1831   b   Samuel b 1837; untraced
   c   Nancy b 1837; possibly twin; comes next in census, may be alone

Robert R Dow adaieca, shoemaker of Seabrook m Oct 13, 1850,

Nancy F Edmunds (Edwards in d rec) b Chester May 20, 1833, d Seabrook Mch 10, 1905, dau of Gardner and Elsie. Children:

  a Augusta A d Seabrook Mch 31, 1871, ae 19
  b Orrin B b Nov 7, 1854; d Seabrook Nov 2, 1903, shoemaker unm
  c ——— Our informant says there were 2 sons

Aaron Dow adaif. That he outlived his father is indicated, but there seems to be no place for him among the Aarons who are found later in Seabrook or among the Pittsfield Dows, his immediate kin. We are compelled to leave him untraced.

Phineas Dow adaig seems to have been the pioneer of the family to Pittsfield. Of Chichester, he m Deerfield Dec 4, 1780, Taberthy (Tabitha) Page of Northwood. She descends from Robert Page immigrant on same boat as Henry Dow in 1637. They traded actively in land until 1803. His homestead was lot 76, a little westerly of Jenness Pond. The 1790 census gives him 1a, 3b, 2c, only two sons being known:

  a Daniel b 1785 (census)   b David
  c (guess) Aaron Dow m Sept 15, 1811, Betsey Kinney, both of Center Harbor
  d Hannah, dau of Phineas. See sub bcdaaa

Daniel Dow adaiga seems to have inherited the homestead; 1st wife not found; m 2nd Nov 5, 1847, Diana Kelley b Meredith, d Northwood Dec 1, 1857, ae 31, dau of Richard and Ann W (Goodwin), by whom 2 children. They appear in 1850 census, which mentions but 3 children. In later years the 2nd family lost sight of the 1st

  a Benjamin Franklin (always called Frank) b 1826, by census
  b William d in young manhood c Rebecca d unm
  d Dolly m ——— Thompson e Mary Jane grew up and m
  f Louisa m Timothy Langley g Abigail d unm
  h Sarah d unm i Emily E b 1849; m Albert Joy of Pittsfield
  j William; in 1921 carpenter of Pittsfield; m but only child d young

Frank B Dow adaigaa, carpenter, d widower Belknap County farm Nov 8, 1905; m 1851 Mary Ann Dearborn b Derby, Vt, 1827, d Laconia July 16, 1900; lived mostly in Gilford. In d rec of son, she is called Mary Switzer b Vt, possibly her mother's name. At least 3 children:

  a James Pierce b Gilford 1854
  b Benjamin F b Moultonborough 1862; d Gilford Apr 20, 1883
  c Charles Henry b 1859(?)

James P Dow adaigaaa, farmer of Plymouth, later laborer of Gilford and Laconia, m Aug 4, 1877, Nettie Shores, ae 19, d childless Nov 25, 1878, dau of William and Hannah of Campton; 2nd Laconia Sept 20, 1882, Lilla A Chase. A characteristically garbled Laconia rec gives James T Dow b Pittsfield 1856, laborer of Laconia, m Mary A Dearborn b New Hampton 1866. Mary Dearborn is his mother and Lilla the wife. She got a divorce; he m 3rd (her 3rd, twice div) Feb 2, 1901, Ada Maria Goodwin, ae 44, dau of Samuel and Susan F (Taylor). He d Lakeport Jan 6, 1913. Children:

b   Ellen M b Laconia Jan 19, 1885; d Gilford July 13, 1891
c   Frank B (known as Jr) b Lakeport 1887
d   Susie Etta d Sept 9, 1891, ae 6 mos, 1 day
e   Arthur B b 1894, laborer of Pembroke, m June 9, 1915, Edith Mary Campbell,
     ae 22, dau of Watson and Cora (Tobin).

Frank B Dow adaigaaac, laborer of Campton, then of Lakeport, m 1st ——; div; m 2nd Dec 13, 1909, Ednah E Locke, ae 18, dau of Fred W and Laurette E (Foote). Children:

b   —— dau b Laconia Nov 30, 1911   c   —— son b Ashland Dec 22, 1913

Charles H Dow adaigaac has appeared only from own rec m; ae 51, div, m 2nd Cambridge, Mass, Feb 20, 1910, Ethelene Ruth Parker, ae 22, dau of Edwin J and Agnes (Munroe).

Locality is our only evidence to consider him identical with Charles H Dow, boatman of Moultonborough, m Ellen (or Anne, both in rec) Fogg; having at least 2 children, b Moultonborough:

a   Charles E b 1882   b   Benjamin F b 1893

Charles E Dow adaigaaca, marine engineer, m Dec 25, 1907, Myrtie L Bickford, ae 26, of Meredith, dau of Moses F and Anna

Benjamin F Dow adaigaacb, teamster of Moultonborough, m Dec 1, 1917, Evelyn Davis Shawpenny, ae 18, dau of Eugene and Mary Ann (Eastman)

David Dow adaigb was perhaps the 1st born, as census says b N H 1782-3. In 1850 farmer of Moultonborough, assessed $1,600, with dau, but no wife. He m Dec 11, 1806, Betsey Brown, both of Moultonborough. He had only one son:

a   Betsey b N H 1812   b   Daniel P b about 1817

Daniel P Dow adaigbb m Pittsfield (int pub Moultonborough May 30) Oct 29, 1841, Abigail E Goodwin, b 1823 both of Moultonborough. She d wid Moultonborough 1908 where both appear in 1850 census. Children, all b Moultonborough:

a   Benjamin Weymouth b 1843   b   Jeremiah Kendall
c   Frederick R b 1849; is not recalled by brother, hence d 1850 or is error
d   Sylvia d ae about 15 mos

Benjamin W Dow adaigbba, farmer of Moultonborough, lives 1923 retired Center Harbor; m Aug 28, 1864, Sarah E Wentworth b Somersworth Feb 26, 1848, d Moultonborough Sept 11, 1909, dau of Clark and Harriet (Carnes). Children:

a   George K   b   Benjamin R b Mch 22, 1867
c   Irving E b Aug 5, 1868   d   Joseph W b 1866, by m rec
e   Ella M b Oct 22, 1870   f   Hattie A b Jan 1, 1884; unm at home

George K Dow adaigbbaa, traveling salesman of Peoria, Ill, m Ft Wayne, Ind, Dec 23, 1896, Anna Madge Williams. Children:

a   Gertrude b Dec 24, 1897   b   Katherine b Jan 27, 1899
c   Dorothy b June 9, 1911

Benjamin R Dow adaigbbab, baggage master of Dover, returned to the homestead; m Jan 3, 1893, Eva E Huston, ae 20, dau of Samuel and Jane E (Pierce).   Children:

a   Edith b Feb 16, 1894   b   Ethel b June 30, 1895; d young
c   Lizzie E b Nov 15, 1899   d   Evelyn L b Aug 17, 1905
e   Helen I d Dover Mch 31, 1913 f   Gladys b June 28, 1911

Edith Dow adaigbbaba m Oct 3, 1921, Charles Banfield

Lizzie E Dow adaigbbabc m Sept 4, 1920, Volney Ackerman.   Children:

a   Eva b Aug 6, 1921   b   Freda b Nov 3, 1922

Irving E Dow adaigbbac, mill worker 1889, shoemaker 1890, grocery clerk 1892, carpenter 1896-8, m Oct 31, 1889, Abbie Swazey Trask, ae 22, dau of Ancil and Maria (Otis).   Children:

a   Erwin W b Dover July 21, 1890; d Moultonborough July 21, 1912
b   Florence Blanche d Dover Nov 21, 1896; ae 4-8-12
x   Emma Elizabeth b Dover June 28, 1890 (date error)
c   Minerva Monroe b June 20, 1896   d   Thelma A b Apr 19, 1898

Joseph W Dow adaigbbad, shoe shop operative, belt maker of Dover, m May 27, 1899, Charlotte W Foster, div, ae 28, dau of James and Charlotte (Yates) Meaney of Eng.   She d June 24, 1910; he m 2nd Aug 15, 1921, Martha J Leitch of Cambridge, Mass.   They moved to Brooklyn, N Y.   Children:

a   Pearl C b Aug 14, 1901   b   Mildred E b Feb 1, 1904
c   Weymouth F b May 1, 1906 d   Stewart Leitch b Oct 9, 1922

Ella M Dow adaigbbae m Oct 14, 1889, J Fred Goodrich of Moultonborough; d Apr 8, 1904.   Children:

a   William F b Oct 4, 1890; m Brenda Swan; dau Marion
b   Clarence E b July 3, 1892; d ae 15 mos
c   Arthur E b Mch 2, 1895; m Alice M Richardson
d   Ransom E b June 13, 1897; m Florence Coff of Wolfboro

Jeremiah K Dow adaigbbb appears in census as farmer and cook. He adopted a son:

a   Henry E, laborer, by recent directory

Lois Dow adaih m Apr 12, 1797, Abraham Green, son of Jonathan and Margaret (Tilton).   He d Pittsfield 1812, she surviving.

Levi Dow adaii was of Seabrook all his life, must have had some good traits, as there has been a Levi in direct line ever since.   A Salisbury rec shows a payment to him for labor 1783; no military rec appears in rolls.   Census of 1790 shows him, wife and son over 16.   His wife Lois m 2nd (his 3rd or 2nd) Jacob Dow adgxf, her dau Rhoda m his son Elihu.

a   Levi b 1774, his father being then only 22
b   Rhoda, clearly very much younger

Levi Dow adaiia is little known.   Family tradition has it that he m Mary Dow, unplaced, but cannot well be a 1st cousin.   She m 2nd Dec

5, 1825, Mark Cilley and had by him a son Mark. Clearly, then, she must be much younger than her 1st husband. Same family tradition says there were several children by Levi, but no rec are extant. One son is certain:

   a Levi b probably 1800 to 1805, probably not 1st born
   b Josiah F (a guess)

Levi Dow adaiiaa was recalled to mind by the elderly Seabrook gentleman who recalled the adaie line and who even named Levi's children, altho not in order. The 1850 census comes to the rescue: Levi was a fish dealer of Newburyport, with wife Mary M b N H 1806. Children, all b N H:

   a Jane b 1831 (1841?); d Newburyport May 26, 1915, unm
   b Susan b 1844; m —— Beckman   c Zachaeus b 1846; untraced
   d Charles E b 1839; untraced
   e Levi A b Seabrook Sept 9, 1839 (census, 1842)
   f Josiah H (Josiah F is right; H is census error)   g Samuel P b 1847

Levi A Dow adaiiaae, when weighed in the final balance, may stand safely. He d Amesbury Nov 14, 1899; m Hannah Minan (probably Moynahan) b Ireland. He enlisted Newburyport Nov 17, 1861, 8th Mass inf, transferred to 30th Mass, in which his brother was. His term expiring, he re-enlisted Jan 2, 1864, and at Port Hudson volunteered for the "forlorn hope," a well known episode. He was a good soldier throughout, but after a few drinks was quarrelsome. In a drunken row with another soldier, an officer interfered and Levi struck him. For this he was imprisoned, pardoned after the end of the war, but given a dishonorable discharge. He then settled in Amesbury, where his children are now worthy and respected citizens:

   a Charles E b 1873; hatter, unm   b William, untraced
   c Eugene F b 1879; hatter, m Elizabeth Parker; 1 child
   d Levi J b 1883; hatter, m Hannah Moynahan; 2 children
   e Arthur J b 1885; hatter, unm   f Mary dec   g Caroline dec

Levi J Dow adaiiaaed differs in Amesbury rec from family rec as given above; b 1881; m Amesbury Nov 6, 1907, Elizabeth A Burke of Amesbury, ac 27, dau of Henry and Sarah (Chisnell). A dau:

   a Virginia b Amesbury Oct 11, 1908

Josiah F Dow adaiiaaf; probably named for Josiah F, tentatively adaiiab, enlisted 30th Mass from Newburyport; promoted to corporal for valor in the field; was at Winchester, Fisher's Hill, Cedar Creek; wounded, returned to service; mustered out July 5, 1866. Subsequently watchman of Newburyport jail; d Mch 31, 1917, leaving 3 sons, 3 dau. No sons living 1922; dau:

   a Sadie m —— Ritcherson   b Jennie m —— Morse
   c Ellen m Meleglen

Samuel P Dow adaiiaag, fisherman of Newburyport, d July 12, 1920; m Hannah Bowen, now with son.   Children:

a   William A b 1883; of Newburyport, unm, boat builder
b   Samuel P b 1886, fisherman of Newburyport; m Margaret Griffin

Josiah F Dow adaiiab.   A man of this name was a guard in Concord State's prison 1834.   A Josiah F Dow int pub Newburyport Aug 18, 1846, Sarah J Parker of Cornish, Me.   Dr Josiah F Dow of Concord with wife Sarah J Barker had a 1st born Lynn 1847.   Coincidence of name and of the places Lynn and Newburyport make it highly probable that all three rec apply to the same man and that he is of the ill-traced adaiia line and that a nephew was named for him.   The title Dr means little.   Self-constituted doctors were very numerous in those days.   A son sure, dau probable:

a   George F b Lynn Jan 19, 1847
b   Sarah Frances (dau of Josiah) m Feb 11, 1874, Aaron Shute Currier of Concord

George F Dow adaiiaba served 4 years in 27th Iowa inf; mill weaver, later janitor of Ashland, N H; d Ashland June 21, 1896; m Mary E Blanchard d Ashland Aug 10, 1909, ae 56-7-29, dau of Edward K and Sarah (Dustin) b Holderness.   One son found:

a   George E b 1876

George E Dow adaiiabaa mill operative of Ashland, m June 5, 1897, Hattie Vallie, ae 17.   Children:

a   Tressie Emma b Oct 21, 1898   b   Albert E b Sept 7, 1900
c   Sam E b Aug 7, 1903   d   Richard E b June 2, 1906
e   —— son b and d June 13, 1907   f   —— dau b Jan 20, 1909

Lois Dow adaiic, b Seabrook about 1796, is surely older than Levi, her brother.   She d Salisbury Aug 29, 1851; m Charles Gove b Feb 23, 1792, son of Levi and Mary (Chase).   He was a Baptist.   Only child:

a   Levi Dow b Seabrook about 1830; m Caroline Bragg; 1 dau

Zebulon Dow adaij is obscure because every one in his environment was obscure, but he was long confused with Zebulon ahbaaa of Epping, Alice wife of one and Abigail wife of the other dying about the same time, each having a dau m —— Creighton.   Zebulon was heir to his uncle Noah, receiving a house and some money.   He m by Rev Sam Langdon Dec 8, 1785, wid Abigail Bragg, whose maiden name has not appeared.   She survived many years, living in Hampton Falls in comfortable circumstances.   Census 1790 shows them of Hampton Falls 1a, 2b, 1c.   There must have been 2 sons who d young enough to be forgotten, for family tradition is firm that there were only 2 sons, and 2 sons were b after 1790.

a   Rhoda b 1796 by family statement; probably b before 1790. She m Josiah
    Shaw of Hampton; 4 children,—Jeremiah F, Asa, Elizabeth, Hiram. Jerem-
    iah F d 1846, m Mary Ann Lord of York, Me. Dau Abby m Mch 9, 1861,

David Creighton of Hampton Falls, son of James, and the young couple
settled in Maine.   Wid Mary Ann m 2nd Zebulon Dow adaijb
b   Zebulon b July 4, 1800   c   Joseph b 1804

Zebulon Dow adaijb d May 23, 1873; m Mary Ann Lord b 1825, d
Aug 31, 1877.   They were a well-mated couple, the favorite amusement
of both being hard work.   They first lived where Seabrook railroad
station now is; swapped real estate to considerable advantage and finally
bought at a bargain the Weare mansion in Hampton Falls from Polly
Dow adkdbd, no longer willing to maintain it.   Here Zebulon and Mary
Ann worked harder than ever.   She could dig a ditch or plough a field as
well as any man.   For several years she contracted to supply milk to
Boston and collected and hauled to the station, handling the full cans
with ease.   Children:

a   Ellen Maria b Mch 27, 1849
b   Delilah Frances b 1851; m George L Gove, div husband of Mary M Dow
    adaimbbe
c   Abby b Apr 30, 1851; not in family rec; must be twin and d in infancy
d   Mary Elizabeth b July 15, 1856; m May 8, 1878, Charles M Perley of Ipswich.
    Children,—Lawrence d in infancy, Helen m —— Adams

Ellen M Dow adaijba d July 24, 1905; m Aug 23, 1886, William H
Brown, a Scotchman, 7 years her junior, son of William.   The mansion
was used by them as a sanatorium for nervous patients.   He remarried
Sept 3, 1906.   Ellen left the mansion to her dau:

a   Helen Deborah m Charles W Birtwell. Son Roger b May 19, 1901

Delilah Frances Dow adaijbb m George L Gove, farmer and
butcher of Seabrook, son of Albert N and Nancy B (Tuttle).   Children:

a   Helen E b Sept 5, 1877; m Philip W Richards
b   Harold Albert b about 1880; m Clara Bernice Sylvada; 4 children
c   Edith Marion b Oct 16, 1890; a physician

Joseph Dow adaijc, shoemaker, m about 1837 Sally b 1800.   Children, by census:

a   Julia A b 1838
b   Lucy Jane b Oct 1840; d Dec 21, 1864; m Abram Dow adhchaa
c   Joseph b 1847; d June 29, 1851

Zopher Dow adail m So Hampton church May 17, 1790, Hannah
Eaton.   Name found as Jopha, Zopha, etc, but never Zophar.
On Hampton Falls tax list 1791 only.   Cordwainer, he moved to
So Seabrook and had considerable family, descendants today shoemakers
of So Seabrook.   One child only found:

a   Reuben b Sept, 27 1917

Reuben Dow adaila evidently moved to So Hampton, where the
family is hard to distinguish from the adaai line.   This Reuben m Amesbury Dec 15, 1812, Hannah Hackett.   He evidently d by 1850, for census
gives Hannah alone b Mass 1794.   In 1813 they were living in Salisbury.
They may have had a large family, but only one can be surely placed:

a   Reuben b Mass 1813

Reuben Dow adailaa of Salisbury m (int pub Nov 7, 1846) Sarah Ann Richardson b Mass 1822. Perhaps there was another Reuben of the adail line; more likely that Reuben made a 2nd m, for Reuben Dow and Jennett Walton had a son old enough to marry in 1877; Reuben and Sarah appear in 1850 census, laborer of Salisbury, with dau Julia and Sarah. Reuben Dow, widower, laborer of So Hampton, d of intemperance Feb 1861. Probably the three are identical. If so, a considerable family. With Reuben in 1850 was Nancy Dow b N H 1783. Her relationship is not obvious. Children:

a   Dorothy. So Hampton rec: Dorothy, dau of Reuben Dow, bap Nov 9, 1743.
    Date must be doubly wrong. No Dorothy is known
b   Julia b 1847   c   Sarah b 1849; these in census
d   Ira F, son of Reuben
e   Edmund M, known to be brother of Ira F
f   Amos V b Kingston, son of Reuben and Jennett

Ira F Dow adailaad m Catherine Dow adkfbbcl. In 1915 he was still living in Waltham, Mass. A child:

a   Augusta A b May 3, 1873; d Seabrook Feb 14, 1895

Edmund M Dow adailaae was living Newburyport 1918, but no family appeared in directory. To a letter of genealogical inquiry he returned without comment a newspaper clipping about a Cambridge Dow, absolutely unrelated and unknown to him.

Amos V Dow adailaaf m Mch 1877 Emily Dow b and of Seabrook. She is unplaced. Rec of this whole line are in a very fragmentary state.

Mary Dow adailxx. The next name in 1850 census to adailaa is Mary Dow b Me 1805. Presumably wid, with children:

a   George b Mass 1838   b   Ezra b Mass 1843; both untraced

Zachaeus Dow adaim, cordwainer of Hampton Falls and Seabrook, has much the largest posterity of the Seabrook Dow. Upon him to a greater extent than the other brothers who remained in Seabrook fell the inheritance of the finer qualities of Judah Dow; to his posterity has remained the best of the Seabrook Dow. Zachaeus is in the Hampton Falls tax list 1789-92. His wife Janna in deeds or Jane in m rec bought Apr 30, 1792, about 4 acres of Seabrook land from David Dow, joyner. This may be any of three Davids; and the land became the homestead. Zachaeus bought five acres in Seabrook Nov 2, 1812, from Jacob Felch of Kensington. He was living widower in 1850. Next to him in census stands Julia A Dow b 1841, who has not yet been recognized. Reliable family rec give the children, who are not found in town rec. This large family constituted probably a fourth of the disconnected Seabrook Dows until the work of Miss Mary J Greene, a splendid achievement, arranged them with a completeness found in few other branches:

a   Isaiah b 1791 (census, 1795); d June 1873
b   Tristram b 1792; d Nov 1, 1868
c   William b 1794   d   Jane b 1797; d Oct 23, 1870
e   Zacchaeus   f   Susan E (Susan R in rec m)

Isaiah Dow adaima lived neighbor of Zebulon Dow adaijb, near the site of the present railroad depot; property assessed 1850 at $300; m Feb 20, 1816, Mary Ann Felch b Nov 18, 1791, d Jan 2, 1879, dau of Daniel of Seabrook. This was the first intermarriage, there being many subsequent, with the posterity of Daniel Felch, first Felch to live in Seabrook, a fisherman. Census does not give her, but gives Jemima b 1800, not found otherwise. Children, by sure family rec:

a John Plummer b 1817   b Miriam Jane b Aug 1820; m Tristram **Dow**
c Josiah Felch b 1824; d Apr 26, 1849, unm
d Thomas d in childhood
e Sophia Ann b Jan 3, 1831; d Jan 9, 1871; m Emery Brown
f Sarah Felch b 1833   g Emeline b 1836; m Charles Barnard

John P Dow adaimaa, farmer, d July 7, 1883; m Mch 21, 1847, Susan J Walton, a 2nd cousin, b Jan 1829, d Oct 17, 1856, dau of William of Seabrook; m 2nd Mch 10, 1858, Mary Jane Butler b Feb 1833, d Nov 23, 1883, dau of Michael and Mary A (Fretson) of Nova Scotia. He inherited the homestead. Children:

a John William Walton b Oct 14, 1848
b Adelaide Adelia b Aug 2, 1851; d Jan 22, 1892
c William Swett b 1852   d Abbott, twin, d in infancy
e Rebecca J b 1855; d in infancy   f —— dau b May 10, 1859
g Susan Jane b Mch 1860; m Frank Field; 1 child d in infancy
h George Hubbard b June 1862; d Dec 28, 1894; farmer of Seabrook, m Dec 25, 1888, Emogene Boyd, ae 22, dau of Daniel and Sarah. No children

John W W Dow adaimaaa, shoemaker, m Jan 3, 1870, Anna Evelyn Dow adaimbid b Oct 3, 1853; d Nov 29, 1907. Children:

a Marietta b Sept 4, 1870   b Elias Howe b Dec 17, 1871
c Sarah T H b Jan 6, 1873; m Charles O Smith
d Melissa b Jan 23, 1875; m William Prescott
e —— d Mch 8, 1880, ae 3 days

Marietta Dow adaimaaaa m Mch 15, 1891, Charles Bell Brown of Hampton Falls; moved to Seabrook. She is much interested in Dow genealogy and well versed in local rec. Children:

a Eugene Russell b July 3, 1892; d Sept 27, 1918, unm
b Marjorie Dow b Sept 11, 1894

Elias H Dow adaimaaab m Sept 28, 1899, Villa Dow adaimbbda; live in homestead inherited from great grandfather. Children:

a William Winship b Feb 11, 1890
b Harry Walton b Sept 5, 1891; d Mch 18, 1893
c Carroll Webster b Jan 16, 1896

William W Dow adaimaaaba, shoe worker of Seabrook, m Feb 29, 1908, Ina M (Jura, Exeter rec) Dow adgcadaaaaa; div; m 2nd July 31, 1917, Irene Grace Donley, ae 21, dau of William W and Alice (Doughty). Children:

a Evelyn   b Tyler E b Exeter Dec 23, 1908

Carroll W Dow adaimaaabc, shoemaker of Seabrook, m Dec 9, 1916,

Ruby B Fowler b Nov 19, 1895, dau of Jacob Salonius and Huldah (Dow) adgxfccd. Child:

   a Reginald Webster b Aug 19, 1917

Sarah T H Dow adaimaaac m 1897 Charles O Smith of Seabrook; d Mch 7, 1903. Children:

   a Elijah b Feb 18, 1898   b Sadie Dow b Mch 1, 1903

Melissa Dow adaimaaad m William Prescott of Mansfield, Mass. Children:

   a Jennie E b Feb 1899   b John Dow b Dec 11, 1900
   c Faith McKinley b Feb 1902   d Helen b July 1904
   e Gladys b Aug 1906   f Lennox b Sept 1909

Adelaide A Dow adaimaab m Sept 29, 1869, Abram Dow (unplaced) of Seabrook d June 9, 1902. Children:

   b Herbert Lester b July 23, 1870   c Leonard Jasper b 1876
   d Andrin J b Salisbury May 24, 1883; killed in railroad accident Nov 12, 1912
   e Jesse Morgan b June 2, 1884; lives Mass; has a child

Herbert L Dow adaimaabb m Oct 1, 1898, Alice Mary Walton, ae 18, dau of James L and Ellen F (Barton) of Seabrook. They lived Wakefield, Mass; he d Seabrook Oct 15, 1920. Son:

   a Clyde Walton b Wakefield Sept 18, 1907

Leonard J Dow adaimaabc lives Seabrook; m May 18, 1901, Fannie E Gynan, dau of Nicholas and Miriam R (Fowler). Children:

   a Avetta b Dec 19, 1905   b Leonard J b Feb 19, 1908
   c Gynan b July 17, 1909

Jesse M Dow adaimaabe b Seabrook m Marion Stewart b Wakefield. Child:

   a Lloyd Alexander b Wakefield Sept 12, 1910

William S Dow adaimaac lives Newburyport; m July 13, 1874, Sarah R Killburn, dau of John. Dau:

   a Angeline Thurlow

Sophia Ann Dow adaimae m Emery Brown of Seabrook. Children:

   a Clara Augusta b Jan 25, 1851; m David A Whittier of Hampton Falls; had
      the Stacy L Nudd adhcdad homestead
   b Eugene b Apr 5, 1854; d July 4, 1908

Sarah F Dow adaimaf m Apr 23, 1854, Joseph Taylor Weare b Dec 3, 1828, son of Taylor and Mary (Redman); lived Hampton. Children:

   a Ella Maria b Jan 17, 1855; m James Henry Jenness; went to Colo
   b Charles Austin b Mch 13, 1857; lived Hampton; m Kate Julia Pritchett
   c Rosie Bell b Aug 20, 1859; m John Wesley Richardson of Andover, Mass.
   d Annie Laurie b Dec 17, 1864; m Edgar Deal of Hampton
   e Alice Sarah b Aug 24, 1867
   f Josephine b June 1872; d June 20, 1879

Emeline Dow adaimag m May 17, 1862, Charles Barnard of Salisbury; moved, probably to Amesbury. Children:

a Mary Abbie   b Charles

Tristram Dow adaimb lived Seabrook; d Nov 4, 1868; m Oct 4, 1813, Rachel Fowler d Apr 5, 1870, dau of Abraham. Children:

a Tristram b 1814   b Newell b 1817; d Oct 28, 1882
c Sewall B b 1820   d Phineas B b July 11, 1821
e Zelpha   f Hannah b Oct 26, 1826; d Jan 2, 1903
g Betsey Jane   h Dennis b Apr 9, 1831   i Levi b Sept 12, 1833

Tristram Dow adaimba d Mch 20, 1880; m Oct 26, 1843, Miriam J Dow adaimab. Her family objected to the match on account of cousinship, but Tristram after two years wooing gave an ultimatum of having the girl or going to sea. She d Nov 12, 1882. Of ten children, six married:

a Laura E b 1844; d Feb 1, 1860
b Zelpha Ann b Oct 9, 1846; m John Alvin Dow adhcdaa
c Lydia J b Oct 1848; d Apr 22, 1851
d Josiah Felch b Jan 2, 1851; d Jan 14, 1851
e Mima L b Jan 21, 1852; d Oct 3, 1909
f Lucy Adelaide b 1855   g Emma Jane b 1857
h Charles J b Oct 27, 1859; d in infancy
i James W b 1862   j Annie C b 1864

Mima L Dow adaimbae m Mch 29, 1874, George C Locke of Seabrook, son of Jeremiah A. Children:

a Elnora L b Feb 26, 1875; d Apr 19, 1880
b Laura Jane b Aug 9, 1877; d Apr 23, 1880
c Inez A b Nov 22, 1884; m Otis Eastman
d Mary L b Oct 22, 1889; m Harold C Felch
e Luella B b Dec 22, 1892; m ——

Lucy A Dow adaimbaf m 1873 Ivory W Chase d Apr 4, 1901, son of Thomas of Seabrook; she d before 1918. Children:

a William T b 1874; m ——   b Fred L b 1876; m Fannie Janvrin
c Lowell A b 1878; m Mary J Beckman
d Lena M b 1881; m Henry W Knowles

Emma J Dow adaimbag m Aug 6, 1875, Charles F Jones of Hampton Falls; neither living 1915. Child:

a Arthur

James W Dow adaimbai, shoemaker, m Apr 18, 1883, Josephine M Walton b 1865, d 189-, dau of Cyrus and Rosanna; m 2nd Hampton Falls July 2, 1888, Lillian S Perkins, ae 21, dau of Charles G and Nancy (Gove) of Seabrook; moved to Newburyport about 1898. Children:

a Earl W b Aug 30, 1883   b Pauline b Feb 7, 1890
c —— dau b June 6, 1892   d —— son b July 13, 1897

Earl W Dow adaimbaia m Lynn May 10, 1906, Alicea F (Taylor) Nason, ae 22, dau of Frank and Julia. Children, b Nahant:

a Dorothy Delsey b May 28, 1906   b Doris Mae b Aug 28, 1908

Annie C Dow adaimbaj m Apr 23, 1884, Smith Davis of Salisbury; live Amesbury; 2 dau:

    b   Julia M b 1887; m Amesbury Sept 1, 1910, Foster L Clapham, ae 24

Newell Dow adaimbb, railroad flagman at Seabrook, d Oct 28, 1882; m Mch 18, 1841, Nancy Walton d Mch 27, 1897, ae 76, dau of Daniel and Nancy (Brown).　Children:

    a   Alfred Newell b Oct 25, 1841　　　b Esther A b Aug 15, 1844
    c   Julia E b Nov 1848; d Mch 3, 1851
    d   Warren Woodbury b Jan 5, 1851; d June 3, 1912
    e   Mary M　　　　　　　　　　f Angelia b and d 1857
    g   Alroy C b Jan 15, 1861; d June 9, 1902
    h   Annie Newell b 1863; m Apr 8, 1881, Timothy C Crowley of Portsmouth; 1
        child d in infancy

Alfred N Dow adaimbba d Aug 13, 1909; enlisted 3rd N H; disch June 23, 1862; Seabrook Council of Veterans is named for him; m Nov 1, 1862, Ellen F Butler, dau of Michael and Mary (Fretson).　Child:

    a   Annie Newell b Sept 12, 1863; d May 1, 1864

Esther A Dow adaimbbb d Dec 17, 1918; m Nov 6, 1859, Francis Beckman of Seabrook, veteran of Civil War.　Children:

    a   Frank　　　　　　b Louisa b 1864; m James Wright; 2nd Edsyl Churchill
    c   Lemuel S b Aug 14, 1866; m Sallie A Knowles
    d   Clara d young　　e Laura m —— Dennett; 2nd —— Smith
    f   Eugene Hale m Addie Barton　　　g Lillian b May 1873; d May 3, 1891
    h   George m ——　　i Leon E b 1878; m Mazie Rowe; 2nd ——

Warren W Dow adaimbbd m Arvilla Beal, dau of Winship and Emily J (Walton); m 2nd Rhoda Ann Dow granddau of adgxf; lived Seabrook village.　Children:

    a   Villa b 1873; her mother dying, she was taken by grandparents and known as
        Villa Beal; m Elias H Dow adaimbdc
    b   Lena Woodbury b Aug 3, 1875; m Dec 21, 1891, Charles Brown of New London,
        N H; children,—Dora, Gertrude
    c   Mamie Newell b June 21, 1878; unm; children,—Daniel Dow b Aug 26, 1900,
        Ruth Woodbury b Feb 4, 1903, Lena B Raddin b May 3, 1911, Rhoda
        Augusta Raddin b 1913
    d   Daniel b Nov 23, 1883 (surely error, not in family rec)
    e   John N b Nov 30, 1883; d Oct 20, 1902
    f   Arthur W b Nov 6, 1886; d Jan 29, 1890
    g   Henry B b May 29, 1890; veteran of France 1918
    h   Lemuel F b Nov 1, 1895; d Jan 29, 1899

Mary M Dow adaimbbe m Jan 15, 1870, George L Gove of Seabrook, son of Albert; he got divorce, m 2nd Delilah F Dow adaijbb.　She resumed her maiden name; m 2nd July 21, 1885 (his 2nd) (adaimbai) Charles G Perkins of Hampton, who moved to Seabrook.　He had by Nancy Gove, 1st wife, Lillian, Flora, Myrtle.　Children:

    a   Ernest L (Gove) b 1870　　　b Harry D (Dow) b about 1884
    c   Corydon N (Perkins) b 1885; m Bernice Caswell
    d   Augusta b July 23, 1890
    e   Percy L b Sept 27, 1894; m Emma P Littlefield

Ernest L Gove adaimbbea, left with father, rejoined his mother as soon as possible and legally took name Dow; station master at Seabrook; m 1886 Anna Maud Chase b Seabrook 1868, d June 22, 1903, dau of Jeremiah and Esther Ann; 2nd Aug 6, 1912, Mrs Mazie Beckman adaimbbbi, div, dau of Jeremiah and Mary (Walton) Rowe. Children:

a Daniel Ernest b Apr 8, 1887; d in infancy
b Esther E b Feb 7, 1893 c Norman Russell b July 28, 1900

Esther C (sic in rec) **Dow** adaimbbeab m Salisbury Aug 19, 1910, James H Pike, ae 22, son of George C and Mary L D (Pike)

Harry D Dow adaimbbeb m May 4, 1907, Bertha Caswell, dau of Henry and Lola M (Eaton). Children:

a Lola May b July 12, 1908
b Caroline Ellen b Aug 14, 1912; d Oct 25, 1913
c Alfred Newell b June 8, 1916

Alroy C Dow adaimbbg, shoemaker of Seabrook, d June 9, 1902; m Mch 22, 1884, Ida May Felch b 1869, dau of Frederick F and Nancy L of Seabrook. Children:

a Roscoe F b July 30, 1884   b Charlotte b Apr 28, 1898

Roscoe F Dow adaimbbga m Amesbury May 11, 1903, Alberta Rines, ae 22, dau of Albert and Fannie (Davis). Child:

a —— son b Newburyport Feb 6, 1905

Sewall B Dow adaimbc m (int pub Dec 26, 1846) Almira P Robinson of Newburyport b Bath, Me, 1828, d Amesbury 1885. He d 1880; they lived in the part annexed some years ago to Amesbury. Children:

a Philena b 1848; m ——   b Granville S
c Crystodell b Jan 8, 1859; m —— Smith   d —— prob d in infancy
e Laura b Feb 28, 1865
f Charles Archie b May 9, 1872

Granville S Dow adaimbcb m Emma C Twombly of Gilmanton, 4 children; m 2nd Clara Fogg, no children:

b —— son b Seabrook Aug 29, 1877
c Everett Gardner b Salisbury May 10, 1883; untraced
d Lena E m, ae 16, June 2, 1904, George B Eaton of Seabrook, ae 24

Laura Dow adaimbce of Amesbury m 1884 William Ellsworth Butler, son of Robert and Ellen Knight (Lamprey); settled in Hampton. Children:

a Howard Ellsworth b July 6, 1886   b John Wesley b 1892

Charles A Dow adaimbcf, metal worker of Newburyport, m —— Fogg, sister of adaimbcb; 2nd after 1900 wid Etta H Beadley, ae 44, dau of Daniel B and Lydia C (Dole) Nutting of Portsmouth.

Phineas B Dow adaimbd, fisherman, d Jan 28, 1893; m May 31, 1845, Mary Ann Felch b Aug 26, 1826, d May 29, 1898, dau of Elias and Elizabeth (Boyd). Children:

a Phineas A b Dec 17, 1845; shoemaker, d Oct 9, 1868, unm
b Daniel F W b July 19, 1847; d Oct 1849

c   Elias H b Oct 26, 1849; d Oct 10, 1867; unm
d   Daniel W b Dec 3, 1851; d July 1863
e   Anna Evelyn b Oct 3, 1853; d Jan 3, 1870; m John W Dow adaimaaa
f   Melissa b June 20, 1856; d Apr 22, 1878, unm
g   Harriet E b Oct 20, 1858   h   John H b Oct 3, 1860; d Nov 1861
i   Lizzie F b Mch 31, 1862; d Dec 14, 1903; m Frank W Ordway; no children
j   Hannah M b July 6, 1865; d July 1872
k   Betsey J b Apr 16, 1869; m Apr 2, 1885, Arthur W Randall; 1 son, 1 dau

Harriet E Dow adaimbdg d Salisbury Nov 15, 1901; m Charles E Jackman of Salisbury.

Zelpha Dow adaimbe m Nov 13, 1843, Daniel Felch; 2nd July 6, 1866, John Twombly of Raymond, N H. No children.

Hannah Dow adaimbf m Nov 17, 1844, Jacob Fowler 3rd; 2nd Robert Beckman. Children, by 1st husband:

a   Margaret Ann   b   Mima Jane   c   Jacob Salonius

Betsey J Dow adaimbg m Nov 9, 1848, James Fowler; 2nd Apr 4, 1864, Thomas Flanders. Children, by 1st husband:

a   Augusta   b   Tristram   c   James   d   Betsey

Dennis R Dow adaimbh m Oct 14, 1848, Polly Ann Beckman of Seabrook d Newburyport, ae 69, dau of John and Abigail (Walton). They moved to Newburyport. Children, b Seabrook:

a   Drusilla b 1849   b   Amos G   c   Manfred D b 1852
d   Charles A b Nov 12, 1859 (perhaps error, perhaps identical with next)
e   Charles O b Oct 1860; d Jan 12, 1873   f   Alfred E b 1861-2
g   Lettie J b May 24, 1869; m Frank Moody; 2nd Sam Truesdell

Drusilla Dow adaimbha of Seabrook m Mch 17, 1864, Lewis S Lamprey b Dec 27, 1841, son of Daniel and Hannah P. She d June 19, 1883; he m 2nd Carrie E Brown. Children of Drusilla:

a   Lettie J b May 24, 1864; d 1887
b   Marietta b Aug 3, 1867; m George B Blake, son of George A
c   Daniel Perley b July 14, 1869; m July 2, 1892, Annie J Graves of Elgan, Me
d   Howard E b Feb 24, 1876; m 1895
e   William E b Oct 26, 1878; m 1897   f   Lewis T b Mch 9, 1882

Amos G Dow adaimbhb m Mch 3, 1877, Harriet E Gove, both of Seabrook; lived Salisbury and Newburyport. Children:

a   Charles Austin b Aug 6, 1877; married; untraced. Four Chas A Dow are in
      Newburyport directory
b   Chester Key b Aug 6, 1877; married; untraced   c   Zaida

Zaida M Dow adaimbhbc of Newburyport m Jan 7, 1904, John Allen Winchester, ae 30, son of James A and Emma E (Tibbetts). Children, b Newburyport:

a   —— dau b July 11, 1904   b   Helen Gove b Jan 21, 1906

Manfred D Dow adaimbhc m Sept 5, 1876, Mary B Eaton, ae 23, of Seabrook; now living Salisbury. Children:

a   Manfred Lewis b Newburyport 1877
b   Dennis Franklin b Salisbury June 5, 1879

Manfred L Dow adaimbhca of Salisbury d Oct, 1918; m Aug 16, 1906, Bessie C Fowler of Seabrook, ae 14, dau of Adna B. Children:

   a Alfred Ellsworth b Jan 26, 1907   b Dorothy March b Mch 2, 1915

Dennis F Dow adaimbhcb m Mary Callahan of Gloucester; live Salisbury; children:

   a Alice Gertrude b July 6, 1901   b Ervin Franklin b Oct 23, 1902
   c Manfred Cotton b Oct 19, 1904
   d Murl Randolph b Mch 11, 1908; d Jan 14, 1915
   e Percy Glover b Sept 24, 1909   f Dana Frederick b Oct 14, 1912
   g Randolph Clement b Mch 29, 1916   h Eleanor Mara b July 8, 1919

Alfred E Dow adaimbhf of Salisbury and Newburyport m Ida Ruddock. Child:

   a Lula May b May 12, 1880

Levi Dow adaimbi of Seabrook d Sept 5, 1902; m Oct 5, 1851, Mary Abigail Beckman of Seabrook; 2nd Mch 26, 1858, Martha F Souther, ae 18, of Seabrook d Oct 15, 1918, ae 78-10-23. Children:

   a Josiah F b Mch 1, 1852
   b Abbie C b 1854; m George G Small; 9 children
   c Daniel W b May 19, 1858; d 1863
   d George L b Nov 12, 1859; d Apr 6, 1917, unm
   e Jennie b May 16, 1863; d Mch 16, 1889; unm
   f James W b 1866   g Herbert b June 3, 1868
   h Bertie F b June 4, 1869; d June 28, 1898, unm
   i *Emma A b Nov 25, 1870*   j *Minnie Maud b 1871*
   k Hannah Zoa b Apr 1873; m July 4, 1890, William J Price; 2nd Charles Gray; no children   l Willard Alvin b and d 1875

Josiah F Dow adaimbia m Nancy Janvrin of Seabrook; d June 24, 1905. Children:

   a —— b May 1, 1878; d young
   b Cora M b 1875; m Sept 30, 1892, Charles A Beckman; 10 children
   c Talbot J b 1879
   d Bessie L b July 31, 1884; d Jan 22, 1905; m Clarence Blaisdell of Salisbury, ae 28, son of Calvin D and Mary E (Eaton)

Talbot J Dow adaimbiac, shoemaker of Seabrook, m Feb 24, 1906, Evelyn Beckman, ae 17, dau of Edgar and Hattie M (Janvrin). Children:

   a ——   b Bessie May b Sept 22, 1908; d Oct 18, 1908
   c Katherine Evelyn b Apr 23, 1909 (1910?)
   d Mildred Stanley b July 26, 1911
   e Agnes S b Mch 28, 1913   f Florence Talbot b Mch 7, 1915

James W Dow adaimbif (known as 2nd), shoemaker of Seabrook, m May 15, 1890, Sadie A Murphy b Tilton, N H, 1871, dau of Michael and Sarah J. Children:

   a Jennie b Apr 7, 1891
   b Levi C b Oct 22, 1894; wounded and gassed Chateau Thierry 1918
   c Lillian Maud b June 12, 1898; m Elmer C King
   d Henry Archie b Dec 24, 1899; marine in late war
   e Emma Pearl b Dec 24, 1899; m George W Ross Jr. Son George Levi b Oct 5, 1917

f   George Russell b Jan 18, 1903   g —— dau b and d Aug 13, 1904
h   Granville S b June 1, 1906   i Martha Rachel b Nov 20, 1907
j   James Murphy b July 21, 1912   k Bessie Sadie b Oct 22, 1914

Jennie Dow adaimbifa m Haverhill Apr 7, 1910, George Warren Merrill Jr, ae 21, son of George W and Hattie D (Reiley)

Minnie M Dow adaimbij m May 30, 1894, Irving N Perkins, son of Jonathan O of Hampton; lived Seabrook.   Children:

a   Henry O wounded at Chateau Thierry
b   Frank A b Jan 19, 1897; soldier in France
c   Bertie Lee b June 27, 1899   d   Raymond b Apr 12, 1901

William Dow adaimc, sailor of Newburyport, returned to Seabrook; d May 24, 1869; m Oct 28, 1818, Sarah A Eaton b Pittsfield, d Mch 8, 1878, ae 78.   Family rec, apparently error, gives m 2nd Sarah Merrill.   Children:

a   Susan Jane d Oct 6, 1903, ae 86-11-6; m Nov 13, 1838, Abram Brown, both of
    Seabrook
b   Rhoda R
c   Lorilla d June 18, 1907; m Oct 13, 1846, Andrew J Merrill of Seabrook; 2nd
    John Eaton
d   Betsey F d 1875, ae 49; m July 6, 1854, Jacob Dow adgxffaa
e   John Merrill b 1827
f   Eleanor M b 1829; d Dec 2, 1907; m Feb 1, 1848, Joshua M Eaton
g   Eliza Ann b 1836; d Dec 30, 1915, ae 77-11-27; m John N Walton
h   Isaiah b 1838; d May 9, 1869, crippled and weak minded
i   Emeline B b 1840; d Aug 26, 1912; m May 19, 1860, Daniel B Follansbee

Rhoda R Dow adaimcb m Newburyport Jan 11, 1844, Samuel D Hoyt b Chichester July 14, 1821, master mariner of Newburyport, son of Ephraim and Jemima.   Newburyport rec give 2 children:

a   George Stephen b Oct 3, 1844   b   Charles Alfred b Jan 19, 1849

John M Dow adaimce, cordwainer of So Seabrook, d June 11, 1902; generally known as Skete Dow; late in life was tried and acquitted on charge of murder; m June 17, 1851, Lydia A Eaton.   Children:

a   Elizabeth b 1853; d 1865   b   David F b June 29, 1859
c   John M d Mch 5, 1859, ae 7 mos
d   Abbie J b 1861; m Gilman Eaton; 2nd Lewis A Knowles; 3rd John M Beckman
e   —— dau d young
f   Lizzie G b 1867; d Nov 21, 1899; m Nov 24, 1882, Charles W Eaton
g   John F b Nov 12, 1872

David F Dow adaimceb, fisherman and shoemaker, m June 4, 1880, Zelphia A Fowler of Seabrook, dau of John and Maria; moved from Seabrook.   Seven children, 5 mentioned in family rec:

a   —— b Oct 25, 1880 (to David F and Lydia, State rec)
b   Daniel C b Mch 8, 1881; d Mch 20, 1885
c   Lizzie G b 1882; m May 16, 1899, Sidney A Fowler
d   Wildemina b Apr, d Sept 20, 1882
e   Wildemina b 1884; m Mch 14, 1901, Frank M Janvrin
f   David C b May 9, 1885 (State, not family rec; see below)
g   —— dau b Nov 10, 1887   h   Sarah E b Aug 2, 1889
i   Carrie H d Amesbury Apr 3, 1907, ae 15

Wilda M Dow adaimbcebe m Frank M Janvrin. Children b Newburyport:

  a Walter Edward b Apr 17, 1904   b —— son b Jan 21, 1906
  c Frank M b Apr 13, 1909

Walter B Dow adaimcebe appears unmistakably in own rec; m, ae 23, son of David F and Zelphia Fowler, Salisbury, Nov 7, 1908, Mary E Dow, ae 23, both of Seabrook, dau of Henry H adkffbbja and Liona G (Eaton). Further untraced

John F Dow adaimceg m Oct 16, 1893, Ella H Souther, ae 16, dau of Robert dec and Ida B; div, she m 2nd James L Eaton. He did not remarry. Children:

  a Robert H b 1894   b ——
  c Cora Ella b Aug 30, 1899; m Feb 21, 1915; John Warren Jones; div; m 2nd, Dec 25, 1918, Charles H Souther, both of So Seabrook

Robert H Dow adaimcega m Feb 22, 1914, Ella M Jones ae 18, dau of Frank W and Lillian M (Randall). More than 1 child:

  a Lillian Hayes b Sept 24, 1914

Jane Dow adaimd m Oct 20, 1823, Hubbard Locke b 1802, d Dec 1875, son of Simon and Mary (Dow) adggbd. Eight children, of whom:

  a Abbie m Edward Park   b Lydia m Elihu Dow adgxfbf

Zachaeus Dow adaime, shoemaker, m Salisbury Nov 6, 1831, Betsey L Brown b Seabrook 1806, d Mch 6, 1869, dau of Thomas and Abigail. Perhaps only child:

  a George Falls b July 6, 1834

George F Dow adaimea of Seabrook d Sept 7, 1907; m Adeline J Felch b Aug 23, 1838, d Nov 3, 1903, dau of Thomas, fisherman, and Sally (Brown), both of Seabrook. Children:

  a Julia d Seabrook Mch 4, 1866; b Oct 23, 1863
  b Sylvana m Oct 13, 1877, Amos H Ross of Yarmouth, N S; dau Nellie G, m 2nd Lewis A Robinson and lives (1922) on homestead
  c George Percy b July 28, 1871; unm

T HAT farm, belonging to Joseph Dow ad, which lay nearest to Hampton was the inheritance of his 2nd son:

John Dow adb m Hampton Nov 26, 1696, Hannah Page, who presumably became a Friend either at marriage or as soon afterwards as the Friends were safely established. She is bed of our key; the Hingham family. John (1) Page m Mary Marsh, dau of George, immigrant. Joseph (2) Page bap Hingham Mch 5, 1647-8, m 2nd Martha Dow be, wid of Joseph Heath. This couple are the ancestors of the large Quaker Dow family of Maine, almost all the Maine Friends originating in the Hampton district.

Joseph Dow, Hist Hampton, was a little disturbed by his discovery that a son Jonathan was b May 2, 1695, to John and Sarah Dow. This is our Dow family d of Newington

Children of John and Hannah Page:

a   John b 1698   b   Hannah b 1700 (neither rec extant)
c   Judith b Nov or Dec 21, 1702; m June 4, 1740, John Purington, Quaker of
        Seabrook
d   Martha b Mch 2, 1704; m Feb 15, 1725-6, George Conner, late of Salisbury,
        then of Hampton, son of John dec and Elizabeth
e   Benjamin b Aug 10, 1706; m Abigail ——; d Hampton Falls 1748; surely
        without children
f   Sarah b Oct 23, 1709
g   Rachel b May 20, 1712; m Mch 1, 1728-9, Richard Collins of Newbury, Quaker
h   Phoebe b Mch 4, 1718

So far as the Author can ascertain, not one of this family is today among the Friends, altho they were for 150 years consistent.

John Dow adba moved to Kensington; d 1767; m Apr 20, 1731, Patience Swett, dau of Moses and Mary (Hussey). Children:

a   Huldah b Mch 9, 1732   b   Moses b Jan 7, 1734
c   Hannah b Dec 31, 1735   d   Mary b Apr 28, 1738; d young
e   Patience b Apr 7, 1740; m Stephen Brown b Nov 19, 1724, d Oct 24, 1786, son
        of William and Ann (Heath)
f   John b Mch 2, 1743   g   Paul b Oct 8, 1746

Huldah Dow adbaa m Nov 29, 1749, Jonathan Green, son of Jeremiah and Dorothy of Kensington; d after 1770; he m 2nd Oct 21, 1778, wid Abigail Perkins, by whom son Winthrop d Kensington Oct 30, 1790. Huldah's children:

a   Jonathan b Apr 5, 1751; [d?]1776; m Phebe Sargent
b   Levi b Mch 27, 1753; d 1833; m Judith Chase; 2nd Sarah Cortland
c   Abraham b Mch 26, 1755; d Aug 21, 1815; m his step sister Abigail Perkins
d   Simon b Apr 16, 1757; d Jan 10, 1838; m Abial Chase; 2nd Sarah Allen
e   Moses b Oct 28, 1760; d Dec 28, 1817; m Hannah Page
f   Mary b June 23, 1763   g   Stephen b Mch 1, 1766; m Mary Page
h   Huldah b Jan 26, 1770; m Micajah Page

Moses Dow adbab, venerable patriarch of Maine Quakers, m Hampton Dec 8, 1756, Hannah Gove d 30: 9 mo: 1799, dau of Jonathan and

Hannah (Worthen). They moved to Dover where he was admitted to meeting 2: 12 mo: 1759. A few years later they with a considerable party pushed on to Berwick, Me, founding a strong Quaker colony. He d Berwick 31: 10 mo: 1816. Berwick town and Friends rec seldom agree in dates, town rec probably compiled later. Census of 1790 gives Moses la, 3b, 3c, easily reconcilable with rec:

    a   Pelatiah b 11: 5 mo: 1759: d 11: 10 mo: 1792
    b   Jonathan b 26: 9 mo: 1762
    c   Mary b 20: 1 mo: 1765; m 23: 8 mo: 1787, John Buffum d Jan 9, 1812;
          moved to Vassalboro
    d   Hannah b 29: 5 mo: 1769 (1767?)
    e   John b 18: 5 mo: 1769; d 15: 9 mo: 1770
    f   John b June 4, 1771   g   Moses b 5: 4 mo: 1773
    h   Paul b 22: 9 mo: 1775   i   Richard b 22: 7 mo: 1777

    The ms of Edgar R Dow gives without dates additional children,—Hosea, Huldah,
    Patience. If existed, probably d young; more likely cited in error

Jonathan Dow adbabb moved July 23, 1785, to Falmouth, about 1798 to Harlem, later China, Me, where a strong Quaker colony was established. This township was first settled by church people in 1774. Jonathan m 21: 5 mo: 1788, Huldah Beede d 1792, dau of Jonathan and Ann of Poplin, N H; m 2nd Berwick 23: 7 mo: 1793, Abra Wentworth, dau of John and Hannah of Rochester. Census 1790 gives then of Vassalboro 1, lb, lc. N E Gen Reg 1909 gives him m Alexa Winthworth; other rec say Abia, Ahra and Alexandr. Friends rec give b of children, but no more:

    a   Moses b Vassalboro 15: 8 mo: 1789
    b   John b Vassalboro 5: 4 mo: 1797
    c   Richard b Harlem 10: 4 mo: 1799; untraced or confused with adbabi
    d   ——   e   Elijah b Harlem 2: 5 mo: 1801; d Oct 2, 1816
    f   Daniel b Harlem 18: 5 mo: 1805; untraced

Moses Dow adbabba is untraced. When Jonathan and Alexa transferred their membership in 1808 from Harlem, their certificate named all the children except Moses, who was then 19. Perhaps he was bound out. In Palermo nearby there lived a Moses Dow to great age; d May 6, 1879. With him lived Mary Dow and Jane Dow, one his wife, other his sister. Now, adbabba had no sister of either name. Moses is still remembered in the vicinity from his poverty and lameness, having two clubbed feet. He had a large family, one being Charles, who moved to Camden. A search in 1923 failed to find him. Hannah B Dow of Palermo m (int May 7, 1870) may be a dau, but the larger family of Palermo Dow was not related.

An elderly resident of Palermo recalls that the 1st born of Moses was named Frank. Moses also had a dau,—Mahala, said to be named for her mother. If this is so, Mary and Jane were presumably daughters of Moses.

John Dow adbabbb m Mary Meader and is known to have had 4 sons, 5 dau. It is vaguely stated that he had sons John Meader b China 1816 and Benjamin, but there is no definite trace. Beyond reasonable doubt there is a considerable posterity of adbabb, much now in our Maine disconnected chapter, but not a single member is traced. A rec which presumably belongs here is: Moses W Dow of Brooks m Belfast Aug 24, 1856, Maria H Jellison of Waldo.

Mary Dow adbabc m Berwick 23: 8 mo: 1787, John Buffum d 7: 1 mo: 1812, son of Joshua and Elizabeth. His 1st wife was Hannah Rogers. Mary's children:

 a Peace b May 30, 1790; d 14: 3 mo: 1811
 b Huldah D b Feb 12, 1794; m Aaron Varney
 c Zerviah b Feb 6, 1797; m Simeon Varney

Hannah Dow adbabd m Sept 22, 1796, David Gove b 1767, d 1805, son of David and Martha (Hoag); transferred from Berwick meeting to Weare, N H. Children:

 a Anna b Jan 25, 1797; m Eliphalet Paige, son of John and Hannah (Page); 8 children
 b Hannah b Nov 24, 1798; m Capt Samuel Reynolds of Portland, son of Joseph and Abigail (Pinkham)
 c Hiram b Feb 23, 1800; physician; m Mary Sargent Neale; div; m 2nd 1848 Mary Ann Thurber
 d Charles Dow b Feb 2, 1802; m Mary Richards of Goffstown; 2nd Lavina S Ham; 6 children
 e Ruth b 1805; m Hollis Witt of Henniker; 2 children

John Dow adbabf m Feb 22, 1797, Zilpha Lincoln b Lincolnville, dau of Isaac and Lucy of Bristol. She d June 15, 1826; he m 2nd 1829 Jane Hussey of Dover, wid, dau of Moses and Priscilla Bickford. She was a traveling Quaker preacher, well known throughout the two States. The family moved many times from one meeting to another. In the Berwick minutes is still preserved the copy of John's dismissal from Vassalboro: 25, 3 mo, 1803. To the monthly meeting of Friends at Vassalborough. John Dow having requested a removal Certificate to your Monthly Meeting for himself and family, we therefore certify you that he and Zilphia his wife are members of our Monthly Meeting and we recommend them with their children Hannah, Otis, Mary and Oliver, who are also members. Joshua Jenkins, Clerk.

The family finally settled at Branch Mills, pioneers of the place, a hamlet being made by clearing the forest. A 30-mile horseback trail to Augusta, marked by blazing the trees, was for some years the only outlet to civilization. Children:

 a Hannah b Feb 5, 1798
 b Otis Little b Berwick May 11, 1799; d July 10, 1888
 c Mary Buffum b Berwick May 25, 1801 d Oliver b Vassalboro Dec 27, 1802
 e Isaac Lincoln b Vassalboro Dec 5, 1804
 f Huldah Beeda b Harlem Feb 12, 1807 g Rhoda Little b May 15, 1809
 h Abigail Lincoln b Mch 15, 1812; d May 1, 1887
 i John Meader b June 8, 1814 j Sarah Lincoln b Oct 16, 1820

Hannah Dow adbabfa d Mch 7, 1839; m Harlem Jan 1, 1818, Tobias Jones, son of Edward and Mary. Children:

 a John D b William c Isaiah d Francis e Edward
 f Mary Ann m —— Roundy

g Sarah Ellen of Bangor m Calvin Reynolds, 4 children; 2nd T C Smart
h Charles E

Otis L Dow adbabfb, wheelwright of Rockland, m Sept 15, 1828, Jane B Young b May 13, 1804, d Oct 13, 1848; probably m 2nd, for the 1850 census gives wife Mary b Me 1800. Hist Thomaston mentions him, giving partial list of children, adding two not belonging to him:

a Adeline E b Sept 21, 1829; d Lowell, Mass, Mch 10, 1864
b Sarah Jane b Apr 8, 1831; d Houston, Tex, Oct 24, 1866; m (int pub Sept 14, 1852) Joseph H Yeaton of Waldoborough
c Edwin Otis b Sept 20, 1833; stock raiser of Warren, Me; untraced
d Harriet Stilson b Oct 2, 1836; m George Dyer; d Shasta, Calif, Mch 19, 1875
e Herbert J b Mch 20, 1838; wheelwright of Rockland; wounded 1862 in 4th Me; d Rockland Mch 19, 1875; m Bristol Feb 11, 1868, Josephine Thompson of Round Point, dau of E N. She obtained div; d Augusta Sept 24, 1893, ae 53. Children,—Harriet, Stilson and Nellie.
f Weston Wesley b May 21, 1840, carriage maker, m Belfast Nov 27, 1867, Jane N Havener; untraced; not living for many years
g Byron J b Nov 21, 1842
h Ella Frances b June 15, 1845; m Fred H Berry of Rockland; neither living
i Charles H M b July 17, 1848; d East Vassalboro Mch 13, 1850

Byron J Dow adbabfbg d Portland Jan 25, 1909; m Rockland Nov 18, 1864, Julia E Green b Camden, d Rockland Feb 3, 1908, ae 60-9-14, dau of William and Julia K (Start) b Scotland. Children:

a Fred B b Camden Mch 15, 1866
b Weston W b Holden Nov 30, 1869; d Bangor Sept 12, 1870
c Edwin O b Northport Apr 18, 1872; 29 years with Maine Central R R
d Frank G b Holden June 12, 1873

Fred B Dow adbabfbga, barber, d Dec 26, 1896; m Rockland Oct 30, 1890, Nettie L Gregory. Child:

a Hazel L b Rockland May 16, 1895

Edwin O Dow adbabfbgc m Rockland June 12, 1894, Mrs Nellie G (Ingraham) Flint, dau of Thomas H and Rebecca A (Healey). Child:

a Mildred A b Rockland Feb 8, 1896

Francis G Dow adbabfbgd, barber, d Portland Jan 31, 1914; m June 4, 1898, Jennie Ruth Godfrey, ae 20, dau of Charles D and Lucy (Waterman) of So Thomaston; div, she m 2nd Boston Apr 12, 1905, Linwood S Hall, ae 30. Francis m 2nd Portland Oct 12, 1903, Clyde Faulkner, ae 22, dau of Thomas W and Annie J (McCulloch). Child:

a Ella Frances b Portland Mch 2, 1904

Mary B Dow adbabfc d May 29, 1846; m China June 23, 1830, Elijah Winslow of China, son of William and Phoebe. Child:

a Zilpah Jane b Apr 29, 1831; d St Albans 1903-4; m Benjamin Shepard; 2nd Daniel Foss

Oliver Dow adbabfd d June 13, 1874; m 1831 or 1832 Elizabeth Milburn b 1810 Wardell Parish, Durham, Eng, d Milltown Aug 8, 1857, not a Friend. This family followed the milling towns. Children:

a John W d Sept 1, 1834
b Isaac Washington b Petticodiac, N B, May 7, 1833

c   Sarah Jane b Grand Menan Feb 8, 1835
d   John Oliver b Milltown Nov 15, 1837
e   Isaiah Lincoln b June 3, 1839   f Mary Elizabeth b Apr 6, 1842
g   Edwin Jeremiah b Milltown Apr 1, d Apr 6, 1842
h   George Willard b July 1, 1849

Isaac W Dow adbabfdb, captain in Civil War, d Neosho Falls, Kan, Sept 27, 1913; m Dec 18, 1872, Mary J Connor b Dec 31, 1833, d Apr 14, 1895. Child:

a   Frank Manning b Mch 4, d Sept 21, 1874

Sarah J Dow adbabfdc d New Hampton, Iowa, June 20, 1907; m Milltown June 8, 1856, Henry Harrison Inness b St Stephen's N B, 1833, d Neosho Falls Dec 23, 1893. Children:

a   Eliza Hill b Milltown Mch 6, 1857; m Neosho Falls Sept 31, 1881, Daniel Donald McDonald. Children,—Donald Inness, Sarah Inness, Reed Inness, Barnes Sibley, Ainsworth Duncan
b   Nellie b Milltown July 17, 1863; d July 19, 1865
c   Frank Wentworth b Milltown Apr 3, 1867; d 1867

John Oliver Dow adbabfdd went west; d Neosho Falls Feb 12, 1905; m Mch 28, 1865, Mary Catherine Mann b Hillhall, Bald Eagle Co, Pa, June 27, 1843; living Neosho Falls 1918. Children:

a   Sarah Jane b Beech Creek, Pa, Apr 30, 1866; m Neosho Falls Nov 10, 1886, George Phillips b Tinmouth, Vt, Mch 31, 1843; living 1918 El Dorado, Kan
b   Laura Mason b Beech Creek July 15, 1868; m Neosho Falls Nov 29, 1892, Elmer E Wilson b La Salle Co, Ill, Mch 29, 1863; no children; live Raton, N M. She furnished almost all the adbabfd line
c   Alice Amelia b Nov 2, 1871; d Aug 5, 1872
d   Eva Covert b Oct 3, 1872; d Mch 20, 1874
e   Oliver Buffum b Mch 13, 1875
f   Bessie Edith b July 20, 1878; of Neosho Falls
g   Lizzie Inness b Apr 23, 1882; m Raton Sept 17, 1905, Eber Ellsworth Odell b Mattoon, Ill; live Joplin, Mo
h   Lowell Blaine b Apr 18, 1885; d Sept 24, 1887
i   Catherine Lenore b May 21, 1888; nurse and physician's asst Neosho Falls

Oliver B Dow adbabfdde of Neosho Falls m Mary —— of Dewsbury, Yorkshire, Eng

Isaiah L Dow adbabfde, veteran of Civil War, master builder, built more than half the houses of Danforth during his 40 years residence; d Danforth Apr 7, 1918; m Sarah Maxwell (1 child); 2nd 1871 her sister Emily Judson Maxwell b Orient May 1853, d Danforth Sept 11, 1916, a Methodist. Children:

a   Willard Jefferson (called William) b Aug 20, 1866
b   Omar Washburn b Sept 29, 1877
c   Elva Leila b Jan 10, 1881; d Apr 24, 1912; m Allen Hall; child,—Beatrice Nathalie b June 17, 1906

Willard J Dow adbabfdea m Bangor July 18, 1890, Lottie Hillman of Haynesville; div; m 2nd May 17, 1918, Frankie May Sears of Cutler, div, ae 38, dau of Benjamin and Susan E Davis. Child:

a   Sarah Frances b July 13, 1893

Omar W Dow adbabfdeb, in 1915 mail carrier of Houlton, m June

7, 1907, Mrs Mary Geneva Smith b Hodgdon Apr 22, 1878, dau of James R and Sarah A (Merrill) Rouix. No children

Mary E Dow adbabfdf d May 30, 1914; m St Stephens, N B, Jan 19, 1861, John Alexander Inness, cousin of George Inness, artist. Children:

a Walter Edwin b Milltown May 18, 1862; d Mch 30, 1904
b Carrie May b May 29, 1864; m James Wallace McClure
c Abbie Alexander b Feb 11, 1867

George W Dow adbabfdh, carpenter of Guthrie, Okla, m Ella —— b Apr 7, 1844. One child:

a Frank C

Frank C Dow adbabfdha moved to Los Angeles about 1918; m May 27, 1903, Hattie Sears b Williamsburg, Ky, May 2, 1885, dau of George and Eliza. Children:

a Ralph S b Guthrie Mch 2, 1904   b Harold b Jan 19, 1906

Isaac L Dow adbabfe d Apr 8, 1918; m China Sept 4, 1830, Mary Jane Hussey b 1810, of Dover, N H, a Friend. Children, b Branch Mills:

a Charles Edwin b Mch 9, 1832; d Jan 5, 1905
b William Mellvill b East Vassalboro Jan 15, 1834, carpenter, d Nov 6, 1912; m May 18, 1856, Ellen M Buffum of Palermo d Palermo Feb 7, 1897, ae 67-8-27, dau of William N and Mary G (Worthing)
c George Lincoln b June 11, 1836; d June 30, 1892
d Everett Newton b Aug 17, 1837; d Mch 5, 1839
e Amanda Jane b Sept 4, 1839; d June 26, 1903
f Everett Milton b Jan 10, 1842; d May 12, 1903
g Newton Russell b Apr 12, 1844; d June 9, 1862
h Roscoe Greenleaf b Sept 4, 1846; d Sept 11, 1871
i Elwood Weston b Oct 30, 1852; d Aug 3, 1888
j Ella Adelaide b Aug 3, 1854; d July 24, 1907, unm

Charles E Dow adbabfea, carriage maker, d China Jan 5, 1905; m Mary Roxana Worthing d Palermo Jan 2, 1905, ae 68, dau of Hiram and Ally (Marden). Children:

a Allston Marden b July 18, 1867   b Frank Newton R b Feb 9, 1869

Allston M Dow adbabfeaa, plumber of Augusta, d Oct 5, 1919; m Danvers, Mass, Apr 30, 1890, Katherine Elizabeth Doyle b Kenmore, Ire. Child:

a Bernard Charles b Augusta Oct 29, 1892; plumber, m Mch 31, 1918, **Barbara** Susie Stevens of Oakland, dau of Herbert and Maud S (Young)

Frank N R Dow adbabfeab m Feb 23, 1893, Nellie M Robinson of China, ae 17, d May 3, 1894, without children, dau of Lorenzo B and Clara (Lane)

George L Dow adbabfec d Boston; enlisted at China; m China June 18, 1858, Almira Pullen Babcock; all his family Free Will Baptists. Children:

a Fred Burton b China Mch 18, 1859
b Villa Gertrude b Sept 3, 1860   c Eva Augusta b Sept 5, 1862

Fred B Dow adbabfeca d Pittsfield Apr 3, 1920; m Boston Oct 12, 1884, Jessie Mabel Connor Worthen of Branch Mills b China Oct 28, 1865, dau of Ensign and Eunice. This Quaker branch generally changed the spelling to Worthing. The couple settled 1889 in Pittsfield. Children:

a   Marion Eunice b Boston Sept 27, 1888
b   (adopted) Lulu Cushing m Harold Crawford

Villa G Dow adbabfecb m Sept 12, 1887, Jacob Norton Tarbell of Meddybemps; moved to Pittsfield May 1909. Children:

a   Arthur Elwood b June 14, 1888, clergyman; m June 25, 1912, Mabel Ethel
      Frost
b   Gladys Elmira b Jan 21, 1891; m Dec 26, 1911, Verne Leighton Shorey of
      Pittsfield. No children
c   Earle Norton b May 29, 1893; sgt in France, promoted to Lieut for gallantry
d   Ruth b July 20, 1899; d Nov 3, 1899
e   Sterling Dow b Jan 21, 1891
f   Eva Gertrude b July 24, 1904; d Oct 3, 1907

Eva Augusta Dow adbabfecc, teacher of Boston, m June 4, 1903, Jesse Crossman Connor of Pittsfield d Dec 28, 1908, without children; lived 2 years in Glendale, Calif. She returned to Pittsfield, is much interested and has been an important helper in this Book.

Amanda J Dow adbabfee d 1918 (1903?); m 1871 (his 2nd) William E Pinkham of China b Nov 11, 1833, son of John and Mary (Coleman). No children.

Everett M Dow adbabfef, carpenter, d May 12, 1903; m Sept 29, 1867, Mary Cinderella Black. Children:

a   Edgar Everett b Jan 5, 1869; d Apr 3, 1893
b   Bertha Alma b Aug 6, 1872
c   Elva Leila b Apr 29, 1878; d July 2, 1896
d   Clifton Osma b Aug 5, 1881   e   Earl Raymond b July 30, 1887

Bertha A Dow adbabfefb m Jan 1, 1901, Frank L Chadwick of So China. Child:

a   Hugh Elden b Augusta Oct 7, 1904

Clifton O Dow adbabfefd, farmer of Palermo, has with him by recent directory his mother and brother Earl L; m Oct 23, 1902, Hattie May Dodge of Palermo, ae 19, dau of Edmund T and Hardie (Bradstreet). Child:

a   Edmund Everett b China Apr 5, 1904

Earl R Dow adbabfefe, laborer of China, later undertaker, m Jan 4, 1911, Margaret Belle McLean of Baddeck, Cape Breton, waitress, ae 25, dau of Donald and Christie (McRae). Children:

a   Milton Edwin b Feb 9, 1912   b   Christine Cinderella b Aug 11, 1917

Elwood W Dow adbabfei m June 29, 1874, Nellie O Bridgham. Child:

a   Percy La Forest b Mch 17, 1877

Percy La F Dowe adbabfeia m Emma Jacobs of Somerville, Mass (child and mother d together); 2nd June 2, 1915, Florence Bertha Hollis of Arlington.   No children.   A civil engineer of West Somerville

Hulda B Dow adbabff m China Sept 13, 1831, George H Collins, son of Paul and Mary adbace.   Children:

   a   Warren Otis b Dec 7, 1837; d Dec 1914   b   Zilpha Angeline

Rhoda L Dow adbabfg b China, d Jan 2, 1911, almost 102 years old, with one exception the longest lived Dow herein recorded.   As a whole, the Quaker matrons of New England have lived longest, and this is notably the case when they have had large families.   Presumably their placidity of disposition favors longevity.   She m May 2, 1834, Thomas Farr b Litchfield Nov 23, 1806, d Feb 25, 1866.   Children:

   a   Lincoln Dow b Mch 12, 1835; d Jan 14, 1883; m Nov 30, 1860, Hannah Maria
       Bailey
   b   Mary Ellen b July 30, 1838; d Aug 30, 1867, unm
   c   Cynthia Maria b Feb 23, 1844; m June 2, 1869, James Nelson Jones, son of
       Silas and Lois, d years ago. Children,—Carroll Nelson, Leroy Farr. In 1927
       Mrs Jones lives Haddon Heights, N J, with one son, the other living next
       door. A very lovely character, she has always been greatly interested in
       this book

Lincoln Dow Farr adbabfga d Camden, N J; his wife d Rome, Italy, Nov 4, 1912.   Children:

   a   Edward Lincoln b Manchester, Me, Oct 25, 1861; m Wenonah, N J, July 28,
       1885, Mabel Ruth Greene b June 30, 1862, d Apr 26, 1899; m 2nd Nov 12,
       1901, Bertha Wallace Farr b June 3, 1878. Five children by 1st wife, six
       by 2nd
   b   Edith May b Winthrop, Me, Oct 9, 1863
   c   Clifford Bailey b Vineland Apr 17, 1872; grad Haverford and Univ of Penn
       Medical; m Katharine Elliott; 5 children
   d   Clara Emily b Vineland Aug 18, 1874; grad Bryn Mawr

Abigail L Dow adbabfh m 4 mo: 1837 Rev Isaiah P Rogers d June 20, 1852, son of Jeremiah and Dorcas; 2nd Sylvanus Laighton.   Children, by 1st husband; all from China Friends rec:

   a   Mary b 25: 4 mo: 1838; d 31: 3 mo: 1865; m Henry Winslow
   b   Martha A b 10: 10 mo: 1839; d Aug 1, 1885
   c   Charles Byron b 13: 3 mo: 1842; killed Gettysburg July 3, 1863
   d   John Wesley b 11: 6 mo: 1843; d Washington, D C, 1: 9 mo: 1865
   e   Emma F b July 13, 1845   f   Ellen A b Feb 27, 1850

John Meader Dow adbabfi, brought up as a wheelwright, bought a 100-acre farm two miles from Brooks village, on what is called Dow's Hill; d May 22, 1899; m Elizabeth Magoon b St Albans Feb 29, 1816, d Brooks Apr 2, 1896.   Children:

   a   Marcellus John b Brooks Sept 7, 1845
   b   Henry O b Mch 7, 1847; d Mch 8, 1864   c   Mary Elizabeth b Mch 6, 1850

Marcellus J Dow adbabfia d Feb 7, 1916; m Nov 15, 1873, Abbie Ermina Lane, dau of John and Mary R (Gould) of Brooks; grad Normal Academy, taught in half a dozen towns while studying law; became supt of schools before devoting himself to law practice. Mason, Good Templar, prominent in other fraternal orders. In Brooks was county judge, selectman, representative to Legislature 1907, besides holding many local offices. Outside his own community he became widely known as a prohibition orator and lieutenant of Gen Neal Dow adhccbh. A Congregationalist. Children:

    a Grace Elida b Jan 15, 1878   b Alice L b Jan 28, 1880

Grace E Dow adbabfiaa m July 11, 1906, Leroy A Batchelder of Swanville.

Alice L Dow adbabfiab m Brooks Aug 23, 1905, Earl D Bessey. Children:

    a Charles Dow b Apr 25, 1908   b John Marcellus b June 18, 1910
    c Earle D b Apr 25, 1918

Mary E Dow adbabfic m Albert Joseph Robinson of Billerica, Mass, b Monroe, Me, Aug 29, 1849, d Newton Center Apr 10, 1915. Children:

    a Burton Henry b Amesbury, Mass, Aug 9, 1880; m Florence Lovett of Beverly, Mass
    b Francis Willard b Aug 25, 1888; m Mabel Lovett; has,—Burton Willard b June 14, 1918

Moses Dow adbabg of East Vassalboro m Abigail Cobb b July 13, 1781. Friends' minutes give their children, but none found in 1850 census; all were gone from Maine:

    a William Cobb b 4: 4 mo: 1803
    b Franklin b 27: 11 mo: 1805; m Lynn Quarterly Meeting 4: 3 mo: 1847, Hannah B Breed, dau of Moses and Hannah (d 7: 7 mo: 1859). Untraced
    c Phoebe Cobb b Nov 27, 1807
    d Martin b 10: 4 mo: 1810; went to N Y City; living 1860
    e Mary Ann b Dec 21, 1812; m William Lewis of Bangor, not a Friend. A son Cyrus lived N Y City 1860 to after 1870

William C Dow adbabga moved to Lowell, Mass, d Lowell, harness maker; m Nancy Hussey, Quaker. The 1850 census and Me vital rec garble this family, giving William H Dow, farmer, and Nancy Hussey b Nantucket. Vassalboro 1850 census has a Sarah J Dow b 1833; perhaps belongs here. William C and Nancy had 7 sons, 3 dau. He moved to Lowell, Mass, a harness maker; d there. Younger children not found, rec presumably in Lowell:

    a William Henry b Vassalboro Jan 4, 1831
    b Martin b Vassalboro 1832; joined the gold rush to Calif 1855. In 1885 he wrote: "what they called an honest miner; located 1865 in San Francisco, a merchant, but not as an honest miner—oh no!" He never m
    d Timothy

William H Dow adbabgaa, grocer of Waterville, Me, m Oct 9, 1861, Carrie M Tuck b Phillips Jan 23, 1835. Me rec garbles him, giving d rec: William W Dow, wood and coal dealer of Benton, d married Richmond May 11, 1918. Children:

    a Horace Davenport b Vassalboro Feb 16, 1864; of Waterville, untraced
    b Carrie Adelaide b Somerset Mills July 11, 1866; d Fairfield Aug 26, 1867
    c George Henry b Somerset Mills Jan 4, 1868; untraced
    d William M b Somerset Mills Dec 19, 1869; untraced
    e Mary Edith b Waterville May 29, 1872

Timothy Dow adbabgad. This identity is a guess but circumstances make it altogether probable. B Vassalboro, grocer of Waterville, m Isadore Radcliff b Lowell, Mass. One child found by own m rec:

    a Percy A R b 1869; voice teacher, m July 27, 1898, Edith A Clary, music teacher of Hallowell, ae 25, dau of Charles and Susanna E (Young). Recent directory gives him voice teacher of San Francisco, but he has not replied to letters of genealogical inquiry

Phoebe Cobb Dow adbabgc d Bangor Oct 2, 1878; m East Vassalboro Jan 1, 1829, Cyrus Arnold; moved to Bangor. Children:

    a Francis Edwin b Bangor Oct 5, 1829; Episcopal clergyman; m Philadelphia July 3, 1860, Elizabeth Brinton Hickman of Chester Co, Pa. A dau, Mary Gibbons, is now Mrs Henry B Duncan of Wilmington, Del
    b Anne Elizabeth of Boston, unm
    c Henry Clay; twice m; in Calif 1903; no children
    d —— d in infancy

Martin Dow adbabgd of N Y City m Elizabeth Adams. A son by own rec;

    a Frank M b N Y 1855; m 2nd Billerica, Mass, June 5, 1901, Christine F Radcliffe (her 2nd, div), ae 44, dau of Charles B and Adeline S (Flagg)

Paul Dow adbabh d Berwick June 7, 1816; m Berwick July 1, 1802, Lydia Neal, dau of James and Lydia (Roberts) adhag, Friends. She m 2nd Nov 27, 1817, Nathan Mower of Vassalboro. Children:

    a Eliza b Aug 6, 1803; d milliner China Jan 20, 1893, unm
    b Cynthia b Mch 20, 1805; m 27: 10 mo: 1825, Asa Morrell of Falmouth, son of Peter and Hannah
    c Mary b July 22, 1808; m Peter M Stackpole of Berwick, son of Thomas and Sarah
    d James Neal b Dec 2, 1812; d June 12, 1813
    e Lydia Neal b June 13, 1813; d Nov 21, 1815

Richard Dow adbabi moved 1801 to Vassalboro, 1803 to Berwick. The following is offered:

To Berwick Monthly Meeting. Richard Dow having removed within the compass of your meeting and having requested our certificate, this may inform you that he is a member of our meeting and clear of marriage engagements as far as appears. We recommend him. On behalf of a Monthly Meeting held at Vassalborough 18: 5 mo: 1803. Moses Sleeper, clerk.

Perhaps Richard had been mittened by the Vassalboro girls; more likely he had thoughts of matrimony only after starting Berwickward. In 1806 he was dismissed from the Friends. In 1810 he m by William Hight, justice of the peace, Joanna Stevens of Berwick. While no further has come to light about him, there are three Berwick rec surely of this line, perhaps his own children:

    a David of Berwick int pub Aug 1, 1840, to Susan S Walker of So Berwick; untraced
    b Alvira of Berwick int pub May 12, 1843, to Daniel L Keay of Berwick; untraced
    c Lorenzo b So Berwick July 11, 1822
    Presumably belonging here is: Frances E. Dow of Berwick m Dover Aug 27, 1893, Warren B Hastey of Berwick

David Dow adabia went early to Andover or Lawrence, Mass, and learned the mason trade; was employed all his life as head mason of the Pacific Mills, in charge of construction.   Susan S Walker was a real daughter of the Revolution, recognized by Act of Congress, as was customary in such instances.   The couple lived long in Lawrence and had a large family, which is now well scattered.   The only ones known to the Author are grandsons,—Arthur Dow Prince, of G C Prince & Son, Lowell, and Walter E Dow of Lawrence.

Lorenzo Dow adbabic moved in 1853 to Newfields, N H; for over 40 years in the Swampscott machine works; over 30 years deacon of Congregational church; m May 31, 1848, Elizabeth A Winslow of Nottingham, dau of Colcord and Miriam (Harvey).   He d Sept 22, 1901; she Jan 16, 1909.   Children:

    a   Isophene Kimball b 1852   b   Annie Hilton b 1855; unm

Isophene K Dow adbabica was for about 20 years teacher of grammar grades Claremont, N H, where her sister taught for several years in primary grades, and where both will be long remembered.   A severe disciplinarian Isophene had more than any other teacher in the history of the town ability to train the young mind and retain in after years the respect and love of former scholars.   The two sisters abandoned teaching to care for their aging parents in Newfields.

Hannah Dow adbac of Kensington received a legacy of 250£ O T from her father; m Jan 3, 1759, Samuel Collins, son of Tristram and Judith of Hampton Falls. Four children of this well known Quaker couple married Dows.   Hannah and Samuel went to Weare, thence with 4 oxen and 1,700 Spanish dollars to Durham, Me.   Children:

    a   Mary m Aug 8, 1787, Joseph Spaulding
    b   Patience d ae 85, unm   c   John m Hannah Goddard
    d   Esther b Feb 17, 1770; d Dover ae 87; m May 4, 1797, Edward Douglass;
        settled in Brunswick
    e   Paul m Mary Winslow; d Litchfield ae 93
    f   Judith m Mch 4, 1791, John Douglass; d Brunswick ae 76
    g   Betsey m —— Bryant; remained in Weare
    h   Hannah m Marmaduke Gifford; d Fairfield ae 80
    i   Lydia m Joslyn Allen of Durham   j   Abijah m Dolly Jones
    k   Huldah d Dec 22, 1852, ae 83, 6 mos, unm

John Dow adbaf d Kensington before 1792; was executor of his father's will; m Mch 9, 1769, Abigail (Abiall, Amesbury rec) Dow adhcf d Kensington Oct 19, 1842.   The Kensington Dows, including this line, are poorly traced.   Children possibly others:

    a   John b Aug 11, 1770
    b   Mary b Dec 10, 1771; m 2: 10 mo: 1798, Nathan Green, her 2nd cousin, son
        of Stephen and Hannah of Kensington; lived on the farm where her great
        grandmother was born
    c   Anna b Kensington Feb 8, 1773
    d   Abraham b Kensington July 27, 1774 (rec: d Goffstown Feb 11, 1776, a mis-
        identification); untraced

John Dow adbafa, farmer and life long resident of Kensington, d Nov 7, 1862, ae 92, 3 mos; m Jan 30, 1792, Abigail Phillips d Kensington June 24, 1832, dau of Walter and Content (Hope).   This staunch Quaker couple, who came to Lynn from York, Me, had 8 children, 4 marrying Dows.   John's farm assessed $2,000 in 1850.   Children (census gives only 2):

a   Abigail Ann b Oct 18, 1807; m Dec 26, 1837, Jonathan Fitts, both of Kensington
b   John Gustavus b Kensington Apr 26, 1811

John G Dow adbafab, farmer of Kensington, d Aug 28, 1877; m July 4, 1850, Elizabeth Bowles of Portsmouth, d Portsmouth, occupation lady, Dec 18, 1893, ae 64-4-7, dau of John L and Mary A (Woods).   At least 2 children:

a   Elizabeth L b Oct 24, 1851   b   Abigail Phillips b 1851; d May 8, 1864

Mary Dow adbafc and Nathan Green had:

a   Nabby b 1799; d June 1, 1801
b   John Dow b Apr 21, 1801; d Nov 25, 1809
c   Hannah b Jan 12, 1804; d Mch 8, 1815
d   Nancy b May 5, 1806; d Nov 20, 1886; m William Kinsman
e   Polly b Apr 2, 1809
f   Stephen b June 2, 1810; d Jan 26, 1900; m Charlotte F Chapman; his dau
     Ruth m Henry H Knight abdcebk

Paul Dow adbag m 30: 4 mo: 1779, Lydia Roberts; d soon after, for Lydia m James Neal and dau Lydia m 1802 Paul Dow adbabh

Hannah Dow adbb of Hampton d Kensington 1786; m Dec 24, 1730, Theophilus Paige of Hampton b 1707, d June 12, 1782, son of Amos and Hannah of Kensington.   From this line come a large share of the present day Friends of Weare, as well as an unusual number of clergymen of many denominations.   Children:

a   Daniel m Mary Peaslee; moved to Weare
b   Enoch m Ruth Peaslee; settled in Berwick   c   Nathan m Molly Brown
d   Samuel m Patience Gove; 2nd Mary Johnson; 4th child Judith m Elijah Dow
     adhag of Weare

Sarah Dow adbf d Kittery May 12, 1790; m Hampton Dec 22, 1732, Benjamin Frye b 11: 9 mo: 1701, d Mch 11, 1754, son of William and Harriet (Hill) of Kittery.   Children, b Kittery:

a   Jonathan b Nov 15, 1733; d Jan 1812; m outside the Society; disowned
b   Ruth b Oct 9, 1735; d 1743   c   Rowland b Oct 9, 1737
d   Alice b Oct 22, 1739; d 22: 9 mo: 1807; m Timothy Robinson Jr
e   Ruth b Dec 8, 1743; d 20: 10 mo: 1841; m William Jenkins Jr
f   Silas b Apr 12, 1746; d 8: 2 mo: 1805, unm
g   Judith b Apr 7, 1750; d 14: 5 mo: 1754
h   Judith b Feb 17, 1754; m 1787 Stephen Hussey

Rachel Dow adbg m Richard Collins, lifelong Friends.   Children:

a   Richard b Nov 20, 1739   b   Abigail b Feb 3, 1741
c   Sarah b Dec 13, 1743   d   Phebe b Mch 6, 1745
e   Elijah b Dec 13, 1746

Hannah Dow ade m William Fowler, one of Capt Saltonstall's snow shoe men of 1708. His will made Amesbury Oct 1735, probated 1745. Hist Hampton incorrect in order of children, rec of Amesbury:

a   Hannah b Apr 4, 1692; m Amesbury Apr 7, 1708, John Bagley
b   Mary b Dec 3, 1694; m Sept 18, 1718, Samuel Davis; 2nd —— Downer
c   Thomas b Apr 1, 1698; lived Newton; will proved Jan 1752
d   Josiah b Mch 28, 1704   e   William b Oct 14, 1706
f   Philip b Oct 12, 1709; lived Newmarket; will proved Aug 26, 1767; 7 children
g   Joseph b Apr 28, 1715; all named in father's will

HENRY Dow adf inherited a farm adjoining that of his brothers Joseph and Jeremiah, a large piece of land bought in 1683 being cut into three parts. Part of this was low, swampy and overgrown with elders. Through this swamp crept the Indians in the great raid of Aug 17, 1703, described by Francis Parkman. They were first noticed by Joseph Dow ada, who ran to the nearest blockhouse with the alarm. One of the first victims was Henry Dow's kinswoman, widow Muzzey, a talented speaker among the Friends and greatly respected in the community. She was passing by the swamp, was seized, dragged into the woods, and her brains beaten out with a tomahawk. Ordinarily, the Quakers and Indians got along in perfect harmony, quite a few Indian children living with Quaker families and being educated. This raid was by Canadian Indians, inspired by the French. Henry carried no weapons, nor did his friends. He suffered as much as any from confiscations of property to pay the minister's tax and in fines for refusing to perform militia duty.

Henry m Dec 7, 1694, Mary Mussey b Newbury Nov 23, 1672, d May 18, 1739, dau of Joseph and Esther (Jackman). She became a lifelong minister of the Friends. Henry was the first Dow of Seabrook who realized that the families had grown too large for their lands and that the younger generation should migrate to avoid poverty much more extreme than had yet been met with. To this end, he became an original shareholder in Salisbury, N H, in 1735, one of the earliest upstate projects. Probably he intended to establish his son there, rather than himself, for he himself felt the burden of years. He kept the home farm and d there, will dated Dec 8, 1738, probated Feb 12, 1739. He left legacies to brothers Jeremiah and Samuel. The estate inventoried 509£. The Salisbury, N H, land came 30 years later into possession of his grand nephew, Gideon Dow adggd. Children:

a   Johanna b Oct 4, 1696; d Apr 18, 1736
b   Lydia d Dec 31, 1699; m (int pub Amesbury Oct 17, 1719) Dec 10, 1719, Samuel Gould of Amesbury, son of Samuel and Sarah (Rowell); living 1736
c   Samuel b Jan 22, 1702   d   Susannah b Mch 12, 1705
e   Ruth b June 4, 1707; m 13: 11 mo: 1724, John Morrill, son of John of Kittery, Me. Hampton rec in error that she m 1727 —— Rowe
f   Judith b June 10, 1710; m 16: 3 mo: 1728, John Mumford, yeoman of Newport, R I; lived Narragansett; a dau Sarah b 1729, m Aug 4, 1750, Card Foster of Exeter, R I. Spelled Juda in Salisbury rec
g   Henry b Dec 13, 1711; d Dec 11, 1729
h   Daniel b Feb 4, 1714; almost certainly d young

Johanna Dow adfa m Mch 6, 1717, Nehimiah Heath, sea captain, who m 1st Oct 14, 1705, Mary Gove d Apr 16, 1715, ae 28, dau of John; left 2 children. Upon his 2nd m he retired from the sea and built a house in Hampton Falls; d Jan 14, 1718, with no children by Johanna. She m 2nd July 21, 1719, Aaron Morrill of Salisbury, son of Jacob dec

and Susanna (Whittier). Her grand dau Mehitable Morrill m Jacob
Brown; grandson was Edward A Brown, librarian of Amesbury,
accomplished genealogist, who rescued the family rec of Judah Dow adai.
Aaron Morrill m 2nd having 2 more children.   Johanna's children:

a   Elijah b Oct 30, 1719; m Aug 18, 1741, Anne Hoyt; 2nd Nov 24, 1761, Sarah
       Osgood
b   Theodate b Dec 1, 1721; d young
c   Aaron b Dec 25, 1723; m Hannah ——; 2nd Oct 17, 1754, Susanna Satterly
d   Theodate b Nov 24, 1725; m Jan 13, 1742-3, Jonathan Hutchinson
e   Susanna b Dec 7, 1728; m Nov 17, 1748, Nathaniel Currier
f   Henry b June 30, 1731; m Oct 5, 1756, Eleanor Currier
g   Judith b May 13, 1733; m Jan 9, 1751-2, Nathaniel Brown

Lydia Dow adfb and Samuel Gould: Children Amesbury rec:

a   Mary b Feb 15, 1722   b   Sarah b Apr 5, 1724
c   Mussey b Apr 5, 1727   d   Samuel b June 19, 1729
e   Judith b June 27, 1734

Samuel Dow adfc d Salisbury, Mass, May 9, 1773; had wife Mary.
Family tradition, which has helped the Author much in the Quaker lines,
has failed here.   Samuel was in Seabrook 1738 and from 1771 until his
death.   He might have been there all the time between, but no rec of his
children are there. His name does not appear in Hist Salisbury, N H, and
the vital rec of that town were burned many years ago.   We know that
Gideon Dow adggd owned the Salisbury, N H, property from 1772.   The
Author believes that Samuel and family lived in N H, coming back to
Seabrook two years before his death. In that case the children would be
b Salisbury, N H.   The list of them was inherited by the present Author,
who does not know their authority.   It is a strange coincidence that the
names repeat those of children of Samuel Dow adk, and these two Samuels were badly confused by one Dow genealogist:

a   Sarah; one would expect her b about 1728
b   Jabez; went to Portland, Me. Now, Jabez Dow adkg did go to Falmouth,
       Me. Jabez is untraced; did he exist?
c   Samuel; no doubt of his existence
d   Josiah; another duplicated name with adk line

Samuel Dow adfcc. Epping 1790 census gives a notable coincidence.
Samuel Dow appears 1a, 2b, 3c; that is, 2 sons b later than 1774 and
2 dau. Josiah Dow appears 2a, 1b, 4c. All the other Dow in the Epping
census are accounted for in the ahba and adaab lines.   Samuel and Josiah
are not found in Epping church rec. They were Quakers. Moreover,
Amesbury Friends rec contain Josiah's family.   Perhaps Samuel was
not a permanent resident of Epping. We cannot guess Samuel's sons;
the dau are reasonably certain:

a   Elizabeth m Salisbury May 21, 1769, Joshua Collins, cordwainer of Lynn, son
       of Joshua dec
b   Judith of Salisbury (both specified as dau of Samuel) m July 21, 1770, Jacob
       Collins, cordwainer of Lynn, brother of above. This family of Collins were
       staunch Quakers

Elizabeth Dow adfcca and Joshua Collins had, by Lynn Friends rec:

a Sarah b June 14, 1772   b Hannah b July 26, 1775
c Peace b May 20, 1778   d Ruth b Apr 26, 1780
e Stephen b Mch 26, 1782

Judith Dow adfccb m Jacob Collins; had, by Friends Lynn rec:

a Amos b July 15, 1773   b Mary b Dec 24, 1775
c Reuben b June 28, 1778   d Isaac b July 31, 1785
e Jacob b Dec 7, 1787

Josiah Dow adfcd had, if our identification be correct, 3 sons, 4 dau at home 1790, one son b prior to 1774. Amesbury Friends rec gives him 4 children, all b prior to 1774. This leaves 3 sons not found. Friends rec mention but once Sarah Newton as wife of Josiah. This may possibly be Sarah —— of Newtown, for in 1768 they were living in Newtown. Nothing whatever has been found regarding the lives of either Josiah or his brother. The known children:

a Mary b Apr 4, 1760
b Sarah b Apr 25, 1766; improbably the Sarah m June 30, 1801, Abel Bagley; left a son John
c Josiah b Apr 10, 1768, in Newtown. This rec appears 4 times,—Isaiah son of Josiah, Josiah son of Josiah, Isah, Isaiah. Josiah is right
d John (called 3rd in Friends rec; because of John and John Jr of Epping?), son of Josiah, b New Salem Apr 18, 1770; untraced; perhaps went to Vt

Josiah Dow adfcdc seems to have lived Kingston; one son proved, others reasonably certain:

a Josiah b Kingston July 4, 1803   b Tilotus
c Elvira, tailoress of Corinth, Vt, 1883

Josiah Dow adfcdca, shoemaker, moved to Corinth, Vt; to Newbury, Vt, after 1833; m Anne Webster b Newbury Mch 28, 1802, d Newbury Jan 3, 1875. Only child:

a Henry Keyes b Newbury Nov 9, 1834

Henry K Dow adfcdcaa, farmer of Newbury, owning in 1883 35 acres, was in 1887 a mechanic; m Delia M Jackson; d widower Haverhill, N H, Sept 29, 1913. At least 1 child:

a Abraham L b Newbury 1885

Abraham L Dow adfcdcaaa, railroad fireman of Haverhill, m Concord, N H, Nov 14, 1912, Lillian M Wright, dau of Henry F and Minnie O (Russell). Child:

a Russell Wright b Haverhill Apr 17, 1915

Tilotus Dow adfcdcb of Corinth m Dec 4, 1840, Susan Green, Friend, dau or grand dau of Winthrop Green adbaa, who m 1st Abigail Blake; 2nd Susanna Dearborn of Weare d Sept 25, 1810.

Ruth Dow adfe m John Morrill of Kittery; moved to Berwick.
Children, Berwick Friends rec:

a Miriam m Aug 24, 1744, Ebenezer Hussey
b Hannah b 26: 4 mo: 1731; m Moses Purington
c Peace m Dec 1, 1748, Gideon Warren. In town rec these 2 marriages are re-
      versed
d Keziah   e Pelatiah   f Mary   g Susanna
h William Pepperell   These 5 d young

It is with the utmost chagrin that the Author is compelled to leave
this Quaker line so poorly traced.

QUAKERISM began in this country about 1665 with a great growth which persecution gives and threatened to convert the country. So long as Quaker martyrs hung from gallows or languished in jail, their numbers increased. In half a century there was no more martyrdom, but persecution on all sides, mostly petty, from which no one stood aloof, but often seriously impoverishing, continued. So long as it continued, the Quakers increased their numbers and continued to dream of conquering the world for universal peace. By 1725 persecution was ended; there was nothing more than a sort of social ostracism. Then, the Quaker body recognized that there was no more net growth. They began to regard themselves as a remnant and a peculiar people; right they thought, in their own convictions, but no longer gaining by proselytizing. There was over a century of this isolation, of constant combat to prevent going outside the Society, of attempting to restrict marriages to the limits of the Society. Two great schisms occurred inside the Society. These tended to reduce greatly the numerical strength of the Quaker body. In 1725 the danger to the Seabrook Quakers was the withdrawal of their own children to escape the social ostracism which compelled poverty.

Jeremiah Dow adg lived through and in his person typified the culmination of the Quaker movement. In his young manhood every person in his community was Quaker and regular attendance at all meetings, either for worship or business, was universal. He lived to see the loss to Quakerism of every one of his children, to see himself left absolutely alone, deserted, impoverished almost to the point of pauperism, to see the uncared-for home in which he died at the age of about 96. There was no one left to record his death.

Almost all his vital records are extant and not a few of his vicissitudes. Returning at 7 from exile with his parents, he worked the next 13 years on his father's farms. He m ae 19, Apr 5, 1697, Elizabeth Perkins b Apr 9, 1676, dau of Abraham Jr and Elizabeth (Sleeper). This marriage was in line with his whole life. Abraham Perkins Sr had come from Wales, was the father of New Hampshire; m Mary Wise, dau of Humphrey, who came himself to America a few years later. Abraham stood high in Hampton, marshal in 1654, selectman 8 years in all. His son Abraham had m the dau of another Hampton pioneer, but was one of the twelve original Quakers and with Joseph Dow ad the leader into the new colony of Seabrook. In the great Indian raid Abraham Jr was killed by tomahawk on his own door step. The records of Jeremiah Dow appear as of Hampton, Hampton Falls, Salisbury and Seabrook. All these refer to a single place, his inherited farm near the Salisbury border. It was far from being the best farm which Joseph left. It had a fresh water

swamp and much overgrown waste ground. As times went, it would
support four occupants; but Jeremiah supported a large family as well
as caring for others. Every one of his brothers possessed more business
ability. Jeremiah tilled his farm, seeming to stake everything on his
faith alone. He realized that his crop was not to be harvested in this
world. He was the freest giver, taking the least for himself. Tall, lean,
taciturn, severe, frowning on all which is usually considered innocent
pleasure, his house was, no doubt, a cheerless place, one which his children escaped from gladly. The helpless old maid, the orphan stayed.
In Meeting one spoke if the Spirit moved, otherwise remained silent. It
always moved Jeremiah to sit in silence under his broad-brimmed hat,
to criticize no one for differing on some point of faith or works. His became a patriarchal figure, greatly respected by the right-minded, but the
right-minded grew fewer and fewer.

Until Joseph ad died, all went fairly well. That able man was able
to fend off all harm and the even more powerful Capt Henry Dow ab saw
to it that no man injured his brother's family. Trouble began in 1701,
when the authorities decided to levy forcibly upon the Quakers for their
share of the Minister's tax. No Quaker would pay for the support of
what he considered the greatest of abominations,—a hireling ministry.
There was a poll tax, from which one was free by serving in the militia.
Consequently, every man of proper age served in the militia. The Quakers were willing to pay this poll tax, but the authorities decided to administer fines for refusing to perform military service. In 1701 "Isaac
Morrill Jr, constable for the previous year, did take from Jeremiah Dow
a quart pot, a pair of fire tongs, a tray, and a cake of tallow to satisfy the
hireling minister, Caleb Cushing, for preaching." The constable levied
forcibly also on the neighbors, seizing guns so generally that there was
almost none left in the community at the time of the great Indian raid
of 1703. Not that the Quakers would have then used their guns; they
merely ran to the block houses. There was no legal process; one could
mulct a Quaker at will. "Taken from Jeremiah Dow of Salisbury one
cow valued fifty shils without showing any warrant due by ye Clark of
ye train band which Clark said was for not appering to traine & being
wanting there seven days." At the same time a cow was confiscated
from Henry Dow adf for the same reason.

At a town meeting some wags nominated Jeremiah for the office of
Constable, well knowing that he would not take any office, especially one
which required the use of physical force. The point of the jest lay in
the Statute that any one elected to public office and refusing to serve
should, unless a satisfactory substitute was produced, be fined 5£.
Happily in this instance his cousin Simon volunteered to take the office
and no one dared to trifle with Simon Dow. It was 1721 before these
multings ceased.

Meanwhile matters were going from bad to worse at home. As

poverty increased, he "bound out" his sons as fast as he could. The social life of inner Seabrook had not become a beautiful one. Drunkenness and irresponsibility were everywhere. The home of Joseph Dow ada was part of the new Seabrook. Charity Dow, his sister, sweet pure Quakeress, took refuge with Jeremiah, so did his aged mother. There grew up a lad in Jeremiah's home, reputed to be Jeremiah's own son. This lad was the closest of lifelong associates of Judah Dow adai, the baby of Joseph's family. One of his nephews killed a man in self-defense but it was in a drunken row and he was hanged for it. Two of his sons enlisted, to the neighbors' satisfaction. Part of the farm was sold to pay debts. Wife and sister died; all the children departed. A legacy came in 1768 from Samuel Dow, his brother, but even this was tied up for five years until the old man was dead. The children of Jeremiah:

a Mercy b Mch 11, 1698; d 1741; int pub to John Page 10: 26: 1717
b Jeremiah b Jan 9, 1700   c Jonathan b Dec 21, 1701
d David b Dec 17, 1703   e Abigail b Dec 19, 1705
f Ebenezer b Jan 31, 1708   g Gideon b Nov 20, 1710
h Patience (Pasiance in rec) b Jan 19,1712: int pub 12: 25: 1731, to Oneysyphorne
     Page Jr
i Elizabeth b Mch 1, 1715; m Oct 31, 1734, Joseph Perkins, son of Benjamin and
     Lydia (McCrease). Sister and brother Gideon m own cousins
j Hannah b Oct 24, 1716; m Sept 16, 1736, Jonathan Thrasher of Hampton
x Elihu b 1700-1709 (Cf sub adgx)

The lines of the older children are particularly obscure.

Jeremiah Dow adgb, home carpenter, d Salisbury Dec 11, 1725, leaving 2 infant children. No rec of wife found:

a Gideon b 1722   b Mary m John Page of Hampton

Gideon Dow adgba of Salisbury appears only in b rec of son:

a David b 1746; untraced. Hist Hampton possibly errs in giving a **David Dow** d Jan 10, 1755, as aed; might be adgbaa

Jonathan Dow adgc appears only in b rec of son:

a Joseph b 1724 (mother's name not in rec). Hist Hampton has lost its grip on the Quaker lines of Seabrook

Joseph Dow adgca cannot be the Joseph d Salisbury Dec 8, 1780, but must be he who m Dec 9, 1747, Rhoda Eaton b Mch 15, 1725, dau of Benjamin and Sarah (Morrill). David B Hoyt, Old Families of Amesbury and Salisbury, is inclined to doubt the Author's identification. Mr Hoyt wrote always without having had access to any Seabrook rec. So far, about a dozen cases of disagreement have been settled by discovery of proof in Seabrook, and in each case the Author has been right, having had all of Hoyt's evidence in advance. Therefore, the Author remains positive. Jan 15, 1748, this couple became members of the Salisbury church, formal repudiation of the faith of their grandsires. They moved to Chichester, but probably comparatively late in life, surely after 1766. Children, mostly Hampton rec:

a Rachel b Nov 30, 1748; m July 12, 1771, John Hilyard of Hampton Falls
b Sarah b Nov 20, 1750   c Samuel b Aug 18, 1756
d Joseph b Nov 9, 1759. This date perhaps error, for Joseph, son of Joseph, bap
   Oct 25, 1759. Also cf date of next
e Rhoda. Chichester d rec, no date; Rhoda Dow b Hampton May 6, 1760. If
   1761, all would be easy
f Perley b Aug 12, 1763
g Jabez b Apr 12, 1766; int pub Feb 2, 1784, to —— (Rec defective)

Samuel Dow adgcac. After many years of study, the Author is as uncertain of this line as he was in the beginning. A dozen known facts cannot be merged into one identity without discrepancies. Samuel Dow b 1760 is a Revolutionary pensioner 1850 in Chichester. Samuel Dow of Bow appears in 1790 census as 1a, 1b, 2c, quite plausible. That census places with Bow all the Dows of Pittsfield and Chichester. Samuel Dow of Bow made his will Oct 13, 1803; probated Nov 14. Samuel Dow of Bow m Jan 22, 1784, Betty Maxfield of Chichester. Samuel Dow of Bow m Epsom Dec 27, 1786, Sarah Fellows of Chichester. Now, a strange coincidence: John Dow of Bow m Oct 20, 1786, Abigail Fellows of Chichester. The same John Dow is in Bow 1790 census 1a, 2c. What John is this, and what was his connection with Samuel? Odd if two unrelated Dows of Bow m two Fellows girls of Chichester about the same time. The easiest guess is that Samuel m twice.

Further discrepancies appear. The will of Samuel Dow of Bow was administered in 1803 by James Ordway and inventoried $577.19. The family Bible of William Dow says he was born June 1, 1785, the son of Samuel and Sarah. This date does not fit. Moreover, William had an older half brother. Family tradition has it that William had several half brothers or sisters. Of course, the family Bible may not have been begun in the time of a 1st wife. The family tradition that William was executor of his father's will is patently error, for he was but 18. We know that William had an own brother and own sister. Again, we must assume. We give the children:

a Plummer. Family tradition has it that he was a farmer of Enfield with a family
   of his own when he cared for a baby son of his half brother William. As no
   such Dow appears in Enfield rec, we doubt the place and even doubt the
   correctness of the name. He is of course untraced
b William b June 1, 1785 (family Bible entry)
c Jonathan   d Betsey

William Dow adgcacb and his posterity are clear in every detail. He first appears as a farmer of Sunapee, N H, on the Newport road; a free will Baptist, very religious, and greatly in request when farm work was "exchanged," as used to be the custom, being a famous worker. He d Aug 1849; m Sept 22, 1808, Nancy Crowell of Newport b July 19, 1788; 8 children; m 2nd Apr 1, 1836, Lydia Baker of Fishersfield; 1 child; 3rd

Dec 27, 1838, Lucy Tandy; 2 children; 4th Feb 16, 1848, wid **Ruth** Morse of Concord. Children:

a Samuel b Mch 3, 1810
b Emeline b Dec 29, 1812; d in infancy
c Emeline b Dec 30, 1815
d Nancy Maria b Mch 31, 1819
e Eleanor C b May 29, 1821
f Carlton b Dec 9, 1823; d in infancy
g Fanny b Dec 23, 1825
h Hazen b Jan 28, 1829; farmer of Newport, moved afterwards to Galesburg, Ill; no children
i ——, d in infancy
j William Bradford b Feb 7, 1841
k Parker Tandy b Nov 25, 1844

Samuel Dow adgcacba m Lempster Sept 2, 1834, Lovina M Tenney b New Ipswich May 12, 1814, d Apr 24, 1880, dau of Samson and Sarah (Parker); moved about 1840 to Galesburg, Ill. Children:

a —— dau b Mch 5, 1836; d in infancy
b Samuel Alvus b Feb 5, 1837; physician in Australia; untraced
c William Sampson b Mch 25, 1842; grad Lombard Univ; d Mch 21, 1863
d Andrew Gregg b Jan 16, 1845
e —— dau b Mch 16, 1849; d in infancy
f Helen Lovina b Aug 25, 1852; d June 4, 1854

Andrew G Dow adgcacbad, for many years in carriage business in Galesburg, d Aug 19, 1903; m Dec 4, 1872, Flora A Prindle. Children:

a Mabel b Aug 7, 1875
b Ednah Lavinia b Nov 19, 1880

Mabel Dow adgcacbada of Galesburg m Feb 7, 1900, Frank L Conger of Galesburg. Child:

a Barbara Lois b Aug 13, 1902

Ednah L Dow adgcacbadb of Galesburg m June 3, 1903, James Moir. Children:

a Elizabeth Dow b Mch 23, 1905
b Nancy Jean b Oct 23, 1908

Emeline Dow adgcacbc. There are in Newport 3 disconnected records which seem to belong to the adgcac line somewhere. Elizabeth Dow b 1810 occurs in 1850 census between two adgcac names; perhaps wid. Samuel Dow m Feb 23, 1812, Lydia Berry, both of Newport; it is quite gratuitous to place him here. Louisa Dow of Newport m Sept 8, 1834, Abel R Hinckley of Augusta, Me; she might easily have come from Me and not be of adgcac at all. Emeline Dow m Apr 11, 1838, Isaac Bradley Hurd b Newport June 28, 1815, son of Levi. Children:

a Nancy b Nov 3, 1839; d Feb 10, 1840
b Carlton b Oct 7, 1842; druggist and bank president of Newport; m Claremont 1871 Marietta Garfield; no children
c Nancy Maria b Jan 7, 1845; m Wallace White
d Elizabeth Ann b Apr 5, 1848; m Dennis Gardner
e Fanny Melinda b Oct 1, 1850; d Jan 5, 1866

Nancy Maria Dow adgcacbd is in all probability the Harriet Maria Dow of Newport m Feb 6, 1851, Avriel Gunnison of Newbury.

Fanny J Dow adgcacbg m Sunapee Dec 1, 1855, George S Muzzey, both of Newport. A dau:

a Fannie E m Newport 1899 Allen B Gould

William B Dow adgcacbj, orphaned in childhood, was brought up by his mother's relatives; veteran of Civil War; was farmer of Acworth and Langdon; in 1921 had an attractive farm just south of Saxton's River, Vt, with a milk route; m Weathersfield, Vt, Feb 5, 1868, Almira P Farr, who in 1921 shared his home.　Much interested in his genealogy. Children:

a　Ernest Elmer b Acworth Feb 27, 1869; unm
b　Ethel Mina b Langdon May 29, 1871
c　Ida May b May 6, 1873　　　d　Charles William b Apr 1, 1875

Ida M Dow adgcacbjc m Saxton's River June 12, 1901, Emery E Porter; d Jan 2, 1907, leaving 2 dau, in 1921 with their father in N S.

Charles W Dow adgcacbjd m Haverhill, Mass, Nov 25, 1903, Ethel A Spackman, ae 20, dau of William J and Naomi (Badmington).　Dau:

a　Ruth Ethel

Parker T Dow adgcacbk went for a few years with his half brother, then brought up with his brother William; m Goshen Feb 17, 1869, Marcia E Stevens; for many years widower in Mill Village or with his dau in Newport; d in 1922.　Children:

a　Alfred E b 1871; carpenter, m July 3, 1912, Agavine A Garabedian, ae 30, b
　　Asia Minor, dau of Agnsh A and Susan; d Mch 2, 1914; no children
b　Grace E　　　c　Jessamine E; both unm of Newport

Jonathan Dow adgcacc m Feb 8, 1813, Eliza Atwood, both of Newport; lived Croyden and Sunapee.　Possibly considerable family, but only one child found:

a　Jacob H b Aug 25, 1821

Jacob H Dow adgcacca, carpenter of Wendell Hill, and by 1856 of Bristol, d Hill Apr 20, 1884; served through the Civil War.　Every year he met at the G A R encampment William B Dow and they became close friends, but never knew they were related.　Jacob m Feb 14, 1839, Irene Angell of Sunapee and Wendell; 2nd Newport Mch 30, 1843, Mary Ann Stevens of Sunapee and Wendell; 3rd Oct 22, 1858, Charlotte L Holden, dau of Ira.　Her d rec: wid of Jacob H, d Franklin Feb 3, 1912, ae 81-4-11. We cannot explain a Newport rec: Jacob H Dow b 1823, m Newport July 14, 1868 (her 2nd) Dorothy Holden, ae 28, dau of Joseph of Hill and Sanbornton.　Hist Bristol gives children, without dates:

a　Irene b Sunapee; m Mark Towle of Haverhill; moved to Hammond, Ind
b　Sarah m Charles E Smith of New Hampton; moved to Hammond
c　John; probably d young
d　Luella m and d New Hampton.　One of these dau was b Sunapee May 27,
　　1852
e　Mary A m —— Cheney of Newport　　　f　Arthur A b Bristol Sept 1, 1859
g　Horace E b Bristol Dec 18, 1861; m Chicago Feb 18, 1885, Rose Eagan; moved
　　to So Omaha, Neb
h　Edward Everett b Oct 20, 1864; m Kate Carneys; moved to Hammond,
　　thence to Larkin, Kan; thence to Redlands, Calif; an undertaker.　Children,—Jessie, Hazel C, Fern, Everett

   i Alice A b Nov 20, 1867; m June 1894 Charles P Sargent of Gilmanton **and**
     East Concord
   j Donna E (State rec, Donna Isabel, 5th child) b July 8, 1870; m Mch 20, **1897,**
     Wallis L Smith of Buxton, Me; moved to Gleasondale, Mass

Arthur A Dow adgcaccaf, machinist of Franklin, m June 4, 1881, Ida
Belle Wadleigh b Sanbornton 1862, dau of Gustavus B and Abbie (Eaton);
div; m 2nd Nov 7, 1907, Annie M Gove, ae 36, dau of James A and Lavina A (Howe) Heath of Wilmot, wid of William Ellsworth Gove; both
living Franklin 1915.   Child:

   a Mabel E b July 18, 1883; m Lester Hobart Maclinn b Groton Aug 3, 1883, son
     of George Darling and Hannah (Darling)

Joseph Dow adgcad.   Instead of clearing up on new evidence, the
situation becomes more obscure.   Joseph Dow came from Seabrook to
Pittsfield; m Pittsfield Feb 18, 1783, Sarah Berry b Rye, then of Chichester, bap 1761, dau of Timothy and Mary (Tucker); she m 2nd Chichester Mch 27, 1805, Thomas Lake of Pittsfield.   This Joseph had
(*fide* a grandson) a cousin, Jonathan Dow of Chichester.   There is
reason for thinking this a lost line of adg.   Joseph Dow m Epsom Nov 6,
1786, Rhoda Ring of Chichester, and he seems to be the true adgcad.
The names of the Chichester Dow seem to have been duplicated throughout.   Our informant says that this Joseph had brothers,—William (who
has not appeared) and Samuel, who d at sea.   If this last be correct, it
throws all the more doubt on the identification of Samuel, called herein
adgcac.   That all are of adg line, probably adgb, is almost certain.

   To Joseph and Rhoda only one child is known:

   a Joseph b Pittsfield about 1787

   There were at least 2 more children and the gap of about 13 years
indicates that this is far from all:

   b Betsey, dau of Joseph, b Chichester Aug 27, 1800
   c Rhoda, dau of Joseph, b Chichester Dec 23, 1802; unm 1850

Joseph Dow adgcada, farmer and shingle maker, lived and died
Pittsfield; m Oct 29, 1806, Sarah Marden, m rec giving both of Chichester.
Not found in 1850 census.   In d rec of son mother is called Hannah, perhaps a careless error in Canterbury.   This couple had 3 sons, 4 dau, all
b Pittsfield. In Pittsfield records under various dates are quite a number of Dows, but none safely attributable.   Three younger are surely
recognized:

   a John b 1807   d Sarah Marden b about 1814
   e Elizabeth b May 28, 1818   f Joseph b May 24, 1819

Sarah M Dow adgcadad of Concord m July 31, 1834, William Mc-
Daniels of Canterbury (rec both in Canterbury and Epsom) b Apr 7,
1806, son of Nehimiah and Martha (Glines).   Children:

   a Joseph m Cynthia Dearborn
   b Elizabeth m Oct 19, 1859, Martin V B Streeter
   c Tristram
   d Henry W b July 29, 1843; d May 15, 1910; m Susan Bailey of Franklin

Elizabeth Dow adgcadae, living 1890, remembered the facts of grand parents as given above; m Oct 25, 1839, John Hutchins of Canterbury; moved to East Concord.   Of children:

a   John C b Feb 10, 1841; railroad engineer, m Carrie B Curtis; 3 children
c   Issara b Jan 28, 1848; m Nov 30, 1870, Warren H Ring; 4 children
d   Ellen M b Oct 15, 1849; m Charles Staniels of Chichester

John Dow adgcadaa; identification reasonably safe; was a blacksmith who came to Weare from Chichester; m Weare July 4, 1830, Lydia Shaw, dau of Jonathan and Mary (Weed); apparently moved soon to Bradford, hence the passing mention in Hist Weare. He d soon after 1832; his wid m 2nd Dec 2, 1849 Zachaeus Jackman of Bradford.   Doubtless, only child:

a   Horace M b Bradford May 2, 1832

Horace M Dow adgcadaaa, farmer of Bradford and Hopkinton, d Hopkinton Apr 2, 1910; m Bradford Jan 27, 1857, Elizabeth M Murdough (Eliza E and Musclough in various rec), ae 18, d Hopkinton Apr 7, 1912, dau of William and Caroline S (Ayer).   Children:

a   William H b Bradford 1858
b   Sarah Georgianna b Nov 9, 1861; m Fred O Howlett of Bradford
c   Lydia M b Dec 4, 1863; m (Lilla M) of Bradford Aug 22, 1883, James F Hoyt of Hopkinton
d   Horace A b May 14, 1866; d young
e   Carrie E m —— Crosby of Manchester
f   Mary B b Aug 12, 1874; m J H Connor of Henniker; dau Marion S at school 1908
g   Horace A; 1908 bookkeeper in Boston

William H Dow adgcadaaaa, butcher of Manchester, later painter of Exeter, m Henniker June 2, 1885, Nettie M Daniels, ae 27, dau of George S and Sarah (Chase).   In 1888 he was laborer of Bradford; 1892 mechanic of Goffstown.   Children:

a   Ina M b Weare Mch 7, 1888; m William W Dow adaimaaba of Seabrook
b   —— son b Goffstown Nov 25, 1892

Joseph Dow adgcadaf, farmer of Canterbury, d Feb 6, 1897; m Feb 26, 1839, Abigail Heath Carter b Canterbury Mch 11, 1816, d Jan 21, 1894, dau of John and Nancy (Sargent); m 2nd Aug 10, 1894, wid Mary F Perkins.   Children:

a   George P b Apr 24, 1839; d Mch 11, 1842
b   Gilbert F b Mch 3, 1841; vol 4th N H; mustered out Feb 18, 1864; re-enlisted; captured; in Salisbury prison; transferred to Deep Bottom, Va; d of hunger and wounds Dec 19, 1864; bur at Annapolis
c   George M b May 27, 1843; d Oct 27, 1872, farmer of Canterbury, unm
d   Orrin b Oct 24, 1845; d Oct 30, 1846
e   Joseph F b Apr 20, 1849; d Jan 21, 1853
f   Sylvester J b Sept 3, 1852
g   Mary P b Oct 15, 1855; m Nov 9, 1881, Thomas E Simpson of Deerfield b Feb 10, 1856, son of Joseph; child,—Samuel W b Deerfield Aug 15, 1883

Sylvester J Dow adgcadaff, mason of Canterbury, moved before 1881 to Topeka, Kan; d Bow Aug 3, 1891; m Canterbury Sept 6, 1879,

Eliza Butterworth b Eng, dau of Abel S and Martha.   She m 2nd William L Kimball of Cheney, Kan.   Children:

a Jay Henry b July 8, 1884
b Ada May b Sept 3, 1885; m Dec 19, 1905, Abram E Valentine of San Bernardino, Calif; son,—Melvin Dow b May 18, 1910

Jay H Dow adgcadaffa of San Bernardino m Nov 1906 Lynne Roberds.   Child:

a Dorothy M b Jan 29, 1909

Perley Dow adgcaf m Feb 11, 1784, Dorothy Brown of Seabrook. Perley Dow appears in 1790 census Chichester 1a, 2b, 3c.   Four children in 6 years is quick work.   Apparently 3 of them d young, for Perley Dow, mariner, d Readfield, Me, his will filed by wid Dorothy Jan 19, 1797. Will mentions 1 child:

a Rhoda

Wid Dorothy Dow m 2nd —— Lake.   We note the recurrence in this line of name Rhoda and Lake

Jabez Dow adgcag disappears with the defective rec of 1784.   Presumably he went to Chichester with his brothers.   The name Jabez recurs in China, Me, the settlement of which began 1774.   Recurrence of name Perley is strong evidence that the children of Jabez turned up in China, there before 1820.   By this time the place was busy with mills devoted to handling lumber and paper.   It is an unavoidable inference that Jabez adgcag had 3 sons, perhaps more dau:

a Jabez b Mass 1789   b John b Me 1797   c Daniel b Me 1805

Jabez Dow adgcaga appears in 1850 census farmer of China; assessed $7501; wife Sally b 1794; both d China, bur local cemetery.   Census gives children, doubtless complete, but a 3rd generation cannot be picked out of the few disconnected data:

a Perley b 1817; d China after 1880, unm
b Charles E b 1820; m and left only child,—Frances Belle m China Feb 1886 Frank D Healey; 1923 of Cambridge, Mass; 2 sons
c Atlanta E b 1822; d Liberty, Me; m (int pub Belfast Aug 4, 1855) Willard L Maddocks
d Martin A b 1824; d Augusta, unm
e Lorenzo b 1827; d married Fairfield; untraced. He appears in 1850 census farmer of Vassalboro
f Franklin b 1829; d in Calif; untraced
g Betsey E b 1833; m Belfast Nov 24, 1855, Alexander H Maddocks; d Vassalboro
h Relief b 1838; living Me 1920; m —— Brier

Caroline E Dow, wife or wid, hotel proprietor, d China Apr 25, 1899, b Liberty, ae 70-4-26, dau of John and Sally Knowlton.   Presumably she was wife of Charles E Dow

John Dow adgcagb, farmer of China, assessed $500; wife Mehitable b 1795.   Children, by 1850 census, all untraced:

   a Elijah b 1826   b Dudley b 1831   c Harriet b 1837

Daniel Dow adgcagc, farmer of China, assessed $1,200; wife Mary b 1807.   Children, by census, all untraced:

   a Horace b 1827
   b George b 1830.   He appears in 1850 census shoemaker of Vassalboro
   c Sarah b 1836   d Ellen b 1843

WE admit that for a red-blooded lad or vigorous young man the home of Jeremiah Dow, Quaker, was a cheerless place, all work, no play, all poverty, no pleasure. Many men are over-pious; they drive their children to the other extreme.

David Dow adgd was long lost genealogically, because the records of So Hampton in early days were worse than poorly kept. An old family rec of his wid furnishes the clue to set matters right. He acquired in some way a farm in So Hampton and is the David, farmer of So Hampton, m Salisbury 1753 Naomi Carr. There is a Jonathan Dow, seemingly of adg line, who m Seabrook Dec 14, 1775, Anney Worth, but he does not belong to adgd. David left the Friends; paid minister's tax. He d soon after having an only child and his wid m adke, taking her son with her:

    a   Robert b So Hampton Aug 11, 1754

Robert Dow adgda (b rec specifies both parents) enlisted Apr 20, 1775, Capt Stephen Merrill, Col Caleb Cushing, served until Nov 14, or longer. No rec of m is found, but in rec of children he is of Salisbury with wife Sarah. Nothing about his personality has been found. The 1790 census finds him 1a, 4b, 2c. This means that three younger sons are genealogically lost, altho there are many disconnected to choose from. The two known ones:

    a   Robert b July 23, 1776; untraced   b   Martha b Oct 1, 1778

Ebenezer Dow adgf, like his brother Gideon, rebelled at the pleasureless home life. Not apprenticed to a trade, he helped cultivate the homestead. He m early, as was the custom, Oct 24, 1730, Lydia Ranlit (Runlet in int). This So Hampton family has defied genealogical tracing. She was always a consistent Quaker. After 1735 he disappears absolutely from Hampton Falls rec, but may not have gone far, as he was back in 1759, having 7 or more children. Tradition speaks of him as anything but religious, a wild and reckless man. He seems to have had no occupation except farming. At Hampton Falls Apr 12, 1759, he and brother Gideon enlisted at half pay for the Canadian campaign. One may wonder a little at the motive impelling a middle-aged man to leave wife and seven small children to go to a war in which he had no interest, and a long journey necessarily full of great hardship and danger. If there was a promise of a land allotment, a motive were easy found. Perhaps he merely sought freedom from home restraint. Gideon died during the campaign. Ebenezer came back somewhat sobered. He rejoined his family; he never followed the Friends, and one son was very like him. The others were influenced by the mother and continued in the Society.

The next that appears of him is in Lee 1765. He and son Jonathan signed the petition that Durham be set off as a separate parish. Not that they were affected religiously; a church was the only meeting place and, while the Lee church was miles away, one might seldom greet a neighbor, unless in passing by. Thus Durham began, it being early settled as Oyster River. Nothing further appears of him or Lydia, whether they lived to see the settling of New Durham or of Hollis, Me. There is slight evidence that Lydia was the survivor. Of the children, only the first three have absolute rec. Others are sure, two are based on place and association:

> a Abigail b Aug 4, 1731   b Jeremiah b Apr 12, 1733
> c Jonathan b Aug 13, 1735; these 3 by Hampton Falls rec
> d Ebenezer
> e Ann; both authenticated fairly, but place and date unknown
> f John; wholly conjecture based on coincidence of name and Quaker associations
> g Moses, better authenticated, by place, religion and associations

Jeremiah Dow adgfb. The Author, like most genealogists, began with earliest known facts and worked downward as far as facts permitted. Thus, after many years, he had a single line from adgfb to date and a mass of smaller lines to be placed conjecturally. The late Edgar R Dow had not the present-day libraries. He was a letter writer; he begun with living Dows and worked until he got back as far as possible. At last he found, 1884, a descendant, genealogically inclined, who had studied all possible family sources and was able to bring back a host of Dows to an earliest known ancestor, Jeremiah. In 20 years Edgar Dow could not find the identity of Jeremiah. In 1923 the Author received the great aggregate of scraps which Edgar had kept. From these, adding his own knowledge, it was easy not only to establish the connection, but to find the wife and every child of adgfb. He was of Little Falls, Me, in 1790, the census giving him 2a, 2c. The oldest children had married and gone. Jeremiah Jr was 1a, 1b, 2c. Ebenezer Dow was 1a, 2c, his older ones married and gone. Ebenezer Jr was 2a, 2b, 6c. Samuel was 1a, 2c. Jeremiah and his brothers were settlers of Hollis when it was an uncleared forest. Jeremiah had also been an early settler of New Durham, its pioneers coming direct from Durham. He was at one time of Tamworth.

His wife was Martha Goodwin; when and where they were married is not known. She is unknown genealogically. Her family gave the name to Goodwin's Mills, a hamlet of Hollis. In later life she was of So Tamworth. The list of children is authoritative, altho dates are lacking:

> a Hannah   b Betsey   c Abraham d unm   d Samuel
> e Jeremiah   f Ebenezer   g Charles   h David
> Order of birth probably correct

Hannah Dow adgfba m Daniel Evans, tanner and shoemaker of New Durham. Both d New Durham. Children:

> a Lydia m Joseph Palmer of Tuftonborough; 4 or 5 children
> b and c ——, sons

Betsey Dow adgfbb (Elizabeth) m William Eastman, both of Tamworth.

Abraham Dow adgfbc is not to be confused with his nephew, Abraham Dow of Saco, Me, adgfbfb.

Samuel Dow adgfbd appears in the 1790 census of Little Falls. His movements thereafter are complicated by errors, one of which is giving Hollis, N H, instead of Maine. His being at Vassalboro, Me, is open to much doubt. It is certain that he was a farmer of Hollis moved comparatively late in life to Gilmanton. His wife was Hannah Wadleigh. This name is interchangeable with Wadlin in Hollis; there were several intermarriages with Dow. If he lived in Vassalboro at all, it was around 1797. He d Gilmanton 1807 and his wife a year later. Such family as there was scattered quickly and soon lost sight of each other. We have proof of two children, but there were probably more:

  a Abigail A b Me 1781; she appears unm in Vassalboro 1850 census. It is probably absurd to make this identification, but the 1790 census calls for a dau
  b Jacob b Hollis Aug 7, 1797 (his son wrote Vassalboro as his birthplace; perhaps complete error)

A more trustworthy account comes from another source. Samuel adgfbd went from Hollis to New Durham and farmed it there for several years before buying the Gilmanton farm. He had only one dau, but had either two or three sons besides Jacob. These sons:

  c Moses   d Stephen

Jacob Dow adgfbdb was a farmer of Gilmanton, later buying a farm in Barnstead; d Barnstead Feb 26, 1883 (son gives May 20), his wife surviving. The rec gives m 1st Sarah Swain b Gilmanton Feb 1, 1795, d Gilmanton Apr 5, 1864. Also, Jacob Dow m 2nd Nov 6, 1864, Sarah Swain, ae 69, dau of William and Sally (Nelson). Errors like this are not rare in official rec. We think there was but one Sarah Swain. That there were three children is proven:

  a Theophilus S b Moultonborough July 12, 1828
  b Charles W b 1840; shoemaker, enlisted; d Falmouth, Va, Dec 19, 1862, unm, ae 22-4-27
  c Sarah E m Gilmanton Nov 30, 1863, Peleg D Perkins; d Sept 15, 1883

Theophilus S Dow adgfbdba, farmer of Barnstead, inherited the homestead; m Mch 5, 1856, Emma N Cole b Quincy, Mass, Apr 17, 1839, surviving him. He d Barnstead Jan 22, 1913. His letter of 1887 mentions no children

Stephen Dow adgfbdd. We have no proof whatever of this identity. Census 1850 Orrington, Me, gives b Me 1801, laborer, realty $100; wife Eliza b Me 1801. Children:

  a Samuel b 1836; untraced   b Elizabeth b 1839
  c Sarah b 1841
     The next name in census (no others in Orrington) seems akin: Joseph Dow b Me 1824, cooper; wife Elizabeth b Me 1830. No children in 1850

Jeremiah Dow adgfbe was always a consistent Quaker. He was living New Durham when he m Jan 15, 1786, Elizabeth Perkins of Rochester. She was not a Friend, was dau of Solomon, grand dau of Joshua, that Perkins family at the time being considered among the "First Families of Dover." In 1850 census Elizabeth is given as b Nottingham 1766, and Jeremiah b 1763. In 1850 the couple were living in Rochester, called farmers but with no land. Both lived to unusual age and were finally living with a married dau.

For a year or so Jeremiah lived with his father-in-law, who gave as a wedding present a lot of wild land in Hollis, Me, just beginning to be settled. Jeremiah decided to utilize the gift; leaving wife at her father's he journeyed to Hollis and one of the few neighbors (Jeremiah never told his name) pointed out what was ostensibly the Perkins lot. Jeremiah worked several weeks to clear it and get it ready for building and for planting. Then he learned he had been deceived. His informant had pointed out a lot owned by himself, the Perkins lot being somewhat distant. Jeremiah made a mild request for some payment or satisfaction, but was laughed at, the dishonesty esteemed a shrewd Yankee trick. There were several Quakers in town by then but they showed little sympathy, Jeremiah having married "outside the Society." So, Jeremiah without another word set out to clear the right lot. When this was done and a house built he went back, got his wife and returned to Hollis just in time to get into the 1790 census. They stayed until there were 4 babies. Then Jeremiah got a farm in Tuftonborough, sold out in Hollis and started. Susan Perkins Dow, the family historian, was a baby on this trip, which took two days. An ox cart was rigged with boarded sides covered with bed quilts. An especially heavy bed tick was the cart floor. Ample food had been cooked in advance and herein mother and babies rode in utmost comfort through zero weather, Jeremiah walking alongside. Tuftonborough was their home until very old age came on. Children:

a   Polly   b   John   c   Solomon
d   Anna b Apr 12, 1794   e   Stephen (b Hollis Mch 7, 1793)
f   Dolly   g   Jeremiah b Sept 1, 1800
h   Susan Perkins b Hollis July 22, 1806   i   Hannah   j   David
k   Mary d unm

Polly Dow adgfbea, b at the Perkins home in Rochester, m Nathaniel Evans. A son:

a   ——, a Joseph, scalded to death in infancy

The grieving parents then moved to Tuftonborough, where they had 11 more children:

b   Eliza m John Kimball of Dover; several children
c   Mary became a Free Will Baptist; m James Cheney; a family in Springvale, Me
d   Ann m George Wooster of Plymouth, Mass; 2 children d in infancy
e   Adeline m Jesse Taylor, Georgetown, Mass; 6 children
f   Jeremiah m Abigail Ridley; after various enterprises, kept a boarding house in Boston; several children

g Belinda m ——— Sias; m 2nd ——— Thurston of Ossipee; a family
h Benjamin m Mary Neal of Dover; had a family in Lynn, Mass
i Lorenzo; d leaving children
j Estwick; went south and became a Confederate officer; had a family in Virginia
k Samuel Dunster; left 2 children
l Susan m Orren Quint of Sanford; d in Calif without children

John Dow adgfbeb moved to Lancaster, N H; tanner, shoe maker and preacher, d he without children; m June 26, 1816 Polly Swan. In 1850 farmer of Wolfboro, realty $2000.

Solomon Dow adgfbec m Lydia Sullivan, whose brother m his sister. His children not well traced: he d Lynn of tuberculosis Feb 17, 1848, ae 55. Children:

a Mary   b James S m Abbie Shackley   c Sarah d young
d Bradley (rightly Benjamin Bradley)   e Lyman m Lydia Twisden; 1 child
f Ann Eliza m William Batchelder of Lynn; children,—Willie, Carrie, Lyman
g George W

Mary S Dow adgfbeca m (int pub Lynn Aug 28, 1842) Henry Atkins b Claremont. A dau:

a Mary Esther m Sandwich 1871 William H Estes

James S Dow adgfbecb, b N H 1819, appears in 1850 census as rock mason; wife Abigail b Me 1818. She was Abigail Shackley m Dec 15, 1840. Children, all b Mass:

a Mary A b 1842; d in infancy   b Clara Augusta b June 21, 1844
c Charles E b Mch 9, 1846; d canker Aug 2, 1846
d Sarah F b July 24, 1847

Benjamin B Dow adgfbecd m Oct 21, 1849 Caroline Gibson of Lynn. Two children, neither living 1887:

b ——, son b Portsmouth, N H, Jan 30, 1855

George W Dow adgfbecg of Lynn m (int pub Jan 9, 1848) Jane Bennett of Sanford, Me. Children:

a Arvilla d May 12, 1848
b George H d Dec 4, 1849, ae 1, 7 mos   c Ida

Anne Dow adgfbed m Apr 22, 1818, Nathaniel Hoit (generally Hoyt) both of Tuftonborough; moved to Rochester, thence to Edinburg, Me. Six children:

a Augusta   b Lafayette
c Almira m Albert G Angell of Providence, R I; 1 child
d William had a family in Me   e David went to Los Angeles
f Lizzie m Marcellus Hodgkin; went to Los Angeles

Stephen Dow adgfbee is said by family rec to be twin with Anna, but official rec does not concur. He apparently inherited the homestead; d Dover Sept 7, 1883; was a carpenter; m 1st Feb 26, 1819, Elizabeth Severance of Tuftonborough; m 2nd Nov 12, 1840, Hannah Parke of

Rochester (family gives Pierce, in error); m 3rd Abby Brown of Sandwich. Children:

    a John d in infancy   b ——, d in infancy
    c Philena m James H Grant; no children
    d Christiania A of Tuftonborough m Newmarket Dec 22, 1848, George Butler of
        Durham; 1 child, Charles Edward b Mch 4, 1853, m Emma Hays
    e Tryphena b 1830; m Wolfboro 1850-3 Joseph Hodgdon of Tuftonborough; no
        children
    f Selenia m Henry Obrien of Woburn, Mass; no children
    g Stephen Franklin b 1837; d ae 17

Dolly Dow adgfbef m Stephen Sullivan. Home not given in family rec. Children:

    a Lozetta m Joel Ham of Rochester; children,—Granville Sylvester b Natick,
        Mass; Joel Addison b Danvers
    b James D m Hannah Ham; lived Georgetown, Mass; children,—Lozetta m
        Edward Kneeland, William Henry unm, Sarah unm, Ida May m —— Wallis,
        Sanie Belle m Rollins Bessey
    c Lyman Sylvester d ae 9
    d Nancy m Charles Bisbee of Lynn; only child Nancy
    e Susan m (his 2nd) Charles Bisbee; had Fred, Elma, Josephine m John Regan,
        Charles, Inezetta, Minnie m James Snellen having child, Charles, —— d in
        infancy
    f Lydia m William Larrabee; only child Clara m Charles Wesson
    g George of Bangor, Me; no children
    h Stephen Frank m Janette Matthews; children,—Frank, Ida May, Etta, George,
        William
    i William Henry d in infancy

Jeremiah Dow adgfbeg, farmer and mechanic, moved with his brother David about 1820 to Middlesex, Vt. He d Berlin, Vt, Apr 12, 1862. In Middlesex they m the two dau of George Phelps, a Revolutionary veteran from Conn, who lived to 104. Jeremiah m Nov 9, 1821 Parnel E Phelps b Mch 4, 1804, d Montpelier May 21, 1872. There were 13 children in all, some d in infancy:

    a Elisha, not mentioned by a niece
    b Betsey Maria b July 10, 1822   c David Perkins b Jan 26, 1824
    d Jeremiah probably d young
    e Martha Irene b Montpelier Dec 2, 1835
    f Clementine m Fann Horton; m 2nd Amos Allen; no children
    g William   h Lorenzo   i Loretta d unm
    j Lewis; not found in Vt rec, but had son a Arthur who lives "out west."

Betsey Maria Dow adgfbegb d Aug 8, 1858; m July 17, 1841, Reuben L Munson b Oct 27, 1819, son of Reuben; she divorced him 1855; he enlisted 1861 with fine record in 2nd Vt. Children:

    a Clinton De Witt b Duxbury June 14, 1842; d July 27, 1842
    b Homer Castellan b Oct 8, 1843; d Aug 30, 1873
    c Helen Phemy Paulina b Montpelier Aug 21, 1845; m Julius Hill; div; m 2nd
        Paolo Sgobel, an Italian; no children

David Perkins Dow adgfbegc, designer of Norwich, Vt, m Mch 3 1847, Rebecca W Sargent b Ill July 2, 1824, dau of Amos and Anna (Cheney). In 1857 he was railroad conductor of Strafford, Vt. Children:

    a Clara A b 1848; living 1922 N Y City, unm
    b Carrie Alpharetta b Dec 25, 1857; not living 1922

c Edwin D b 1862; went to N Y; conducted successfully a small chain of restaurants. One was a favorite resort of visitors to the American Museum and was often used by the Author. He retired, living 1922, unm

Martha I Dow adgfbege m Sept 9, 1852, Jacob Cummins Spear b Washington, Vt, Apr 15, 1830, d Montpelier May 25, 1887. She joined her son in Peabody, Mass. Children:

a George E b Lowell May 20, 1853; lives Peabody; m Dec 11, 1875, Nettie E Reynolds
b Charles F b Berlin Feb 17, 1857
c Clara E b May 21, 1860; d unm
d William H b Mch 13, 1867
e Minnie E b Montpelier Apr 8, 1873

William Dow adgfbegg enlisted with his brother Lorenzo and fought throughout the War. Both died a few years later, Lorenzo presumably unm. William married and became a factory worker in Lynn, Mass, dying and leaving an infant only child:

a Harry Lee b Lynn Aug 26, 1866

Harry L Dow adgfbegga, painter, moved to Manchester, N H, and followed his trade in many towns; m Corinth, Vt, Sept 1884 Georgianna Bigelow b Montpelier. He was brought up by his uncle Lewis A Dow of Peabody. Soon after the birth of his youngest child he and his wife separated, the children all going with their mother, and they heard little subsequently of their father, who d Peabody 1913-4. Children:

a Lillian Augusta b Sept 14, 1885   b William Allen b Feb 21, 1888
c Asa Lee b Mch 1, d July 20, 1890
d Earl H d Hooksett Aug 4, 1892, ae 4 mos, 10 days
e Clarence Lorenzo b Oct 9, 1893; m Cambridge Oct 1915 ——; now of Reading; 7 children
f Ethel May b Manchester Oct 1, 1896; m Nov 1913 Frank Perry Jones; lives 1924 Methuen; 3 living children

Lillian A Dow adgfbeggaa m Medford or Cambridge Apr 22, 1906, Alan Richards b Windsor, Vt, Jan 26, 1884; now railroad clerk of Boston son of Andrew McClary and Inez Ellen (Bartholomew). Children:

a —— son b and d Apr 2, 1907   b Doris Lillian b July 21, 1908

William A Dow adgfbeggab, now of Malden, m 2nd May 1923 ——

Lewis Dow adgfbegj is untraced; by a remarkable coincidence a Lewis A Dow from Nova Scotia lived in Peabody soon afterwards. adgfbegj had a son, Walter or Arthur, both names given by kinfolk, who went "out west."

Susan Perkins Dow adgfbeh m Rochester Oct 12, 1828, Samuel Dunster, son of Jason and Mary (Meriam) a descendant of the first president of Harvard College. A scholarly gentlemen, he aided his wife in research of the adgfb line, as well as his own. They moved to Providence, R I. Both living 1890. Children:

   a Mary Susan b Aug 9, 1830; d 1832
   b Mary Susan b Jan 27, 1833; m Dec 25, 1849, Joseph E Smith; survived him
   c Edward Swift b Sept 2, 1834; a physician
   d Caleb Emery b July 27, 1836; d comparatively young
   e Eliza Annie b Oct 24, 1838; m William Taylor Baker of Chicago

Hannah Dow adgfbei d Rochester 1842; m Nathaniel Randall of Rochester d 1846. Children:

   a Betsey J m —— Trickey of Rochester
   b Mary A m Oralenna Stoddard of Providence, R I; living Andover, Vt, 1886; 5 children
        -
   c Almira R m —— Twombly of Rochester; left 1 dau
   d Jeremiah lived and d Rochester   e Horace, of Haverhill, Mass, in 1886

David Dow adgfbej went to Middlesex, Vt, 1820; m 1830 Betsey E Phelps. He was a farmer, lost on steamer Westfield in N Y harbor 1871, pushed overboard during its burning. Children:

   a Sarah Ann b Duxbury Oct 29, 1833; m Montpelier Sept 2, 1850, William M Turner; 11 children
   b Charles m Mary Hayes of Middlesex; only child Jessie b Brooklyn, N Y
   c Lester K, veteran of Civil War, d Plainfield, Vt, after 1915, unm
   d Truman M d Civil War, unm
   e Maryetta m Edward K Richards of N Y; dau Edna Earl m James G Huff of Brooklyn; m 2nd Charles W Auburn of N Y; dau,——Ella and Edith
   f Mortimer D b 1846; has been for 50 years farmer of Williamstown, Mass, unm
   g Susan M b 1848; m Edward H Richardson; m 2nd George E Kellogg, a Brooklyn policeman; widowed 1896, she joined her brother in Williamstown; no children

Ebenezer Dow adgfbf is in one family rec b Hollis, another Waterloo, Me. The dates estimated vary from 1765 to 1770; former nearer right, as in 1790 he had 1 dau. He m about 1789 Hannah Page b 1765, d Lowell, Mass, 1853, of the original Page family of Ormsby, Eng. (Cf account of immigration 1637, sub a), of the Quaker branch. Ebenezer and wife were always consistent Quakers. Most of their lives were spent on their farm in So Tamworth, where he d 1844. Of 7 children, 6 matured:

   a Lydia m —— Simpson, veteran of 1812
   b Abraham b Me 1795 (1850 Census)
   c David b Waterloo Mch 22, 1793   d William b about 1800
   e Benjamin P   f Ebenezer b So Tamworth June 18, 1811

Abraham Dow adgfbfb is not mentioned in family rec, and identification not absolutely proven. He lived Hollis, moving to Saco. It is possible that two Abrahams are confused. Abraham of 1850 census has wife Sarah b Me 1801, two children given. Abraham Dow m Jan 19, 1817, Eleanor Wood, both of Saco. In 1850 called farmer, but with no land. It looks as though there were 1st and 2nd wife.

Late in 1927, while this section of the book was in proof his entire line was proven. See Appendix, sub adgfbfb.

Albert Dow adgfbfba b Hollis, d struck by train Old Orchard Beach Oct 2, 1897, married, ae 69-0-21, retired. Albert Dow, moulder of Saco, m Mary A Tripp b Westport, Mass. She d wid Saco Sept 24, 1911, ae 80, dau of Warren and Celia (Bliss). One child found:

   a Ulysses G b Saco (one rec gives Lawrence, Mass) 1869

Ulysses G Dow adgfbfbaa, moulder of Saco, m Jan 20, 1894, Mattie A Langley, ae 24, dau of James H, sea capt, and Mary A (Mitchell). Children:

   a Raymond b Saco Sept 27, 1894
   b N Emerson (Ned in recent directory) b Saco Nov 9, 1895

David Dow adgfbfc m Tamworth Dec 10, 1816, Deborah Gilman b Oct 1, 1792, d Boston Aug 9, 1875, dau of William and Polly (Gilman). He d East Cambridge Sept 13, 1875, was a merchant of Boston. Children:

   a Susan Gilman b May 29, 1818; d Oct 29, 1834, unm
   b Eliza Ann b Oct 12, 1819; m Dec 1845 Le Roy Hackett; m 2nd Benjamin S Hoyt
   c Charles H b Tamworth June 4, 1826

Charles H Dow adgfbfcc was 1881 with a mercantile agency 81 Milk St, Boston; retired 1908, returning to Tamworth; d Tamworth Apr 9, 1914; m 1st Oct 1850 Sarah Elizabeth Hunt b Braintree, Mass; m 2nd Annie Stearns Butterfield (Butterworth in one rec) b Boston Feb 20, 1843, dau of George and Matressa F (Lull); she survived him. Children:

   a Charles M b Braintree; unm in 1881
   b Sarah F b Braintree; m —— Crossett of Boston; living 1908

Benjamin P Dow adgfbfe of Tamworth m Jan 20, 1823, I—— W Boynton of Meredith. About 1847 he went to Mich or Minn; left several sons, one of whom was a Boston merchant. Further untraced.

Ebenezer Dow adgfbff, generally called Eben, was a capt of militia, proving that he left the Friends. He d Dec 3, 1859; m Sept 11, 1834, Harriet Newell Mason b So Tamworth Oct 6, 1815, living 1882. They moved to Indiana, where Evansville grew up around them. He was there a carpenter. Children:

   a Harriet E m Oct 11, 1853, William E Mason of Tamworth and Evansville, apparently her cousin
   b John Lincoln b So Tamworth Jan 8, 1839
   c Anna m Charles Vrie, teacher of Denver, Colo
   e ——, son probably d young

John L Dow adgfbffb, physician of Evansville, m 1st Apr 23, 1865, Irene Gray d Ft Branch Nov 3, 1876; m 2nd Oct 4, 1877, Lucie Woodbury. Children b near Evansville in army posts:

   a Bessie H b July 10, 1868   b Richard Arthur b Apr 13, 1870
   c Gertrude E b Oct 25, 1872   d Fredda b Sept 23, 1876

William Dow adgfbfd b 1798 (rec says Lyman, Me) is possibly but improbably confused with a contemporary William of Lyman, who may not have existed. Census of 1850 shows him farmer of Lyman, realty assessed $3,000; wife Isabella b Scarboro 1804. Children, from census:

a Clarissa b 1827   b Serena b 1834   c Sewell b **1836**
d Edward b 1839   e Orlando b 1841; the family almost untraced

Clarissa Dow adgfbfda d Newton, Mass, 1893, ae 66; m Benjamin Franklin Fuller b Newton May 26, 1824, d Northampton, Mass, Sept 5, 1900, son of Benjamin and Susan (Jackson). Child:

a Adele J b New Haven, Conn, 1853; m Jan 6, 1885, Alfred G Fearing b Wareham, Conn, 1857

Orlando Dow (not surely adgfbfde), merchant and postmaster of Kennebunk, m Dover, N H, Jan 18, 1900, Sadie G Emmons, ae 28, dau of Eliakim and Caroline.

Charles Dow adgfbg m (int pub Sept 17, 1790) Martha A Gordon, both of Little Falls. In spite of rec, he was of So Tamworth. The Gordons intermarried a number of times with Dow, especially of Hollis. The young couple bought a farm on the Buzzell road, Hollis, the part soon set off as Dayton. Both lived to ripe old age and the house was recently standing. They were farmers and, there being no convenient meeting, soon drifted from the Friends. They had ten children, losing 2 in childhood from scarlatina; those maturing were (order at random, except that John was eldest, Daniel youngest):

a John b 1795 (possibly older d young)
b Alvan b 1806?   c Abigail   d Amos b 1797
e Andrew b about 1800   f Jeremiah   g Samuel b 1802
h Daniel. From them come almost all the Biddeford and Saco Dows, the drift being naturally down the Saco Valley to places where there was business

John Dow adgfbga. It is possible that two Johns, almost contemporary, were in Lyman. He was a trader of Lyman; no realty in 1850, wife Susan b Me 1794. Children, from 1850 census:

a Elizabeth b 1823
b Francis, blacksmith b 1825, with wife Frances b 1829, untraced
c Hezekiah b N H 1827, wife Miranda b N H 1828. All others b Me. **Hezekiah** appears in Biddeford 1849 directory as mason, otherwise untraced
d Adeline b 1830   e John b 1833   f Miriam b 1835
g Charles b 1847, untraced   h Ellen b 1842

John Dow adgfbgae, blacksmith of Lyman, m Abby L Young. One child found:

a Kate D d Lyman Apr 17, 1896, ae 31, 7 mos, unm

Alvan Dow adgfbgb. Biddeford 1850 census, written in pencil, gives Anchen Dow b Me 1806, farmer assessed $1,700, wife Lydia b Me 1806. This must be our Alvin. Children, by census:

a Charlotte b 1833   b Robert b 1835, untraced   c Abby b 1839

Amos Dow adgfbgd, in Biddeford 1850 census farmer assessed $2,000, m Miriam Wadlin b Me 1801. Children, by census:

a   Jason b 1826, untraced   b   Amos b 1829, untraced
c   William H b 1831

William H Dow adgfbgdc, farmer of Biddeford, d Sept 19, 1912, ae 74-4-18; m Lydia A Lowell d Biddeford Oct 18, 1914, ae 81-2-20, dau of Harrison and Mary (Hooper).   There were many Dow intermarriages with this old Me family.   Ten children:

a   Eugene L   b   Ida C b Aug 4, 1865   c   Martha
d   Rose m Frank Gilpatrick; 4 children
e   Byron A b 1866; of Biddeford m Dover, N H, Nov 13, 1889, Ethele Huff, ae
     17; not living 1922
f   Almer d young   g   Alice m —Hazelton
h   Clarence L b 1872   i   Horace M; now of Freeport, L I
j   Fred W b Biddeford 1876

Eugene L Dow adgfbgdca m Apr 12, 1879, Sarah T Hicks of Biddeford, still recalled by neighbors as the prettiest girl in town.   They soon went to N Y City, but separated, he dying a year after, she 2 years later. Only child:

a   Edward Hicks b N Y Sept 20, 1881

Edward Hicks Dow adgfbgdcaa was brought up in N Y, being told little or nothing about his father's people.   In 1921 he had never known any person named Dow, but, getting into contact with the Author, a search in Biddeford established his identity.   He is of Torrington, Conn; m Oct 22, 1906, Julia Ann Latham.   Of 4 children, 2 survive:

a   Edward Hicks b July 20, 1909   c   Philip McCook b Sept 10, 1914

Byron A Dow adgfbgdce d Lynn, Mass, June 19, 1897.   They had 4 children:

a   Florence Ethel b Aug 27, 1891; m Ray C Howland of Newport, R I; 1 dau
b   Elsie Louise b Aug 22, 1893; m Arthur D Fulton of Hopedale, Mass, where her
     mother now lives
c   Bessie Edith b Jan 28, 1895; teacher of the deaf, Philadelphia
d   Grace Edna b Aug 28, 1896; m Henry C Bridge of Medfield, Mass; 1 dau

Clarence L Dow adgfbgdch, painter of Biddeford, now Amesbury, Mass, m July 8, 1899, Olive N Tarbox, ae 30, b Lyman, dau of Orlando and Ann (Jordan).   In 1902 he was a Biddeford ice dealer.   One child:

a   Lowell Jordan b July 24, 1902; in 1923 in Univ of Maine

Fred W Dow adgfbgdcj, painter of Biddeford, now occupies the homestead; m June 17, 1915, Nellie B Hood, ae 17, b Lowell, Mass, dau of Charles H and Arabelle (Green).   No children.

Andrew Dow adgfbge m Jan 25, 1825, Lydia Cleaves, both of Hollis. At least 2 children:

a   George F b Biddeford 1828   b   Robert F b 1834

George F Dow adgfbgea d Lewiston Sept 11, 1906, ae 82; m 1st Caroline Staples, by whom 3 children; m 2nd Delia Mowers b Gardiner, d Lewiston Mch 21, 1906, ae 68-6-1, dau of Thomas P and Mary Ann (Forbush).   Children:

a   Carrie   b   Ella   c   Oswald, untraced
d   George W (A in m rec) b Biddeford 1862
e   Fred N   f   Willis M, untraced   g   Albert H b 1867
h   Irving W b 1879

George W Dow adgfbgead, electrician of Lewiston, m Manchester, N H, Apr 25, 1900, Eva M Wright, ae 27, of Lowell, Mass, dau of James H and Elizabeth (Longmore)

Fred N Dow adgfbgeae, farmer of Lewiston, previously shoemaker, m Linnie Etta Smith of Auburn.   Children, perhaps others:

a   Forest Arthur b 1887   b   —— b Lewiston May 31, 1897

Forest A Dow adgfbgeaea, farmer of Minot, m Oct 2, 1913, Christine Leland of Minot, ae 25, dau of Walter E and Eliza (Sawyer)

Albert H Dow adgfbgeag, shoe cutter of Lewiston, d Feb 5, 1899, ae 31-8-4; m Grace L Clark.   Of children:

b   Elenor Welch b Lewiston Dec 9, 1894

Irving W Dow adgfbgeah, farmer of Lewiston, m Aug 12, 1903, Lillian M Bradstreet, ae 23, dau of R Thomas and Rovenia (Parker). Children:

a   —— b Feb 10, 1904
b   Alice May b Lewiston Aug 2, 1911; d Sept 26, 1911

Robert F Dow adgfbgeb, farmer of Biddeford, d Feb 28, 1901, ae 66-4-18; m Sarah A Staples of Biddeford d Feb 14, 1901, ae 67, dau of Joseph and Sarah (Dolloff).   Perhaps other children:

a   (?) Oren J d July 29, 1865   b   Edward S b Biddeford 1866

Edward S Dow adgfbgebb, farmer of Biddeford, d Saco June 6, 1905, ae 39-0-21; m Sept 11, 1893, Nellie Edith Hill, ae 18.   She m 2nd Wilbur O Dow adgfdabbc.   Children by Edward S, all b Biddeford:

a   Gladys Winnifred b Aug 7, 1896   b   Sara Martha b Apr 8, 1898
c   Robert Wilbur b Mch 24, 1900   d   Lawrence Edward b Jan 9, 1902
e   Ralph M b May 29, 1904

Jeremiah Dow adgfbgf, farmer of Biddeford, m Phoebe Young b Me 1802.   Children,—only 3 traced:

a   George H b 1829   b   Eunice b 1832   c   Charles b 1833
d   Daniel b 1835   e   Miriam b 1836   f   Joseph W b Mch 10, 1839
g   Elijah b 1840   h   Asbury b 1843
i   James A b 1847; all living 1850

George H Dow adgfbgfa at 2nd m gave ae 70, the usual fib; b Biddeford, m 2nd Hanover, Mass, Sept 6, 1902, Mary A (Power) Radout, ae 52, her 2nd, dau of John and Charlotte (Bentley)

It seems probable, but we lack proof, that he was George Henry Dow, who m Marie Abigail Manchester. Her family is best known on and near Bar Harbor. They separated when their only son was a child and the family kept no trace of him. Two children:

a   Herbert Manchester b Portland
b   Annie May m —— Redick of So Portland; left two sons, Daniel and William,
    all now dead

Herbert M Dow adgfbgfaa. Rec of son gives his wife as Sarah Doyle b Portland. This is error. He met and married in Honolulu 1884 Sarah Crandal Lyle of Halifax, N S. They finally separated legally. Seven children, all b Honolulu, all living 1924:

a   Abigail Marion b 1885; now high school teacher of Honolulu, unm
b   Herbert Manchester   c   Annie Lois, now of San Francisco
d   Thompson Faxon   e   Charles Rose
f   Mildred May   g   Helen Marie

Herbert M Dow adgfbgfaab, laborer of Standish, then machinist, then steamship officer of Portland, m Standish Dec 18, 1906, Della Brackett of West Buxton. They are now div. Five children, all living 1924:

a   Alton C b Standish Dec 9, 1907   b   Herbert M b So Portland Dec 21, 1909
c   Marion Geraldine b So Portland Apr 30, 1911
d   Reginald Edwin b Standish July 26, 1919

Thompson F Dow adgfbgfaad appears in recent directory as fireman of Portland, home So Portland; m Mildred Binford Brown b Cape Elizabeth. Children:

a   Thompson Faxon b Portland Dec 1, 1915   b   Harriet Benita

Charles R Dow adgfbgfaae of San Francisco m Dec 1923 Gladys Gorgas.

Mildred M Dow adgfbgfaaf m Sept 1917 Charles Stanley Allen of Augusta, Me; now of Breckenridge, Tex. Child:

a   Robert Hugh b Jan 13, 1924

Helen M Dow adgfbgfaag m 1917 John P Dean of Tacoma, Wash; div and now of San Francisco.

Charles Dow adgfbgfc, farmer of Biddeford, d Apr 5, 1902; m 1878 Mary E Hill, who survived. Presumably more than one child:

a   Frank B b 1889

Frank B Dow adgfbgfca, blacksmith of Biddeford, m Jan 1, 1916, Lulu W Thompson, ae 19, dau of Rev Augustus B and Flora M (Benner).

a   Ethel Burtina b Biddeford Nov 2, 1916
b   Donald Augustus b Dayton Nov 22, 1917
c   Flora Mae b Dayton Sept 9, 1919

Joseph W Dow adgfbgff in 1921 farmer of Biddeford, m Mary Frances Dow adgfb-, his cousin

James A Dow adgfbgfi, carriage maker of Amesbury, Mass, m Feb 5, 1874, Ella F Marden, ae 18, of Portsmouth, N H, now living with her son in Biddeford, member of D A R.   Children:

a   Joseph B b Scarborough Oct 11, 1878
b   Ernest Hillgrove b Scarborough Jan 24, 1880

Joseph B Dow adgfbgfia, grad Boston Univ Law School 1905, lawyer of Biddeford and Saco, m June 20, 1911, Marion E Goodwin.   No children.

Ernest H Dow adgfbgfib, railroad engineer of Somerville, Mass, m Aug 10, 1901, Katherine Wilson Cameron, ae 22, b Glasgow, Scotland, dau of Thomas and Elizabeth (McCresson).   Child:

a   Marion Louise b Portland Nov 9, 1902

Samuel Dow adgfbgg b Hollis, m Sophia Knight.   Children, by 1850 census:

a   Lucinda b 1826; in 1905 Dayton directory
b   Samuel Knight b Hollis June 25, 1828   c   Sophia b 1831
d   Hannah S b Dayton Nov 25, 1835; d, music teacher of Saco, 1918
e   Caroline b 1838   f   Melissa b 1841

Saco directory gives Caroline A and Hannah S (latter d 1918) but the name just above them is Dorothy G Dow b Dyer.   Perhaps last name is accidental juxtaposition.

Samuel K Dow adgfbggb, grad Harvard 1854, began law practice in Chicago; his first clerk being Melville E Fuller; the firm became Dow & Fuller until the junior was appointed Chief Justice of U S Supreme Court.   He m about 1855 Frances E Hill of Biddeford d Chicago.   Of 9 children, those who survived him:

a   Frederick W   b   Mrs Orrin L Evans   c   Mrs G R Walker
d   Harriet   e   Mrs D W Wilkins

Harriet Dow adgfbggbd m Frank Johnson, vice president of American Tobacco Co, lives N Y City; only child:

a   Marie Dow

Daniel Dow adgfbgfd of Goodwin's Mills m Caroline Dyer b Hollis. Perhaps other children:

a   Francis A b Goodwin's Mills 1859

Francis A Dow adgfbgfda, photographer of Concord, N H, m Eugenia P Lyon b Sherman, N Y, 1854.   Two children found:

a   Rose Caroline b Bradford, Pa, 1889; m Kennebunkport, Me, Oct. 8, 1910, Walter Horace Kimball, ae 27, son of Fred Willis and Lizzie E (Smith)
b   William Alfred b Concord Aug 21, 1894

Daniel Dow adgfbgh is presumably the Daniel, farmer b 1814, d Kennebunkport Jan 13, 1894; no other data

David Dow adgfbh, farmer of Swift River, Tamworth, m Lydia Young d of tuberculosis. Children, presumably b 1791 and onward:

a   Moses   b   James d Tamworth, probably unm
c   Aaron   d   Daniel, untraced   e   Alva d tuberculosis

Moses Dow adgfbha. It is pure guess to regard him as Moses B Dow b Me (so 1850 census says) 1791; shoemaker without realty; wife Sarah b Me 1804. Name Lorenzo suggests Methodist convictions. Possibly a 1st born m by 1850. Children by census:

a   Lorenzo b 1832   b   Harriet b 1836   c   Abra E b 1838
d   Charles H b 1841   e   Mary T b 1849

Charles W Dow adgfbhad (initial H in census easily may be error) shoe worker of Rochester, N H, either m twice or there are two of same name. By Sarah A Smith b Acton, Me:

a   Ralph W b Sanford 1869

By Augusta Styles:

b   Jean Irving b Rochester 1871; electrician of Lynn, Mass, m Jan 19, 1893, Nellie May Waldron, ae 22, teacher, b Hartland, Me, dau of Charles and Sophronia (Ward)

Ralph W Dow adgfbhada, shoe worker of Sanford and No Lebanon, m Dec 29, 1892, Mabel L Cowell (Crowell in one rec) b Lebanon 1874, dau of Q C and Hattie A (Smith). Children:

a   Neil McAllister b Rochester Apr 13, 1894
b   Ralph K b Springvale Dec 16, 1895; d Sept 15, 1896
c   Ruth b Springvale Dec 25, 1897
d   Mabel Abigail b Revere, Mass, Oct 20, 1906

Neil McA Dow adgfbhadaa, civil engineer asst of Saco, m Nov 16, 1914, Marion Harriet Milliken, ae 19, dau of Ezra C and Laura (Morse) of Scarboro.

Aaron Dow adgfbhc is here from the account given by Mrs Dunster. He first appears in Salem, Mass, as a steam doctor (Thompsonian system), much criticized by the medical men of the place. Unfortunately one day he scalded a child to death, whereupon he hastened to Boston, where in 1828 he was keeping an intelligence office. In 1835 he was in Newburyport as a botanist doctor, then headed west. He turned up in Green Valley, Calif, where he made a fortune as a spiritualist. He got possession of and edited the "Banner of Light." He d Calif while waiting for the "earthly grand windup." He had 2 children b Boston, untraced.

There are few disconnected Aaron Dows. Perhaps adgfbhc m rather young. At least some Aaron m Sept 15, 1811, Betsey Kinney, both of Center Harbor. In spite of wording of rec, he may not have lived himself in Center Harbor.

Altho members of the adgfd line came down the Saco valley, there are a number of fugitive records probably belonging to the adgfb. For convenience in indexing, we put them here:

Frances Dow adgfbi b 1834 and **Sarah Dow** b 1823 boarding in Saco 1850.   May be identical with Sarah E Dow m Horatio Dunn. Child, Walter H b Dayton 1856; m Oct 13, 1881, Annie A Chipman.

Caroline Dow adgfbj of Lyman m Norwich, Conn, 1844 (1824?) John Hill of Hollis.

Charles Dow adgfbk, ship carpenter in Biddeford 1849 directory may be Charles m Mary Elizabeth Goodale d wid Kennebunk Jan 31, 1913, ae 73, 2 mos, b Wells, dau of George H b Vt and Louisa (Hatch).

This family was proven in 1927.   See Appendix adgfbfb.

John Dow adgfbl, farmer with no land, of Biddeford by 1850 census; b 1825; wife Mary b 1826.   No children in census.   Probably identical with John Dow m Mary G Gray (wid?) d Biddeford Dec 27, 1901, dau of Jotham and Mary (Gray) Moulton.   One child found:

    a   Roswell W d Biddeford Feb 23, 1902, ae 57, 10 mos, unm

Thomas Dow adgfbm m Lydia Gooch; known only from d rec of a son:

    a   George M b 1827. He d widower Biddeford Nov 20, 1897, ae 70-3-5, carpenter. Perhaps identical with George Dow in 1850 census farmer of Biddeford b 1827, assessed $1,000; wife Mary b Me 1828. No children in census, but may have been later

William F Dow adgfbn m Mary Frances Wadlin d Biddeford July 3, 1916, ae 86-7-24, dau of Jeremiah and Lucy (Goodwin) of Dayton.

William H Dow adgfbo b Dayton about 1840, d before 1912; m Mary E Alley b Lynn or Marblehead, d Dayton Oct 11, 1912, ae 70-7-10. Two children found:

    a   William H b Dayton 1873   b   Forrest d Dayton Mch 19, 1892, ae 15-0-22

William H Dow, farmer of Dayton, m July 4, 1918, Helen Hyman, ae 28, div, dau of James and Mary Ella (Bradbury) Eaton of Buxton. Children:

    a   Ernest Henry b Dayton Dec 23, 1918
    b   Selden Lovett b Dayton Aug 15, 1920

George A Dow adgfbp (Cf adgfbm), living 1918, m Isabel B Gooch d Portland Feb 27, 1918, ae 52-1-6, b Kennebunkport, dau of William H and Mary J (Murphy).

adgfbq.   Lyman 1907 directory has **Mary E Dow, Mattie I Dow, Alice Dow.**

Jonathan Dow adgfc. A family Bible exists with entries in his own hand, continued by a son. He m So Hampton May 24, 1764, Lydia Huse d Feb 19, 1793. This indicates that he and his father may have been much of the time in So Hampton. He was his father's own son, never connected with the Friends. A wild youth, he was always a good fighter, a a hard drinker, wanderer and venturesome. In Wheelock he seems to have accumulated considerable property. In 1765 he was of Durham with his father and there also 1775, signing the Association Test. One child was b Exeter, another Merrimac. In Gilmanton he was very much at home and his Revolutionary service was from there. He was evidently in close comradeship with the Gilmanton Dows of the ahba and adaab lines. He is probably the Jonathan of Lee 1a, 1b, 2c in the 1790 census. He d Aug 22, 1805, probably in Lee. In 1777 and off and on subsequently for many years he was in Wheelock, Vt, then a trading post on the edge of civilization, trading with the Indians. Very likely he took furs for whiskey, the most profitable form of Indian trade. While nominally illicit, this traffic was general. His family were divided subsequently between Wheelock and Gilmanton:

    a Perkins b Lee Mch 8, 1765
    b Olive b Jan 20, 1767   c Betty b Dec 4, 1768
    d Beniah b July 25, 1770   e Anna b July 22, 1772
    f Jonathan b May 17, 1774; d Nov 30, 1778
    g David b Apr 6, 1776; d Dec 5, 1778
    h Simon b May 21, 1778; d Wheelock 1804. Entry of d not in family Bible;
          found in Wheelock
    i Jonathan b June 16, 1780   j David b July 12, 1782
    k Lydia b June 28, 1792; d June 4, 1805. This entry made by father

Perkins Dow adgfca appears in Wheelock history until 1813, on the tax list each year from 1793, was a town officer 1800 and 1803. Tradition says that he moved to Gilmanton in 1813, but absence of his name there argues he had neither wife nor children.

Olive Dow adgfcb (said in m rec b Gilmanton) m Gilmanton Apr 11, 1786, Nathaniel Thompson b Apr 21, 1765, son of Nathaniel and Elizabeth (Stevens).

Betty Dow adgfcc m Belmont Mch 15, 1789, Jonathan Dow Jr, both of Gilmanton. It was for years the fashion for Gilmanton folks to be married in Belmont. They appear in 1790 census 1a, 1c, but Jonathan (called 3rd) is not positively identified.

Beniah Dow adgfcd, while with his parents in Wheelock 1777 suddenly disappeared and if ever again known to his parents, it was over 20 years later. It was a spring morning and there had come to town a party of Indians from Newfoundland. They also suddenly disappeared and it was supposed they had kidnapped the lad in hope of ransom. When couriers were sent after them, such a start had been made that the errand was in vain. Beniah in later years said that he went with them from choice. He told his story many hundred times in his old age and it never varied materially. Where he lived for the next five years he was not sure. He contentedly lived the Indian life and gained much reputation in his tribe as a hunter and athlete. A good jumper was most highly esteemed in Indian circles and Beniah was the best in his tribe. His first contact with civilization was at Quebec. He must have been there for some time, for, while his Indian friends were unable to count above ten, he himself learned to read, write and cipher. From the Indians he learned to make a raw moose hide boot of great serviceability and this knowledge supported him in later life.

At one time he left the tribe and took some position in Quebec, staying six years. But the wanderlust was frequent or constant. He started one day with Joseph Macure, a Frenchman, to Kingsport, P Q, to track deer in the snow. Three were encountered, of which Beniah shot two. A party of Indians had been tracking the same deer and soon came up, much disappointed. As they were of a friendly tribe, they were invited to stay to eat the game and go on for more deer. They stayed together for seven years. Beniah returned to civilization in Machias, Me, or Grand Menan. He met Joanna Mitchell and they were married. It is said that she was a Spanish woman and her name was anglicized. This is probably romance; she was b 1777 in Maine, probably of American parents. She was a good wife and mother. She alone could handle Beniah when in his cups.

Cambello Isl was in 1783 allotted to the United States, but for many years it was without government, its defences too good to warrant attempt at seizure. Young Admiral Owen of the British navy used it as a sort of pocket borough, having a legitimate title to most of its land. He took no rent from tenants,—merely he barred Methodists and Catholics, all others welcome with no moral qualifications required. He even issued a paper currency of his own. Naturally, the place became the refuge, first for tories, then for a pirate gang, outlaws. Beniah became a favorite with the Admiral, entrusted with money matters, collecting what revenues there were. He was able to hold his own with the gang, from his strong arm and deadly accuracy with a knife,—an Indian accomplishment. He fought and conquered with hands alone a vicious stallion. He had only one real man fight. An Irishman had arrived, giant in stature, and aspired to become the leading bully. As a challenge he kicked Beniah's dog over the cliff. The rest is Cambello history.

After some years Beniah took account of stock. His wife liked respectability and a baby had come. He had managed so that, while others may have had paper, he had hard silver,—2,000 Spanish milled dollars. He decided to make a run for civilization and, spying one day a passing schooner, he and family rowed out and got aboard. The $2,000 were in a couple of canvas bags. The schooner, bound for Portland, was wrecked; the silver went to the bottom. The party got safely ashore with hand luggage only and four silver dollars which Beniah had in his pocket. Work was found at once. Beniah never used the dollars. His son, Rev Huse Dow, bequeathed them, one to each of his four sons, the most precious legacy he had. Three of them are known in 1923; the fourth should belong to Maj Alexander Dow U S A, but that gentleman has never replied to many letters of genealogical inquiry.

Beniah settled in Paris, years later taking up land in gore no 1, Woodstock, where he and his wife finally died, he ae 81-6-5. Fortune never came his way again. He subsisted by making from house to house his famous moose hide boot, but as soon as he had earned a dollar he quit until next day. He was robust almost to the day of his death, good hearted, kindly, inoffensive, generous to a fault, but when in liquor (often) and crossed was worse than ten wildcats. A piece of personal property saved from the shipwreck was a drinking cup of china (now an heirloom), its blue inscription:

"Come drink and let us sing together,
In spite of wind and weather.
Come, here's to all ye honest men,—
Drink deep and drink again."

No doubt Beniah drank deep and often, but he carried it well. At Gray there was a haunted house, in which no tenant would stay. Incited by a promise of considerable reward, Beniah organized a party to lay the ghost. The latter, perhaps terrified by Beniah's reputation, confined himself to night noises, from which Beniah located it in an old dry well in the cellar. The party decided at once to excavate the well bottom to find the skeleton of the murdered man from whom all ghosts arise. But first they must wait for reinforcements for which one of the party went to town. They arrived in the shape of two gallons of whiskey. They then dug quickly. At the end of several days nothing had been heard from them and a rescue posse was formed. Beniah and companions were in the well, the toes of each toward the center, each asleep. The demijohns were empty. The ghost never reappeared.

In Paris there was a lawyer whose name was George, but nicknamed Gouge, for his practices. A solemn conclave decided that Gouge had cheated one of the gang and must be "licked." Beniah was chosen as able to do an artistic job. When Gouge got out of the hospital, Beniah was arrested, tried and found guilty. A stiff jail sentence seemed imminent, when 61 men came forward and demanded the same sentence, claiming to be equally *particeps criminis*. Public opinion came to the rescue; Beniah was released and Gouge left town.

In later years Beniah stayed a little longer each day in the chimney corner, inclined to tell stories. He had had much danger, some narrow escapes. Once, he admitted he was positively afraid. It was at night when he chanced not to have a pine knot. At a repeated noise, his dog

bristled up and refused to go out.   A hostile tribe was known to be in the
section.   He sat for the rest of the night with primed rifle over his knee.
In the morning all was well; there were catamount tracks all around, the
beast having stayed long.   The Indians always camped in one spot until
the last morsel of game was eaten.   They began with the choicest parts
of the deer but never quit until they had boiled the very bones for soup.
Then the squaws would locate the next deer that they had buried under
the snow.   The camp would be transferred alongside.   After each feast
they went hungry until the next game was killed.   Athletic games were
often intertribal.

The children of Beniah and Joanna:

a   Huse b Jan 25, 1801; d May 24, 1842
b   Olive b Apr 23, 1802; d Sept 13, 1806
c   Eliza b Dec 24, 1804; d May 11, 1847
d   Simon b May 24, 1806; d Sept 19, 1806
e   Annie b Sept 17, 1807; d Sept 7, 1842; m Levi Andrews
f   Jane b Oct 12, 1809; d Jan 3, 1854; m Cyrus Andrews
g   Beniah b Oct 12, 1809; d Jan 27, 1876
h   Olive b Dec 8, 1811; m (his 2nd) Levi Andrews
i   Pamelia b July 2, 1813
j   Dardama b Apr 25, 1815; d Sept 2, 1842

Huse Dow adgfcda was the only member of the family to become a
Methodist and a democrat.   Upon conversion he became a circuit rider
around several towns with his home in Jay.   Pay was very small, he was
kept on horseback five days a week with hardships which wore him out
at 40.   He m Zilpha Drake b Winthrop Mch 6, 1805, dau of Alpheus and
Sybilla (Fairbanks), a young belle with many beaux for a small town.
She preferred the poor young preacher, making a splendid wife and mother
of a hungry Methodist family.   Many Indians were around Jay and they
came to Aunt Zilphy for many favors.   One day she loaned her iron
cooking pot to a squaw; as it was not returned three days later, she sent
her young son Simon for it.   Simon found it, but in the pot, hide, hair
and all, was Zilphy's favorite and superannuated dog.   In 1850 she was
left more or less lonely, as all her sons started for California to seek gold.
She lost an eye through erysipelas.   She was an old woman when she m
2nd John Hamilton.   They lived together in Canton, Ohio, for a couple
of years, but neither had any money.   They had to separate, he going to
his relatives, she to hers.   They corresponded regularly for the rest of
their lives.   His letters invariably began "Respected Madam" and ended
"Yours respectfully."   Her later days were in Maine.   Children:

a   Lorenzo b Sumner July 10, 1823, at which time Lorenzo Dow ahgge was at the
       height of his fame as a revivalist
b   Simon   c   William Mitchell   d   Edwin Clinton b Aug 22, 1835

Lorenzo Dow adgfcdaa grad Kent's Hill Academy and had the
scholarship given to oldest sons of Methodist ministers in Wesleyan Univ;
grad 1848.   In 1850 he went to California but all four brothers soon came
back.   In 1853 he was elected president of a college in Alabama; m Eliza-

beth Pinfield of Middletown, Conn. She d Feb 1862; he m 2nd Oct 1862 Mrs Sabrina H Anderson, nee Smith, of Fayette, Me, a fine singer and author of a book on artistic singing. She d May 25, 1893. Lorenzo's anti slavery views soon cost him his Alabama position; he came to New York, moving next year to Topeka, Kan. He was its first mayor and a territorial judge. He returned to N Y because he had invented a waterproof cartridge adopted by the Government. He allied himself with the Winchester Arms Co of New Haven. There he invented a type-setting machine which promised wonderfully until it was killed by the superior Mergenthaler. He d 1899. Children:

a Grace Elizabeth b July 12, 1859; d 1864
b Florence b Feb 17, 1864; m A Blair Thaw of N Y; living 1923
c Alexander b Jan 6, 1868; grad Stevens Institute; was president of Dow Type Setting Machine Co. Later of Detroit and many other places. In 1918 was commissioned major in regular army to wind up some business affairs

Simon Dow adgfcdab d at the home of his son, Greeley, Iowa, Feb 5, 1916; lived 44 years in Malta Bend, Mo. As sheriff he exchanged many shots with the James gang, including Jesse himself. To his children by 2nd wife he never mentioned his 1st wife or oldest child, neither known to them by name. He m 2nd Jane Kinsley, school teacher, by whom 2 children; m 3rd Sarah Kinsley, teacher, her sister; 2 children; m 4th at Malta Bend Mary Maxson; 2 children:

a —— b Harry d in infancy c Charles Guy b July 6, 1860
d Victor Eugene e Fanny Sarah
f Nellie, now Mrs Belt of Coffeyville, Kan g Clarence, now of El Paso, Tex

Victor E Dow adgfcdabd is editor of the Greeley, Iowa, Home Press; m Sept 23, 1896, Sadie Verona Chapman. They keep one of Beniah's silver dollars. Children:

a Merl Eugene b Nov 21, 1897; d Aug 2, 1901
b Huse Ard b Apr 28, 1899 c Florence Ardine b Aug 24, 1906; d Aug 4, 1909

Fannie S Dow adgfcdabe d Nov 1909; m Earl Smitherman of Kansas City; left sons,—Clyde and Roy.

William M Dow adgfcdac d Feb 20, 1902; sgt in the Civil War, his three brothers being captains; was at Gettysburg; one time deputy sheriff of Franklin Co; then deputy collector at Portland under Gen Anderson bcdbcca; an active contributor to various magazines on many topics. He m Mehitable Thayer Libbey b June 21, 1827, d Jan 10, 1913, dau of James and Betsey (Thayer) of Gray. In d rec her mother is wrongly given as Mehitable Low. Children:

a William H b Danville Oct 22, 1854
b James A b Gray (all younger b Gray) May 16, 1857
c Lorenzo Everett b Dec 11, 1858
d Hettie C b Sept 5, 1862; m 1918 Lanville Webster of Gray
e Charles Libbey b July 27, 1864 f Grace P b Sept 8, 1867
g True M b Mch 30, 1872; d Nov 27, 1880

William H Dow adgfcdaca m Clara W Pennell.   Gray 1909 directory gave him mail carrier, with children, at school:

a   Ralph P b 1889; teacher, m Tamworth, N H, July 19, 1911, Evelyn B Bartlett, ae 20, dau of Elroy G and Emmogene (Evans)
b   Philip Huse b Aug 22, 1892; m Gertrude Gooding of New Bedford, Mass
c   Nettie C

James A Dow adgfcdacb, farmer of So Portland, d Oct 21, 1918; m Annie McCool b Sept 11, 1858.   Children:

a   Charlotte Mehitable d ae 3
b   William James b July 5, 1891; studied art in Philadelphia, winning a foreign scholarship; since 1918 commercial artist in N Y City; unm 1923. He aided much on his own direct line in this Book: m July 30, 1924 Sylvia Castle Hurlburt, dau of William E

Lorenzo E Dow adgfcdacc, grad Gorham Normal School; in 1881 teacher and part owner of a Montclair, N J, school for boys; later of Boys High School, Brooklyn; the superintendent of schools Homer, Mich; entered Hillsdale College, grad 1887; a trustee 1900; studied law Northwestern Univ; admitted to bar 1891; senior partner of Dow, Cummings & Ingersoll 1908; republican and Free Will Baptist. It is a fact that no son of Huse Dow remained Methodist or democrat.   Lorenzo E m 1890 Lillian Kirkwood d 1892; m 2nd Eldora Lockwood Smith of Calif.   One dau:

a   Dorothy Lillian b Feb 2, 1892; m —— Libbey

Charles L Dow adgfcdace, merchant of West Pownal, m Alice S Merrill.   Children:

a   Ella m and has family
b   Lorenzo L, clerk of Pownal, m Jan 23, 1914, Alice M Martain, ae 21, teacher, dau of Charles and Alice E (Boothby)
c   Mehitable b July 19, 1895
d   John Neal b Oct 2, 1897; d (Merrill Neal) Cleveland, Ohio, Oct 7, 1918, unm
e   Egbert b July 7, 1900   f   Elizabeth b Sept 14, 1901
g   Olive b Feb 27, 1909
h   Grace Phyllis b Sept 22, 1914; d Oct 11, 1918

Edwin C Dow adgfcdad settled soon after 1850 in New Haven, Conn, living there 1923; was captain present at Gettysburg; practiced law, for many years a city judge, until age forced his resignation.

Not having seen his brother Simon for over 30 years, Edwin decided to take a vacation to look him up.   Alighting at a small Kansas town, he inquired from a taciturn driver the way to the hotel.   The ride was in silence.   At the hotel he learned that the driver was the sought brother.

He m 1st Jan 13, 1858, Hester D Barnes d Jan 26, 1904; m 2nd May 6, 1905; Harriet A Griffing.   Children;

a   Zera b Aug 3, 1859; m and has sons,—William, Arthur and Gardner
b   Edwin   c   Harry Barnes b July 31, 1866
d   Mae Barnes b May 28 1874; m E A Munsell of New Haven; dau,—Dorothy

Beniah Dow adgfcdg, farmer, progressive man of considerable ability, m Anna H Briggs b 1816. He m 2nd wid —— Whittle; 3rd wid Mary Ann (Raines) Grover. Children:

   a   Benjamin K b 1835   b   Moses D b 1836
   c   Greenleaf G b Jan 1, 1838; d So Paris Sept 27, 1920
   d   Emily b 1840; m Dec 28, 1856, Joshua Kendall; 5 children; now only one
        living,—Mrs Nellie Littlehale of No Paris

Benjamin K Dow adgfcdga, farmer of Paris, d Strafford, N H, at his son's home, Apr 25, 1918; m Feb 1, 1857, Mary A Kendall b Mch 13, 1841, West Milan, N H. Children:

   a   David Briggs b Paris Dec 31, 1857   b   Simon Henry b Nov 13, 1863

David B Dow adgfcdgaa, well known clergyman with many parishes in Me and N H, now lives Rochester, N H, with his son; m Abbie J Churchill b West Paris, dau of Kingman and Loretta (Andrews). Children:

   a   Henry Kingman b No Paris 1884   b   Hattie C b Monticello Apr 5, 1886
   c   Ada M W b Bucksport Apr 27, 1891 d   Esther N b Guilford Nov 27, 1899

Henry K Dow adgfcdgaaa owns the Rochester newspaper, whose policy of pay and be paid, of excluding write-ups, and of general independence gave it more than local reputation; m June 6, 1912, Ruth Lightbody, ae 20, b Vassalboro, dau of Samuel, druggist, and Eunice (Jepson). Only child:

   a   Mary Emma b Dover Mch 21, 1917

Simon Henry Dow adgfcdgab, often known as Henry S Dow, moved to Vt, then to Leominster, Mass, real estate and insurance agent; m Ellen Davis d Manchester, Vt, without children; 2nd (by family rec) Robie Putnam, by whom 1 child. Her d rec: Robie A Woodward b Landgrove, Vt, d No Paris Dec 20, 1901, ae 39, 3 mos, dau of Charles D and Lucy (Pease), both b Vt. He m 3rd Nov 12, 1905, Edith A Hastings, ae 30, dau of Henry and Eliza M (Jewett). She survives in Leominster. Child:

   a   Ethel d young in Paris, Me

Moses D Dow adgfcdgb, farmer, d married, Sumner Sept 9, 1919, ae 83-2-13; m Paris Nov 24, 1859, Susan F Chandler b Buckfield Feb 1, 1840, d Sumner Mch 7, 1865; m 2nd Nov 10, 1867, Lucy A Trask b Hartford Mch 9, 1842, dau of Amasa and Arvilla (Tilson). Children:

   a   Charles d in childhood
   b   Hattie M b Paris Dec 8, 1861; now Mrs Bessey of Bryant's Pond
   c   Etta M b Paris Mch 27, 1870; d unm

Greenleaf G Dow adgfcdgc saw more than the others of his grandfather and preserved best his traditions, altho in later years he let his imagination run and claimed relatives of all lines of adgfc to a point which cost the genealogists years of trouble, as his narrative was at first taken

fully for granted. He could have written a large volume on the subject
of Beniah, full of valuable Indian lore. He was a farmer of Durham.
returning finally to So Paris. He m 1st May 1, 1858, Lucinda A Farrar b
Buckfield June 23, 1836, d Bethel Jan 8, 1894, dau of Nathan and Susanna
(Brock); m 2nd Jan 1, 1896, Nettie B Bowie, ae 26, dau of Melvin and
Olivia D (Larrabee). She d Mch 18, 1908. Children:

a Evalina (Elvira Ann) b Sumner Dec 28, 1859; m Sept 6, 1885, J H Briggs of
   New Gloucester; 1 child now Mrs John Wright of So Paris
b Ida M b Sumner May 2, 1863; m Nov 16, 1881, George E Stevens of Woodstock,
   son of Oren (physician) and Ellen (Davis) of Oxford, Me. Children:
   Ward J b Nov 4, 1884; Bertha A b May 28, 1886
c Frank Lafayette b Paris Jan 10, 1868
d Mildred E b Durham Nov 18, 1897

Frank L Dow adgfcdgcc inherited the farm; m Mch 17, 1892, May
Isabelle Cummings b Sept 14, 1875, dau of Maurice and Eda May (Le
Baron) of So Paris. Children:

a Lafayette Frank b Oct 27, 1893   b Arthur Greenleaf b July 23, 1896

Olive Dow adgfcdh, living 1887, m Mch 18, 1827, Levi Andrews, b
Jan 23, 1810, farmer of Paris. Children:

a Oliver S b Sept 16, 1828; m Rose Gilkey; of Minn; 3 children
b James F b July 7, 1833; m Lizzie Rice; of Manchester, Iowa
c Everett D b May 10, 1839; m Amanda M Curtis; of Paris; 1 child
d Isabella A b Sept 22, 1842; d May 30, 1871; m Oct 25, 1860, Francis Grovenor;
   3 children
e Ella R b Sept 16, 1849; m Jan 30, 1871, John H Dowrst of Brooklyn; 2 children
f Ida W b Mch 16, 1852; m Dec 25, 1879, H A Fuller; of Paris; 2 children

Pamelia Dow adgfcdi m Joseph Dunham b May 13, 1805, son of
Asa and Lydia (Cobb); had strong ideas regarding devotion to home and
children, of whom many came. A thoroughly intelligent woman, she read
the newspapers regularly, but when, after 40 years of married life, she
visited her sister-in-law Zilpha, it was her first experience outside her
native village.

Jonathan Dow adgfci was a lifelong resident of Wheelock, Vt,
continuing the trading business begun by his father. The late Greenleaf Dow allowed his imagination to run until he himself believed that
Jonathan accumulated $2,000, crossed the White Mts on horseback,
settled in Avon, Me, re-discovered his brother Beniah and reunited the
family. This was based on an unrelated Jonathan Dow who was of Avon
and on various Dow who came to Maine with much silver. There is no
evidence that Beniah Dow adgfcd was ever again known to his family
after his disappearance at age of 7.

Jonathan d Wheelock Jan 30, 1842; was known as Capt Jonathan
Dow Jr. Perhaps the military title was inherited, as he does not appear
in the 1812 war rosters. He held occasional town offices and was one of

the most influential citizens; m Martha W Hoyt and late in life made a 2nd m. Children, all b Wheelock by 1st wife:

<blockquote>
a Joseph b Mch 3, 1803; d 1809   b Ira b Aug 14, 1809; d Apr 6, 1885

c Joseph b Sept 24, 1811; d Nov 22, 1868

d Simon b July 28, 1813; d Feb 12, 1851; m Fidelia Coe d Aug 7, 1849; no children; was a hotel keeper, at one time of Haverhill, Mass

e Galusha b Mch 12, 1816; d July 16, 1881   f Jonathan b Mch 24, 1818

g Lydia Maria b May 7, 1820   h Sophia E b Apr 27, 1823

i Hiram b Dec 26, 1825; grad Medical college; located in Halifax, Nova Scotia; became a British subject and served in N S Parliament. The late Greenleaf Dow may have had some vague knowledge of this, but he certainly confused Perkins Dow adgfca with John Dow (bcdgb line), who was a member of New Brunswick Parliament. Hiram d Aug 30, 1884, a distinguished operating surgeon of Fredericksburg; never married
</blockquote>

Ira Dow adgfcib appears in 1850 census farmer of Wheelock, assessed $2,737; m Apr 8, 1835, Martha Morgan, dau of Stephen and Anna (Gibson).   Children:

<blockquote>
a Laura Ann b July 28, 1835; d Jan 29, 1855, unm

b Martha b Mch 3, 1842; d July 22, 1872; m Nov 3, 1862, Joseph H Ingalls; children,—George B, Laura M m 1892 William H Brown

c Jonathan (Jonathan J by 1850 census, Jonathan E by ms Hist Wheelock) b May 3, 1844; d May 21, 1897

d Emma b 1846; living 1860, but not recalled 1881 by members of the family
</blockquote>

Jonathan E Dow adgfcibc appears in 1850 census farmer of Sutton, assessed $3,300; m Nov 29, 1866, Amy Richardson Nelson, dau of Samuel and Lucy (Richardson).   Only child:

<blockquote>
a Arthur L b Feb 10, 1868; d Apr 18, 1889
</blockquote>

Joseph Dow adgfcic appears in 1850 farmer of Wheelock, assessed $800; m May 4, 1836 (May 11, 1835, State rec), Mary C (Marcy in several rec) Chase b Aug 7, 1814, d Feb 3, 1876, dau of John and Betsey (Carter).   This family of Quaker stock came from Boscawen to Sanbornton, thence to Wheelock.   After Joseph's death, his whole family moved to No Conway, N H.   Children:

<blockquote>
a Martha b Mch 14, 1837; d Apr 5, 1873; m Aug 27, 1853, Daniel Harvey Ward

b Eliza Bradley b June 7, 1839; d Jan 24, 1897; m Nov 24, 1860, Benjamin Smith of Tamworth; children,—Frank Edwin b Jan 9, 1862; Mary Helen b Sept 3, 1864; Addie Dow b July 12, 1869; d Feb 1892; Grace d Apr 1883

c Helen Maria b Sept 16, 1840; d Feb 18, 1914; m 1st Dec 17, 1864, Isaac Edwin Merrill of No Conway; m 2nd Sumner Hill; child,—Louise Dow (Merrill) b Dec 31, 1881

d Hiram Harvey b July 6, 1847   e Julia Hodgdon b May 5, 1852; d Nov 13, 1863

f Addie Ward b June 30, 1854
</blockquote>

Hiram H Dow adgfcicd d Dec 23, 1911; m Oct 20, 1870, Clara E Barnes of No Conway, ae 19, dau of Albert and Almira H (Seavey).   He was a hotel proprietor of No Conway.   Children:

<blockquote>
a Marion J b Aug 11, 1871; d July 21, 1872

b Helen Merrill b Feb 26, 1874   c Albert Barnes b Aug 27, 1876
</blockquote>

Albert B Dow adgfcicdc, hotel keeper, later telegrapher of No Conway, m Oct 21, 1903, Helen M Eastman, teacher, ae 22, dau of John L and Nanny L (Bessey).   Children:

   a Arline b Feb 22, 1905   b ——, dau b Dec 6, 1906
   c Elizabeth b Jan 29, 1915

Addie Ward Dow adgfcicf m Jan 2, 1876, James Lewis Gibson of No Conway; in 1923 wid living No Conway and Atlantic City.   Children:

   a Frances Louise b Aug 21, 1879; m Aug 21, 1907, Ernest Roliston Woodbury of Castine, Me; 3 children
   b Harvey Dow b Mch 12, 1882; grad Bowdoin; m Carrie Curtis of Newtonville, Mass; came to N Y to become president of Liberty Nat Bank, then president of N Y Trust Co; now one of the leading national financiers

Galusha Dow adgfcie d July 16, 1881; m Oct 28, 1848, Drusilla Darling, dau of Reuben D and Hannah (Chandler); was of Wheelock 1845, farmer of Sheffield 1850; hostler in 1860, later hotel keeper.   Census of 1880 finds Drusilla house keeper of Lyndon.   Children:

   a George C b 1845; m Grace C Weymouth
   b Fidelia M (Delia) b Dec 6, 1849

George C Dow adgfciea moved to Wasioga, Minn, where his mother and sister also passed their old age.   He had sons:

   a Clifford L   b Harry

Delia M Dow adgfcieb m Oct 27, 1874, Elmore E Cleveland.   Children:

   a Mabel Darling b May 30, 1875   b Henry Elmore b June 30, 1880

Jonathan Dow adgfcif became a hotel keeper of Conway; m Elizabeth Thompson of No Conway.   Children:

   a Louise   b Frank, untraced

Lydia M Dow adgfcig m Horace Merrill.   Children:

   a Emily   b Sarah   c Elizabeth   d Simon   e Amos

Sophia E Dow adgfcih d May 30, 1883; m 1st Apr 15, 1840, Abel Park, by whom 7 children; m 2nd Nov 21, 1877, Asa Ladd.   A large posterity with many still in Wheelock.   Children:

   a William   b Hiram   c Myron   d Simon   e Frank
   f Luella   g Mary

David Dow adgfcj lived to maturity in Wheelock; moved after 1808 to Skowhegan, Me, where he d Aug 17, 1862; m Elizabeth French b Epping, N H, Dec 1, 1784, d Skowhegan May 14, 1867.   Had 2 sons, 3 dau, of whom:

   a Hannah E b Mch 13, 1806   b John b Wheelock Oct 2, 1808
   c Jane b Woodstock, Me, Nov 14, 1814
   d Edgar; apparently lived to advanced age; left a dau,—in 1881 Mrs Aldear Hinton of Hartland, Me

Hannah E Dow adgfcja m Nathaniel P Ames, shoemaker of Canaan. Children:

- a Frances b Mch 1827; m A Herrin of Skowhegan; 4 children
- b David b 1829; m H Ireland; 6 children
- c Hórace b Dec 26, 1831; m Oct 23, 1852, T Barnes; 5 children
- d Elizabeth b June 16, 1834; m A Gray; 1 child
- e Perley b Mch 1837; m B Barnes; 8 children
- f Augustus b 1839; m —— Bragg; 3 children
- g Aratus b Dec 24, 1841; m —— Eldridge; 5 children
- h Edgar b Jan 30, 1844; m S Gleason; 4 children
- i Helen b 1847; m C Barnes; 4 children

John Dow adgfcjb, farmer of Plymouth, d July 11, 1884; was capt militia 3 years; in Legislature of 1849; m Dec 5, 1839, Hannah Jordan b Danville, Vt, Nov 17, 1816. Children, all b Plymouth:

- a Alvesta b May 24, 1841; d Aug 25, 1841
- b Emily b Jan 13, 1843; m May 5, 1867, A D Sherburn of Maine, Iowa
- c Edgar R b Jan 10, 1846   d Moses J b Apr 6, 1848
- e John S b Mch 13, 1851; moved to Valley, Kan; untraced
- f Nancy J b June 8, 1853; m Oct 26, 1873, John F Longley of Plymouth; 3 children
- g Sumner b May 13, 1856   h Sarah C b Nov 17, 1859; unm

Edgar R Dow adgfcjbc, merchant and deputy sheriff of Newport, Me, m Nov 8, 1870, Augusta M Dudley b St Albans 1850. Children:

- a Edna Maria b Newport July 11, 1876
- b Guy Stewart (Stuart) b Nov 21, 1878; untraced

Moses J Dow adgfcjbd, farmer of Plymouth, m Sept 18, 1872, Anna E Paine b Plymouth Aug 11, 1848. Children:

- a ——, dau b Dec 11, 1875; d in infancy
- b Mittie A b Mch 6, 1878   c —— son b and d May 10, 1884
- d Dora E b Apr 6, 1886

Sumner Dow adhfcjbg moved to Eureka, Kan, then bank cashier of Emporia, Kan; m May 27, 1884, Mary A Howard b Terre Haute, Ind, Nov 6, 1861. Directory of 1915 gives her wid of Emporia with 2 children:

- a Kate Sumner b Aug 24, 1885; teacher unm in 1915
- b John b after 1888, in which year Sumner Dow wrote his few words of genealogy; in 1915 student

Jane Dow adgfcjc m Aug 30, 1836, Joseph W Pooler, farmer of Canaan, b Feb 7, 1811. Children:

- a Willis b Sept 20, 1837; m 1867 Mary A Seeley; 4 children in Gualala, Calif
- b John F b May 6, 1839; m Apr 29, 1864, B E Franklin; moved to St Charles, Minn
- c Leslie b Apr 11, 1842; d Oct 4, 1847
- d Abbie F b Sept 23, 1843; m Dec 21, 1862, B E Berwise; 3 children
- e Philena b Mch 8, 1845; d Sept 24, 1847
- f Coolidge b Nov 8, 1846; d Oct 2, 1847
- g Sidney L b June 18, 1851; m Sept 2, 1875, L E Richardson; 2 children in Skowhegan

One of the pioneers of Hollis, Me, was brother of Jeremiah Dow, already considered:

Ebenezer Dow adgfd was probably b 1737 and the place was not improbably So Hampton.   Of his life until 1790 nothing is known.   That he m before 1774 is shown by the 1790 census of Little Falls, which gives him 2a, 2b, 6c, i e, with 3 sons and 5 dau, or 6 dau, if he were a widower. If he continued Quaker is not known, at all events he probably was out of the Society by the time he came to Hollis.   When he d is not known; name of wife never found.   Not one child can be proven.   There was, however, a large Dow family of Hollis which must descend from him and they spread through Lyman, Buxton, Dayton, and to some slight extent down the valley to Biddeford.   The 3 sons can be placed with reasonable certainty, the many girls are genealogically lost.   Except for possible omissions in the adgfb line all the local untraced or disconnected Dows belong here.   The sons:

    a   Daniel b before 1774
    b   John int pub Hollis Apr 3, 1812, to Betsey Gordon
    c   Oliver, in business for self 1822

The division of children of the first two is wholly by guess.

Daniel Dow adgfda appears positively only once; he joined the Hollis Methodist church 1809, being called Captain.   For convenience, we attach as many as possible of the children to him:

    a   William b (say) 1810   b   Ebenezer; his wife b 1814
    c   Daniel b (by census) 1812

William Dow adgfdaa is known only by mention in d rec of son: may be the true adgfbfd.

    a   Simon Black b 1836 by d rec, which gives Hollis or Strafford, (N H)

Simon B Dow adgfdaaa m Newmarket, N H, Sept 6, 1859, Loisa L Gordon (sic in rec, but she was Lucinda Day Gordon b Kennebunkport). He enlisted 1861 from Hollis; after the war he was for many years a mill watchman in Biddeford; d Jan 1, 1898, ae 61.   Inquiry in Biddeford has failed to elicit the 4 older children:

    e   Susia M b Biddeford July 15, 1892; m (as Lurie May), mill operative, Oct 21,
         1917, William Edwin Dow adaabfdi: Further untraced

Ebenezer Dow adgfdab appears in 1850 census as farmer of Dayton; assessed $3,000; wife Sarah Drew b Me 1814.   Census gives 2 children, unlikely that there were more:

    a   Lydia b 1837   b   Albert b 1839

Albert Dow adgfdabb, farmer of Dayton, d, married, Jan 2, 1896, ae 56-11-17; wife was Fannie Hill.   Children as found by own m rec:

    a   Walter E b 1868   b   Bartlett A b 1870
    c   Wilbur O b 1873   d   Arthur b 1877

Walter E Dow adgfdabba, engineer of Dayton, m June 25, 1902, Lucinda I Smith, ae 26, dau of Albert and Mary E (Cummings) of Dayton.

Bartlett A Dow adgfdabbb, blacksmith, m May 3, 1902, Hettie F Cole, teacher, ae 26, dau of Oliver and Elsie A (Hill), all of Dayton. Children:

    a Kenneth B b Dayton Sept 10, 1902   b ——, dau b Biddeford Jan 16, 1907

Wilbur O Dow adgfdabbc, painter of Dayton and Biddeford, m Sept 11, 1907, Nellie Edith Dow, wid ae 31, adgfbgeda, dau of George W and Martha (Dearborn) Hill.

Arthur Dow adgfdabbd, jeweler of Dayton, m Sept 22, 1905, Sarah Marian Chase, ae 26, teacher of Standish, dau of John L and Sarah (Spear). Children:

    a Dorothy d Portland May 17, 1909, ae 8 days
    b John Chase b Portland Dec 19, 1914

Oliver Dow adgfdc is, we must admit, arbitrarily placed. His first appearance is in Buxton, where in 1822 he bought out the lumber business of his employer, subsequently succeeding, as in 1850 his assessment was $7,000. He m about 1832 Harriet Taylor b Me 1809, dau of Amos and Nancy (Haley). Libby Gen has this family badly garbled, calling her Sarah Haley. She b Waterboro. Children, of whom 5 in 1850 census:

    a Mary J b 1834; d Buxton Mch 3, 1907, ae 72-3-2, unm
    b Harriet b 1838   c Cornelia b 1841
    d Julia A b 1845; m 1868 George B Libby b Mch 8, 1841, son of Jonathan Jr and
        Matilda S (Bacon). Libby Gen says Jonathan was a cooper and partner of
        E Dow
    e Oliver b 1848; untraced
    f Amanda F b after 1850; m Dec 31, 1873, Charles Albert Libby b Portland Dec
        10, 1844, hostler of Biddeford

Daniel Dow adgfdac, farmer of Biddeford, assessed in 1850 $400; wife Mary b Me 1806. Four children in census

    a Franklin b 1836; untraced   b George b 1838; untraced
    c Elmin (sex?) b 1843   d Webster b 1846; untraced

David Dow adgfdd (for cenvenience in index). Hist Saco Valley gets us into a mixup, saying he m (no place) June 25, 1846, Sarah H Edgcomb; she m 2nd June 24, 1876, Ezra Tyler. This connects with:

William Dow (b 1848), carpenter, married, d Buxton Dec 12, 1896, ae 48-6-9, son of Daniel, ship carpenter, and Sarah Edgcomb, both b Bath. Again:

Sarah A Dow d Biddeford June 24, 1906, ae 84-6-8, dau of Edgcomb and Sally (Watson) Haley. Of previous occurrence of name Sarah Haley.

Sophia Dow adgfde stands alone in Buxton census, b 1826.

Oliver Dow adgfdf b 1821, blacksmith of Hollis, assessed $4,000; wife Sarah b Me 1822.   Census gives one child:

a   Amanda b 1845

William M Dow adgfdg appears in Hollis 1907 directory, but never replied to letter of genealogical inquiry.   Children, from directory:

a   Adyn   b   Elsie   c   Hazel   d   Allen

William M Dow Jr adgfdh appears in Dayton 1905 directory. Others in same directory: Mary E Dow, Percy E Dow, Nellie E Dow.

Ann Dow adgfe (no other identity possible) is resurrected by De-merritt Gen; of Durham m Samuel Emerson bap Sept 10, 1741, son of Solomon and Elizabeth (Burnham).   He m 2nd Lois McCoy, by whom 4 children.   By Ann, order not accurate:

a   Joseph   b   Catherine
c   Abigail m June 23, 1825, Davis Demerritt
d   Anna m 1809 Robert Hill of Lee

The recurrence of name, Solomon Emerson, is the only evidence by which to place the next:

John Dow adgff, chair maker, not a member of the Friends, d Weare, N H, Dec 12, 1825.   Hist Weare errs doubly, saying he b Rowley and came to Weare 1769.   Our theory is that he was a younger son and left Durham in youth with a companion of the Emerson family, that they aimed seaward and reached Rowley.   John m (int pub Gloucester May 28, 1774) Lucy Brewer.   Next year he enlisted from Rowley and was making Ipswich his home in 1777.   The date of their coming to Weare is indicated by bap rec as not earlier than 1780 and not later than 1798. Children, correct by Weare and Ipswich:

a   Polly. B rec not found, but must be twin or not oldest. Hist Weare gives her
     oldest
b   Lucy bap Ipswich Oct 22, 1775   c   John bap Ipswich Aug 17, 1777

Polly Dow adgffa m Weare Nov 17, 1803, Marden Emerson, son of Marden and Nancy (Carr).   Children:

a   Marden m 1827 Lydia M Eaton   b   Solomon
c   Jesse b 1810; m Harriet Drake   d   John L d unm
e   Mary Jane m 1842 Daniel Barnard

Lucy Dow adgffb m Oct 11, 1798, John Peaslee, both of Dunbarton. The adgff line now becomes close to the Friends.   They moved to Ipswich; she d July 16, 1843.   Children:

a   John b Nov 3, 1801   b   Lucy Dow b Oct 31, 1805; m Hazen Colby
c   Mary E b Aug 6, 1807; m Rodney E Presby
d   Susan C b May 14, 1811; m Thomas Davis

John Dow adgffc was of Weare 1830; became farmer of Canaan, d there.   A local history says he came from Hopkinton, error unless Hopkinton was a way station. He m, ae 31, Weare Nov 27, 1805, Hannah Worthen, ae 25, dau of Samuel, farmer, and Deborah. These people were Quakers. Children:

a Samuel d Canaan Oct 29, 1884, ae 78-5-21   b Helen
c Mary S m Aug 9, 1831, Daniel B Locke; moved to Warner
d Hannah   e Lucy d Canaan Sept 24, 1877, unm

Samuel Dow adgffca m Aug 15, 1830, Sarepta Sargent, both of Weare; a farmer; census 1850 finds him with no land and no wife, but mentions one child:

a Malinda b N H 1832

Helen Dow adgffcb m Oct 20, 1831, William Dinsmore of Foxcroft, Me; moved to Manchester, N H. A child:

a Mary Dow m 1st—Colburn; 2nd Manchester 1887 William Perkins

---

Moses Dow adgfg. We must have a Dow, early settler of New Durham, old enough to have a grandchild by 1827. We know that the only early Dows of New Durham were the adgf members. We find a fugitive rec: Moses Dow of New Durham inherited for his wife part of the estate of Col Thomas Wallingford, reputed to be one of the richest men in the State. Elsewhere we find that Col. Wallingford, merchant, d Aug 4, 1771, ae 74. Another heir was a Wentworth akin to Ahra Wentworth adbabb. Here is clearly a Quaker connection. In adgfb, Quaker line, we have two untraced Moses Dows, but both are too young by at least a dozen years to fit either requirement, altho one of these was known to live for some years, at least, in New Durham. As no one has searched the early parish rec of New Durham, the town rec being worthless, the only working hypothesis is to give another son to Ebenezer Dow and Lydia Ranlit. As the next known name is Jeremiah, the thing is all the more plausible. What family had Moses we know not. The earliest known member of a long line is:

a Jeremiah, probably b before 1800

Jeremiah Dow adgfga m Mary Hall, both of New Durham. They had a large family, some of whom no doubt are in the mass of upstate disconnected rec. Only three are recalled, and order not known:

a ——, a dau m and moved to Battle Creek, Mich
b Samuel Hall b New Durham Dec 1827
c Lorenzo b New Durham Nov, 1835; wanderer, following many trades; d laborer, widower, New Durham Jan 20, 1899; no further rec

Samuel H Dow adgfgab moved to Boston and Cambridge, Mass; m here about Jan 1851 Catherine Lucretia Manson b Biddeford, Me, Nov 7, 1832. They bought a farm in Vermont, but moved to New Hampton, N H. He enlisted while in No Tisbury, Mass, altho having 6 children. Invalided, he bought a farm in Campton, N H, but July 19, 1864, he was chosen 1st Lieut in the new 18th N H, Col Thomas L Livermore. Disch

Mch 13, 1865, he became a well known farmer and sugar maker of Campton, deacon in Baptist church.   In 1903 he moved again to No Tisbury, Mass, to be near relatives.   Apparently others from New Durham went to No Tisbury.   Here he d 1908.   His wid went to live with her son in Gallatin, Mo; d Feb 1917.   Children:

    a Walter H b Westboro, Mass, 1852
    b Mary E b No Tisbury 1854; m William Chase, carpenter of No Tisbury; d 1915 without children
    c Ernest Wentworth b Campton Apr 12, 1856   d   Winnie Robbins b 1858
    e Jeremiah b No Tisbury 1861; killed by playmate 1867
    f Lucretia b 1864; d Bowling Green, Mo, student instructor in Pike College

Walter H Dow adgfgaba, carpenter, farmer, merchant, butcher, breeder of fine horses, etc, of Campton, moved about 1896 to No Tisbury; d July 30, 1904; m 1st Campton May 30, 1878, Clara Ann Osgood b Sept 18, 1846, dau of Luther and Eliza (Sanborn); m 2nd Nov 5, 1896, Mary Otis Swift, wid ae 47, dau of Otis and Mary C (Chase) Tilton. Children

    a ——, son b and d Campton May 2, 1879
    b Luther Osgood b May 21, 1880; d Sept 23, 1900, unm

Ernest W Dow adgfgabc had a busy life. Grad Colgate and Newton Theological Seminary; ordained evangelist Louisiana, Mo, Feb 1884; Ph D 1893; taught at Knoxville, N Y, thence, as president, to Pike College, Bowling Green, Mo.   Next, vice president of Lexington Ladies College, then McCune College at Louisiana.   Then a pastorate for 3 years at Troy, N H, then several years at Oak Bluff, Mass.   In the east was president of the Baptist Y P U of N H 1897-8, editor of Baptist Weekly Missionary; Chaplain of Sons of Veterans, N H.   In 1899 back west as president of Pierce City College; 5 years later president of Southwest Baptist College, Bolivar, Mo.   Two years later he took a pastorate in Osceola, Mo, then in Caente, New Bedford and West Midway, Mass. Buying the buildings of the Grand River College at Gallatin, Mo, he used them as a private college for young ladies until they were burned in 1918; then taught school in Liberty, Mo, until his death.   He m 1st Oct 10, 1883, Blanche Hinman, dau of Grover Snow and Helen (Vedder); she d Mch 31, 1889; he m 2nd Dec 25, 1890, Carrie Ann Reneau b Clarksville, Mo, 1871, a teacher associated with him, dau of James Polk and Martha (Mulheren).   Children:

    a Helen Kate b Knoxville, N Y, Aug 17, 1884; grad Smith College 1907; A M from Univ of Chicago, has taught in many places; in 1921 professor of Latin and dean of women, Simmons College, Abilene, Tex; m 1924 —— Baker
    b Ernest Hinman b Dec 6, 1886; d 1892
    c Grove Samuel b Bowling Green, Mo, Oct 7, 1888
    d Blanche Hinman b Feb 9, 1893; grad Smith College 1913; in 1921 instructor in French Missouri Teachers College; unm
    e Neal b Troy Feb 9, 1896; d July 1902
    f John Reneau b May 3, 1898; grad William Jewell College; aviator 1918
    g Ernestine b Sept 4, 1904; 1921 in William Jewell College
    h Elizabeth Nason b New Bedford Oct 28, 1909

Grove Samuel Dow adgfgabcc, grad William Jewell College 1909; A M Brown Univ; grad student in Harvard and Univ of Chicago, was professor of Sociology Baylor College, Tex, from 1919. In 1921 he published a book on Sociology for general use. This became quickly recognized as a master work and has placed him at the head of his branch of study. It gave offense, however, to the conservative and ultra orthodox and led to his resignation from his professorship into a much broader field. He m Aug 17, 1914, Olive Brashers of Bolivar, Mo. Children:

   a Grove Samuel b Charlotte, Mich, May 5, 1916
   b Evelyn Hinman b Waco, Tex, Feb 18, 1920

Winnie R Dow adgfgabd, grad Hamilton Female Seminary, m Elmer Swift, foreman of a shoe factory, Middleboro, Mass. Children:

   a Fred E b 1884; 1 surviving child   b Arthur Howard; 4 children in Me
   c Bradford Elmer; teacher in Boston   d Lucretia m Ralph Chipman of Boston

IT is but natural and wholly pardonable that the Author of a Gen- ealogy should become a little more prolix in treating his own par- ticular line of descent.

Gideon Dow adgg m Nov 12, 1735 (int pub Oct 25), Lydia Perkins b Nov 1, 1714, dau of Benjamin and Lydia McCrease). She was his cousin, Quaker, altho she permitted the baptism of her children in church. Gideon had been a wild lad and grew more reckless as time went on. The playless rigidity of his father's home was hateful, but when, soon after marriage, he got a farm of his own its work grew more and more distasteful. As his family increased, it produced compara- tively less.

Gideon paid minister's tax to avoid annoyance but he had as little use for church as for meeting house. His sons were apprenticed as early as practicable. After 25 years of married life he sought relief or novelty by enlisting at half pay with a considerable company of Hampton Falls men for the Canadian campaign. All these got half pay.

Gideon was twice the age of the average recruit. N H Rev Papers: Province of New Hampsh'r Coll: Weare's Regiment Recd of Capt Sam'll Leavitt muster master & Pay master to the forces raised for the Canada Expedition the respective sums set against our names being in full for bounty, Cloathing and half pay allowed by the Governur Council & Assembly.

Hampton Falls April 28: 1759

Mens Names	Sum paid	Time of enlistment	—— half pay
Gideon Dow	6-1-6	April 5	Guidan Dow

Province of New Hampsh'r

This may certifie that the several men Contained in the foregoing list were enlisted into his majestys Service for the Canada Expedition 1759 on the date Set against their respective names Thomas Cilley ex- cepted

Sworn before   Anth'y Emery Just's Pacis

Hampton Falls may 12: 1759

Dow, Hist Hampton, states Gideon d in the army 1756. This is merely error of date. He d by 1760. His wid Lydia continued 12 years in Seabrook, then accompanied her son Gideon to Salisbury, N H. Chil- dren:

    a   Daniel b Oct 9, 1738 (Seabrook rec). Salisbury rec gives July 19, 1739, that being the date of David the 2nd born. The Author thinks the date should be 1736. D B Hoyt, Old Families of Amesbury and Salisbury, insists that the 1st born was Samuel bap July 30, 1738, and doubts the existence of Daniel. Mr Hoyt's Samuel cannot even be adfec. As is frequently the case, Mr Hoyt argued without any knowledge of Seabrook town rec, which became accessible to the Author years after Mr Hoyt prepared his volume

   b   David b July 19, 1739. Mr Hoyt finds no rec of his existence and doubts it.
       Seabrook rec reveal his whole career
   c   Mary b Mch 23, 1741; bap Aug 1, 1742
   d   Gideon b Jan 7 (Jan 3, Hampton Falls rec), 1745; bap Aug 25, 1745
   e   Jeremiah b June 3, 1749; bap 1752
   f   Lydia b Feb 28, 1752; bap June 17, 1752

Daniel Dow adgga was apprenticed early and appears no more in Seabrook; is probably the Daniel of Newburyport, following the sea; wife Catherine. Children, Newburyport rec:

   a   Susanna bap Oct 28, 1765   b   Betty bap July 7, 1767
   c   Catherine bap Oct 4, 1769

Catherine Dow adggac m Newburyport Dec 1, 1792, Samuel Corning. Newburyport rec shows 1 child:

   a   Samuel b Mch 9, 1797

David Dow adggb m Nov 3 (int pub Salisbury Oct 1), 1763, Rebecca Brown. Probably David the joiner who sold 4 Seabrook acres to Janna Dow adaim; paid minister's tax 1761-73; will dated 1811 names all children, appoints son Jeremiah executor. Oct 13, 1824, Rebecca petitioned for her "thirds." Children:

   a   Nathan b July 11, 1764
   b   Betty b Jan 7, 1766; m —— George; called Betty George in father's will
   c   Daniel b Oct 7, 1767
   d   Molly b Apr 19, 1770; m Simon Locke; son Hubbard is also adaim, adgxfbca
   e   David b Aug 22, 1772   f   Lydia (called Cushion in will)
   g   Jeremiah   h   Sarah unm in 1811   i   Rebecca unm in 1811

Nathan Dow adggba m Salisbury May 20, 1789, Jane Chase. Father's will fails to mention name or sex of 2 children:

   a   Lydia b Oct 1773 (sic Gove Gen; right date must be after 1789)

Lydia Dow adggbaa d Seabrook Jan 10, 1864; m Enoch Gove b Seabrook about 1765, son of Enoch and Huldah (Green). He d about 1825, leaving 4 young children:

   a   Nathan Dow d young
   b   Lucy m Joseph French of Salisbury-Seabrook; 2 children
   c   Lydia Dow b Apr 21, 1814; m Joseph French; moved to Gloucester, Mass;
       she lived to 102; 3 children
   d   Huldah Jane b 1820; m Lowell Brown of Seabrook; moved to New London,
       N H; 5 children
   e   Nathan   f   Annie Lummus b Aug 23, 1824; m Samuel Clifford; 4 children

Daniel Dow adggbc inherited 2 acres; some Daniel Dow was administrator in Seabrook 1823. He presumably moved away; unsafe to guess any connection later.

David Dow adggbe, carpenter and boat builder of Seabrook, d Dec 13, 1850; m June 13 (int pub Apr 24), 1801, Hannah Merrill of Seabrook b May 22, 1776, d Manchester Aug 27, 1857. Children:

   a   Harriet b Apr 25, 1802; int to Noyes Webster pub Sept 20, 1834
   b   Betsey M b Nov 24, 1805; m Salisbury Dec 27, 1831, Ezekiel F Webster
   c   Sarah b July 26, 1808   d   Mary C b Oct 18, 1810

Betty Dow adggbb m —— George. Salisbury gives Ebenezer George of right age with wife Betsey. Children:

a   James b Oct 2, 1794   b   Miriam b Apr 19, 1796   c   Polly b Oct 11, 1798
d   Betsey b Mch 13, 1799; error in date rather than identity
e   Nathaniel b Mch 11, 1801   f   Azor O W b Sept 8, 1909

Lydia Dow adggbf d Nov 6, 1810; m Apr 1, 1799, Capt John Newmarch Cushing b May 3, 1779, son of Benjamin and Hannah (Hazeltine) of Salisbury. A sea captain, moved 1802 to Newburyport. Children:

a   Caleb b Jan 17, 1800; grad Harvard; m Caroline Elizabeth Wilde
b   —— d in infancy   c   Lydia b 1806; d 1851

Jeremiah Dow adggbg seems to have been in Seabrook 1824; unsafe to attach any further rec to him

IT may be that in this broad land all men are born free and equal, but they cannot remain so with differing abilities, free competition and unequal environment. The first settlers of Hampton had an almost equal chance at the start, for the land allotments were fair and, if one man came with a little more cash than another, that became equalized in a few years. The second generation was also well provided for and became but little unequal, as one of greater ability rose a little higher than his fellows. The 3rd generation was less fortunate, as population increased. In the whole community there was room for not over a score of the best minds to rise above the common lot of the farmer or fisherman. All but the minister. a few manufacturers and a few store keepers had to farm, at least as a side issue. The public officials got nominal pay only. Each citizen had to raise a little cash, for taxes, utensils, a few articles of wear. Meanwhile, the cost of living had on the whole increased. Farm products had not. Besides, each farm had to support at least twice the population it did originally. Currency nor commerce had come Hampton way. Its very site had been selected for its abundance of salt grass. Its harbor was well nigh worthless. Portsmouth and Newburyport took all the shipping. To escape practical starvation, the youth of Seabrook, Hampton and elsewhere nearby, had to take to the manufacturing towns, to go to sea or become shoemakers. As soon as the Indian menace was removed from the interior, the best minds of Seabrook decided that the greatest promise of the future lay in pioneering. The less ambitious were those who remained at home, working for little more than board and lodging, but getting a taste of the effeteness which, in its primitive way, had already come to the old settlements. The loafer of 1750 merely worked about twice as hard as men did a century or so later. The posterity of Joseph Dow, landed magnate if he chose to be, soon found itself among the poorest. Emigrate or starve was recognized by Henry Dow adf while he was still prosperous.

The land of Salisbury, N H, a hillside slope with poor soil over granite rock, comparatively poor site even for inland New Hampshire, was settled, as its name indicates, by younger sons from Salisbury, Mass. Here, there was never an organized Quaker colony. Henry's family finally decided to return to former haunts and the original grant was traded to a cousin.

Gideon Dow adggd had been a shipwright's apprentice and after his father's disappearance became the mainstay of the family, providing for mother, sister and perhaps one brother. It is vague family tradition that he came to Salisbury, N H, in 1767. He seems to have bought the adf land in 1772. He had m a Greeley girl, whose kin were pioneers of Salisbury. The Greeley farm adjoined the Dow farm. The Horace

Greeley line passed through here on the way to N Y State. The Webster farm adjoined the Dow farm on the other side, and here Daniel Webster was born, playmate of the Dow boys. Hist Salisbury mentions no Dow between Henry, the grantee, and Gideon in 1776. He signed the Association Test and volunteered May 27, 1776, in a home reserve force whose object seemed to be to guard against a possible invasion from the north rather than to enter the N Y or seacoast campaigns.

Just as he had been an unselfish family protector in his youth, Gideon the old man was dictatorial, almost intolerably so according to 20th century notions, just but always severe. He had many idiosyncracies, one of which was that he should eat no salt. For 60 years there was a separate bread-baking for his especial use. When children had grown up and gone away, Gideon and his wife had no further incentive to work the farm. They sold it and made a home with the most energetic of the sons, in Plainfield, N H. Here both passed a comparatively easy old age. Both d 1826; buried side by side in the original cemetery by the north border of the town. Some years ago both gravestones were glassed in to guard against further encroachments of time and weather.

So Hampton rec contain a duplication:

Gideon Dow m Sarah Greele (entry looks like Creele) Oct 8, 1767
Gideon Dow m Sarah Greeley Jan 8, 1770.

Sarah Greeley was dau of Ilsley and Sarah (Morrill). There is evidence that a 1st born d in infancy. Probably the 1770 entry should be b of this child. Actual rec are not extant; list here from family sources

a	Insley b Aug 28, 1772	b	—— dau b 1773; d in infancy
c	Jeremiah b Oct 31, 1774	d	Lydia b Aug 28, 1776
e	Daniel b 1778	f	Hannah b 1780	g	Polly b 1782
h	Nancy b 1784	i	Benjamin b 1786	j	Betsey b 1788
k	Rebecca b 1790	l	Lucinda b 1793; d ae 2

Insley Dow adggda followed his True kinsman to Corinth, Vt, buying a farm on which he lived and died; was well remembered by his niece Fannie Dow who visited him in 1814. He m Apr 12, 1798, Susanna Brown of Corinth. Children:

a   Daniel b June 9, 1799
b   Lucinda b May 18, 1801; m Jan 20, 1822, Lyman Washburn
c   Lydia b Dec 28, 1803   d   Insley b May 23, 1807

Daniel Dow adggdaa inherited the farm; m Corinth Mch 4, 1830, Sophronia Rowland; 2nd Sept 5, 1836, Lydia Robie b 1778, descendant of the pioneer Robies of Hampton. In 1850 his farm assessed $1,500; with him lived Jonathan Roby, probably a nephew. Children, by census:

a   Susan b 1831; m Corinth Jan 7, 1851, Sulliman Taplin
b   Sophronia C b 1837; m Oct 2, 1858, Charles R Brigham, both of Claremont,
    N H; dau,—Jennie A m —— Crosby; 2nd 1894 Charles L Bailey
c   Mary A b 1839
d   Sarah b 1842; m Aug 12, 1867, Joseph Knight of Corinth
e   Olive b 1845

Mary Anzolette Dow adggdaac of Newburyport, Mass, m (his 3rd) July 24, 1895, Joseph Kimball Darling b Corinth Mch 8, 1833, d Oct 25, 1910, son of Jesse and Rebecca (Whitaker). His 1st wife was her cousin, dau of Joseph and Mary (Robie) Knight. He served as corporal in Civil War and was lawyer of Corinth.

Insley Dow adggdad m Corinth Feb 5, 1840, Sarah Newhall. They soon moved to a farm near a lake not far from Cleveland, Ohio. In later life he became rather well-to-do and influential. Probably at least one more child than appears here:

  a Arthur Chase
  b Mary E in 1924 Mrs Keeley wid of Pasadena, Calif
  c Ebenezer   d Nathaniel; both d without issue
  e Stella, in 1922 Mrs Curtis J Judd of Boston

Arthur Chase Dow adggdada became a man of large business affairs, at some time of Boston. He d about 1911. After 1880 he owned a butter and cheese manufacturing and commission business in Chicago. He was probably not the oldest child, born in Ohio about 1850. He m 2nd Chicago 1891 Anna S Letton, now of Chicago, member of D A R, dau of Theodore W and Mary C (Field). One child by 1st wife. His cousin Fred H Dow adggdcic grew up with his Chicago business and succeeded to it, but the two never knew their close relationship. For that matter, there is no evidence that Insley Dow ever met his two cousins living not far from Cleveland, Ohio. Children:

  a Florence E m Dana Estes Jr of Boston
  b Arthur Chase; held positions in Chicago, mostly clerical or secretarial; in 1923 insurance agent of Los Angeles; married, has a dau, Mary Elizabeth
  c Ruth Mary; m S White of Winnetka, Ill

Jeremiah Dow adggdc supported his parents in old age, just as they had supported their mother. At age of 21 he had taken his slender savings and parents' blessings, joined a party to found Salisbury, Vt, out of the wilderness. Jeremiah was as easy-going as his father was dictatorial. He became obsessed with the idea that he could better himself by frequently swapping farms, and thus had at least seven in succession in Morristown, Milford, Pomfret, Vt, and Plainfield, N H. The first Plainfield farm was near the Meriden border, had a clay subsoil and was quite stony. He swapped this for a farm on the Plains, selected because it was easier to hoe. That it was a sand bank was ignored.

Altho he had a large family he listened to the call of 1812 and enlisted, backed up by his wife. He contracted in the service what was called chronic asthma, really valvular heart trouble, and from this was unable to lie down for over 20 years, sleeping in a chair. In 1910 this chair stood exactly as he left it. He received a small and much needed pension. He deeded in old age his farm to his son for maintenance for himself and wife. The deed is holographic and mentions $300 penalty for violation of its provisions; specifies the room to be his, bed and bed-deng for self and wife, the cow (provided he or his wife did the milking), use of a certain horse or successor thereto, a particular buggy and sleigh, a certain wood lot for pocket money.

To mild-mannered, long suffering Jeremiah Dow came a better half of the most resolute kind, with a touch of red in her hair, and whom, did she decide upon a course of action, no convulsion of nature could check. She was Kesiah Sessions, dau of Resolved and Elizabeth (Childs). Resolved appears 4 times in Vt Rev rolls, paid 6s as speed horseman Mch 9, 1781, at Ft Fortitude, 4 days and mileage under Capt John Throop; (as Solvad) 14 days and 20 miles under Capt Edmund Hodges; repairing Ft Bethel 3 days from Aug 10, 1781, Capt Bartholomew Durkee.

Kesiah had decided views on bringing up children. In each feather bed (Kesiah raised geese for the feathers) were lodged 2. Did they squabble on a winter night, Kesiah took from the shed an icy crowbar and laid it down the exact middle. A story since told of almost any one is attributed to her. One day Jeremiah had started afoot for the village and had progressed half a mile when he heard the fish horn used for emergencies or to summon distant workmen to dinner. He trudged back and was greeted:

"Jeremiah, you forgot something."   "Well."
"Jeremiah, you forgot to kiss me."

Next Sabbath Jeremiah remained on his knees an unusually long time: For, had he not blasphemed last Tuesday?

Kesiah's grandparents were Simeon and Sarah (Dana), d ae 96 and 94 respectively, pioneers to Pomfret from Pomfret, Conn. Sarah's brother was an original grantee of Lebanon, N H. Materials for a Hist of the Sessions Family fail to find this line. In the copy in the library of the Sons of the Revolution, Los Angeles, the Author has inserted the complete line.

Children of Jeremiah and Kesiah:

a   Lewis b Nov 1, 1799; d July 29, 1803
b   Fannie b Aug 27, 1801   c   Prentis b Morristown Dec 8, 1803
d   Dennis b June 19, 1806   e   Eliza b June 13, 1808
f   Hiram b Oct 10, 1810   g   George b Nov 24, 1812
h   Henry b May 16, 1815   i   Lucius Harmon b Aug 5, 1820

The farm in Plainfield passed out of the possession of the family in 1912, its barrenness having other tillers. It had been a poor support and about 1821 the situation was exactly the same as in Seabrook in 1737. Most of the family must emigrate or starve. The oldest son was the only one to realize this.

Prentis Dow adggdcc had the advantage of unusual physique, so was able to lie awake and read long into the night. Many the time Kesiah had risen at midnight and angrily snuffed out his candle, for the boys had to be up and at their chores before sunrise. In 1819 a party organized to go to Michigan. Prentis arranged with some of its members

to work his way with them.   He took $14 the share saved up for his in-
heritance, and a blessing, but, being the oldest, he received also his father's
watch, truly typical, sterling but an unreliable time keeper.   In Michigan
they carved a town out of the forest.   Prentis Dow was its first school
master; was comparatively well read and able to lick any two pupils
simultaneously.   Opportunity, the good lady, soon knocked at his door.
Prentis noticed from the first the wisdom of establishing close friendly
relations with the Indians who came regularly with furs to sell to the
Cleveland dealers who came with manufactured goods once a year.
These merchants soon noted that Prentis Dow bought furs out of season
to better advantage than they could.   He soon had a well established
business.   The merchants invited him to come to Cleveland, promising
backing in a mercantile career.   In a few years he made a partnership with
Irad Kelley, son of a pioneer of the Western Reserve.   They married
sisters.   The business was primarily dry goods, but grew to jobbing and
wholesaling.   Being well looked upon at the bank, they could often re-
discount at a profit endorsed notes.

He m Nov 29, 1832, Lucretia Martha Pease b Sept 5, 1815, of a Western Reserve pioneer family.*

*The Mayflower line of Lucretia M Pease: William Bradford, Governor, m Alice
Carpenter Southworth; Maj William Bradford m Alice Richards; Alice Bradford m
1680 Rev William Adams b 1650; Alice Adams m 1701 Rev Nathaniel Collins b 1672;
Ann Collins b Dec 20, 1702, m Enfield, Conn, Sept 13, 1723, Ephraim Terry b Enfield
Oct 25, 1701; Mary Terry b Enfield Jan 1, 1723-4, m Enfield Nov 29, 1739, Ebenezer
Pease b Enfield 1719; Ebenezer Pease Jr b Enfield May 8, 1747, m Enfield July 15, 1771,
Hulda Pease b Enfield Mch 4, 1752; George Pease b Enfield 1776, d Cleveland 1845, m
Goshen, Conn, Oct 15, 1797, Esther Thompson, d Cleveland 1860, leaving a large family.
The Kelley Gen begins with the family in Conn.   It really originates in this country
with the Kelleys of Isles of Shoals, N H, from which they spread upstate, frequently
intermarried with Dow (for names, consult index).   One member, a sailor, settled in Conn.
Esther Thompson gets the benefit of the labors of a Thompson who pursued his
line into England, devoting many years to it.   Her line, going backward: Stephen
Thompson b New Haven Apr 20, 1737, d Hudson, Ohio, 1830; m Goshen Jan 3, 1760,
Mary Walter b May 27, 1742; Gideon Thompson b New Haven Dec 25, 1704, d Hart-
ford May 21, 1759, m New Haven Jan 9, 1729, Lydia Punderson; Samuel Thompson b
New Haven May 12, 1669, d Goshen Mch 26, 1749, m New Haven Nov 14, 1695, Re-
becca Bishop; John Thompson b Lenham, Kent, 1632, d New Haven June 2, 1707, m
Helena ——; Anthony Thompson b Lenham Aug 3, 1612, d New Haven 1698; Henry
Thompson was son of Thomas of Sandwich, grandson of Thomas of Sandwich, this
Henry b Lenham Oct 20, 1648, m Dorothy Honeywood d Lenham Feb 5, 1748.   She was
dau of Robert Honeywood of Charing m Mary Atwater of Roylston.   Robert was son
of John Honeywood d Charing 1557, m a dau of —— Barnes of Rye.   Mary Atwater of
Roylston was dau of Robert of Wye and Roylston m a Miss De Brocas.   She was a
dau of a younger son of the baronial De Brocas family, whose line is published to Alfred
the Great.
The original parchment genealogy prepared by Venerable Bede for Alfred the Great
is still preserved in Westminster.   This traces Alfred's line to Adam, much as the lines
of the Irish kings are traced.   The Irish lines favor Shem, why not Japhet we do not
know.   The Alfred line is Adam, Seth, Enos, Cainen, Malaleel, Jared, Enoch, Methu-
saleh, Lamech, Noah (whose wife's name, by the way, is Norida), and Sceaf.   This last
was born in the ark, at least so Bede says.   From him the names become immediately
Saxon: Bednig, Wala, Hathia, Itermod, Sceldwea, Bean, Tetwa, Geata, Godulf, Fin,
Frithwulf, Frealaf, Frithwald, Woden, Bealdeag, Brand, Freothregar, Fearwine, Wig,
Gewis, Esla, Elesa, Cerdic, Cymric, Ceanless, Cuthwine, Cutha, Ceowald, Coenred,
Ingels, Eoppa, Edfa, Albmund, Egbert, Ethelwulf, Alfred. It has escaped the notice of
many students of this clearly fabricated document that the 48 generations occupy
exactly 4,800 years of orthodox chronology.

The Pease family were intensely Presbyterian; Prentis Dow a nominal Congregationalist of Quaker stock. Why the couple went to an Episcopal church to be married, all their descendants bap Episcopalian and Prentis and wife active church members in it all their lives, was never explained to the Author by his grandparents. Two children came.

    a   Robert Kimball b Cleveland July 2, 1835 (named for Robert Kimball of Mer-
        iden, N H, a lifelong friend, one of the builders of the Boston & Albany R R)
    b   William Pease b June 4, 1837; d Aug 19, 1838

Within five years of his arrival in Cleveland Prentis Dow was a well established man on the road to wealth and controlling several businesses, including a paper mill in Cuyahoga Falls. He planned a bank. Mindful of his brothers on the barren Plainfield farm, he sent for them, and all came except Hiram, who was established as a physician. It was his plan to place a brother at the head of each line of controlled industry. It did not work, and only one brother continued with him. Alexander Mitchell controlled for the Scotch bondholders what is now the Chicago, Milwaukee & St Paul R R. He put Prentis Dow in charge as trustee. In 1861 he abandoned Cleveland, for President Lincoln needed a trusted confidential agent in the great gun factory established in Windsor, Vt. In spite of the pecuniary sacrifice, Prentis accepted this gladly. It was 4 miles from his old home. Trips to Washington were only about 3 times a year. At the end of the war, his varied interests, railroad and banking, necessitated his living near N Y City; he lived in East Orange, N J, and Fordham, N. Y. At the latter place, he boarded. Financial difficulties forced his landlady to withdraw. Rather than give up his comfortable quarters, he bought the establishment. After a year in Europe, the grand tour, he decided to retire, his son well established. He chose Claremont, N H, 14 miles from the old Plainfield home. To this place he imported all the help from Fordham, two maids being in his family nearly 40 years, the others soon establishing themselves in Claremont. There was one house in town which he wanted. He bought a cottage which backed against this and waited. The house was bought at auction a year or so later. It was the Tappan mansion, a replica of a Virginia Colonial, built by Abolitionist John Tappan in 1839, and filled with mahogany much of it traceable back to Colonial times. The adjoining cottage was turned over to two sisters from Plainfield, soon to be joined by a brother returned from Ohio. One room in the mansion was long known as the Bishop's room; it was always kept in readiness for Bishop W W Niles while in town on his diocesan rounds. During the last year of Grandfather's life the Author was in High School and a daily visitor. The score of the daily games of dominoes, seven up, euchre, backgammon, etc, was over 2,000 that year. On a winter's day he drove a spirited span somewhat too long in the keen wind; dying Mch 25, 1885.

His wid survived until Nov 10, 1900, to idolize the grandchildren. At the age of 70 she broke her hip, which inconvenienced her for several months. After discarding crutches, she took to a cane, but soon discarded that because it did not look becoming. Fifteen years later she fell down a flight of 21 stairs and apparently came out unhurt. As she had favored for 30 years a heart disease, the shock told upon her and she d six months later. At the time of her marriage she transposed her name and was always known as Martha L Dow.

Robert K Dow adggdcca grad Kimball Union Academy, as did his father; his young manhood coming during the stay in Windsor, Vt. A couple of vacations were spent in the office of Carpender & Vermilye, N Y City. The railroad at Windsor was the Vermont Central, poorly run, unprofitable, generally in bankruptcy. It was R K Dow's original ambition to control this railroad. He did not do so for the sole reason that other more profitable railroads always offered themselves. But, it shaped his whole career. His profession was a doctor of sick railroads.

He began in N Y with his father in more or less general banking and security business. A prosperous railroad never appealed to him. It was always a road in or near bankruptcy. As such, he took it, nursed it, never left it until it was prosperous. At one time he became the *de facto* head of the Philadelphia & Reading. He bought one day as an individual speculation the entire Long Island R R, turning over during the same day a one-third interest to each of two close associates. For many years he ruled the Mobile & Ohio, Memphis & Little Rock, was associated in control of the Richmond & Danville, Iowa Central, East Tennessee, Virginia & Georgia, and many others. He put together the many bankrupt links into the N Y, Susquehanna & Western, extending it into the coal fields. The ups and downs of big business fascinated him and were many. Losing millions and making millions were alike a pleasure.

After his father located in Claremont, he decided to do the same, theorizing correctly that in the quiet of the country he could map out his plans with long foresight and during short stays in N Y put them into execution. He decided that more than 2 weeks in the feverishness of stock market circles warped one's judgment, made one attach too much importance to transient matters, dangers or promises. As a matter of fact, he never took a great business loss except when he broke his rule and stayed more than a fortnight in N Y. Up to about 1889 it was often profitable to build new railroad in territory which had great need of communication. From 1870 onward he did much of this. Often great tracts of virgin timber, coal and iron, lay easy of development but several hundred miles from a railroad. He became a busy organizer to buy such lands, where the population was often about 1 per square mile, build a railroad through them, finance the road until population came and it became self-supporting. In old times States, counties, municipalities helped much by granting land to the railroad or taking its bonds. After 1889 the business was abandoned. It was public policy to look on; if the road failed, the builder was ruined; if the road was a success, new laws regulating rates, wages and what not, virtually confiscated the property and the builder was ruined. In Georgia the Chattanooga, Rome & Carrollton was successfully built and established as a permanent, profitable concern. In Arkansas lay for 300 miles hundreds of thousands of acres, each acre purchasable at 50 cents to $1.50, on each at least one black walnut tree worth $50, if transported as far as the river bank. Throughout this wilderness are now dotted a hundred sturdy towns. R K Dow had a steady policy regarding land grants. He sold to bona fide settlers at almost nothing, gave them credit for tools and a year's supply of food and gave 20 years to pay.

In 1894 he became permanently lame from a broken hip, thereafter went to N Y less often and stayed longer. It was for 30 years his practice to go almost every Monday and return each Saturday midnight. To most men this would be killing in a year. There were no conveniences, and the trip averaged almost 10 hours. He throve under it because he was able to sleep standing up, if he could lean against a wall. In 1912 he could go back and forth no longer and retired altogether to the Claremont home, where he had a library of about 10,000 volumes selected on no particular plan and for no particular purpose, but rich in all kinds of reference books and favoring books not generally found in public libraries. From 1869 to 1908 he lived in a house bought by himself. Then the family moved to the Tappan mansion.

He m East Orange, N J, May 3, 1865, Susan Frances Piercy b Jan 10, 1845, d Feb 22, 1880, dau of Alexander and Elsie (Dupuy); 2nd Cuba, N Y, March 6, 1884, Mary Emily Smith b Cuba Dec 8, 1855, living 1927, dau of Robert and Mary C (Windsor).

The Piercy line is not traceable. One Jacob Piercy was a soldier in Lord Howe's army. He deserted up the Hudson to the American lines, was accepted as a recruit, made a good record and was a pensioner in N Y State 1824. He succeeded in m a dau of his captain, Jeremiah Ballard, and was grandfather of Alexander.

Elsie Dupuy was descended from Nicholas Depuis and his wife Catharine (Reynard) DeVos. They were Huguenots who fled from Artois to Holland and thence to New York, by the ship "Pemberton Church" in Oct, 1662. Their second son Moses was a pioneer in what is now Ulster County. Elsie Dupuy was born in Ulsterville, Ulster County, Sept 12, 1813, died Orange, N J, Jan 20, 1848. The Chauncey Depew line is from the third son of the immigrant.

Children of R K Dow

a Prentis b Jan 13, 1867; d ae 15   b Robert Piercy b N Y Feb 24, 1869
c Francis Randall b Sept 25, 1870; grad Williams 1892; d Spokane, Wash, Apr 4, 1895, unm
d Jessie Anderson b Aug 28, 1872; grad Tufts Medical School; practicing physician or globe trotter; unm. Both named for friends of grandfather Dow
e John Winthrop b Dec 30, 1874

f   Susan Frances b May 1, 1878; since her father's death sole occupant of the
    homestead; unm
g   Mary Windsor b Dec 21, 1884; grad Smith College; d June 22, 1916, unm
h   Elizabeth Sheldon b June 1, 1887   i —— son b and d Sept 9, 1898

Robert Piercy Dow adggdccab, grad Williams 1891, entered general brokerage business N Y City, drifted into journalism; one time financial editor of the Commercial Advertiser and Morning Advertiser; wrote considerably on economic subjects; from 1911 did a security business on his own account.   Is best known as a scientific student, given to Museum uplift, member of the principal museums and scientific societies, specializing in entomology; for years editor of the publications of the Brooklyn Society.   After 26 years business, he retired Dec 1918, coming to Hollywood, Calif, becoming member of the Society of Friends; devoting himself to this Book.

He m Nov 7, 1898, Mabel Ruth Burbank of Claremont b P Q Mch 14, 1872, dau of Jason Charles and Edna Maria (Willey), descendant of Gov Leete of Conn colony.   No children.

John W Dow adggdccae, grad Harvard 1897, A M 1899, taught many years in High School work in many places, Tacoma, Wash, to Augusta, Ga; one time professor of Chemistry in University of Georgia and city chemist.   In 1919 he retired permanently to his large country place, Reading, Vt.

He m Dec 13, 1901, Flora Belle Wheeler, dau of James P and Evelyn M (Parker), descendant of Oliver Wheeler minute man 1775 of Concord and Acton, Mass.   Children:

a   Frances Wheeler b Oct 30, 1906; 1923 at Kimball Union Academy, 3rd gener-
    ation attending this famous school; m Alfred Robinson McEwen of
    Tarrytown, N Y, one child, Margaret Wheeler McEwen
b   ——, son b and d Sept 29, 1909   c   Robert Kimball b Apr 25, 1911

Elizabeth S Dow adggdccah m 1918 Horace Lewis Rockwell, patent attorney for the Sullivan Machinery Co; they took the original Prentis Dow house.   Now of Hartford, Conn.   Children:

a   Henry Lewis b 1919   b   Horace Ensign b 1921   c   Richard b 1922
d   Constance b 1924

Fannie Dow adggdcb never married.   For the 26 years that the Author remembers her she devoted every possible hour to her flower garden, up to a fortnight of her death, Mch 5, 1894.   In 1820 or thereabouts every young woman was expected to be a good housekeeper and cook, as well as a good mother.   If she had been a good housekeeper, the Dow genealogy would have had another line; if she had been a good cook, this Book never would have been written, for Aunt Fannie made it possible.   As it was, she never married.   The hard worked farmer needed his supper, promptly and with certainty; would run no chance of coming home at sunset to find the tulips all planted, but the dough neglected and fit only for the swill pail. Not that she lacked desire to be a good house-keeper, not that she did not resolve never to fail again; but other ambitions always intervened. That is why the biscuit dough fell flat. It took only a short time to plant some particular thing, but one weed led to another, and so on until too late. She was sorry, but that did not restore supper. Therefore Fannie's job became more and more attending to grandfather Gideon, for this could be done in the garden, where he liked to sit and tell of old times. Therefore, after his death, Fannie with little spare horse and light buggy went visiting more and more, long trips, seldom taken unless one was going to stay.

The records of Salisbury, N H, were many years ago taken to Concord to be compiled into a complete State vital statistical bureau. While this was finally accomplished, it was at first a political job. The records were stored for years in a wooden building, untouched. They finally burned, irretrievably lost. When, in 1888, the Author's father inspired by Edgar R Dow, sought to elucidate his own line, there was a gap of two generations. Therefore he daily sought Aunt Fannie, pencil and paper in hand. He jotted down her fugitive memories of visiting days and her grandfather's reminiscences. One thing Father could not understand. The place Salisbury was mentioned for almost every generation. There was no distinction between Salisbury, Mass, N H and Vt. One recollection was always clear to Aunt Fannie, the sound of the cannon at the Battle of Lake Erie. All others came haltingly and at intervals; her memory could not be forced or jogged. The result was a mass of little scraps of paper with a dozen words or so to each. Father never cleared them up. The Author found them many years later and has finally interpreted the very last.

"Grand'ther Gideon had a brother Jeremiah who went to Strafford."

Now, the genealogist of the adgge line had failed in 20 years to identify his Jeremiah. This proved it. "Jeremiah was superintendent of the copperas works at Shrewsbury." This is his son.

"Uncle Daniel had a 2nd wife with very black eyes; she had children. His 1st wife named her boy for grandfather; he died in Brandon maybe 10 or 15 years before the war."

"Uncle Insley was good; he married Susan Brown up in Corinth; they 2 boys and 2 girls when I visited them. I think they went to N Y State."

To the repeated question who was her grandfather's father, she never could reply; she generally suggested Jeremiah. Finally: "I don't know, but he m a Perkins girl." This jibed with Salisbury rec and proved the line. She never mentioned Seabrook, always Salisbury.

Aunt Fannie, Aunt Eliza and Uncle George lived together in the Middle St home, a short block from the Congregational church, which all attended regularly, as had their grandparents. The Author's father instructed a local physician to drop in once a month under guise of a social call, but really to look over health conditions. One day the doctor suggested, Aunt Fannie being 91, a little stimulant now and again, perhaps a little glass of sherry with dinner. Aunt Fannie flatly refused. She had seen many go down to drunkards' graves, and it always came from taking the first glass. The Author's father, ever dictatorial, sent over a case of good sherry and a peremptory command. Aunt Fannie obeyed but never without a prayer in her bedroom that she should be spared the drunkard's grave.

Uncle George wore his hair long over his shoulders, was absolutely bald on top and liked his after dinner nap. The Author considered long how the flies must love to slide down that polished pate. It was the work of a minute to get out the oil colors and a little turpentine, Uncle not waking, to paint a fine spider to keep them away. In the parlor, never lived in, used only for marriages and funerals, was a dish of broken candy, to be doled out piece by piece.

Thanksgiving day was the annual reunion, always at Grandfather's house. With the Cornish cousins, there were generally 17, with 3 helpers in the kitchen. The menu was invariable; no wine except what father brought. Grandfather bought Angelica a bottle at a time and loathed it. There was a turkey at one end, a baked ham at the other. About midway was a dish of scalloped oysters. There was mince pie, pumpkin pie, plum pudding with choice of hard or boiled sauce.

Dennis Dow adggdcd told his brother frankly that he was not a success at business, was a farmer. So, he bought a farm in Dover, now No Olmstead; was county supervisor and a fairly successful man. His grave carries a G A R marker. He m Clarissa Howard of Vt d Oct 28, 1845, ae 39-4-4; 2nd Lucretia Spencer of Dover. He was greatly devoted to a dau named for his brother's wife. On the 10th anniversary of her death, his son and son-in-law went squirrel hunting, ignoring Dennis' remark of impending trouble. When they returned they found him hanging dead in his barn. Lucretia d Mch 9, 1887, ae 70, 5 mos. Children, by 1st wife:

    a Charles Henry b Dover Oct 28, 1835
    b Martha Lucretia b Nov 24, 1862, ae 22-8-22
    c Jeannette Latham m Wilbur Bently of Dover; moved to Cuyahoga Falls;
        children,—Louis, Alice. Apparently she m 2nd —— Oatman of Cleveland

Charles H Dow adggdcda, corporal in 150th Ohio, d Cuyahoga Falls May 19, 1884; m Aug 21, 1869, Mary J Parsons b Dover Dec 7, 1843, dau of Sidney and Eliza (Coe). Son:

    a Howard P b May 4, 1870; m Carrie Burdick; moved to Pittsburgh, unt

Eliza Dow adggdce was in middle age when she m July 12, 1854, William Sumner Deming of Cornish b Aug 7, 1800, son of William and Sarah (Hall). He d within a year, leaving to her the fine farm which she entrusted to her brother L Harmon. In 1868 she came to Claremont; d June 1, 1892.

Hiram Dow adggdcf grad Dartmouth Medical School, practiced West Thetford, Vt; m Nov 3, 1835, Elizabeth Hurd Clement b Croyden, N H, dau of Solomon and Lucy (Carroll). Her father was a large property owner, having several water powers, a soap stone mine, etc, but lost everything by the 1857 panic. Hiram enlisted as private in 6th N H, detailed as asst surgeon, stationed in No Car; returned invalided in 1865 to the homestead farm; d Oct 24, 1873. His wid survived nearly 30 years. Children:

   a Flora E b Jan 4, 1837; d May 27, 1837
   b Solomon Clement b Goshen, N H, Apr 7, 1840
   c George H b West Hartford, Vt, July 28, 1847; hotel clerk Windsor, d June 10, 1872, unm

Solomon C Dow adggdcfb carried on the homestead farm until his death, Feb 7, 1901; m June 10, 1868, Addie M Fitch of Claremont, N H, who survived. Children:

   a George Herbert b Dec 11, 1869   b Florence Elizabeth b Sept 22, 1877

Sol Dow and his cousin Robert K were boys together in Plainfield, the older adventurous and designing much mischief, the younger mild and willing to follow whithersoever the leader went. Sol had a very small voice and his meekness was much imposed upon. An itinerant tin peddler was his especial *bete noire*, using to declaim sonorously: "Sol, Saul of Tarshish, where art thou? And Saul lifted up his voice and cried, *Here I be, Lord.*"

Sol's final independence was the result of sudden inspiration. His mother gave him 10 cents, bidding him to run 4 miles to Windsor and buy molasses. · Returning with pail full, he met the village bad boy and a colloquy ensued: "What ye got, Sol?"

"Molasses; going to have gingerbread tonight."

"Bet ye ain't." "I be, etc." With the final word the bad boy picked up a handful of road dust and threw it into Sol's pail. Moments passed, anguish, tears, imprecations; then the inspiration. Suddenly Sol lifted his pail, clapped it over the boy's head, it fitting closely over the ears. Still weeping, he arrived home and told his tale. Aunt Elizabeth hunted up uncle Hiram and got another dime; Sol ran back to Windsor. After he had eaten his gingerbread, he sauntered over to ask the bad boy how much it hurt to sit down after his interview with his father in the wood shed. It did hurt.

In one respect Sol was like Job and they usually came in a place which made it agony to sit still in church. One day the boys crossed the river to pick blackberries. The bark on a log was loose and slipped. As Robert rowed Sol back across the river, Sol shrieked without ceasing, "I'm dead, I'm dead." "No, you ain't, Sol, if you were, you couldn't holler so."

George H (Bert) Dow adggdcfba, house painter of Claremont, m 2nd May 19, 1916, Florence Wood of Claremont. No children.

Florence E Dow adggdcfbb m 1902 Fred G Foster of Kenmore, N Y. Children,—Mabel A, Thomas D, George E, Raymond H, Elizabeth G, Arthur G.

George Dow adggdcg managed the paper mill in Cuyahoga Falls until his son was old enough to succeed him; m Aug 25, 1838, Caroline Beebe b Middletown, Conn. After her death he gave up business and came to the Middle St house in Claremont, devoting himself to his grand nephews and nieces until he d Mch 20, 1893. Only child:

  a George Lewis b July 20, 1843

George L Dow adggdcga became manager of the paper mill; no children by 1st wife; m 2nd a Miss Zerbe of Cuyahoga; went to Chicago; filled various positions of secretarial nature. Children:

  a Robert Beebe b 1881; architect of Denver, Colo
  b Florence b Dec 8, 1886; d in Iroquois Theatre fire

Henry Dow adggdch undertook the banking end of his brother's business in Akron, Ohio, then Chicago; became manager for S M Swenson in Houston, Tex; later with Phoenix Bank, N Y. Health failing, he returned to the Plainfield homestead; d Mch 23, 1864, unm.

Lucius H Dow adggdci spent a few years in Cleveland but came back and bought a Cornish farm near the Plainfield border. The death of his brother in law left a much better farm without a cultivator, so Uncle Harmon sold his own, lived on the other until his death. General farming was still the rule when he began. A farm once mortgaged never gets free, in New Hampshire. One cannot compete with hand labor on rocks and thin soil with the level prairies where steam plows handle a thousand acres. So, after sundry vicissitudes, Uncle Harmon devoted his farm to butter-making only and achieved some success. He was a founder of the Cornish creamery which took 1st prize at 1893 Chicago World's fair. He also had agencies for the sale of farm machinery and acted as local wool buyer for several Vt mills until a democratic tariff drove them into bankruptcy. He m Lucilla A Smith of Grantham b 1832, d Mch 2, 1863, dau of Cyrus and Hannah (Abbott); 2nd Mch 6, 1866, Isabella M Tracy b 1846, d Mch 2, 1894, a remarkable woman who at 28 became stepmother of five children, all of whom lived long to revere her memory.

The 200-acre farm in Cornish was a second home to the Author, who knew and loved every acre from the beech grove at the highest point, across the hay meadow, with its brook too small for aught but fingerling trout, up the bare pasturage on the north side. Beyond that lay the earliest cemetery of Cornish. In 1880 many stones were readable, but by 1909 not a single stone showed inscription. There were three fine seasons in Cornish,—maple sugar time, autumn, when it was lawful to shoot partridges, and midsummer. In sugar time all had to work carrying sap buckets, but in the boiling shed one might make sugar wax in the snow

as much as he liked. In midsummer one had to work quickly to get in
the hay, if a shower threatened, but there was always raspberry pie for
breakfast. The highway was a side road up a very long steep hill, a
passing wagon such a rarity that all invariably stopped to see whose it
was; but the land was good and the hay stood high.

At supper Uncle Harmon read aloud from the semi-weekly paper and
commented with a breadth of knowledge which seemed marvelous to the
Author. The labor and devotion of Aunt Belle never flagged. Sometimes
there was extra help in the kitchen, sometimes not. In haytime there
were always many extra hands to cook for. Around the barns there was
a host of pigeons, ownerless parasites on the grain bins. The Author
suggested the desirability of a pigeon potpie but was always put off by
Aunt Belle with an indefinite "some other time." Venturing one day to
disobey, he brought in a score of pigeons carefully plucked, cleaned and
larded with salt pork, of which there was always an unlimited supply in a
barrel. Aunt Belle smiled and thereafter pigeons, squirrels, partridges
were always welcome. Many years later the Author realized that to keep
a house clean, cook for ten, wash and care for five children and pluck
pigeons might crowd the daylight hours. Aunt Belle felt like going to
bed at 8 P M.

Sunday was a great day in Cornish. Food for the entire day was
cooked Saturday, leaving only coffee to be boiled at sunset. The minister took a day off from farming and conducted two services, with Sunday
school and an hour for dinner between. In the Author's day the minister
was Mr Brick House Jackson, to distinguish him from the White House
Jacksons, unrelated and further down the road. He believed in predestination, but was always ready to pray for rain. The high-backed
pews were ample to hide in and play our innocent games unseen. At
midday the men swapped cattle and women discussed affairs of great
moment. Toward sundown we drove home realizing what is the end of
a perfect day.

Children:

a Abbie Frances b Oct 10, 1853; m June 27, 1876, William Harvey Harlow of
   Cornish. Son, Harmon Leroy, grad Kimball Union Academy, now runs the
   homestead farm
b William Deming b Sept 10, 1857   c Fred Henry b Sept 25, 1859
d Mary Ella b Aug 9, 1861; m June 1885 Will G Cain M D of Marlboro, N H;
   no children
e Martha Lucretia b Aug 30, 1863

William D Dow adggdcib tried farming in California a few years
but came back to the homestead, inheriting it on the death of his aunt;
m Hattie A Weld of Cornish b July 11, 1863, d Sept 12, 1889, dau of
Hiram A and Alice (Hamblett); 2nd Nora E Crosby of Andover, N H,
dau of Gilman and Eleanor R (Lear). She d 1919. Children:

a Hattie E b Aug 7, 1896
b Maurice Harmon b Nov 27, 1900; took 3rd State prize 1916 for results in his
   own potato patch
c Lucelia Eleanor b Mch 31, 1904   d Prentis b Mch 29, 1907

Fred H Dow adggdcic, grad Kimball Union Academy, went to Chicago, where his cousin Geo L Dow offered him a position until he found what he liked. On the way to business each morning he passed the butter and cheese house of A C Dow & Co; he went in, found the head of the firm, asked for a job, saying that he was brought up on a butter farm. He has now succeeded to the business; lives Plymouth, Wis, to run the cheese factory, while his son manages the Chicago business.   He never knew until the Author told him that he and A C Dow adggdada were at all related.   He m June 4, 1884, Mattie Gamble of Chicago.   Child:

   a   Harmon James b Feb 28, 1885; married; has a dau

Martha L Dow adggdcie m Nov 25, 1885, Lewis J Quimby of Claremont.   Children:

   a   Ruth I b Jan 17, 1887; m a missionary; d 1915 in China, without children
   b   George F b Oct 12, 1889; now married

The others of the adggd family soon scattered, generally to places where vital statistics are not easy of access.

Lydia Dow adggdd d Brandon, Vt, 1845; m Osgood True.   Children,—Amanda, George, Lydia, Daniel, Nancy.

Daniel Dow adggde, farmer of Washington, Vt, m Pembroke, Mass, Dec 11, 1805, Jane Waters; m 2nd and moved to Schoharie, N Y (rec of 2nd m and children not found), where he became quite prominent, cornet of militia, president 1813 of Washington Benevolent Society.   Child:

   a   Gideon b 1806; d Brandon, Vt, not much later than 1850, probably unm

Hannah Dow adggdf m Truman Freeman of Hanover, N H; moved to Brockport, N Y.   Children:

a Hannah m —— Lowry of Fowlersville	b Minerva	c George
d Daniel e Lucinda f Mary	g Norman L of Springfield, Ill	

Polly Dow adggdg m Daniel Freeman of Hanover, N H

Nancy Dow adggdh d young at Schoharie, whither she went with her brother.

Benjamin Dow adggdi m twice; 2nd wid Colston of Ascutneyville. This was in his 80th year.   A child by 2nd m d in infancy.   He was famous in his section of Vt as a hunter and a horse breaker, at 80 could ride any horse in the country; once knocked down an intractable stallion with a fist blow.   By 1st wife 2 children:

   a   Benjamin b 1814; untraced.   His father d at his home about 1869, Janesville,
       Wis.   Author has failed to locate any rec or reminiscence
   b   —— a dau

Betsey Dow adggdj d Oct 13, 1858; located near Batavia, N Y; m Moses True of Lebanon who came as agent of a great land owner.   He afterwards dealt enormously for his own account.   At time of his death he owned only his home place. His children found stacks of deeds, all representing properties bought and resold.   Children:

a Amelia Fifield m —— Chaddock; left a dau   b Stella M
c Nancy

Rebecca Dow adggdk m Feb 2, 1817, Ephraim Kinsman of Cornish Flat, N H, son of Ephraim and Mary (Hall). She d July 4, 1855. Children, a grandchild in 1923 postmaster where his great grandfather lived:

a William M b Nov 17, 1817   b Francis S b Mch 2, 1820
c Julius A b Jan 8, 1822   d Gideon Dow b Mch 23, 1824
e Minerva b Mch 21, 1826   f Lewis Dow b Mch 15, 1828
g Charles A b Apr 5, 1830   h Mary L b July 24, 1833
i Martha J b July 24, 1833

JEREMIAH Dow adgge m Dec 20, 1777, by Timothy Upham, clergyman at Deerfield, Rachel Chase b Poplin, N H, Dec 28, 1857, d Strafford, Vt, Apr 9, 1846, dau of Thomas and Mary (Dow) adhaac. At this time she was a Friend, he not. No rec is found of her dismissal and it is probable that in Vermont they drifted into the village church, there being no accessible meeting house. For several years the young couple lived in the Quaker part of Pittsfield. Some time after 1791 they arrived at Strafford, Vt, making a permanent home in the forest south of the village. Here he was a farmer, dying Jan 22, 1837.

Benjamin F Dow made an effort many years ago to trace his own ancestry and the quest was continued by his son Dr Frank F Dow adggeiba. They had Jeremiah's family Bible, but never got farther back. The Author of this Book was finally found and had proof of the needed identity, giving to Dr Dow all the forbears to 1520. Dr Dow then worked all the harder and finally succeeded, as he thinks, in tracing every descendant. Unfortunately he was always too busy to help the Author and in 1927 not one word on the adgge line has ever reached him from this source, Dr Dow having suffered a serious stroke of paralysis.

Dr Dow, when a lad, was instructed by his father to start from a point near the Connecticut River and follow upward a little brook which was well marked with red iron oxide and to report what he found at its source. It was a hard all-day tramp for the youngster, almost pathless. The brook finally ended in a tiny red spring, nothing else to be seen. It was near sunset, so that after many minutes he was relieved to spy in a clearing a hundred yards away an unpainted house farm. He knocked at the door and told a woman who he was. It was his great Aunt Sarah, and there were pancakes for supper. Next day his father came.

Forty years later one of the aunts visited Rochester, N Y and Dr Dow suggested a memory of his childhood visit. On her return she was to examine two large stones on the cellar floor. These were found to be the original marble gravestones of Jeremiah and Rachel, taken up to make way for better ones, stored in the cellar and forgotten.

At least six of the children b Pittsfield:

a   Lydia b Aug 1, 1778; d Oct 7, 1867
b   William b Jan 25, 1780   c   Mehitable b Feb 12, 1782
d   Nancy b Oct 12, 1784   e   David b Aug 15, 1787
f   Daniel, his twin, b Pittsfield   g   Chase b May 7, 1791
h   Jeremiah b May 7, 1791   i   Asahel b Strafford Oct 7, 1795
j   Sally b Oct 7, 1797; m Feb 1, 1820, Samuel C Clark of Atkinson, Kan; m 2nd
     Aug 8, 1826, David Wells of Strafford

Lydia Dow adggea m Jan 6, 1796, Joseph Preston of Strafford. A dau:

a   Bathsheba m July 23, 1845, Rev John Bayles Libby b July 21, 1820, son of
     Isaac Lotan and Adeline C (Burton)

William Dow adggeb m Clarissa ——. At least one child:

a George W P b Feb 8, 1846; untraced

Mehitable Dow adggec m June 20, 1805, Oliver Clark of Thetford.

Nancy Dow adgged d Thetford Sept 15, 1856; m Aug 28, 1805, Noah Ellis b Dec 9, 1777, son of Matthew. Children b Thetford:

a Rachel b May 16, 1806	b Lydia b Jan 7, 1808	
c Warren b Dec 29, 1809	d Sabra b 1812	
e Chase Dow b 1814	f Dyer b 1816	g Mary Ann b 1818
h Sarah Ann b June 21, 1822	i Adaline b Jan 23, 1829	
j Harriet b Sept 10, 1830		

David Dow adggee m Jan 15, 1811, Dolly Day of Lebanon, N H. They settled in Batavia, N Y, where he d Apr, 1882. Children:

a Emilia b Aug 11, 1814
b Aurilla b Feb 1, 1818. One of them m J F Kenyon of Batavia
c Henry b Sept 22, 1821; was sgt of 8th N Y cav; apparently left an only dau, Sally m —— Clark, whose dau m Maj George F Robinson, Ft Union, N M

Daniel Dow adggef remained in Strafford; m Polly Day, Dolly's sister. Children:

a Asa Day b Aug 11, 1808; untraced
b Mary b June 20, 1810; m Oct 20, 1830, Aaron Buzzell Jr of Strafford
c Charles b July 6, 1812
d Emily b Mch 4, 1814; m John Alger of Strafford
e Enoch b Feb 2, 1816   f Royal b July 14, 1817
g William b Jan 16, 1819
h Sophronia b Aug 10, 1820; m Aug 1, 1841, Smith Morrill of Strafford
i Elias B b Aug 21, 1827

Royal Dow adggeff m and had a son, perhaps others:

a Benjamin Franklin

Benjamin F Dow adggeffa (known as Frank) m Mary E Powers b Sou Woodstock, Vt, Apr 8, 1853, d May 16, 1897, dau of Hiram, miller, and Sarah (Morgan); came to Claremont, N H, 1892. His dau m B E Small of Claremont. Altho well past 70, Frank chafed much at the in-activity of life with his dau and in 1923 was cultivating a farm which he had bought in Sou Cornish, N H.

William Dow adggefg. Either he or a brother had a family, there being 3 grandchildren:

a Herbert G, foreman, m, no children; William E, employe; ——, dau m, all living Claremont

In 1922 Mrs Herbert G Dow at the request of the Author prepared the data of her husband's immediate line and sent it to Dr Frank F Dow. Hence the Author has to leave it lamentably defective.

George W Dow adggefgx m Ida W——; moved 1920 from Tunbridge, Vt, to Claremont. She d June 12, 1924, ae 75-4-15, leaving husband, sons Herbert G and William E, daughters Mrs. Eda Claflin of

Claremont and Mrs Etta Bryant of Randolph Center, Vt; 8 grand-children and 6 great grandchildren.

Charles Dow adggefc m Phoebe —— d May 3, 1844, ae 25; m 2nd Oct 2, 1843 (date, not identity, wrong), Philinda Bradbury of Strafford. Children:

    a Hellen b Dec 6, 1838   b Mary b Aug 19, 1841
    c Phebe b Apr 22, 1843

Enoch Dow adggefe m Caroline ——. Children:

    a Jennette B b Mch 20, 1841   b Jerome C b Strafford 1843

Jerome C Dow adggefeb, mechanic of Manchester, N, H, m Nov 8, 1863, Sarah S Onthank, ae 17, b Charlestown, Mass, dau of William B and Lucetta; untraced.

Elias B Dow adggefi m Dec 14, 1851, Aurora Russell of Strafford; untraced.

Chase Dow adggeg inherited the homestead; d May 1, 1868; m Dec 26, 1815, Lucy Walker b Dec 27, 1793, dau of Major Freeman and Elizabeth (Chandler). She d Nov 8, 1880. Children:

    a Alvira b Sept 26, 1816; m (Elvira W) Dec 25, 1838, Andrew A Gove of Strafford;
         moved to Minnesota Jc, Wis
    b Simon Chase b Oct 26, 1818
    c Lucia b Feb 25, 1822; m Aug 7, 1849, Major Oel A Buck, veteran of Mexican
         War, of Washington, D C
    d Chester B b Feb 12, 1825
    e Frances Ellen b May 4, 1833; m Levi W Bliss

Elvira Walker Dow adggega m Andrew Allen Gove b July 28, 1812, d Minnesota Jc May 29, 1892, son of Enos Sanborn and Mercy (Eastman). Children:

    a Lucy Ellen b Feb 10, 1840; m Frank Coon; 11 children
    b Juliette b Apr 11, 1846; m —— Lindley; 4 children
    c Solon Chase b Jan 23, 1850; m Lillie V Searle; lived Milwaukee; 5 children
    d Belle b Aug 4, 1852; d Sept 9, 1878
    e Curtis b Dec 26, 1857; m ——; d Jan 11, 1887

Simon Chase Dow adggegb m Mch 11, 1844, Mary Bliss Morse of West Fairlee; went west in 1849, finally locating on a farm at Alma City, Minn. She d Jan 9, 1892; he d Faribault Feb 27, 1914. Children:

    a Frederick M b Chelsea, Ill, Dec 1, 1848
    b Marcella C b Lind, Wis, Apr 22, 1850

Frederick Morris Dow adggegba of Janesville, Wis, m Apr 2, 1876, Mary Emma Waterbury b Woodstock, Ontario, July 11, 1858. Living 1924 at the home of a son, Olympia, Wash. Nine children:

    a Harry Goodger b Alma City Dec 16, 1877; m Cherokee, Iowa, July 1903 Nona
         Winifred Hull; now postal traveling clerk of St. Joseph, Mo. No children
    b Marcella Buyrl b Oct 12, 1879   c Calvin Lawrence b Aug 1, 1881
    d Sylvia Chase b Janesville May 18, 1882
    e Walter Simon b Smith Mills, Minn, Apr 11, 1886

f   Wallace Silas (twin); service in France 1918; m May 30, 1920, Frances Suther-
    land and moved to Pasadena, Calif. She d Dec 31, 1923; no children
g   Edith Louise b Alma City Sept 26, 1887
h   Lura Mae b Oct 6, 1891; grad San Jose Normal School; now teacher in Calif;
    unm
i   Frederick Waterbury b May 19, 1900; m Olympia, Wash, July 9, 1823, Carolyn
    Smith of Ft Bragg; now in Olympia State Bank

Marcella B Dow adggegbab m June 26, 1901, Clayton Leon Kennedy, now County Auditor of Mankato, Minn. Children, b Mankato:

a   Gordon Douglas b Dec 10, 1904   b   Harold Leon b Aug 16, 1918

Calvin L Dow adggegbac m Feb 26, 1906, Delia Ann Munch b
Lovington, Ill, July 23, 1882; d Oakes, N D, July 27, 1908; m 2nd
Wahpeton, N D, Sept 28, 1909, Mary Estelle Robertson.   Now a rancher
of Olympia. Children:

a   Alfred Jesse b Dec 14, 1907   b   Marcella b Dec 14, 1907
c   Donald Dwight   d   Marie Emma b Aug 22, 1912
e   Phyllis b June 1915   f   Frederick

Sylvia C Dow adggegbad m Morgan Hill, Calif, Feb 12, 1909,
Frank Leslie Merrill, in 1924 cement contractor of Sierra Madre, Calif.
To her thanks are due for the exactness of the narrative of three genera-
tions of her line. Only child:

a   Harold Wayne b Sierra Madre June 12, 1911

Walter Simon Dow adggegbae m Santa Cruz Jan 16, 1909, Emily
Alberta Page of Morgan Hill, Calif. Cement contractor. Children:

a   Kenneth Irwin b Mch 4, 1910   b   Alberta Emma b June 18, 1911

Edith Louise Dow adggegbag m Mch 27, 1912, William Fredrick
of Lampson, Wis; moved to Sierra Madre Nov 1923. Children:

a   Lura Mae b Aug 21, 1913   b   Howard William b Oct 6, 1918
c   Dean Russell b Apr 3, 1921

Marcella C Dow adggegbb m Apr 9, 1871, Alfred Smith Grant of
Morristown, Minn. He d; she m 2nd Charles Sargent. Living 1924
in Minn. Children, by 1st husband:

a   Edna Lois b Jan 27, 1875   b   Arthur Dow b Oct 26, 1877
c   Harry Carlton b Mch 30, 1880   d   George Harrison
e   Alfred Smith

Chester B Dow adggegd inherited the homestead; florist and prop-
agator of fine plants; m Concord, N H, Jan 1, 1851, Ellen Kibling b
Strafford Jan 22, 1834. Children:

a   Carrie Ella b Sept 11, 1851
b   Nellie Sophia b June 28, 1853; m Mch 18, 1879, Fred French Chaffee b Jan 29,
    1855, son of John Willard and Lomacy (French).

Jeremiah Dow adggeh d Jan 7, 1868; m Jan 3, 1820, Polly Perkins
of Strafford; became superintendent of the copper works at Shrewsbury,
Vt. Children:

a   William Chase b Nov 3, 1820   b   Lucius b Apr 13, 1823
c   Luman b Sept 1, 1826; left children   d   Mary M b June 24, 1835

William C Dow adggeha of Shrewsbury m Jan 10, 1843, Julian Greason of Shrewsbury. Untraced.

Lucius Dow adggehb, trader of Cuttingville, Vt, m Medford, Mass, Dec 28, 1847, Rebecca Stillman Sprague b May 20, 1826, d Apr 17, 1849, dau of Isaac and Rebecca (Cutter); m 2nd Dec 12, 1849, Garafilia Mohalby Sprague, her sister. No rec of children.

Mary M Dow adggehd of Shrewsbury d Nov 12, 1868; m (his 3rd) Sept 25, 1865, Rev Hiram P Osgood b Dec 15, 1823, son of John C and Jane (Pratt).

Asahel Dow adggei was a successful woolen manufacturer of Bethany, N Y; d Fowlersville Dec 7, 1866; m May 5, 1818, Dolly Blaisdell b Jan 19, 1801, d Nov 9, 1870, dau of John and Rebecca (Kendall). Children:

a   Betsey D b Mch 15, 1819; d Aug 5, 1883; m Sept 14, 1841, Russell Hawkes of Watseka, Ill; dau Viola b Mch 20, 1843
b   Benjamin Franklin b Jan 12, 1820   c   John Blaisdell b Nov 17, 1821
d   Amanda E (Auranda, Vt rec) b Feb 26, 1823; d June 16, 1903; m May 14, 1847, Perez Brown; children,—Perez b Feb 8, 1848, d Dec 22, 1869; La Motte b Apr 5, 1851; d 1871
e   Daniel b Oct 2, 1824; d Bethany Oct 11, 1845
f   Rebecca B b Feb 17, 1826; m Apr 11, 1849, Almond Marsh; went to Watseka, Ill; children,—Ida b Mch 19, 1853, m —— Smith; Olive b Oct 22, 1857, d Feb 20, 1864
g   Sarah C b Apr 5, 1828; d July 26, 1860; m May 9, 1854, Elias Eastman
h   Asahel b Feb 14, 1830; d Strafford July 2, 1832
i   Louisa E b Mch 19, 1832; m Oct 27, 1853, Arthur Polhemus of Old Mines, Mo
j   Asahel C b May 26, 1834
k   Emma M b Bethany June 29, 1836; m Jesse Smith of Denver, Colo; only child Daisy
l   Luman Frary b July 28, 1838
m   Adelaide G b May 23, 1840; d Chicago Oct 18, 1881; m Hiram Ludden; only child,—La Motte
n   Henry G b July 7, 1843

Benjamin F Dow adggeib d Buffalo Feb 28, 1901; m Sept 5, 1848, Caroline W Capron b Oct 17, 1829, dau of Clark Lyman and Martha (Fowler). In 1851 he began to manufacture threshing machines in Logansport, Ind, and soon, as Dow & Fowler, built another large plant in Fowlersville. This was completely destroyed by fire in 1882 just as an order for 100 machines had been booked. A new plant was improvised, so that work on the order began in 3 days and in 8 days 85 hands had been re-employed. Citizens of Peru, Ind, intervened and subscribed $10,000 bonus if the plant would locate there. This was done at cost of $50,000, Benjamin's brother Luman F being a partner. The Fowlersville plant was kept as an auxiliary. In the end the properties were sold to the farm machine combination. Mr Dow was able in later life to take a wide interest in affairs in his part of the state; was an organizer and a director always in Buffalo, Rochester & Pittsburg R R. In 1884 Robert K Dow adggdcca inspected the property with a view to absorbing it for the larger Reading system and learned to put high value on the counsels of his new found kinsman.

Children:

a Frank Fowler b Fowlersville Apr 16, 1851
b Caroline Bell b Dec 15, 1856; grad Vassar 1880 *summa cum laude*; in 1922 Dean of Y M C A training school, N Y City; never m
c George Churchill b Mch 13, 1864; grad Rochester University 1887; manufacturer of Buffalo; m May 22, 1901, Eva C Carr b Fenton, Mich, May 1, 1866; no children
d Charles C b Mch 4, 1866; d Jan 23, 1869
e Helen Louise b Nov 24, 1869; d Mch 4, 1903

Frank F Dow adggeiba grad Amherst 1874; for a number of years was his father's partner, altho graduated in medicine. He later was an operating surgeon of Rochester; m Sept 19, 1877, Harriet E Brown b Wheatland Jan 14, 1852, member of D A R, dau of Volney P and Sarah (Avery). In 1921 he was incapacitated by paralysis.

While in college his professor of geology remarked that, as a general principle, when any one saw a mountain top which no one else wanted, it would be well to buy it. Ten years later Dr Dow was fishing in the north part of the State and encountered just such a hill top, buying it for a few dollars an acre. He then almost dismissed it from his mind. Fifteen years later a stranger called upon him offering to buy the hill for $10,000. Dr Dow decided to look before he leaped and took another fishing trip, taking along a diamond driller. The stranger finally paid about $90,000 for the property, full of fair grade iron ore.

Children:

a Leland Brown b Wheatland Mch 2, 1880
b Fayette Brown b Peru, Ind, Aug 25, 1881
c Amoret Brown b May 1, 1889; d Feb 10, 1892

Leland B Dow adggeibaa m Rochester May 18, 1907, Edith Longfellow Vaughn, dau of Richard Fairfax and Mary (Longfellow). Child:

a Leland Brown b Apr 13, 1908

Fayette B Dow adggeibab m Denver, Colo, June 18, 1913, Annie Lloyd Thomas, dau of Lloyd and Annie (Schley).

John B Dow adggeic m Sept 21, 1846, Lucia Dolly Lincoln b Bethany, N Y, Feb 21, 1826, dau of Col Cornelius J and Zeralda (Foster), moved to Ann Arbor, Mich. Children b Scio, Mich:

a Hattie A b Mch 3, 1852; m July 21, 1879, Charles Baxter
b Chase L b Jan 11, 1856; m Sept 15, 1881, Mary Wahr; lived Ann Arbor

Hattie A Dow adggeica d Ann Arbor Sept 19, 1911; no children.

Clare Lincoln Dow adggeicb d Apr 14, 1908; m Mary Wahr, dau of Gottlieb of Ann Arbor. Only child:

a Lucia Caroline b Nov 5, 1885; m July 5, 1905, Harry McCain; only child,— Harry A b Jan 7, 1907

Luman Frary Dow adggeil enlisted as private in 13th N Y, served in building the defenses of Washington; disch for disability, recovered, raised a company in 10th N Y, went as 1st Lieut, promoted to captain at close of war; was wounded at Antietam and Fredericksburg. At the close of the war he returned to the threshing machine works. He m Feb 10, 1864, Minnie E Sackett b Oct 9, 1839, d Rochester Oct 22, 1904. When the machine works sold out he moved to Grand Forks, N Dak, soon running for Governor on the Socialist ticket. A recent directory gives him a cement contractor in Denver, Colo. Children:

a Ellie May b Fowlersville May 17, 1865; of Minneapolis
b Lillian Maude b Apr 16, 1867; of Minneapolis
c Horace Sackett b Oct 10, 1869; m July 7, 1897, Martha Murch; of Minneapolis; no children
d Charles Sumner b Dec 8, 1871; m Sept 25, 1895, Elizabeth Parsons of Grand Forks; 1 son, 1 dau
e Willard Clare b May 21, 1874; lives Kenmore, N Dak; m Oct 25, 1899, Beulah Robinson; 1 son

Nellie May Dow adggeila m Apr 3, 1912, Theodore A Ryan; now of Chicago; no children:

Lillian Maude Dow adggeilb m Nov 28, 1912, Frank Edwin Smith; now of Detroit; member of D A R. No children.

Horace S Dow adggeilc and Martha (Murch) have an adopted son:

a Roger Wilson

Charles S Dow adggeild has 2 children, b Grand Forks:

a Lillian May b May 10, 1896; m John Landon Laycock of Grand Forks
b Edward Parsons b Aug 27, 1897

Willard C Dow adggeile has a son:

a Chester Robinson b Larimore, N D, Jan 31, 1907

Henry G Dow adggein enlisted in 3rd N Y cav, served until commissioned Lieut 16th N Y cav; served throughout the war; never wounded; afterwards lived in Kan; untraced.

Asahel C Dow adggeij d Hillsdale, Mich, 1871; m Apr 18, 1855, Mary L Calkins, b June 4, 1831. Only child:

a Edd C b May 31, 1858

Edd C Dow adggeija m Mch 8, 1881, Juna Pierce b May 30, 1862. Child:

a Elmer Asahel b July 7, 1883

Elmer Asahel Dow adggeijaa, railroad man of Tucson, Ariz, his wid mother with him; m Feb 14, 1911, Arta I Cochran b Oct 20, 1885. Children:

a Homer Eugene b May 2, 1912   b Mary L Hall b Sept 16, 1915

Sally Dow adggej by Samuel C Clark had:

a Aurora   b Prentis

Lydia Dow adggf m (int Mch 20) Apr 6, 1773, by Rev Sam Perley, Jacob True b Mch 26, 1748, son of Ezekiel and Mary (Morrill) of Salisbury Plain.   Ezekiel was son of Dea John True and Martha M (Morrill). John True was son of Capt Henry and Jane (Bradbury). Henry was son of Henry, immigrant, who m dau of Capt Robert Pike. Lydia and Jacob followed her brother to Salisbury, N H, where they had 6 children, one being a pioneer of Corinth, Vt, influencing the going there of Insley Dow adgga.

d Ezekiel m Mary True; pioneer of Corinth

Patience Dow adgh m Oneysiphorus Page, whose name is seldom spelled twice alike. (See Page family sub adb.) Salisbury rec show 2 children:

a Sarah b Mch 10, 1732   b Winthrop b Jan 28, 1733-4

ELIHU Dow adgx. His great grandson, a man of more than average attainments, lifelong resident of Seabrook, well posted in its traditions, stated that he was told by his grandfather Jacob, son of Elihu, that Elihu was son of Jeremiah Dow adg. The Author knows that Elihu was brought up as a son of Jeremiah, and for this reason, his place in the letter key. It is possibly correct, but all of Jeremiah's children appear in extant b rec. Elihu and Judah Dow adai were as close to each other as two men can be. Judging from m date, Elihu was b by 1705. He was of So Hampton 1748; taxed regularly in Hampton Falls until Seabrook was set off; back in Hampton Falls 1763. Hid d rec not found, nor a will. He paid no minister's tax, hence was at least nominally a Quaker. He m May 6, 1728, Mehitable (Cilley) Eaton, wid of Thomas, dau of Thomas, sister of Eleanor who m Bildad Dow adah. Their posterity is closely identified with Seabrook and was in fragmentary shape until put together by the spendid work of Miss Mary J Greene of Hampton Falls. Children:

a   Hannah b Nov 24, 1728 (a departure from certain Quaker standards)
b   Mary, twin   c   Joseph b Mch 22, 1729-30
d   Miriam b Feb 12, 1731-2   e   Tabitha b Aug 19, 1734
f   Jacob b Feb 6, 1737-8   g   Kesia, his twin
h   Jemima b Mch 8, 1739-40

Hannah Dow adgxa (dau of Elihu of S Hampton) m Amesbury Oct 13, 1748, John Jones Jr, son of John, yeoman, and Susanna. Salisbury rec have 2 younger children:

e   (perhaps) Mehitable b Oct 30, 1760   g   Elizabeth (a twin) b Sept 25, 1763

Mary Dow adgxb, said by Gove Gen b 1727 and of Kensington, m Dec 22, 1752, Obediah Gove of Kensington, b Hampton Falls Sept 2, 1723, son of John and Ruth (Johnson). They moved to Weare. He was a Quaker and refused to sign the Association Test. Children, all b Kensington:

a   Mary b Dec 19, 1754; m Apr 17, 1776, Richard Bean, son of Jeremiah and
      Abigail (Prescott); 10 children
b   Obediah b Oct 10, 1756; d Weare July 1814; m Sarah Nichols; 10 children.
      Their oldest dau, Mary, m Asa Dow adahc of Weare
c   Nathan b Feb 8, 1758; veteran of Revolution; m Rhoda Prescott; 8 children
d   Patience b Jan 25, 1760; m Levi Bean; 7 children
e   Elijah b July 8, 1762; m Susan Jewell; 2nd Elizabeth Jones; 7 children
f   Enoch b Oct 10, 1764; m Hannah Dearborn; 10 children
g   Ruth b Oct 7, 1766; m Jonathan Burbank of Brentwood; 10 children
h   Hannah b Sept 11, 1768; m Green Chase; 6 children
i   Anna b Aug 1, 1773; d Aug 1836, unm

Joseph Dow adgxc appears regularly in Hampton Falls tax list; probably is he who d Salisbury Dec 3, 1780. Further unknown, except by inference:

a   Joseph (son of Joseph) b Salisbury May 20, 1753. This Joseph drops out of
      sight genealogically. Probably the Joseph mustered out R I Aug 1778, ser-
      vice 25 days, Capt Moses Leavitt, Col Moses Nichols

Jacob Dow adgxf. His gravestone still stands, calls him Capt, military rec not found. Was a substantial citizen of Seabrook; will dated 1813, probated 1820, makes son Elihu executor and residuary legatee, son Robert $40, sons Tristram and Edward Dearborn $100 each, to wife Lois half interest during her widowhood and "furniture of her own to do what she likes with." As Lois had furniture of her own, she must have been a wid. This is important. Jacob m 1st Sept 13, 1770, Mary Dow of Seabrook, unplaced; m 2nd Lois Weber of York, Me. A descendant now living states that he m Lois Dow, wid of Levi. This, of course, is adaii. Either, this was a 3rd m, or, more likely, Lois Weber was wid of Levi Dow. Our original informant says Lois had considerable family by 1st husband. This is probably correct. A later informant says Lois had but one child, Rhoda m Elihu Dow adgxfb. This cannot be, for the name Levi was continued without interruption in every generation of the adai line. Lois had 3 children by Jacob; marriage was probably in 1803. Others by 1st wife:

a   Robert b Mch 14, 1776 (son of Jacob and Mary)   b   Elihu b May 1778
c   Jacob b June 7, 1780 (in rec, 4th child; if correct a 1st born d young)
d   Tristram (Trustom, mother Louese, in rec) b Jan 30, 1804; will provides he
    shall be maintained until 14, then bound out to some mechanic
e   —— son d in infancy
f   Edward Dearborn, named for a popular Seabrook physician, godfather to many

Robert Dow adgxfa was a puzzle for many years, there being 3 contemporaneous Roberts in Seabrook. Greeley Gen gave to Robert and Sally (Brown) 3 children, barely mentioning names of parents. This was with appearance of finality. Nothing appears regarding their life in Seabrook. It remained for Miss Mary J Greene to find their gravestones and confirm that they had 14 children. Smithtown cemetery shows Robert Dow d Mch 13, 1843, ae 66; and Sally, wife of Robert Dow d Sept 24, 1857, ae 80. One child d in infancy; others:

a   Jacob b 1798; d Sept 1882, ae 84
b   Elihu (called Jr) b July 1800; d Feb 7, 1864
c   Mary b about 1803; m Oct 6, 1822, Isaac Brown (cf adgxffb)
d   Simeon E b 1805-6; m Aug 19, 1827, Susan E Dow adaimf
e   Betsey b 1807; m Apr 24, 1825, Samuel Eaton of Weare
f   Robert b 1807 (census says 1816, probably correct); m Nov 1, 1836, Ruth True
g   Christopher E b Nov 12, 1812; of Atkinson, d Dec 29, 1886
h   Andrew E b by 1813
i   Ben, probably Benjamin b 1815 (or possibly 1807); untraced
j   Jane b about 1817; m Sept 19, 1847, Simeon L Eaton
k   Rhoda m Jesse Worthley; son,—Robert Dow b Salisbury Apr 13, 1844
l   Lowell Brown b 1820; d Aug 17, 1824
m   Charlotte b July 15, 1822; m Nov 26, 1841, John A True of Salisbury

Jacob Dow adgxfaa, farmer of Seabrook, m Jan 27, 1822, Sarah A (Sally) Eaton of Salisbury b Pittsfield 1799, dau of Jonathan and Sarah. On the same day Sarah Dow of Seabrook m Jabez Eaton of Salisbury. We cannot place this couple, probably akin. Stones in Smithtown cemetery say Jacob Dow d Dec 1, 1882, ae 85, 5 mos; and Sarah A, wife of Jacob Dow, d Mch 8, 1878, ae 78. Census of 1850 gives him laborer b 1785

and Sally b 1781, obviously errors.   Realty assessed $1,000.   In 1849
Jacob appears as joiner.   Will dated Nov 16 (probated Dec 13), 1882,
mentions 4 children.   If others had left posterity, they presumably would
have been mentioned:

   a   Thomas Arnold b Oct 1822   b   Lowell Brown b Sept 1824
   c   Albert M b Nov 4, 1826
   d   Edward E d Jan 21, 1835, ae 1 year, 5 days; buried alongside parents
   e   Charles S b July 1836
   f   Francis Byron b (to Jacob, joiner, and Sarah A) June 23, 1849; must have d
      without issue

Thomas A Dow adgxfaaa, shoemaker of Seabrook, realty assessed
$300 in 1850, d June 14, 1886, ae 63-8-5; m Lydia Ann Walton b Apr 25,
1826, d Mch 29, 1899, dau of Daniel and Nancy (Brown).   Children:

   a   Charlotte Ann b 1846; m Jan 5, 1865, Henry Brown
   b   Sarah A b 1847; m Tristram L Dow adgxff
   c   Emma M (probably Emma L) b Sept 19, 1851
   d   Alvah Leroy b Oct 15, 1856
   e   Annie Arnold b 1859; m May 21, 1887, John T Janvrin; 2nd Dec 24, 1898,
      Henry C Seamans

Emma L Dow adgxfaaac d Sept 23, 1905; had a son Andy P b Sept
5, 1868, d shoemaker unm Dec 22, 1913 or 1915; m Dec 3, 1885, Samuel
Boyd; 2nd Oct 14, 1891, Franklin Merrill, by whom 2 children.

Alvah L Dow adgxfaaad, carpenter of Seabrook, d Nov 14, 1920;
m May 1, 1883, Mary Lydia Bragg b 1859, dau of Daniel and Julia A of
Seabrook.   At least 3 children:

   a   Anna M m, ae 17, Nov 17, 1900, Thomas F Owen
   b   Anthony d May 31, 1906, ae 19-8-28   c —— son b Sept 25, 1897

Lowell B Dow adgxfaab d Apr 1, 1894; m June 27, 1854, Eliza A
Dow adgxfdd b July 10, 1834.   Children:

   a   Frank B b 1857   b   Annette True

Frank B Dow adgxfaaba m 1872 Martha J Knowles; he d; she m
2nd 1886 Mark Leslie Dow adgxfaff.   Frank's children:

   a   Annie Lowell b Mch 24, 1873; d Oct 26, 1909; m Charles F Dow adgxfebc; 5
      children
   b   Frank Herbert b 1875   c   Clara M b 1876

Frank H Dow adgxfaabab, mason of Seabrook, moved to Haverhill,
Mass; m Sept 2, 1893, Maggie S Charles; a son b Seabrook Dec 29, 1894.

Annette True Dow adgxfaabb d before 1919; m Charles Hull of
Salisbury.   Children:

   a   Maud E   b   Nettie D

Albert M Dow adgxfaac d June 10, 1899; m Kesiah Collins d Feb

4, 1901, ae 55, 4 mos, dau of Samuel. A sketch of Albert M is in Hist Rockingham Co. Children:

a Jacob Franklin   b Charles E b 1861
c George C b Oct 25, 1867
d Hulda M b Sept 9, 1870; m June 3, 1893, Jacob S Fowler adaimbfc; dau Ruby B m 1916 Carroll W Dow adaimbaaabc
e ——— dau m ——— Gynan

Jacob F Dow adgxfaaca, expressman of Seabrook, m Aug 28, 1875, Abbie V Eaton, dau of Caleb and Louisa J. Children:

a George L b July 10, 1878   b Albert M b Nov 3, 1880

George L Dow adgxfaacaa, merchant, teamster, grocer, m Sept 18, 1902, Lenora A Boyd, ae 16, dau of William L and Viola F (Fowler). Children:

a Franklin L b Mch 16, 1903; d Jan 7, 1905
b Abbie F b Jan 16, 1905   c ——— son b Mch 3, 1913; d young

Albert M Dow adgxfaacab, merchant of Seabrook, m Oct 3, 1903, Anga V Osborne, dau of George W of Weare and Mary F (Fowler). Children:

a ——— dau b and d Jan 17, 1904   b ——— dau b May 27, 1905

Charles E Dow adgxfaacb of Seabrook, m July 2, 1881, Gertrude F Gynan d Nov 21, 1884, dau of Nicholas and M R of Halifax, ae 22; m 2nd Hampton Falls May 1, 1886, Betsey A Eaton, ae 22, dau of Caleb and Louisa J. Children:

a Dova W b Apr 10, 1882; unm in Haverhill Aug 7, 1899
b ——— son b and d Nov 21, 1884
c Jessie B b 1887; m June 1, 1907, Claude E Adams adgxfbebe; dau Agnes L b Nov 25, 1907

Dova (probably Dora) **M Dow** adgxfaacba m May 24, 1905, Ralph L Hayes, ae 21, son of George H and Hattie B (Marsh).

George C Dow adgxfaacc, shoemaker of Seabrook, m Nov 15, 1885, Albertia G Bragg, ae 20, dau of Daniel. Children:

a Gertrude Emma b Mch 7, 1886; m Mch 12, 1910, Frank P Goss; ae 20, son of Frank M and Ellen C (Perley). Children,—Raymond b Feb 14, 1911; Ellen A b Apr 25, 1913
b George Ellsworth b 1889

George E Dow adgxfaaccb of Seabrook m Mch 12, 1910, Lulu A Eaton, dau of Charles E and Lucy (Perkins). Child:

a Pauline Della b May 2, 1917

Charles S Dow adgxfaae, farmer of Seabrook, d Mch 16, 1906; m Lizzie I Gynan b Nova Scotia. Children:

a Emma Josephine b 1865-6; d unm
b Louise H b Nov 25, 1867; d Feb 17, 1884   c George H

Elizabeth Lavender Gynan, ae 58, dau of John A and Elizabeth (Deering), m 2nd Georgetown, Mass, Mch 11, 1909, Daniel Webster Spofford, ae 74.

George H Dow adgxfaaec, machinist, m Portland, Me, Oct 19, 1908, Catherine M Holker, ae 29, of Newburyport, dau of William and Alcena M (Bartlett). Recent directory shows him in Newburyport. These 3 children are mentioned in father's will. Children b Newburyport:

a   Catherine b Jan 4, 1909   b   William Holker b Jan 26, 1910
c   ——

Elihu Dow (Jr) adgxfab, trader, m Loudon Dec 26, 1824, Charlotte Eaton of Pittsfield (not in 1850 census); in 1850 seaman of Seabrook, realty assessed $800.

Probably Elihu spent most of his life away from Seabrook. He made a 2nd m, for Sally Collins, wid of Elihu Dow, dau of Tristram and Ruth (Eaton) of Seabrook, d Malden, Mass, Oct 15, 1902, ae 85-1-17. A dau, perhaps more:

a   Huldah A b 1827; living 1850

Mary Dow adgxfac m Oct 6, 1822, Isaac Brown of Seabrook. At least 2 children:

a   Jacob Dow b Seabrook 1864
b   Ruth Ann m Daniel B Dow adgxffb

Simeon E Dow adgxfad, carpenter, m Salisbury Aug 19, 1827, Susan E Dow adaimf; lived Seabrook; will names Nelson, Simeon, Jennette and 6 grandchildren:

a   Philip C b 1828   b   Meribah m Thomas Boyd   c   Alfred b 1830
d   Clarissa b Nov 1835; m Salisbury Mch 18, 1860, William H Walton of Seabrook;
      d Aug 29, 1864; 1 child d in infancy
e   Melissa b 1834; d young   f   Nelson P b Seabrook 1840
g   Simeon J b 1842; Civil War veteran; moved upstate; untraced
h   Sarah J b 1844   i   Susan Jeannette b Nov 2, 1852

Philip C Dow adgxfada, shoemaker of Seabrook, d Dec 12, 1869, of tuberculosis; m June 29, 1854 Rhoda (Eaton) Brown of Seabrook, dau of Jeremiah of So Seabrook. Children:

a   Melinda
b   Gertrude of Newburyport m Portsmouth May 26, 1900, James Arthur Beckman adkddgja

Alfred Dow adgxfadc (whose middle initial appears as B, M and N), carpenter of Seabrook, m Sarah J Felch. At least 2 children:

a   Alfred Frank b Seabrook Feb 7, 1891, ae 27, 9 mos, unm   b   Susan

Nelson P Dow adgxfadf, shoemaker, later merchant of Seabrook, d Feb 26, 1885; m July 9, 1867, Sarah B Marston, ae 30, dau of Joseph; dying childless, he willed to her the homestead.

Sarah J Dow adgxfadh lived Seabrook; m Feb 10, 1861, William True Eaton.   Children:

a   Melissa Dow   b   William E

Susan J Dow adgxfadi m Portsmouth Oct 22, 1868, George Franklin Huntington, Quaker, carriage painter of Amesbury.   They and four children drowned 1882 while crossing to Newburyport in a small boat. Children:

a   Herbert Ellsworth b Mch 6, 1869; of Amesbury
b   Nellie May b July 14, 1870; drowned
c   Carrie b Oct 14, 1872; d Feb 25, 1882
d   George Daniel b Jan 20, 1874; went to Calif
e   Lillian Maud b June 9, 1876; m Lawrence W Pierce
f   Arthur b Nov 3, 1877   g   Grace b May 9, 1880; both drowned
h   Nettie b June 11, 1881; drowned

Robert Dow adgxfaf, farmer of Salisbury, m Ruth True b Mass 1820.   This line amplified from Greeley Gen.   Children, all b Salisbury:

a   Caroline A b Nov 18, 1838
b   Moses True b Oct 28, 1841; living 1850; untraced
c   Sarah P b 1843   d   Samuel Melvin b 1852
e   Robert Edgar b 1854   f   Mark Leslie b 1857
g   Herbert Allen b Dec 23, 1864; m A Loffy of Salisbury; no children

Caroline A Dow adgxfafa m Salisbury June 21, 1866, William Hook French b Feb 11, 1832, son of Josiah and Hannah (French).   Son:

a   William H b Salisbury Mch 12, 1870

Sarah P Dow adgxfafc m Salisbury Apr 26, 1862, John Moody b Mch 13, 1841, son of Joseph; d Apr 9, 1872; he m 2nd Mch 27, 1873, Juda Jackman.   Sarah's children:

a   John Wesley b Nov 26, 1862   b   Alden True b Oct 1, 1864
c   Addie Sarah b Oct 31, 1866; m Jan 2, 1886, W S Rowe of Salisbury

Samuel M Dow adgxfafd m Newburyport Nov 29, 1875, Annie L True of Hudson, N Y.   Child:

a   Melvin b Salisbury Nov 27, 1876; untraced

Mark L Dow adgxfaff, farmer of Salisbury, m Mch 9, 1886, Martha J Knowles, ae 29, adgxfaaba, dau of Charles and Ardesia; wid of Frank Dow.

Robert Edgar Dow adgxfafe, blacksmith of Salisbury, m Sept 4, 1874, Flora M Knowles, ae 16.

Christopher E Dow adgxfag, wheelwright of Atkinson, d Dec 29, 1886, ae 74, 29 days; m Feb 5, 1835, Rachel E French b 1814, dau of Elias and Hannah E (Carter).   She d Salisbury Dec 9, 1854; he m 2nd Salisbury Ednah Pike b May 5, 1836, dau of Otis and Ednah (Deal). Some Mary Dow b 1836 living with them 1850.   Children:

a   Charles Wesley b Sept 29, 1836; d Dec 20, 1855
b   Edwin Augustus b Aug 7, 1842; d Salisbury Apr 11, 1879; m Addie B Smith;
    presumably no children

    c Charles Irving b Nov 14, 1856; carpenter of Atkinson, m Sept 1, 1884, **Ida S**
       Mason, ae 20, dau of S Bailey and Julia

Andrew E Dow adgxfah appears 1850 census as fisherman of
Salisbury, realty $1,000; m Salisbury Dec 12, 1838, Louisa Pike b Mass
1819. Three children, by census:

    a Charles Franklin b Salisbury Aug 1, 1840
    b George b 1844; untraced   c Elizabeth b 1849

Charles Franklin Dow adgxfaha m Margaret A Brown. A dau
by own rec;

    a Lottie L b 1879; m Amesbury Jan 19, 1901, **Harry E Hewett b Lawrence, ae**
       22, son of Edward A and Mary A (Long)

Charlotte E Dow adgxfam d Newburyport Nov 11, 1880; m Nov 26,
1841, John E True of Seabrook. Children:

    a Ploomy A b Mch 1, 1844; d Newton Feb 4, 1880; m July 13, 1862, George B
       Merrill; 2 children
    b Ruth b Jan 9, 1846; m Edward G Pearson of Melrose; 1 dau
    c Andrew Clement b Newburyport Oct 19, 1850; m Clara Squier of Nev; lived
       San Francisco; 3 children

—— **Dow** adgxfa line m Anna Gynan (Guinan in 2nd m rec). She,
ae 38, dau of Philip R and Frances M (O'Brien), m 2nd Boston Feb 23,
1902, Otis P Brickett, ae 52.

Elihu Dow adgxfb, cooper of Seabrook, d Aug 24, 1853, ae 75, 3
mos; m Rhoda Dow b 1786, his step sister. A ms calling her Rhoda
Eaton with 1 child is wholly error. All the gravestones still stand in
Smithtown cemetery. Rhoda, wife of Elihu, d Apr 17, 1876, ae 93, 1 mo.
Children:

    a Rhoda b 1808; d Jan 6, 1835, unm
    b Hannah b 1809 (1819 census); d Aug 2, 1853, unm
    c Charles b 1812 (1815 census); d Feb 26, 1850, unm
    d Oliver b 1815   e Elihu b Feb 6, 1822
    f Jacob b 1824; d Apr 13, 1846, unm
    g Sewall B b 1827; d Nov 27, 1847, unm

Oliver Dow adgxfbd. Family rec says he d unm Feb 26, 1850, but
census says d tuberculosis and next to him is apparently a dau:

    a Isabell b 1848; d consumption Sept 1849

Elihu Dow adgxfbe appears in 1850 census seaman, realty $800; in
later life farmer, then retired, with a comfortable home, a man of some
standing, high character and good mental equipment. It is remarkable
that he should have apparently inherited the family Bible of Judah
Dow adai; it is remarkable, too, that the lines of adai and adgx have intermarried in all generations and been more closely associated than any other
lines. Elihu m Lydia Locke b Salisbury Feb 6, 1824, d Sept 28, 1899, dau
of Hubbard and Jane (Dow). Thus Lydia is also adaimdb and adggbdb,

perhaps thus inherited Judah's Bible. Such heirlooms are most apt to be inherited by female lines. Children:

a   Charles A b Dec 13, 1850; d July 7, 1870
b   Lydia Locke b Aug 17, 1851
c   Rhoda E b Feb 10, 1867; d Feb 14, 1899. State rec: Rosa E Dow d Feb 5, 1894, ae 27, 5 days, seems the same badly garbled
d   (doubtfully belonging here) Julia A d Seabrook Oct 7, 1895, ae 52, unm

Lydia L Dow adgxfbeb m June 24, 1873, Edwin Adams of Newburyport; living Newburyport 1921; inherited the homestead. Children:

a   Charles E b 1875; d 1896
b   Elihu T m Anna M Johnson; lives Seabrook homestead
c   Herbert Quincy m Helen Prior
d   Gertrude M m Benjamin Endicott Evans
e   Claude E b 1886; m Jessie B Dow adgxfaacbb

Elihu and Claude Adams, shoe manufacturers of Newburyport, conceived the idea that it would be advantageous to have their plant in Seabrook, instead of getting Seabrook labor to Newburyport. They built a fine factory near the homestead. It was burned, but rebuilt; it has been a great regenerative influence in Seabrook.

———————

Jacob Dow adgxfc, heir to an acre of salt marsh and $20, is genealogically lost. Probably he, improbably adaaaab, m Sarah Jones. Rec of son says both b Rumney but this is doubtless careless error. At all events they settled in Rumney and had at least 1 child:

a   James P b Rumney Aug 11, 1813; farmer, d Meredith Feb 26, 1895. Further untraced

Tristram Dow adgxfd was drowned 1851 while on a fishing trip to Prince Edward's Isl; m Sept 20, 1824, Hannah Bragg of Salisbury b 1804. Children by family rec agree with census, but latter more reliable as regards dates:

a   Tristram L b June 6, 1826 (1836 census)
b   Zelphia b 1829; m Amesbury Sept 20, 1846, John Christian adkfbbba; dau Zelphia Ann b Salisbury Mch 23, 1847
c   Lucinda b 1832; m Enoch E Felch
d   Eliza b 1834; d Aug 14, 1898; m Lowell B Dow adgxfaab
e   Adeline b 1844; m Salisbury Jan 22, 1864, George Chase
f   Edward Dearborn b 1847; d childless Mch 28, 1870
g   Mary b 1849; m John Newell Boyd; 2nd Richard T Keene

Tristram L Dow adgxfda, cordwainer of Seabrook, d June 13, 1911; m Salisbury Feb 26, 1862, Sarah A Dow adgxfaaab. Children:

a   Hattie L b Mch 31, 1863; m July 6, 1879, Frank Merrill (Morrill, State rec)
b   Scott A b Mch 25, 1865
c   Sally A d 1866, ae 13 mos, apparently twin
d   Tristram E b 1869   e   Mabel T b Feb 5, 1872
f   Alvah H b Oct 1, 1875   g   Lowell B b Aug 8, 1877; unm
h   Chester B; untraced

Scott A Dow adgxfdab, shoemaker of Seabrook, d May 14, 1903; m Climena Eaton (her 2nd), ae 27, dau of Samuel C and Apia Ann, Achsah

A, Roxy Ann (all in rec) (Brown). She d Oct 28, 1887; he m 2nd July
12, 1891, Louisa B Sargent, ae 25, dau of Owen Perry and Mary (Sally,
Sargent Gen) A (Eaton). Children:

   a Everett S b June 16, 1886   b Carl A b Nov 6, 1894
   c —— dau b Sept 13, 1896

Everett S Dow adgxfdaba, shoemaker of Seabrook, m Sept 22, 1906,
Alice M Fowler, ae 16, dau of Lowell and Christina (Eaton); div; m
2nd Mch 23, 1909, Lizzie M Fowler, ae 16, dau of Charles A and Margaret
E. Children:

   a —— son b Sept 10, 1907   b —— son b May 17, 1910
   c —— son b Apr 1, 1911

Carl A Dow adgxfdabb, U S Coast Guard of Salisbury, m Aug 6,
1911, Christie Berry, ae 19, dau of Charles and Mary (Hayden) of Haverhill, Mass; 2nd Mch 5, 1915, Sadie L Geldart, ae 26, dau of John W b
Eng and Ellen D (Spofford). No rec of children

Tristram E Dow adgxfdad (called Tristram 3rd) m Feb 14, 1891,
Hattie M Knowles, dau of Lewis E and Ann. Children:

   a Eula Evelyn b Aug 5, 1891; m Amesbury June 7, 1910, Edmund Buck, ae 22,
      b Northfield, Vt, son of Henry H and Cora (Beane). Two children
   b —— son b Sept 21, d Sept 25, 1899

Mabel T Dow adgxfdae m Apr 21, 1888 Edward F Felch; he d;
she m 2nd William Stacy Walton, son of William. Three children by
1st husband:

   a Myron B b 1889; m Feb 20, 1909, Sarah M J Perkins
   b Ernest F b 1891; m Oct 23, 1913, Sadie B Johnson
   c Ralph F b 1893; m July 18, 1914, Viola Hersey
   d Edwin (Walton) b Aug 6, 1897   e Tristram Heyes b Mch 15, 1901
   f Jonathan L b June 6, 1909   g Frank Royce b Feb 5, 1916

Alvah H Dow adgxfdaf lives Seabrook; m Sept 15, 1893, Susia M
Eaton, ae 20, dau of Samuel C and Achsah A (adgxfdab) (Brown). Three
children:

   a —— dau b Sept 15, d Oct 9, 1893   c —— dau b Dec 28, 1908

Edward D Dow adgxff b 1806 (known as Dearborn Dow), carpenter
of Seabrook, d Aug 13, 1880; m Jan 6, 1830, Rhoda Collins d July 26,
1872, ae 74, dau of Tristram and Lydia; m 2nd (her 3rd) Hampton Falls
Sept 5, 1875, Mary Walton, ae 64, b Salisbury, dau of Samuel. Children,
possibly others:

   a Jacob b Apr 29, 1831   b Daniel B b Nov 3, 1833
   c Jonathan S b June 30, 1836   d Samuel, probably d young
   e Betsey L b Dec 25, 1859, Seth Flanders of Salisbury

Jacob Dow adgxffa, cabinet maker of Seabrook, d widower Oct 26, 1887; m June 27, 1854, Betsey F Dow adaimcg. Nine children:

a Samuel E b Dec 3, 1854; d Nov 30, 1897, shoemaker, unm
b Edward D b Dec 2, 1858; untraced   c Willey H d 1863, ae 18 mos
d Lavilla b 1862-3
e Clinda E (family rec). State rec gives Clitidia, 5th child, b 1865-6, dau of
    Jacob S, shoemaker, and Betsey L. M rec gives Kilinda K, dau of Jacob and
    Betsey F, m May 10, 1885, David W Blake. Also m May 23, 1897, Joseph
    J Pelon (Belon, State); 2 children
    Charles J b Apr 27, 1868; d May 25, 1869
g Abbott C b Mch 23, 1870   h Charlotte b Nov 25, 1873
x One child not found

Abbott C Dow adgxffag m Mch 8, 1902, Mary L Eaton, ae 17, dau of Almon and Mary (Wright); moved to Mass; no further rec.

Charlotte T Dow adgxffah m Ipswich Nov 18, 1910, Howard N Jewett, ae 38, son of Newell M and Sarah E (Washburn).

Daniel B Dow adgxffb, shoemaker of Seabrook, d Nov 9, 1902; m Oct 3, 1854, Ruth Ann Brown, dau of Isaac and Mary (Dow) adgxfac. She m 2nd Dec 17, 1917, Alfred C Short, 39 years her junior. This unique interval of 63 years between marriages followed a disagreement with her children regarding her support. Children:

a Rhoda Ann m Warren W Dow adaimbbd
b Alfred Newell b Oct 11, 1858   c Daniel F b 1861
d Charles F b Mch 1866   e —— son b June 7, 1870
f Fred S b 1875   g Emma F b Jan 5, 1879

Alfred N (called Newell) **Dow** adgxffbb, carpenter of Seabrook, m July 22, 1880, Helen F Fowler, ae 19, dau of Richard and E M of Bath, Me. Children, perhaps others:

a Harry E b 1884   b Nettie H b Oct 29, 1887

Harry E Dow adgxffbba, teamster of Seabrook, m June 14, 1905, Gertrude H McAllister, ae 18, dau of John D and Adeline (Eaton); div; m 2nd Feb 6, 1914, Martha A Perkins, ae 18, dau of Freeman and Esther A (Souther). Two children by 1st wife; not found.

Nettie H Dow adgxffbbb d Apr 27, 1911; m July 20, 1909, Samuel A Brown, son of Charles C and Emma L. Children:

a Helen Courtland b Mch 7, 1910   b Harry C b Apr 9, 1911

Daniel F Dow adgxffbc, shoemaker of Seabrook, m Aug 20, 1881, Hannah A Merrill, ae 17, dau of Frank S and Martha J.

Charles F Dow adgxffbd m July 14, 1889, Annie Lowell Dow adgxfaba d Oct 26, 1909; 2nd Dec 18, 1917, wid Maude H Foote, dau of Wesley A Janvrin. Children:

a Flora May b Jan 8, 1890; d Feb 28, 1890
b Flora May b June 11, d Aug 30, 1892
c Helen F b May 10, 1898; m Dec 30, 1914, Charles A Souther; child,—Annie
    Lowell b July 15, 1915
d Son b Jan 14, d Jan 17, 1904   e Ruth E b Aug 25, 1905

Fred S Dow adgxffbf, shoemaker of Seabrook, m Mch 9, 1895, Mildred E Natter, ae 19, b Salem, Mass, dau of Otis and Addie. At least three:

a —— d Nov 28, 1895 b —— son b Apr 24, 1897
x Carroll Erwin b Salisbury Aug 7, 1903

Jonathan S Dow adgxffc, farmer of Seabrook, d Aug 5, 1900; m Hannah J Brown b July 1840, d Dec 30, 1918, dau of Abram and Susan J (Dow) adaimea. Children, perhaps others:

a Charles A b Dec 1856; d Nov 30, 1876, shoemaker, unm
b Abram H b 1860; of Seabrook m Nov 27, 1881, Sarah M Eaton, ae 18, dau of Abner L and Philena R
c Simeon J b Feb 8, 1871

Simeon J Dow adgxffcc, shoemaker of Seabrook, m May 22, 1890, Estella M Buckman, ae 17, dau of James A and Clarissa J; 2nd Aug 27, 1897, Lillian M Eaton, ae 17, dau of Jacob F and Eliza A. Children:

a Melissa E b Aug 5, 1893
b Jonathan S b Apr 17, 1898; d June 20, 1917, unm
c Leroy E b Oct 20, 1900 d Charles b May 15, 1904
e Lunetta P d Sept 28, 1906 f —— son b and d May 12, 1908
g Nancy May b June 13, 1912; d Feb 25, 1914
h Ednah May b Aug 29, 1915

Melissa E Dow adgxffcca m Oct 4, 1911, Frank E Carter. Children:

a Irene Agnes b Aug 20, 1912 b Carlene Frances b Apr 13, 1915

Kesia Dow adgxg appears in Salisbury rec as mateless twin b Sept 3, 1724. Amesbury sets matters right: Kesiah, dau Elihue of Hampton Falls and Robert Collins, son of Tristram and Judith, m Feb 2, 1763. This staunch Quaker family often intermarried with Dow.

J OSIAH Dow adh, weaver, d Apr 18, 1718, ae 39; his inheritance a farm in the part of Seabrook known as New Boston. Greatly esteemed by his father, he was named as executor of his will. Ability, especially business ability, was very unequally divided among the sons of Joseph Dow. Josiah and Samuel were much the abler; Samuel followed the path of least resistance and left the Friends, thus materially widening his horizon. Josiah remained within that body, was a leader of it, working to compel recognition of its members and its merits. Untimely death cut off a man who was a respected councillor even among the churchmen. Fortunately, he had a son who during a very long life upheld the dignity of the body.

His posterity has been of all the lines the most consistent until the general decay of Quakerism about the middle of the 19th century. His is the only line which contains Friends today without a break, one Mass family now in the Society. As a whole the line is more than usually homogeneous, rather high in standards of morals, very seldom containing marked genius, but from which failure through turpitude is unknown. Its best line is one which left Seabrook early and got the rejuvenating energy of a pioneering environment. Of intermarriages in a small circle of families there was fully as much as in other lines. A majority of the early marriages were with the original Quaker families of Seabrook, Gove, Chase, Purington, Green, Collins, Brown. We have noted in the ab lines that a great majority of early marriages were with other pioneer families of Hampton until every one in town could trace blood relationship with every other one. We note also among the non-Quaker Dows of Seabrook, a majority of marriages, even to today, have been with Eaton, Felch, Fowler, Walton.

No doubt, an influence lasting through nine generations was the moral standards maintained in the family in Seabrook at a time when the local standards were at their lowest. No doubt, the exceptional abstention from drink during the half century when drunkenness was a daily custom has affected the morale of the family as a whole for over a century.

Josiah m (int pub Sept 22) Oct 6, 1710, Mary Purington, dau of James by his 1st wife Elizabeth. This couple came from York, Me. After her death, James located in Seabrook; m Lydia Mussey of the well known Quaker family. He was lost at sea, ae 55, but the Friends rec do not give any date. Children:

a Winthrop b Sept 20, 1711   b Abraham b May 29, 1713
c Abraham b May 2, 1714. Both Abrahams appear in rec; either one d almost at birth, or there is an error and there was only one Abraham
d Elizabeth b May 8, 1716
e Anna b Apr 18, 1718, the day of her father's death

Winthrop Dow adha, cordwainer of Seabrook, was one of the earliest in that trade, patriarch of the Seabrook Friends for many years. His name appears on many documents, witness of the will of John Dow adb, very frequently as appraiser of estates. His religion barred him from political preferment. He and the other Seabrook Friends refused to sign the Association Test. He m Rachel Gove, dau of Ebenezer and Judith (Sanborn), by whom 1 child; m 2nd June 30, 1741, Elizabeth Green b July 23, 1724, d July 23, 1818, dau of Jeremiah and Dorothy (Conner). He appears in 1790 census 1a, 4c, perhaps including some grand dau. He d Seabrook Aug 6, 1802. Second, 3rd and 4th child appear in Book 2 Hampton Falls town rec, all others in Book 1. No reason to think the list incomplete:

a Mary b Apr 8, 1734
b Winthrop b Oct 15, 1742. Winthrop Dow m Seabrook by Rev Sam Perley June 8, 1773, Mehitable Scelley (more often Selley, later always Cilley), niece of the wives of Elihu Dow adgx and Bildad Dow adah. Apparently Winthrop's father disinherited him and named a younger son Winthrop, quite in line with the character of the stern Quaker father. Winthrop appears in Seabrook 1790 with wife and no children
c Abial Green b Oct 21, 1744; unheard of later
d Josiah b Oct 28, 1746
e Dorothy b 1747 or 1748; m (Dolly) Dec 11, 1769, Richard Gove, son of John and Hannah (Worthen) of Seabrook
f David b Apr 9, 1749   g Elijah b Aug 4, 1758
h Winthrop b Feb 14, 1760   i Ann b 1762; d May 24, 1835, unm

Mary Dow adhaa of Hampton Falls (there being no Seabrook yet) m June 22, 1752, Thomas Chase, son of John of Hampton and Anna (Rundlett). As their dau Rachel m Jeremiah Dow adgge, this line becomes of double interest:

Aquila (1) Chase m Elizabeth Preston. John (2) Chase m Elizabeth Bingley, dau of Elizabeth; 2nd Lydia Challis, John (3) Chase (by 1st wife) b about 1680, m his 2nd cousin Abigail Chase, had 6 children.

Thomas (1) Chase, brother of Aquila, was pioneer of Hampton; his son Thomas was the first Quaker Chase. James (2) Chase m Elizabeth Green, dau of Judge and Councillor Henry (1) Green (see under ab). Abigail (3) Chase b Aug 27, 1681. John (4) Chase, son of James and Abigail, m Mch 27, 1729, Anna Rundlett (antecedents untraced).

Children of adhaa:

a Nathaniel b June 9, 1753; m Mary Brown
b Amos b July 12, 1756; m Huldah Dow adahb
c Rachel m Jeremiah Dow adgge   d Winthrop m Anna Dow adhafh
e Anna   f Dolly m 1790 Elijah Brown of Weare

Josiah Dow adhad, farmer of Seabrook, d Nov 13, 1827; m 1773 Judith Hoag div wife of Edward Gove of Seabrook, 12 years his senior. She d; he m 2nd Apr 25, 1775, Lydia Gove, his step dau, b May 21, 1753. Nevertheless, the family continued in the Friends. Josiah's will provides for wife Lydia and 3 grandchildren:

a Judith b June 26, 1775   b Betty b Dec 26, 1779
c Winthrop b Mch 24, 1782   d Abraham b Jan 1, 1785

Judith Dow adhada m Oct 24, 1798, Samuel Challis, Amesbury Friend.   Children:

a   Ruth b Aug 7, 1799   b   David b Mch 3, 1801
c   Josiah Dow b Dec 19, 1802

Betty Dow adhadb d Weare July 17, 1859; m Oct 26, 1804, John Chase b Aug 20, 1782, d Apr 7, 1853, farmer, several times selectman of Weare.   Children:

a   Nathan G b July 17, 1806; m Anna Gove; went to Iowa
b   Lydia G b Jan 3, 1808; m Moses Gove; went to Iowa; 4 children
c   Phoebe H b Mch 4, 1810; m 1845 Enoch Green M D; lived some N H town
d   Josiah Dow b Nov 13, 1811; m Aug 23, 1838, Mary C Breed b Oct 1, 1811, d
      Weare Dec 12, 1886; farmer, teacher, supt of schools; 3 dau
e   Molly B b Aug 2, 1813; d June 23, 1833
f   Hannah G b June 21, 1817; m 1837 Simon Green Gove of Weare; 4 children;
      lived Minneapolis

Winthrop Dow adhadc m Feb 18, 1808, Susanna Chase of Weare; moved 1824 to Lincoln, Vt, where 3 cousins of the Gove family were among a considerable party founding a new Quaker settlement.   There were meetings at Lincoln and Starksborough.   Friends rec have not yet been searched and the list of children was furnished by Mrs Chivey C Dow:

a   Sarah C   b   John C   c   Chivey Chase b 1818
d   Daniel V   e   Winthrop Phila (one family rec says by a 2nd wife)

Sarah C Dow adhadca.   Gove Gen gives Sarah Dow b Oct 31, 1807; identity seems safe in spite of discrepancy of dates.   At all events, **Sarah** Dow of Lincoln d Jan 20, 1880; m Nov 18, 1827, John Gove b Lincoln Mch 14, 1806, son of Winthrop and Judith (Gove).   Children:

a   Laura b Feb 24, 1828; d Apr 12, 1829
b   Albert F b May 2, 1830; m Isora Sherman of Bristol; 4 children
c   Winthrop b Feb 12, 1833; m Lucinda Sumner of Bristol; 1 child
d   Mary Dow b Nov 16, 1834; d Dec 27, 1842

John C Dow adhadcb m Mercy Farr.   Rec gives John L Dow of Lincoln m Huntington Jan 8, 1827, Mary Farr.   She m 2nd Judge William W Pope of Lincoln.   Tombstone rec: Mercy D, wife of Wm W Pope, d Oct 1, 1892, ae 76, 6 mos.   These 2 dates do not fit; latter certainly right.   Two children found by tombstone rec:

a   Alson, son of John C and Mercy Dow, d Oct 13, 1840, ae 2-10-25
b   Edwin C d Dec 14, 1861, ae 19-0-10

Chivey C Dow adhadcc, farmer of Lincoln, owned but 4 acres in 1883; famed in his time as a bear hunter; m Abigail Lydia Butterfield b Vt 1824, dau of James and Lydia (Barnes).   A Bristol, Vt, newspaper in 1917 stated she had just celebrated her 99th birthday by finishing a patchwork quilt, the work of many years.   The Author wrote at once and received a reply from her, who was almost blind, and dictated to her daughter.   She d 1923.   Her letter said there were 3 grandchildren and

4 great grandchildren, but did not name them, nor specify to which children they belonged.   Children, rec in 1850 census:

a   Edwin C b 1842; soldier d Camp Griffith, Va, unm
b   Janet Sherman b 1844   c   John C d Oct 16, 1847
d   John C b 1848
e   Flora Alice b 1850   f   Fred L, twin

Janet S Dow adhadccb m Oct 4, 1862, Gurdeon Tucker b July 17, 1835, son of Rev Joshua and Anna S (Crook).   Children:

a   Edna A b Feb 17, 1866; m Nov 12, 1890, Charles S Dow adhadcea
b   —— son b and d Dec 25, 1871   c   Eugene M b Sept 2, 1878

John C Dow adhadccd lived near the old home; m Elva Barstow (or Barlow), dau of Charles.   Children:

a   Elizabeth   b   Roy   c   —— d in infancy

Flora A Dow adhadcce d 1923; m Wallace Varney; 1 child; div; m 2nd William Briggs, farmer of Bristol; in 1917 mother living with them.

Daniel V Dow adhaded is not found in 1850 census; had no grandchildren.   He d Yates Center, Kan.   A placeless, garbled Vt rec indicates 2 dau:

a   Susan C   b   Estelle A

Winthrop Phila Dow adhadce, farmer near Lincoln, not found in 1850 census; b Oct 13, 1839, d Dec 27, 1896, m Feb 1860 Matilda Buttles d Nov 1873; 2nd 1874 Ruby Alger d Dec 25, 1896.   Children:

a   Jennie C b Aug 18, 1861   b   Cora A b Aug 21, 1863
c   Charlie S b June 27, 1867   d   Kate Lulu b Aug 29, 1869
e   Ervine Lavinia b Nov 25, 1875
f   Guy W b Oct 25, 1877; d Mch 6, 1897
g   Ruth Bessie b June 5, 1880; d Feb 26, 1890
h   Clinton Sanford b Dec 11, 1882   i   John Chivey b Dec 23, 1884
j   Samuel C b Mch 17, 1889; d Feb 28, 1897
k   Grace May b June 18, 1890; d 1903
l   Lali Ida b Aug 15, 1894; d Aug 29, 1896

Jennie C Dow adhadcea m Nov 3, 1880, Sanford J Johns; 2nd Walter B Palmer.   Children, by 1st husband:

a   —— dau b and d same day
b   Nellie Matilda m Walter Labounty; dau,—Margaret Nellie

Cora A Dow adhadceb m June 1891 George Harrington; 2nd Will Adams.

Charlie S Dow adhadcec, farmer of East Charlotte, Vt, m Nov 12, 1890, Edna Anna Tucker adhadccba.   Children:

a   Beulah Janet b July 1892; teacher of East Hardwick
b   Bessie May b Feb 14, 1895; m May 16, 1921, Arthur J St George; dau,—Ruth Elizabeth b May 7, 1922
c   Roy Winthrop b Nov 28, 1898; d July 5, 1911

Kate L Dow adhadced m Feb 12, 1891, Arthur Cronk.

Ervine L Dow adhadcee m Eugene M Tucker adhadccbe; div; m 2nd George Santau.

Clinton Sanford Dow adhadceh m Retta Birkett. Children:

a Ruby Louise   b Marion

Abraham Dow adhadd d Seabrook Feb 6, 1822; m Weare Oct 25, 1809, Dolly Chase of Deering b Feb 2, 1787, d 9 mo: 29: 1843, dau of Amos adhaab and Elizabeth (Kimball). Children:

a Lydia Gove b Apr 5, 1812; m Mch 11, 1847, John Gove of Seabrook, son of John and Deborah (Nason). No children
b Elizabeth Chase b July 26, 1816; m 10 mo: 10; 1838, Jonathan Gove, son of Richard and Sarah (Morrison)
c Ruth Challis b Mch 4, 1820; m 11 mo: 5: 1846, John Weare Jr, son of John and Lydia of Hampton Falls

Elizabeth C Dow adhaddb lived Seabrook in the Gove homestead built 1713; d May 23, 1870; m Jonathan Gove b Oct 4, 1810, d Oct 17, 1890. Only child:

a Sarah Emma b Dec 29, 1839; d Mch 22, 1895, unm

Dorothy Dow adhae m Richard Gove b Jan 20, 1748-9, d July 1832; lived Seabrook in the old Edward Gove homestead. Children:

a Jonathan m Dolly Gove; Friends of Lincoln; 4 children
b Winthrop m Judith Gove; Friends of Lincoln; of 7 children, 3 bore the middle name Dow. In all over 25 Goves have had Dow for middle name
c Richard, Friend of Seabrook
d Josiah m Delia Gove; Friends of Lincoln; their oldest son m Mary Butterfield, dau of William and Hannah

An interesting line: Winthrop Gove adhaeb b Seabrook 1773, d Lincoln, Vt, 1853; m 1800 Judith Gove, dau of Judith, who was dau of John Gove and Martha (Dow) adaha. Lucy Gove, dau of Winthrop and Judith, b Weare 1803, d Lincoln 1865, m Solomon Varney. Their dau Lydia b Lincoln 1823, d 1889, m 1840 William Butterfield Jr, nephew of bcfiff. Their son Charles G Butterfield m Ella M Batchelder and moved 1894 to Easthampton, Mass. Their dau is Myrtie Alice Butterfield, now a music teacher of Easthampton and an accomplished amateur genealogist. She checked up and corrected all the adhadc line, copied all cemetery inscriptions at Lincoln and gave to the Author sketches and local color of the Quaker settlements at Lincoln and Starksboro made from Weare, almost every member of which is related to Dow by blood, marriage or both.

David Dow adhaf, farmer of Hampton Falls, moved to Weare; d May 2, 1828; m (int pub 12: 17: 1872) Mary Gilman b Aug 16, 1750, d 1815. Census 1790 gives them 2a, 3b, 4c. Children, Amesbury Friends rec:

a Winthrop b Oct 12, 1773   b Betty b Nov 20, 1775
c David b Jan 4, 1777   d Elijah b Feb 25, 1779

e   Dolly b Mch 28, 1781; m 1802 Thomas Davis, son of David Dow m Henniker
    1835
f   Mary b June 2, 1785; m June 22, 1802, Aaron Gove
g   Jonathan b Feb 15, 1788
h   Anna b Aug 14, 1790; m Oct 25, 1809, Winthrop Chase adhaad of Henniker;
    son Jonathan Dow b June 18, 1817; m Weare 1839
x   Polly. State rec gives Polly, dau of David and Mary, m Weare May 1, 1800,
    Samuel Morrison of Henniker

Winthrop Dow adhafa went with his father to Weare; farmer and miller, d Feb 28, 1842; m Dec 31, 1799, Sarah Montgomery b Weare Mch 28, 1774, d Dec 30, 1863.   Children:

a   Abraham b Nov 28, 1800   b   David b Sept 9, 1802
c   Mary b Mch 25, 1805; m Dec 26, 1833, James Howe of New Ipswich, shoe-
    maker; moved back to Weare
d   Nancy b July 5, 1807; d May 25, 1883
e   Winthrop b Aug 29, 1810   f   Hannah b Dec 6, 1812
g   William Montgomery b May 2, 1815   h   Josiah b Nov 16, 1817

Abraham Dow adhafaa in 1850 farmer of Washington, N H, assessed $2,000; moved to Weare; d July 2, 1878; m July 21, 1824, Lucretia Caldwell b 1800, d July 28, 1884, dau of Daniel and Mary (Paige).
    Children:

a   Julia A b May 19, 1825   b   Clarissa H b Oct 1, 1826
c   Mary A b 1826; in 1850 census
d   Daniel R b Aug 23, 1834; d Mch 30, 1836
e   Caroline E b Dec 25, 1836; d July 30, 1853

Julia A Dow adhafaaa d Aug 1, 1858; m Oct 29, 1850, Henry Train. Children:

a   Ansel   b   Arthur H of Fitchburg, Mass

Clarissa H Dow adhafaab m Jan 28, 1847, Joseph Clark Jones b Washington May 25, 1825; son of Charles and Abigail (Seaverns); no children. He was captain of militia and several times selectman of Washington; m 2nd Mrs Mary F (Carr) Morrill.

David Dow adhafab succeeded to the Weare farm and sawmill; in 1850 crushed one of his legs; confined to a chair 24 years; d Dec 13, 1874; m Oct 23, 1827, Rhoda Shaw b Jan 8, 1806, d Sept 4, 1853; m 2nd Aug 16, 1855, Mrs Sarah J Taylor b East Tilton Nov 20, 1811.   Children:

a   John Quincy b Feb 22, 1829   b   Sherburn b June 18, 1831
c   Elijah b June 1, 1834   d   Sarah J b Apr 7, 1836; d June 26, 1853
e   Charles b Chichester Feb 2, 1839
f   Almon b July 21, 1841; d Aug 27, 1863, in 16th N H
g   William Henry b Dec 29, 1843
h   James Irving b June 29, 1849; d Aug 15, 1869; slipped while a child, crippled
i   Irving (not lastborn) d in infancy

John Q Dow adhafaba, machinist of Weare, d Feb 6, 1911; m 1854 Sarah Jane Dow adhagbb d Weare Mch 5, 1911.   Child:

a   Charles Larin b Seabrook 1861

Charles L Dow adhafabaa m East Deering Mch 23, 1884, Carrie E Carter, ae 19, dau of James P and Nell (Blaisdell). Children:

a Hannah Jane b Weare May 9, 1884   b Archie C b Fitchburg 1887

Archie C Dow adhafabaab m Hillsboro Sept 12, 1908, Mabel F Patten, ae 19, dau of William and Louise (Currier).

Sherburn Dow adhafabb, machinery manufacturer of Fitchburg, d Dec 9, 1882; m Dec 31, 1854, Harriet A Young, both of Pembroke; 2nd Asenath H ——. No rec of children

Charles Dow adhafabe, railroad engineer of No Weare, d Deering May 11, 1893; m Dec 19, 1868, Laura A Emery b Deering May 1, 1839, d Epping Mch 1, 1901, dau of Jonathan Rounds and Ruth (Diamond). No children.

William Henry Dow adhafabg, machinist, d widower Weare June 13, 1906; wife not stated; no rec of children.

Winthrop Dow adhafae, farmer of Weare, assessed $2,000 in 1850; m May 28, 1840, Betsey L Downing b Deering May 23, 1817, d Aug 28, 1871. Children:

a Sarah E b Sept 12, 1841; m Dec 19, 1878, James Henry Wallace of Weare b Feb 8, 1838
b James W b Dec 10, 1851; d in infancy
c Frank C b Oct 12, 1853; d Aug 29, 1854
d J Herbert b Dec 20, 1856; d July 8, 1868

Nancy Dow adhafad of Weare d May 25, 1883; m 1827 Reuben Smith d Pike's Peak, Colo, son of William and Jane (Montgomery). Children:

a Sarah L b 1835; m 1861 Albert S Fisher
b Mary J b 1839; m John T Hutchins
c George W b 1843; d Sept 10, 1855

Hannah Dow adhafaf m Nov 17, 1836, John W Chase b Jan 30, 1813, d Oct 25, 1877, son of John and Sarah (Harmon). Children:

a Alfred W b 1840; d Apr 30, 1877   b Sarah E b 1847; d Sept 7, 1863
c Frank W b 1853; d in infancy   d George S b 1854
e Sarah M b 1858; m 1878 Oliver E Branch

William M Dow adhafag appears in 1850 census shoemaker of Washington; realty assessed $1,000; later machinist of Lawrence, Mass; d Mch 30, 1866. Census 1850 gives a William B Dow b N H 1841 in this family; unrecognized. William M m Dec 14, 1839, Mary Jane Goodale b Deering Oct 23, 1819, d Lewiston, Me, Apr 7, 1897, dau of Jonathan and Lucy (Locke). Children:

a Wesley W b Mch 8, 1841; d Aug 11, 1863, unm
b Albert F b Feb 3, 1844   c Emma J b Apr 12, 1846
d Ella M b May 7, 1849; m July 10, 18—, Lucius E Hoyle of Rochester, N Y; children,—Maria, Milton, Isabella

e   Mary L b Mch 20, 1854; m Mch 21, 1877, George W Putnam of Providence,
    R I; children,—Alice, Frank
f   Frank W b Oct 10, 1857; d July 14, 1877, unm

Albert F Dow adhafagb, corporation president of Fall River, Mass,
d 1922; m Jan 4, 1871, Mary Adeline Everett.   Only child:

a   Walter E, succeeded to his father's business, Fall River

Emma J Dow adhafagc, living 1922 Berkeley, Calif; m Apr 18,
1866, George D Armstrong of Lawrence.   Children:

a   Byron Wesley b May 24, 1867; of Greenfield, Mass; 2 children
b   Edward Dow b Sept 22, 1872; in 1922 of Hercules, Calif; grad Harvard; 4
    sons
c   Helen Standish b July 30, 1877; m Joseph Dawson Sinkerson of Berkeley; 1
    dau
d   Emma Dow b Feb 28, 1882; grad Smith College; m Herbert Oakes; 1922 of
    Belmont, Mass; 1 dau

Josiah Dow adhafah, farmer of Weare, d Mass Mch 31, 1901, m
May 9, 1844, Sarah Peaslee b Apr 12, 1818, d Apr 26, 1897, dau of Abner
and Betsey (Patch).   Children:

a   Mary E b 1845; d May 20, 1848
b   Minerva E b Jan 10, 1847; m Charles Shackford of Boston, Mass; children,—
    William J b Jan 9, 1870; Albion C b Mch 27, 1874
c   Clara b Jan 29, 1850

Clara Dow adhafahc m 1869 Charles Blood.   Children:

a   Frederick E b Nov 14, 1870   b   Frank b Jan 27, 1876
c   Clara b July 10, 1887

Betty Dow adhafb m June 10, 1799, Simon Brown, who came to
Weare from Seabrook, son of Enoch and Betty.   Children:

a   Eliza m William Smith of Henniker
b   Mary m Joseph Hussey of Henniker
c   Simon m Weare 1827 Mary A Getchell; served 1820 in Seminole war
d   David m Weare 1827 Lavina Dudley; left a son George

David Dow adhafc of Weare d Apr 13, 1856; farm assessed $1,700
in 1850; m Jan 1, 1806, Jemima Robbins b Stow, Mass, 1799, d July 10,
1867.   Helen A Dow b 1841 in this family 1850.   Children:

a   Daniel Gilman b Aug 1, 1806
b   Ruth b Apr 2, 1808; m 1830 Sumner Stanley
c   Lewis b Dec 9, 1809; d Sept 10, 1837, unm
d   George A b Dec 27, 1811   e   Mary Ann b Jan 7, 1814
f   Moses b Nov 18, 1816; d Nov 9, 1832
g   Adeline Robbins b May 1, 1817; m 1840 Thomas Stearns of Hollis
h   Almeda b Dec 24, 1818; d Feb 18, 1846
i   Ceba H b Feb 6, 1822   j   Cynthia H b Feb 6, 1822

Daniel G Dow adhafca of Weare d Sept 21, 1875; m Mary Eliza
Chase.   Children:

a   Harriet Melissa b Aug 15, 1827   b   Amos Chase b Henniker Dec 20, 1829
c   Daniel Gilman b Mch 19, 1832; m 1857 Jennie Van Loan Raymond; untraced
d   Edward Chase b Deering Oct 11, 1834
e   Ann C b July 15, 1837; m Nov 7, 1856, Gilbert P Hill of Bedford

Harriet M Dow adhafcaa m 1856 Lawrence Keiley b May 20, 1831.
Children:

  a Jennie M b Apr 3, 1857   b Willie L b Nov 14, 1865; d Aug 13, 1875
  c Mamie A b Dec 2, 1869; d Oct 14, 1884

Amos C Dow adhafcab, tinsmith, d widower Apr 3, 1900; m Sarah
Jane Nichols d Oct 27, 1899, dau of Henry and Mary (Chase); at one time
official of Boscawen, lived Pembroke and Laconia.   Possibly he m twice,
for d rec of 1st born gives mother as Jane Morse.   Children (at least 5):

  a Frank b Manchester, N H; d Lawrence, Mass Nov 14, 1903, ae 50-9-0, bur
     Laconia.   Not stated if married
  b Fred (2nd child, State rec) b Pembroke Apr 30, 1858; untraced
  c Edward b 1866   d George Alvin b Laconia 1870

Edward Dow adhafcabc, tinsmith of Gilford, m May 11, 1887,
Lizzie M Johnson.

George A Dow adhafcabd, spinner, later tinsmith of Laconia, m
Mch 29, 1890, Annie M Whitton, ae 16, dau of Joseph J; div; m 2nd
July 15, 1905, Mary (Dryer) Henry, div, ae 34, dau of Henry and Mary
(Clark).   Children:

  a Amos Chase b Feb 20, d Sept 18, 1892
  b Mildred Hazel b Feb 13, 1893
  c Marion Francilla b June 5, 1895; d Lakeport Oct 20, 1912

Hazel Marie Dow adhafcabdb, b Gilford, m Worcester, Mass, May
20, 1909, Richard Massey, ae 25, b Turkey, son of Pashere and Melliceka
(Sheame).

Edward C Dow adhafcad, mechanic and blacksmith, m Henniker
Mch 7, 1869, Roanna E Chase, ae 24, dau of Eli and Hannah of Weare,
d May 1879 ae 24, 5 mos; m 2nd No Weare Aug 27, 1881, Emily A Webber
ae 31, b Warner.   Children:

  a Herbert E b Apr 13, 1870; d Deering Mch 7, 1871
  b Fannie E b Mch 5, 1888; d Jan 2, 1891

George A Dow adhafcd m Weare Oct 2, 1839, Nancy W Keniston
(Keneson, State rec) of Pittsfield d Northwood Feb 6, 1887, dau of Samuel and Lois (Chesley);   blacksmith of Concord;   no rec of d or children

Mary Ann Dow adhafce m Oct 15, 1835, John Lyman Green b
Weare May 14, 1810, son of Simon and Naomi (Tewksbury); moved to
Starksboro, Vt, a Quaker colony; later to Spring Valley, Minn.   There
he d June 1887, she Jan 17, 1889.   Children:

  a Ellen b Sept 27, 1836; m Abner Lyman
  b Sewall b Apr 11, 1839; d 1856
  c Franklin Homer b May 26, 1841; d Aug 9, 1913; m Anna Neill
  d George b July 18, 1843; d 1860
  e Emma b 1847; d June 1877; m Henry C Roberts
  f Wesley b Jan 2, 1849; d before 1900; m Sarah Canfield
  g David Edson b Apr 22, 1852; d Mch 1, 1914; m Rosetta Babcock

Cynthia H Dow adhafcj m Apr 29, 1845, Enos Hoyt of Weare, son of John 2nd Mary (Baker); 2nd Charles G Thayer. Children, all by 1st husband:

   a Francelia M b Mch 6, 1847; m 1864 Hazen Colby of Manchester; 2nd Henry Kendall
   b Charles F b Dec 11, 1849; m Mary Paige   c Flora b Oct 9, 1851
   d Clara b Aug 17, 1854; m Robert Young
   e Lilla F b Nov 8, 1859; m John Raymond
   f William H b June 23, 1860; m Anna Fielding

Elijah Dow adhafd, farmer and shoemaker of Weare, d Dec 15, 1827; m May 30, 1804, Hannah Chase b Dec 31, 1785, d Feb 15, 1809, dau of Nathaniel and Mary (Brown); 2nd Apr 10, 1910, Eunice Robbins b Stowe, Mass, Aug 4, 1781, d Weare July 5, 1870. Children:

   a John b Dec 28, 1805; d July 5, 1810
   b Hannah b Dec 20, 1807; m Sept 23, 1829, Josiah Dow adhaeb
   c Greeley b Feb 6, 1809; d Dec 25, 1815
   d Dorcas Neal b Dec 25, 1810   e Mary Chase b Dec 20, 1812
   f Nathan C b Dec 19, 1814   g Greeley Elijah b Sept 18, 1818
   h Peace Chase b Dec 17, 1821; d Nov 29, 1896, unm
   i Levi Hoit b Dec 17, 1821   j Ann Catherine b Sept 20, 1825

Dorcas N Dow adhafdd m Oct 13, 1833, Harrison Crafts b Oct 27, 1802, of Washington, Vt; moved 1857 to Bradford, Vt. Children:

   a Mary Susan b Feb 18, 1835; d Aug 1836
   b Aurora Rosina b Aug 3, 1836
   c Henrietta b June 24, 1838; d Apr 2, 1839
   d Melina Atwood b Feb 22, 1840   e Pliny Earl b Apr 3, 1842
   f Warren Levi b June 6, 1846   g Emily Ann Webster b Oct 26, 1849

Mary C Dow adhafde m Mch 27, 1832, Horace Tucker b Henniker Jan 21, 1809, d Apr 5, 1866; 2nd June 23, 1870, Burton Wadsworth d Feb 24, 1877. Children:

   a Lucy Maria b Henniker Nov 2, 1832; m Nov 11, 1852, B Frank Philbrick of Weare
   b Charlotte Mary b July 1, 1835; m Apr 3, 1856, William H Smith of Henniker
   c Eliza Jane b Dec 27, 1837; m Oct 13, 1857, Walter B Barnes of Henniker
   d Greeley Dow b May 1, 1841; lived Henniker
   e Orlando Horace b Mch 11, d Sept 6, 1852
   f John Smith b Mch 15, 1856; m Mch 15, 1875, Louisa Simonds of Keene

Nathan C Dow adhafdf, farmer of Weare, in 1850 shoemaker, assessed $500; m Feb 27, 1840, Mary E Leighton b Farmington Oct 26, 1813, d Weare Oct 30, 1862, dau of John and Mary (Furber); 2nd Jan 7, 1864, Abigail O Hussey b Henniker May 20, 1817, d Weare Aug 8, 1903, dau of Daniel and Elizabeth M (Osborne). Children:

   a Luella E b Oct 25, 1850; d Sept 2, 1852
   b John Leighton b Feb 6, 1852   c Luella E b Jan 1, 1857

John L Dow adhafdfb, farmer of Weare, m Nov 21, 1882, Lizzie J Sweet b Bay Verte, N B, Nov 10, 1855, d Dec 25, 1883, dau of Joshua C and Jane (Richardson) Goodwin; 2nd Sept 21, 1898, Jessie Sawyer, ae 26, b Minot, Me, dau of Albert L and Abby M (Campbell). Child:

   a —— son b and d Dec 25, 1883

Greeley E Dow adhafdg d Aug 28, 1907; in 1850 farmer of Weare, assessed $1,400; m June 9, 1847, Lydia B Holder b Bolton July 20, 1825, d Dec 4, 1914; moved 1852 to Bolton, Mass, where a colony of the Friends still exists. Children:

    a   Sarah Holder b Apr 13, 1848; m Edward Sawyer of Berlin; 1 child d in infancy;
        she d Apr 10, 1888
    b   James G b Aug 4, 1849; d Dec 29, 1918; m Aug 24, 1870, Maria Montgomery
        living 1923; only dau d Dec 20, 1877
    c   Alfred b Apr 29, 1851   d   George Edward b Dec 10, 1854
    e   William Henry b Aug 20, 1857

Alfred Dow adhafdgc has been 44 years a farmer; celebrated 1922 his golden wedding; a consistent Friend in the meeting which was founded over a century ago; m Nov 27, 1872, Alice M Wheeler of Bolton, for 50 years pastor at Bolton. Children:

    a   Alfred Walter b Mch 12, 1875; m June 12, 1904, Hannah Busk b Finland, ae
        31, dau of Herman and Johanna (Oldricka); d Oct 17, 1919; only dau b Apr
        2, d Apr 3, 1912; now of Berkeley, Calif
    b   Susan Lydia b Jan 24, 1877; teacher; since 1919 principal of Bolton Junior
        High School; unm
    c   Stephen Arlon b Apr 4, 1884
    d   Mary Alice b Oct 18, 1881; teacher; invalid at home since 1914

Stephen A Dow adhafdgcc of Berkeley, Calif, m May 1, 1912, Stella Brownell of New Mexico. Children:

    a   Arlon Brownell b June 12, 1913   b   Margaret Carolyn b Sept 20, 1916
    c   Marianna b Jan 19, 1919

George E Dow adhafdgd of Berlin, Mass, d Feb 28, 1917; m June 8, 1887, Alice Lillian Wheeler b Nov 8, 1863. Children:

    a   Sarah Helena b Sept 13, 1889; 1923 a high school teacher Monte Vista, Colo
    b   Ruth Nancy b July 2, 1893; in 1923 high school teacher Fall River, Mass

William H Dow adhafdge, blacksmith and lumber dealer of Bolton, m Nov 8, 1881, Ella P Powers b Bolton Oct 1, 1858, d Jan 5, 1891; 2nd C A Echert, b Arlington 1852. Children:

    a   Edna E b Oct 23, 1882   b   Esther Powers b May 9, 1886
    c   Aaron W b Jan 1, 1891

Edna E Dow adhafdgea m 1913 Charles Maguire. Children:

    a   Katherine Aileen b Feb 10, 1914   b   Jean Edna b Sept 23, 1915
    c   Ella Powers b Dec 27, 1916   d   Edith Charlotte b Nov 15, 1918

Esther P Dow adhafdgeb m —— Norman: a son:

    a   Philip; in 1923 in Mass Agric College

Aaron W Dow adhafdgec m 1916 Abbie Mank. Children:

    a   Richard b Aug 6, 1916   b   Fanny Elizabeth b July 7, 1919
    c   George Stanley b Feb 25, 1922

Levi Hoit Dow adhafdi, miller and farmer of Weare, m Nov 18, 1849, Aurora M Waite b Newport Sept 23, 1826, d Mch 29, 1902, dau of Thomas; took a prominent part in local politics, 6 years selectman, generally representative to Legislature, supervisor, or some other town or county office.   Children:

    a   Charles H b Sept 11, 1852.   News clipping Oct 9, 1896: "The body of Charles Dow, who disappeared last Tuesday, was found in the river today.   He was 44 and unm.   It is not known whether it was accident or suicide." State rec gives: Charles H Dow, laborer and Elsie (Eaton) b Weare 1861 a dau,—Gladis b Aug 6, 1887
    b   Nellie M b June 23, 1855   c   Emma L b Dec 3, 1857
    d   Herbert L b May 30, 1860; d Weare Jan 31, 1889, unm
    e   Nelson L b July 31, 1862   f   Alfred C b Feb 9, 1865
    g   Ida M b Mch 28, 1867; m 1887 Charles W Thorndyke b 1866, son of William and Sarah A (Osborne)
    h   William b Aug 31, d Sept 11, 1870
    i   Mabel E b Oct 28, 1874; d June 21, 1888

Emma L Dow adhafdic m Apr 12, 1874, Fred O Downing b 1852, son of Oscar and Susan (Cochran).   Children:

    a   Olive F b Sept 28, 1877   b   Herbert A
    c   Bessie E b Mch 6, 1883   d   Elsie T b 1887

Nelson L Dow adhafdie, laborer, d suicide Sept 4, 1898; m May 16, 1883, Lizzie J Rogers, dau of Jeff and Sarah M (Chase), m 2nd Weare May 12, 1898, Thomas F Gilbert.   Children:

    a   Harry L b Aug 21, 1886   b   —— son b Nov 11, 1888

Harry L Dow adhafdiea, farmer of Weare, m Dec 23, 1912, Gladys L White, ae 17, dau of Arthur M and Minnie (Stevens).   Child:

    a   Rosamond Ellen b May 11, 1914

Fred C Dow adhafdif, farmer of Weare, moved to Kansas but returned; m Nellie Rogers b Loudon 1873.   Children, 1 missing:

    a   Archie Chase b No Weare June 12, 1893
    b   Emma Bell b Aug 24, 1894   c   Mabel Aurora b Nov 4, 1896
    d   Levi Jeff b Mch 10, 1899   e   —— b and d June 2, 1907

Ann C Dow adhafdj m Feb 26, 1852 (his 2nd), Harrison Philbrick, carpenter and farmer of Plymouth, b Weare Aug 4, 1822, son of David and Eunice (Clark).   Children:

    a   Hattie Emily b June 22, 1854; m Apr 11, 1874, George S Pierce of Colston, Calif
    b   Sylvia Celestia b Oct 23, 1856; m Dec 11, 1880, A T Whittemore of Concord
    c   Willis Florian b May 9, 1859; m Apr 16, 1887, Lunna Gilbert; of Plymouth
    d   Belle Aurora b Sept 19, 1863; m 1904 David G Lowell

Dolly Dow adhafe m Thomas Davis, son of Thomas.   Two children b Weare, a number of others after they moved to Henniker, of whom:

    a   Levi M b Nov 8, 1807   b   John D b Feb 20, 1809
    c   David Dow m Henniker 1835

Mary Dow adhaff moved to the Quaker colony at Lincoln; m there June 2, 1802, Aaron Gove adahad. We note that fully half their family left the Quaker ranks.   In all the New England colonies of the Friends the same process was going on.   New recruits to the denomination were few.

The members of any colony had become closely related from a long series of intermarriages between a dozen families. When it came time for the young members to marry, the choice was limited. It was seldom that a Friend could induce his or her fiance to join the Society. The result was generally disownment. In addition, the emigrants to the west or nearer, unless they were numerous enough to form a colony of themselves, were forced by every association to join whatever religious persuasion was prevalent at the new home. Thus the Quaker colonies of Vermont disappeared entirely. The children of Mary (Dow) Gove:

a Jonathan Dow b 1803; m Dolly P Gove of Lincoln; 3 children
b Rhoda Breed b Mch 12, 1805; m John Brown of Bristol; 2 children
c David Dow b Dec 27, 1807; m Diantha Meader; 4 children; moved to Minn
d Squiers b Dec 9, 1809; m Louisa Colby; 2nd Clarissa (Kelton) Durfey; 7 children
e Winthrop b 1811; d 1826
f Martha b July 1813; m Lowell Brown; disowned
g John b July 7, 1815; m Maria Tucker; 2nd Lydia Tucker; disowned
h Anna C b 1818; m William Follansbee of Starksboro; disowned
i Charles C b 1820; m Sarah Abbott; 3 dau
j Elijah Dow b 1827; m Louisa Maria Emerson; disowned; moved to Texas

Jonathan Dow adhafg founded the Dow family of Henniker, which town attracted many Quaker families of Weare; d 1815; m Dec 23, 1807, Sally (Sara, rec) Plummer. Children:

a Squire b 1808   b Joseph Plummer b Oct 1812
c Jonathan b Dec 5, 1814

Squire Dow adhafga, farmer of Henniker, d Feb 25, 1879; m Nov 10, 1831, Cynthia Page b 1816. Children:

a Melissa J b Feb 19, 1832
b Sophia P b Jan 17, 1834; m July 8, 1852, Robert Harriman of Lansingburgh, N Y

Melissa J Dow adhafgaa m (Melvina T) Hopkinton Nov 27, 1854, Benjamin Flanders, both of Hopkinton. A son:

a Walter H m Hopkinton 1889; 2nd Manchester 1897

Joseph P Dow adhafgb, paper manufacturer of Henniker, d Aug 22, 1881; m Apr 18, 1841, Eliza Ann Davis b Weare. Children:

a Mary E b 1854; d Feb 28, 1873; m Mch 29, 1871, John A Burnham of Lyndeboro
b Jennie S b Aug 31, 1860; m (Sarah Jane) July 22, 1875, Frank P Moore; a son,—Guy B

Jonathan Dow adhafgc of Henniker m Sept 29, 1836, Anna R Peaslee of Weare b Sept 5, 1817, d Hopkinton Jan 11, 1895, dau of James and Mary (Colby). Children:

a Ann Maria b Dec 6, 1838   b George W S b Mch 9, 1841
c —— d in infancy Jan 11, 1844   d Jackson P b Feb 17, 1845
e John F b Aug 11, 1852
f Mary E b Mch 24, 1857; m Henniker July 25, 1883, Van R Paige

Ann M Dow adhafgca m Jan 1, 1858, John L Garland b N Y City. Children:

    a Fred J m Francestown 1885
    b Hattie M m 1893 Fred M Gordon of Franklin

George W S Dow adhafgcb, farmer and kit manufacturer of Henniker, m Newbury Nov 7, 1862, Mary L Hoyt, ae 19, b Henniker, dau of Nathan and Susan. Children:

    a George H b Mch 5, 1865   b William E b Apr 7, 1868
    c Charles Henry b Nov 10, 1871
    d Orrin H b Aug 19, 1873; 1908 shoe shop worker, Reading, Mass
    e Fred B b Feb 21, 1878
    f Blanche M b Apr 9, 1880; m —— Flanders of Lebanon
    g Percy Duncan b Mch 10, 1885

George H Dow adhafgcba m Oct 6, 1891, Annie B Morse, ae 21, dau of Herbert and Katie (James); 1908 carpenter of Manchester, 1917 carpenter of Henniker.

William E Dow adhafgcbb, shoemaker of Henniker, 1900 laborer, 1915 teamster, div from 1st wife, m 2nd Bradford Dec 25, 1898, Neva B Colburn, ae 23, dau of Josiah B and Belle S (Colby). Child:

    a —— dau b Sutton Mch 9, 1900

Charles H Dow adhafgcbc, meat merchant of Henniker, m Nov 6, 1897, Lucy E Melvin, ae 16, b Sutton, dau of Elgin and Florence (Presby). Children:

    a Clayton Henry b Apr 7, 1899   b Mildred A b Jan 6, 1905
    c Lucille F b May 8, 1906   d —— dau b Dec 18, 1908; all Henniker
    e Mary Florence b Dec 22, 1910   f George Washington b Oct 21, 1916

Orrin H Dow adhafgcbd m Catherine M Driscoll of Reading, Mass; 2 children b Reading; seems to m 2nd, for rec gives 3rd child to Orrin P. and Sadie E Jennings, both of Haverhill:

    a Norbert Orrin b Feb 18, 1901   b Mary Katherine b Sept 18, 1903
    c Bernard Russell b May 16, 1905

Fred B Dow adhafgcbe m Mch 9, 1900, Rookie T Ripley, wid ae 27, of Concord; 1900 manufacturer of Henniker; 1908 conductor of Hudson, N Y.

Percy D Dow adhafgcbg, laborer of Henniker, 1908 surveyor of Henniker; 1915 salesman of Lebanon; m Apr 21, 1906, Ethel M Keddy, ae 19, b Halifax, N S, dau of James U and Mary (McCabe); 2nd Bessie V Heath b 1895. Children:

    a Elsie May b Nov 3, 1906   b Eula Bonnie b Jan 19, 1915

Ethel Maud Keddy got div; m 2nd Barre, Mass, Nov 22, 1910, Thomas W Dorsey, son of John and Julia (Gleason).

Jackson P Dow adhafgcd d Henniker Sept 25, 1910; m 1863 Hannah Jane Hoyt (Hoitt d rec) b June 10, 1840, d Aug 23, 1910, dau of Nathan and Susan (Ward). Children:

 a Arthur Walter b Mch 11, 1864 b Edward b Nov 15, 1866
 c Charles Jonathan b 1872

Arthur W Dow adhafgcda, 1896 stage driver, 1908 mechanic, 1915 constable, m (Walter A), laborer, 1885 Minnie M Halliday b New Boston 1868; 2nd West Hopkinton Sept 30, 1896, Anna Caroline Carr b Hopkinton Feb 28, 1872, d Hopkinton June 28, 1911, dau of Frank H and Mary A (Chandler). Children:

 a Myrtie Mabel Halliday b Apr 10, 1885 b Robert Bruce b June 25, 1899

Edward Dow adhafgcdb, shoemaker of Henniker, m May 22, 1889, Izetta W Cate, ae 17, dau of Daniel S N P and Nellie E (Ashworth); div; m 2nd May 5, 1897, Edith M Sturtevant, ae 22, dau of Herbert and Hattie M of St Johnsbury, Vt. Child:

 a Flossie, at school 1918

Charles J Dow adhafgcdc, farmer of Henniker, m Hopkinton Nov 19, 1893, Clara E Cutler, ae 18, b Hudson, Mass, dau of James and Caroline (Stuart).

John F Dow adhafgce, farmer of Henniker, d widower Mch 9, 1911; m Jan 3, 1878, Roxy L Rowley, ae 28, b Mich, of Henniker, dau of Madison and Sarah (Lewis). Children:

 a Walter Jonathan b Sept 8, 1879; laborer 1915
 b Elmer A b July 14, 1882; farmer 1908

Elijah Dow adhag of Weare d Mch 6, 1836; m Dec 12, 1791, Judith Page b Aug 21, 1766, d Apr 30, 1865, dau of Samuel adbbd dec and Mary of Kensington. Children:

 a Hannah b Jan 16, 1798; m Weare July 13, 1823, Levi Brown of Deering
 b Josiah b Apr 5, 1805

Josiah Dow adhagb, farmer of Weare, d Sept 30, 1889; m Sept 23, 1829, Hannah Dow adhafdb d Weare Apr 22, 1896. Children:

 a Lucinda H b Sept 9, 1832
 b Sarah Jane b Sept 8, 1834; m 1854 John Quincy Dow adhafaba
 c Elijah b Aug 4, 1836 d Aura A b July 5, 1838
 e Eliza C b Feb 5, 1841
 f John Duane b Aug 21, 1847; mechanic, m 1872 Abbie F Cram b Nov 26, 1851, d Weare Feb 9, 1876, dau of Moses and Abial (Gove); a son d young; she m 2nd her cousin John F Cram

Lucinda H Dow adhagba d 1887; m Feb 27, 1856, William T Morse b Oct 23, 1823, son of Jeremiah and Clarissa (Marshall). Children:

 a Bylon L b May 22, 1860 b Aura A b Feb 27, 1862

Elijah Dow adhagbc, farmer of Weare, m Lynn Sept 11, 1871, Eliza A March, ae 30, dau of Eldad and Lydia of Henniker; 2nd Aug 8, 1877, Eliza J Carnes, ae 18, dau of George. Child:

  a Orrin Duane b July 27, 1879; d unm

Aura A Dow adhagbd m Jan 1, 1859, Moses Hanson Clement b June 29, 1839, son of Jonathan Dow adhcbf and Cynthia (Hanson). Child:

  a Julia Emma b Sept 29, 1859

Eliza C Dow adhagbe m (his 2nd) Apr 30, 1863, Moses H Clement, her brother-in-law. Children:

  a Loren Dow b Sept 4, 1865; m Weare 1887
  b Orison b Aug 1, 1867; d Mch 28, 1868
  c Archie W b Jan 31, 1870; m Hillsborough 1891
  d Arthur b Dec 13, 1874; d Oct 9, 1876   e Fred Dow b Oct 5, 1877

Winthrop Dow adhah, farmer of Weare, d May 24, 1835; m 1787 Mary Dow adhcca d July 18, 1825. Children:

  a Anna b July 3, 1788; d 1852
  b Ezra C b Apr 11, 1790; d July 11, 1793
  c Dorcas b Dec 11, 1792; d 1814   d Ruth Gage b Dec 8, 1794
  e Abraham b Aug 5, 1797   f Ezra b Jan 7, 1802; d 1887
  g Lydia b Sept 15, 1805; d 1814

Ruth G Dow adhahd m 1823 Thomas Thorndyke Wilson b 1797, son of John and Mary (Wilson), wheelwright of Concord, moved 1840 to Weare. Children:

  a Henry b 1824; d 1878   b John b 1826; d 1885
  c Wilson b 1828; d 1899
  d Mary Dow b 1830; d 1865; m 1851 Edward L Gove
  e Charles H b 1833; d 1911
  f Lucy P b 1835; d 1917; m 1863 Lindley H Osborne
  g Anna D b 1838; m 1867 Wilson M Page of Chappaqua, N Y; children,— Clarence W m Amy Titus Shotwell, Helen T m Edward Haviland, Albert W physician m Rachel Mason, Charles T m Helen Hobson

Abraham Dow adhahe is the cousin mentioned in Autobiography of Gen Neal Dow as visiting Boston with him and thrashing a party who attempted to impose upon him as a greenhorn. After leaving Weare he taught school in Concord; with money saved there he opened a grocery store in Portland, Me. A few years after marriage he sold this out and bought a farm in West Gorham, where he spent the rest of his life. He m 1826 Jane Adeline Steele of Portland b 1804, d 1881. Children:

  a George Winthrop b 1827; d after 1900   b William Everett b 1831; d 1858
  c James Osgood b 1834; d after 1900
  d Edward Steele b 1836; d 1897   e Mary Elizabeth b 1842; d 1877

George W Dow adhahea and three brothers left home in youth, headed west; went first to Kansas; m 1858 Mary Mabel Coates d 1872-3; 2nd about 1875 Esther Rector; 3rd in Georgia a wid who survived him; a wanderer all his life; caught by the Calif gold fever; returned in a few years to Maine. Thereafter many places in the south, in many businesses. Children, by 1st wife:

a Alice Adeline b 1859; d 1876   b William Steele b 1860; d in infancy

William E Dow adhaheb located in Minn; d Cannon Falls, unm.

James O Dow adhahec, civil engineer, later cattle drover with a market in Red Wing, Minn; m 1857 Angeline M Moody d soon after b of only child; 2nd Nov 13, 1866, Mary Charlotte Hawkins. Children:

a Henry b Portland, Me   b Charles Everett b Aug 30, 1867; d 1894, unm
c Etta Frances b June 29, 1869   d Minnie Louise b July 31, 1871
e Mary Adeline b Aug 10, 1873   f Grace Josephine b Feb 21, 1879
g Fannie Isabel b Sept 10, 1881

Henry Dow adhaheca left home in youth, went to Chicago, next settled in San Francisco; m Leora May Jones of Chicago. They separated 1907; she d San Francisco Mch 6, 1922. Children:

a Clifford Jack   b James Osgood   c Fremont Adrian

Clifford J Dow adhahecaa lived in orphan homes most of the time until he was 12; then a few years with his mother; enlisted in the navy at 17; learned radio; settled 1919 in Maui, Hawaii; has become the best known radio amateur in this country; was the first to catch a message from N Y; replying with a message caught in Minn and relayed to N Y; in 1923 is returning to U S. One child:

a Clifford Jack b 1920

Etta F Dow adhahecc m Apr 9, 1889, Lloyd Wooders of Red Wing. Children:

a Neal Dow b Jan 8, 1892   b Marie Adeline b May 15, 1898

Minnie L Dow adhahecd m James H Drew of Osage, Iowa. Children:

a Charles Kenneth   b Robert   c Richard Earl   d Joseph
e Catherine Jane

Mary A Dow adhahece m Oscar Seebach of Red Wing.

Grace J Dow adhahecf m 1903 Arthur Wilford Wing of Seattle, Wash. Children:

a Ivan   b James   c —— dau b 1917

Edward S Dow adhahed went to Kansas; returned to Portland while still a young man; moved to Falmouth; d Feb 1, 1897, blacksmith, boat builder, carpenter, violin maker; m Portland 1862 Octavia Ann Starling. Children:

a Jane A b 1863   b Julia E b 1867
c Marietta b 1869; d 1884   d William E b 1874

Jane A Dow adhaheda m 1884 John P Hall; lives So Paris, Me; furnished much of the data of the whole adhahe line, which had not been in earlier Dow genealogies.   Children:

    a   Ray Philip b 1885; m 1916 Oena May Whyte; traveling inspector
    b   Marian Frances b 1886; teacher Junior High School, Milton, Mass
    c   Harold Everett b 1897; grad Colby 1917; teacher of languages

Julia E Dow adhahedb m 1887 Edgar H Merrill of Woodfords. Child:

    a   Chester Arnold, b 1888, electrician of Limerick, m 1917 Lillian Matthews

William E Dow adhahedd, grocer, later railroad superintendent of Falmouth, m June 6, 1900, Mabel Ethaline French b Oxford, ae 20, dau of Winfield and Fannie M.   Children:

    a   Edward French b 1901   b   Hilda Elizabeth b July 27, 1904
    c   Edith Josephine b Mch 10, 1906

Ezra Dow adhahf, farmer and tanner of Weare, assessed 1850, $3,000; member of Legislature 1853-4; d Dec 29, 1887; m Aug 3, 1830, Elvira Jane Eaton b Nov 6, 1805, d Weare Jan 8, 1861, dau of Jacob and Jane (Goodwin).   Children:

    a   Mary Jane b 1831
    b   Lydia Ann b May 5, 1835; d Weare Dec 16, 1908, unm
    c   Dorcas b 1837; d 1840   d   Harriet B b 1840; d 1841
    e   Miranda J b Mch 6, 1845; d Weare May 12, 1913, unm

Mary J Dow adhahfa m Aug 10, 1857, Thomas McConnell, tanner of Enfield, b Pictou, N S, Mch 2, 1822.   Children:

    a   Ellsworth Dow b Enfield May 15, 1861; of Minneapolis
    b   George H b Franklin Sept 11, 1871; of Franklin

The adhc line is so well traced that the few disconnected records of Weare are presumably all adha or adah lines. To facilitate ultimate recognition such are collected here.   Elijah Dow adhafac grew to maturity, left dau.

Hannah Dow adhai m Daniel Paige. A son:

    a   John m Weare 1790. Cf adbb

Martha A Dow adhaj b Weare or Franklin (both in rec) m Weare Nov 21, 1846, John Andrews of Weare. A son:

    a   Nelson Harrison m Lyme 1875

Mary E Dow adhak m Samuel Hussey b Feb 22, 1833, son of Andrew and Judith (Gove); lived Berwick, Weare, Bradford; Quakers. Suggests adbab line.

Katherine Dow adhal m Mch 25, 1842, Thomas Eaton b 1818, son of Thomas, both of Weare. No children.

Betsey Dow adham m Weare Aug 12, 1810, Robert Clough, both of Weare.

Josiah Dow (2nd) adhan m Mary (Dow?). A child:

a   Clara E m June 13, 1880, Alonzo Brant, both of Weare

Sarah A Dow wid adhao b Sanbornton Nov 18, 1811, d Weare July 17, 1890, dau of Anthony C (b Sanbornton) and Mary (b Deerfield) (Chase) Hunt.

Abraham Dow adhc, farmer of Seabrook, inherited equally with his older brother the mental and moral characteristics of his father, continuing through a third generation the ideals sought for Seabrook by its original community of the Friends; was a prominent preacher and man of influence; d 1784, will proved Feb 18; m May 5 or July 3 (earlier date perhaps int), 1735, Phoebe Green b June 19, 1715, d July 20, 1816, dau of John and Abial (Marston). It is a notable fact that the greatest longevities recorded in this Book are of Quaker matrons, especially those with rather large families. Phoebe lived 81 years in one house; left 260 descendants, including a 5th generation; was a remarkable woman in character. Children:

a   Josiah b Sept 15, 1736; d young (rec not found)
b   Jonathan b Nov 28, 1737   c   Jedediah b Apr 22, 1739
d   Benjamin b 1742
e   Judith b Mch 12, 1745; m May 17, 1766, Samuel Collins, blacksmith of Lynn, son of Zacchaeus, whose family has intermarried often with Dow
f   Abial (Abigail in will) b Apr 7, 1748; m Mch 9, 1769, John Dow adbad
g   Anna b Jan 1, 1756 (State, 1750, more probable)
h   Abraham b Jan 26, 1757 (State, June 30, 1751)
i   Mary b 1759 (probably several years earlier)

Jonathan Dow adhcb, Quaker preacher, continued for the 4th generation the original ideals of the Seabrook Friends, but realized that a new environment was needed; he located in Kensington; moved 1768 to Weare. The brothers bought full shares in Weare settlement at the same time, Jedediah being the first to move there. There does not seem to have been at any time in Weare any political distinction between Quakers and others. Jonathan was soon elected selectman and served a very long series of terms in the Legislature. His speech of Jan 15, 1788, in opposition to the existence of negro slavery led to its prohibition by the State constitution; he was a member when the Federal constitution was ratified. During his career the Friends of New Hampshire reached their greatest numerical strength and breadth of influence. He d Apr 30, 1814; m Berwick Nov 4, 1760, Keziah Roberts b Jan 27, 1739, d Nov 27, 1826, dau of Stephen and Keziah of Dover. Children:

a   Phoebe b Sept 11, 1761   b   Stephen b Mch 28, 1764
c   Judith b Jan 7, 1766
d   Anna b Feb 29, 1768; m Nov 26, 1795, Levi Hoag, son of Nathan and Miriam of Stratham, both dec
e   Mary b Aug 14, 1774; m Oct 21, 1793, David Green, son of Daniel and Rebecca of Kensington
f   Keziah b May 26, 1776-7; m Carlton Clement

Phoebe Dow adhcba d Henniker Feb 15, 1819, m Dec 23, 1782, Humphrey Peaslee of Weare, son of Moses and Mary (Gove) of Newton; settled in Deering.   Children:

a   Keziah m 1811 Abraham Chase   b   Mary m Dudley Chase
c   Jonathan m Sally Hook   d   Stephen   e   Nancy d young
f   Abraham m Eliza Alcock   g   Humphrey m Abigail Atwood
h   Obadiah   i   Nancy   j   Patience
k   Phoebe m Nathan W Bailey

Stephen Dow adhcbb, farmer, tanner, merchant of No Weare, d July 26, 1842; m Sept 14, 1791, Peace Neal d 1793; 2nd Aug 3, 1797, Lydia Gove b May 31, 1779, d Nov 11, 1832, dau of Daniel and Miriam (Courtland) (Cartland in Gove Gen.)   He moved to Woburn 1841. Children:

a   Peace Neal b Feb 24, 1798
b   Abraham b May 1, 1799; changed his name to Alfred
c   Judith Phillips b Aug 20, 1801   d   Jonathan b Aug 29, 1803
e   Mary Green b Aug 11, 1806   f   Stephen b Jan 13, 1809
g   Moses Gove b June 7, 1811   h   James Neal b May 5, 1814
i   Lydia Gove b Nov 17, 1816   j   Benjamin Franklin b July 2, 1819
k   Emma Maria b Jan 30, 1824

Peace N Dow adhcbba d Como, Ill, Jan 29, 1847; m 1819 Stephen P Breed, tanner, b Jan 30, 1796, d 1871, son of Enoch and Martha (Mower); lived Weare, Concord, Alton, Ill.   He returned and for his last 15 years was station agent at No Weare; m 2nd wid Anna (Green) Huse.   Children:

a   Lydia Ann b Feb 2, 1820; m John Roberts
b   Dana Farrar b Jan 14, 1823
c   Mary Dow b May 17, 1825; m Frank Cushing
d   Eliza Frances b Nov 28, 1830; m Lorenzo Hapgood
e   Caroline Silsby b Dec 14, 1839; m John H Paige

Alfred Dow adhcbbb moved to Alton, Ill; d Oct 1, 1875; m 1832 Betsey Neal Hall b May 20, 1807, d Como July 1839; 2nd 1843 Caroline S Silsby b June 1819.   Children:

a   Mary Eliza b Portland, Me, Oct 3, 1833
b   Ellen Maria b Nov 27, 1835; lived Alton and Woburn, Mass; d Mch 3, 1923
c   Julia b Portland Sept 28, 1837; d Woburn June 15, 1913; many years teacher
     in Alton

Mary E Dow adhcbbba d Brooklyn, N Y, Dec 13, 1908; m Nov 23, 1854, John Shipman of Brooklyn b July 18, 1825, d July 21, 1908. Children:

a   Isabelle b Sept 12, 1855; d Aug 12, 1874
b   Alfred Dow b Sept 10, 1857   c   Caroline b Apr, d Aug 1859
d   Frederick William b Mch 18, 1863

Judith P Dow adhcbbc d Woburn Sept 9, 1877; m 1820 Enoch Breed 2nd b Aug 8, 1795, d Dec 13, 1866, son of Ebenezer and Lydia (Bassett); moved to Woburn 1849.   Children:

a   George Newell 1821-48; m Anna Johnson   b   Clarissa 1827-38

Jonathan Dow adhcbbd d Sept 27, 1893; m Aug 1, 1830, Harriet Chase b Nov 16, 1809, dau of Charles and Fanny (Whittle); 2nd Matilda L Brown. Children:

a   Harriet b Nov 14, 1831   b   Annette m 1856 Thomas Gray
c   Ellen Delilah (Ellen Celende) b Sept 19, 1844
d   Mary m ——; left children,—Lulu and Guy

Ellen C Dow adhcbbdc m June 27, 1861, Joseph Vowels Beers b 1819, d 1867; 2nd 1877 Franklin Doremus Beebe b May 15, 1854, d Jan 8, 1917. They lived St Louis, Mo. After his death, no member of the family surviving, she used what little money was left to enter a St Louis Home for the Friendless, where she now (1926) resides. Children:

a   John d 1863, ae 5 mos   b   Nathan Lee b Aug 20, 1868; d May 27, 1884
c   Mabel b Nov 5, 1870; d Feb 8, 1913; m John W Weston; no children

Mary G Dow adhcbbe d Wakefield, Mass, Nov 1871; m Goffstown May 5, 1836, Hial Plumley Cram hotel keeper, b Sept 27, 1807, son of Daniel and Lydia (Hadley); lived Weare, Woburn, Boston, Wakefield. Children:

a   Charles Choate b 1841; d 1863
b   Emma Dow b Apr 27, 1842; d Sept 7, 1843

Stephen Dow adhcbbf of Weare, Portland and Woburn, d Boston Jan 4, 1887; m May 24, 1836, Celende, dau of Gen Thompson, b Feb 13, 1816, d Nov 1, 1890. Children:

a   Ellen Thompson b May 28, 1838   b   Alfred Abijah b Apr 6, 1841
c   Harriet Josephine b Mch 30, 1843
d   James Henry b Feb 4, 1845; d Woburn July 26, 1846
e   Julia Thompson b May 2, 1847   f   Stephen Henry b Sept 12, 1848
g   Edward Augustus b Sept 29, 1857

Ellen T Dow adhcbbfa d Woburn Apr 20, 1904; m William T Barrett of Northfield b May 26, 1838, d Jan 29, 1863; 2nd July 6, 1865, George Frank Ellis d Jan 17, 1891; dau,—Mabel Thompson b Apr 15, 1867, m Aug 29, 1888, Heber B Clewley.

Alfred A Dow adhcbbfb d Woburn Nov 20, 1891; m Sept 23, 1862, Carrie Swift Ellis of Woburn b Cincinnati, Ohio. Children:

a   Alice Gertrude b Aug 25, 1864
b   Willard Alfred b Apr 16, 1866; d Woburn Mch 30, 1906; m Susan McIntire
      b Sept 14, 1867
c   Edith Celende b Mch 10, 1868; d Shoreham Jan 18, 1891; m Aug 27, 1888,
      William Brown b 1863, d Nov 24, 1897. No children
d   Frederick Thompson b June 23, 1877
e   Julian Ellis b July 6, 1879; secy of a Birmingham, Ala, corporation; m —— in
      1926

Alice G Dow adhcbbfba m Nov 22, 1886, Everett Griffin Place b Oct 19, 1863, d May 9, 1899, son of Griffin and Adeline (Cummings);

2nd Apr 12, 1910, Harry Putnam Davis, son of Horace and **Hannah** (Bruce). Children:

  a Alfred Griffin b Sept 29, 1887   b Gertrude b May 17, 1889
  c Everett Eugene b May 8, 1891
  d Edith Dow b Nov 22, 1893; d Jan 10, 1894
  e Edith Marion b May 24, 1897

Frederick T Dow adhcbbfbd, real estate operator of Birmingham, Ala, m Dec 2, 1908, Maud Melina Skinner b Mch 4, 1880. Children:

  a Barbara Skinner b Jan 27, 1920   b Frederick Thompson b July 3, 1923

Harriet J Dow adhcbbfc d Woburn Mch 24, 1870; m Nov 11, 1863, William Henry Winn b Burlington, Mass, Feb 8, 1840, son of William and Abigail (Parker); he m 2nd Elizabeth June Pollock. Harriet's child:

  a William H b and d Mch 25, 1869

Julia T Dow adhcbbfe d Woburn May 14, 1880; m Sept 1, 1868, James William Churchill Pickering of Manchester, N H. Children:

  a Herbert Dow b Apr 23, 1870   b Josie Belle b June 25, 1872
  c Harry Edward b Nov 18, 1874   d Nellie Gertrude b Mch 18, 1875
  e James William Churchill b May 22, 1878; d 1880

Stephen H Dow adhcbbff d Swampscott Aug 19, 1879; m Oct 24, 1869, Emma Tryphena Thompson of Woburn b Aug 23, 1849, dau of Abijah. Children:

  a Henry Abijah Thompson b July 7, 1871
  b Carl Stephen b Aug 13, 1874
  c Emma Minette b Dec 31, 1875; m Oct 24, 1914, Frank Herbert Knight **grad** Bowdoin 1894
  d Louis Hackett b June 3, 1878

Henry A T Dow adhcbbffa of Needham, Mass, m Apr 5, 1898, Mary Celende Whitcher b Oct 29, 1874, d Apr 17, 1901; 2nd June 6, 1904, Etta May Willard b May 29, 1874, dau of Joel W and Ermina V (Young). Children:

  a Henry Kenneth b Feb 19, 1900   b Lois Willard b Sept 24, 1905

Carl S Dow adhcbbffb, grad Harvard B S 1897; author of a number of text books on mechanics; lived Auburndale and elsewhere; d Worcester, Mass, June 9, 1925; m June 12, 1900, Eva Eulalia Strout b Sept 15, 1875, dau of Melville and Marilla (Spooner). Child:

  a Katherine b Chicago Sept 13, 1903

Louis H Dow adhcbbffd lived Woburn; moved away some years ago; m Apr 22, 1908, Margaret Alice Locke ae 23 b Ludington, Mich, dau of George A and Atlanta (Sibley). Children:

  a George Stephen b Dec 27, 1911   b Jennie Thompson b Sept 10, 1919

Edward A Dow adhcbbfg of Woburn m Feb 17, 1885, Annie E Le Clair b Aug 21, 1859. Child:

  a Ruth Harodine b Aug 9, d Aug 18, 1889

Moses Gove Dow adhcbbg d Oct 31, 1891; m Oct 5, 1834, Harriet Purrington b Weare June 7, 1811, d Norway, Me, Apr 12, 1843; 2nd June 6, 1844, Ellen Maria Lowell d Deering, Me, Dec 25, 1874; 3rd Apr 25, 1876, Betsey Noyes Harris b New Sharon, Me, Jan 27, 1831, d Portland Oct 20, 1892, dau of Nicholas H and Maria (Ford). An honest and very likable man, he was somewhat of a rolling stone, with a great variety of occupations and making many ventures in several States, merchant of Portland, hotel proprietor, proprietor of a sanatorium, exploiter of a mineral spring, etc., etc. Many times he was very close to making a fortune. He lived fairly well, died poor, made and kept a great number of friends, to whom he was quite ready to give but from whom very reluctant to ask. Children:

   a Letïtia Gove b July 10, 1838; d Portland Dec 31, 1854
   b Marion Wallace b July 30, 1842; d Deering Dec 20, 1851
   c Celende Thompson b July 30, 1842; d Woburn Oct 16, 1842
   d Frank Lowell b May 24, 1845
   e Henry Oscar b June 14, 1847; d Springfield, Mo, Jan 9, 1881; m 1877 Roxanna Onstott, who m 2nd his brother Herbert G
   f Gertrude Gove b Mch 28, 1857   g Herbert Gruby b July 8, 1860

Frank L Dow adhcbbgd, 25th Me vols, commercial salesman of Chelsea, Mass, and Portland; m Nov 27, 1878, Idella Theresa Robinson b Portland July 4, 1857, d Aug 13, 1906, dau of Luther B and Sally Barstow (Stetson). After his wife's death he was librarian of Nat. Soldiers' Home, Me, until his death in 1922. Children:

   a William Chenery b July 3, 1881
   b Ellen Marie b July 3, 1881; d July, 1881

William C Dow adhcbbgda, clerk, floor walker, insurance agent, etc, of Portland, m Apr 27, 1903, Grace Enid McAdam b Halifax, N S, dau of William and Louisa M (Poole). Children:

   a Frank Chenery b Dec 18, 1903   b William McAdam b May 6, 1910
   c Byron Gove b Jan 20, 1916   d Richard Poole b Aug 29, 1917

Gertrude G Dow adhcbbgf m James Naylor; div 1896; 2nd Dec 21, 1896, Frank Adams Pennell; 3rd Ralph S French. Child:

   a Herbert Oscar b 1880

Herbert Gruby Dow adhcbbgg of Los Angeles, Calif, m Aug 4, 1882, Roxanna (Onstott) Dow; div July 17, 1901; m 2nd Aug 20, 1910, Nellie Maude Loomis b Sept 8, 1886. Children:

   a Marie b Nov 15, 1888   b Nadine, twin

James N Dow adhcbbh, ae 18, entered a store in Waterville, Me, later in Norway, then joined his brother Moses in Portland; next had charge of a construction gang building the Chicago & Alton R R. The lure of Calif calling him, he dammed Feather River for power, but a flood swept down his dam and he returned east to make a fresh start; became a successful manufacturer of morocco leather in Woburn; town treasurer 1883; trustee of local savings bank; d Aug 6, 1887; m Biddeford Me, outside the Friends, Aug 11, 1853, Ellen Sophia Beeman b No Bridgeton Aug 12, 1828, d Woburn Apr 20, 1909. Children:

    a   James Neal b Nov 9, 1854; d Apr 14, 1857
    b   Herbert Beeman b Mch 7, 1858

Herbert B Dow adhcbbhb grad Harvard 1879, becoming that year principal of Proctor Academy, Andover, N H; taught 1881-3 Orange, N J; returned to Andover; M A Dartmouth 1884; moved 1887 to Woburn, Mass, where he has lived ever since. He taught mathematics in Harvard, but some years later accepted the position of actuary to the New England Mutual Life Insurance Co, which he now holds. His aptitude for highly complicated actuarial problems have made him regarded as the dean of the profession.

He renders a striking example of how much work can be systematized to fit into days of only 24 hours long. He has control of 52 clerks, but likes to put his personal attention and o k to every matter he can. At home he was executor of his aunt's (Mrs Charles Choate) will and is trustee of the home for the aged established by her; has served as executor for a number of members of the family. Is President of the Board of the Woburn Public Library; vice-president Woburn Five Cents Savings Bank; secretary of executive committee of Woburn Hospital; chairman of Finance Committee of Co-operative Bank; trustee of his Masonic Lodge; clerk for over 30 years of the First Unitarian Parish; and serves in quite a number of other matters of trust. It may be readily understood that he has little time for politics, but he found time in 1918 to go to the Texas border, care for and bring home his son, who had contracted typhoid while in the army.

While at Andover his active interest in genealogy was begun, he being the pioneer of Dow Genealogy as far as he knew. As a matter of fact, Edgar R Dow of Portland, Me (coincidently, also an actuary), began a year or two earlier. In 1912, when the Author of this Book began, the collection of Edgar was slightly the larger,—about 6,000 to 7,000 names,—but each had over 2,000 names which the other did not. Their methods of working were radically different. Edgar worked wholly by personal letter writing. Herbert liked to devote much time in the long vacation given by schools to search of probate documents, realty deeds, etc, and in consequence his collection was the much more authoritative. He had also a rare insight to connect the right parents with the right children. For fully 30 years he was regarded as the one man to whom all queries in Dow genealogy should be referred and he never failed to reply to a letter or inquiry, the total of which ran into the thousands. Stress of work compelled him to slow up a little on this hobby and inquiries were shifted somewhat from him to the Author. In 1926 he is again hard at work, checking, revising, adding to prepare this Book for publication.

A bushel or two of letters have passed between him and the Author and the relations between them are such that the feeling of gratitude is very keen indeed.

It has been his intention for many years to bequeath his self-indexing card catalogue of Dow and every one intermarried with Dow to the Genealogical Society. His system in making this enormous catalogue (containing every name added by the Author) differs somewhat from the one usually employed by genealogists, but seems to the Author to be the finest existing in the matter of clarity and labor-saving.

He m Jan 1, 1883, Vanie Buck Robinson b Sept 9, 1850, dau of John and Abby (Buck), who presides over the home in Woburn. Children:

    a Ethel Robinson b Aug 4, 1884   b Roland Beeman b Feb 12, 1889

Roland B Dow adhcbbhbb, business man of Boston, served 1918 on the Mexican border; m Sept 11, 1920, Marguerite Smith, dau of Charles Willard and Sarah Lillian (Thompson) of Woburn. Is now asst Actuary N E Mutual Life. Children:

    a Richard Thompson b Nov 3, 1921   b Prescott Robinson b Sept 25, 1923

Lydia G Dow adhcbbi of Woburn m Sept 14, 1840, Charles Choate b Sept 16, 1806, d Feb 15, 1883, merchant of Boston; no children. She d Apr 5, 1904, leaving her homestead as an endowed home for aged persons. Her nephew Herbert B Dow was executor of her will and is trustee of the home.

Benjamin F Dow adhcbbj d Portland Oct 28, 1904, at one time partner with his brother James N; m Mch 26, 1845, Judith Richardson Rogers b Sept 18, 1824, d June 23, 1861, dau of Artemus and Lydia; 2nd Oct 17, 1866, Laura Jane Lapont b 1846; div 1900. Children:

    a Frank Henry b Sept 28, 1846   b Frederick Augustus b Aug 27, 1867
    c Charles Choate b May 26, 1868   d Henry Oscar b Sept 16, 1870
    e Jennie Agnes b Nov 29, 1885

Frank H Dow adhcbbja of Boston d Revere Feb 6, 1901; m Jan 6, 1873, Clara C J Follett b Oct 21, 1854, dau of Joseph H and Elizabeth Edith. She d Apr 22, 1891. Children:

    a Rogers b Nov 24, 1873; grad Harvard 1896; law school 1899; lawyer in Boston; unm
    b Elizabeth Edith b Jan 5, 1875; d Andover, Mass, Feb 9, 1911; m Dec 5, 1895, Nathan Chipman Hamblin
    c Lydia b Aug 8, 1877

Lydia Dow adhcbbjac m June 29, 1905, James Francis Butterworth, ae 37, son of James F and Mary F (Webber).

Frederick A Dow adhcbbjb of Swanton, Vt, m Apr 15, 1891, Mary Lavinia Carman b Kane, Ill, Aug 19, 1871; moved to St Louis. Children:

    a Hazel Lavinia b Feb 29, 1892   b Frederick Lapont b Apr 7, 1893

Charles C Dow adhcbbjc, 1917 real estate operator N Y City, m Alton, Ill, May 30, 1888, Medea Elizabeth Gates b Speedwell, N Y, Feb 18, 1866. Child:

a   Josephine Medea b May 31, 1889; now married

Henry O Dow adhcbbjd of Springfield, Mo, moved to El Paso, Tex; m Apr 13, 1891, Mary Ellen Purcell b June 16, 1871, dau of Thomas William and Ellen (White). Children:

a   Gertrude Ellen b Jan 8, 1892   b   Genevieve Laura b Jan 23, 1894
c   William Harry b Sept 9, 1896
d   Benjamin Franklin b Oct 17, 1898; d Apr 15, 1899

Jennie A Dow adhcbbje (identity assumed) m John W Stevens. Child, b Newburyport:

a   Kenneth Walter b May 12, 1905

Emma M Dow adhcbbk of Woburn d East Boston Dec 15, 1873; m June 28, 1848, Benjamin Pond, lawyer of Boston b Feb 6, 1822, d Nov 21, 1889. Children:

a   Clara Baldwin b Apr 21, 1849   b   Lucius Augustus b Dec 26, 1850
c   Charles Choate b Jan 12, 1853   d   Benjamin Fetty Place b Jan 27, 1855
e   William Whiting b Aug 22, 1858   f   Emma Sumner b Feb 22, 1860
g   Washington Gregg b Nov 22, 1862   h   Annie Moriarty b Aug 13, 1865

Judith Dow adhcbc m Weare Oct 15, 1788, John Phillips of Lynn, son of Walter and Content (Hope). Four of the 8 children of this staunch Quaker couple, who came to Lynn from York, Me, m Dows. They lived Lynn. Children:

a   John b Nov 29, 1789
b   Jonathan Dow b Mch 3, 1791; m (int pub Jan 24, 1819) Nancy F Lee; has
     posterity
c   Stephen b Nov 19, 1792; d Nov 7, 1817
d   Anna Dow b Aug 22, 1794   e   Walter b Oct 13, 1796
f   Judith b Mch 8, 1798; int pub Mch 19, 1826, to Hiram Pond
g   Hannah b June 23, 1799; m 17: 11 mo: 1819, Benjamin Hood
h   George (twin) b Feb 17, 1805; int pub Apr 26, 1840, to Elizabeth Silsbee

Keziah Dow adhcbf m 1797 Carlton Clement; 2nd Richard Clement. Children:

a   Jonathan Dow   b   Richard   c   Squire S   d   Keziah

HIST Weare, N H, gives a good account of its early days, of pioneer life, carving farms and hamlets out of the forest, for some years fully as inaccessible to civilization as Hampton had been in 1644. In fact, Hampton had been the more accessible, since it could be reached by water, while stumps had to be grubbed out to make all roads from Weare. The town was not settled by Quakers; in fact, the Dows were the first Quakers there. Jonathan and Jedediah Dow bought each for rather less than $250 an original lot with full common rights. Following them came several cousins and within 10 years No. Weare was a well established Quaker settlement, almost all coming from Seabrook. In fact, New Seabrook would be a deserved name. This region soon became the largest of the Quaker communities in the State.

Jedediah Dow adhcc arrived 1772, a middle-aged, energetic man, with 4 children. Jonathan had been established 4 years. Jedediah at once built a log house and cleared a farm around it. There was not yet a carriage road out. Three years later the brothers built for common occupancy the first 2 story house in town. Jedediah was blacksmith as well as farmer and had no idle hours.

The Indian menace lasted only a few years; an occasional captive was made for camp work or ransom. The Quakers followed their usual plan of non-resistance and got along rather better than others. One man returned one day to his home to find it raided and his wife kidnapped. She had been bound and kept in the woods in charge of a one-armed squaw. While secured, her husband and a relief party passed by near enough to have heard her voice, but the squaw stood with tomahawk uplifted and she dared not speak. A few days later she was rescued. Wild beasts were for many years fatal to pigs and hens and occasionally dangerous to man. A bear too old to hibernate is an ugly customer in winter. Such a one Jedediah met one day in a narrow path, not seeing it until the bear had snatched his hat from his head. Jedediah had his woodsman's axe and after some fencing managed to disable a paw, after which he got in the fatal blow on the head. Even bear meat was valued food. Weare fare was simple in the extreme; bean porridge a staple; wheat too readily salable for much home consumption. No grist mill existed for several years; each family pounded its corn in mortars hollowed out from rock maple wood.

Jedediah d, ae 87, May 10, 1826, living his later years with his dau Mary, who continued a Dow by marriage. His 1st wife was Mary Dow adbad, killed by a stroke of lightning a few days after marriage; m 2nd Dover Nov 3, 1763, Dorcas Neal b June 21, 1740, d May 18, 1810, dau of Andrew and Dorcas of Kittery. They were pioneer Friends in Maine and the family intermarried with Quaker Dows several times. Jedediah's

home was near the Weare meeting house, taken down to build a bigger
one on the same spot, the third building being still standing.   Unhewn
stones are the rule there and under two were laid Jedediah and his wife
in unmarked graves in the rugged environment of their own making.
Children, 4 b Seabrook, 3 Weare:

a   Mary b Apr 19, 1765; m Winthrop Dow adhah   b   Josiah b Sept 2, 1766
c   Ruth b Sept 1, 1768; m Benjamin Gage. Children,—John; Hannah m ——
    Clements; Mary m Joseph Mountford of Portland, having Addie, Wallace,
    Jennie, Fanny
d   Abraham b Dec 31, 1774; d 1793 of a nose bleed
e   Jedediah b Apr 26, 1777   f   Jonathan b Oct 31, 1782

Josiah Dow adhccb, oldest of three able brothers, was 6 when he
came to Weare and about 24 when he left to seek his fortune.   He read
every book he could get and at 20 was chosen to teach school.   In summer
he was the usual farmer, but learned tanning.   Neal Dow speaks of the
tanbark road in front of the Weare home.   In 1790 he went to Falmouth
and joined his brother-in-law in a tanning business, teaching school
during winters. He built a house, which still stands, on the bank of the
Presumscot about 5 miles from Portland.   The meeting house, now
taken down, was just across the river, its yard filled with the unmarked
graves of 3 generations.   Either at meeting or in the school Josiah met
the girl he married, seven years his junior.   The Allens were well-to-do
Friends living in a house still standing, about a mile away but in plain
sight of his own home.

Isaac Allen, a slight man not in rugged health, wore the knee breeches
and broad brimmed hat of the Friends but in youth had been a man of
carnal warfare.   He told little of his experience in this line, but had
probably been at the siege of Louisburg.   His wife was Abigail Hall b
Feb 12, 1740, d Feb 12, 1825, dau of Hate-Evil Hall, descendant of John
Hall b Eng 1617, came to Boston and finally to Dover.   She was well
remembered by Gen Neal Dow, especially as sitting in the chimney
corner smoking her pipe. The grandson imagined his abhorrence of tobacco dated from then.   Josiah had chewed tobacco from the time he
was 25 until he was about 70, then gave it up as "nasty stuff."   The
Allens had 7 children, of whom Dorcas was 6th b Aug 28, 1773.   Dorcas
and Josiah were married Feb 3 1796, in the meeting house, Hate-Evil
Hall, then 90, being present and, with 24 other witnesses, signing the
marriage certificate.   The couple moved at once to a house he had bought
in Portland on Congress St, near Green, on which a store now stands
owned by the family.   Four years later they moved to another house,
in which they passed the remainder of their lives.   Just prior to his marriage Josiah had started a tannery of his own, which prospered until it
was discontinued in 1874 by his son and grandson, then by far the oldest
business in Portland.   The firm was Josiah Dow & Son from Neal's
21st birthday; it weathered every panic, altho the business grew to be
a large one, importing hides and needing from time to time no small

credit. It was discontinued because Neal Dow was devoting himself wholly to national affairs and Col Fred Dow had too many other irons in the fire.

Josiah was born, lived and died a Quaker, but he was human. He was 9 and was casting bullets for his hunting rifle when a company of militia, including relatives, came by and took not only his bullets but his lead and mould. Later he regretted he had not cast enough to win Bunker Hill, that being the troop's destination. At the outbreak of the Civil War his sentiments were slightly more orthodox; he might not fire shot and shells, but "would try the effect of some hot water, but I would heat it very hot." One time he was assaulted by a man he had been forced to discharge. He did not strike back, merely grabbed the offender by the collar, pushed him against a wall and held him there in spite of constant blows until he was thoroughly tired and compelled to beg Josiah's pardon.

He was an organizer of the Merchant's Bank of Portland and a director from the first, 1824, until compelled to retire by the infirmities of age; also a director in a number of other corporations. Somewhat isolated during his last years, he retained a keen interest in the affairs of the day up to a few weeks before his death. He was greatly dissatisfied with the national administration in 1860 for its unpreparedness in allowing batteries to be built facing Ft Sumpter. He voted always, Federalist, National Republican, Whig, Free Soiler and Republican, but through infirmity could not vote for Lincoln in 1860. He served several terms in the Legislature and held a few city offices but always with reluctance and from a sense of duty. His health began to fail about the time, past 80, he fell on the ice and broke his hip. Thereafter he was always lame. His wife also broke her hip and died at 78, July 8, 1851. He himself kept as busy as possible at the tannery. One day when over 90 he offered, in the absence of a teamster, to drive the express wagon to mill to get meal for the horses. Returning, the wagon seat slipped, throwing him backward among the meal bags, from which on account of his lameness he could not readily extricate himself. The faithful old horse stood still. An acquaintance passing by, not recognizing the old man covered with meal, helped him up and remarked:

"It's a pity that a man of your age should get so drunk as to be unable to sit up."

"Drunk," snorted Josiah, "if when thou art my age thou canst sit up, drunk or sober, thou'lt be smarter than I think for."

He d ae 94, 9 mos, June 1, 1861. In all his life neither his personal character nor his business integrity was ever questioned by a breath of suspicion. His was a venerable figure, in honor second to none among the Quakers; in influence in the upbuilding of Portland second to none. The 1850 census finds him with wife and dau Harriet; realty assessment $10,500. Children:

a Emma Mead b Jan 4, 1800   b Neal b Mch 20, 1804

c Harriet b May 21, 1806; d Feb 22, 1869; all her life an invalid, altho able to share actively in the social life of the home

Emma M Dow adhccba d Sept 12, 1851; m Neal D Shaw of Baring, Me. Only child:

a Harriet m J F Barnard

Neal Dow adhccbb d Portland Oct 2, 1897; m Jan 20, 1830, Maria Cornelia Durant Maynard b Boston June 18, 1808, d Portland Jan 13, 1883; on the Governor's staff 1841; Col and Brig Gen U S A 1861; presidential candidate 1880; twice mayor of Portland.

During the presidential campaign of 1880 the Author was a lad of 11 in a thriving New Hampshire town, much interested in the issues of the day and retaining a vivid recollection of happenings. This campaign brought to him his first knowledge of the existence of a Neal Dow and at that formative age impressions are always the most lasting. The impressions of Neal Dow were as unfavorable as his political enemies wished to convey and unfavorable impressions seem always to cling most persistently. It was a much hotter campaign than 1876, when the Democrats won, only to be cheated out. The republican machine, fat with 20 years office holding, was desperate, the odds all summer slightly favoring the Democrats. It was felt that a very few votes might overthrow a candidate for Congress and almost as few might alter the electoral vote. As a matter of fact, Neal Dow polled a much smaller vote than was usual for the Prohibition candidate. This was due to the fear of a national overturn. He had a prominence which no candidate of his party ever had before or since. The Democratic spell binders said little of him. The Republicans were instructed everywhere to stop at no vituperation of the intruder.

Gen Benjamin F Butler came in invariably for a joke. No one seemed to fear that his few votes would be taken from one party rather than another. Political vilification was at its greatest freedom in 1880. Things said then passed unnoticed, altho they would send a speaker to jail at present. The Cleveland election changed all that.

It was not, the speakers generally asserted, that Neal Dow was vicious or criminal, altho by criminal negligence and ignorance he had needlessly sacrificed thousands of lives in the War. It was not that he acked ability, but it was of a peculiar and harmful sort, that he was a visionary and impractical dreamer, a marplot, too narrow to make aught but a muddle of public matters, that he was rich by inheritance, not by brains, and thus irresponsible, not needing to count the cost of any national trouble his peculiar lunacy might bring about. This is the stuff we were told in 1880. Even then we might have been more incredulous, but most of the New York and Boston papers gave no better impression, tho in more guarded language.

Orators were instructed to go easy on the matter of drinking, merely to point out that it was not a national issue and was either local or even individual. This was a matter of great importance to our town, which was "dry." Liquor paid a good share of our taxes. Twenty saloons ran openly; the proprietor of each was arrested and fined $25 on the first of each month. "I do not care," cried one orator, "if Neal Dow does not want to take a drink; that is his privilege. I do not want to drink, myself; I never do. But I do protest that because some man does not want to take a drink he has no right to impose his prohibition upon the choice of any other man. If this should be, then we should be no longer free and equal and the constitution go for naught." Our local view was that, if happiness lay in a quart of rum, it should be taxed to the utmost but not prohibited. Drunkards should be locked up if troublesome; if not should be fined for the public benefit.

How many of us have ever given the matter thought enough to disabuse ourselves of those impressions of 1880? Prohibition finally came, but Neal Dow was forgotten. Who, outside of Maine, listened to laudatory obituaries in 1897? *Nil de mortuis.* It is true that in Maine many still revere his memory as by all odds the most unselfish real statesman the State ever produced. Most of us have forgotten that in 1918 Neal Dow was a more potent influence than during his life. The very politicians who berated him in 1880 voted not only a prohibition law but an amendment to the Constitution, not wishing it but afraid of the votes of women and the silent parties. Neal Dow drew up almost every phrase of the Volstead law, all but the loopholes vainly left.

He was the only son, born when his father had barely developed a promising business. When he came of age his father was wealthy for those days, with a fine business, a bank director and owning much forest land. During the next 35 years the family fortune increased greatly, but even at this it was not great as fortunes are considered in recent years. Beyond doubt, Neal Dow between 1830 and 1870 multiplied the property several times. In other words he became rich, but not by inheritance. He had a good asset in his physique, wiry and of great endurance. His education was good but was largely self-acquired, first at the local Quaker school, then at Portland Academy, finally with his sister Harriet at the Friends Academy at New Bedford, Mass. This was a long journey by Sea. He was a grown man when the first railroad was built from Portland to Boston. His first trip between the two points took 12 hours and the passengers had to walk at times to enable the train to make the grades. His father did not think favorably of college, altho Neal much wished it. Instead, he applied himself to study at home, reading medicine and history and practicing debate. To become traveled, he first took a horseback trip to the old home in Weare, thence through the White Mountains. For business training, his father bought for him a third interest in a forest tract in Aroostook Co, which Neal surveyed, plotted and sold profitably to settlers. June 1825 he started on his grand tour, to Dover, thence to Boston, where he had business to attend to, then suddenly for business exigencies back to Portland. Starting afresh, he visited Weare and took his cousin Abraham Dow adhahe to Boston with him. From Weare he staged it through Vermont to Saratoga, Poughkeepsie, Utica and Buffalo. Thence to Niagara and by water to Montreal. Next to Albany and New York City, through the streets of which, he says, hogs and poultry roamed freely. A trip to Philadelphia followed, thence by stage to Providence, Boston and home. The whole trip lasted only two months.

Business career immediately followed, becoming equal partner and giving the business his daily superintendence for 27 years. From the first his income sufficed for his unextravagant wants and by 26 he felt justified in establishing a home for himself. He m Maria C D Maynard of Scarboro b June 18, 1808, the youngest of her family. Her father, John Maynard, was descended from John Maynard of Framingham, immigrant about 1660. The grandfather and great uncle had been Revolutionary officers. Her mother was Mary Durant b St Croix, W I, of a Huguenot family which settled in Conn 1633. Mrs Dow presided over the home for 43 years, devoted to a large family, acting as hostess in a household which entertained much. After their wedding they went directly to a house which Neal had built, across the street from his father's, in which they lived the rest of their lives. Six months later they started by carriage on a belated wedding trip, visiting relatives of each in N H and Mass. In all their lives, when apart, letters passed daily; after Mrs Dow's death her husband's letters were found carefully filed together. There were many separations, one when Neal was in the army and Libby prison, another when Mrs Dow went to Minneapolis to care for an invalid son.

Mrs Dow was a member of the Congregational church and never a Friend. By this time the Friends had begun to be a little more lax about marrying outside the Society. The Autobiography touches very lightly on Neal's withdrawal from the Friends, laying it entirely on military affairs. In 1841 he became an officer on the Governor's staff, nominally only, a military position. A committee of the Friends waited upon him and suggested that he resign his military title or withdraw from the Society. He did neither, merely automatically ceased to be a member. By this time the Friends had lost at least half their membership throughout New England.

From 1830 the business career of Neal Dow was about what is to be expected from a diligent, able man, imbued with old-fashioned Quaker notions of thrift and integrity. Fifty years later, in the height of political abuse, not one whisper was ever, could ever be directed against his business integrity or his family life. The tannery became too small a field for ambition. Timber lands in the unsettled portions of the State were incidentally necessary to the tanning business and afforded by far the most promising speculations, as the country was growing rapidly. Only once or twice did a great commercial crisis, like the panic of 1857, endanger large holdings of these lands; once the whole credit of a combined syndicate was taxed to its utmost. At 29 he became director of the bank, continuing for over 40 years. He became trustee of a savings bank and president of the Portland Gas Co. A railroad being a public necessity, he pledged most of his means and credit toward the construction of the Maine Central R R, altho refusing its presidency. He was a director in a considerable number of railroads, manufacturing and commercial corporations. By 1857 he could no longer afford to give daily attention to business details. This is the actual business career of the man assailed in 1880 as a scatter-brained irresponsible, wealthy by inheritance.

His interest in public life began before he heard the oration of Daniel Webster in 1825 at the laying of the corner-stone of Bunker Hill Monument. He was in Washington, guest of Senator Hannibal Hamlin, met and discussed affairs with such noted, hated free-soilers as Salmon P Chase, William H Seward, Charles Sumner. He had talked, too, with Andrew Johnson, the young representative from Tennessee, and with the leaders of the opposition, Henry Clay, John C Calhoun, Alexander H Stephens. Stephen A Douglas, Lincoln's opponent, was in the Senate but young and little known. He was past middle life when James G Blaine first came to Portland, when Thomas Brackett Reed was a school boy. His first vote was cast for John Quincy Adams and he believed that the election of Andrew Jackson would prove a national calamity. In the campaign of 1832, opposed to Jackson, not believing in Clay, he took refuge in the short-lived Anti-Masonic ticket. He supported Harrison, of course; in 1844 he could not support Clay, the Quaker instinct revolting alike against duelling and slavery. In 1848 he favored Van Buren as the Free Soil candidate, and in 1852 worked for Gen Scott. He was one of those who waited to establish the new party and was a charter member when Gen John C Fremont was chosen to lead a forlorn hope. After 1860 he supported the Republican administrations until in 1880 he became the candidate of a party largely of his own creation, existing previously as a name, hardly as an influence.

A State political party committed to "temperance" was founded Feb 1834 and of this he was a charter member and delegate. Little by little his personal effort was to free local politics from national issues, leaving it in position to make its chief issue the repeal of the license laws governing the sale of liquor. This had been a city issue, it was before long forced to the front as the leading State issue. The first bill to prohibit the sale of liquor came before the Legislature of 1839; similar bills introduced each session gained increased support. Most of these State-wide bills were drawn by Neal Dow, modified as considered advisable by friends of the cause. In 1849 the entering wedge was driven, forbidding the sale of liquor at fairs and cattle shows. This was the first statute in the U S providing fine and imprisonment for liquor-selling. In 1850 these penalties were increased, with little opposition, for the liquor adherents thought that by throwing this sop to growing public opinion danger of Statewide prohibition would be greatly lessened. The tug of war was to come, however, only a few years later. He had received votes for nomination as Mayor in 1847; in 1851 he was nominated and elected by the largest vote ever cast in Portland, altho by no means the largest plurality,—quite the reverse. From the moment of his inauguration, Apr 24, the policy became to empty the almshouse by closing the saloon, this being constantly declared to be the effect and cause. The war in the Legislature was pushed with the support of the Portland delegation. An act for the suppression of drinking houses and tippling shops became a law that very year and except for two years has been ever since the Maine law, known world wide and the term impossible of conception in any other connection. Free Soiler vote was unanimous for it, Whigs and Democrats 63 to 50. The mental calibre of local politicians in that day was not great,—witness a speech made by a Senator Cary of Aroostook Co, who had been a member of Congress, entrusted with law-making for 30,000,000 people. "This new manifestation of the spirit of fanaticism originated in the city of Portland under the auspices of that prince of fanatics, the present Mayor of that city—embodied the ultra notions of the wringnecks of that city, of whom the Mayor is chief. Has the Legislature of Maine, and a Democrat Legislature too, become so lost to dignity and self-respect, as to sit here the registrar of the inquisatorial edicts of the temperance fanatics of Portland, headed by its popinjay Mayor, a Whig abolitionist of the most ultra stripe (interesting light on slavery in politics in Maine in 1851). I met the Mayor the other day on the stairway. He is a pretty little dapper man, goes well dressed, wears a nice blue jacket and a fancy vest and his hat cocked on one side of his head. He succeeded in getting his bill reported by the committee, word for word and letter for letter, as it was prepared for them. I do not expect to make any impression on the Senate. I do not belong to the powers that be. I train in a different company. I do not expect to have any influence in the party until the reign of niggerism and fanaticism is over. A few years ago the jackdaw Mayor of Portland, this man with the fancy vest, who got up the precious document the Legislature is called upon to register, was at the head of the nigger movement in that city. He was formerly a Federalist, but federalism alone was not low enough for his instincts, and he joined the abolition movement; but even abolitionism was not strong enough for his diseased palate, and he has added temperancism to his former stock of humbugs. Is this Federal-abolition wringneck to be allowed to dictate to a democratic Legislature what enactments it shall pass? Talk with the Mayor. Does he pretend to be a Democrat? No. He never had and never can have a Democratic feeling or pulsation.   He is a Federalist at heart, of the alien and sedition law stripe. Why should he, the Lord Mayor of Portland, come down here with his rum bill, all cut and dried, for this Legislature to enact into a law? Was it for any good to the Democracy? Why, all he cares about is to overturn the democracy of the State and put himself at the top of the heap by heading this wringneck temperance movement as he headed the abolition movement.   We have two kinds of bees, one small but not handsome, but useful, the honey bee.   A swarm of this sort of bees has a king bee or queen bee, bigger than any of the rest.   The mode of making him is said to be this: they take the largest maggot they can find and by some sort of process not fully understood continue to grow it into a bee of immense size, and install it as the king or queen bee, whom all the little bees fall down and worship.   The temperance fanatics have imitated the example of the honey bee in this respect. They have taken the Mayor of Portland, and by some process blown him up into a king bee, bigger than all the other bees in the hive.   There is also another kind of bee, called the bumble bee or humble bee, a very big and pretty bee. It has a fine coat with pretty colors, and makes a great noise.   In fact it keeps up a tremendous buzz, buzz, buzz, wherever it goes.   The House has been frightened into the passage of this bill by the buzzing of a bumble bee.''

Governor Hubbard, a physician and worthy man, signed the bill after listening to great pressure on both sides.   Thereafter for seven years Portland and the whole state were in constant turmoil over its enforcement or its evasion, its repeal or its continuance, setting up or throwing down officials as opposed to or in favor of it.   The same process is national in 1923.   There were no party lines except as a cloak.   In 1852 the law was safe but Dow defeated for re-election as Mayor.   His Democratic opponent was Judge Albion K Parris, man of the highest character, national and judicial experience.   Gov Hubbard was re-elected by an increased plurality, but followed by a Governor decidedly opposed to the law.   In 1853 Dow was not renominated, the local Whig party being in two factions,—Dowites and anti-Dowites, colloquially the Ramrods and Schiedam Schnapps.   The Whig nominee, former Mayor Cahoon, not opposed to the Maine law, was elected.   In 1854 the Whigs made no attempt at a nomination.   In 1855 the newly founded Republican party nominated Neal Dow for Mayor and he was elected by a majority of 46.   The Governorship was thrown into the Legislature, there being no majority, and the outcome of this was the repeal of the Maine law, lasting for two years.   Before this a remarkable riot in Portland caused a great sensation.

The Maine law provided that in each town or city a suitable agent should be appointed under bond to sell liquor for medicinal or mechanical purposes and no other.   The stock of liquor throughout the State was soon greatly reduced. It was provided that reasonable time should be given to sell all stocks of liquors to go outside the State. Wholesalers at once complied and went out of business; retailers either did likewise or ran the secret "speakeasies." To provide for a medicinal supply, Mayor Dow, chairman of a committee for the purpose, bought a stock for about $1,600, which was to be sold by the local agent from a store owned by the city in the basement of the city hall. An anonymous broadside was then circulated widely: "A T T E N T I O N, C I T Y MARSHAL. While the city authorities are busy searching private houses for demijohns and jugs of liquor, it is, perhaps, not strange that they would overlook wholesale importations into the city of what are probably impure liquors intended for sale. We are credibly informed that $1,600 worth of liquors have recently been purchased by a citizen of Portland, and brought into the city in violation of law, and are still kept here illegally. Why doesn't the marshal seize and destroy? The Mayor of the city has no more right to deal in liquors without authority than any other citizen. Where are our vigilant police, who are knowing to the above facts, and who think it their duty to move about in search of the poor man's cider, and often push their search into a private house, contrary to every principle of justice and law? Why are they so negligent of the weightier matters and so eager for the mint and *cumin*? We call upon them by virtue of Neal Dow's law to seize Neal Dow's liquors and pour them into the street. The old maxim reads: *Fiat justitia ruat coelum*," which means, "Let the lash which Neal Dow has prepared for other backs be applied to his own when he deserves it."

Three citizens, one formerly a distiller, applied for and obtained a warrant for the seizure of the city stores and it was handed to the proper city officer for execution. The officer found truckmen present, come to haul the liquor away, for what reason does not seem clear. He found the liquors all marked as the property of the city and tallying with the invoice. He thereupon left to consult the city marshal and county attorney. Returning, he made formal seizure of the property, leaving it in the store. Meanwhile, the crowd surrounding the building had increased and become turbulent. The police tried to disperse them and did not succeed; two companies of militia were then called upon. The captain of one of them refused to expose his men to the mob unless they were properly armed and equipped. This encouraged the rioters. The police by use of revolvers maintained their position inside the building into which the mob was trying to force its way. The Mayor, sheriff of the county and one militia company arrived, the riot act was read by Mayor and sheriff. The militia company was stoned until only eight were left in line: the second company then arrived, firing several warning volleys, then dispersed the mob by bayonet. One rioter was killed and several wounded, either by militia or police.

This ended the riot; its political side was followed up vigorously. One coroner's jury found that the deceased came to his death by a gunshot—by some person unknown acting under the authority—in defense of city property from the ravages of an excited mob, unlawfully congregated for that purpose, of which the deceased was found to be one. A second coroner sat at once with jury which brought in a verdict placing the responsibility for murder or manslaughter on Neal Dow and asking the grand jury to act.

All facts were published in every newspaper throughout the country. Excitement in Portland continued great. The grand jury refused to act. The city council took matters into their own hands and appointed a non-partisan committee of 17 to make a full investigation. This committee unanimously decided upholding the city authorities. The only legal proceeding was on the matter of the liquors still under seizure. They were promptly returned to the city. Counsel was eminent, Nathan Clifford, ex-Attorney General of the United States for the writ and U S Senator William Pitt Fessenden for the defense.

Nevertheless, the parties who instigated the broadside and the riot gained much of their point. Neal Dow did not run again for Mayor. That year the Maine law was repealed. Its friends did not push its re-enactment; leaving it to observation of the practical results of license vs no license. Neal Dow was elected without opposition to the Legislature of 1858 but never again accepted public office. After two years the law was re-enacted without the aid of a lobby and in 1882 it became a constitutional amendment. Neal Dow divided his time between traveling through this country and Great Britain, always with undivided purpose of furthering prohibition laws, and attending to his business in Portland, his directorates being many.

The criticism of his military career was at one time severe, until the facts were made perfectly clear. He was 57 when Sumpter fell, and nothing farther from his thoughts than military service. As a bank director his influence was great, perhaps the leading one, in inducing financial institutions to lend their credit to the Governor to finance a response to Lincoln's call for troops. Possibly the account in his Autobiography is perfectly fair: "But immediately after the attack on Sumpter I was forced to prepare for the possibility of joining the ranks, as the only way to prevent my older son, Fred, who I thought was not as well able as I to endure the hardships of army life, from going off with the first troops from Maine. On the evening of the day of the call of the President for 75,000 men he enlisted in the first military company of the State which volunteered. Because of his poor health I refused my approval, at the same time promising him that if the war continued he should go if I did not, reminding him that we could not both leave home. The next day I offered my services to the Governor in any capacity in which I might be useful, and the same day began the study of Hardee's Tactics."

That part of the country which entered the Confederacy had been looking forward for years for the outbreak which actually came. The trained officers, supplies, munitions were all in the south. Rank and file had been drilled and only a minority had to be taught how to handle a gun. The north had the weight of numbers, but not 10 per cent had ever used a gun. All munitions, supplies, everything had to be made. The trained officers were not 1 per cent of those needed. The whole country did what Neal Dow did,—started to read Hardee's Tactics. Dow became the best read military man in New England, thoroughly posted on fortifications.

He was promptly commissioned Colonel and ordered by the Secretary of War to raise a battery of artillery for 3 years service. He called for volunteers in Portland and 2,000 responded; of these 600 had to be attached to other regiments. Thus the 16th Me came into existence and after camping near Augusta started Feb 13, 1862 for an unknown destination. They went by rail to Boston, thence by sea arriving at Ship Island Mch 20, attached to the department of Maj Gen Benjamin F Butler. May 20 Dow received his commission as Brig Gen; service followed in command of Ft St Philip, Pensacola, then of the defenses of New Orleans and Carrollton. May 30, the brigade started for Port Hudson, its first field service. A battle was in progress when it arrived, with Gen W T Sherman in command. This was an outlying part of the Vicksburg unit, dependent upon its base. Both Gen Banks and Gen-in-chief Hallock concurred that, if Vicksburg fell, Port Hudson could not hold out. This was found to be true. Vicksburg fell July 8 and Col Gardner at Port Hudson surrendered without another shot.

Unfortunately, independent proceedings against Port Hudson were not postponed, altho the northern troops were not attacked nor in danger of attack. The place had splendid natural defense and no frontal attack could be made except over open country swept by the best artillery and rifle barrage the south could afford. Dow's brigade was centered at a farm house seven miles away. Gen Dow accompanied Gen Sherman on many reconnoissances without being able to see clearly the enemy position or estimate its strength. By direct approach there was an open plain of over 500 yards, a gulch into which the enemy had the exact range, then the nearby defenses, ditches, ramparts, sharpshooters. But, as is now well known, many movements throughout the war were on orders from Washington politics, compelled by men who had never seen a battle front. Some such order came here and now, far above the head of Gen Sherman, above Hallock. It was peremptory: "Port Hudson must fall tomorrow." Without discretion, all of Sherman's division had to share in an assault direct and without possibility of success. Dow's brigade, the 6th Mich, 128th N Y, 26th Conn, 15th Me, had to cross the wide, open plain. This it did and reached the gulch. The biggest gun in Port Hudson was manned by a New Yorker, who, caught south at the opening of the war, saved himself and aided the north by manning a gun and deflecting his aim. Even at this, the loss did not stop at decimation;

a comparatively small number finally retired to safety. The attack was abandoned. As already said, Port Hudson surrendered a month later without a shot. Gen Dow had a wound on the arm from a spent bullet and a ball through the thigh.

How or why the next blunder is even more incomprehensible. Altho very weak from malarial fever, as well as wounds, Dow remained to convalesce at a plantation house several miles in the rear of his former headquarters, far inside the Union lines. From here he applied for and hoped to get a transfer to the Army of the Potomac. Nine days before the fall of Port Hudson, June 30, 1863, a squad of cavalry, riding unopposed, even unseen, swooped down on the plantation house, captured the convalescent general, who was absolutely unaccompanied. No Union troops were in sight or hearing, nothing to disturb six uniformed Confederate cavalrymen. In fact the entire rear was unguarded and a company of cavalry could at any time rake it from end to end and get away before resistance could begin.

Next day he was put on a horse and started from camp Logan toward Richmond, put first in the Marbleyard prison at Jackson, Miss; thence to Montgomery, Ala, finally to Richmond and the notorious Libby prison. From here he was taken to Mobile and two months later back to Libby.

Why these transfers is not said. It is charged that Gen Dow was a troublesome prisoner, disregarding his paroles to observe and go about as freely as possible. At all events he was able to see that the whole south was almost spent, has no reserve power, must give up the war before long from exhaustion. The only Confederate officer of like rank held by the Union was Brig Gen Fitzhugh Lee. Mch 16, 1864, the two were exchanged. Neal Dow was sent to Washington and returned to Portland on 30 days leave.

After the war, his entire activity was in furtherance of his views on liquor prohibition, for at least fifteen years a speaker all over the country, a vigorous and polemical writer. The campaign of 1880 was the culmination of his activity. In 1884 he supported his lifelong friend, James G Blaine, but without activity in his canvass. In 1888 he left the Republican party. The time of life had long since come when men generally rest. After 1888 he followed the easy path of life at home and with friends. He had no specific illness, only the natural, not unwelcome, dissolution which comes to the normal person after the full life span. A week before his death he was unable to dress, fainting while attempting it. Then to his bed until the end, Oct 2, 1897. His children:

a   Louisa Dwight b Mch 23, 1831; m Dec 12, 1860, Jacob Benton of Lancaster, N H. No children
b   Edward b Sept 20, 1833; d Sept 18, 1835
c   Emma Maynard b Apr 5, 1836
d   Henry Neal b Apr 3, 1839; d Sept 29, 1840
e   Frederick Neal b Dec 23, 1840
f   Maria Cornelia b Nov 10, 1842; d Oct 12, 1905

g Josiah b Sept 29, 1845; d Oct 4, 1847
h Frank Allen b July 23, 1847; d Minneapolis Dec 13, 1865, where he had gone in search of health
i Russell Congdon b May 30, 1850; d Aug 11, 1852

Emma M Dow adhccbbc d Feb 22, 1918; m Apr 27, 1859, William Edward Gould b June 9, 1837, d Apr 16, 1919, son of Edward and Althea (Chase). For many years cashier of First Nat Bank, Portland; retired to Brookline, Mass, active member of the New England Genealogical Society, editor of the publications of the Chase-Chase Association, and authority on the genealogy of Gould and Maynard. About 1916 he wrote of a Chase Genealogy left with him, the work of a lifetime, which was going begging, not even acceptable as a gift to the larger libraries because it was not indexed. Children:

a Alice Maynard b Sept 4, 1860; m 1892 Everett W Pattison of Conway, N H
b Neal Dow b Jan 7, 1863
c Herbert Chase b Oct 5, 1865; d Aug 13, 1866
d Conrad Wieser b Sept 15, 1871; d Oct 29, 1871
e Margaret McClellan b July 5, 1874

Frederick Neal Dow adhccbbe, Col on the Governor's staff, was admitted to partnership in Josiah Dow & Son, as his father had been before him, and was its head for about ten years; was 7 years Collector of the Port; is president of the Casco Nat Bank; owns the Express, the leading newspaper; always high in the Republican organization of the State, prominent in Portland political and social life; promises to share the longevity of his line. He m Oct 22, 1864, Julia Dana Hammond b July 18, 1839. Children:

a Maria Cornelia Durant Maynard b 1865
b William Hammond b Dec 25, 1866
c Marion Durant b 1870; m 1895 William C Eaton; 1 dau

William H Dow adhccbbeb, business manager of the Portland Express; one time president of Portland Common Council, is identified with the industrial, social and political life of Portland. He is a strong believer in full middle names, as he has known and sometimes confused mail with 27 William H Dows in Maine. He m June 16, 1897, Kate Turner Wade, ae 25, dau of Leander A and Mary F (Turner). Children:

a Katherine Maynard b May 1, 1900   b Neal b May 11, 1907

Maria C Dow adhccbbf d unm Oct 12, 1905. After the death of her mother she assumed the responsibility of the care of the home and of hostess and companion to her father; was long secretary of the Y W C A of Portland, prominent in the national body of the W C T U, a lifelong devotee of charitable and philanthropic work; made especial study of reformatory work in this country and Europe.

Dorcas N Dow adhccd m Nov 8, 1797, Moses Hodgdon b Aug 22,

1773, d Sept 18, 1841, who stood 6 feet 4 and weighed about 250; a prominent citizen of Weare.   Children:

 a John b Oct 8, 1800; m Margaret Amelia Leggett; prominent lawyer of Weare
 b Abigail Breed b Nov 28, 1802; m Asa Hanson
 c Mary b Aug 27, 1804; d Mch 1851
 d Susanna b Aug 8, 1806; d Mch 9, 1829, unm
 e Anna b Apr 30, 1809; m Nathan Sawyer
 f Dorcas Neal b July 25, 1811; m Daniel Sawyer   g Moses Austin

Jedediah Dow adhccf d Portland Dec 25, 1843; held various offices in town and city government; had various occupations; in d rec of son is given as butcher; m Sept 5, 1802, Nancy Glazier b Nantucket, d Portland May 3, 18—.   Children:

 a Jedediah b Aug 14, 1803; d Havana, Cuba, July 3, 1823
 b Major John b Dec 15, 1805; d Oct 1808
 c Jane H b Apr 19, 1810 d Eleanor M b Nov 21, 1814
 e Charles Fitch b Mch 27, 1818
 f Jonathan Bulcher b Aug 4, 1821; d Mch 26, 1839
 g Albion K Parris b Dec 7, 1822
 h George H b Dec 2, 1826

Eleanor M Dow adhccfd m Jabez M Knight of Portland.   A dau:

 a Eleanor J D b Portland July 8, 1852; m Roxbury, Mass, Oct 20, 1885, George Cushman Owen b Sept 6, 1848, son of George and Ellen Louisa (Merrill)

Charles F Dow adhccfe, engineer of Cape Elizabeth, m Nov 6, 1842, Emeline Mead Richards b Falmouth Jan 13, 1822.   He d widower Dec 10, 1893.   Children:

 a Jedediah b Portland Oct 11, 1844; m Apr 25, 1871, Annie Devine; lived Pa; untraced; had several children, including a son, Charles T
 b Annie G b Sept 5, 1849; m Oct 20, 1868, Frank S Libby of Scarborough; 2 children
 c Charles F b Cape Elizabeth Jan 11, 1859; d Oct 10, 1861

Albion K P Dow adhccfg was named after a renowned statesman, altho the census takers knew him not, for the Portland 1849 directory gives him Alvin H P, seaman, and the 1850 census Almi H P; his wid mother lived with him.   He m after 1850 Mary E—; enlisted and d Salisbury prison, No Car, Dec 9, 1864.   Only child:

 a George Albion b Portland Aug 27, 1857

George A Dow adhccfga, capt in Portland Light Infantry, d Oct 20, 1891; m Ida L —— of N B; 2nd Elizabeth —— d 1904.   No rec of children.

George H Dow adhccfh, rigger of Portland, d widower Jan 2, 1914; m Jane Linton b St Andrews, N B, d Portland Oct 28, 1895, ae 67-7-17, dau of John and Martha (Greeley).   Only child:

 a Kate L b Mch 26, 1852

Kate L Dow adhccfha m Dec 24, 1873, Samuel J Knowles of Portland; living in Portland 1924; only child:

 a James Edgar of Portland b May 23, 1875; m Mary Earley; 2 children

Jonathan Dow adhccg, for many years sea captain, settled down in Portland; m 1807 Phoebe Greeley. Portland's first Mayor dying in office, Jonathan was elected for the unexpired term. He had some literary taste, and wrote a dozen papers which he called the Jack Downing Papers, the name being a modification of his own. He did not wish his authorship known and even got young Neal Dow to copy the ms so that the printer would not recognize the hand. The printer was Seba H Smith. Jonathan did not continue the work; Smith wrote a few additions and hired a well-known New York writer to do the rest. He had no children but adopted a boy, Hiram.

Hiram H Dow adhccga d Portland Oct 13, 1893, ae 88, 11 mos, b Portland son of Christopher ——— b Conn and Mary (Thomas) b Kittery. His wife, by d rec of a son, was Alice M Pearson. Hiram appears in 1847-8 directory as candle manufacturer, but the family has not been found in 1850 census. Four children are mentioned in an obituary and 2 sons found by own rec. All b Portland:

    a Charles D b 1837   b Hiram Augustus b 1837 (twins apparently)
    c Mrs J Neal Read   d Mrs Preston O'Brion

Charles D Dow adhccgaa, druggist of Bangor, m Freedom, N H, June 5, 1859, Lucy S Wilson, ae 21, of Yarmouth. Age does not quite agree with a C D Dow, traveling salesman of Portland, d Farmington, N H, June 5, 1893, ae 51, and, as our Charles D survived his father, the identity is improbable. No mention of children.

Hiram A Dow adhccgab, cattle and horse dealer, d Feb 22, 1908, ae 71, 5 mos; m Portland June 11, 1867, Caroline P Clark d Jan 14, 1920, ae 71-0-21, dau of Elliott F and Mary A (Frye) of Hollis. Three children found by own rec:

    a Cora E d Portland Aug 11, 1911, ae 42, unm
    b Augustus E, survived his father; appears in recent directory his wid mother
        with him, horse dealer
    c George S, traveling salesman, d Portland June 24, 1912, ae 39, 6 mos, unm

Alice Dow adhccgac m (his 2nd) James Neal Read b Windham or Coventry, Conn, Aug 17, 1820.

Widely divergent is the history of the two sons of Abraham Dow, Quaker preacher, who elected to stay in Seabrook, from the two who went to Weare.

Benjamin Dow adhcd, husbandman of Seabrook, m Sept 24, 1776, Lynn Quarterly Meeting, Hannah Phillips, dau of Walter and Content (Hope); 2nd Mch 16, 1808, Harriet Silsby, dau of Henry and Hannah of Lynn, Quakers. If more details were available, Benjamin would make a fine subject for story or psychological study. His piety genuine and deep, honesty sound, thrift more than great, business acumen good, narrow, domineering, wholly unable to see any view point except his

own, losing year after year whatever winsome qualities he ever had,
thoroughly unlovely in his old age. His house was a one-story, rambling
affair, with an ell which he built for his son when he married. Local
tradition has it that this house was moved from Seabrook into Hampton
Falls by merely moving it across the road. The fact is that the ell was
so moved and became the homestead of another generation. Benjamin
d Jan 28, 1835, will dated Oct 28, 1834; probated June 10, 1835. His
wife's bequest was the use of two rooms and various small items of
personal property. She timidly asked the court what she would have if
she did not accept the provisions. The court immediately granted her
"thirds." To grandsons Abraham, Edward and Walter P were given
$1 each. Bequests were made to dau Hannah Wells and granddau
Eunice Wells. The considerable residuary estate went 2-3 to grandson
Benjamin and 1-3 to granddau Mary Ann. Children:

   a Benjamin b July 1777   b Hannah b June 1784

Benjamin Dow adhcda d Nov 11, 1833; m Apr 6, 1800, Hannah
Gove b 1785, d Feb 1, 1848, dau of Winthrop and Elizabeth (Ring)
Quakers. Benjamin suffered under the terrible handicap of being his
father's son and inherited something of his narrowness. Always under
a thumb from birth, never able to break away, never able to get a home
of his own, living with wife and family in the ell built for him by his father,
having to account for almost every movement, he d in that semi-slavery
before his father. His father even had him adjudged a common drunkard
and got himself appointed guardian of his property,—value $970. The
narrow hand of his father also blighted Hannah Gove, to whom was
willed "an estate during her widowed life in the house where she now
lives—also a comfortable support as long as she remains his widow."
As Hannah was then 50 with no aim in the world except to care for her
5 children, the precautions seem superfluous:

   a Abram b Oct 15, 1800   b Edward b Mch 19, 1804
   c Walter Phillips b Dec 18, 1806
   d Mary Ann b Aug 1809; m July 30, 1839, Stacy L Nudd akecaha. No children.
      He owned a seashore hotel, where they lived summers, spending winters in
      Hampton Falls. Their first home was the ell moved across the street;
      this they sold and bought the homestead of Abraham Dow adhcha south
      of Falls River. By thrift she amassed considerable property; was a good
      and not at all narrow-minded woman. Her nephew being denied a home
      by his father, who disapproved his marriage, Mary Ann took in the young
      couple, shared her home as long as she lived and made the nephew her heir
   e Benjamin b Nov 10, 1813; changed his name, but without legal action, to
      George Franklin Dow

Abram Dow adhcdaa m Aug 18—; drowned at sea; his wid remarried. Only child:

   a Weare b about 1825; grew up and in the vague tradition of the Falls "went
      west or somewhere." Untraced

Edward Dow adhcdab m Seabrook Dec 30, 1846, wid Jennette
Thompson, by whom 1 dau; 2nd Cory, Pa, ——, by whom 2 dau. Under

the new environment he prospered and had no inclination ever to revisit his boyhood home.   Dau by 1st wife:

    a Emma m —— Cox; 2 dau

Walter P Dow adhcdac, taxed from 1830 in Hampton Falls, moved
to Amesbury; d Amesbury Oct 24, 1871; m Seabrook Apr 13, 1835,
Belinda Smith of Hampton Falls b 1809, d Amesbury Dec 25, 1882.
Children:

    a Hannah Phillips b 1835; m Albert Noyes of Newburyport; 1 dau
    b Lucy Ann b 1838; m James Dow adk line; 2 sons, untraced
    c Lewis Phillips b 1840; d Amesbury ae about 15
    d Mary Lucinda b Seabrook July 8, 1844; m May 24, 1862, John C Berry of
       Pittsfield; 1 dau; 2nd Sewall Felch of Salisbury; 2 sons; living 1920 in
       Salisbury
    e Elvira Gove b 1844; m Walter W Flanders; 2nd George Loney; d without
       children
    f Adelaide Arvilla d young   g Ellen Augusta d young
    h Emery W b Salisbury

Emery W Dow adhcdach lived Amesbury; d July 2, 1904; m Rose
Williams of Lynn; 5 children; 2nd Carrie Norton, by whom 1 dau
living 1921.   Older 5 have left Amesbury, untraced.

George F Dow adhcdae d Apr 2, 1874; m (Benjamin Jr) May 2,
1839, Elvira Ross of Salisbury b Apr 14, 1816, d Red Oak, Iowa, Jan 1,
1882.   In boyhood called Bennie, greatly to his dislike.   His will is
signed Benjamin.   A blacksmith, he also farmed the homestead and
grew rich by spending little.   Realty assessment 1850 $6,000.   Children:

    a John Alvin b Feb 11, 1840
    b Martha Ann b May 14, 1841; d Aug 13, 1884; m Peter G Tilton of Hampton
       Falls d Sept 22, 1885; no children
    c Hannah Maria b July 2, 1843; d Feb 7, 1916; m James Monroe S Tucker d
       Aug 21, 1914; no children; they bought the homestead from the other
       heirs
    d Mary Ellen b Nov 9, 1849
    e Sarah A b May 14, 1852; d May 23, 1917; m Charles Henry Tucker; lived
       Amesbury; no children

John A Dow adhcdaea d Sept 22, 1911; m Zelpha Ann Dow adaim-
bab d 1884.   Both were very young, he had accumulated nothing.   His
father refused to receive the young couple and they had no home.   His
aunt, Mrs Mary A Nudd, took them into her home and made him her
heir.   Thereafter he cut quite a figure in Hampton Falls.   He m 2nd
Dec 20, 1885, Mary Frances Chase, ae 42, dau of Charles F, blacksmith
of Hampton Falls.   His father willed him $5, remarking that he was
already well provided for.   Children, by 1st wife:

    a Helen M b Aug 20, 1864   b Mary S b May 29, 1868; unm of Salisbury
    c George F, now of Salisbury, unm

Helen M Dow adhcdaeaa m June 28, 1888, John Arthur Moulton
of Hampton b Aug 8, 1860, son of Daniel Y and Martha A (Brown).
Children:

    a Jessie A b May 3, 1889   b Martha

Mary E Dow adhcdaed m Thomas Horace Dearborn d Apr 19, 1916, son of John and Mary A (Towle); moved to Red Oak, Iowa; living 1921. Children:

    a   Helen Towle b Aug 4, 1879   b   Frances Ross b May 11, 1881
    c   John Tilton b May 15, 1883
    d   George Tucker b Aug 3, 1886; d Nov 26, 1892

Hannah Dow adhcdb inherited a piece of marsh land, $500 and, at her mother's death, half the household furniture; m 1: 2: 1809, Moses Wells of Hampton Falls, a Quaker, owning an inn on the high road to Boston, much used in coaching days. Hannah d Hampton Mch 10, 1860. Children:

    a   Eunice, inherited her grandfather's watch; d unm
    b   Hannah Phillips grew up and m   c   Abbie d unm
    d   Sarah Phillips m John H Gove, a man of much force of character. His lifelong
        friend and kinsman, John Greenleaf Whittier, found the Gove home his
        favorite retreat in later years and died there; under its famous elms he wrote
        much, especially the poems dealing with early Quaker history. One child,—
        Sarah Abbie, unm, spends her summers in the homestead, attends the Ames-
        bury meeting house, following the simple ancestral faith of the first meeting
        house of 1702

Judith Dow adhce d before 1802; m Samuel Collins of Lynn, son of Zachaeus and Elizabeth (Sawyer). Four children found in Lynn rec, perhaps more between:

    a   Zachaeus b May 23, 1768; m 20: 11 mo: 1793, Theodate Farrington; had
        posterity
    b   Content b Jan 27, 1770; d Sept 24, 1790, unm
    c   Ezra b Aug 24, 1780; m 17: 11 mo: 1802, Eunice Basset, dau of Isaac and Mary
    d   Nancy, twin, m 18: 5 mo: 1803, Daniel Johnson, son of Nehimiah and Lydia

Abraham Dow adhch d 1828, his estate administered by his son, Sam George, and John Philbrick of Seabrook; m (int pub Aug 10, 1779) Dorothy (Dolly) Green of Kensington b Mch 17, 1758, dau of David and Ruth, half sister of David Green adhcbe. Abraham, a blacksmith of Seabrook, bought a farm just south of the Falls and set up a forge on it. This land, an original grant about 1638 to Capt Christopher Hussey (*Vide sub* ab), was sold by Abraham's son to Mrs Mary A Nudd and became the homestead of John A Dow adhcdaaa. Children:

    a   Abram (so signing, bap Abraham) b 1783
    b   Ruth d Dec 14, 1866, unm

Abraham Dow adhcha moved to Hampton when he sold the homestead and was lost sight of by the Hampton Falls kin; said d 1834, but probably m late and had:

    a   Abram b Hampton 1842

Abram Dow adhchaa, corporal in the Winnacunnett Guards, disabled and disch after a year's service, returned to Seabrook; m Nov 3, 1863, Lucy Jane Dow adaijaba d Dec 21, 1864, ae 24, 2 mos. Only child:

    a   Joseph A b Dec 21, 1864

Joseph A Dow adhchaaa, shoemaker of Seabrook, m Nov 19, 1904, Alice J Eaton, ae 27, dau of Abner L and Phylena (Fowler).

Mary Dow adhci m Benjamin Phillips of Lynn, son of Walter and Content (Hope); their posterity still numerous in Lynn. Phillips Gen does not follow up this line. In the copy in the library of Sons of the Revolution, Los Angeles, the Author has inserted another generation. Children:

    a Walter b July 7, 1783
    b Content b Oct 23, 1784; m (int pub Aug 18, 1805) Joshua R Gove
    c Benjamin b Mch 6, 1786   d Abraham Dow b Jan 22, 1788
    e Mary b Nov 11, 1790; m Aug 3, 1818, Daniel Farrington Jr
    f Anna b Jan 17, 1793   g Abigail b Dec 11, 1794
    h Sarah b Jan 4, 1797   i Phebe b Dec 4, 1798
    j Jonathan b July 12, 1800

Elizabeth Dow adhd m May 15, 1735, Jonathan Hoag of Newmarket, son of Jonathan and Martha, Quakers, whose posterity have married several times into Dow. Hist Hampton Falls: "In Seabrook lived the mother of Hussey Hoag, a Revolutionary soldier. She is said to have sold her son for a quintal of fish and to have lived to 105. In after years the son never recognized his mother on this account. With her lived an old lady named Dow, said to have reached nearly the same age." Her identity is not recognizable, probably wid. While their ages are greatly exaggerated, they surely lived to great age, as Quaker matrons often do. In every New England village there is some such derelict. Perhaps Elizabeth was poor and let some family better able to care for her son. In the Author's home town there was a couple of aged spinsters, regarded as witches and criticized for their use of tobacco. It was their habit to use a cane with pointed nail in the end and spear all cigar butts they found. They had very beautiful house plants, which they fed with tobacco decoction. Just as sound are the prejudices regarding the mother of Hussey Hoag.

Anna Dow adhe m 20: 12 mo: 1737, Jedediah Morrill (Morrell in rec) b Kittery Aug 29, 1711, d 26: 2 mo: 1776, son of John and Hannah. He m 1st Dover 1: 10 mo: 1734, Elizabeth Jenkins: 3rd 28: 1 mo: 1762, Sarah Gould. Anna d No Berwick May 12, 1761. Children:

    a Abraham b Dec 26, 1738; m Elizabeth Lewis; 2nd Sarah Nichols
    b Josiah d Litchfield, Me; m Oct 25, 1764, Hannah Webber
    c Winthrop b Dec 20, 1744; m Susannah Lewis
    d John m Sarah Varney; 2nd Elizabeth G Baker
    e Peace m 1783 Daniel Perkins of Wells, Me

SAMUEL Dow adk by the terms of his father's will was taught the weaver's trade. He also learned, perhaps from his father, the art of surveying. His chain and compass are still kept as heirlooms by his descendants; these may have belonged to his father, but more likely were bought by himself. He studied mathematics and compiled an almanac extensively used by his neighbors, who chose from it the right days for certain plantings, setting hens and other routine of farm life. This almanac was calculated for 25 years, Samuel saying that by then he would be dead or the world would have come to its end. He inherited a farm at the New Plantation, but July 11, 1718, bought a better from Richard Sanborn Sr. In the deed he is called Samuel of Salisbury, but his lands were in what is now Seabrook, well above the border. An interesting deed is one dated Aug 20, 1711, by which Henry, Jeremiah, Josiah and Samuel Dow sell a piece of Hampton land. It was the last piece in Hampton kept in the ad line.

From the time he reached manhood, Samuel was not enthusiastic about the Friends. He saw service at Ft William & Mary Oct 16 to Nov 1708. His marriage seems to have been at the Friends meeting house 2: 11 mo: 1711, Sarah Shepard b Haverhill Aug 11, 1689, dau of Samuel and Mary (Dow ba) of Salisbury,—Shepard of Salisbury or now living in ye Provins of Newhampsher. There is reason for thinking that he and his wife considered for 17 years the matter of becoming church members and formally leaving the Friends. Unless Sarah Shepard had become nominally a Friend, we cannot understand how she could be married at the meeting house. Mary had been duly bap in Haverhill; there is no evidence that Samuel ever was. Four older children were bap in west parish, three younger at a slightly earlier date in east parish. The oldest dau was bap and owned the covenant Mch 17, 1728, ae 16. None of the Shepards appear among the Friends. Probably Sarah favored the change and Samuel was not especially unwilling.

Samuel's d rec is not found; it was in 1777, for his will was probated Exeter June 10, 1777. It was dated May 20, 1768; so that a legacy to his unfortunate brother Jeremiah came too late. He had been thrifty and able. The inventory showed £1750-17-10. The will mentions sons Jabez, Joseph, Josiah, dau Sarah Clough and Mercy Adams. Son Abner must have d without issue:

a   Sarah b Oct 26, 1712   b   Abner b July 25, 1715; bap Aug 4, 1728
c   Mercy b Nov 27, 1717; bap Aug 4, 1728
d   Josiah b Mch 25, 1719; bap Aug 4, 1728
e   Joseph b Feb 10, 1721   f   Samuel b Mch 15, 1726
g   Jabez b Aug 12, 1727; the 3 bap together July 19, 1728

It is rather remarkable that the four sons went their several ways, probably never meeting again.

Sarah Dow adka m Apr 25, 1734, Samuel Clough of Salisbury. Two Samuels of Salisbury had wives Sarah, one with children from 1716; but there is no chance that any children herein belong to the older:

a   Mehitabel b Nov 3, 1737
b   Samuel b Mch 10, 1739-40; d June 4, 1756
c   Miriam (to Samuel & Sarah Brown, clearly error) b Apr 25, 1742; m (int Jan 17, 1764) William True Jr
d   Abner b May 24, 1744
e   Sarah b Apr 11, 1748; m Nov 17, 1771, Samuel Dudley of Gilmanton
f   Jonathan b May 26, 1750; m Dec 10, 1776, Mary True
g   Josiah b Nov 26, 1752; bap (Isaiah) Dec 3, 1752
h   Daniel b June 6, 1754
i   Anna b Feb 1, 1756; m Dec 4, 1782, Daniel Dudley of Barnstead

Mercy Dow adkc m (Marse in int) Apr 28, 1737, Archelaus Adams. Hoyt, Old Families, errs in giving her d 1741 with 2 dau. Descendants of William Adams (Essex Historical Series) is right that Mercy d Salisbury Sept 2, 1784. Children:

a   Sarah b Jan 19, 1737-8; d ae 90; m Jan 23, 1755, John Merrill Jr
b   Mary b July 13, 1739; m Dec 5, 1758, Ebenezer Tucker
c   Betsey b Jan 21, 1742; m Aug 21, 1760, Joseph Flanders Jr of Greensboro, Vt
d   Zilpha b Nov 17, 1743; m July 1770 Jonathan Ring
e   Joseph b Apr 9, 1745; m Mary Currier; moved to Salisbury, N H
f   Samuel b Nov 5, 1747; d Feb 3, 1748
g   Samuel b Jan 13, 1749; shipwright, d Salisbury
h   Abigail b June 18, 1752; m ——— Stevens
i   Mercy b June 14, 1755; d young   j   Archelaus b June 14, 1755
k   Stephen m and left 2 children   l   Mercy b Feb 16, 1759

Josiah Dow adkd left Seabrook to buy a farm in Kensington; d Oct 20, 1805; m Jan 24, 1744-5, Mary Wadleigh b Dec 29, 1719, d Apr 2, 1795, dau of Joseph and Abigail (Allen) of Salisbury. Census 1790 shows them alone, all the children married and gone:

a   Sarah b Dec 6, 1745   b   Joseph bap Aug 2, 1747
c   Anna b Dec 2, 1748   d   Benjamin b Dec 16, 1750
e   Richard b Mch 22, 1753   f   Mary b Feb 28, 1758; d July 20, 1760
g   Polly b 1760   h   Mary b Jan 2, 1763; d Mch 5, 1789

Sarah Dow adkda appears in Hist Union, Me, but with b date Dec 7, 1747, error. She m Oct 30, 1775, Samuel Sibley b Feb 23, 1751, original settler of Meredith, Me, on a tract owned by his father, a pioneer of Union. He was short, his wife tall. At the wedding a young woman, not fancying this inequality, seized a wooden oven lid, about 2 inches thick, and pushed it against his heels. He stepped upon it and thus the pair stood at equal height during the ceremony. Meredith was primitive, at first their nearest neighbor being 3 miles distant. Samuel was away lumbering much of the time, but Sarah was a hardy pioneer. One night a neighbor staying by to guard the house shot and wounded a bear found eating corn. Sarah pursued the wounded bear, caught it by the leg as it was clambering over a log and cut its throat with a jack knife. Children:

a   Josiah Dow b 1779; d ae 15 mos
b   Hannah b Feb 7, 1780; m (his 2nd) Jeremiah Gove of Hampton Falls, son of Joseph and Susanna (Pevere); son John C b June 13, 1824

    c Richard b 1782; m Polly French of Newmarket; rafter, drowned in a squall
    d Mary b Mch 1, 1784; m Paul H Stanton of Bartlett; 4 children
    e Sarah b Sept 16, 1786; m July 3, 1806, William Robinson of Sanbornton; wid, returned to Meredith, cared for her parents in old age
    f Benjamin b Mch 7, 1790; m —— Hilliard; moved 1817 to Woodstock, Ohio; not heard from by parents for 23 years; 4 children
    g Nancy b Feb 1792; d ae 17 mos

Joseph Dow adkdb is dismissed by the genealogist of the adkde line with the statement that he was a Major in the Revolution, m a Miss Healey, had a son Warren b 1773, named for a near relative, Maj Joseph Warren of Bunker Hill fame. While little has found its way into print about him, there need be no such dismissal of his jovial, eccentric and well known personality. He m Dec 13, 1770, Mary Healey, dau of Stephen and Sarah of Kensington. That he won his majority by merit is certain. Husbandman of Kensington, ae 28, he enlisted June 3, 1775, promoted to corporal, received $4 allowance for an overcoat; 1777 asst muster master R I, Capt Joseph Parsons, Col Senter; 1777 promoted to Lieut. The rolls seldom give data of higher officers. After the war he returned to Kensington; his wife d Nov 13, 1780, ae 29; he m 2nd Feb 25, 1785 (Kensington rec) or Oct 1, 1784 (Hampton Falls rec), Elizabeth dau of Gov Meshech Weare. He moved to his wife's home in Hampton Falls 1795. In his regiment he had been superior officer of James Monroe, afterwards President. The latter visited Maj Dow in Hampton Falls 1817, writing that he looked forward with much pleasure to renewing the army acquaintance. The Major had a reputation as a wag and during the president's visit bewailed the change of the times which had left him the under dog. *Eheu, tempora mutantur.* For many years he dispensed hospitality from the Weare mansion. His eccentricities were wholly of the genial sort and he certainly laughed with glee over his thought that any one must be crazy, if a genuine Dow, and that any Dow claiming to be sane must be an imposter. A man of leisure, of sufficient income, he traveled much around the region, passing the time of day and making a joke to be greeted with laugh and verbal repetition. The home was shared by his wife's sister Hannah and her husband, John Porter. Hannah d ae 95, the Major himself at 82, Dec 19, 1829. Census 1790 shows him 1a, 3b, 3c. Children:

    a Stephen b June 28, 1771; d fever Dec 23, 1781
    b Weare b Mch 8, 1773; d scalded Jan 6, 1774
    c Weare b Oct 10, 1774; d unm Hampton Falls June 24, 1813; will signed May 28, probated July 19. He owned a large tract of land in Ohio. His bequests included brother, sister, father, cousin Furber Dow adkddgb. Rev Jacob Abbott, his executor, received his library, of unusual size and merit
    d Polly b Dec 2, 1776; bap Molly Dec 14, 1776; often signed Mary
    e Joseph Warren b Apr 8, 1779
    f Meshech Weare b Aug 8 1787; d Dec 1, 1812

Polly Dow adkdbd. This sprightly daughter of the Revolution, who never married, will always live in Hampton Falls traditions. Member of the Congregational church, she was active in town life. In 1823 she appears as presenting colors to the Haverhill Light Infantry, making a stirring address. Late in her father's life she took into the home Sally Healey, an unm cousin who lived to 92. In 1864 she sold the mansion to Zebulon Dow adaijb, who came from Seabrook to occupy it, while Polly and Sally moved into smaller quarters. She d Jan 10, 1868.

Joseph W Dow adkdbe was the only Congregational clergyman to come from Hampton Falls; took a parish in Tyringham, Mass, d there Jan 9, 1833; m May 12, 1812, Emily Peabody b June 24, 1780, d childless Feb 1813; 2nd Sarah Kimball m 2nd Aug 8, 1848, Silas Hardy, widower, carpenter of Bradford, ae 66, son of Henry and Rachel (Danford). Children:

a   Sarah Peabody b July 4, 1816; int pub May 15, 1836, to Putnam Perley
b   Elizabeth Weare b Oct 25, 1818; m Haverhill Sept 20, 1842, Charles B Hall
c   Mary Healey b Oct 12, 1820
d   Harriet Pamela b July 17, 1822; d Apr 6, 1835
e   Susan Huntington b Nov 28, 1828

Benjamin Dow adkdd, lifelong resident of Kensington, receipted for £4-10-0 enlistment bounty and served in the same company as his brother; was mustered out as captain; m Feb 1, 1780, by Rev Jeremiah Fogg, Ruth Fellows of Kensington, dau of Jeremiah and Ruth (Row). She d Aug 18, 1842, ae 87, 10 mos. Benjamin d of dropsy Mch 15, 1808, leaving an estate of $6,617.86. Son Richard executor. Nov 29, 1811, wid Ruth received her dower, the rest cut in 7 equal parts. May 27, 1811, Robert Prescott was made guardian of Jeremiah and Wadleigh, minors over 14. Census 1790 finds Benjamin 1a, 1b, 4c. Children:

a   Benjamin d Nov 18, 1780, infant
b   Anna bap by Rev Jeremiah Fogg May 26, 1782; d (Nancy) Nov 18, 1862, unm
c   Richard bap Nov 7, 1783; b Oct 31, 1783
d   Olive d Oct 11, 1812, ae 27, of typhoid; brother Benjamin administrator
e   Sophia b Mch 27, 1788; d consumption Nov 25, 1807
f   Benjamin bap June 12, 1791; d from a scythe cut Oct 4, 1852
g   Newell d Kensington Nov 14, 1875; ae 81, 11 mos
h   Wadleigh d Salem, Mass, July 29, 1845, ae 50; m Newburyport July 10, 1825, Zilpha Stetson. No recollection of children by our informant in this line.
i   Jeremiah bap May 19, 1799

Richard Dow adkddc d Apr 10, 1861; m Kensington Jan 25, 1809, Jemima Worthen b Kensington Nov 2, 1783, d Dec 22, 1867, at her daughter's home, No Hampton, dau of Enoch and Jemima (Quimby), granddau of Maj Ezekiel Worthen. The couple moved 1817-8 to a farm over the Exeter line, assessed 1850 at $4,500. Children:

a   George b Kensington Oct 29, 1809; d Exeter Mch 30, 1890
b   Charles d Kensington Aug 8, 1883, ae 72, 2 mos
c   Mary W d Exeter Sept 16, 1833, ae 18, 4 mos
d   Nancy b Exeter; d No Hampton Mch 24, 1889, ae 68, 6 mos
e   Benjamin Worthen b Exeter Sept 24, 1826; d Exeter July 16, 1909

George Dow adkddca, farmer of Exeter m Mch 4, 1868, Sophia R Davis, wid of —— Robinson of Exeter. Children:

a   Mary Worthen b Mch 19, 1868; m June 28, 1888, Henry G Durgin of Portland, Me; living Exeter 1921

   b   Ellen A b July 24, 1870; m Jan 31, 1894, George E Jones of Concord, Mass
   c   Addie F of Dow's Hill, Exeter, m June 23, 1909, Eugene Donovan

Charles Dow adkddcb lived many years Lowell, Mass; m Exeter Oct 16, 1832, Elizabeth L Badger of Kensington. Said to have had family.

Benjamin W Dow adkddce, farmer of Dow's Hill, Exeter, m No Hampton Apr 8, 1857, Sarah A Locke b May 21, 1831, d Jan 22, 1921. Children:

   a   Josephine Plummer; teacher of Boston, spends her summers at the homestead;
         unm; furnished the adkddc line
   b   Charles H

Charles H Dow adkddceb, lawyer of Boston, in Cambridge Sept 23, 1896, Mary Esther Fulton of Folly Village, N S; 2nd June 22, 1905, Ina F Capen of Spencer, Mass, dau of Herbert H and Edith M (Parkhurst). Children:

   a   (by 1st wife) —— son d young   b   Doris b Sept 12, 1907
   c   Richard b Dec 11, 1910; d Mch 15, 1911
   d   Benjamin Capen b Nov 18, 1913
   e   Joan b Nov 29, 1914; d Jan 8, 1918
   f   Richard Worthen b Nov 9, 1916
   g   Carolyn b Apr 15, 1919; d Mch 3, 1920

Benjamin Dow adkddf, farmer of Kensington, assessed 1850 at $3,000; wife Nancy b N H 1785. The name immediately following is Francis Dow b 1840 N H. He is unknown, if a younger son, d soon after. Benjamin lived near the Exeter line; wife Mary d Kensington Jan 20, 1862, ae 67. There seems no possibility that two Benjamins have been confused. Mary was probably 2nd wife. Family rec mentions only 1 child:

   a   Newell b 1822

Newell Dow adkddfa (called Jr, on account of his uncle) became a shoemaker in Seabrook; m Oct 25, 1846, Betsey Knowles. Lost sight of by the Kensington kinsfolk. He must have m 2nd, for Newell Dow Jr m Seabrook June 10, 1863, Sarah A Knowles, both of Seabrook. Newell hanged himself Aug 30, 1878.   Children:

   a   Newell F b Apr 1846; soldier d diphtheria Mch 17, 1864, unm
   b   (to Newell Jr and Sarah) —— dau b Feb 28, 1865

Newell Dow adkddg d Nov 14, 1875; m Sarah A Chase b Jan 1804, d Kensington Oct 5, 1891, dau of Daniel and Sarah. He bought from his father-in-law a farm adjoining his father's.   Children:

   a   Weare b July 12, 1823; d smallpox Concord Feb 26, 1846
   b   Furber b June 2, 1825; d Aug 27, 1863
   c   Charles C b Nov 16, 1827; d Sept 26, 1885
   d   Jeremiah b Dec 28, 1829; d July 21, 1893
   e   Newell b Mch 18, 1832; d Aug 8, 1838
   f   Sarah E b Dec 12, 1834; d Oct 10, 1918; m Norris Robie.   Children,—Charles
         and Carrie E still live on the farm bought by Josiah Dow adkd
   g   John F b Oct 30, 1837; d Mch 7, 1848

h Benjamin b Dec 30, 1841; d Feb 11, 1909, unm
i David Sewall b Dec 30, 1841; d July 17, 1842
j Carrie C b Apr 24, 1845; m June 7, 1873, Robert Beckman of Seabrook; in
   1919 was the only survivor of her family. A son James Arthur m Portsmouth
   1900

Furber Dow adkddgb, carpenter of Kensington and Exeter, d Aug
27, 1863. Untraced, except for a son:

a —— son b Exeter Sept 24, 1857

Charles C Dowe (sic) adkddgc, farmer of Kensington, m Sarah C
Locke b Hopkinton. Children:

a Willie N b Kensington 1862   b Mary E b Nov 8, 1865
c Ellen M b Nov 8, 1865; m (Nellie M) July 4, 1885; Wilbur K Parker of Salem,
   Mass
d Minnie C m June 27, 1887, C Eugene Janvrin of Hampton Falls

William N Dow adkddgca, 1887 farmer of Kensington, 1892-5
shoemaker of Exeter, m Hattie B Weare b Hampton Falls 1865. Children:

a Charles Layforest b Apr 19, 1887
b George W b Jan 19, 1889; d Hampton Mch 11, 1891
c Harry Chester b Exeter June 15, 1892; d Oct 27, 1894
d —— dau b Exeter June 15, 1892
e Nellie b Kensington Sept 24, 1899

Charles Forrest Dow adkddgcaa m Merrimac, N H, Oct 17, 1910,
Viola Emily Grocut, ae 24, dau of John W and Nellie (Murphy).

Jeremiah Dow adkddgd d Kensington July 21, 1893; m May 17,
1852, Almira B Palmer, both of Kensington. State rec give 2 children:

a Julia b Jan 7, 1855. Lynn rec gives Julia A Dow, adopted dau of the couple;
   m Mch 22, 1907, Arthur W Sanborn. May be identical; more likely Julia
   d and the adoption was of a much younger girl
b Charles A b Kensington May 21, 1857

Charles A Dow adkddgdb, shoemaker of Kensington, m Seabrook
Nov 18, 1882, Estella McQuillan adaieaad, ae 23; moved to Seabrook.
At least 1 child:

a —— son b Seabrook July 10, 1883

Jeremiah Dow adkddi grad Dartmouth Medical School; practiced
medicine in Hiram, Me, many years until his d. He d Erving, Mass, at
his son's home Aug 19, 1875; m 2nd Oct 1849 Jane Ingalls b West Baldwin
June 3, 1816, d West Baldwin Sept 29, 1901, dau of David and Polly,
pioneers of Baldwin. Census 1850 gives them, assessment $1,500, and
children:

a Edmund b 1838   b James b 1843; untraced

Her own d rec at Baldwin gives Jane dau of David W and Sarah
(Sherburn) Ingalls. Son James in untraced, but a Baldwin rec: Clinton
Dow m Oct 6, 1884, Mary E Gatchell, both of Baldwin. This seems
referable to this line.

Edmund Dow adkddia, for many years confidential clerk for a Mr Rankin, merchant and manufacturer of Erving, who came from Hiram Me, lived in Lowell and finally went into the grocery business in Waltham. Wife was Myra P b Bridgeton, Me.   Children:

a   Nellie b July 11, 1871
b   Frederick Elmer b Jan 16, 1874.   Recent directory gives a Fred E Dow janitor of Waltham

---

Richard Dow adkde, private under Capt Henry Elkins, Portsmouth Nov 23, 1775, was an original settler of Wakefield, N H, deed dated Apr 10, 1782.   This land has never left the family and is now the summer home and reunion place.   He was deacon of Wakefield church; d Feb 17, 1836; m Dec 17, 1777, Mercy Coffin of Epping, dau of Enoch.   Children:

a   Richard Furber b Sept 12, 1778   b   Enoch b Aug 16, 1780
c   Josiah b Dec 27, 1782
d   Benjamin b Apr 8, 1785; m 1810 Mary Proctor; no children
e   Asa b Mch 24, 1788
f   Mary Coffin b May 28, 1791; d Galena, Ill, Sept 18, 1841, unm
g   Sarah Barber b Sept 8, 1793; m 1815 Samuel Yeaton. Children,—Samuel, Enoch Dow, William Barber
h   John b May 28, 1795; school teacher in Nor Car; d unm, young
i   Eunice Norris b June 20, 1788; m Josiah Gould
j   Thomas Leavitt b Oct 22, 1800; seaman on the Patterson; drowned Texas Roads Apr 4, 1822

Richard F Dow adkdea, farmer of Wakefield, d Apr 29, 1820; m 1808 Susan Parsons b Parsonsfield Jan 17, 1788, d Wakefield Aug 2, 1837, dau of Thomas and Lucy (Bradbury).   This line accurate in Parsons Gen:

a   Asa Parsons b Aug 28, 1809; d Landgrove, Vt, Oct 9, 1832, unm
b   Susan Maria b Dec 31, 1810; d Wolfboro Dec 4, 1844; m George Brigham Farrar of Wolfboro, son of Joseph and Mehitable (Dana)
c   Enoch Coffin b May 26, 1812
d   Richard Furber Hamilton b Dec 12, 1815; d June 4, 1816
e   Eunice Gould b Mch 30, 1817
f   Thomas Usher b May 6, 1819; d Philadelphia Sept 7, 1835, unm

Enoch C Dow adkdeac d Rochester Jan 4, 1876; grad Bowdoin Medical School; practiced Tuftonborough and Rochester; m Nov 4, 1831, Roxana Poland of Hartford; 2nd Nov 18, 1841, Martha Moore Palmer of Tuftonborough b Nov 12, 1813, d Oct 18, 1861, dau of Joseph and Lydia (Evans); 3rd Jan 27, 1863, Lucy Ann Tibbetts b Nov 21, 1831, dau of Leonard and Lucy (Cross).   Probably only child:

a   Enoch Coffin, evidently succeeded his father, for Rochester rec: Sabrina L, wid of Dr Dow, dau of Nicholas and Olive (Boston) Styles, b Oct 27, 1835, d Rochester Oct 18, 1906

Eunice G Dow adkdeae m Wakefield Apr 18, 1837, Jeremiah Harris Banks b Dover Mch 9, 1813; d Springfield, Mass, Aug 27, 1867.   Children:

a   Henry Harms b Jan 13, 1838; m Emma Wells
b   Ella Maria b Mch 2, 1844; m Charles Chauncey Morrill
c   Jennie Florence b 1855; d 1859

Enoch Dow adkdeb, tailor, d Salem, Mass, June 12, 1816, ae 36; m Oct 6, 1805, Mary Brooks d ae 34 May 1815.   Newspapers of the day called him one of our most worthy citizens. A prominent Mason, buried with masonic and military honors.   Children:

  a Mary b 1806-8; m ——— Coddington; 2nd Rev Septimus Page
  b Caroline Abigail b 1808-10; m William Northasse
  c Lucia Ann Coffin b 1810-12
  d Charlotte Elizabeth b 1812-4; int pub Sept 25, 1835, to David S Bartlett of
     Newtown

Josiah Dow adkdec, clerk, then store owner of Salem, m Jan 5, 1806, Rebecca Maria Phippen b Dec 7, 1783, dau of Samuel.   She was born in the house in which she continued to live for 4 years after marriage, d Wakefield July 7, 1875.   Her family was originally Penn of Eng, one Philip Penn contracting the name.   They moved 1810 to Boylston St, Boston, having outgrown the merchandizing possibilities of Salem. Here he established the first department store in Boston, called Dow's Long Store because it extended through the block with entrances on each street.   This was such a success that Josiah decided to retire in 1819 to Wakefield.   After six years, deciding to resume, he bought a home in Nassau St, Brooklyn, N Y, and became an importer in N Y. His specialty was the East Indian trade, in which he had made connections before he left Salem.   Owning or chartering ships and maintaining agents in the east by the year, he could sell as cheaply as any one else could import.   He soon developed into one of the most prominent merchants in old N Y.   Good sketches of him are in Hist Brooklyn and Hunt's Old N Y Merchants.   In Brooklyn he avoided political life, but was active in civil and educational affairs; one of the founders of the Brooklyn Lyceum in Washington St, now the Brooklyn Institute of Arts & Sciences; founder of the Young Ladies' Seminary in Hicks St.   In Wakefield he built and endowed an academy attended by students from all parts of the country.   Having amassed a substantial fortune and having a son to continue the business, he retired 1840 to Wakefield, buying out the other heirs to the homestead. Here he d Nov 2, 1850. The library on Chinese and Oriental Art in the Essex Institute, Salem, Mass, was begun by him.   Children:

  a Samuel Phippen b Oct 5, 1806; d Jan 5, 1824
  b Rebecca Maria b Dec 30, 1807; d Apr 8, 1828
  c Richard Weare b Aug 14, 1809; lost Jan 14, 1840, on S S Lexington burned in
     Long Island Sound
  d Josiah Coffin b Aug 14, 1809; d Canton, Ill, May 1, 1833
  e George Worthington b Feb 12, 1811   f Horace Holly b Jan 3, 1813
  g Charles Alexander b Dec 7, 1814; d Concord Apr 12, 1900, senile dementia
     patient for 43 years
  h William Henry b Aug 30, 1816; d Havana, Cuba, June 23, 1839
  i Francis b May 21, 1818; d Jacksonville, Ill, 1846; no children
  j Harriet b Nov 2, 1819; d July 10, 1904, unm
  k Ann Augusta b Jan 16, 1822; d Jan 27, 1822
  l Ellen Almira b Mch 8, 1823   m Sarah Ann b Apr 9, 1825
  n Adeline b Mch 25, d Mch 28, 1827

George W Dow adkdece d Brooklyn Mch 4, 1884; merchant continuing the business of his father; m Nov 12, 1833, Anna De Bevoise Prince b Brooklyn July 7, 1816, d Wakefield Jan 1, 1905, dau of Christopher (long a captain in the East India trade) and Anna (Duffield). Children:

a   Anna Maria b Oct 20, 1834; d July 29, 1835
b   Josiah b Feb 12, 1835   c   George Prince b Sept 16, 1837
d   Anna Prince b July 28, 1839; unm; living 1923 with her brother in Charlestown
e   Rebecca Maria b Jan 24, 1841; d Sept 10, 1842
f   Margueretta Duffield b Feb 4, 1842; d Nov 24, 1843
g   Amelia b and d July 16, 1843   h   Abbot Low b Feb 10, 1845
i   Susan Rockwell b Dec 19, 1846
j   Maria b May 21, d June 27, 1849
k   Benjamin Prince b Oct 15, 1850; d Feb 14, 1851
l   Samuel Phippen b May 14, 1852; d July 1, 1852
m   Benjamin Prince b Dec 31, 1854; d Feb 25, 1878
n   Richard William b Oct 12, 1856; long attached to the Episcopal diocese of N
      H; 1923 rector of St Luke's, Charlestown, N H. Unm

Josiah Dow adkdeceb m Dec 1860 Katherine W Downing b Salem, d Germantown, Pa, May 28, 1891, ae 54, 9 mos, dau of Thomas and Nancy (Brown). Children:

a   Mary Pickering   b   Katherine Phippen b Aug 12, 1864
c   George Worthington b Nov 19, 1866

Katherine P Dow adkdecebb m Sept 22, 1896, John H Garvin of Wakefield. Children:

a   J Howard   b   Josiah Dow

George W Dow adkdecebc m May 6, 1896, Alice Maud Osborne d Mch 14, 1908; 2nd Apr 23, 1910, Leila Aileen Joyce. No children.

George P Dow adkdecec d Topsfield, Mass, Nov 14, 1916, farmer; m Dec 13, 1866, Ada Bingham Tappan, dau of Rev Daniel and Abigail (Marsh). Children:

a   George Francis b Jan 7, 1868   b   Grace Tappan b Apr 28, 1871
c   Eugene Marsh b Jan 13, 1876
d   Adeline Marsh b Jan 17, 1879; of Topsfield, unm

George Francis Dow adkdececa, secy many years until 1919 of Essex Institute, Salem, lives in the homestead; held various town offices and was representative to Legislature. His published works exceed 100 titles on local history and genealogical subjects, member of many historical and museum associations. Unm.

Grace T Dow adkdececb m June 16, 1907, Samuel Conley ae 45, son of James H and Annie G (James) of Topsfield. No children.

Eugene M Dow adkdececc, carpenter and contractor of Topsfield, m June 5, 1907, Daisy Louise Dow adkgdegb of Rowley, Mass. Children:

a   Muriel Elizabeth b July 13, 1908   b   Florence Marsh b Sept 8, 1911

Abbot L Dow adkdeceh, merchant and importer, d N Y City May 5, 1914; m Oct 14, 1869, Cornelia Suydam Herriman; 2nd Feb 14, 1905, Carola Helena Sanford. Children:

a   Margaret Herriman b Jan 18, 1871; m Oct 8, 1896, Ernest Greene; 3 children
b   Cornelia Herriman b Nov 4, 1872; m June 7, 1905, by Rev Richard William Dow, Charles Foster Bancroft; 2 children
c   Caroline b May 2, 1874; m Feb 13, 1906, Dr P Hansen Hiss, who d without children

Susan R Dow adkdecei m May 15, 1872, James W Lovering of Cambridge, Mass. Children:

a   Annie Dow b Feb 20, 1874; unm 1917
b   Arthur b Aug 13, 1875; m Gladys Tappen
c   Cornelia Herriman b Nov 24, 1876; d unm
d   Joseph b Aug 29, 1879; twice m
e   Eleanor b Aug 29, 1881; unm 1917
f   Susan Rockwell b 1883; m Harry Hooper

Horace H Dow adkdecf m 1838 Mary Ann Niles. Children:

a   Ellen Almira d young   b   Horace Henry d Dec 1874; ae 23

Ellen A Dow adkdecl m 1845 Abiel Abbot Low, leading merchant and Brooklyn philanthropist; d Jan 25, 1850, leaving 2 sons, 2 dau, of whom:

d   Seth b 1850; d 1917; Mayor of Brooklyn; Mayor of Greater N Y; pres Columbia Univ; trustee American Museum of Nat Hist; etc

Asa Dow adkdee d Apr 9, 1858; in 1850 merchant of Wakefield, owning $2,000 realty; m Wakefield Oct 13, 1815, Lucia Ann March Coffin b Newburyport Oct 13, 1798, d Wakefield May 16, 1882, dau of David and Lucia (Lunt). In later years lived Boston and N Y. Children:

a   David Coffin; not in 1850 census; untraced
b   Ann March m Sept 16, 1843, Philip Pike of Manchester; dau Hattie
c   Albert Lafayette b Wakefield Apr 21, 1820   d   John F d young
e   Henry d young   f   Harriet d young
g   Sarah Elizabeth m 1848 Salchell Weeks

Albert L Dow adkdeec appears in 1850 census as night watchman of Somersworth; m Jan 1, 1846, Charlotte Ann Melcham b Wakefield Feb 1, 1827; survived her husband, d Somersworth Oct 18, 1886, dau of Joseph and Rachel (Horn) both b Wakefield. Children:

a   Helen Augusta b Sept 5, 1848   b   John Albert b Berwick, Me, July 14, 1855

Helen A Dow adkdeeca m June 26, 1873, Christie Leander Lord of Gt Falls, Me. Children:

a   Kirke Abbot b May 18, 1874   b   Eugenia Maud b July 22, 1878
c   Charlotte Lucia b Mch 8, 1880

John A Dow adkdeecb m Oct 2, 1881, Allie Minetta Shepard b Hancock, N Y, Nov 20, 1861; in 1885 inspector for Standard Oil Co, N Y, with no children. Untraced.

There is no reason to think that the adke line is smaller than its predecessors, but for 30 years it was as poorly traced as any in this Book. Vital records of its earlier years in Salisbury are unusually defective and from Deerfield are worse yet. In 1922 the Author received from Miss Alice Osborn Dow adkedjb an account set down from memory by an aged aunt, which omits no member of adked line and helps straighten out the whole. Nevertheless, the senior line is left in skeleton shape, comparatively few rec ever found.

Joseph Dow adke, farmer, bought a farm by or over the Salisbury border; m about 1756 Naomi (Carr) Dow adgd, who brought with her her infant son Robert. D rec of either not found, but they never left the homestead. Children, possibly not in right order:

a   Jacob b about 1757; lived Deerfield
b   Israel b Oct 10, 1761; lived Deerfield
c   Caleb b Salisbury 1763 (from d rec)   d   Josiah b Salisbury May 7, 1774
e   Polly m Mch 28, 1793, Jonathan Fallington; 1 dau,—Polly
f   Naomi   g   Mehitable   h   Joshua b Salisbury

Jacob Dow adkea m 1784 Charlotte Langley, first of many intermarriages with this family. Perhaps a disconnected family of Lee belongs to them; others appear provedly in Epsom. Deerfield rec are obscure. Probably more than 4 children:

a   Abigail b 1790; known only by mention in 1850 census, name occurring next to Josiah
b   James b Deerfield 1792-5 (m rec does not give age)
c   ——, a son. This merely because Epsom 1850 census gives Nancy Dow b 1793 (guessed to be wid) with (apparently) son Joseph b N H 1837, otherwise unknown
d   Esther d Deerfield Mch 29, 1886, ae 88, 8 mos, dau of Jacob and Charlotte Longley
e   Josiah b Deerfield 1812; d Deerfield Nov 16, 1867. No proof that b and d rec belong to same man

James Dow adkeab. Proof only of m and 1st born; either he or oldest son moved to Epsom; m Aug 15, 1816, Betsey Robinson of Epsom. She must be the Mrs James Dow d Epsom May 28, 1861. Presumably more children than herein:

a   John Robinson b Feb 1817   b   True Langley

John R Dow adkeaba, farmer of Epsom, d widower suicide Apr 23, 1887; m Feb 28, 1845, Hannah E Fogg b N H 1827. Rec of son Geo A gives mother Lucinda, may be error, may be 2nd wife. Children, list uncertain:

a   John D b Epsom 1846; d Epsom Nov 8, 1867; m Nov 7, 1865, Lizzie E Libby, ae 22, dau of Erah and Olive (not found in Libby Gen); probably no child
b   Aura A b 1848; proved by census
c   James O d Epsom Aug 22, 1858, identity conjectured
d   Emma M b Epsom Aug 3, 1860
e   George A b Epsom July 4, 1862 or 1863 (both dates in duplicated rec). Some John R Dow d Epsom Oct 30, 1863; may be confused
f   —— child b Nov 3, 1864; conjectured as Nellie B, dau of John R, m Oct 23, 1887, Charles F Brown, both of Epsom

True L Dow adkeabb. No proof of identity, but must be of this line. Lived Deerfield; m Mehitable —— of Deerfield. State rec has a curious garble, evidently belonging here: Mehitable Dow m June 9, 1830, True Langley; son Jacob m 1885. One child found, b 11 years after m (if 1830 is right?), indicating probability of others:

  a Jacob b 1841 (date from m rec)

Jacob L Dow adkeabba, name correct in b rec of son, but m rec gives James L. Surely m twice, 1st Hannah J More, both of Deerfield; 2nd Oct 17, 1885, Myra C Brown, ae 24, dau of Benjamin and Martha (Fownes); d, farmer of Deerfield, Epsom Jan 1, 1889. Three children found:

  a Rinaldo H b July 14, 1860
  b George E b Deerfield Mch 31, 1880; untraced
  c —— son b Apr 5, 1886; untraced
    He had also a dau, in whose m rec mother is given Myra Coffin:
  d Mabel b Deerfield 1886; of Haverhill, Mass, m June 18, 1904, Aime J Descoteau, ae 31, son of Desire and Elizabeth (Gautier)

Rinaldo H Dow adkeabbaa d Deerfield Dec 28, 1880, ae 27 (date presumably 1887), son of Jacob L and —— (Moore); wife was Mary E b Jamaica Plain, Mass. One child found:

  a Rinaldo E b Feb 13, 1879; d Deerfield Jan 11, 1887

Josiah Dow adkeae m July 9, 1829, Hannah Langley, both of Deerfield. In census she b N H 1804; apparently at 17, he m a woman 8 years his senior. In 1850 farmers, assessed $1,500; no children; but 1 child is proved:

  a John N b Nottingham 1846, son of Josiah and Hannah (Langley), mechanic, d Nottingham July 18, 1873, unm

---

Israel Dow adkeb d Deerfield Feb 1, 1823; m Salisbury (int pub May 13) 1784, Olive Abbott b Salisbury Apr 4, 1764, d Wilmot, N H, Dec 16, 1839. His will probated Feb 13, 1823, is our authority for children, not necessarily in correct order:

  a Jacob b Dec 25, 1784; unt   b Rebecca b Jan 19, 1796 (m rec)
  c Joshua   d Joseph   e Mehitable   f Nancy b 1797
  g Israel b Mch 15, 1800 (family Bible)   h Naomi   i Hannah

Jacob Dow adaaaha, cooper and carpenter, lived Deerfield and Raymond; d Groveland, Mass, Feb 20, 1864, at the home of a dau; m Nov 9, 1809, Judith Bartlett b Deerfield Mch 28, 1785, d Raymond May 30, 1852. Two sons, 5 dau:

  a Israel b Salisbury Jan 18, 1815   b Jacob b about 1818
  c Sarah Bartlett b Raymond 1819; m Nov 3, 1846, Nathaniel G Knowles of Northwood
  d Abby B of Raymond int pub July 7, 1847, to French Ordway of Amesbury
  e (conjecture) Apphia F m Raymond June 29, 1843, Henry Heart
  f Nancy b 1829; only child to appear in 1850 census
  g Hannah m Thomas Burbank of Groveland, Mass

Israel Dow adaaahaa moved to Manchester, employed in a cotton mill; an important invention by himself was profited by and he became an important officer with lifelong position. He m July 1, 1846, Lavinia Hobbs of Somersworth b Sanford, Me, July 22, 1822, d Sept 24, 1896. He d Brattleboro, Vt, Aug 24, 1898, while on a visit to a dau. He served in the Legislature 1857-8, senator 1883. A portrait, fine-looking and venerable, occurs in Stearns Hist New Hampshire. Identity of Jacob Dow as son of Capt Elijah Dow proved too late in 1927 to permit proper placing. Children:

a   Ansonnette d Manchester Oct 9, 1851, ae 14 mos
b   Julietta b Manchester Nov 11, 1852; d Sept 30, 1861
c   Perry Hobbs b July 8, 1854
d   Edna M m Oct 13, 1881, John H Morse of Worcester, Mass, later of Brattleboro;
      1 dau
e   Herbert d 1866

Perry H Dow adaaahaac, officer in one of the large Manchester mills; m 1879 Susan Chadwick Cook of Provincetown, Mass, b Sept 10, 1855, dau of Harvey and Susannah (Peabody); representative to Legislature 1889, senator 1891. Children:

a   ——son b Apr 11, 1880; untraced   b   —— son b 1882; untraced
c   Bertha F d Manchester Dec 20, 1884, ae 6-3-22
d   Clinton Israel b Apr 12, 1886

Clinton I Dow adaaahaacd, with the Amoskeag Mills, Manchester, m Sophia Russell b Honesdale, Pa, 1887. Child:

a   Priscilla Russell b Feb 7, 1916

Jacob Dow adaaahab (Jacob B in rec of son) m Dec 22, 1842, Sarah A Dearborn, both of Raymond. Census gives 2 children:

a   Edwin H b 1844; untraced   b   Samuel Alonzo b 1847

Samuel A Dow adaaahabb moved to No Hampton while quite young, opened a grocery store; m Dec 23, 1869, Emily A Marston, ae 23, of No Hampton. At least 6 children:

a   Fred Leland b 1873 (m rec)
b   Mabel J b May 30, 1875; m June 27, 1890, Haven S Berry of No Hampton
c   Lottie Florence b May 24, 1878; d Portsmouth Jan 4, 1899
d   —— dau b May 29, 1881   f   J Russell b Apr 8, 1886

Fred L Dow adaaahabba, grocer of No Hampton, m Oct 27, 1896, Gertrude Eliza Robinson b Jan 21, 1871, d Portsmouth Apr 22, 1907, dau of John William and Roxa Jane (Traverse) (Travis in dup rec); 2nd Dec 31, 1910, Christiana Perkins, ae 31, dau of James H and Mary C (Goodwin) of Rye. Child by each wife:

a   Gordon Sumner b Sept 24, 1905   b   Gertrude b Portsmouth Feb 17, 1912

J Russell Dow adaaahabbf, grocer of No Hampton, m Oct 9, 1907, Grace I Wright, ae 27, dau of David and Margaret (Adams).

Hannah Dow adaaahag was a tailor of Groveland, Mass; m there Thomas Burbank, farmer of Groveland, son of Nathan. Her father d at their home. Children:

a Hannah m A Boynton; moved to Utah	b Matilda H	c John
d Caroline A e Marinda J d young	f Marinda J	g Laura R

Rebecca Dow adkebb m May 25, 1814, Abraham B Cilley b Mch 12, 1795, d same day as his wife Mch 23, 1873, son of John and Hannah (Elliott) and grandson of Cutting and Martha (Morrill) Cilley of Northwood. Children:

a Mary Jane b Sept 16, 1814; d Oct 7, 1818
b Samuel B b Mch 20, 1816; d May 26, 1874; m May 11, 1843, Sarah C Dow adadabbe
c Mary J b Nov 28, 1818; d May 3, 1842
d Olive b Sept 18, 1820; d Jan 27, 1823
e John b Oct 15, 1822; m Martha Cilley, dau of Jonathan Elliott Cilley of Northwood
f Naomi b June 15, 1824; d Jan 28, 1872; m Sept 14, 1843, Nathaniel D Caswell; 1 child,—Charles
g Olive b Aug 9, 1826; m Apr 28, 1845, Clark Bryant
h Martha b June 3, 1828; m June 29, 1847, Charles H Hill
i Abraham B b Apr 7, 1830; m Jan 30, 1849, Julia A Cilley of Nottingham
j Hannah b Feb 7, 1832; m Feb 6, 1849, George H Knowlton of Northwood; d May 9, 1876; 1 son Alvin
k Joseph P b Apr 3, 1841; m June 11, 1875, Jennie Robinson; no children
l Rebecca J b Dec 23, 1842; m Sept 8, 1822, Isaac Foss of Strafford

Joshua Dow adkebc d Deerfield Apr (will probated May 2), 1832; m 1825 Abigail ——. Children, from will:

a Sally B   b Mehitable L   c Moses B

Sarah B Dow adkebca, b Andover, m Isaiah Langley b Deerfield. Children:

a Mary A m Allenstown 1898 John F Bartlett   b H B m Pembroke 1894

Moses B Dow adkebcc, cooper, moved to Hooksett; m Almira P Philbrick b June 20, 1827, dau of Josiah and Sarah (Quimby); she living Manchester 1915 with dau Sadie C. Children:

a Georgianna B b Danville Sept 29, 1845   b Sadie C b July 8, 1848; unm

Georgianna B Dow adkebcca of Manchester m Aug 12, 1871, Woodbury, Quimby Sargent, grocer of Manchester. Children:

a Eugene W b June 8, 1872
b George Ernest b May 9, 1876; d Mch 29, 1877
c Ethel G b Feb 18, 1878   d Edith M L b Apr 7, 1881

Joseph Dow adkebd. The only likely identity we know is Joseph Dow, said by Richmond Gen b Aug 5, 1786, a traveling merchant who settled in Winthrop. All the marriages in his family are with names familiar to Salisbury, Mass. He d Apr 23, 1860; m Oct 24, 1809, Abigail Richmond b Winthrop Jan 24, 1787, d Oct 23, 1856, dau of Nathan

(Rev veteran) and Mary (Streeter). This Richmond family came from
Middleboro, Mass. Children:

a   Rosanna W b Turner Dec 25, 1812
b   Thirza Leavitt b Winthrop Nov 27, 1814
c   Rosilla H b Oct 3, 1816   d   Betsey F b Dec 15, 1818
e   Lavina C b Nov 4, 1827; m Oct 3, 1849, Josiah C Beal
f   Charles L b 1828; d Dec 23, 1856   g   Henry W b May 16, 1832
h, i, j Perley, Marcia, Joseph S d in infancy

Rosanna W Dow adkebda m Nov 24, 1836, Daniel Marston.
Children:

a   Lena C b July 27, 1840; m Feb 13, 1860, J F Bonney
b   Mabbie b Sept 18, 1843   c   D W b May 31, 1848
d   George b Oct 2, 1854

Thirza L Dow adkebdb m Feb 4, 1838, Josiah F Prescott, son of
Jedediah Jr and Sarah (Merrill). Children:

a   Daniel Marshall b Nov 18, 1838; 1st Lieut 15th Me; m July 1859 Zelpha True
b   Joseph Pernham b Nov 26, 1846; d Aug 26, 1867

Rosilla H Dow adkebdc m May 1, 1838, Erasmus D Prescott,
brother of Josiah. Children:

a   Edwin Augustus b May 16, 1842; killed in action July 18, 1864
b   Emma Foster b Oct 14, 1853; m Mch 4, 1877, Eugene H Shepard of Phillips

Betsey F Dow adkebdd m Dec 4, 1842, Martin S Kelley. Children:

a   M S b Apr 6, 1845   b   A G b Aug 16, 1846   c   Ada b Apr 4, 1848
d   Rosa b May 1850   e   Hattie b May 1856   f   Charles b 1859

Mehitable Dow adkebe m Dec 30, 1817, Andrew Freeze Langley
of Wilmot and Danbury b Jan 23, 1795, son of Isaiah and Charlotte
(Emerson). No children.

Nancy Dow adkebf d June 11, 1882; m (his 2nd) Andrew F Langley.
Children:

a   Isaiah b 1822; d May 26, 1908; m Polly Currier
b   Mehitable m Morrill Currier, Polly's brother
c   Olive Jane b 1831; d July 28, 1916; m Alonzo Wilkins
d   John L b 1838; d Mch 31, 1916; m Nov 5, 1877, Hattie S Pettingell

Israel Dow adkebg of Deerfield m Dec 25, 1823, Abigail Cram b
Raymond 1800; moved to No Wilmot; farm assessed 1850 at $1,500; d
Oct 28, 1883. Children:

a   Isaiah C b Aug 15, 1824   b   Israel b Wilmot Jan 5, 1826
c   Olive b Nov 6, 1827; d Sept 23, 1862
d   Lucinda b Dec 26, 1829   e   Melinda b May 17, 1831; d Jan 19, 1900
f   Hannah b Apr 17, 1833   g   Abigail b June 6, 1835; d Nov 27, 1884
h   Nancy L b Feb 27, 1838; m Jacob S Dutton of Concord; living 1919; a son
        Edward W m 1889 and 1894
i   Jonathan b Dec 11, 1841; d May 10, 1842   j   John, twin, d at b

Isaiah C Dow adkebga d May 19, 1899; machinist of Bedford, assessed 1850 at $1,200; wife Almira b Canada. Children, all living 1919:

a   Mira J b 1848; m E N Knapp of Middletown, N Y
b   Mrs G M Clemson of Middletown   c   Mrs Lucy Beach of N Y City
d   Mrs Fred L Blendinger of Plainfield, N J

Israel Dow adkebgb d No Wilmot Dec 8, 1857; m 1852 Abi P Fisk, dau of Jeremiah. Only child:

a   Frank H b No Wilmot July 18, 1853

Frank H Dow adkebgba went at 21 to Corning, N Y; m Caton, N Y, Sept 15, 1875, Mary E Davis, dau of Daniel and Ruth (Bates), from Mass. He d Dec 20, 1916. Children:

a   Harry Israel b Aug 9, 1878
b   Jessie R b May 18, 1885; teacher of Hudson, N Y; furnished 3 generations of this line, from which Author readily connected with main tree

Harry I Dow adkebgbaa lives on the home farm, Caton; m Oct 15, 1908, Josie Weaver. Children:

a   Charles Frank b Jan 17, 1910   b   Howard Frederick b Jan 4, 1915

Olive Dow adkebgc b Danbury, Vt; m Joseph Fogg b Wilmot, Bridgewater, Bristol, Vt, in as many rec. Children:

a   Ida E m Lebanon 1876 Fred M Brown
b   Israel Dow, merchant of Claremont, m 1884 and 1896
c   Joseph H of Claremont m 1886
d   N Mary m —— Randall; 2nd Eugene Putnam of Claremont

Melinda Dow adkebge b Northwood; m Daniel Perkins. Only child:

a   George W D d Wilmot married July 13, 1915, ae 61-10-4

Caleb Dow adkec m Kensington Mch 2, 1784 (Kensington rec Feb 7,—probably date of int), Anna Cram of Seabrook. Caleb appears as executor 1819, of whom not found. In 1808 or a little before a Dow family came from Kensington and occupied the Blake homestead on King St, Hampton Falls; mentioned in Hist Hampton Falls as the "Woodchuck Dows." This nickname arose from their retiring disposition. They worked industriously, but at the approach of any one scurried away like a woodchuck into its hole. As tax list from 1809 carries Caleb and Elijah, the identity is certain. A family rec recalls all the children, only 2 found in vital rec. Census 1790 gives 1a, 1b, 4c. Order not accurate:

a   Mehitable   b   Caleb b about 1785   c   Enoch
d   Elijah m Nov 16, 1818, Sally Shaw, both of Kensington. No children known; he not in 1850 census. She d old age and opium Kensington Mch 17, 1860, ae 74
e   Nancy d young   f   Ruth   g   Betsey   h   Charlotte
i   Eunice   j   Nancy   k   Lyddy (Lydia)

Caleb Dow adkecb m Apr 24, 1812, Mary Perkins; moved to

Wolfboro, where 1850 census finds him alone. One child found, surely 1st born:

a True Perkins b Wolfboro Aug 1812

True P Dow adkecba, farmer and carpenter of Moultonborough, assessed $600 in 1850; d May 1888, ae 75-9-7; m May 9, 1842, Eunice Carney Brown b 1822, d wid Moultonborough Oct 20, 1901, dau of Paul, farmer b Ossipee, and Mary (Neal). Twelve children in all:

a George Edgar b Moultonborough 1843
b Henry T b 1845 (census); untraced
c Lewis A b Tuftonborough June 7, 1850
d William Lawton b Moultonborough June 25, 1852. Census gives 1849; probably two of same name, one dying in infancy
e —— dau b Mch 6, 1852; a dau is Priscilla M
f —— dau b Nov 5, 1853; one is Lizzie S m Jan 5, 1881, Frank E Farrell of Farmington
g James B b Aug 15, 1853. James B b May 24, 1859; probably two of same name, 1 dying in infancy
h —— son b Oct 15, 1855; Lorenzo d Nov 8, 1870, unm; the same?
i Susan E b Moultonborough July 26, 1861
l (specified as 12th) Minerva A b 1863-4; m Farmington Apr 26, 1884, John F Corson

George E Dow adkecbaa d Derry Feb 9, 1903, ae 69-3-11; lost a leg in 2nd N H; carpenter of Sanbornton, moved to Moultonborough; m May 16, 1863, Julia Ann Nelson (Wilson, Morrison, in errors) b Goffstown Oct 30, 1842, d Tilton Jan 4, 1894, dau of Moses and Mary Ann (Morrison). Children:

a Charles Edmund b Moultonborough Apr 13, 1864
b Anna Augusta b Feb 2, 1866; d Tilton Oct 31, 1886; unm
c William Henry b Tilton Aug 1, 1869
d Mary Albertina b July 1, 1875   e Catherine Evelyn b June 18, 1877
f Ernest R b July 7, 1883; d Tilton May 8, 1890

Charles E Dow adkecbaaa, carpenter, then mill operative of Tilton, d Jan 12, 1909; m May 14, 1884, Emma E Hawes d Tilton Mch 2, 1909, dau of James M, machinist and Emily (Brown) b Northfield, Vt. One child found:

a Harry E b Tilton Oct 8, 1886; mill operative of Tilton, m Dec 7, 1907, Maude M Webster, ae 20, dau of Adelbert C and Jennie (Stevens)

William H Dow adkecbaac, machinist of Portsmouth, m (William b Tilton, ae 31, should be 21) Marguerite Palmer, ae 29, b Pictou; 7 children; 2nd (William M), merchant of Chelsea, Mass, Oct 24, 1904, Margaret Hedderman, ae 24, dau of William H b Ireland and Mary F (Harihan). Children:

a —— dau b Portsmouth Apr 27, 1892
b Ernest Arnold b Portsmouth Nov 17, 1893
c George Frank b Portsmouth Aug 25, 1895; d July 20, 1898, ae 2-9-3
d George b May 25, 1897   f Marion Clyde b Apr 6, 1901
g Grace b Feb 17, 1904   h Clinton Austin b Mch 15, 1905
j Raymond Parker b Dec 9, 1906

Lewis A Dow adkecbac, carpenter of Farmington, d before 1899;

m Aug 17, 1870, Margaret M Page, ae 19, of Milton, dau of George and Jane. At least one child:

a William A b Middletown 1871 (from m rec)

William A Dow adkecbaca, machinist of Manchester, m Feb 9, 1899, Eveline I Monbleau, ae 29, dau of Oliver and Mathilde (Bougois) of Canada. Children:

a Bertina Emma b Mch 10, 1901   b William A b Nov 7, 1903
c Inez Gertrude b Apr 16, 1907

William L Dow adkecbad moved 1895 to Bristol, factory foreman; m. Feb 9, 1879, Sadie Fergeson, dau of Ivory and Rhoda (Philpot). State rec has: Will S Dow m Sadie F Percher, ae 23, dau of Leroy and Rhoda B.

Priscilla M Dow adkecbae m Laconia Apr 10, 1868, Frank Pierce Burleigh b Alton Nov 19, 1847, son of Samuel Randall and Eunice Kelly (Coffin).

James B Dow adkecbag, farmer of Moultonborough, d Feb 4, 1914; m Dec 27, 1884, Lizzie E Garland, ae 17, dau of Charles F. She not in 1908 directory, which gives children:

a Etta M b May 22, 1885; m —— Bickford; a dau b Nov 16, 1902
b Berenice E
c Leroy E b Feb 19, 18—; machinist of Manchester; d Center Harbor 1918,
      corporal, of wounds received in France
d Harrie Ellsworth b Jan 26, 1890; teamster of Moultonborough
e Arline A b May 11, 1894   f Francis P b Sept 11, 1896
g Ernest H b Sept 6, 1898   h Ellis M b May 19, 1901

Ruth Dow adkecf is probably she who m (int pub Salisbury, Nov 29, 1817) Hampton Falls Jan 13, 1818, by Rev Jacob Abbott, John Flanders of Salisbury.

Charlotte Dow adkech is almost surely she who m Mch 1811 (date questionable) Samuel Fogg, preacher of Winthrop, Me, a place where a kinsman of hers was located. Children:

a Samuel D b Mch 5, 1818; m Maria A Cushing
b Katherine C b July 18, 1822; m Marcellus Houghton of Winthrop
c Abigail b Jan 25, 1825   d Ruth A b May 4, 1832

Eunice Dow adkeci must be the Eunice int pub (Hampton rec) Oct 6, 1827, to Daniel M Page of Hampton. Salisbury rec gives her m Oct 6, 1827, David H Page.

Nancy Dow adkecj is possibly the Nancy who m 22: 7: 1812, Daniel Morrison, son of Abraham and Mary. To this couple Salisbury rec gives 4 children:

a Alexander Clark b Dec 24, 1812   b Alfred b Apr 2, 1819
c Sarah Ann Bagley b Sept 30, 1822
d Edward Gove b Mch 31, 1825 (This name throws doubt on identity)

Lydia Dow adkeck may be the Lydia of Hampton Falls, m **Apr 9** 1816, John Blaisdell Jr of Kingston. Children:

a John L m Newton 1872
b Diana Pillsbury m Daniel Bailey Short b 1811; 3 children

Josiah Dow adked d Lyndon, Vt, Aug 9, 1845. The full data of his line are due mainly to the study of Miss Alice Osborn Dow adkedjb. He m Loudon May 30, 1799, Ann Osborn (Anne, Anna and Osburn in various rec) b Loudon Feb 2, 1782, d Lyndon Sept 2, 1835, dau of Jacob, an early settler. He was a farmer, first in Salisbury, moving about 1804 to Pittsfield and about 1807 to Wheelock, Vt. They settled finally in Lyndon before 1823. Children, 3 b Salisbury, 1 Pittsfield, 3 Wheelock:

a Nancy b Mch 16, 1800   b Joseph b Nov 25, 1801
c Mary b Dec 3, 1803
d Abigail O b June 23, 1805; d Wheelock Nov 26, 1875; unm. For many years a tailor of Wheelock; lost the use of her legs from excessive use of calomel
e Hannah b Dec 22, 1808; d Newburyport May 6, 1890; m Lyndon Nov 17, 1831, Ira Mcquillan, merchant of Newburyport (cousin of adaieaad). No children
f Eliza O b Apr 11, 1811; associated with her sister in Wheelock; d Reading, Mass, Dec 11, 1888, unm
g Julia F b June 14, 1814; d Lyndon Mch 19, 1823
h Laura b Aug 30, 1817; d Hathorne, Mass, July 2, 1902; m Lowell Oct 11, 1840, Henry C Brooks; child,—Inez d young
i John Osborn b Jan 2, 1820; d Mch 17, 1823
j John Osborn b Apr 25, 1822
k Julia Malina b June 17, 1825; d Salisbury, N H, Apr 12, 1841; m Barnet, Vt, Dec 5, 1840, Reuben Dow adkehf; child,—Charles d Gloucester, Mass, young
l Emeline Augusta b Danville, Vt, Feb 20, 1829; d Gloucester, Mass

Nancy Dow adkeda d Amherst, Mass, Nov 21, 1861; m Lyndon May 9, 1824, Reuben Miles. Children:

a Julia m —— Avery; 2nd —— Cargable of Chicopee; 2 dau
b Adeline d unm
c Aurilla m —— Halen of Belchertown; 1 son   d Miranda
e Marcus Tullius Cicero, married, d in army
f Mark Hill   g John, located Hartford, Conn
h Anna m and had 2 children   i Reuben d in army

Joseph Dow adkedb d Lyndon Dec 19, 1833; m Gilmanton Dec 28, 1827, Charlotte Dow (unplaced). Belmont rec gives her of Tuftonborough, him of Andover, Mass. No children

Mary Dow adkedc m Nov 20, 1840, Francis J Crowder; moved to Wis; d May 10, 1860. Children:

a Emeline m Edward Harndon of Whitewater; 1 son
b Mary m —— Sears of Iowa; 8 children

John O Dow adkedj d Reading, Mass, Feb 22, 1897; practiced medicine many years in Harvard and Reading; m Springfield Apr 15, 1857, Frances A Phelps b Nov 25, 1840, d Reading Nov 11, 1902 (for her line see Descendants of John White, vol 3). Children:

a Emma Frances b May 17, 1859; m Reading June 14, 1882, Frederick William Tarrant of Rochester, N H. Child,—Mildred Frances b Reading Mch 30, 1892

b Alice Osborn b Sept 14, 1864; grad Wellesley College; taught in Everett and elsewhere; in 1922 of Hyannis, Mass; unm
c Agnes Louisa b Sept 15, 1866; d Feb 24, 1868
d George Farwell b Mch 27, 1869
e Anne Eliza b Springfield Oct 19, 1872; d Oct 20, 1873
f Edith May b Sept 4, 1876; m Reading Apr 15, 1902, Edwin R Scheck

George F Dow adkedjd, grad Harvard Medical School, practicing physician of Reading, m Haverhill, Mass, Sept 25, 1900, Gertrude May Thresher of Dolgeville, N Y. Children:

a John Aldrich b Aug 11, 1902   b Richard Phelps b May 14, 1907

Emeline A Dow adkedl d Gloucester, Mass; m Newburyport **Aug 21, 1852**, Sherman J Carter b Oct 25, 1831, son of Jeremiah and **Sally** (Woodman). This family came from Boscawen, N H, all the children identified with Gloucester:

a Sherman b Apr 26, 1854; m Cora Edmands; 1 dau
b John D b July 3, 1856; m Nellie Ingalls; considerable family
c Fred O b Sept 28, 1860, m Jennie Clark; 2 children
d Emma F b Sept 16, 1863; m —— Palmer

Naomi Dow adkef m Jan 13, 1791, Abel Clough of Salisbury; moved to Gilmanton; 2nd —— Adams. Family rec does not mention oldest two, found in Salisbury rec:

a Aaron b June 19, 1791; d Aug 14, 1817, Abra Greeley
b Josiah b Feb 27, 1793   c Joseph   d Isaiah   e Hiram
f Hazen   g Benjamin
h Cynthia m —— Hunkin; possibly garbled recollection of adkehh

Mehitable Dow adkeg m So Hampton Dec 19 (int pub Salisbury Nov 30), 1793, Benjamin Brown of Salisbury b Aug 14, 1771; moved to Northwood; 2nd Stephen Watson. Only child,—Benjamin (Brown).

Joshua Dow adkeh, wheelwright of Salisbury-Seabrook, d Jan 3, 1835, ae 57; m about 1800 Nancy Eaton. A ms giving Joshua m 1794 Nancy Cram wholly error. Children, complete by family rec:

a Joshua   b Jacob   c Israel   d Benjamin   e **William**
f Reuben   g Nancy   h Cynthia
i Susan (Sukey) b Mch 4, 1819
j Zelpha b Nov 25, 1821 (Oct 9, 1820, Salisbury rec); int pub Jan 7, 1843, to John L Brown of Seabrook
k Eunice b Mch 9, 1824

Joshua Dow adkeha m (int pub Salisbury July 10, 1830) Lydia Hunkin of Sanbornton; apparently moved to Me. One child found:

a Albert M b Andover, Me, 1844; farmer of Littleton, N H; m Nov 28, **1868**, Edna F Russell, ae 17. Untraced

Jacob Dow adkehb may be he who d Salisbury Jan 15, 1847, **ae 46, 6** mos; almost surely he who m May 11, 1825, Mary Merrill (Morrill Seabrook rec, surely clerical error), both of Seabrook. Children:

a Stephen b Nov 8, 1826
b Mary Abigail b Sept 24, 1828; m Nov 5, 1844, William Dow Jr of Newburyport (unplaced)

  c Martha Ann b July 23, 1830
  d Phoebe M b Apr 22, 1832; m Oliver P Crocker
     Their son Henry F R Crocker, ae 28, m Amesbury May 4, 1903, Sadie A Smith,
        ae 23, dau of John and Susan C (Dow,) latter unplaced
     She appears as Susan F Dow m John Smith and a dau Anne F b 1884, m Ames-
        bury June 12, 1910, William Andrew Butters
  e George b Aug 1, 1834; d May 25, 1837
  f George William b Sept 6, 1837; untraced; possibly he who enlisted (Concord
        rec) 1861 Co I, heavy artillery
  g Margaret Ann b Nov 24, 1839; m June 5, 1856, Wells H Eaton of Seabrook
  h Ezra Lowell M b Salisbury 1843

Stephen Dow adkehba, shoemaker of Salisbury, m Apr 20, 1848,
Rebecca J Curtis, ae 18, dau of Philemon and Sarah.   Census 1850 gives
just above them John G Dow, laborer, b 1790.   Next name following is
Eunice Dow b 1827 (adkehk??).   Only child:

  a Christina (Justina, census) b 1849

Ezra L M Dow adkehbh, painter of Newburyport, d Salisbury
Mch 2, 1905, ae 62, 8 mos; m Roxanna Annis d Salisbury May 31, 1905,
ae 52-2-3, dau of William F and Dorothy (Williams).   Apparently this
a 2nd m and he m 1st Nellie F Ryan, by whom a son:

  a Leon L b 1880

Leon L Dow adkehbha m Lynn Apr 6, 1901, Elizabeth I Thompson,
ae 19, dau of George A and Ida M (Buzzell).   A dau:

  a —— b and d Aug 30, 1901

Israel Dow adkehc m Salisbury (int pub Apr 13, 1834) Betsey
Smith b N H 1797.   Salisbury rec give 3 children; all mentioned in 1850
census; no other data found:

  a James Morrill b Dec 23, 1835   b Enoch Smith b Apr 26, 1838; untraced
  c Aaron Morrill b May 20, 1840

James M Dow adkehca must be the James m Lucy Ann Dow
adhcdacb; d before 1889; left 2 sons, untraced.

Aaron M Dow adkehcc, farmer of Salisbury, m Seabrook Oct 25,
1869, Clara M Dwight, ae 25, dau of Henry L and Sarah Ann (Dow) of
Seabrook.   At least 1 child:

  a Arthur C b Salisbury 1872 (m rec)

Arthur C Dow adkehcca, laborer of Salisbury, m Seabrook Jan 22,
1891, Nellie F Gove, ae 18, dau of Edward A and Annie J (Brown) of
Lynn.   She m 2nd Charles C Bragg.   Children:

  a —— son b Seabrook Dec 1, 1891
  b Arthur d Seabrook June 5, 1900; ae 10 mos, 10 days

Benjamin Dow adkehd.   Possibly all following rec apply.   Benjamin Dow d Salisbury Feb 28, 1835.   Benjamin Dow 4th m Feb 24,
1826, Hannah Souther, both of Seabrook.   Benjamin Dow m Apr 21,
1833, Marriam Brown of Seabrook.   Salisbury rec seemingly more ac-

curate: Benjamin Dow of Salisbury m Apr 21, 1833, Miriam H Brown of Seabrook. She m 2nd Jan 15, 1840, Oliver Eaton, both of Seabrook. To Benjamin and Miriam, presumably posthumous:

a —— dau b Oct 11, 1835

William Dow adkche. There were at least four Benjamin Dows in the locality of almost the same age. There were at least three contemporaneous William Dows. William Dow m Mch 22, 1826, Hannah Morrill. This must be: Mrs Hannah Dow b May 1, 1800, dau of Benjamin and Abigail Morrill, d June 20, 1833, ae 32. Hannah Dow, wife of William, d Aug 20, 1834; surely some other William. It is probably William Dow adkehe who of Salisbury m (int pub June 28, 1834, Amesbury rec) Margaret Brown. We presume this is 2nd m. He cannot be the father of William b 1822, who m Mary Abigail Dow adkehbb. To William and Margaret:

a —— child of William (not stated what William) d Dec 21, 1834
b Mary Abigail b Sept 4, 1835; some Mary Abigail d ae 9

Reuben Dow adkehf m his cousin Julia M Dow adkedk. One child only.

Nancy Dow adkehg (Nancy W in int) is presumably the Nancy m Caleb Moulton b about 1808, son of Joseph and Olive (Bragg) of Seabrook. They moved to Gilmanton, where he became quite well to do, tanner, farmer, cattle trader. She d; he m 2nd a Mrs Wright of Northwood. Nancy's children:

a Charles F d in young manhood
b Susan A m Nathan Batchelder of Gilmanton
c John S of Gilmanton

Cynthia Dow adkehh must be the Cynthia P and Cynthia C who m May 20, 1833, George W Hunkins, both of Salisbury.

Susan Dow adkehi. Altho age does not quite fit, she seems to be Susan d Seabrook Aug 21, 1894, ae 76-5-12; m (int pub Nov 2, 1838) Richard Smith of Seabrook. At least 2 children:

a Elbridge d Seabrook June 28, 1907, ae 58, 8 mos
b Lydia E m Seabrook 1859 Francis M Bennett

Eunice Dow adkehk of Salisbury m Seabrook [dau of Jacob and Nancy (Eaton), partial error] (rec also Hampton Falls) Dec 10, 1854, George F Eaton of Haverhill, Mass.

Samuel Dow adkf d May 15, 1812, ae 84 (Salisbury rec, apparently 4 years wrong); m Kensington May 15, 1756, Ann Wadleigh. Presumably he is the Samuel Dow 3rd of Salisbury who hired a substitute for the Crown Point expedition 1756. He is said, however, to have fought at Bunker Hill.   He had a farm over the Salisbury border, perhaps bought, perhaps inherited.   A third child probable:

    a   Sarah b June 15, 1758   b   Aaron b Jan 12, 1761
    c   John, a close kinsman and, like Aaron, a sailor

Aaron Dow adkfb is said to have started with his father for Bunker Hill, but it is doubtful whether he got there, being but 14.   Private at Winter Hill, Capt Sam Huse, Col Jacob Gerrish, Nov 11, 1777, to Apr 4, 1778.   He d 1812; m Nov 21, 1782, Elizabeth Goodwin b Nov 16, 1764, dau of Henry and Sarah (Marten) of Amesbury.   Children, all Salisbury rec:

    a   Samuel b Feb 14, 1783   b   John b Jan 8, 1785
    c   Betsey Goodwin b Mch 18, 1787; m June 26, 1809, Jonathan Perkins of Ken-
          sington; 2nd Aaron Palmer
    d   Aaron b July 23, 1789   e   Jabez
    f   Jenny b Jan 12, 1796; m (Jane in int) Feb 14, 1816, William O Bennett

Samuel Dow adkfba m Salisbury July 25, 1805, Judith Eaton (Jedida in int).   Hist Sanbornton gives her Dorothy.   He was killed Salisbury Apr 16, 1809, falling from a house frame.   Twin dau:

    a   Nancy b Jan 25, 1807
    b   Susan m Nov 29, 1827 (1838, Salisbury rec), Samuel Felch

Nancy Dow adkfbaa m Nov 9, 1828, Samuel Kendrick Jr of Ames-bury; lived Amesbury.   Children:

    a   Mary Ann b Oct 3, 1830   b   Cyrus Eaton b Dec 23, 1831
    c   Benjamin Dow b Mch 29, 1835

John Dow adkfbb, sometimes in jest called Colonel, hence mistaken by one of our genealogists for col of 4th Mass.   He was more often Elder John Dow, from a *sui generis* piety, rather than any church con-nection, albeit a man of great piety.   An enthusiastic convert to the second adventist belief, he was from time to time a traveling preacher. He published a small volume of hymns devoted to it, a local imprint with few copies now known.   He m June 23, 1805, Betsey Downs (Downer, rec) b Hampton 1794 (obvious error in rec), d Salisbury Dec 31, 1867. They lived at Gill's Corner, Salisbury Plain, where he had a shop for boat building, carriage making or general carpentry.   His sons worked with him.

    Religious fervor in old Salisbury was occasionally carried to extremes, especially when mixed with Medford rum, of which John and his sons were very fond.   As he wished to get sober by Saturday (his Sabbath), it became necessary to begin potations by Monday morning or before.   This practice caused more or less trouble for himself and entire family.   All were kindly, good-natured, helpful when sober, but most of the time were wholly playful.   Their idea of play was invariably assault and battery. One day the sons attacked and beat up thoroughly an inoffensive citizen of Amesbury, who complained at once to the local authorities.   The boys had been arrested many times before and had gotten off probably too easily. This time Elder John also had too much rum and announced to the deputy sheriff that not only would he refuse to surrender the offenders but would shoot full of holes any one attempting to make an arrest. The single-handed deputy returned to Mills Village and reported. Sheriff Gilman and militia captain Buswell called for volunteers to uphold law and order. The Dow rebellion included an army of 3, barricaded in the shop, and returned as many shots as the whole posse. The fort was finally carried by assault and, when the smoke cleared, it was found that Samuel Dow had been shot through the hat. This time all were properly punished. Dow's Fort is still a name in Salisbury annals. A local bard celebrated the event in an epic, not suited to Sunday School recital, hence left in manuscript. The poet d 1918, ae 91 and toward the end could remember but little of his composition. An elderly lady had preserved a few stanzas, but she refused,—would not repeat them for worlds. Salisbury and family rec nearly agree on the children:

a Paulina Smith b Jan 8, 1806; m Eben Whittemore of East Livermore, Me. A dau Nancy took quite an interest in her family genealogy
b Eliza b Nov 1, 1807; m Mch 16, 1828, Joseph Christian of Salisbury. A son John m Zelphia Dow adgxfdc
c Samuel b June 3, 1810   d   John b Seabrook Apr 29, 1813
e Sophia b 1815; m (int pub Oct 29, 1836) George Winch. Salisbury gives 1 child,—George Francis b Jan 23, 1838
f Sarah Mills b Nov 1, 1817; m Jan 23, 1842, William Storey
g Lorenzo b Jan 11, 1821; d in boyhood
h Edward b May 18, 1823; d May 25, 1824
i Laura Ann b Sept 3, 1824; m July 9, 1841, John G Colby d Sept 10, 1846; 2nd Daniel Harrigan
j Joseph Warren b Dec 2 (or 31), 1828

Samuel Dow adkfbbc, the terror of Salisbury, cooled his martial ardor as the years progressed and became a boat builder in Salisbury Plain; d 1872; m Apr 7, 1831, Mary Greenleaf of Amesbury b Seabrook 1811.

Samuel and John shipped, one time, on a schooner to New Brunswick, but had a disagreement with the captain and beat him up. Realizing that the consequences of such act at sea were serious, they seized a boat and rowed quickly ashore. They gave a fisherman a shilling to take the boat back again and started afoot overland for Salisbury. In East Livermore they stopped 2 months, for haymakers' wages were high. On another occasion Samuel asked for a job from a Newburyport boat builder who did not happen to know him. On being asked whether he could cut a trunion, he borrowed the man's glove and a broad axe. After testing the axe with his thumb, he laid a piece of wood on the glove and cut a perfect trunion without scratching the glove.

The list of children is badly garbled in Salisbury, but the compilation of Edward A Brown, Amesbury librarian, is quite accurate:

a Elizabeth b June 25, 1832; d Feb 9, 1904

b John b Sept 20, 1833; d Newburyport Apr 7, 1911; m 1858 Lavinia Currier b
   Newburyport 1833. No rec of children. He served in navy during Civil
   War, afterwards manufacturer of billiard tables, Newburyport. Made some
   attempt at collecting his own genealogy, copying all the pertinent gravestone inscriptions in the several towns
c Abraham Greenleaf b Sept 25, 1835
d Napoleon Bonaparte b Sept 2, 1839 (Sept 3, 1838, Salisbury rec)
e William Henry Harrison b Feb 11, 1841; d Oct 17, 1863; unm
f Josephine b Aug 4, 1844; d Salisbury Sept 2, 1884; m Exeter Jan 1, 1863,
   Wallace W Flanders d Amesbury Dec 2, 1911
g Julia A b Dec 31, 1864; m July 18, 1865, Amasa Pike; both living 1918. Their
   son Elmer E Pike m Feb 8, 1903, Alida Gravel
   Elizaa b Apr 4, 1849; d Mch 12, 1913; m Edwin J Merrill
   Franklin Pierce b Jan 11, 1852
   Catherine b Nov 8, 1856; m Ira F Dow ada——

Abraham G Dow adkfbbcc, living Newburyport 1918, at least 1
child:

a Edward H b Lincolnville, Me, Mch 7, 1857; traveling salesman, d Keene, N
   H, Mch 24, 1913. No other rec

Abraham G Dow m Alwilda Ames. It is barely possible that there
are two of this name, for the span is long from 1857 birthdate of a son to
1878, date of another. A son:

b Frank A b Cape Elizabeth, Me, 1878 (date may err, as his wife was on face of
   rec 13 years his senior); of Newburyport m Sept 19, 1904 (her 2nd), May A
   Bryant, ae 39, dau of Frank K and Mary (Jewett)

Napoleon B Dow adkfbbcd moved to Seabrook, married and had
a son:

a Frank P b 1869; probably only child

Frank P Dow adkfbbcda, clerk, subsequently merchant of Seabrook, m Sept 16, 1888, Nellie M Small, ae 17, dau of Perley and Hilda.
Fifteen children:

a —— son b Feb 3, 1889   b Elsie B b Apr 12, d Aug 9, 1890
c —— dau b June 1, 1891   d Persie F b Sept 30, 1893
f —— son b and d May 19, 1897 g —— son b June 10, 1898
h —— dau b Nov 30, 1899   i —— son b May 12, 1901
j —— dau b Aug 30, 1903   k — son b Dec 19, 1904
l —— dau b Nov 21, 1906   m Alice Longworth b Mch 4, 1908
n Frank C b June 29, 1910   o —— son b Mch 21, 1913

Franklin P Dow adkfbbci m Etta Francina Goodwin of York, Me;
living Newburyport 1919. A Joseph Dow at same address may be
adkfbbj. Children:

a Etta F m Oct 5, 1895, Clifford A Millen of Seabrook; 3 children, 1 married by
   1919
b Willard Frank b Salisbury July 17, 1879   c Everett Howard, unm
d Pearly Albert m Clementina Bussell; 3 children   e Eva Maud, unm

Willard F Dow adkfbbcib, foreman in West Springfield, lives
Chicopee Falls; m Boston Dec 21, 1903, Edna Day Thurlow b June 16,
1880, d Sept 19, 1916, dau of Justus and Cynthia (Reed); 2nd Aug 1,
1918, Gertrude Carpenter b Brattleboro Sept 13, 1879, dau of Darwin

Erasmus and Katherine J (Morse), wid of Robert Hitchcock Kibber. Child:

  a Willard Elbert b Springfield Nov 1, 1904

Perley A Dow adkfbbcid of Salisbury m, ae 22, Feb 11, 1907, Clementine E Buzzell, ae 17 of Newburyport, dau of Maurice A and Alice P (Cheney). Of children:

  a —— son b Springfield May 10, 1907
  b Raymond Perley b Salisbury Apr 29, 1909

John Dow adkfbbd also settled down into an industrious citizen of Salisbury; m Feb 22, 1834, Lavinia Jackman b 1820 of Amesbury. Children:

  a Mary Barnard b July 20, 1835; m Charles Morrill
  b Albert Freeman b Aug 28, 1838; m Sarah Hawthorne
  c Caroline J b 1842; m Samuel Collins
  d Almira W b 1845; m William Taplin
  e Dorothy G b Oct 10, 1847; m Jeremiah Eastman
  f David M b 1851; m Florence Griggs

Albert F Dow adkfbbdb. The identity of following seems sure, altho both generations must have married very young: To Albert L Dow and Sarah F Hawthorn, a dau:

  a Sarah L of Nashua m June 7, 1876, George W English of Lowell. Rec gives England. Their son Albert G m Amesbury Apr 13, 1903, Mary Agnes Peaslee

David M Dow adkfbbdf. That he m Florence Griggs comes from a family narrative. If so, he m 2nd Theresa Sweeny, to whom 3 children appear, b Lynn:

  a William Albert b 1880
  b Harriet Louise b 1882; m Amesbury June 26, 1903, Thomas H Westlake, ae 21, son of Henry and Mary (Hopkins)
  c Lottie M b Lynn 1886

William A Dow adkfbbdfa of Amesbury m Oct 4, 1902, Bertha Elsie Whelpley, ae 21, b St John, N B, dau of Wilmot and Henrietta (Golding). Children:

  a William Arthur b Apr 17, 1903   b David Albert b July 1, 1906
  c John Carleton b Mch 21, 1908

Lottie M Dow adkfbbdfc b Lynn; m Amesbury Dec 25, 1909, Robert P Lee, ae 27, son of Joseph and Anne (Pickering).

Joseph Warren Dow adkfbbj. In almost all lists of children of adkfbbc occurs Joseph N Dow without date; perhaps garbled for Josephine. More likely only one, also appearing as Joseph A. He m Mary E Beckman and moved to Seabrook. Children known only by own rec:

  a Henry H b Feb 29, 1860   b Joseph A b 1861
  c Mary E d Mch 18, 1868, ae 1, 7 mos
  d John W b 1872   e Charles S b Oct 25, 1872

Henry H Dow adkfbbja m Aug 13, 1881, wid Liona D Fuller, ae 22, dau of Thomas and Betsey J Eaton; 2nd, widower giving his b date 1863, Mary F Goldmore, ae 39, div (her 3rd), dau of Norman and Rachel McLeod.   Children:

    a Henry E b Salisbury 1882
    b Mamie b Seabrook July 29, 1883; m Walter B Dow adaimcdbf

For possible misidentification cf supplement *sub* adaabf

Henry E Dow adkfbbjaa; m June 28, 1905, Mabel E Kennedy, ae 22, dau of Matthew and Margaret A.

Joseph A Dow adkfbbjb, shoemaker of Exeter, m Feb 5, 1881, Avesta S Small, ae 19, dau of Perley and H A.   July 11, 1897, she joined the Exeter Baptist church.   Children:

    a John J, printer by 1908 directory
    c Mabel L b Jan 4, 1884; shoe shop operator 1908
    d Laurence P b May 1, 1886; iron founder
    e Helen M b May 1, 1886; m Fred Eldridge; has Helen M, Mabel
    f Llewellyn b Sept 2, 1887
    g Perley A, water tender of Portsmouth, m Mch 7, 1913, Marion H Page, ae 17,
        dau of Frank and Julia (Huntington)
    h —— d Aug 22, 1892, ae 5 mos   i —— son b June 24, 1896

John Joseph Dow adkfbbjba of Lynn m Brockton Nov 25, 1908, Eva Ethel Miller, ae 21, dau of Westley and Mary (Pickett).

Llewellyn Dow adkfbbjbf, shoe shop operator of Exeter, m (Louis b 1883, rec) Exeter Dec 25, 1907, Clara Sawyer, ae 16, dau of Caton and Carrie (Glover).

John W Dow adkfbbjd, clerk of Seabrook, m Feb 2, 1892, Joanna Leehy, ae 21, b Ireland, dau of Thomas and Mary.   Children:

    a —— dau b Sept 26, 1892   c Margret A b July 22, 1898
    d Susie Beckman b Oct 15, 1901; d young
    e Grace E b June 24, 1903; d Dec 24, 1905
    g Susie B d Dec 22, 1916, ae 4-2-7

Charles S Dow adkfbbje moved to Exeter, back to Seabrook by 1905; m Newburyport Dec 24, 1899, shoemaker, Helen F Merrill, ae 17, dau of Frank and Vienna.   Child:

    a Charles Harold b Newburyport Nov 28, 1902
    b Samuel Tilden b Newburyport Dec 16, 1904
    c —— dau b and d Oct 20, 1905

Aaron Dow adkfbd.   Probably the Aaron who m Sanbornton Sept 8, 1811, Mariam Eaton, dau of William and Betsey (Eaton).   Hist Sanbornton insists that he came from Weare, but perhaps has confused adaif or adaahx.   Census of 1850 finds Aaron "gentleman" and Miriam. The next names in the census list are Sarah and James G (below), but age makes it improbable that they belong here.

    a Cyrus b 1832 (found only by own d rec "son of Aaron")
    b Sarah b 1847   c James G b 1849; otherwise unknown

Cyrus Dow adkfbda, farmer, div; d Lynn, Mass, June 2, 1894, ae 62.

Somewhere here belongs a brave man:

Cyrus P Dow adgfbdx; his mother was Caroline Long and he was adopted in childhood by a man named Tenney. Enlisted, wounded, returned to service, promoted to corporal, mustered out 1865; became a florist of Sanbornton; m Conway Aug 17, 1865, Delia E Harford b Tamworth Jan 14, 1843, d Laconia Dec 14, 1912, dau of Warren and Sophia (Gannett). Children:

   a Cyrus G b Franklin 1869; m Boston Apr 3, 1905, Pallen (Patten?), ae 26, dau of William and Anne E (Thornton)
   b Mary A b Franklin; d Laconia Oct 20, 1883, ae 13
   c Laura Estella b Nov 1, 1877; m Arthur Francis Clough b Franklin Sept 8, 1877, son of Thomas Van Buren and Maria R (Gale)
   d Grace M b Dec 9, 1884; d Laconia Apr 5, 1885

Betsey Goodwin Dow adkfbc had 1 child by each husband; during 2nd widowhood made her home with brother Jabez, East Livermore, Me:

   a Mary m —— Hanson   b Aaron, grew up in Me

Jabez Dow adkfbe while a lad attempted to jump a ditch with a scythe in his hands; when found was half dead from loss of blood, but refused to have his leg amputated, as the doctors claimed was necessary. This leg was ever after several inches shorter. Nevertheless, it is said of him that he could build more brush fence in a day than he could walk back. He never learned to read or write, able to sign his name mechanically, but generally making "his mark." He m early,—Salisbury Oct 10, 1815, Betsey Chase b Salisbury Jan 11, 1799, d East Livermore Jan 1855, dau of James and Mary (Tucker). Census 1850 gives her wid with the younger children, the homestead assessed $1,900.

By the time he came of age Jabez had surveyed his environment and drawn various deductions. The necessity for working prevented his gaining an education, and now he considered it too late; he became particularly anxious that his children should acquire as much learning as was reasonably possible. The liquor question was even more important. Drink was a daily necessity to his kin and neighbors. It took all their spare funds and they got little or no pleasure from it. So, Jabez decided to cut it out, even the hard cider which had cost only the labor of making it. Finally, the atmosphere of Salisbury did not seem conducive to ambition. So, Jabez bought a farm in East Livermore. It must be conceded that his posterity has remained above the average, possibly the cause and effect herein noted. Children:

   a Nancy Chase b 1816; d 1817   b James Chase b Mch 29, 1818
   c Martha Follinsby b 1820; m 1838 Amos Hobbs of Farmington, Me. He lost a leg quite early in life and d long before his wife, who lived to extreme old age. Children,—Dorillus and Curtis M. The latter continued his father's small manufacturing business (see Hinds Gen). Dorillus in 16th Me, missing after first Battle of Gettysburg; family learned much later he d Oct 1863 in Bellisle prison

d Francis Lyford b Brentwood Dec 9, 1822
e Susan Watson b 1825; m 1842 William Smith of Jay, whose sister m her brother.
   A large family, including James Chase who lost his right hand in the war and
   Justus Jesse, for years a contractor in N Y City
f Charles F b 1827; d 1828   g   Charles Hawes b 1830; d 1837
h Sarah Elizabeth b 1832; m Lyman Black of Chesterville; outlived her husband
   many years; d about 1915; son Wallace of Farmington, Me
i Charles Curtis b 1835
j John William b 1835; m 1857 —— Ellsworth; enlisted 26th Me; came home
   invalided; d a few years later; no children

James Chase Dow adkfbeb was promised a cow by his father if he
would abstain from drinking; educated Farmington Academy and Parsonsfield Theological Seminary; became a Baptist minister; in 1843
missionary to Midnapore, India, where 3 of his children born; returned
broken in health 1848; 1850 census finds him farmer of Buckfield;
children correct as per list; some time later bought a farm in Dover,
Minn; after 1880 bought a farm near De Smet, So Dak; returned to St
Charles, Minn; d May 14, 1899.   He m June 25, 1843, Hannah Gould
Bacon b Wilton, Me, Mch 15, 1825, lived her widowhood with dau Sarah
in Winona; d Mch 7, 1905.   Her grandfather, Silas Gould of Barnstable,
Mass, enlisted at 15, at Bunker Hill, at siege of Boston; re-enlisted in the
field in Durkee's Conn reg, in the Battle of Long Island, in the retreat
across New Jersey, crossing the Delaware with Washington;   his term
expired but he stayed and fought at Battles of Trenton and Princeton.
After the war he came to Wilton, Me; lived until 1842.   Children of
James C:

a Maria Wakefield b Jan 12, 1845; m 1867 G F Doolittle of Owatonna, Minn;
   living 1922 Chicago; 1 son
b Sarah Elizabeth b Apr 4, 1848; d Nov 13, 1913; m Dr L G Wilberton of Winona,
   who survives; 1 dau; 1 son George in 1918 with 20th engineers in France
c James Jabez b Feb 15, 1848 (this date or preceding error)
d Hannah Bacon b Buckfield Dec 31, 1849; m Thomas W Sidway of Jamesville,
   Wis; 1 son, 1 dau
e Julia Emma b East Killingly, Conn, Oct 9, 1852 (her father pastor there); d
   East Livermore Oct 14, 1857
f Emma Catherine b East Livermore Dec 13, 1855; m 1872 Calvin Carter; d
   Oct 13, 1877; 2 sons; 1 dau
g Frederick Neal b Jan 24, 1857; m Mary Glover; 1921 of De Smet, So Dak; 3
   dau
h Julia Frances b Aug 13, 1859; kept house for her brother James J since the death
   of his wife; succeeded 1921 as superintendent of the State school for the
   blind at Faribault; unm
i Elmer Chase b July 18, 1861; d Northfield, Minn, Feb 27, 1908; m Mary G
   Miller, who survives; 1 son, 2 dau
j Josiah Willis b Feb 18, 1864; d Ft Smith, Ark, Mch 1911; m Elizabeth ——;
   1 son
k Horace Albert b Dover, Minn, Nov 22, 1866; m Mrs Anna Newell; lived
   Kendall, Wis; murdered Olathe, Kan, 1922; no children
l Edwin Ruthven b Dec 21, 1869; m Mary ——; 1 son, perhaps 1 dau.   Traveling evangelist of Wheaton, Ill, he never answered letter of genealogical
   inquiry with return postage enclosed.   In recent directory at same address:
   Miss Florence Dow

James Jabez Dow adkfbebc after his return from India
picked up a country school education and studied with his father; at 14
teaching school, at 15 prepared for college.   He enlisted 1863, not yet

16 but well grown, in 2nd Me cav; leaving Me in 4 feet of snow directly for southern Louisiana.

They had comparatively little fighting, but shared in the Red River campaign and against Mobile. During the year 5 were killed in action, but 41 out of 100 died, mainly from fevers. At the close of the war they were held for weary months, expecting to be sent to the Mexican border. Disch late in 1865, he joined his father in Minn, unable to do much for several years on account of illnesses contracted in the Louisiana swamps. After 3 years recuperation, he entered Carlton College, just opened in Northfield, Minn, taking A B in 1874. The other of the 2 graduates was Myra Amelia Brown b Fitchburg, Mass, May 19, 1849, d Faribault Jan 22, 1908. He is a member of Phi Beta Kappa, M A, and L H D. After one year as supt of schools, he took up work with the blind and has made this his whole study since 1875; supt of school for the blind established by the State at Faribault. His especial field has been with children born blind and he has world wide recognition as an authority. In 1916 he spent a vacation in Me, seeing many relatives for the first time in 30 years. In 1919 he retired, his place taken by his sister Julia. He d 1927.

Some time between 1880 and 1890 he conceived the idea of a Dow genealogy, as the outgrowth of attempting to trace his own direct line. He sent out blank forms to as many Dows as he could find, working much as did Edgar R Dow, but he never was able to unravel the confusion between Samuel Dow adk and Samuel adfc, making a composite of them and giving to the net result about half the children of both. Abandoning the task in disgust, the valuable correspondence was stored in a garret and long since lost. Children:

a Charles Francis b Dec 3, 1875; d Faribault Apr 3, 1901
b James Chase b Sept 22, 1877; m but no children; electrical engineer Great Falls, Mont
c Mary Amelia b Oct 18, 1879; d May 21, 1892
d Harry b Sept 21, 1881; d Dec 11, 1882
e George Brown b Oct 19, 1884; d Feb 11, 1887
f Myra Catherine b Mch 23, 1888; d Feb 17, 1889
g Margaret Whitney b Feb 27, 1892; grad Carlton College; musician and teacher of Faribault
h William Gould b Sept 30, 1895; grad Univ of Minn 1916; 2nd Lieut of Engineers France 1919

Francis L Dow adkfbed, farmer of Jay, Me, d Jan 28, 1893; m Feb 3, 1844, Melinda Knowles Smith b Livermore Jan 29, 1817. It is said that for years their descendants held an annual reunion, but (strange to say) not one of a dozen letters of genealogical inquiry has ever been answered and all data herein are from Me vital statistics. Children:

a Horace F b Amesbury, Mass, Oct 16, 1846; d Apr 4, 1847
b Charles F b July 25, 1848   c Horace M b Oct 12, 1850
d Everett C b Jay Aug 4, 1856   e Wallace L b Nov 11, 1860

Horace M Dow adkfbeda living Livermore Falls 1915; of Jay, m May 30, 1886, Eliza A Howland d Apr 11, 1911, ae 45, dau of Joseph and Cordelia (Searles); m 2nd (carpenter) Dec 17, 1913, wid Ella Corliss

Heckler, Christian Science practitioner, ae 52, dau of David Bailey and Eliza H (Smith) Corliss.

Charles F Dow adkfbedb, commercial traveler of Boston, m Manchester, N H, July 19, 1878, wid Ann A Deland, ae 33; d Pelham, Mass, Oct 23, 1911. They had at least 1 child, for:

a   Ella F b Londonderry, N H, 1882; m Lowell, Mass, Oct 27, 1902, Arthur F Hammond, ae 25, son of Stephen F and Annie (Sargent)

Everett C Dow adkfbedd of Jay m June 30, 1883, Maria Corine Hunt. Children:

a   Clinton Hunt b 1886   b   Pearl
c   Francis S b 1888   d   Lucy M b June 24, 1892

Clinton H Dow adkfbedda, shipping clerk of Portland, m Aug 20, 1917, Bertha Hazel Bell, ae 27, teacher of Waterford, dau of Frank Lester and Clara Elmira (Cheever). Children:

a   Gertrude Bell b Jan 18, 1918   b   Charles Clinton b Apr 16, 1919

Francis S Dow adkfbeddc, farmer of Jay, m Sept 4, 1919, Ruth P Jackson b 1892, wid, dau of Edward F and Mary H (Parsons) Holden. Child:

a   Margaret Sylvester b June 14, 1920

Wallace L Dow adkfbede, farmer of Jay, m Sept 7, 1892, Addie S French, ae 19, teacher, dau of N S and Mary (Stanley). Children:

a   Leon F b Nov 11, 1893   b   Miriam L b Aug 15, 1895
c   Robert b May 2, 1910

Charles C Dow adkfbei, farmer of Wayne, m Caroline Ellsworth b Avon, d before 1903. He d Feb 9, 1919, at the home of his son, who d 3 days earlier, both exhausted by influenza. Children:

a   Dorillus Winfield b June 16, 1866   b   James Henry b 1862 (m rec)
c   Cora Caroline; in 1919 teacher of Waterville, unm

Dorillus W Dow adkfbeia, 28 years traveling auditor of Me Central R R, d Portland Feb 6, 1919; m Carrie Wall b Augusta, d Portland Nov 9, 1902, ae 36, 4 mos, dau of Horace and Sarah (Stevens) Merrill; 2nd Oct 2, 1907, Mary Frances Haskell b Cape Elizabeth 1875, music teacher, dau of Alfred Edwin and Lydia Frances (Johnson). Children:

a   Carroll Winfield b Portland Jan 2, 1894
b   Florence Edna b July 24, 1895; m Calvin Crossett
c   Frances Winifred b 1909; in high school 1921; compiled her line 3 generations

James H Dow adkfbeib, in 1903 asst supt State school for boys; 1919 farmer of Wayne; widower, m 2nd July 10, 1903, Abbie Louisa Farrington b Holden, ae 33, dau of Zenas and Ella F (Rowe). Children:

a   Ruth Ellsworth b Apr 19, 1904   b   George Farrington b July 22, 1905

John Dow adkfc. For many years he was a slight memory, for a century an almost forgotten legend, considered by many as never real. In 1921 he is found and becomes an episode in American history.

In the spacious garret of Jabez Dow's house in East Livermore were many keepsakes and curiosities brought from Salisbury to Me,—shells, curios from many lands, all suggestive of a traveler by sea. Among them was a box of old letters and a powder horn. The latter was elaborately carved. The lettering was JOHN DOW. The decorations were sketches of harbors, not nearby, but of distant ones, Pacific and So America. James Chase Dow used to play with this on rainy days, but not yet able to read the letters, asked his father about them. Jabez merely replied grimly that they were from the pirate. Some years later the house burned and the relics were lost. Thirty years later James Chase Dow told what he could remember of these things to his son James Jabez, who in later years was inclined to doubt the whole matter. John Dow wrote from a prison in Jamaica, telling of his audience with the Governor, adding facetiously that he was living at the Governor's expense, if not at his table. Finally he wrote that he was to be hanged the next day.

This John Dow was a sailor. Aaron Dow, to whom the letters were probably written, was also a sailor until he came back to the farm; we presume they were brothers. John became a minor officer. During the war of 1812 the U S issued many letters of marque and reprisal and many privateersmen scoured the sea. John became one of these. The papers of such matters were lost when the British took Washington, so we cannot tell whether John then commanded his own ship. At all events he was in command of a boat when he was captured at sea and taken to Jamaica for trial. He was executed at Kingston, Jamaica. The Jamaican archives are difficult of access, but the date was about 1814.

There is no possibility that he left a posterity.

THE junior branch of the adk line left Salisbury before 1755 and has ever since been identified with Maine, a majority of its members still there. Edgar R Dow, the first genealogist of the family, was of this line and gave to it especial attention. Only about 100 names have been added by the present Author.

Jabez Dow adkg m (int pub 8: 11: 1750) Dorothy Wood of Salisbury b Dec 10, 1727; rec in Salisbury fails to mention parents. After the birth of two children they moved to Falmouth, Me, where he bought a truck farm. In 1790 census 1a, 2c, the rest grown and gone away:

a Abner b Aug 28, 1751   b Samuel b Apr 22, 1753
c Sarah b Mch 2, 1756; d young   d Joseph b Mch 17, 1758
e Jabez b July 17, 1760; lost at sea in Rev navy
f Jonathan b Nov 20, 1762; d Dec 24, 1773
g Sarah b Aug 20, 1766   h Mercy b July 5, 1771; d Nov 19, 1773

Abner Dow adkga, shoemaker of Falmouth, was among the first ten to enlist May 12, 1775, Capt David Bradish; made 4th corporal; mustered out as 4th sgt; re-enlisted as master gunner of artillery; commissioned 1st Lieut Jan 1, 1777, serving 34 months; as captain Oct 1779. His commissions are now family heirlooms in Portland. He was in Col Timothy Bigelow's 15th Mass, transferred Jan 1, 1781, to 9th Mass; fighting 1780 before West Point. Mass rolls do not mention termination of service. N Y rec of Officers contains an annoying entry,—Capt Abner Dow cashiered Aug 9, 1781. This sound strange, coming at the very end of the War, his career having been uniformly excellent. Apparently Edgar R Dow found this entry, but did not pursue it. The Author appealed to Washington and there is no such rec, no court martial, no proceedings of any sort. It seems to be a clerical error; at worst it seems that, the war being ended, he did not wait for acceptance of his resignation before leaving for home. At all events, he received a great welcome in Falmouth and for the rest of his life was greatly respected and honored for his war services. He received in 1783 his allotment of 160 acres. He settled in Pearsontown; m July 27, 1782, wid Martha (Sawyer) Hinckley d Standish 1794. Census 1790 gives them 2a, 2b, 2c, unintelligible, as he could not have a son of 16. Vital statistics not kept, rec from family:

a Abigail b 1783   b Samuel b 1785; d young, presumably
c Mercy b 1787   d Elizabeth Hinckley b 1789
e Seth Hinckley b Standish Aug 3, 1790

Abigail Dow adkgaa m James Benson, weaver b Eng Feb 20, 1772, immigrant of Nov 16, 1800. Children:

a Martha b Gray 1810; m William H Roberts of Portland
b Mary   c Susan b —— Frost; had,—James, Edward, Mary Susan
d Joseph m Maria Adams

e Arthur M b Sept 21, 1821; d Gorham Jan 2, 1905; m Elizabeth Lowell; currier, tanner, street commissioner, trustee of savings bank, etc. Dau Sarah m —— Usher
f Elizabeth m —— Nickerson; dau Ella m —— Nash

Mercy Dow adkgac d Oct 1869; m Luther Topping. Children:

a Mary b Standish Dec 3, 1807; changed her name to Tappan; d unm
b Elias b Baldwin Aug 1809; d July 1831
c Dolly m George Clement of Gorham
d Martha D d Gorham Mch 26, 1880; m John Higgins
e Elizabeth d in infancy   f Samuel   g Elizabeth
h Lydia d in infancy   i Lydia   j Sybil
k Nancy b Feb 1828; d West Gorham Apr 11, 1910; m 1852 George Crockett; sons,—Charles E, Nelson H
l Caroline M b Dec 31, 1831; d Nov 9, 1895; m Charles E Jordan of West Gorham

Elizabeth H Dow adkgad d Gorham July 29, 1875; m Richard Pottle b Nov 7, 1776, d Nov 5, 1835, son of William of Stratham, N H. No children.

Seth H Dow adkgae d West Baldwin Mch 25, 1841; m 1814 Harriet Sanborn b Baldwin Dec 9, 1794, d Turner Aug 23, 1884; a cooper. Children:

a Angelina b Aug 6, 1815; m Alden Bean; d tuberculosis Portland Jan 16, 1841
b Edwin b Oct 5, 1817   c Martha Sanborn b July 5, 1819
d Stephen H b Portland July 20, 1822   e Emily G b Mch 24, 1825
f Alexander P b Apr 27, 1827   g Abbie S b Feb 23, 1832
h Mary Frances b Jan 23, 1838; d Dec 16, 1839

Edwin Dow adkgaeb d July 18, 1888; m Apr 28, 1844, Adeline S Atwood b New Gloucester Aug 27, 1815, d Portland Oct 26, 1897, dau of Solomon. He was a cooper and operated somewhat in Portland real estate. Many stories are told of his ability to do the work of two ordinary men. In a week he made by hand from the rough lumber 65 syrup barrels, each with 14 hoops. On a Saturday he made from white oak in the rough 11 kerosene barrels. As a citizen he was held in high esteem. Children:

a Frank E b Mechanic Falls Nov 19, 1845
b Imogene R b Durham Feb 9, 1849; d No Woodstock Jan 27, 1854
c Charles Leroy b Durham Oct 6, 1850
d Ella Tucker b Aug 1, 1852; d Apr 18, 1854
e Edgar Randolph b Oct 3, 1854   f George Eugene b Sept 13, 1856

Frank E Dow adkgaeba m June 1, 1878, Sarah O Ames; got divorce Nov 22, 1886; printer, found drowned Oct 29, 1902; no children.

Charles Leroy Dow adkgaebc, interior decorator of Denver, Colo; in 1923 Long Beach, Calif; had for a few years Edgar R Dow as partner; m Jan 29, 1879, Eliza M Williams b Sept 1851, dau of Ezra T. Children:

a Wallace Leo b Dec 26, 1881; d Sept 3, 1882
b Neal b Aug 4, 1886; d June 16, 1887

Edgar R Dow adkgaebe, b Mechanic Falls; d Portland Feb 17,

1909; no children; m Oct 15, 1878, Ella Lufkin b No Yarmouth Apr 25, 1858, d Portland Aug 30, 1914, dau of Asa A and Almira (Dennison).

An accountant in a Portland Insurance company, Edgar was the pioneer in Dow Genealogy. ˙Like almost all others, he began through his interest in tracing back his own direct line. Early in 1881 he had conceived the idea of tracing the entire Dow name in America, little knowing the extent of such task. He was able to get without error the names in the three earliest generations of both a and b lines. With this foundation, he worked mainly as a letter writer, sending a form to be filled by every Dow whose name he could obtain. In those days other genealogists who could help and exchange information were few. The great libraries of today either did not exist or were almost inaccessible to him. His weakest point was in having to jump at conclusions in the 4th and subsequent generations to connect the right son with the right father. Nevertheless, these errors were all of the kind easy to correct in later years. He was a persuasive genius of unlimited patience, getting replies to his inquiries, while the other workers (notably the present Author) failed in that department. It often took an exchange of half a dozen letters to get facts complete which might have been done in the first letter, had the subject of inquiry had any knowledge of what is required by a good genealogy. His health failed more or less completely and he abandoned the work for about seven years, going to Denver. On his return to Portland he attempted to take it up again, but was able to do little. His letters show plainly his ambition to publish a Dow Book. His manuscript gave about 6,000 names properly arranged. A second manuscript contained about 3,000 names arranged in lines of several generations, but having a gap. There was, in addition, a large folio of original letters, often with data of 4 or 5 generations, which he was wholly unable to connect.

His original completed part added about 2,000 names new to the Herbert B Dow collection. His unadjusted work was considerably over 6,000 names, and when this was edited in 1923, the additional knowledge made over 90 per cent connectible. One thing especially has made his work indispensable to his successors. Most of his names came out of family Bibles and thus had exact dates. Similar information gleaned from wills and deeds had no dates, and many workers inserted approximated dates for working convenience. Such guesses were often terribly misleading. A very good-natured man, he gave to every inquirer all the information which he could acquire and, no doubt, informed a thousand persons for the first time of their genealogy to 1637.

George E Dow adkgaebf, practicing dentist of Portland, prominent in Maine Dental Association, d 1921; m Carrie E Smith b London, Eng, Sept 15, 1856. He rescued his brother's manuscripts and made occasional entries, chiefly to keep the adkga lines up to date. Realizing that the present Author meant business and that the Book might eventually see publication, he forwarded the manuscripts, which have been copied complete. These manuscripts, by the way, contain the only research known into the Lufkin family.   Children:

   a Leroy Eugene b July 5, 1875
   b Edwin Francis b Nov 20, 1879; d Jan 22, 1907
   c (adopted) Harriet J Smith (Harriet J S Dow) b Nov 17, 1899

Leroy E Dow adkgaebfa, civil engineer in Govt employ of Portland, m Jan 17, 1905, Ethel Bartlett, dau of Charles Jr and Catherine J D (Willis) of Roxbury, Mass.   Child:

   a Shirley Ethel b June 16, 1909

Martha S Dow adkgaec d Turner Mch 17, 1880; m Nov 21, 1847, Charles H Littlefield b Topham Aug 22, 1818, d Turner Aug 31, 1879, harness maker.   Children:

   a —— son b Sept 28, d Nov 6, 1850
   b Albert L b Sept 1, 1853; d Dec 11, 1855

Stephen H Dow adkgaed, cooper of Portland, d Mch 20, 1882; m Martha A Snell b 1830, d Jan 30, 1905. The grandfather of Martha and Clarinda was a Revolutionary veteran, an original settler of Turner, the homestead still known as Snell's Hill.   Children:

   a Clara b June 23, 1850   b Emma b Feb 8, 1852
   c Lillian b Hebron Feb 20, 1857; d Portland Apr 11, 1902, unm
   d Albert Littlefield b Hebron Feb 22, 1859
   e Fred Eugene b Portland Jan 14, 1862

Clara Dow adkgaeda m William A Lowe, plumber of Portland. Children:

   a Charles E b Feb 13, 1870; d Apr 10, 1872
   b George B b Oct 21, 1871; d Nov 18, 1880
   c Eleanor Dennis b May 1887; m Aug 12, 1908, Clinton Wesley Graffam

Emma Dow adkgaedb m Edgar E Rounds of Portland, business man, holding a number of municipal offices.   Children:

   a Alice Beulah b Feb 4, 1880; m Walter S Crandall
   b Gertrude Mary b 1881; d Dec 10, 1885
   c Arthur Harold b May 1887; d June 1903
   d Gertrude Alester   e Edgar Dow

Albert L Dow adkgaedd m Oct 11, 1886, Clara Jane Stevens b Young America, Ill, Feb 5, 1862.   Children:

   a Stephen Hinckley b Aug 4, 1888   b Walter Edward b Oct 29, 1890
   c William Albert b May 21, 1893   d Lorena Maud b Apr 21, 1896

Walter E Dow adkgaeddb is probably untraced. A Walter E Dow, farmer and teacher of Woodland, m Hattie Everett, is probably disconnected. A child:

   c (3rd, rec) —— dau b Mch 13, 1918

Stephen H Dow adkgaedda, plumber of Portland, m June 5, 1911, Gertrude Owen of Portland, ae 24, dau of Charles Fred and Lizzie A (Wilbur).

Fred E Dow adkgaede m Aug 24, 1903, Grace W Clement b Gorham July 16, 1875, only child of Charles J and Emna L (Rand).

Emily G Dow adkgaee d Oct 26, 1882; m William Small of Waterford. Children:

a   Mary Frances b Turner July 30, 1847; d Oct 23, 1864
b   Rebecca A b May 1, 1850; d Nov 4, 1870; m George O Keith of Auburn; son
       Frank b Oct 21, 1870
c   Martha Maria b No Woodstock Oct 24, 1852; m Sept 10, 1873, Welcome B
       Beal of Newton, Mass. Children,—Herbert A b Bridgeton May 2, 1876;
       Maud E b Waterford July 24, 1877
d   William M b East Baldwin Sept 26, 1854; m Clara A Staples. Children,—
       Walter S b Sept 30, 1878, d June 5, 1880; Edith May b July 21, 1880
e   Flora A b Portland July 22, 1856; m Jan 22, 1878, George B Bradford of Turner
f   John C C b Bethel Feb 10, 1860; m Georgianna Elizabeth Horr; 2nd Marion
       L Horr; 6 sons, 4 dau

Alexander P Dow adkgaef, farmer of Turner, in 1850 cooper of Portland, d May 11, 1897; m Clarinda S Snell, b Jan 31, 1827, d Mch 5, 1908, dau of Eleazer and Martha (Drake). Children:

a   Ada J b Apr 12, 1857   b   Arthur C b Jan 11, 1860
c   Alton E b June 11, 1862
d   Edwin W b Apr 4, 1864.   Directory 1906 shows the 3 sons farmers of Turner,
       all unm

Ada J Dow adkgaefa m Sept 30, 1877, Archelus W Sawyer of Buckfield b Greenville Mch 28, 1838. Children:

a   Wilfred A b Sept 14, 1878
b   Nellie L b Dec 16, 1879; m Mch 11, 1902, W Hathaway of Turner
c   George L b Feb 2, 1882
d   Mabelle Florence b Buckfield July 29, 1884; m June 26, 1909, Clarence Henry
       Robinson
e   Clara E b Dec 6, 1885
f   Edith J b Dec 16, 1886; m June 2, 1904, A G Hayes of Richmond
g   Percy G b May 13, 1888; m Alice Bertha Williams of Turner
h   Flora E b Oct 24, 1889   i   Alexander Dow b May 7, 1891
j   Archie W b June 11, 1894   k   Emily A b May 7, 1899

Abbie S Dow adkgaeg d Ansonia, Conn, May 10, 1921; m July 12, 1851, William Spencer b Gray Feb 13, 1825, d Sept 17, 1888, factory foreman of Ansonia. Children:

a   Emma J b Turner Apr 30, 1852
b   Ida M b Jan 1, 1854; m Frank F Vandercook b Aug 14, 1856
c   Eva M b Oct 28, 1856; m July 12, 1876, Lewis J Cook of Ansonia. Children,—
       Lewis W b July 18, 1877; Ernest V b July 9, 1878, d Aug 16, 1879; Ruby
       May b Brooklyn, N Y, Mch 3, 1881, m Richard Hurlburt

Samuel Dow adkgb. Edgar R Dow hunted long and diligently for traces of this soldier; his ms has many pencil marks,—as: d 1812? m a Miss Hobart?, etc. Maine rec end with his enlistment 3 days after his brother, in the same regiment. Mass rolls show he receipted for pay Aug 11, 1775.

Samuel went to Boston. Some, probably all, the following belong to him. Samuel Dow, blacksmith of Boston, complained 1786 that he had been unable to collect pay due to him while in the Quartermaster's dept 1776-7. The N H pension list carries Samuel Dow in 1840, b N H, ae 87, living with William B Harding in Boston. Age agrees and Samuel was born Seabrook, N H. Boston directory for 1789 and 1796 give Samuel Dow, blacksmith, shop on Nassau St assessed $600; house in Frog Lane. This Samuel was constable 1796-7. Samuel Dow of Boston m Jan 17, 1782, Elizabeth Holden. Samuel Dow of Boston m June 12, 1799, Sally Turner. Boston vital statistics show no Dow b before 1800. Census 1790 gives Samuel Dow Boston 1a, 1b, 4c. So far, it all looks like the same Samuel, twice married, with 3 dau, 1 son. It looks as though he was living 1840 with a married dau. Useless to speculate on the missing son.

Joseph Dow adkgd of Falmouth, private Oct 2, 1776, to Mch 24, 1780 (brother Jabez in same company); m (int pub Apr 26, 1782) Lucy Sanborn b Hampton, N H, Oct 19, 1755, d Standish Sept 1, 1836. Standish 1790 census gives them 1a, 2b, 2c. Children:

    a   Susannah b Dec 1783   b   Jabez b Mch 13, 1785
    c   Jonathan b July 29, 1787; d Mch 20, 1866
    d   Joseph b Oct 22, 1790   e   Abner b Nov 20, 1792

Susannah Dow adkgda m Daniel Hasty b May 3, 1780, d 1863, son of William and Martha (McLaughlin), who came from Rye, N H.

Jabez Dow adkgdb d Standish Oct 31, 1868; m Dec 23, 1810, Lucy Sanborn b Standish Sept 1, 1789, d Standish Oct 4, 1854. Children:

    a   Wilson b Jan 19, 1812   b   Susan b Mch 18, 1816; d Nov 25, 1839
    c   Almira b Aug 27, 1818; d Nov 5, 1897, unm
    d   Lucy H b Oct 12, 1820; d Aug 7, 1825
    e   Matilda b July 5, 1823   f   Benjamin A b Aug 31, 1825, untraced
    g   John J b Jan 29, d Feb 8, 1829

Wilson Dow adkgdba of Standish d Sept 12, 1893; m Jan 4, 1838, Catherine McDonald Nason b Hollis Apr 18, 1817, d Feb 9, 1894, dau of Robert and Catherine (McDonald). Children:

    a   Charles H b Mch 20, 1840; untraced
    b   Susan M b Nov 20, 1843; d Oct 21, 1851
    c   Edgar P b Aug 6, 1846   d   Herbert W b Feb 9, 1854
    e   Margaret D b Feb 5, 1859

Charles H Dow adkgdbaa. It seems probable that it is he who enlisted 1861 from Sheepscot; may be the Charles Dow d regimental hospital, Va, who enlisted from Sheepscot. Unlikely that he is the Charles H Dow disconnected of Richmond, Me.

Edgar P Dow adkgdbac of Portland m Clara B Mason d Portland Aug 10, 1907. Children:

    a   Alice B, teacher of Rangeley and elsewhere, m Nov 5, 1905, Andrew Jackson of
        N Y City

b   Wilson Everett b Standish 1885; m Sept 18, 1915, Anna Mackin, ae 32, dau
    of John T and Ellen (Hewes)

Herbert W Dow adkgdbad, farmer and merchant of Standish, m
Lizzie E French.   Children:

a   M Pearl m —— Brooks   b   Vera E

Jonathan Dow adkgdc d Standish Mch 20, 1866.   Fragmentary
rec indicate 2 children:

a   Edmond M   b   ——, father of May E Dow b Feb 19, 1875

Edmond M Dow adkgdca m, ae 28, 2nd Sept 3, 1864, Anne L Rich
of Standish, ae 20, d Sept 3, 1865, dau of Luke and Miranda (Libby); he
merchant, she seamstress.   Perhaps children by 1st wife:

a   Fannie M b Sept 3, d Sept 17, 1865

Joseph Dow adkgdd d Apr 24, 1875; m Catherine Rounds of
Buxton; 2nd Lydia Thompson Cole of Cornish.   Children, by 1st wife:

a   Harriet Rounds b Aug 20, 1818; d Dec 20, 1848; m Carsten Roes d Dec 3, 1886
b   Emeline b June 9, 1821; d Mch 11, 1885; m John Hasty d Feb 1, 1886
c   Rachel Ayer b Sept 19, 1824; d Jan 9, 1899, unm
d   Eliza Irish b Dec 28, 1826
e   Mary Rounds b Nov 27, 1828; d Feb 2, 1908; m William Chaplin
f   Benjamin Ayer b Oct 23, 1832
g   Oliver b Dec 3, 1837   h   Alphonso L b 1847

Eliza I Dow adkgddd m Mch 19, 1851, Charles Wesley Boothby of
Lancaster, Mass, d Jan 4, 1858.   She d May 30, 1916.   Children:

a   Ella Frances b Sept 12, 1851; of Standish 1920, unm
b   Catie Elizabeth b Aug 22, 1853; d July 10, 1861
c   Emma Elvira b Jan 27, 1856; d Feb 19, 1910; m Horace E Allen
d   Charles Wesley b Nov 27, 1857; of Cumberland Co; m Nellie A Libby d Apr
    14, 1916

Benjamin A Dow adkgddf, farmer of Standish, vet of Me 17th
Inf, d June 8, 1913; m Mary E Handy b St Andrews.   Children:

a   John Franklin b Hollis 1865; d Standish Mch 2, 1916; untraced
b   Addie M d May 11, 1898, ae 30   c   Arthur L b 1869

Arthur L Dow adkgddfc, laborer of Standish, m Jan 22, 1905, Etta
J York, ae 14, d July 19, 1916, dau of Mellen A and Lovina (Wiggin).
In 1915 he had a bicycle repair shop.   A son:

a   —— b Westbrook June 15, 1913

Oliver Dow adkgddg of Standish d July 8, 1905; m Harriet Augusta
Chase d Nov 20, 1909, dau of David and Hannah (Phinney).   Children:

a   Howard K b Mass
b   Edna V M b Mass; d Standish June 30, 1898, ae 22-2-20

Howard K Dow adkgddga, chauffeur of Standish, m Feb 9, 1910,
Alice C Gray of Standish, dau of Rufus E and Ada (Flood).   Children:

a   Pauline Augusta b Nov 9, 1910; d Oct 5, 1911

b   Paul Wielding b Aug 17, 1912   c   Kenneth Rufus b Mch 10, 1914
d   William Lawrence b Nov 16, 1915   e   Virginia Alice b May 25, 1917

Alphonso L Dow adkgddh d Westbrook, carpenter, div; d 1909, ae 62, 5 mos; apparently m twice:—Jennie Handy b N S, of Boston; 2nd Maggie D ——.   Children:

a   Joseph L b 1868, painter of Westbrook, m Nov 20, 1894, Ida Ann Babb, ae 21, dau of —— and Elizabeth Babb
d   Edgar C b 1897, clerk of Portland, m June 19, 1920, Martha Elfreda Newcomb of Cumberland, ae 26, dau of Alexander and Amelia (Allen)
e   Harry S b Sept 22, 1899   f   Leslie M (both b Standish) Jan 20, 1901

Joseph L Dow adkgddha evidently m 2nd Elizabeth Caldwell (also Conway in rec) b Lawrence, Mass, for two children appear:

a   —— son b Mch 13, 1900   b   —— son (both b Westbrook) Aug 5, 1902

Abner Dow adkgde of Baldwin d Dec 7, 1850; m 1817 Frances Thompson b Standish Mch 17, 1794, d Gorham Sept 29, 1873; realty assessed $2,000 in 1850.   Children:

a   Franklin I b July 16, 1817   b   Susan; m or d by 1850
c   Frances S b Mch 27, 1819; m (int pub Apr 21, 1844) Frederick Todd of Rowley, Mass
d   Deborah T b Sept 6, 1821 (1830, census)
e   Benjamin L b Oct 21, 1822; d May 27, 1824
f   Alfred A b July 2, 1827 (1829, census)   g   Leander Abner b May 23, 1832

Franklin I Dow adkgdea d Oct 1, 1848; m Mch 14, 1847, Harriet J Staples.   Presumably no children

Deborah T Dow adkgded, described as a woman of unusual beauty, m Jan 1, 1851, Sylvanus R Yates, farmer of West Baldwin; d ae 95, 6 days, having held for some time the gold headed cane voted to the oldest man in town.   Children:

a   Frank E b Oct 5, 1851; of Gorham; m Apr 28, 1880, Georgianna Noble
b   William H b Sept 11, 1858; of Bartlett, N H
c   Charles L b Feb 19, 1861; of West Baldwin
d   Fannie Etta b Mch 5, 1866; m —— Spring of Brownfield
e   John Abner b Mch 2, d Mch 19, 1870

Alfred A Dow adkgdef, farmer of West Baldwin, d Sept 11, 1896; m Apr 5, 1852, Ophelia P Cram b Standish Oct 1, 1835, d Feb 22, 1919, dau of Joseph and Mary (Weeman).   Children:

a   Marshall Clinton b Dec 1, 1856; farmer of Lodi, Calif; 4 children; never answered letter of genealogical inquiry
b   Alfred V b Feb 4, 1859
c   Frank E b Sept 2, 1871; d Oct 12, 1880
d   Joseph A b Nov 2, 1873; physician of West Topsham, Vt; untraced

Alfred V Dow adkgdefb, proprietor of Mt Cutler hotel, d Sept 11, 1896; m Mch 17, 1880, Cassie Gray.   One child found:

a   Owen Oscar b 1885

Owen O Dow adkgdefba, teacher of Hiram, d July 12, 1919; m

Hiram Jan 1, 1912, Mildred Roselle Sherman, teacher, ae 21, dau of Orra E and Georgia A (Mitchell). Children:

   a Donald Sherman b Scarboro Jan 3, 1912   b ——, dau b Apr 17, 1915

Leander D Dow adkgdeg, butcher and farmer of Gorham, m Apr 3, 1857, Mary Ellen Haven b Hiram Apr 25, 1836, d July 29, 1878. Children:

   a Phoebe P b Baldwin Oct 7, 1858; d Feb 1, 1877
   b Hattie May b Nov 27, 1860
   c Ellen H b Sept 29, 1865; m (Nellie H) Newington, N H, Oct 19, 1892, Fred C
      Googins
   d Fred Todd b July 23, 1867   e Laura P b May 1, 1870, Gorham
   f Daisy Louise m Eugene M Dow adkdececc

Fred T Dow adkgdegd, in 1915 civil engineer of Bangor, m Sept 4, 1893, Marion Antoinette Reed, ae 24, b Buckport, d Bangor Oct 17, 1915, ae 45-10-30, dau of Capt George W and Sara (Treat). A dau:

   a —— b July 15, 1904

Jabez Dow adkge served as private, Capt Benjamin Hopper, sea-coast service 8 mos, 25 days from Feb 29, 1776; re-enlisted; drowned. Doubtless unm.

Sarah Dow adkgg d East Baldwin Aug 10, 1845; m 1788 Richard Pierce, lumberman, b Ipswich, Mass, Sept 1756, killed by upset of cart Standish July 17, 1810. Children:

   a Susan b Nov 29, 1789; d Standish 1813
   b William b June 7, 1892; d Standish, lumberman and militia captain, June 23,
      1836; m May 1823 Mehitable Charles b Fryeburg Dec 1, 1797, d Standish
      Jan 9, 1842; 5 sons, 2 dau
   c Samuel b Aug 10, 1794-5; of West Baldwin, d Mch 16, 1842; m Aug 1826
      Rachel Lowell
   d Dolly b Mch 1797; d 1799
   e Dolly b Dec 31, 1800; m July 3, 1823, David Brown Jr
   f Annie b Apr 19, 1803; d Baldwin Jan 15, 1885; m Jan 25, 1825, Capt Reuben
      Brown d Nov 25, 1875

UNAVOIDABLY, the destinies of the younger children of Henry Dow, immigrant, were completely altered by the marriage of his widow to Richard Kimball of Ipswich. It involved the complete separation of the two families, which almost never met again genealogically. True, the distance by air line is but 11 miles. Passage by land was practically impossible. By water it was more than a day's journey. There was no regular post and people had neither time nor money to write letters depending on the kindness of some traveler for delivery. The two halves of the family were as far apart as they would now be if one was in New York, the other in Los Angeles. The oldest son of Margaret Cole Dow was 20 when she married and, as his patrimony lay in Hampton and as he was self-supporting, he quite reasonably elected to remain in Hampton.

Daniel Dow ae m at 32, rather later than usual in those times, 13: 9: 1673, Elizabeth Lamprey, dau of Henry and Gillyen of Hampton. It was a brilliant marriage. Gillyen's mother had been an heiress in England, receiving as dowry a metal bound wooden chest placed on one end of the scales. Gillyen's mother sat on the other and her father poured in gold pieces until the scales balanced,—112 lbs. This chest is now in possession of the children of Morris Lamprey of St Paul, Minn. Daniel Dow was of a very different way of thinking, of mode of life, from his brothers. He took no part in civic affairs, does not even appear by signature in any political or church movement, not even constable, not even on any church committee, when at least three were appointed for a task as simple as moving a stove in or out of church. In fact he did nothing to warrant mention in Hist Hampton. It is quite notable that his posterity almost invariably intermarried in a small circle of the pioneer families. There was almost from the first a little local aristocracy and the tribe of Daniel Dow seldom went outside it. Daniel was thrifty;— in 1667 he added to his estate from the luckless Nathaniel Boulter 2 1-2 acres of planting ground west of the Southe acre, with one share of the Cow Common and one of the Great Ox Common. "Goodman" William Fuller, immigrant of 1635, dying childless, his property was divided among relatives and friends. One recipient was "Elizabeth, now wife of Daniel Dow."

Following a custom still not infrequent in New England to this day, he made no will but deeded all his property to his children during his life. This deed, recorded Apr 10, 1710, gave land "unto my well beloved son—David Dow, my home and barn and houselot where I live, etc; and to my son Henry Dow 2 shares of the great Ox Common of Hampton; and to my daughter—Mary Dow, 20 shares, etc, etc." Wife is not mentioned, evidently dead before 1710. Children:

a Elizabeth b Jan 28, 1675; d Nov 29, 1731; a ms gives m Reuben Gore Dearborn, seemingly error

b   Hannah b Sept 13, 1676   c   Mary b Dec 7, 1678; d July 30, 1749
d   David b Mch 20, 1680   e   Henry b 1683; bap June 26, 1698

Hannah Dow aeb d June 13, 1733; m Jan 10, 1695, Dea John Dearborn Jr b Sept 2, 1673, d Mch 19, 1746, son of John and Mary (Ward). Children:

a   Ann b Oct 22, 1695; d July 30, 1718; m Joseph Philbrick; no children
b   Joseph b Apr 9, 1699; d Dec 9, 1700
c   John b Mch 28, 1703; d Mch 24, 1754; m Anna Sanborn; 10 children

David Dow aed inherited the homestead and was regarded by his father as his well beloved son and heir, proving that at the age of 30 he was not deficient mentally or morally.   Yet, from that moment the man drops absolutely out of sight,—the unsolved mystery of the whole 3rd generation of Dow.   In the table of births Hist Hampton gives d Jan 10, 1755.   This rec seems to belong to a lad of two generations later. How could any man live in Hampton for many years, a land owner and member of a most prominent family, and escape notice to the Historian of Hampton?   David must have moved away, as did his brother.

The logical way of procedure is to search other towns for disconnected Dows, possibly children of David.   Hist Hampton always loses its grip over Dows who moved to adjoining towns.   Only one candidate is found, a man who had Salisbury and Hampton connections, who was in youth in or near Greenland:

a   Amasa; rec not found; b presumably about 1704

Amasa Dow aeda by inference, first appears as int pub Sept 14, 1728, to Hannah Briant of Greenland.   Oddly, this is Salisbury rec. Also, Salisbury rec: Amasa Dow int pub June 28, 1729, to Lydia Robey of Hampton.   Whether Hannah Bryant d, was jiltor or jiltee, we know not.   Rec errs in giving Lydia Robey of Hampton.   She was then of Kingston; m Kingston Aug 4, 1729.   The rest of Amasa's career is a tale soon told.   His will probated 1730 names a son:

a   Amasa b Kingston Jan 17, 1729-30

Amasa Dow aedaa is traced occasionally.   Kingston rec has an error, Amasa m May 2, 1742, Elizabeth French.   The truth of this garble is clear in Kingston church rec: Amasa Dow bap May 2, 1742.   The next rec is accurate: Amasa Dow m May 16, 1750, Hannah Buswell. They left Kingston after 1755.   Amasa is in the Canterbury tax lists 1767-72, as Amaziah (amazing spelling was then frequent).   In 1772 Amasa and Samuel, his son, were among the petitioners for a separate town and parish of Loudon, the nearest church being 13 miles away. His last appearance is in the 1790 census of Bow, Emersay Dow 1a, 2c. This census credits to Bow many inhabitants of Loudon, Pittsfield and Chichester.   Kingston rec prove 2 children but the census indicates a 3rd, the oldest dau being m and gone long before 1790.

a   Sarah b Kingston Mch 31, 1752; bap June 7, 1752; m Bow Nov 19, 1776, Richard Clough

b   Samuel b Kingston Mch 22, 1755; bap Kingston Apr 30, 1755
c   (a wild guess) Mareba L Dow of Bow m Dec 20, 1791, Joel Varnum

Samuel Dow aedaab seems to have associated closely with his father, appears in Bow 1790 census 1a, 1b, 2c. This indicates 1 dau and a son b later than 1774. All else concerning him must be conjecture. He cannot well be the Samuel, pensioner in Chichester 1840, for he was born 1760, according to pension rec. There was a considerable number of Loudon Dows, probably many descending from aedaab, but the fragmentary rec permit no reliable continuation. Samuel continues a favorite family name there.

Three unconnected Loudon records possibly belong here:

Deborah Dow aedb of Loudon m Nov 27, 1806, Ebenezer Bean of Barnstead.

John Dow m Mch 9, 1835, Susan Jackson, both of Loudon.

Meshech Dow m Nov 22, 1835, Rachel Johnson, both of Loudon. He lived a few years in Northfield, making linen wheels and shuttles; an odd character called there "Old Shuttle Dow."

Henry Dow aee, husbandman, acquired an attractive farm on Dow's Hill, Hampton, but did not live long to enjoy it; d June 4, 1727; m Aug 8, 1723, Martha Sanborn. He served under Capt James Davis in the 1712 scouting campaign against the Indians, drawing pay for 2 weeks, 1 day at 6s per week. Second child reasonably certain:

a   Daniel b Jan 27, 1724
b   Martha. This name appears twice in Hist Hampton; once with question mark. She d No Hampton Mch 10, 1770; m Aug 12, 1741, Jeremiah Moulton, son of Robert and Lucy (Smith). Child,—Martha b Aug 29, 1750

Daniel Dow aeea can be reconstructed from fragmentary vital and legal rec; m Nov 27, 1749, Rachel Brown bap Sept 5, 1736, d Mch 26, 1807, dau of Joshua and Rachel (Sanborn). Daniel and Rachel sold Hampton land July 3, 1755, to Nathaniel Batchelder. This date marks their removal to No Hampton. Family not found in 1790 census. Will dated 1784, probated 1790. Children, all named in will:

a   Elizabeth rec not found
b   Rachel b Sept 7, 1756; m Dec 12, 1783, Ezekiel Knowles of Deerfield
c   Simon b June 7, 1759
d   Miriam b Mch 21, 1762; m Aug 23, 1790, John Leavitt of No Hampton
e   Abraham Brown b Aug 30, 1767

Simon Dow aeeac, husbandman of No Hampton, m Nov 25, 1788, Love Mason of No Hampton b 1772. Will, probated Feb 27, 1805. Children, named in will:

a   Daniel b July 13, 1791
b   Elizabeth; possibly the Eliza m June 24, 1813, Stephen Page of No Hampton
c   Miriam b May 21, 1795; m June 27, 1819, Luther Leavitt of No Hampton
d   Rachel b Nov 3, 1801

Daniel Dow aeeaca, farmer of No Hampton, d Apr 6, 1869, ae 78; m Jan 9, 1821, Lucinda Marston of No Hampton.   At least 3 children:

a   Daniel M (often David M in rec) b June 4, 1821
b   Miriam b 1826; m Moses Shaw b Aug 11, 1824, d Jan 15, 1875, son of Benjamin
    and Abigail (Leavitt). Duplicate rec gives his mother Sarah Nudd. No
    children
c   George A b July 10, 1831

Daniel M Dow aeeacaca m Martha —— d soon after b of child; 2nd Apr 21, 1845, Abbie L Hobbs of No Hampton d wid Oct 19, 1885, ae 63-11-5, dau of John and Mary (Batchelder).   At least 6 children:

a   Daniel O b No Hampton Feb 4, 1844   b   Martha A b Mch 14, 1846
d   Frank P b Mch 21, 1852; farmer of No Hampton, d Aug 27, 1876, unm
e   Lucinda E b Oct 10, 1856
f   Abraham C b Jan 31, 1862; Abram C in m rec

Daniel O Dow aeeacaaa m Ellen O Donnell.   At least 2 children:

a   Frank Paul b Newton, Mass, 1876; m Nov 26, 1903, Susie Cestella, ae 27, dau
    of Henry and Mary (Nester)
b   Clara Agnes b Newton 1880; m June 21, 1905, Thomas Quinn, ae 24, son of
    Michael and Mary (Killen)

Frank P Dow aeeacaaaa and Susie A Cestella had; b Newton:

a   Dorothy Elizabeth b Sept 18, 1905   b   Norman Francis b Feb 15, 1910

Abram C Dow aeecaaf m Lawrence, Mass, June 22, 1899, Addie F Tuttle, ae 23, of Stratham, dau of Jacob B and Mary E (Home).   Children:

a   Lena Mary b Apr 7, 1906   b   —— dau b May 1, 1907

Abraham B Dow aeeae m Aug 17, 1806, Love Dow, both of No Hampton. She is his brother's wid.   Children, all b No Hampton:

a   Simon b Mch 17, 1807; untraced   b   Margaret b Oct 11, 1811
c   George b Mch 16, 1817

Margaret Dow aeeaeb m John Dow Lane, son of John and Sarah (Dow) abbeacc.   Two children, one Sarah E b Apr 12, 1846, m—Stevens

George O Dow aeeaec, farmer of No Hampton, m May 2, 1847, May Esther Philbrick b Sept 17, 1825, d May 4, 1877, dau of Jonathan abdccba and Abigail (Marston).   Children:

a   Margaret Anna b 1848; m Sept 23, 1872, Thomas E Marston of No Hampton
    1 son
b   Mary Abby (Abbie Mary, m rec) b 1849; m Sept 12, 1874, Erastus Bloomer
    Jewell of Stratham; 2 sons, 1 dau,—Alice May b Stratham June 12, 1877, m
    June 12, 1902, James Lewis Coe of Newfields
c   George Edgar b June 29, 1854

George E Dow aeeaecc, farmer of No Hampton, d Hampton Apr 5, 1883; m Dec 24, 1873, Fannie Wesley Jenness, ae 18, dau of Wesley of Rye: 3 children; she m 2nd Sept 26, 1887, Henry J Brown b 1862, son of William and Henrietta (Downs).   Children:

a   Hattie W b June 22, 1874   b   Nellie M b Mch 29, 1876
c   George Edgar b 1883

Hattie W Dow aeeaecca m July 2, 1893, Frank C Brown b July 1864, whose brother m her mother.   Children:

  a Doris Julian b Dec 16, 1897   b Perley William b Mch 23, 1900
  c Alan Francis b Nov 10, 1901

Nellie M Dow aeeaeccb m Rye Oct 6, 1893, Ezra B Philbrick; moved to Maine.   Children:

  a Jennie May b July 26, 1896   b George Oliver b Oct 10, 1897
  c Benning b June 18, d Sept 9, 1899
  d Josephine Marjorie b July 22, 1900   e John Ezra b Feb 26, 1902

George E Dow aeeaeccc, painter of Salem, Mass, m July 20, 1911, Helen V Hamilton, ae 27, div, dau of William O and Mary A (Nealor) Dennis.

WE have noted, with much interest to ourselves, at least, the tendency of all Dow lines so far toward marriages confined in a great majority of instances to a small circle of families. This is most marked in the ae line, five generations allying exclusively with other pioneer families of Hampton. The tendency is almost as complete in all the ab lines who remained near Hampton; a dozen other pioneer families supplying most of the marriages. In the ad lines those who remained Quaker married comparatively little outside Perkins, Hussey, Phillips, Collins. The non-Quakers of Seabrook did likewise, Eaton, Brown, Walton, Felch supplying most of the names. This tendency toward inbreeding was absent from the ah lines, Ipswich being a larger place, with other larger towns nearby, giving a much wider range to natural selection. In all this line there are almost never more than three marriages with the same family. The exception is the line of Epping and Gilmanton, about 30 intermarriages with Gilman. In the long run this seems to have had little effect on posterity, numerically or in personal ability. One is apt to think that hereditary influences follow a name, rather than the female lines. True, characters often persist in a family, unaltered from father to son, regardless of the influence of the mothers. A Dow of the 9th generation has but 1-512 of the blood of the immigrant. Gideon Dow's mother was a Perkins and grandmother was a Perkins. Clearly, his posterity have twice as much Perkins in them as they have Dow. The old Scotchman was no more in error than most of us, when he remarked:

"Had I kenned one of my sons would be a doctor, the other a minister, I never would have had auld Jeannie Cosh for their mither."

Resemblances are more apt to follow localities than blood. A whole town comes to look more alike, as well as act more alike, than a whole family divided up among a dozen towns.

Altho Richard Kimball, wheelwright of Watertown and Ipswich, became a very rich man, as times went, accumulating an estate of over £4,000, and altho he naturally desired that it should go to his own blood, he was a little "near," as the New Englanders say. He made a prenuptial contract with Margaret (Cole) Dow, whereby she should have £40 in her own right and "all the stuff she brought with her." Both d about the same time, she Mch 1, 1675, so there was no widow to spend his accumulations in riotous living. True, he brought up his step children and taught the boys a trade, but his legacies were not fortunes. To Thomas Dow ah, who needed nothing, he left 40s, payable a year and a half after his death. To Mary Dow af he left the same, altho she never married and was maintained always by her brother. To Jeremiah Dow ai he displayed his wildest extravagance,—£15 when the latter became of age.

Mary Dow af went to Ipswich, outlived her parents many years; d Ipswich Oct 16, 1731, ae 88, provided for in the will of Thomas Dow ah.

Hannah Dow ag m 1670 Jonas Gregorie of Ipswich; d childless Feb 2, 1671. Jonas m 2nd May 10, 1672, Elizabeth Healey, dau of William (2) and Sarah (Brown).

Thomas Dow ah, Ye Wheelwright of Ipswich, was a prolific ancestor equal to his half brother Joseph. The two have a much larger posterity than all other Dows of eight families combined. The brothers differed much. Henry ab was a public character always, Joseph ad devoted his best self to his religious association. Daniel ae did nothing. Thomas built his life closely around his home and his business, avoiding publicity either civil or church. He was a soldier when required, publicly unknown otherwise, except as occasionally surveyor of highways and for ten years tything man. He went to church, as did every one; no one could afford to stay away. He and Jeremiah ai had seats together in the new meeting house 1710. Ipswich commons were divided 1693, the share of Thomas being 6 acres. He was a keen judge of real estate and a successful speculator. His name appears often as witness to deeds and to wills. Of 9 children, he lost but 2, and many grandchildren were maintained under his roof.

Twenty-seven years ago his shop, then a crumbling ruin, existed on the edge of present Ipswich City. It was then visited by Joy W Dow and Arthur W Dow, both descendants, driven to the spot by Harvey Nourse, authority on Dow temperament (see quotation in preface). Said Joy, many years subsequently: "I had studied genealogy hard for over 20 years, Arthur never except when I stirred him up. I took a very little piece, but Arthur *took a whole brick*."

Thomas is noted in all the genealogical compendiums, his career well known, yet almost no one has noted the discrepancies in his vital statistics. Hoyt, Old Families, noted but offered no correction. Hampton rec is clear that he was b Apr 28, 1653. Savage Genealogical Dictionary. gives him m 1663. Original entry of m not found. Hall Gen gives 1675; N E Gen Reg (vol 6, p 250) 1673. The actual date was prior to June 1668. It may be noted that in the list of children of Henry Dow a, there is a gap of nearly ten years. Herein is the error. The date is not wrong by a single figure; it could not be 1643, for instance. Men of his time married mostly when 21 to 24. He was born soon after 1644. The name of his 1st wife is given Wall as frequently as Hall. James Hall of Hampton m 2nd wid Mary Tuck, dau of James Philbrick. His homestead adjoined the Tuck lot to the north and that of Thomas Webster, subsequently sold to Oliver Towle. His farm was west of Robert Page's, north of Taylor's River. He d Oct 3, 1659, leaving 4 dau,—Mary m John Marston, Elizabeth m Thomas Harvey, Hannah m Benjamin Moulton.

Sarah m Thomas Dow. In Exeter Registry of Deeds: Tho Harvey and wife Elizabeth and Sarah Wall, sister of said Elizabeth, convey land in Hampton Aug 20, 1663. Acknowledged by Sarah Wall, now wife of Thomas Dow June 25, 1668. Another: Apr 3, 1669; Tho Harvey & wife Elizabeth, dau of said James Wall, and by Sarah Wall, ye present wife of Tho Dow. Savage's error lies clearly in taking the date of the deed, not its acknowledgment. These acknowledgments were made when Sarah came of age, this was 1668, she having been married just previously.

No doubt, they lived in Ipswich from the first. When she d is uncertain. Ipswich earliest rec are almost *nil*. Early Inhabitants of Ipswich gives Feb 14, 1680. Hoyt, Old Families, Feb 7, 1680-1, and Hoyt is as careful as any one. No authority is quoted. There was only 1 child. Thomas m 2nd in 1684, name of bride being Susannah. This is only known from the mention in his will. Her identity is the subject of many queries for over 30 years in the genealogical periodicals. If the rec is extant, which is more than doubtful, it is too garbled for recognition.

He enlisted, Capt Samuel Appleton, for the Narragansett war; was in camp when it burned, losing his belongings. For this he was indemnified in £2-10-0, paid May 1676, or over a year later. For the attack on the swamp fort he was in the center of the line. He charged with the rest but fell with a bullet through the knee. The fort was carried. He and 20 others were taken by boat to Road Island to recuperate. Thereafter he was always lame but it was not until Apr 1684 that he filed a petition to be excused from drill on this account.

Thomas was impressed with the conviction that land of his choosing was the best form of property for his posterity. For many years he traded actively in Ipswich, often together with Jeremiah ai, a less venturesome speculator, but more often alone. Not only Ipswich town lots, but farms, water front, shares in new tracts, anything promising. A farm in Rowley is notable, for when he sold it he reserved the right to cut firewood for his own and children's lifetime. This incident served to locate his son John, genealogically missing, who availed himself of the privilege in 1729. In 1715 the proprietors of a large tract in Windham Co, Conn, advertised very low prices for bona fide settlers, with long credit. It is probable that Thomas himself visited the place, which became the home of three of his sons.

He d July 12, 1728, will probated 13 days later. It had been made Nov 15, 1720, and provided for wife Susannah, who had d Aug 29, 1724. Most of the property had been distributed as land before he died. The whole property was about £4,000. Sister Mary was to be maintained for life. Dau Hannah was to have the household goods, but she had married and moved away 7 years previously. Legacies of £50 in corn or cattle were made payable 1, 3, 5, and 7 years later to John, Ebenezer,

Thomas, Jeremiah. John received a special legacy of £10 payable in 10 years. Ephraim was executor and residuary legatee.

A crown act resulted unexpectedly to Ephraim's benefit. In 1730 grants of land were made, after many years delay, to veterans of King Philip's War, or their heirs. Five or six such tracts were granted, as more and more claimants were proved. The allotment for Thomas Dow was in what is now Buxton, Me. Ephraim Dow proved his claim and in 1735 the land was in the name of Nathan Simonds. Probably Ephraim sold it without ever seeing it.

Children of Thomas ah:

a Daniel b 1669 to 1671   b John b Apr 24, 1685
x —— stillborn about 1688   c Ebenezer b May 26, 1792
d Thomas b Nov 29, 1694
e Hannah b Oct 3, 1697; int pub June 23, 1721, to Abijah How
f Jeremiah b Dec 12, 1699   g Ephraim b Jan 26, 1701-2
h Benjamin b July 30, 1706; not in father's will

Daniel Dow aha is not found in deeds, hence probably lived with his father; d Ipswich Apr 5, 1725; m (int pub Apr 23, 1715) Exercise Jewett d Dec 18, 1724. No children. His will was made before starting on a trip to Boston. He returned safely, but d unexpectedly 2 months later. It begins: In the name of God amen. The first day of March one thousand seven hundred and twenty five I Daniel Dow of Ipswich in the County of Essex in the Province of Massachusetts Bay in New England cordwainer being in good health of body & of perfect mind and memory thanks be to God for itt being now bound on a voyage to sea and not knowing the place where nor the time I shall be called out of this World do make and ordain this my last Will and Testament. That is to say principally and first of all I give and Recommend my Soul to the hands of God ——. He left £30 each to brothers John, Ebenezer, Thomas and Ephraim; books and spinning wheel to sister Hannah.

John Dow ahb seems to have lived in Newbury, Ipswich and Rowley, as his vital data are generally found in all three. A small law suit over right to cut firewood finds him of Rowley 1727 on a piece of land bought many years before by his father. It is quite certain that his oldest two children were b Rowley. He was of Rowley when he receipted for legacies from father and brother. What was his trade we do not know; his children spent most of their early years with grandfather Dow in Ipswich. He seems to have been a widower for 11 years. His 1st wife Mary d Ipswich Sept 1724. Her identity has not been found. Int pub Ipswich Nov 1725 to Elizabeth Smith. She may be b Apr 3, 1703, dau of Daniel and Elizabeth (Paine); or b Apr 13, 1704, dau of Nathaniel and Elizabeth (Fuller). No marriage of either is found. It is very doubtful whether she m John Dow, at all events there was no issue. He m (Newbury rec) Jan 29, 1735, Elizabeth Moody, both of Rowley. A

son was born, John d 1738; Elizabeth m 2nd Feb 4, 1739-40, Benjamin
Morrill of Andover, Mass, and took her infant son thither.   Children:

a Benjamin b Apr 27, 1712   b Moses b Sept 5, 1714
c Isaac b Mch 13, 1716   d Elizabeth b Mch 11, 1718
e Mary b June 4, 1721; int pub to Sylvanus Lakeman Jr Nov 30, 1745, son of
     Sylvanus and Mary (Lull).   The couple are not found anywhere
f Miriam b Mch 10, 1722-3
g Ebenezer b Newbury Nov 12, 1737 (rec in 3 towns)

FOR nearly twenty years D Webster Dow of Melrose and No Epping followed industriously the search of genealogy. He had married Alice Burleigh Dow of Epping, like himself of an old Epping family, and to determine their relationship was his goal. Almost all old Epping rec were burned many years ago, the exception being the rec of second church. Altho he had access to many family Bibles and traditions, he came soon to a point beyond which he could not get. Mrs Dow's line easily went back to Zebulon Dow, Revolutionary soldier, who m Alice Elsie Burleigh. His own line stopped at Daniel Dow, Revolutionary soldier. There was a vague tradition that Zebulon was son of John. But, what John? There were about five in Epping. Only one is found in any vital rec: Lieut John Dow, gentleman, d Epping 1775, leaving wid Judith. He assumed that Zebulon and Daniel were brothers, altho 18 years apart.

This mystery which defied all Dow searchers was solved in 1917 by a happy discovery of John Mark Moses, a keen student who wished to find a will of Beniah Dow adada. None being found in Exeter, he went to Concord. Incidentally he searched the rooms of the N H Historical Society as never before. Here he found a bound manuscript of the late Gov Samuel Plumer, who at one time considered writing a history of Epping. He got only as far as transcribing the town rec and those of 2 churches. His rec are the very ones which have been lost. He seemingly did not know of rec of the second church. The vital statistics in the ms are from 1678 to 1842. They are imperfect, many seem not to have ever had original entry. They give, however, the data needed to prove the identities sought.

Benjamin Dow ahba. The ms proves that Benjamin was father of Lieut John and Daniel. It also proves identity, as Benjamin and Elizabeth were charter members of church in 1748. Elizabeth is ahbd, then keeping house for her widowered brother. Benjamin settled in Epping not many months before 1748. How or where he spent his married life, what was his trade is not known. His brother Isaac had settled 1742 in Amesbury; his brother Moses and his sister Miriam have never appeared. He had 2 sons and had at least 3 more children by 1755. His 2nd m must have been very close to 1748. She was not an Epping girl and that her name was Sarah is known only from real estate deeds. No trace of 1st wife has ever appeared. The Plumer ms gives his death: 1786 (year blurred, but probably correctly given), ae 65, Benjamin Dow. Also in Plumer ms: 1811, ae 83, widow of the late Benjamin Dow, & noted midwife. Benjamin's 1st born was but 7 years younger than she. Wm G Nichols of Griffin, Ga, inspected every deed in Exeter bearing the name Dow. As Benjamin was a constant land speculator, his career is now easily followed. His first purchase was in 1749; by 1758 he had bought 11 parcels and sold 2. This proves he was comparatively well to do by the time he reached Epping. Two purchases were of expected inheritances, each with a life intervening. His homestead farm finally amounted to 210 acres. In 1758 he sold 2 plots which he had owned for 5 years. He then made a purchase most notable in the history of the Dow family,—from Samuel Gilman Jr a slice of the newly organized town of Gilmanton, N H. Much of this land was inherited by his son Noah and Gilmanton became the home of more Dows than any other town in this country. This deed contains another remarkable circumstance,— witnessed by Benjamin A Dow, otherwise wholly unknown. There is no tenable hypothesis about him. In 1758 Benjamin transferred to his son John a homestead bought 2 years previously from Samuel Gilman Jr. In 1774 he deeded to son Daniel land of equal value, being half of his own 140 acre homestead. The three pieces adjoined and were kept by the sons all their lives. That Benjamin deferred his gift to Daniel indicates that Daniel lived elsewhere until 1774. There were no later real estate transactions. It is improbable that any children were b later than 1755. The list:

a John. Plumer ms gives: John, son of Benjamin, b 1735
b Daniel. Plumer gives: Daniel, son of Benjamin, b 1737. This date agrees with Daniel's enlistment papers
c Noah. Rec of Epping second church seem to have been transcribed, the writer taking liberties in condensation, stating Noah, Rachel, and Josiah were bap prior to Dec 25, 1755. This may or may not mean that they were bap at the same time
d Rachel; maybe b 1752; no other rec
e Josiah, probably bap in infancy
The possibility of sons Nathaniel b 1758 and Benjamin b 1759 is discussed under adaab

John Dow ahbaa, generally called Jr, an older John Dow in town being adaab, was little known until the discovery of the Plumber ms, rec of second church, Exeter deed and his own inventory made reconstruction easy. He d at 40, Nov 1775, having promised a notable career. The Plumber ms says: "John Dow, son of Benjamin, bold, active, enterprising man & very ambitious, Lieutenant of Militia, of good understanding and great decision of character." He had grown enormously stout, could easily button his vest around 4 of his children.

He m at 21, but rec not found. Hist Newfields says Judith Gilman m a Dow of Epping. There is here a little break in the Gilman Gen. Judith was dau of James by a 1st wife. Lyford Gen gives Eliza Lyford, descendant of Francis Lyford and Gov Paul Dudley, m James Gilman. James Gilman in his will bequeathed to Judith Dow all the clothing that was her late mother's (Hannah Leavitt's), all his cattle and sheep not otherwise disposed of. It seems that James Gilman neglected to make a will after his 2nd m. This will was probated July 1779. Elizabeth Gilman at once makes application to the court for relief. This is surely Eliza Lyford. She represents that her late husband James Gilman had left her destitute. The court at once granted her petition and presumably Judith had to relinquish her legacy. Judith was a good woman of business. John Dow d intestate and unexpectedly, still involved in heavy speculations. He owed money and the estate had not enough personal property to pay it off. We note that he owned 16 notes of hand. No value is placed upon them in his inventory. They could not have been worthless, probably they were not collectible at short notice. Judith applied for permission to sell some of the real estate, and while the court had her petition under advisement, she married Timothy Jones, her neighbor, recently a widower, with a dau Eleanor to be added to Judith's large flock.

John Dow was a more daring land speculator than his father. He had doubled the size of his homestead; had backed the founding of new communities upstate. He took an original share in Tamworth, N H, and was one of the largest original proprietors of Sanbornton. Tamworth hung fire for about 20 years. Sanbornton prospered quickly. In 1771 John was one of the three to survey the town, laying off the lots for individual ownership. He bought and sold freely, but there is no indication that he ever intended to leave Epping. Speculation in shares of new towns was about the only form of speculation in those days. Fluctuations were lively, sometimes astonishing.

If old tenor were worth present sterling John Dow would have been a very rich man for his time. His estate was inventoried by Joseph Sias, afterwards Revolutionary captain and father-in-law of Josiah Dow ahbae, and David Folsom:

Homestead farm about 215 acres	£13330
Dwelling house thereon	£1000
Two barns	£800
The sixth part of a saw mill in Epping	£140
35 a of land in Nottingham at a place called Clark's Mill	£350
1-6 part of a saw mill thereon and utensils	£140
96 acres of land in Sanbornton being part of the assigned right of Jonathan Chase	£1800
55 acres of land in Sanbornton being part of lot which David Bean buts	£600
1 right of land in Tamworth, purchased	£50
Total, old tenor	£24244
Lawful money	£1212

(The Author did not make this wrong addition.)

His personal estate:

3 yoke of oxen, 5 cows, 4 2-year olds, 6 yearlings, 1 horse, 10 sheep, 5 swine.

1-2 of a gundelow in partnership with Moses Dalton (a flat-bottomed freight boat, of which Dalton was skipper).

16 notes of hand.

1 Suit Blew cloth. 1 Brown coat. 1 Blew Sattute (surtout). 1 Silver laced Hatt. 2 shirts. 3 Pare Stockins. 1 pare Splatterlashes. 1 Sword and belt. 1 Blew coat and jacket. 1 velvet jacket and plush Briches. 1 bever hat. 3 wiggs. Shoes and boots. Silver shoe buckles. Etc, etc.

As we have said before there were a number of John Dows in Epping. All the bap rec of children specify "of John," mother's name never given. Therefore we cannot be absolutely sure that all the children listed here belong to ahbaa. We are merely reasonably certain:

a   Zebulon; rec not found; enlistment says b 1757
b   James Gilman bap Nov 23, 1761; d young? See below
c   John bap Apr 18, 1762   d   Judith bap Aug 2, 1764
e   Elizabeth bap July 13, 1766   f   Hannah bap July 31, 1768
g   Sarah bap May 13, 1770   h   Benjamin (twin), rec not found
i   James Gilman bap July 19, 1772. It is reasonably certain that Gilman Dow of Walden, Vt, 1805, was he. Cf adaabdd in Book and adaabdd in Supplement.

Zebulon Dow ahbaaa d Epping Dec 20, 1843. A family statement that he was the oldest Revolutionary survivor in N H is nearly correct. He enlisted 1st in Capt Clark's Epping company 1775; a year later under Capt Daniel Gordon, serving over a year; receipted at Saratoga 1777 for a month's pay. After the war he returned to his excellent farm; m Alice Elsie Burleigh of Epping b Apr 10, 1763, d Oct 20, 1842. M rec not found; date probably about 1785. Of children, rec of only 2 are found, rest as given in Zebulon's will, dated May 1, 1819, and never changed for the 24 years following. Quite probable that 1 or more d young:

a   John b Mch 16, 1791   b   Benjamin b 1796 (family rec)
c   Suky, called Suky Dow in will; m (as Susan) long before 1843 Peter Sanborn of Concord, N H; 2 sons
d   Judith; 2nd wife of Joseph H Hilton ahbabi
e   Sally m —— Creighton of Lee

John Dow ahbaaaa of Epping served as Ensign 1812, m Dec 11, 1814, Nancy Plumer, niece of Gov Samuel, b Mch 3, 1795, d Dec 29, 1879. In 1850 his farm assessed $5,500. Children:

a   Samuel Plumer b Oct 9, 1815
b   Elizabeth Plumer b Aug 4, 1819; d Dec 19, 1824
c   Warren Quincy b Oct 5, 1822; d May 1, 1856. Census of 1850 shows him engineer of Portsmouth, alone. Family rec says he left wife and children. Could not be more than 2. Untraced
d   Lorenzo b Gosport Jan 14, d Jan 18, 1826
e   Annie Elizabeth b Oct 2, 1827; living N Y City 1918; m Nov 19, 1851, John Haven Cheever of Boston. Children,—Charles A b 1852, d 1900; Elizabeth S b 1855; John b 1859, d 1913; Gertrude b 1863, d 1908, m John E Cowden; Durant b 1867

Samuel P Dow ahbaaaaa, farmer and lumber merchant of Gosport and Epping, d Epping Dec 9, 1875; candidate 1857 for State senator from Gosport; m Aug 24, 1847, Sarah Josephine Towle b Lee Oct 3, 1827, d Jan 3, 1890, dau of Gardiner and Elizabeth (Fogg). Children, all in Newmarket:

    a Fanny Plumer b Dec 11, 1848; d Aug 12, 1863 (Frances P, State rec)
    b George Quincy b Oct 14, 1850; d Epping Dec 3, 1896; lumber dealer, m Mch
        9, 1883, Lydia D Morse, ae 27, b Bradford, Mass, dau of George F and
        Henrietta P. No children
    c Alice Burleigh b Oct 11, 1852; m Daniel Webster Dow ahbabjia
    d Grace Plumer b Feb 6, 1869; m Harry Hill Young. No children

Benjamin Dow ahbaaab. It is remarkable that the Epping Dow genealogist never mentioned his existence, also remarkable that he, a man of wealth and prominence, executor of his father's will, lifelong resident of Epping, should not be even mentioned in town vital statistics. Census 1850 finds him b 1805 (obvious error); wife Susan b N H 1798; farmer, realty assessed $6,000. Census shows a child:

    a Lavina b 1824; untraced

John Dow ahbaac. We are here apparently hopelessly confused, 3 Johns of about the same age and circumstances in Epping. In 1885 Freeman Augustus Dow, mariner of San Francisco, unm, corresponded at length with Edgar R Dow of Portland. He reported that Miss Laura E Dow of So Lee, N H, was an authority on this family. He stated with utmost positiveness that his ancestor John was brother of Zebulon Dow ahbaaa, and this is strengthened by the circumstances that John named one son Zebulon. He stated, moreover, that John moved to Newmarket, thence to Gilmanton, where he lived, a pensioner, to extreme age; that by a 1st wife he had 3 sons; m 2nd Rebecca Knox, by whom 4 sons, 1 dau.

This may be absolutely correct. The rec shows that John Dow arrived in Gilmanton 1776; that Sept 25, 1776, he was on the roll of Capt John Moody, Col John Badger, with travel allowance 320 miles; afterwards in Col Stickney's reg. Enlisted July 14, 1779 Capt Ezekiel Worthen; disch Jan 9, 1780. The pension list shows that this John was a pensioner in Gilmanton 1850. Gilmanton vital statistics are fragmentary and give no item attachable with plausibility. Census of 1850 gives John Dow, farmer, b N H 1758, wife Rebecca b N H 1784. This must be Rebecca Knox.

John Dow ahbaac was bap 1762; perhaps he was b 1758. If so, all well. There is just this element of doubt. It is just possible that Freeman A Dow, trying to find his own ancestry, groped among the various Johns and jumped at the conclusion of ahbaac. Three sons by John's 1st wife are given. These are unknown. There is at least one more Benjamin in Gilmanton than is accounted for. The son John is lost in the multiplicity of John Dows. The son Gilman is evidence of the Epping connection.

However, the children of John, by the list of Freeman A Dow:

    a John   b Benjamin
    c Gilman; none living 1885; these by 1st wife; b presumably 1782-93

d   Zebulon   e   Freeman, untraced   f   Everett
g   Augustus, living Syracuse, N Y, 1885; untraced
h   Ann, became Mrs Brown of Ward's Corners, Buchanan Co, Iowa
x   John

Zebulon Dow ahbaacd.   D rec of a dau gives him b Epping, d rec of a son gives b Newmarket.   In 1850 census he is of Gilmanton, name immediately following Jonathan Dow adabig.   He apparently lived Gilmanton until 1856, moved to Laconia, d Concord insane asylum Jan 6, 1895; m Jan 7, 1843, Almira Gilford of Gilford d Laconia Dec 18, 1897, ae 77, 5 mos, dau of Jonathan, cabinet maker, and Betsey (Davis).   Children; 4 by census:

a   James M b Gilmanton 1844   b   Charles b 1845; untraced
c   Susan b 1846   d   Woodbury b 1848; untraced
e   Mary E, mill operative, d Laconia Oct 23, 1892, ae 39, 6 mos
f   Elbridge G b Gilmanton Aug 1856
g   Cora F m Mch 25, 1882, T Henry Newell of Laconia

James M Dow ahbaacda (b Meredith by 1st m rec, Laconia by 2nd m), farmer of Laconia, m Feb 23, 1857, Amanda M Davis, ae 23, d Laconia Jan 25, 1879, dau of Nathaniel and Nancy of Gilford (date surely error for 1876-7); m 2nd (her 2nd) Sept 30, 1880, Maria A Fennell, ae 22.   Children:

a   Ida B (to James M and Amanda) b May 3, 1877
b   Frederick J (he and rest to James M and Maria A) b Lowell, Mass, 1881
c   Walter F b 1883   d   Charles M b Ford's Village, Mass, 1886
e   Elmer L b Graniteville, Mass, 1887

Frederick J Dow ahbaacdab, painter of Laconia, d accident Aug 16, 1910; m Mary E Goff b No Andover, 1884, dau of Samuel and Agnes (Lee).   Children:

a   Harold Russell b No Andover Jan 14, 1906
b   Frank W b Aug 27, 1908; presumably d in infancy
c   Irene Goff b May 26, 1910

Walter F Dow ahbaacdac car inspector of Laconia, m May 23, 1910, Mary June Bourge, ae 21, dau of Alfred and Maria L (Millette).   Child:

a   Bernard d Laconia Aug 1, 1913, ae 2 days

Charles M Dow ahbaacdad, electrician of Laconia, m Apr 3, 1907, Lele E Muzzy, ae 28, dau of John and Levda (Estey).

Elmer Dow ahbaacdae, laborer of Laconia, m Ada Weeks b 1882.   Child:

a   James Elmer b Laconia Nov 25, 1909

Elbridge G Dow ahbaacdf, mill operative, d Laconia Nov 10, 1884; m Annie Healey b St Johnsbury, Vt, 1861.   Child:

a   Elbridge b Gilford Aug 22, 1881; untraced

Everett Dow ahbaacf, b Epping 1818, stone cutter of Quincy, Mass, m Wealthy Rich b Strafford, Vt, d Quincy 1855.   He d Quincy May 10,

1866. The 1850 census agrees in respect to children, but gives Everett b Me 1821 and Wealthy b Vt 1821.

Four sons, 2 dau:

a John d in infancy
b John E b 1847, Mass, living 1885 Danvers, Mass; at least 1 son
c Ella I b 1849, m —— White; living 1885 Providence, R I
d **Freeman Augustus** b Quincy May 30, 1851
e Sarah d unm   f Eugene; untraced; not living 1885

John E Dow ahbaacfb has so far been found only in rec of son; m Caroline E Ropes. A son:

a Waldo Hayward b Danvers 1882; m Beverly Aug 21, 1907, Nettie Clark Morgan of Beverly ae 22, dau of William C and Susan A (Clark)

Freeman A Dow ahbaacfd went to sea and lost touch with his family. In 1885 he was mariner of San Francisco; m soon after; d at sea, leaving 2 young children:

a Harold Stanley b San Francisco May 11, 1890; drowned Feb 19, 1914; m Hildur A ——; no children; she m 2nd and has a child
b Myrtle; in 1923 in Los Angeles Co hospital training school

John Dow ahbaacx. Until reading the 1885 letters of Freeman A Dow, the Author identified ahbaac with the John Dow of Epping known as "Little John," to distinguish him from ahbaaaa. Plumer ms gives: Mch 8, 1815, ae 50, 1st wife of John Dow, dau of Thomas Noble of Lee. It is not at all impossible that this is ahbaac, the m to Rebecca Knox occurring 1815-6. Plumer ms gives: John Dow of Epping m May 12, 1823, Ruth James of Northwood. This cannot be the same John. Still another unknown John appears, but without discovered date, for Sally, wife of John Clough of Strafford, signed a receipt for a dower provision to John Dow, executor of John Dow. Evidently some Sally m John Dow who had a son John and before her husband's estate was fully administered had a 2nd m. Until we can disentangle the two Johns, we call (for convenience) John, now either identical or confused with ahbaacx. There follow, however, in Epping rec some children of John, mother not stated. The 1st born sounds identical with the 1st born of Freeman A Dow's account,-all the more so, as there was a dau Laura:

a John. D rec says b 1784; census gives b 1798
b —— dau of John, son of John, d 1810, ae 21
c Samuel B. D rec gives b 1791, son of John
d —— dau of John, son of John, d 1810, ae 20
e —— Miss Dow, dau of John, d 1814, ae 20
f Hannah, dau of John Dow, wife of Samuel Collins, receipted to John Dow Jr, exr; otherwise unknown; rec devious
g George Washington, son of John Dow Jr, grandson of John Dow, d Apr 17, 1826, ae 7 mos

John Dow ahbaacxa, farmer, d Epping 1865, ae 81; m Nottingham Jan 1, 1831, Harriet Plumer d Epping Dec 17, 1871, ae 71. No b rec of children extant, some found from own d rec and 1850 census:

a John B b N H 1836

x   Joseph C P.   Census gives him here, b 1824; unknown
b   Laura Ann d Epping June 20, 1888, ae 66-3-28, unm.   Sounds like the Laura
     E Dow of Freeman Dow's narrative
c   William H, farmer, d Epping Nov 2, 1876, ae 51, unm

Just below the name of John B Dow in the 1850 census occur three names which we cannot place:

Nina Dow b N H 1767 (presumably a wid); Susan Dow b N H 1824; d June 1849; Frank Dow b N H 1849; d Sept 1849

John B Dow ahbaacxaa, carpenter, d Epping Mch 27, 1878; m Epping Jan 16, 1867, Sarah E Sanborn d Epping Dec 19, 1901, dau of Henry Jr and Nancy (Stevens).   One child found:

a   Edith E b Epping June 25, 1877

Samuel B Dow ahbaacxc d Epping Jan 28, 1866, ae 77; m Apr 9, 1822, Polly Peale, both of Epping.   No proof of child, but recurrence of name indicates a son:

a   Samuel Dow Jr m May 3, 1846, Ann Maria Abbott, both of Epping.   Census
     1850 gives Samuel H Dow b N H 1822, farmer, no wife.   This leads us to
     infer that Ann d within 4 years of marriage, leaving no living child

Judith Dow ahbaad m David Jones b Colchester, Conn, Jan 23, 1752, son of Joshua and Elizabeth (Blick).   He d 1838; she d Lowell, Mass, 1840.   They joined a numerous colony of original settlers of Canaan, N H.   Children, perhaps others:

a   John d ae about 20   b   Hannah b Aug 7, 1795
c   Eleanor, her twin   d   Betsey

Hannah Jones ahbaadb m Jasper Jones, kinsman, of Lebanon d 1819-20, leaving 4 children.   She m 2nd Lieut John Gilmore, an Englishman from Canada; d Lowell, Mass Feb 23, 1873.   Children:

a   Sarah Maria b Feb 20, 1812   b   Mary Ann b Sept 15, 1813
c   Judith b 1816   d   Eleanor b Jan 22, 1819   —
e   Hannah (Gilmore) b Aug 25, 1830; d old age Washington, D C
f   Elizabeth b Jan 29, 1832   g   John b July 23, 1833
h   James d young   i   Jane b Feb 15, 1836, living Washington 1921

Elizabeth Gilmore ahbaadbf m Lowell Feb 23, 1873, William H Wight b Mch 14, 1832, d June 27, 1910 (James 7, James 6, Joseph 5, Jonathan 4, Jonathan 3, Henry 2, Thomas 1 of Dedham and Watertown). Elizabeth d Mch 5, 1878.   Children:

a   Charles L, now of Honolulu   b   William H G, now of Lowell
c   Margaret b May 18, 1871

Margaret Wight ahbaadbfc m Lowell Dec 3, 1896, William G Nichols.   They live Griffin, Ga, where he manages a large cotton mill, but have a summer home in Hampton, N H.   Interested in tracing his wife's line, he has aided the Author greatly, making needful excerpts from every deed in Exeter in which the name Dow appears.   These supplied all the local color of the ahbaa line and set many matters right in Plaistow (bcbeb line).   Children,—Elizabeth, Rhoda, Abby, William W, Mary.

Hannah Dow ahbaaf m Deerfield Aug 27, 1785, James Nelson, both of Alinstown.

Elizabeth Dow ahbaae m Gordon Burleigh d Jan 30, 1823; moved to Dorchester. Children:

    a   John b Dorchester Apr 10, 1786; a Boston policeman
    b   Thomas m Elizabeth Doten of Canaan, N H; 2 dau
    c   Benjamin b May 10, 1778; m Mary Norris
    d   Joseph b May 10, 1788; d ae 21   e   Sarah m Wales Dole of Canaan
    f   Elsie m Joseph Howard of Vt   g   Betsey m Nathaniel Wilson of Canaan
    h   Joshua m Mary Holt of Dorchester   i   Caleb, twin, d ae 4
    j   Judith m Daniel Pattee of Canaan bcfiex   k   Gordon m —— Fox of N Y

Benjamin Dow ahbaah went with the Burleighs to Dorchester; became justice of the peace and a man of much local influence; m Mch 4, 1802, Alice Burley (Burleigh), both of Dorchester. She d Dorchester Mch 1, 1826. In 1850 census the only Dow family in town was that of her son John. There was, however, Susan Dow b N H 1775, owning $1,300 realty; presumably a wid from Epping. Benjamin's children from town rec, presumably complete:

    a   Benjamin b July 8, 1803   b   Mary b June 10, 1805
    c   Joseph b May 12, d Aug 16, 1807   d   Joseph P b June 28, 1808
    e   John b June 15, 1810   f   Louisa b May 30, 1812

Benjamin Dow ahbaaha appears only in vital statistics, not found in 1850 census; m Mch 15, 1831, Charlotte Storrs of Lebanon b July 5, 1808. Children:

    a   Constan (sic in rec) b July 22, 1832
    b   Henry P b Oct 1, 1834; d Aug 22, 1839
    c   Charlotte A b Nov 4, 1839; presumably the Charlotte T of Haverhill in 1850
        census

Constant S Dow ahbaahaa appears in 1850 census laborer of Enfield. wife Ellen E b N H 1832. No further rec.

Joseph B Dow ahbaahd (sic in m rec, probably correct, for Burleigh) m (by Benjamin Dow, J P) Nov 30, 1835, Mary A Burley (Barley in rec, surely clerical error) d May 8, 1862, ae 44-3-28, dau of Edward and Mary. They moved to Orford, where he was a merchant; m 2nd Susan K Ford b Canada; apparently moved to Thetford, Vt, after 1866. Children:

    a   Edwin b Orford 1842 (spelled Dowe)
    b   Lucretia H b Feb 14, 1848; d Mch 5, 1865
    c   Charles M b Orford June 29, 1864; untraced
    d   Florence M b Orford; m May 29, 1884, Isaac N Ellsworth of Wentworth; 2nd
        Silas C Chamberlain of Lincoln. Children by 2nd husband,—Ernest, Paul
    e   Harry M b Thetford, Vt, 1868

Edwin B Dowe ahbaahda of Bedford m Lebanon Sept 5, 1863, A M Howard, ae 20, of Great Falls.

Harry M Dow ahbaahde, farmer of Haverhill, m Sept 1, 1893, Lena M Dolloff, ae 14, d Bath Sept 10, 1897, dau of Daniel and Sarah M. Child:

a   Arthur M b Nov 18, 1893

Arthur M Dow ahbaahdea, railroad employe of Haverhill, m Jan 15, 1910, Lillian L Day, ae 22, dau of Joseph R and Carrie (Humphrey). Children:

a   Harry Weston b Sept 26, 1912   b   Bernice Eleanor b Aug 22, 1922

John Dow ahbaahe appears in 1850 census farmer of Dorchester, assessed $2,500; wife Lucy b N H 1807; farmer of Hebron m 2nd June 15, 1858, Mary McClure of Hebron m 2nd July 1, 1873, Jacob D Sanborn. Child, by 1st wife:

a   John K b Dorchester 1845

John K Dow ahbaahea, carpenter of Dorchester, m May 31, 1878, Ella Florence Merrill, ae 20, dau of G W of Rumney.   She d before 1904. Children:

a   Lenora Grace b Rumney Oct 27, 1878
b   Charles K b Dorchester Mch 11, 1880   c   —— dau b July 12, 1883
d   —— son b Apr 5, 1886; perhaps identical with next
e   George Allen b 1889 (by m rec)

Charles K Dow ahbaaheab m Feb 2, 1904, Lydia Ann Abbott, div, ae 24, dau of Fred S and Jennie (Avery) Downing of Rumney.   Children:

a   Edna Grace b Nov 2, 1905   b   Eva May b Apr 6, 1909

George Allen Dow ahbaaheae, shoemaker of Manchester, m Mch 25, 1908, Annie Josephine St Pierre, ae 26, dau of Joseph and Judith (Tetualt).   She d Manchester Jan 12, 1912; m 2nd Feb 6, 1913, Wealthy Emma Chalker b Canada Mch 25, 1864, boarding house keeper, dau of Joel and Maria (King).   She d without children June 23, 1913.   Children:

a   Mabel Katherine b Jan 1, 1909; d Campton July 23, 1913
b   George Walter b Nov 30, 1910

James Gilman Dow ahbaai.   See Supplement sub adaabf, adaabfe, adbaai.   He went to Gilmanton, thence to Walden, Vt.

———

Daniel Dow ahbab.   So far not one of his children's b rec have been found in Epping, altho he lived there all his life except for a *hiatus* of about 12 years.   Apparently, he m away from Epping and returned there just before the war, receiving the 70-acre gift of his father. Gov Plumer in his ms notes: 1780 (year not certain), ae conjectured, the first wife of Daniel Dow.   The ms notes that the original entries are not wholly legible, and it is evident that the ms entry was after the 2nd m.

If she had been an Epping girl, her name might not have been given, but surely her age would not have been conjectured. He did not stay long to cultivate his patrimony, for he appeared in Haverhill, Mass, to enlist Aug 1, 1775, 5th reg, Capt Jeremiah Gilman, Col John Nixon; at Winter Hill Dec 1775; re-enlisted twice; finally disch Nov 30, 1777. Plumer ms notes his death Sept 18, 1816,—Daniel Dow, son of the late Benjamin Dow, Baptist Society, age disagreeing 2 years with enlistment papers, which gave him b 1737. Plumer ms is quite prone to such minor errors.

Soon after his disch Daniel returned to his Epping farm; m 2nd Mary Grant of Exeter, d June 4, 1831. She was considerably younger than Daniel, and it is doubtful whether she had more than one child, altho the Epping bap rec attributes some to her, now known to be born before 1780.

The homestead has never left the family,—it is now the 400-acre nursery farm of D Webster Dow ahbabjib. Daniel was not satisfied with his old house and built a new one. He was his own architect, not even consulting his wife, for the house had not as much as a single window, and wives generally demand plenty of windows as well as closets. The whole family moved in, but, happily for the health of all, it soon got the reputation of being haunted. The former house had been demolished, so a third had to be built in a hurry. After Daniel died his children altered the haunted house, putting in extra windows to make up for lost time. This structure with massive timbers was the homestead until about 1900. when a more modern house was built alongside, the old timbers being used. Daniel had no eye for architectural beauty, only a keen sense of stability.

His will dated Mch 3, 1816, made his son Noah executor, names 9 children, 3 grandchildren. Family tradition, surely correct, says there were 12 children. Bap rec finds 3, rest from family rec or from subsequent rec:

a Lyford bap Sept 4, 1763; d Apr 7, 1841, ae 78, 5 mos
b Betsey (bap Betty May 20, 1764); called in will Betsey Parsons; m —— Parsons and d old age Ripley, Me; had a son Job of Dover
c Benjamin b May 25, 1766 (family Bible)
d Chandler bap July 3, 1768   e   Asa bap Aug 5, 1770
f John; probably b later than here
g Abigail d Feb 11, 1867, ae 92 1-2; m —— Barker, as she is called Abigail Barker in will
h Sally b Apr 12, 1779 (year wrong); m (int pub Feb 7) Dec 9, 1796, Joseph Robinson of Exeter; d Aug 12, 1825; had a son John
i Polly   j   Daniel b May 18, 1778 (family Bible)
k Noah b 1780 (probably earlier)
l Lucretia; not in will; presumably d young

Epping church has a rec not easily explicable: Nov 6, 1773, Daniel Dow, son of Daniel, bap on his own account only. A family tradition says that Noah Dow ahbabk had an illegitimate son, whom he recognized. This is unlikely of Noah (q v), and it is not improbable that Daniel ahbab was the father of this youngster, who d in young manhood.

Lyford Dow ahbaba.   The Lyford family of Epping is connected with Dow almost as frequently as Gilman;   the recurrence of the name here suggests that the first wife of Daniel was a Lyford.   The gap in the narrative of Daniel's life prior to his return to Epping may be filled by guessing that he went to sea for some years, leaving his first wife ashore at Newbury or elsewhere and that his wife d there.   Lyford left Epping early, as did Daniel's other sons, leaving the homestead to be inherited by the tenth child.   Lyford m Nov 11, 1783, Miriam Morrill, both of Epping.   If identification of their oldest son is correct, he probably lived some years in Newburyport.   His next certain mention is in 1798 as surveyor of highways in Sanbornton.   He is not found in the 1790 census, which mentions an Eliphalet Dow 2a, 1b, 2c.   This is probably error for Lyford.   He m about 1791-2 Eunice Parsons of Epping b about 1770-1, d Dover, Me, 1862, and had by her 5 children.   In 1805 they moved to the Piscataquis Valley, Me.   Parsons Gen does not give Eunice nor her brother Job, who m Lyford's sister Betty and was a pioneer of Ripley, Me.   Lyford was the second settler of what is now Dover, Me, where he lived until Apr 7, 1841.   His sons cleared land while he occupied himself with hauling goods for incoming settlers, having good ox teams.

Mrs Reuben B Edgerly of East Dover began over 20 years ago a monograph of his descendants.   Not knowing Lyford's parentage and getting a clue that he came from Epping, she wrote to D Webster Dow. The unanswered letter fell 20 years later into the hands of the present Author and Lyford's ancestry was made clear.   Mrs Edgerly's work is very complete and careful.   Children; 6 b Sanbornton:

a   Daniel   b and c —— two dau, unknown
d   John b Sept 1793   e   Benjamin b Sept 18, 1795
f   Sarah (Sally) b Apr 12, 1797   g   Betsey G b Sept 3, 1800
h   Lyford b Apr 8, 1802   i   Eunice b Nov 7, 1804
j   Job b Jan 3, 1807; 1st white male b in Dover
k   Deborah (unaccountably skipped in family Bible); recalled by two of her
      brothers as a playmate; surely d young
l   Asa Parsons (the father of Eunice was probably John of Epping, who moved
      upstate)
m   Josiah b Feb 23, 1814

Daniel Dow ahbabaa of Newbury is placed here solely because Lyford had an untraced oldest son and the name Lyford recurs.   He m Aug 13, 1810, Johanna Morse Pettingell of Newburyport.   Census 1850 gives him b N H 1785, merchant of Salem, assessed $2,500; wife Joanna b Mass 1795.   Children:

a   Benjamin Pettingell b Dec 10, 1810; int pub Nov 30, 1838, to Margaret A
      Campbell of Newburyport; member of master mariners' association and for
      many years a deep sea captain; d San Francisco Apr 17, 1869. Census
      1850 gives him merchant of Newburyport, assessed $4,000; wife b Mass.
      1813.   No children
b   Daniel Lyford b Dec 14, 1818; d Sept 29, 1822
c   Abby C b Nov 18, 1820; d Jan 16, 1862; m Nov 18, 1846, Robert Morse, ae
      29, accountant of Boston, son of Robert and Mary (Adams). Adams Gen
      mentions no children

John Dow ahbabad, farmer of Foxcroft (all the sons and sons-in-law of ahbaba were farmers), assessed at $500 in 1850, d Foxcroft Feb 7, 1865; m Mary Chandler b Mch 30, 1797, d Oct 17, 1877. All children b Foxcroft:

   a Sarepta b Jan 6, 1825; d Nov 9, 1862, unm   b Erastus b Oct 20, 1827
   c Ann C b May 28, 1830 d Mary E b Apr 26, 1833
   e Angeline b July 13, 1836 f Henrietta b July 19, 1839

Erastus Dow ahbabadb inherited the farm; d Foxcroft Nov 27, 1907; m Aug 10, 1860, Sarah A Towne b Dec 6, 1828, d Sept 5, 1898. Children, all b Foxcroft:

   a Angie E b June 2, 1861; d Mch 10, 1862 b Mary b E Nov 6, 1867

A lad, Guy Hershey, b 1886, was brought up by Erastus Dow, generally known, even in official records, as a Dow, but he was never adopted and in later years not recognized. He m Foxcroft Apr 25, 1911, Stella Arline Wharff, ae 17, dau of Albert J, tinsmith, and Lizzie A (Bennett). Laborer, he d suicide Aug 2, 1919. Five children, one Elsie Ruth b Guilford July 28, 1916.

Mary E Dow ahbabadbb of Foxcroft; m Aug 8, 1886, Oscar O Shorey b Jan 6, 1860. Children:

   a Ralph O b June 6, 1887   b Edwin B b Oct 30, d Nov 24, 1888
   c Alice H b July 15, 1890; m Mch 18, 1914, Sidney Barchard
   d Herbert E b June 22, 1891   e Alton C b Aug 20, 1893
   f Estella J b Jan 3, 1895; d Apr 27, 1901
   g Sarah R b Feb 20, 1896; d Mch 12, 1896
   h Helen E b Aug 28, 1898   i Maurice E b Apr 13, d May 5, 1900
   j Doris I b Nov 22, 1901   k Thelma I b Sept 13, 1903

Ann C Dow ahbabadc d Foxcroft Jan 25, 1895; m Samuel O Wyman b June 1830, d Feb 3, 1853; 2nd Nov 30, 1855, Levi B Dunham b Apr 6, 1828, d Dec 20, 1908. Children:

   a and b —— 2 dau b by 1st husband, both d young
   c Abbie H b Oct 30, 1856; m June 12, 1886, Charles Merrill, dentist of Bangor, b Nov 29, 1859, d Jan 30, 1913. No children
   d Eben J b July 17, 1859; of Sebec, m Apr 29, 1884, Rose Ewer b Oct 13, 1859. No children
   e Angie b Apr 13, 1863; d Foxcroft Apr 16, 1920; m Oct 19, 1887, Henry B Packard, carpenter, b Jan 24, 1863
   f William H, broker of Detroit, Mich, b Mch 4, 1866; m Oct 29, 1896, Laura Bird b Apr 2, 1874
   g Effie J b Aug 10, 1869; of Dover; m June 22, 1910, William T Merrill b Mch 26, 1862. No children

Mary E Dow ahbabadd d Randolph Jan 3, 1902; m Mch 17, 1853, Orison V Rowe, carriage maker and blacksmith, b Mch 14, 1824, d Aug 23, 1895. Children, all b Dover:

   a Flora F b Feb 10, 1854; of Randolph in 1921
   b Elwin M b Oct 13, 1857; d Aug 25, 1913
   c Willie H b Nov 14, 1861; d Mch 20, 1864

Angeline Dow ahbabade d Mch 3, 1858; m Dec 5, 1857, Amasa Gilman b Oct 3, 1833, d Dec 4, 1916. No children.

Henrietta Dow ahbabadf d Apr 25, 1912; m Feb 14, 1859 (his 2nd) Amasa Gilman. Children, b Dover:

a   Martha A b Aug 28, 1861; m Sept 22, 1885, Charles H Chapman b Sept 9,
     1862, d Feb 5, 1916; now of Charlestown
b   Lettie M b June 26, 1872; m Jan 13, 1894, Elmer W Young of Dover b Nov 1,
     1861

Benjamin Dow ahbabae d Dover Mch 6, 1893; m Sybil Towne, first white child b in Dover, b Mch 6, 1803, d Mch 25, 1896, dau of Eli and Persis (Scripture). Benjamin had a fine farm, assessed $3,000 in 1850. Children, all b Dover:

a   Lorenzo G b Aug 15, 1828   b   Lucretia b Jan 31, 1831
c   Benjamin F b Dec 8, 1833   d   Zebulon b Apr 18, 1836
e   Maria b Feb 4, 1839   f   Increase K b Nov 10, 1841
g   Charlotte b July 19, 1846; d Feb 14, 1850
h   Gilman b Sept 9, 1849; d June 13, 1852

Lorenzo G Dow ahbabaea d Dover Jan 5, 1913; m Oct 2, 1855, Maria A Haskell b Jan 4, 1831, d May 23, 1920, dau of Eliphalet and Johanna (True). Children, all b Dover:

a   Frank L b June 17, 1857   b   Nellie A b Aug 22, 1858
c   John P b Apr 27, 1860   d   George B b Nov 10, 1864
e   Lewis H b Sept 4, 1867

Frank L Dow ahbabaeaa, farmer of Sebec, m Nov 3, 1900, Angie Packard, wid, dau of Jacob and Lucinda (Rand) Grant.

While family rec says no children, it may have been made prior to 1914. Following seems to apply: To Frank S Dow b Sangerville, Govt employe of Philadelphia, and Alice B Packard b Sebec, a 1st born:

a   Packard b Sebec July 22, 1914

Nellie A Dow ahbabaeab m Feb 22, 1886, Lewis I Blood b Mch 28, 1859; moved to Avon, Mont. Children, all b Mont:

a   Lizzie M b Feb 11, d Feb 23, 1887
b   Luella C b Aug 12, 1891; d May 24, 1896   c   Ira L b Aug 13, 1893
d   Everett L b (Dover, Me) Aug 31, 1896; d Nov 9, 1899
e   Charles A b Oct 13, 1898
f   Dora I b Mch 5, 1901; d Jan 10, 1908

John P Dow ahbabaeac, farmer and justice of the peace of Atkinson, lives 1921 Dover; m July 12, 1885, Hattie M Hall b Nov 16, 1863, d Atkinson Mch 13, 1902; 2nd May 27, 1907, Nora L Crommett b Aug 27, 1866, dau of John and Mary Ann (Blake). Family rec say 1 child d in infancy. State rec seem garbled, giving 6th child:

a   —— dau d, ae 4 days, May 29, 1911
e   —— dau b and d May 9, 1921; probably same rec garbled

George B Dow ahbabaead, in 1921 farmer of Dover, appears in family rec m Feb 14, 1907, Grace Maud Clarke b Jan 8, 1880, of Vienna, dau of Nathan W and Ellen (Carter). State rec give a George B Dow b

Dover, farmer of Exeter, m Alice M Blackwell b Corinth and to them 9 children.   This seems 1st and 2nd m:

a ——— b June 28, 1892   c George R b Apr 29, 1894
d Roy m (Roy O b Exeter, farmer of Exeter, m rec) Bangor May 5, 1917, Wilda
    Jane Pratt b Atkinson, teacher ae 22, dau of Wallace and Lillian (Doore).
    1st born,—Richard Donald b Exeter May 23, 1918
g Merl Hervey d Exeter May 12, 1900, ae 3 mos, 15 days
h Albert b Exeter Jan 21, 1903   i   Reginald B b Exeter Apr 14, 1905
j (to Grace Clark) Berenice E b Oct 4, 1908
k ——— dau b Dover June 30, 1911   l   Mildred Louise b Dover Mch 1, 1914

George R Dow ahbabaeadc, b Exeter, mechanic of Bangor, m Oct 2, 1917, Deborah J Michaud, ae 20, b Ft Kent, dau of Joseph M and Melvina (St Amans).   Child:

a   Jane Pauline b Bangor June 28, 1920

Lewis H Dow ahbabaeae, farmer of Dover, m Nov 9, 1903, Lillian G Mitchell b Pasadena, Calif, Jan 15, 1887, dau of Charles W and Rachel (Taggart).   Children, all b Dover:

a Elwin L b Apr 4, 1905   b   Ada M b Sept 12, 1906
c Elmer C b June 9, 1908   d   Stanley L b Oct 16, 1909
e Alice N b Jan 4, 1911   f   Helen E b Mch 16, 1914
g Luella C b Sept 6, 1916   h   Ruth b Aug 6, 1918

Lucretia Dow ahbabaeb d June 25, 1898; m Jan 31, 1854, Hartford J Gould b Apr 8, 1823, d Aug 30, 1886.   Children, all b Dover:

a Gilman F b Nov 9, 1855; of Dover; m Susie E Cross
b Emma F b Sept 19, 1856; m Seth Lee
c Estelle m Henry Fitzgerald of Old Town; now of Washington, D C

Benjamin F Dow ahbabaec d Dover Feb 4, 1894; m Nov 18, 1865, Eliza A Cilley b Apr 29, 1840, d East Dover Mch 3, 1916, dau of Isaac and Betsey (Blake).   No children.

Zebulon Dow ahbabaed d Dover May 21, 1915; m June 28, 1860, Sabrah Ginn b Nov 27, 1831, d Dec 9, 1901, dau of Thomas and Betsey (Lewis); 2nd, Feb 2, 1903, Elzada H Downs, wid, b Feb 1841, dau of William and Charlotte A (Hanson) Ball of Sebec.   Children, all b Atkinson:

a Effie F b Apr 11, 1861   b   Thomas b May 15, 1863; d Mch 15, 1866
c William b Mch 1, 1866; d May 1, 1878

Effie F Dow ahbabaeda m June 27, 1887, Lewis J Drinkwater of Sebec b July 22, 1857.   Children, all b Sebec:

a Etta S b Dec 15, 1889; m Apr 27, 1917, Elmer O Hill b Feb 14, 1890; of Fox-
    croft
b Katie L b Jan 27, 1890; m Dec 31, 1914, Ray P Berce b Feb 11, 1890; of
    Sebec
c Zebulon Dow b Apr 20, 1892; m June 19, 1920, Stella Smith b Oct 19, 1888;
    of Sebec
d Walter b Feb 14, 1894; m Oct 18, 1917, Nellie R Eddy b Aug 17, 1897; of Dover
e Ralph L b Oct 3, 1896; m July 7, 1921, Zola E Sands b Apr 21, 1902; of Dover
f Helen M b May 4, 1898   g ——— dau b 1900; d in infancy

Maria Dow ahbabaee, of Dover in 1921; m July 17, 1864, Hosea B Mayhew b Oct 28, 1836, d Apr 11, 1903. Children, all b Dover:

a Fred A b Oct 30, 1872; of Dover
b Annie C b Apr 6, 1879; m Oct 11, 1916, Albert A McClure b Nov 21, 1858

Increase K Dow ahbabaef d Sebec June 27, 1917; m May 21, 1865, Angelia W Blake b June 13, 1844. Children, all b Atkinson:

a Cora E b Jan 11, 1866   b Wallace b Oct 18, 1867
c Sybil b Mch 29, 1869   d Louise W b Jan 1, 1871
e Benjamin G b July 4, 1873

Cora E Dow ahbabaefa, of Foxcroft in 1921; m June 24, 1890, Clarence E Green b Aug 31, 1863, d Dover Nov 2, 1910; 2nd Nov 10, 1917, Linwood Harmon b Feb 2, 1862. Child:

a Angelia E b Aug 28, 1895; d Feb 1, 9104

Wallace Dow ahbabaefb, 1st selectman of Dover, m Dec 6, 1893, Mabel L Titcomb b Feb 13, 1874. Children, all b Dover:

a Marian T b Feb 21, 1896   b Barbara A b Mch 14, 1898
c Geraldine S b May 12, 1907

Sybil Dow ahbabaefc m Boston, Mass, Nov 5, 1901, Henry Augustus Dunham b Aug 7, 1864, son of Orin C and Charity (Glidden); now living on their walnut ranch, Whittier, Calif. Only child:

a Elizabeth Anna b Nov 16, 1906

Louise W Dow ahbabaefd of Dover m Nov 11, 1891, Herbert D Rowell b Apr 8, 1870. Children:

a Sybil H b Augusta Oct 2, 1893; d Dover June 11, 1902
b Madeline B b Dover July 2, 1899; m Aug 26, 1919, Fred A Packard, step son of ahbabaeaa, b Nov 21, 1890, electrician in navy during the war

Benjamin G Dow ahbabaefe, merchant, for several years postmaster, of East Dover, d Dover Jan 23, 1918; m June 19, 1907, Lena E Morrill b Jan 8, 1882. Child:

a Eleanor G b Dover Apr 10, 1910

Sarah Dow ahbabaf d Dover Jan 11, 1887; m Asa Sturtevant b Feb 28, 1800, d Oct 12, 1853. Children, b Dover:

a William L b Dec 5, 1827; d Dec 8, 1909; architect and builder, m Margaret Carleton b May 5, 1836
b Sarah b July 7, 1830; d Dover Oct 14, 1899; m George Washburn b July 14, 1823, d Mch 15, 1909
c Savilla b Oct 12, 1832; d Foxcroft Mch 24, 1912; m George R Hoxie b Dec 1, 1829, d Apr 3, 1905
d Lewis L b Dec 19, 1835; d Jan 9, 1910; m July 13, 1861, Hannah M Hoyt b Nov 17, 1836, d Boulder, Colo, July 25, 1919
e Ellura b June 6, 1837; d Dover Apr 6, 1917; m Walter Bray b about 1834, d Mch 14, 1877

Betsey Dow ahbabag d Dover Nov 28, 1838; m June 14, 1823, Asher Spaulding b Aug 23, 1800, d Waukon, Iowa. Children, b Dover:

a Gilman b Sept 22, 1824; d Gothenburg, Neb, Dec 8, 1892; m Celia J Waterman of Poland, Me, d Waukon Feb 25, 1912

<blockquote>
b Randall H b Jan 16, 1826; d Jan 18, 1898; m Nov 16, 1851, Calista R Bearce
    b Dec 17, 1833, d Sept 18, 1897; veteran of 20th Me
c Cynthia b Aug 12, 1827; d July 1851
d Deborah Dow b May 15, 1829; d Sibley, Iowa, Dec 10, 1902; m Sept 12, 1869,
    Charles Barnard of Waukon b 1817, d June 23, 1898
e Josiah Dow b May 8, 1831; d Dec 27, 1872; 3 years in 12th Iowa
f Albina b May 8, 1834; d McGregor, Iowa, Dec 20, 1911; m Nov 1856 Leander
    O Hatch of Waukon b Apr 13, 1826, d July 20, 1894
g Martha Ann b Apr 18, 1836; d Makee, Iowa, Dec 9, 1860
h Adna Parsons b May 7, 1838; d Reed City, Mich; m Sarah Phillips
</blockquote>

Lyford Dow ahbabah, farmer of Dover, d May 29, 1871; realty assessed 1850 at $2,000; later salesman; m Mary Sutherland of Miramichi, N B, b Apr 16, 1810, d Dover Sept 20, 1877. Children, oldest two b Miramichi, rest Dover:

<blockquote>
a Charlotte b Apr 11, 1829; d Nov 17, 1846
b Deborah Jane b Mch 23, 1831; d Dec 10, 1857
c Cornelius b Dec 10, 1832
d Jerusha M (Hulda J, census) b July 15, 1834
e James De Wolf b Apr 30, 1836   f Josiah B b May 29, 1838
g Pembroke Sutherland b June 2, 1840
h Charles E b May 12, 1842; d Jan 3, 1845
i Mary O b July 4, 1844   j Hannah b Nov 24, 1848
k Josephine Olivia b Mch 14, 1851
l Calista M b May 9, 1853   m Henrietta P b Oct 3, 1855
</blockquote>

Cornelius Dow ahbabahc, farmer, m Anna S Chase b Sebec; both d before 1905. Of considerable family, 4 found:

<blockquote>
a Lyford P   b Wilson   c Willard H
d Adelbert C b Sept 5, 1865; farmer of Sangerville, d Atkinson Aug 28, 1917;
    m Sept 12, 1906, Edna Maud Pratt, ae 21, b Atkinson, dau of W W and
    Lillian A (Doore)
</blockquote>

Lyford P Dow ahbabahca, farmer of Atkinson, m Jennie S Doore. At least 2 children:

<blockquote>
a Ernest Lyford b 1884   b Doris Belle b Dec 24, 1902
</blockquote>

Ernest L Dow ahbabahcaa, clerk of Foxcroft, m Nov 21, 1908, Ethel Christina Hurd, ae 19, dau of Albert S and Fannie (Clarke). He d merchant Nov 12, 1914. Child:

<blockquote>
a Elnore H b Jan 8, d Feb 5, 1911
</blockquote>

Wilson Dow ahbabahcb, laborer of Dover, m —— b Pa. 1st born:

<blockquote>
a Clara M b Feb 23, 1892
</blockquote>

Willard H Dow ahbabahcc, insurance agent of Dover, m Mannie Trefethan b Exeter. 1st born:

<blockquote>
a Annie M b Dover Dec 9, 1892
</blockquote>

Josiah B Dow ahbabahf, farmer of St Albans, m Maria E Waldron. Directory 1892 gives 3 children, grown and gone:

<blockquote>
a Nina   b Cornelia M   c Victor W
</blockquote>

Victor W Dow ahbabahfc, highway surveyor of St Albans, m B Susan Dow (sic in rec, but). 1st born:

<blockquote>
a —— son b Sept 26, 1907
</blockquote>

Pembroke S Dow ahbabahg, farmer of Dover, appears in 1904 and 1915 directories; m Lizzie Rogers. Children, 1904 directory:

  a Isabelle   b Orman P

Orman P Dow ahbabahgb, farmer of Sangerville, m Oct 22, 1903, Blanche Amazine b Sangerville, ae 20, dau of John and Helen M (Marsh). Child:

  a ——— son b Dexter Nov 5, 1906

Josephine O Dow ahbabahk m Feb 25, 1875, Frank W Judkins, son of Rufus Norris and Sarah (Poor).

Eunice Dow ahbabai d Chilton, Wis, Mch 25, 1883; m Ensign Eldridge b Aug 18, 1800, d May 24, 1858; moved to Wis about 1851. Children, all b Dover:

  a Luther E b Apr 22, 1827
  b Betsey D b July 24, 1828; d Chilton Nov 1893
  c Wilson E b July 12, 1830; d Foxcroft May 10, 1909; m Nov 4, 1856, Sarah A
      Houston b Mch 31, 1833, d May 17, 1873; 2nd Mch 22, 1875, Mrs Angie C
      Brockway b Aug 30, 1838, d May 6, 1920
  d Henry S b Mch 26, 1835; m Dec 31, 1858, Mary Snyder
  e Lucinda b Nov 28, 1840; d Oct 28, 1849
  f Job Dow b June 2, 1847; m Apr 24, 1884, May Babcock

Job Dow ahbabaj, farmer of Dover, assessed $2,000 in 1850, d Dover Oct 19, 1899; m June 23, 1831, Elvira Wyman b Canaan Oct 2, 1912, d Dover Dec 28, 1855; 2nd Dec 27, 1863, Lydia E Lyford b Sebec, Mch 26, 1842, living Dover 1921.   Children, all b Dover:

  a Almon b July 23, 1832
  b Van Ransellear b Aug 31, 1834; d Feb 24, 1863
  c Hellen Maria b May 11, 1837   d Rozilla b May 31, 1839
  e Victoria Jane b Sept 7, 1840; d Feb 26, 1865
  f Llewellyn b June 1, 1843; d July 23, 1844
  g Oscar R b Sept 14, 1845
  h Edgar b Mch 14, 1848; d Apr 20, 1850
  i Edson W b June 10, 1850   j Gilman b Aug 16, 1854; d Apr 9, 1855
  k Ralph b Sept 18, 1864; d Apr 29, 1865
  l Wilson J b Aug 27, 1868   m Helen May b Sept 23, 1874
His wid mother Eunice living with him 1850

Almon Dow ahbabaja, farmer, d Bowerbank Aug 16, 1900; m 1859 Emeline L Patterson b Sebec Dec 10, 1838, d Foxcroft Dec 21, 1920, dau of Lewis and Harriet (Lyford). Children, all b Dover:

  a Katie H b Feb 3, 1861   b Van Rennsalaer b Dec 25, 1862
  c Lewis H b June 20, 1865; d Sept 20, 1866
  d Alfred P b May 22, 1868   e Elvira J b Mch 6, 1872
  f Mabel D b Bowerbank Aug 27, 1879
  g Herbert Ancel b June 26, 1883

Katie H Dow ahbabajaa of Auburn m 1881 William Henderson, carpenter. Children:

  a Hattie Lula b Apr 9, 1882   b Harry C b Oct 10, 1885, Dover

Van R Dow ahbabajab, railroad employe and wool spinner, m Mch 31, 1889, Bessie Douglass b July 4, 1867. Only child:

a Aubrey Douglass b Portland Dec 15, 1895

Alfred P Dow ahbabajad, farmer of Dover, later of Foxcroft, m 1892 Leta M Parsons of Dover b July 20, 1876, granddau of ahbabb. Children, b Bowerbank:

a Leroy P b Sept 24, 1893   b Helen b Jan 22, 1895
c Maurice b June 1, 1896   d Gladys E b Nov 18, 1898
e Theresa M b June 17, 1900   f Elvie A b Feb 10, 1903

Leroy P Dow ahbabajada, chauffeur of Dover, later of Foxcroft, m 1915 Margaret Stoddard b Guilford Nov 23, 1895, teacher, dau of Eugene O and Estelle S (Bursley). Children, b Foxcroft:

a Malcolm Stoddard b Feb 10, 1916   b Alfred E b Feb 25, 1917
c Dorothy M b Sept 24, 1918

Helen Dow ahbabajadb m Sept 1, 1920, Charles W Eldridge b Nov 1892 ahbabaicx; lives Dover. Child:

a Warren

Maurice Dow ahbabajadc, farmer of Bowerbank and Brownsville, has moved to Florida; m Apr 5, 1917, Edna C Thomas b Foxcroft, ae 21, dau of Herbert H and Minnie W (Neal) Chandler. Child:

a L Thomas b Brownsville Jan 12, 1918

Elvira J Dow ahbabajae m Aug 27, 1892, Russell J Emery, hardware dealer of Madison, b Sept 26, 1870, killed deer—hunting 1920. Child:

a Florence L b June 7, 1894

Mabel D Dow ahbabajaf m Edwin S Newell b Apr 15, 1873, d Madison Mch 23, 1906; 2nd Manley Davis; moved to Mellowdale, Alberta. Children, b Madison:

a Ralph T b Feb 2, 1900   b Albert M b Oct 3, 1909
c Evelyn M b May 31, 1911

Herbert A Dow ahbabajag, weaver of Dover, later of Exeter, m Mch 28, 1908, Marion Nellie Thomas, ae 20, dau of Hugh and Annie (Hughes). Children, b Dover:

a Virgil b Sept 10, 1908   b Clifton b Foxcroft Sept 18, 1911
c Frances

Helen M Dow ahbabajc d Mch 11, 1868; m William Houston b Aug 3, 1827, d Oct 21, 1883. Children, b Dover:

a Dell b 1859; d June 15, 1879   b Cora M b 1861; d Mch 11, 1884
c Harry b June 1864; d Portland; m Glencora Lambert

Rozilla Dow ahbabajd d Sebec Sept 7, 1912; m Nov 27, 1858,

THE BOOK OF DOW

Edward J Donald b July 28, 1833, d May 31, 1899; in 1st Me heavy artillery, wounded 1864, disch Mch 20, 1865.   Children:

a   Edgar A b Mch 29, 1860; of Dover; m Mch 31, 1886, Mabel A Henfield; 2nd Sept 27, 1915, Mrs Mary A Dexter
b   Wallace b Sept 27, 1865; d Foxcroft; m May 25, 1888, Carrie Dean b Oct 17, 1866

Oscar R Dow ahbabajg moved to Mich before 1871; living 1918 Sage, Gladwin Co. Sons but not himself appear in recent directory; m May 6, 1865, Helen A Dolloff b Nov 27, 1848.   Children:

a   Herbert L b Dover June 28, 1866   b   Frank b Gladwin Co 1871
c   Fred F b Oct 7, 1874   d   Leila b Mch 13, 1876

Herbert L Dow ahbabajga, garage owner of Gladwin, m July 2, 1890, Effie G Wood b Jan 6, 1867.   Children:

a   Edson W b Saginaw Apr 5, 1891   b   Ethel J b Gladwin Dec 24, 1892
c   Viva L b Aug 1, 1896   d   Irma E b Aug 12, 1909

Edson W Dow ahbabajgaa, machinist of Gladwin, m Beaverton Aug 28, 1915, Hazel Wiley b Sept 13, 1897.   Child:

a   Gerald b Aug 7, 1916

Frank Dow ahbabajgb m Gladwin Feb 18, 1903, Daisy Hutchinson b 1885.   Child:

a   Helen M b Mch 1906

Fred F Dow ahbabajgc m Schoolcraft Aug 27, 1896, Mae Carney b Mch 17, 1874, d Cleveland Apr 17, 1917.   Child:

a   Arlene b Nov 14, 1897; m Cleveland July 9, 1917, William F Lehecka

Leila Dow ahbabajgd of Jackson, Mich, m Thad Haynes, killed on railroad 1912.

Edson W Dow ahbabaji m Sugar Valley, Pa, Sybilla Wirth b Loganton Feb 25, 1850; moved after 1886 to Washington State. In 1928 an active, busy man.   Children, b Loganton, Pa:

a   Jennie Estella b Aug 3, 1875; d Oct 14, 1890
b   Mary Elvira b Jan 3, 1877; d Nov 23, 1904; m Joe Emerick; no children
c   Sarah Delvia b Aug 27, 1879; m James Zerbe; only child,—Floyd
d   Warren Osborn b Nov 16, 1883   e   Robert Wirth b Apr 17, 1886

Warren O Dow ahbabajid is now president of the corporation shipping his own apples,—the Wenatchee brand. He m Ada, Ohio, Oct 31, 1907, Nellie Huston.   Children:

a   Edson b Ada Mch 4, 1910   b   Huston b Wenatchee June 27, 1911
c   Wellington b June 27, 1911   d   Marion William b Nov 14, 1912

Robert W Dow ahbabajie, secy with his brother in the apple business; m Ethel Ferrel of Chicago.   Children b Twisp, Wash:

a   Leonard b July 12, 1914   b   Arden b Aug 25, 1917

Wilson J Dow ahbabajl, architect and builder of Pittsburgh, Pa, m 1891 Mildred C Harmon b Aug 20, 1869. Children:

a   Elsie M b Dover Feb 23, 1892; d Pittsburgh May 28, 1903
b   Helen Ruth b Sugar Valley Feb 9, 1894

Helen M Dow ahbabajm of East Dover m Aug 12, 1896, Reuben B Edgerly b Oct 10, 1872. Her letter of inquiry relative to the identity of ahbaba to D Webster Dow of Epping, written 1892, reaching the Author 1919, resulted in the completeness of the entire line. Children:

a   Carroll D b Nov 4, 1906   b   Kathryn E b Jan 11, 1911

Asa P Dow ahbabal, farmer of Dover, assessed 1850 at $1,200, m Nov 2, 1843, Edna A Clark b Atkinson Nov 28, 1821, d Jan 23, 1908. Asa d Seymour, Wis, Aug 19, 1897.   Children, except youngest, b Dover:

a   Benjamin F b Jan 13, 1845   b   Aurora A b May 27, 1847
c   Florence M b Dec 12, 1848   d   Adelard L b Mch 19, 1851
e   Julia P b Sept 28, 1854
f   Charles K b Chilton, Wis, Mch 13, 1855; d Oct 5, 1857

Benjamin F Dow ahbabala fought through the war in 4th Wis cav; m June 7, 1869, Euphrasia Godding. Not found in recent directory.

Aurora A Dow ahbabalb of Seymour, Wis, m Mch 2, 1866, William H Mangan, who fought through the war in 14th Wis vol inf.

Florence M Dow ahbabalc m Jan 9, 1871, John Downey b May 9, 1840; moved 1913 to Spokane, Wash.   Children, b Center, Wis:

a   Stella A b Nov 12, 1872; m Sept 18, 1900, William J Moser, builder and con-
      tractor of Spokane
b   William B b Apr 22, 1874; farmer of Center, m Apr 9, 1913, Mary E Schwartz
c   Herbert A b Jan 5, 1876; bridge carpenter of Spokane
d   Aurora E b Oct 9, 1877; d Jan 7, 1883
e   Henry E b Nov 20, 1881; traveling salesman of Eau Clair, Wis; m Dec 26,
      1914, Dagny I Jorsted
f   John A b Apr 13, 1884; bookkeeper, stenographer of Spokane
g   Archibald W b Mch 26, 1886; dentist of Spokane, m July 2, 1912, Martha M
      Hickel
h   Florence E b Mch 2, 1890; m Oct 24, 1916, Charles S Zeinaantz, rancher of
      Monrovi, Wash

Adelard L Dow ahbabald is supposed to have gone to Kan; untraced.

Julia P Dow ahbabale d Aug 16, 1890; m Aug 4, 1878, Adelbert J Godding of Mersa, Colo. Children:

a   Walter b Sept 1879; d in infancy
b   Clara E b Oct 7, 1881; m Sept 27, 1911, Rufus Mullet of Englewood, Colo

Josiah Dow ahbabam, farmer of Dover, assessed 1850 at $1,000; m Jan 1, 1842, Emily Augusta Currier b Vienna Oct 21, 1819, d Dover Jan 30, 1908, dau of Edmund and Katherine (Dow) ahbabcb. Josiah d Feb 2, 1898; wid lived with her son Lincoln H.   Children, all b Dover:

a   Edmond b Sept 26, 1843; d Mch 19, 1850
b   Lyford b Feb 23, 1845; d Oct 5, 1849

   c Eunice b Nov 13, 1847; d Oct 9, 1849
   d Catherine b July 20, 1849; d Oct 11, 1849
   e Sarah B b July 19, 1850   f Lucella E b Aug 20, 1852
   g Josiah b Aug 1, 1854   h Savilla A b Oct 11, 1856
   i Lincoln H b Jan 9, 1860

Sarah B Dow ahbabame m Sept 30, 1882, J Harvey Greeley of Sebec b Apr 28, 1824, d Oct 5, 1904.

Lucella E Dow ahbabamf m July 20, 1884, Ormandel M Bither of Charleston b Jan 27, 1847.

Josiah Dow ahbabamg of Charleston m Sept 27, 1876, Carrie M Higgins b Oct 5, 18—. Children:

   a Lillian R b Dover July 2, 1877; m Feb 11, 1909, Elias M Philbrick of Easton
   b Theodore Burt b May 1, 1880   c Guy A b Nov 19, 1884
   d Clarence Leroy b Charleston Sept 17, 1887

Theo Burt Dow ahbabamgb d (T Herbert) Jan 28, 1915, farmer of Dover; m Aug 26, 1903, H Edna Stewart, ae 18, of Dover, dau of Charles E and Irene (Davis). Child:

   a Lloyd L b Dec 18, 1904; d Dec 6, 1909

Guy A Dow ahbabamgc, carpenter of Charleston, later of Augusta, m Oct 15, 1908, Florence E Plumer b July 30, 1887, of Benton, dau of Albert and Emma (Crosby). Child:

   a Margaret Emma b Augusta Mch 19, 1911

C Leroy Dow ahbabamgd, farmer of Charleston. m Sept 28, 1912, Cora Ethel Pearl, teacher, ae 30, b Bangor, dau of David and Ellen P (Hibbard). Child:

   a Clarence P b Dec 4, 1918

Savilla A Dow ahbabamh m July 28, 1897, Zophar Bither of Charleston b Dec 29, 1856.

Lincoln H Dow ahbabami, farmer of Dover, selectman; m Feb 20, 1895, Lizzie E Hall b Sept 13, 1865. No children.

            —————

Benjamin Dow ahbabc d Sebec 1835; m Apr 1, 1787, Catherine Robinson of Exeter d ae 66; moved to Cornville, Me. Of 8 children, 3 d young; one dau became Mrs Smart:

   a Betsey b July 2 1788
   b Katherine b Apr 30 1790; m Edmund Currier; her dau m Josiah Dow ahbabam
   c Joseph Robinson b Jan 14, 1793   ·   d Daniel Lyford b July 6, 1794
   e Polly b Dec 6, 1796   f John Ware b Aug 25, 1799
   g Sally b May 17, 1803; m ——Currier
   h Rice Swan b Aug 9, 1806; said to have posterity

Joseph R Dow ahbabcc appears in 1850 census farmer of Vienna, assessed $2,500; wife Ruth b Me 1796. Children, by census, possibly an oldest gone away:

   a Nathaniel b 1829; untraced   b Adeline b 1830
   c Martha b 1833   d Joseph b 1834. Possibly whole family moved away

Daniel L Dow ahbabcd, lifelong farmer of Vienna, assessed 1850 at $1,500; m Sophronia Eaton b 1800. A Dow family of bcbhd line also lived in Vienna. Children:

- a Langdon H d Concord, N H, after 1850, cabinet maker, unm
- b Joseph B b Apr 18, 1823
- c Blake T d Benton Apr 18, 1898, ae 69; merchant of Clinton. He m a granddau of ahbabf. No children
- d Daniel Eaton b 1831   e Martha J b 1834
- f Adrith b 1836; probably counted twice in 1850 census, for Gardiner gives an Adrith Dow b Me 1836, in family of Josiah T Smart, joiner. Mrs Smart is probably Adrith's aunt. Untraced
- g Rice b 1838; d by 1850
- h Mary b 1840; family rec does not give her; gives youngest child Catherine

Joseph B Dow ahbabcdb d Farmington, widower, retired; m May 18, 1850, Mary Belcher Craig b July 31, 1822, d Mch 21, 1882, dau of Moses and Lois Nelson (Thomas). Cabinet maker of Lowell and Lawrence, enlisted from Farmington in 10th Me inf; promoted to 3rd Lieut; served 2 years, 2 mos. At end of war he became a sugar planter of Louisiana, then in business St Paul and Kansas City; retiring finally to Farmington, he ended his days, an influential, highly respected citizen. Children:

- a Mary L
- b Lizzie D b May 20, 1857; m Capt E H Maverick; children,—Edward E, Lillian M, Dwight D
- c Melvin d ae 3   d Charles d ae 5

Mary L Dow ahbabcdba m Nelson Gould of Farmington, son of David and Hannah (French). Child:

- a Wallace J b Oct 18, 1884

John Ware Dow ahbabcf, farmer and minister, appears in census as John b 1804; m Hannah Fogg b Me or Raymond, N H, 1800, realty assessment $1,200. Children:

- a Sylvester N b 1830   b Charles b 1835; untraced

Sylvester N Dow ahbabcfa b Cornville, farmer, d Skowhegan Sept 21, 1910, ae 80-10-19; m Lizzie H Hawes b Norridgewalk, d Skowhegan Sept 22, 1914, ae 85-0-7, dau of —— and Elizabeth (Vickery). One child found:

- a Frank d Cornville Feb 25, 1898, ae 25-11-15

Chandler Dow ahbabd from Epping family rec d Aug 8, 1851, ae 63, no place or other data given. He m (int Mch 6) June 3, 1790, Abigail Robinson of Exeter. Census taken a few days before the wedding shows him alone in Sanbornton. Census of 1850 shows both in Cornville, Me, he 82, she 80, farmers but without land. Probably they went to Cornville as pioneers as the children were b Me. Presumably considerable family, all grown and gone by 1850, census showing none. Two here are not absolutely proven:

- a Joseph b Me 1798 (from 1850 census)
- b John b Cornville 1804; farmer, widower, d Cornville Aug 20, 1893; untraced

Joseph Dow ahbabda appears in census farmer of Athens, realty assessed $1,000; m Margaret Weston b Skowhegan 1800. Children, from census:

a Catherine E   b Emily b 1829   c Mary b 1831
d Chandler J b Athens 1835   e Ruel b 1838; untraced

Catherine E Dow ahbabdaa, b Athens Oct 6, 1824; m Aug 3, 1855, Joseph Charles Thiot Kinsman, at one time brig gen of Me militia. Children:

a Joseph Charles b May 8, 1856; d Sept 21, 1867
b Margaret Eliza b Oct 22, 1857   c Cassius C b June 5, 1860
d Francis Burnham b Dec 4, 1861; d Sept 6, 1867
e Mary Elizabeth b Dec 29, 1863; d Oct 16, 1864
f Edmund Everett b Aug 23, 1865; d Sept 8, 1867

Chandler J Dow ahbabdad, tailor of Skowhegan, d widower Skowhegan Nov 18, 1916, ae 82-9-6; m May 6, 1868, Ellen S Folsom b Dec 9, 1838, d Mch 9, 1911, dau of Rufus and Mary (Currier) of Cornville. Children, by a local hist:

a Fred C b Mch 9, 1871; m Charlotte L Hammond. Some Fred C Dow, called
     single in d rec; div?; motorcycle agent, d Waterville May 2, 1915, of acute
     alcoholism
b Frank P b Dec 19, 1874; d Nov 1879

Asa Dow ahbabe of Epping m Nov 30, 1793, Molly Noble of Lee. No further rec provable; not found 1850 census. Ages do not fit well with a considerable disconnected Dow family of Lee. One dau quite possible:

a Charlotte b Lee 1797, grew up and m. A Boston Transcript query for her in
     1897 has never been answered

John Dow ahbabf. The Epping family rec of all sons of ahbab, except one, are very meager and so often unreliable as to cause much trouble. He lived N H, coming to Milo, Me after 1807. Census 1850 gives two names almost surely his sons. A granddau m Blake T Dow ahbabcdc, name not found:

a Elijah W b N H 1805   b Noah b N H about 1807

Elijah W Dow ahbabfa appears in Milo 1850 census, assessed $150; wife Hannah b N H 1805. Census gives 1 child:

a Rice S b 1828; untraced. This name, occurring 3 times in ahbab is good proof
     of identity
     Next name in census is Eliza Dow b Me 1818, assessment $1,500. Age forbids
     that she was wid of a son of Elijah W. Two names next following must be
     akin:
b Caroline b 1831   c Emma J b 1845

Noah Dow ahbabfb is found only in d rec of dau; wife Sally Dow (maiden name??) b Sebec. The dau:

a Caroline d Benton Apr 13, 1898, ae 65, unm. Is she the Caroline above?

Polly Dow ahbabi of Epping m Nov 13, 1797, Joseph Hilton b Deerfield Nov 27, 1775, d Feb 6, 1813, son of Col Joseph and Sarah (Thurston), brother of Sally m Daniel Dow ahbabj. Polly d and Joseph m 2nd Judith Dow ahbaaad, by whom 1 child. An excellent Hilton Gen, a life work, was prepared by the late Charles H Hilton of East Andover, N H. His wid Marcia continued it as best she could and took a deep pleasure in giving information as widely as possible to all who sought it. The ms is now in the possession of the N H Historical Society. Children of Polly and Judith, all b Deerfield:

a Polly b Sept 13, 1798   b Joseph b Apr 11, 1800
c Theodore b Mch 10, 1802   d Daniel Dow b Oct 7, 1804; d 1806
e Lucretia D b July 15, 1909

Polly Hilton ahbabia (probably bap Mary Dow Hilton) m Richard Bartlett Jr of Newmarket; had Caroline m Levi Towle of Epping, perhaps others.

Joseph Hilton (Capt) ahbabib d 1890; m Feb 1, 1824, Comfort Dearborn of Deerfield b Sept 10, 1800, d Feb 1881-2, dau of Nathaniel and Susan; settled in Cornville, Me; 11 children.

Theodore Hilton ahbabic m Nov 19, 1823, Polly True Butler b Nottingham June 1804, d Oct 28, 1858, dau of Capt John and Sally (Batchelder); 2nd Nov 14, 1859, Mrs Roxana Young of Hampden, Me, d Feb 21, 1884. He d Sept 22, 1887; settled about 1825 in Cornville; 5 children by 1st wife.

Lucretia D Hilton ahbabie m Jan 12, 1826, G Harvey Marston b Nov 14, 1804, d Mch 17, 1882, son of Gen Samuel and Sally (Robinson); moved 1843 to Racine, Wis; 1858 to Appleton, Wis; 9 children, including 3 Civil War veterans.

Daniel Dow ahbabj lived on the Epping homestead, assessed 1850 at $7,000; m Sept 30, 1797, Sarah Hilton b Sept 30, 1777, d Epping Aug 18, 1812; 2nd June 18, 1813, Mary Haley b Feb 16, 1785, d Dec 5, 1854. Children:

a Mary (Mary Grant?) b Oct 25, 1798   b Stephen b Dec 17, 1801
c Joseph Hilton b May 27, 1803   d Sally b Dec 5, 1804
e Zebulon b Feb 7, 1807
f Elizabeth Ann b Mch 12, 1815; m Epping 1835 Edward Stimpson
g Martha Jane b Feb 21, 1816   h Lucretia b Feb 3, 1818
i Daniel b Mch 10, 1820   j Samuel Haley b May 19, 1822
k Abigail b Oct 10, 1825
l Eleanor Haley b May 19, 1828; m Nov 5, 1855, Albert W Buxton of Bedford, Mass

Mary Dow ahbabja d Princeton, Ill, Sept 21, 1885; m June 6, 1818, Josiah Hills of Nottingham b Oct 15, 1797, d Nov 24, 1826, son of Josiah and Molly (Sanborn). The family moved to Ill after his death. Children:

a Daniel Dow b May 6, 1819; d Berlin Center, Ill, July 8, 1854; m Oct 6, 1846, Frances Clement; 2nd Jan 24, 1854, Hannah Walton Bloxam b Evans, N Y, Mch 10, 1838, dau of Thomas and Phoebe (Rhodes). Only child,—Mrs Eva E Mount, Wyanet, Ill

   b Mary Ann b Nov 15, 1820; d Princeton Sept 7, 1904; m Jan 30, 1850, Orris
       Spencer Phelps b Middlebury, Vt, May 13, 1817, d Princeton Jan 23, or 29,
       1904, son of Burnham and Mary (Hooker). Two adopted children
   c Josiah Edward b July 13, 1822; d May 2, 1833
   d Rufus b Mch 21, 1824; d Princeton Dec 25, 1893; m Feb 3, 1853, Betsey
       Axtell, dau of Hiram and Lucy (Crabtree); 2nd Clara Jenks; 3rd ——; 1
       son Josiah by 1st wife
   e Sarah Hilton b Nov 24, 1825; d Iowa City; m July 3, 1847, Dennis Payson
       Greeley b Enfield, N H, Aug 12, 1823, son of David and Judith (Pattee);
       moved to Dover, Ill; thence to Iowa City. He enlisted as private in 11th
       Iowa vols, promoted to Sgt, 2nd Lieut, 1st Lieut and Capt; in 1904 in National
       Soldiers' Home, Sawtelle, Calif. Two adopted children

Stephen Dow ahbabjb lived Brentwood and Lee; m Lee Feb 19, 1829, Mary R Chace b Epping Mch 10, 1805, d Nov 13, 1840, dau of Josiah and Rachel (Prescott); 2nd Nov 13, 1842, Mary Kelsey b Nottingham Nov 19, 1814, d Feb 27, 1907, dau of John and Mary (Roberts); moved to Providence, R I, after 1859; d Nov 14, 1880. Children:

   a Mary Jane b about 1830; d in infancy
   b Mary Kelsey b June 28, 1844   c Louisa Adams b Oct 1, 1845
   d Kelsey b Mch 20, 1851   e Cordelia b Nov 23, 1859; unm of Providence

Mary K Dow ahbabjbb m Nov 29, 1862, George E Robinson b Aug 15, 1842, d Providence 1881, son of J R and Abby (Stevens); 2nd 1887 George A Wilson b Sheepscot, Me, 1842, son of Alfred and Sarah; moved to San Francisco; living 1904 with her son, John A Robinson, owner of Hotel Knickerbocker.

Louisa A Dow ahbabjbc d Nov 3, 1906; m Brentwood Nov 26, 1868, Charles F Tourtillot b Pawtucket, R I, Sept 17, 1841, d Providence, Feb 21, 1877, son of Jesse and Melissa (Hopkins).

Kelsey Dow ahbabjbd m Nov 27, 1873, Emma Sophia Caler b Nov 25, 1850, d Mch 8, 1885, dau of Jasper and Adaline (Barnard); 2nd Sept 12, 1888, Ervina O Sawin of No Providence b Oct 5, 1855, dau of Dr Isaac and Olive S (Rudlong). One child by 2nd wife.

Joseph H Dow ahbabjc d Charlton, Mass, Aug 29, 1880; m Dec 19, 1830, Betsey Fisk b Heath, Mass, Mch 3, 1803, dau of William and Dolly (Wellington). Children:

   a Amanda Fiske b Worcester Aug 14, 1832; d June 19, 1850
   b Louisa Allen b July 8, 1834
   c Daniel Webster b Nov 18, 1835; deaf mute; living Boston 1904
   d Eleanor Emerson b Oxford May 13, 1837; m July 1856 Turner Sanderson;
       both successful teachers in Oceanus, Fla; later in business Fitchburg, Mass;
       3 children
   e Ellen Mandanah b Worcester Oct 26, 1838; m June 1858 —— Aldrich; 2
       children; separated; living 1904 with sister in Fitchburg
   f William Hilton b Charlton Nov 18, 1840

Louisa A Dow ahbabjcb m Nov 17, 1856, Reuben Wallin of Harriman, Tenn, b Aug 4, 1831. Son:

   a Mortimer Fiske Dow b May 30, 1866; m May 27, 1891, ——; lives Tenn

William H Dow ahbabjcf d Worcester Feb 12, 1875; m Jennie Elizabeth Tupper b Wilbraham Dec 11, 1845, dau of Edwin Lombard and Catherine (Moore); both well known teachers and authors. Only child:

a Edith May b Wilbraham May 19, 1867; m Sept 19, 1887, John T Miniter b Newcastle, Eng, May 2, 1862, d Lowell Sept 5, 1900, son of Milton and Bridget (Mohun); now editor of Boston Home Journal and well known writer; lives with her mother

Sally Dow ahbabjd d Belknap, Ill, 1880; m Dec 15, 1824, Gordon Daniel Lawrence of Epping; moved to Ill before 1850. Children:

a David Merrill b Dec 7, 1825; m; left son and dau
b Sarah Ann b Nov 22, 1827; m William Dearborn of Boston
c Mary Susan b May 7, 1832; d ae 18
d Daniel Dow b July 31, 1834; m Jan 6, 1864, Sarah Frances Prescott b Portsmouth, N H, Sept 16, 1844, dau of Reuben A and Mary E of Mendota, Ill; living 1904 Berlin, Ill, with 6 children

Zebulon Dow ahbabje ran away, went to sea, not heard of by family for many years; d Rutland, Mass, June 26, 1854; m Apr 15, 1835, Sally Wellington b West Boylston Dec 9, 1806, d Dec 8, 1843, dau of Ebenezer and Susan (Gale); 2nd Apr 25, 1844, Dolly D Davis, wid of ―― Turner, dau of Silas and Dolly. Children:

a Elizabeth Davis b Holden, Mass, Dec 23, 1835; m Rutland Oct 20, 1853, Charles H Bartlett b Boston Apr 7, 1828, son of Hosea and Abigail (Tilden); living 1904 Godfrey, Ill; 6 children
b ―― dau b Dec 8, d Dec 9, 1837
c William Hervey b Oct 5, 1846   d Gardner Warren b July 14, 1849

William H Dow ahbabjec d after 1904; m Jan 15, 1872, Amarilla Vose; moved to Waukegan, Ill, sash and blind manufacturer. Children:

a Robert W   b Grace   c Frank E   d Ruth

Robert W Dow ahbabjeca, now head of the business in Waukegan, m Cora E ――. Children:

a Dorothy A d young   b Elizabeth   c William H

Grace Dow ahbabjecb m Waukegan Apr 21, 1897, Howard Patterson Boutwell (now dec) b Sept 30, 1872, son of William Thurston and Eliza Jane (Comings). Children, b Waukegan:

a William Dow b Feb 6, 1900   b Helen Irene b Oct 5, 1902

Ruth Dow ahbabjecd m Walter H Wright (now dec). Children:

a Walter T   b Frank D

Gardner W Dow ahbabjed m Mch 28, 1872, Florence Bailey b Indianapolis Dec 21, 1854, dau of Samuel and Marcella (Sprague); living 1904 Littleton, Colo; 9 children. Untraced.

Elizabeth A Dow ahbabjf d Salem, Mass, Jan 17, 1867; m Aug 1, 1835, Edward Stimpson b Mch 28, 1811. Children, Danvers rec:

a Edward Stearns b Mch 16, 1836
b Sarah Ellen b Feb 28, 1838; m Charles Jacobs

Martha J Dow ahbabjg d Dec 7, 1892; m Henry Bowers of Peabody, Mass. Children,—George, Frank.

Lucretia Dow ahbabjh d July 21, 1901; m Feb 16, 1852, Levi Pierson b Oct 15, 1815, d June 25, 1865; lived Reading, Mass; son,— Frank b Nov 2, 1855, d July 21, 1873.

Daniel Dow ahbabji d Newmarket Mch 11, 1900; m May 8, 1848, Sarah Elizabeth Bartlett of Lee b 1824, d Jan 9, 1890, dau of Josiah and Hannah (True); lived on the Epping homestead. Children:

a   Mary True b Feb 22, 1849   b   Daniel Webster b Sept 15, 1853
c   Ida b May 25, 1858; d May 14, 1873
d   Fannie b Oct 19, 1859; m Sept 22, 1888, Frank Newell French b Exeter Aug
    27, 1860, of Dover
e   Frank b Oct 19, 1859; d Oct 22, 1893; m Lancaster Oct 25, 1882, Martha E
    Sanborn b May 27, 1863, m 2nd J E Kent of Newmarket. Child,—Wesley
    S d Aug 18, 1889, ae 4 mos, 8 days

Mary T Dow ahbabjia m June 20, 1871, Benjamin Matthes, son of Benjamin; settled in Newmarket after 1872. Children:

a   Charles Herbert b June 9, 1872; m 1900   b   Ida b July 19, 1879

D Webster Dow ahbabjib, in business many years in Melrose and N Y City, returned after 1900 to the homestead, his by inheritance. This is now a 400-acre nursery.   From his ms the recent generations of ahbab have been freely drawn.   He m Dec 16, 1879, Alice Burleigh Dow. Children:

a   Daniel Frederick b Exeter Sept 14, 1881
b   Carl Plumer b Melrose May 9, 1887

Daniel F Dow ahbabjiba m Melrose Aug 16, 1916, Helen Blanche Sawyer, ae 24, dau of John E and Lucy (Brazier); 1918 in Govt service, civil engineer of Freeport, L I.

Carl P Dow ahbabjibb of Melrose m July 8, 1906, Kate Adams. Child:

a   Katherine b Melrose Aug 29, 1909

Samuel H Dow ahbabjj d Lynn, Mass, Apr 4, 1895; m Oct 3, 1845, Susan A Watson b 1823, d Oct 6, 1849, of Nottingham; 2nd Oct 30, 1851, Clara A Demerritt of Lee b May 20, 1825, dau of Gen Samuel and Sarah (Torr). Children:

a   Nellie A b Oct 30, 1853   b   Mary H b Mch 16, 1863

Nellie A Dow ahbabjja m Aug 22, 1877, Nathaniel Holden of Lynn. Children:

a   Nathaniel Dow b July 21, 1878   b   Andrew Morgan b June 29, 1880

Abigail Dow ahbabjk m Prince George Co, Md, May 7, 1846, Moses Norris Collins, Lieut Col of 11th N H, killed in Battle of the Wilderness May 6, 1864. Child:

a   Mary Abbie b Md Oct 31, 1847; m Peabody, Mass, Oct 17, 1866, Thomas Lord
    Putnam; son Arthur b July 24, 1867

Noah Dow ahbabk, executor of his father's will, is neglected in the ms of the Epping Dow genealogist and does not figure in Epping annals. It is said that he had a son in Epping by a Miss Cilley, whom he recognized but who d ae 18. This may or may not be true. It will be noted that all other sons of ahbab, except the one who inherited the homestead, emigrated to Maine. We believe that Noah also settled in Maine, perhaps a pioneer, for a Noah Dow b about 1780 was a farmer of Exeter, Me, dying there of old age at the home of a married dau. His line was barely touched upon in the Edgar R Dow disconnected papers and a few continuations have been found in miscellaneous Me rec. He m a Miss Herrin; had 4 sons, 3 dau, order of birth not known:

a David; lived Waite   b John b Exeter Nov 14, 1803
c —— son d unm   d Benjamin d young
e Sally m 1830 Elias Titcomb; had sons,—F W of Houlton; Charles of East
   Dover; —— dau m Calvin Ireland of So Dover
f Charlotte m George Heniston of Exeter   g Celinda m Henry Dearborn

David Dow ahbabka. It is known that he settled in Waite and had considerable family; 1st born was John. There have been many Dows of Waite, presumably of this line. David seems to have been the Capt David Dow of the Aroostook war of 1839.

John Dow ahbabkb d (teamster of Bangor) Mch 9, 1876; m Lydia Libbey, ae 29, d Bangor Apr 29, 1834, leaving 1 dau; 2nd (her sister) Abigail Libbey, dau of Jonathan and Hannah of Livermore; 3rd Oct 17, 1858, Mary A Weed b Bangor Oct 11, 1833, d Bangor Mch 4, 1886. Apparently only 2 children:

a Charlotte L b Jan 1, 1834   b William H b Sept 23, 1860

Charlotte L Dow ahbabkba m Oct 29, 1860, Isaac N Jones b Litchfield Jan 12, 1831, owner of Litchfield stage line. Children:

a Alice Maude b Mch 16, 1864   b Clara Susie b Apr 28, 1865

William H Dow ahbabkbb, grocer of Bangor, m Jan 9, 1884, Abby F Stover b Feb 26, 1864. Only child:

a Alice Mae b Jan 29, 1894; of Bangor, recent directory

———

Joel Dow ahbabkx (for convenience). The only known Dows of Atkinson are of the ahbaba line. The 1850 census shows six families there, apparently with a common ancestor Joel b N H 1780. The name Joel recurs often, and it affords no clue,—no missing Joel known. If this family is Dow at all (and it is not likely, since they are not now recognized by old residents), they must have moved away not long after 1850. We notice that there was in the neighborhood a family of Doore, frequently intermarrying with the ahbaba Dows. This name appears to be a corruption of Dorr. Quite possibly the right name is Joel Dorr and the census

taker is to blame.   Joel, farmer of Atkinson, assessed $600, had wife
Hannah b 1781.   Inferentially the six are his children, all b Me:

    a N D b 1801   b David b 1802   c J C b 1802
    d —— d before 1850, leaving wid Hannah —— b Norway, Me
    e Levi b 1810   f Joel b 1814

N D Dow ahbabkxa, farmer of Dover, assessed $1,600; wife Eliza
b Me 1800.   Children:

    a Wellington b 1828, farmer at home 1850   b Elmira b 1831
    c Julia b 1832   d Oric b 1835   e Joel b 1837   f N b 1842

David Dow ahbabkxb, farmer of Atkinson, assessed $500;   wife
Elizabeth b Me 1800.   Children:

    a Daniel b 1830   b Harriet b 1831   c Flavil (son) b 1832
    d H b 1836   e Dudley b 1841

J C Dow ahbabkxc, farmer of Atkinson with no land, either widower,
or with 2nd wife M A b Me 1831.   Children:

    a Fidela b 1838   b Ellen b 1841   c Seth b 1847   d J W b 1849

Levi Dow ahbabkxe, farmer of Atkinson assessed $300;   2nd wife
Patience b Me 1823.   Children:

    a Wilson b 1834   b Nathan b 1836   c Levi b 1838
    d Jane b 1849

Joel Dow ahbabkxf, farmer of Atkinson, with parents in 1850;
wife Sally b Me 1818.   Children:

    a Eliza b 1835   b James b 1837   c Nancy b 1840
    d Iceley b 1842   e Joel A b 1844   f Sarah b 1849

J C Dow ahbabkxy, carpenter of Foxcroft, assessed $900;   wife
Betsey b Me 1808.   Children:

    a James b 1832   b Louise b 1834   c George b 1836

Noah Dow ahbac.   No will or administration papers of ahba have
been found.   We have seen that 1-3 of his homestead was given to each
of the 2 sons by 1st wife.   Another son Josiah probably inherited the
remaining third.   Noah apparently had for his share the Gilmanton
land.   The old-fashioned, non-genealogical, inadequate Hist Gilmanton
gives little aid.   Noah was the first Dow to reach Gilmanton, 1772.
He m Belmont Dec 2, 1772, Hannah Folsom.   A town Hist calls her
dau of William and Hannah (Gilman); this errs.   William Folsom,
selectman of Newmarket for 20 consecutive years, d 1755; his son Maj
David m Sarah —— and was father of Hannah.

Noah signed the Association Test; in 1777 he enlisted for Ticonderoga, the expedition which turned back after a few days.   In later
years he was always known as captain, perhaps a militia title.   An inn
keeper, he gets a mention as on an important church committee in 1793.

Nothing more about his career has been found. The 1790 census gives him 1a, 3b, 3c. This means 2 sons under 16 and 2 dau. No b rec found in Gilmanton. Folsom Gen, an old work, gives 2, also proven by vital statistics. It is useless just now to speculate on the identity of the younger children.

   a Sally b Belmont Sept 3, 1773   b John b Epping Mch 6, 1776

That John Dow ahbacb is our Jonathan Dow adaabff is well nigh certain. See also supplement.

Josiah Dow ahbae grew up in Epping; appears in muster roll of Capt Clark's Epping Co; later enlisted, Capt Joseph Sias, Col Moses Nichols; mustered out R 1 Aug 5, 1778, service 28 days. He m a dau of Capt Sias, and they went with others of the Sias family to Belfast, Me. Here his wife d, oldest child probably hers. He seems to have returned to Epping.

Some of the Epping Lyfords became original settlers of Canterbury and Josiah Dow may have gone with them. At all events he was the original owner of lot 34, school district 2. This lot was sold by his son after 1844. Here he m 2nd Charlotte Clough (Sarah, State rec) b Canterbury (?) Feb 20, 1766, d Concord Sept 30, 1846. Children, family rec:

  a Martha M m ——— Crockett; living in Mass ae 90
  b Charlotte b Nov 22, 1789
  c Mary Jane; of Hopkinton m Sept 18, 1831, Sias Noble of Lee
  d Tristram Coffin b July 10, 1793
  e Susan Clough   f Jeremiah   g Josiah b about 1798

Charlotte Dow ahbaeb d Dec 4, 1868; m Nov 1, 1815, Joseph Lyford; moved 1836 to Buda, Ill. Children, all b Canterbury:

  a Augustus b May 5, 1816   b Alfred b Jan 28, 1818
  c Caroline b Apr 7, 1824; m 1844 Rufus Craig
  d Joseph b Nov 7, 1828   e Moses b Feb 22, 1831; d Feb 26, 1856

Tristram C Dow ahbaed in 1828 is mentioned as a leading citizen of Canterbury. Soon after 1844 he sold out and moved to Bureau Co, Ill, starting a general merchandise business in Annawan; in 1867 moved to Davenport, Iowa, opening a grist mill, which, greatly enlarged, is still carried on by his descendants. He d Davenport Aug 29, 1875; m Canterbury Oct 19, 1815, Susanna Lyford b June 16, 1798, d Davenport Oct 1875, dau of Joseph and Susanna (Dearborn). Children:

  a Almira b Mch 5, 1817; d May 9, 1879; m and left at least one dau m L S Hawley of Clinton, Iowa
  b Joseph L b Mch 5, 1819; d Jan 8, 1891; lived Wilton, Iowa; untraced
  c Tristram T b Nov 2, 1826; d Mch 28, 1882
  d Josiah b Mch 16, 1828; d Mch 9, 1908
  e John Lyford b May 6, 1830; d July 5, 1899
  f Mary Ann b May 6, 1832; d Sept 10, 1894
  g Lyman b May 16, 1834; d Dec 4, 1857

Tristram T Dow ahbaedc, president of First Nat Bank of Davenport, m June 1859 Mary Stevens, formerly of Canterbury. He began as clerk in a Canterbury store, came to Ill with his parents; opened a general store in Annawan, in which he kept an interest until 1868. Enlisted as private in 112th Ill inf, chosen as Capt; promoted to Major Feb 1863, to Lieut Col Apr 1, 1865; resigned 2 months later and returned to Annawan. For 2 years acting Col of 112th, with Burnside and Sherman, taking part in the latter's march to the sea. He commanded a brigade in several actions and directed the parole of a corps of the army of Gen Joe Johnson. Fought in 7 battles and a number of minor engagements; had one piece of bad luck, captured at Winchester by Morgan's raiders, Col Robert G Ingersoll being a fellow prisoner.

In 1866 he entered the lumber business in Chicago; in 1868 moved to Davenport, building the Crescent Flour mills with 2 partners, one being S F Gilman, his son-in-law. He continued this business until his death. In 1872 Alderman, 1878 Mayor of Davenport; 1872 director, 1876 president of First Nat Bank. Of 4 children, 1 survived:

a —— dau m S F Gilman; a dau m Judge Bollinger of Davenport

Josiah Dow ahbaedd continued the milling business; m Dec 25, 1850, Elizabeth Stevens b Canterbury Oct 4, 1829, d Davenport May 19, 1881. Children:

a Mary E b Concord, Ill, Feb 4, 1852; d May 17, 1858
b John F b Oct 17, 1856

John F Dow ahbaeddb continues the milling business; president of Davenport Savings Bank; m Nancie Sears b Oct 24, 1858, dau of Isaac H and Nancy (Jennings). Isaac was a banker, coming to Davenport from Ballston Spa, N Y. Children:

a George, not now living   b Gilbert T   c John S
d Worrall C; the three now of Davenport

John L Dow ahbaede of Davenport had at least one child:

a Lyford T, now of Davenport

Mary A Dow ahbaedf m July 22, 1856, Jacob Miller, real estate operator of Princeton, Ill, b Annville, Pa, June 15, 1835. Seven children, 3 dying young:

a Byron b Apr 10, 1865; m Ida Medley; moved to Aberdeen, S D
b Victor b Mch 1, 1869   c Viola b Mch 1, 1869
d Mertie b Jan 8, 1874

Susan C Dow ahbaee m Albigence Mead (8th generation in America). Children:

a Darius Johnson m Elizabeth Jennings   b Jerome m Mary ——
c Sarah Eliza m George Warner Weeks
d Mary Jane m Alfred Fife of Pembroke   e Joseph, unm

Jeremiah Dow ahbaef of Canterbury m Nov 27, 1824, Alice Arlin of Northfield. As he gets no mention in Hist Canterbury, he presumably moved away at marriage; may be the Jeremiah Dow, farmer, married, d Northfield Mch 23, 1865, b Northfield May 30, 1795, son of —— and Elsie (Hanson). Minor errors in State rec are too usual to make this unlikely.

Josiah Dow ahbaeg m Dec 27, 1821, Elizabeth H Ham b Mch 27, 1802, dau of John and Polly (Osgood); 2nd May 27, 1842, wid Elizabeth Johnson of Boscawen. Presumably lived Boscawen; untraced

Moses Dow ahbb is unproven after his b rec; it seems useless to speculate on what became of him. He may be the Moses Dow of Newington m Mch 19, 1735, Sarah Phillips of Portsmouth, now discussed under d Dow family. An unexplained rec is: Mrs Sarah Dow d Moultonborough July 25, 1779, ae 86. No posterity attributable. He might have had some of the disconnected Dows of Epping. Most likely of all, he d young

Isaac Dow ahbc appears in Amesbury 1742. No rec found between b and m. He m Dec 9, 1742, Martha Hanniford. She is probably dau of John of Stratham and great aunt of Sally Hanniford abbegf. He was for 18 years blacksmith of Amesbury. May 18, 1760, he and wife obtained dismissal from Amesbury second church to the new church of Sandown. Here he built a new smithy. A short, stout man, he went one day in 1784 to cut weeds in the field beside his shop. Not returning to dinner, his children searched and found him dead, leaning against the fence. Children, b Amesbury:

a Thomas bap Sept 11, 1743
b Elizabeth bap Dec 30, 1744; m May 30, 1764, Abner Whitcher
c Martha b Dec 18, 1744; bap Dec 30; d Feb 11, 1753
d Isaac b Oct 1, 1746; d Feb 8, 1768, unm
e Simeon b or bap 1748; not in father's will; perhaps d young; possibly was at Bunker Hill; vague rec perhaps wholly error
f Ela (Eley, rec) bap Apr 30, 1749
g Anna (Hannah, Barker Gen and Essex Antiq, vol 6) b Mch 8, 1750; bap Mch 10, 1751; m 1776 John Barker, whose sister m her brother; both living Methuen 1788
h Jesse b Aug 8; bap Aug 12, 1753   i Martha bap Aug 31, 1755
j Abigail b Sandown May 25, 1758

Thomas Dow ahbca was apprenticed in boyhood to a shipsmith, brazier and blacksmith of Salem, Mass. He m Pawtucket Falls Feb 28, 1767, Mary Barker b Nov 27, 1743, dau of John and Sarah (Roberts) of Methuen. The Barker family had come from Newbury and owned a great tract of undeveloped land beyond Haverhill. The present city of Lawrence is on that land. Presumably owing to this marriage Thomas located in Methuen, setting up his own blacksmith shop, but he was in close touch with Sandown, his sister Hannah marrying Mary's brother John. Sarah Barker, another sister, m John Ford, of distinguished military record. Thomas was a much taller man than his father, but had the dark complexion characteristic of the line. Mary Barker is described by a granddau as of medium height, skin fair as a lily, and eyes a dark heavenly blue. This pronounced blonde type has recurred occasionally in her descendants, most of whom are dark.

In the preliminaries to the Revolution all the Methuen Barkers and Sandown Dows were active, organization and drilling having begun many months before hostilities. All were so-called minute men, having engaged to leave home for the fight at a minute's notice. Who carried the alarm of the British troops leaving Boston is not known. The Methuen and other contingents met punctually at the Alarm Post, a huge boulder at the edge of Lowell. Maj Samuel Bedwell was in command; John Ford was sgt and Thomas Dow corporal. Parson Bridge was at the alarm post demanding that before the start all should repair to his meeting house, but the men refused. Sgt Ford explained particularly that there was more important business on hand. Some were on horseback, some on foot, the latter speeding up by holding a stirrup. They arrived at Lexington Apr 19 and took part in the fray. The rolls give them 4 1-2 days service on this occasion. The organization was the same at Bunker Hill, arriving to find Capt Reuben Dow bcdea already behind the earthworks. It is family tradition that two or more of Thomas' brothers were at Bunker Hill, but there is no record to substantiate this. It is certain, however, that there were nine Dows in this fight. The only reason the Author has for thinking that Simeon Dow ahbce lived to this time is that family tradition says that one brother, supposedly he, came home after the fight and told an anecdote (which stuck in memory) of his neighbor in the ranks loading and firing as fast as he could and praying incessantly: "Oh, God, help us to fight this battle and give to us the victory."

The Revolutionary rolls seldom give enough to trace the movements of any man through the War. Thomas Dow was at the pre-arranged rendezvous after all had come down the hill together. He appears but twice more in the rolls, under Capt John Calfe, Col Timothy Bartlett, in 1776, and receipting, under Capt Stone, for £1-6-8, travel allowance for Charlestown. His permanent return home was probably in 1777. He had been home, laid up with rheumatism, but had reported again for duty. One knee was always afterwards stiffened from rheumatism.

His business in Methuen had been prosperous and in 1775 he had three apprentices. They left, however, and Mary (Barker) Dow was alone to care for her four children. During the summer all went reasonably well, but before the winter had far progressed they became short of firewood and food. Another baby arrived before Spring. Mary Barker explained that to conserve food she would apportion a supply at each meal and even greater scarcity might follow. Thomas Dow ahbcab was then seven years old. When his mother was housecleaning next spring she found in his room small portions of bread, rice and the like. The youngster had silently saved them against the feared times of greater need.   Continental money did not go far.   Mary Barker paid $80 for a cheese.

Thomas Dow was several years in Methuen after the war; and located where is now Danville, Vt.   He sold his Methuen farm and shop and with the proceeds built in Danville a new blacksmith shop and a public house known as Gore Inn.   The place is still called the Gore, on a point of Danville Village Green.   Here he prospered, serving fourteen consecutive years in the Legislature.   He and Aaron Hartshorne, presumably his partner in the inn, sold (Vt Hist Gaz vol I, p 314) Sept, 1796, for and in consideration of £30 to the County a parcel of land containing 4 acres situated in Danville Green Village, to have and to hold the same so long as the public buildings should remain at Danville. This condition was broken many years ago but no Dow has ever laid claim to the property.

In 1819, two of his children being settled in Yorkshire, N Y, Thomas left these children who had elected Danville for their home and went to Yorkshire.   Here he lived three years, dying Mch 15, 1822, his wife dying the following year.   Their gravestones still stand in Arcade cemetery.   The first eight children b Methuen rest in Danville:

a   Mary b Apr 23, 1768   b   Thomas b Dec 2, 1769
c   Richard b Oct 5, 1771   d   Isaac b Oct 5, 1773
e   Martha b Feb 28, 1776; d East Aurora, N Y, Nov 9, 1829; m Isaac Williams.
     This couple were the original founders of Yorkshire and some of their descen-
     dants still live there
f   Sarah m John Brown; settled in Erie, Pa
g   Betsey b 1779; family rec says m Peter Peasley; State gives: m May 16, 1806,
     Peter Russell
h   Hannah b 1783; m Deweysburgh July 9, 1907, Andrew Martin Jr; settled in
     Canada
i   Elsie b Sept 21, 1792   j   Benjamin b Nov 23, 1794

Mary Dow ahbcaa m James Glines of Danville, b Canterbury, N H, Apr 24, 1766, d Jan 11, 1843.   She d Feb 19, 1845; they moved in 1805 to Stanstead, P Q, giving the name to Glines' Corners.   Children:

a   Mary b Aug 1791; m Theodore S Bangs
b   Nancy b June 2, 1794; m Greeley Dow adaabda
c   Hannah b July 10, 1796; m Zebulon Hunt
d   Samuel b Apr 14, 1797; d 1812
e   Stephen Barker b Apr 28, 1799; m Mch 26, 1827, Sarah Sinclair b Aug 15, 1802;
     a dau Mrs Marion Vesey of Perry, Ohio, lived to be much interested in this
     Book
f   Louisa b Sept 3, 1804; d 1820
g   Moses S b Aug 14, 1807; a well known physician; m Emily Abbott
h   Ira b Feb 1, 1810; d 1813

Thomas Dow ahbcab.   A family rec that he d (place ungiven) Dec 3, 1827, is based on error.   He was for a brief time in 1790 in partnership with a brother-in-law in Wheelock,—census giving Dow & Glines 2a—.   He m Oct 30, 1790, Nabby Daniels b Vt Feb 13, 1770. A family rec calling her Nabby Smith is error.   He was wounded 1812 by a canister shot.   They moved to Danville, thence some years later to Brutus, Cayuga Co, N Y. Here he was blacksmith, farmer, justice of the peace, supervisor and deacon. Following death of his wife he m 2nd a wid Dean, who had 6 unm children. This ill-advised affair soon resulted in a separation. He d Brutus Oct 3, 1849. Children:

a David b Oct 9, 1791   b Smith b Jan 5, 1794
c Adams b May 31, 1796
d Whitcher b 1798; burned to death in sugar bush, ae 5
e Thomas Jefferson b Aug 31, 1800
f Whitcher b Oct 3, 1804   g Helena m and lived N Y City; no children
h John b May 7, 1808   i Stephen b Jan 29, 1810
j Benjamin b Dec 19, 1811   k Christina b Dec 12, 1813; d in infancy

David Dow ahbcaba of Danville m 1st Mch 11, 1813, Apphia Sanborn (Sambon in Danville rec) b Aug 28, 1795, of Sanbornton, N H. Sanbornton rec garbles him as Daniel. After a few years he went alone to Jefferson Co, Ill, to investigate living conditions. A good smith, he made good wages and sent money home frequently, asking his wife to come. She demurred for a long time, as he had been a hard drinker and life with him had been almost intolerable. She finally yielded but had to divorce him in Illinois, returning east with her 2 children, who are genealogically lost. He then m a wid who soon d of cholera; m 3rd Jane Delia Lincoln b May 18, 1819. She bore him 3 children, then divorced him on account of intemperance and m Anson Hobart, who came from N Y State. After his third matrimonial misadventure David turned over a new leaf. He did not marry again; became a Methodist preacher, teetotaler, public speaker and high degree mason; d Jefferson Co Mch 4, 1846. Children:

a Eli J   b Abigail; returned east with mother
c William, untraced   d Eliza Ellen
e Thomas Henry Clay b July 22, 1833

Thomas H C Dow ahbcabac got little schooling and no books from his stepfather; went into a machine shop at 18; lived Yorktown, Tampico and New Bedford, Ill. Perhaps parental example made him an ardent prohibitionist; he voted the Prohibition ticket regularly. Of thorough integrity, he served the community as best he knew. He m Sarah Elizabeth Robinson. Children:

a **Orion David** b Yorktown Sept 14, 1862; of New Bedford 1885; untraced
b Unadilla b Mch 21, 1864; m Dec 31, 1882, Dick Ratliff of Hennepin; 2 children
c William Thurman b Nov 19, 1866; living 1885
d Rose Ella b Tampico Apr 18, 1868; d Sept 5, 1885
e Ptolemy b Nov 30, 1871; living 1885
f Emmabelle b Mch 26, 1875   g Jane D b May 31, 1878

Smith Dow ahbcabb m twice; 1st wife d Weedsport, N Y, 1840; he moved to Mich; d Mich or Weedsport 1869; had 4 sons, 1 dau, of whom:

a Perkins S b July 15, 1825   c Marvin Benjamin; grew up; untraced
d Emily; lived Yorktown, Ill
e Asenath m ---- Reynolds of Cold Water, Mich

Perkins S Dow ahbcabba served 1 year in Civil War; d Oct 1876; m Dec 2, 1846, Lucy E Rifenburg b Constancia, N Y, Dec 23, 1827; she m 2nd —— Dart and moved to San Jose, Calif. Three sons, 2 dau, all artists, all adopted spelling Dowe:

    d   Arthur M b Mch 9, 1854

Arthur M Dowe ahbcabbad, artist of San Francisco, sought his subjects mainly in Mexico; m Nov 20, 1875, Anna Hale b Munich, Germany. Children:

    a   Lucy E b Davenport, Iowa, Dec 6, 1876
    b   Enid May b San Francisco July 14, 1878   c   Claude Lorain b Jan 15, 1880

Adams Dow ahbcabc d Brutus Feb 13, 1874, a farmer; wife a Miss Moffett d long before him. A dau d young; the surviving:

    a   Benjamin F, a whaler, lost at sea
    b   Hiram Augustus b N Y City Aug 27, 1821
    c   Jefferson lived Brutus; 2 children; dau Eliza m —— Roberts
    d   Mary m —— Saxe; 2 children

Hiram A Dow ahbcabcb, farmer of Eaton Co, Mich, d Mch 25, 1863 or 1883; m Aug 3, 1846, Caroline Eaton Watson b Apr 26, 1826, d Hot Springs, Ark, Nov 27, 1882. He enlisted Aug 1861 in 6th Mich; disch for disability Sept 1862. Five sons and 3 dau, of whom:

    a   Hiram Albertine b Bellevue, Mich, June 7, 1851; mechanical engineer of St Paul, Ind; m Apr 13, 1881, Marion M Kelsy b Dec 16, 1857; no children
    b   Samuel M   c   William H
    d   Emma S m —— Matherson of Portland, Mich
    e   Levantha Cordelia   f   Adams George lived Portland, Mich

Samuel Moffatt Dow ahbcabcbb, b Bellevue Aug 11, 1853; well known physician of Detroit; m Olivet, Mich, Apr 13, 1876, Mary Jane Blanchard b Bellevue Feb 27, 1864. Only child:

    a   Arden K b Portland Sept 15, 1877; of Detroit 1884

William Henry Dow ahbcabcbc, b New Buffalo, taught school at 17 to support himself while studying electricity; eventually devoting himself to its therapeutics; a college professor, then manager of a plant in Hot Springs, Ark, accumulating considerable property. Study led to his complete absorption and withdrawal from social life, finally to chronic imbecility. In 1885 he was with his brother, his guardian, in Detroit.

Lena C Dow ahbcabcbe, b Victory, N Y, May 22, 1847; m Dec 21, 1872, Charles Henry Tifft b Nassau, N Y, Nov 13, 1843, farmer of Vineland, N J. Children:

    a   Minnie Lurena b Nassau June 22, 1874
    b   Charles Arthur b Yonkers Apr 1, 1878

Thomas J Dow ahbcabe went while a lad to Rochester, N Y; 6 years after m to Mich, where they pioneered it for 10 years, then to

Tampico. He d Tampico, Ill, May 22, 1828; had developed habitual intemperance, so that his wife left him and lived with her dau Roxana. Miss Marcia Gray of Dorset, Vt, copied the narrative of this family from the scarce pamphlet genealogy of Alanson Gray. He m Rochester May 22, 1828, Susan Gray b Dorset Aug 28, 1806, d Tampico Nov 2, 1887, 5th child of Chauncey and Polly (Borland). Children:

a Thomas Jefferson b Rochester June 29, 1830
b Abigail b Sept 5, 1831; d Prophetstown, Ill, Jan 7, 1864
c George b Brighton, N Y, Feb 22, 1833; cooper, moved to Pittsburg, Ore; m 1864; had a son b Jan 13, 1872; untraced
d Daniel b Ladue, Mich, Sept 30, 1835
e Chauncey b Feb 14, 1837; went to Colo to try fortune in mining; d Aug 1875; unm
f Roxana b Nov 11, 1838; m Oct 20, 1876, Joseph Kemp, cooper of Tampico
g William H b June 10, 1840; d Aug 7, 1884; m Jan 12, 1878, Elizabeth Mills d May 12, 1886; lived Tampico
h Mary D b Nov 15, 1841; m 1st —— Edmunds of Denver; m 3rd —— Cantrell, cattle dealer of Castle Rock, Colo
i Schuyler b May 2, 1843; living Kan 1885; untraced
j Charles N b Tampico Sept 15, 1845

Thomas J Dow ahbcabea left home at 10 and learned the blacksmith trade in Whitewater; m Dec 18, 1852, E A Pratt of Whitewater d in 3 mos; m 2nd Dec 15, 1856, R B Burgess of Kenosha; moved to Racine in 1865; d Aug 21, 1888, for 18 years with J I Case works. Children:

a Carrie b Mch 7, 1858; m Dec 1, 1875, —— Le Ray of Racine d Feb 14, 1880. She d Jan 17, 1879, leaving dau Minnie b Aug 21, 1876, brought up by her grandmother Dow
b Will C b Sept 3, 1860
c Bert W b Aug 9, 1865; in 1889 spring fitter in Case works
d Walter L b Jan 17, 1872; in 1889 in Case engine works

Will C Dow ahbcabeab, in 1889 foreman in Case plow works, m June 1, 1882, Cora Baldwin. Son:

a De Milton b Oct 8, 1884; by recent directory machinist of Racine

Daniel Webster Dow ahbcabed, 1st Lieut 44th Iowa inf, studied law in Morristown, Ill; admitted to bar Iowa June 1859; moved to St Paul, Minn; m Hampton Iowa, Dec 4, 1864, Martha J Carter b Jan 6, 1843, dau of Simeon Hackley and Sarah (Randall) of Hampton, Ia. Children, b Hampton:

a Guy H b Nov 3, 1865, untraced   b Avis b June 14, 1867
c Alma b July 7, 1869   d Abi b Sept 5, 1877

Charles N Dow ahbcabej, for many years R R conductor of Davenport, Iowa, moved 1901 to Omaha; m Ft Dodge Oct 3, 1875, Nora Burke. Children:

a Frank C b Sept 23, 1876; now train master Tacoma, Wash
b Edward Albert b Apr 20, 1879
c Mary Eva b Feb 18, 1887; now of Omaha
d Lucy Faber b Feb 13, 1889; m Russell A Fisher; lives Seattle

Edward A Dow ahbcabejb, in U S consular service, St Stephen, N

B, in 1916, Ft William, Ont, 1917; later using excellent judgment in troubled times in Mex; m Oct 6, 1909, Rose Bush. Children:

a Edward Albert b Dec 21, 1912   b Rose Mary b Apr 30, 1917

Whitcher Dow ahbcabf, b Danville, d Yorktown, Ill, May 30, 1882; m Jan 27, 1828, Eunice Bump b Rutland, Vt, Dec 17, 1806, d Yorktown Nov 30, 1877. A farmer, served as supervisor; was a devoted spiritualist and during his last five years held daily conversations with his wife, who often told him much of what was to happen. He was a fine man, temperate, charitable and honest to the last degree. Children:

a Emily b Mch 5, 1828   b Emeline b Mch 25, 1829
c Benjamin F b May 26, 1831; of Yorktown 1907
d Thomas b June 15, 1833; of Tampico 1907
e Edward Whitcher b Nov 22, 1837
f Henry H b Sept 23, 1839; of Pasadena, Calif, 1907
g Albina b Nov 13, 1841
h Henry Clay b July 10, 1848; of West Point, Miss, 1907

Emily Dow ahbcabfa, b Freedom, N Y, m Mch 20, 1850, Oliver W McKenzie b Moriah, N J, Mch 8, 1825, blacksmith, farmer, merchant, constable, assessor, collector of taxes of Yorktown. Children, all b Yorktown.

a Eliza Ella b Feb 3, 1851; 3 children
b Julius Adelbert b July 14, 1853; d Sept 22, 1860
c Raymond Havens b Nov 30, 1854; 1 child
d Willie Edgar b Oct 20, 1856; d Nov 21, 1858
e Oliver William b July 5, 1857; d July 3, 1863
f ——, dau b Oct 2, 1861; d in infancy

Edward W Dow ahbcabfe d, retired, Rock Falls, Ill, Aug 16, 1905, m Fannie Greenman b N Y Mch 5, 1842, d Rock Falls Apr 1902. Children:

a Ernest Linwood b Yorktown Sept 1, 1861
b John G b Nov 11, 1872; of San Francisco 1907
c Nettie W b Feb 22, 1881; m Gray Terrell of Texas

Ernest L Dow ahbcabfea, physician of Rock Falls, Ill, m June 29, 1890, Winnogene Cope b Sterling Dec 4, 1867. Children, all b Rock Falls:

a Maurice C b Jan 14, 1891   b Dorothy b Apr 26, 1893
c Helen b Feb 5, 1897

John Dow ahbcabh lived Wolcott, N Y; his wife surviving him. A relative recalls little of him except his wide reputation for extreme absent mindedness, which got him into many laughable misadventures. He left at least one child:

a Albina m Job Greenman

Stephen Dow ahbcabi d in Iowa; was justice of the peace, town clerk, postmaster, etc; m twice; left 1 son, 3 dau, one being:

a Effie m —— Whitney of Faulkner

Benjamin Dow ahbcabj. Our rec are slightly confused; one Benjamin, probably this one, farmer, d Jefferson Corners about 1882. Another and contemporaneous Benjamin d Oregon leaving 6 children, one being Julia Ann m —— Brewer

Richard Dow ahbcac d (family rec) Dec 23, 1823, or (State rec) Sept 14, 1825; m Mch 27, 1793, Elizabeth Carr b Danville, d Sept 15, 1825 or 1828. Children:

  a Hannah b Aug 22, 1794   b Moses b Dec 3, 1796
  c Betsey b Mch 20, 1799; d Danville Sept 1823; m Nov 15, 1818, Merrill Pills-
       bury; no children
  d Mary b Nov 21, 1801; d Toledo, Ohio, about 1845
  e Abigail b Mch 20, 1804; d Apr 1824
  f William b Dec 27, 1805   g Cynthia b May 10, 1808
  h Isaac b June 30, 1811   i Juliana b Sept 15, 1814; d Feb 5, 1815

Hannah Dow ahbcaca m Yorkshire 182-- Jacob Vrooman; living 1835 Clymer, N Y. Children:

  a Richard Dow b 1827-8   b Hannah (or Martha) b 1829; m —— French
  d Elizabeth b 1835; m James Upton   e William

Moses Dow ahbcacb m Danville Aug 27, 1820, Pamelia F Pope d tuberculosis Albany Apr 4, 1839, six weeks before her husband of same disease. Children:

  a Gilbert B b Nov 25, 1824   b Henry Putnam b Danville Jan 1, 1829

Gilbert Barker Dow ahbcacba, in 1850 tinsmith with Isaac Dow ahbcach, m May 7, 1850, Mary Dow ahbcacfa, both of Burlington. She d Oct 2, 1857; he m 2nd May 17, 1860, Delia F Scott. Children:

  a Mary R b Oct 2, 1857; m C E Rodgers b Gilbert A b Nov 14, 1863
  c Walter Francis b July 24, 1866; d May 31, 1889

Gilbert A Dow ahbcacbab, physician of Burlington, d Oct 20, 1916; m Aug 26, 1891, Mary Elizabeth Root, who sent to the Author the ahbcac data. Children:

  a Louis Fenner b Aug 19, 1892; Burlington student 1915
  b Katherine Scott b Oct 31, 1894; Burlington teacher 1915
  c Walter Wheeler Bell b Sept 14, 1898; d Oct 4, 1906

Henry P Dow ahbcacbb m Essex, Vt, Sept 11, 1850, Mary A Carpenter, both of Burlington. Children:

  a Mary Kate b Richmond, Vt, Feb 13, 1853
  b Luther Morrill b Magnolia, Ill, Nov 10, 1884, Maria Baker of Compton;
       untraced

Mary Dow ahbcacd m Dec 31, 1820, Moses Merrill of Danville, killed by falling tree Sutton Apr 17, 1854. Of 5 children, 3 buried with mother:

  d Luther C   e Ephraim d about 1854, near Mississippi River

William Dow ahbcacf m Derby, Vt, Dec 2, 1830, Philena R Davis d Nov 5, 1858, from a carriage accident; m 2nd Dec 2, 1839, Louisa

Wilson. Many years ago she wrote all the data she had of ahbcac line and gave it to Benjamin Dow ahbcajg, it finally reaching the Author. Only child:

a   Mary R b Jan 25, 1831; m Gilbert B Dow ahbcacba

Cynthia Dow ahbcacg m (his 2nd) Merrill Pillsbury ahbcacc; in 1854 living Johnson, Vt. Children:

a   Betsey b 1825; d Apr 25, 1898; m Charles Burton Stone b Vt 1821; 2 ch
b   Cynthia m Charles W Davis   c   Helen b 1830
d   Merrill b Sept 1, 1832; d tuberculosis Apr 29, 1853
e   Sylvester Isaac b Albany 1838

Isaac Dow ahbcach d Apr 21, 1859; tinsmith of Danville; in 1850 census with nephew and 6 apprentices; m 1st Castleton Jan 17, 1840, Elizabeth Starr Southmayd d Burlington 1845; m 2nd Burlington Aug 19, 1848, Delia Frances Scott b 1830. Children:

a   Isaac b and d 1841   b   William b and d 1845; d 4 mos after mother
c   Albert Richard b Mch 21, 1849
d   Fannie Gertrude b Apr 27, 1857; m Jan 7, 1880, Walter P Wheeler

Albert R Dow ahbcachc m June 20, 1876, Emma G Carruth. Children:

a   Gertrude C b Feb 2, 1877; m Aug 2, 1897, Cassius D Root
b   Charles S b Feb 23, 1879; m June 28, 1909, Margaret F Bartlett
c   Albert Henry b Sept 17, 1882; d Apr 13, 1884
d   Arthur W b Oct 25, 1886; directory gives him "State editor, Burlington";
    letter of genealogical inquiry unanswered

Isaac Dow ahbcad m Dec 6, 1798, Susannah Carr of Danville, sister of ahbcac. In the three sets of family history developed within this family none has even mentioned the career of ahbcad.

We can make a guess. Isaac Dow, inn holder of Brunswick, who came thither from Boston, Mass, d from overdose of opium May 29, 1822, ae estimated 50. Age fits and no other known Isaac fits at all.

Elsie Dow ahbcai m 1st Ishua, N Y, Dec 29, 1816, William Price b L I Dec 9, 1789, d Freedom, N Y, Oct 1, 1844, son of Stephen and Elizabeth (Hall); m 2nd May 24, 1849, William Eaton Crowley b Mass Oct 30, 1791, d East`Aurora Dec 9, 1867. Elsie d East Aurora Apr 9, 1874. Children, by 1st husband:

a   William Henry b Jan 18, 1818; d Cleveland, Ohio, June 8, 1883; m Oct 6, 1843,
    Martha C Guild
b   Malvina F b May 30, 1820; d Barton, Wis, May 6, 1875; m Dec 16, 1838,
    Darwin E Goodenough
c   Orlando H b Mch 9, 1822; d Cleveland Nov 8, 1877; m Aug 11, 1846, Hannah L
    Robinson. His son Charles R m Agnes R Davidson. Their dau Grace
    Agnes m June 15, 1921, William Barron Rawson of Cleveland, descendant
    of Edward Rawson, first secretary of Mass Bay colony. To her patient
    fondness for genealogical research is due an enormous contribution to this
    Book
d   Martha Caroline b Dec 31, 1826; d Wis Aug 1874; m July 4, 1844, David
    Bailey
e   James Harvey b May 10, 1829; d Dec 4, 1888; m Aug 1854 Francis M Thomas
g   Adaline Elsie b Aug 10, 1832; d East Aurora Dec 11, 1911; m Sept 27, 1855,
    Thomas Williams

Martha Dow ahbcae m Isaac Williams b Jan 9, 1775, d Arcade, N Y, Oct 30, 1849. She d Nov 9, 1829. Children:

a Isaac H b 1798; d Dec 24, 1838; m Sarah Miller
b Albert m Melinda Hackett
c Mary b Mch 22, 1809; d Arcade Sept 22, 187—; m Rev Nelson A Jackson

Benjamin Dow ahbcaj served as private under capts Chiff and Stevens, 40th N Y militia, in war of 1812; m Nov 10, 1816, Lydia Lawrence King b Rutland, Vt, Oct 4, 1798, d Oct 4, 1869; moved to Yorkshire, N Y, thence in old age to Pacific, Wis, where he d Apr 1865. Children:

a Mary Barker b Feb 12, 1820   b Lafayette F b July 20, 1824
c Richard b Oct 10, 1826   d Thomas Wellington b May 19, 1829
e Isaac Newton b June 8, 1832   f ——, dau b and d Mch 8, 1834
g Benjamin b July 2, 1835   h Lorenzo H b Oct 19, 1838
i Lydia A b Yorkshire May 21, 1841
j William P b Dec 23, 1843; enlisted 1861 10th Wis vols; d in service Aug 26, 1865

Mary B Dow ahbcaja d old age; taught school with much success N Y State; m 1848 Everett Bump; became pioneers near what is now Grinnell, Iowa. Children:

a Henrietta Lydia   b Melissa   c Everett Hale
d Thomas Barker of Grinnell   e Shepard Charles
f Mary   g Charles Sumner

Lafayette F Dow ahbcajb d Wyocena, Wis, June 3, 1901, on visit to a dau; m 1849 Louisa Lydia Calkins; became pioneers of Pacific, Wis. Moving to Dakota, he was member of the Legislature and delegate to the So Dak Constitutional Convention. About 1891 moved to Iowa to be near sons, all of whom survived him and are said to have had families. Children:

a Ozilous J   b Owen C
c Eva Alferetta b Pacific; m M Warren Spear; m 2nd —— Hill of Wyocena; again wid; member of D A R
d Charles B   e Mary   f Martha   g Jessie A

Richard Dow ahbcajc d Beaver Dam, Wis, Apr 1863; m Sept 1853 Julia Moshin. Children:

a Lydia Julia b Apr 15, 1854; m —— Ward of Hurley, Dak
b Almedia H b Apr 2, 1856; m —— Welch of Hurley
c Lavinia Sennet b Nov 7, 1857; m —— Hurst of Sioux Falls
d Emma J b Nov 12, 1859
e Richard B b Aug 5, 1862; lived Washington; untraced

Thomas W Dow ahbcajd m 1854 Caroline Fish. Sept 16, 1864, he joined the 16th Wis vols to fill depleted ranks; arrived in time to share Sherman's march to the sea. His reg in reserve when Ft McAllister was taken, but had a fight at and were first to enter Savannah, staying there Christmas and New Year's. Thence by land and sea to Beaufort, in the heavy battle against Johnson at Saulkahatchee, then in long march to Orangeburg, charging the place. Arrived in time to see the burning of Columbia by unorganized veterans whose terms were up but who had not received discharges.   The next was Battle of Bentonville, the hardest they had, but Johnson's defeated army was pursued to Goldsborough, Raleigh (stopping to take the city), to Greensboro, where Johnson was forced to surrender.

This was the end; the regiment reached Richmond and Washington in time to take part in the grand review.   Thomas arrived home in time for the July 4 celebration.   Children:

a   Elvira b Oct 25, 1856   b   Nathan W b De Smet, Dak Apr 25, 1859
c   Bertha C b Mch 17, 1863   d   Chloe T b Feb 24, 1865
e   Edna W b Feb 17, 1876

Elvira Dow ahbcajda m Apr 29, 1879, Ain Bump; now of Gervais, Ore.   Children:

a   Celia E b Apr 7, 1880   b   Charlestown A b Aug 10, 1882
c   Ruth E b May 31, 1888   d   Thomas Wellington Dow b Feb 5, 1890
e   Bertha b Sept 20, 1892

Bertha C Dow ahbcajdc d Nov 1911; m Dec 25, 1881, Thomas Dunn.   Children:

a   Carrie A b Oct 21, 1882
b   Harvey T b Mch 8, 1884; well known illustrator and cartoonist, of Tenafly, N J
c   Roy J b Apr 9, 1885

Chloe T Dow ahbcajdd m Feb 28, 1883, Charleston S G Fuller. Children:

a   Robert C b Sept 30, 1884   b   Claude E b Feb 8, 1886
c   Charleston E b Nov 1, 1892   d   Jack b Mch 5, 1895

Isaac N Dow ahbcaje d La Harpe, Kan, Apr 20, 1899; m 1858 Phebe Daggett.   A pioneer of Columbia Co, Wis, 1849; moved to Grinnell, Iowa, 1860; enlisted at first call in 4th Iowa Cav; served throughout the war.   Wife and four or five children survived:

a Mary   b Frances   c ——   d Loraine   e Beulah

Benjamin Dow ahbcajg was living Kan 1904; excused from war service for disability; m Dec 29, 1856, Sabrina Howard.   Children:

a   Olive Lissett b Feb 22, 1857   b   Lorenzo Truman b Aug 16, 1859
c   William B b Sept 15, 1861   d   Lydia Mary b Nov 15, 1867
e   George Price b Aug 25, 1869   f   Frank Edwin b Nov 4, 1871
g   Carrie Ethel b Aug 30, 1873; d Oct 1876
h   Lewis Hale b June 17, 1876; d Oct 13, 187—
i   Leonard b Mch 1, 1879   j   Pearl

Lorenzo H Dow ahbcajh, veteran of 10th Wis vols, m Apr 7, 1859, Caroline Thurston; directory about 1915 gives her wid of Beloit, Wis; no children.

Lydia A Dow ahbcaji d Portage City, Wis, 1904; m 1st Wyocena, Wis, Jan 1, 1859, Zebria J D Swift b Delhi, N Y, Jan 1, 1833, d Portage, Dec 6, 1886.   Disabled from service, he was foreman of military carpenters at Jacksonville, Tenn. She m 2nd, Portage Sept 30, 1893, Arthur C Flanders. A woman of much sweetness of character, she was for many years State Regent of the D A R. She searched long for members of the ahbcaj line, which had become almost hopelessly scattered. Her discoveries were just before her death made known to Mrs Rawson and thus became the basis of the present narrative in this Book. Children, by 1st husband:

    a Edwin Joseph b Jan 1, 1860; m Sept 27, 1888, Della A Brown; 3 children; of Portage. In 1922 he sent on every scrap of genealogical material left by his mother, including a Revolutionary song since printed in the Sons of the Revolution archives

    b Charles Richard b Dec 21, 1863; m 1886 Maud Alexander; now of Seattle, Wash; 7 children

    c Edith Gertrude b Oct 15, 1869; d Jan 1, 1886

Elizabeth Dow ahbcb m Abner Whitcher. A son:

    c Isaac b Methuen Oct 7, 1770; came to Danville, Vt, 1791; in 1799 physician of Stanstead, P Q

Ela Dow ahbcf appears in rec Eli and Ely; m Mch 3, 1780, Abigail Hoyt b Jan 16, 1761. He was private at Great Island Nov 5, 1775, Capt Robert Crawford, and re-enlisted. Was selectman of Sandown 1786. Census of 1790 gives him 2a, 1b, 3c. The 2nd adult might be father-in-law. Presumably he had 1 son, 2 dau. No rec. An Ela Dow, probably the son, had a dau b Bristol, Vt, July 1, 1821. Abigail Hoyt, dau of Jabez and Abigail (Hazeltine) m 2nd Apr 23, 1823, Eliphalet Worthen b Hampstead, d Sanbornton Jan 10, 1846. Abigail d Hampstead July 11, 1829.

Jesse Dow ahbch, blacksmith of Methuen, enlisted June 6, 1775, Capt John Ford, Col Ebenezer Bridge, serving 3 mos, 10 days; re-enlisted Sept 25, height 5 feet, 10; m Mch 12, 1778, Phebe Palmer. May have lived a short time in Warren, N H, but was of Fishersfield by 1790, where census shows him 1a, 4b, 2c. It is thought that his male line is now extinct. New London has a rec that he d June 20, 1820, but it is error. He and wife went finally to Orange, N H, where he d May 6, 1841; she Oct 19, 1845. Rec of children appear for the most part both in Sandown and New London (equals Fishersfield):

    a Samuel b Aug 4, 1779; untraced after 1790, but surely no posterity in 1887

    b Betty (New London gives Bety b July 14, 1781; Sandown Battey b July 14, 1782; surely the Betsey m Feb 8, 1808, Edward Ide, both of New London

    c Evans b 1786 (m rec gives at Warren)

    d Jesse b New London Oct 20, 1788

    e Phoebe b June 6, 1791

    f Achsah b Dec 13, 1793; m New London Dec 30, 1819, Micajah Fowler of Sutton

    g Asa (no date in rec) probably before 1790

    h Nabe (Nabby) b Apr 23, 1796; m (Abigail) New London Dec 17, 1828, Thomas Cole Jr of Orange. Her parents d at her house

    i Amanda b Sept 21, 1798. Identical with Alvira or there was another child: Alvira Dow of New London m Mch 18, 1832, Daniel B Cole of Orange

Evans Dow ahbchc, blacksmith, m June 27, 1811, Lydia Morgan, both of New London; both living 1850. Two children:

a Lydia b Dec 4, 1811   b John M b Feb 18, 1819

John M Dow ahbchcb, farmer and blacksmith of New London, wrote in 1889 that his only son was last male descendant of Jesse ahbch. He m New London Dec 22, 1842, Lydia B Young b New London, d New London Dec 29, 1892, ae 69, 9 mos, dau of Aaron and Abigail (March). Children:

a Frank O b Feb 23, 1845; at home 1889; m Aug 14, 1866, M E Huntoon; d
   without children
b and c State rec give two sons,—b Sept 22, 1851 and Nov 4, 1853, calling them 4th
   and 5th children; either error or they d young

Jesse Dow ahbchd of New London appears so far only in rec of dau:

a Phylana b New London Mch 6, 1820

Philena Dow ahbchda m Dec 12, 1843, Joshua D Hemphill, son of James and Ruth (Hawthorne) of Grantham. Children:

a Sarah J b Dec 22, 1844; m F B Camp of Newport
b Irene W b June 12, 1846   c Aurora b Oct 28, 1850; m G W Dunbar

Asa Dow ahbchg (spoken of as Ela by his cousin), blacksmith of Springfield, m New London June 5, 1818, Annie Little of Sutton. Children:

a William Little b June 8, 1818; evidently d without issue
b Harriett Newell b Sept 29, 1820

---

ahbcx. Sandown, N H, was always a small place and no Dow family known there except ahbc. A few facts that fit ill together are put here.

Some **Charles Dow** enlisted 1749 for Canada, 7th Mass, Capt John Prescott. This reg recruited largely from N H. With him was Benjamin Dow (barely possible ahba?).

Some Charles Dow had wife Sarah and a dau:

a Rebeckah b Sandown Oct 24, 1739. Now, Sandown was not then organized,
   the name did not exist

Sandown 1790 census gives a Sarah Dow 1b, 2c, perhaps wid with young son and dau.

Neither fits an item of **Charlier Dow** of Sandown, wife Sarah, had:

a Mary b Sandown June 5, 1792

We guess the date of Rebecca should be 50 years later, but nothing would fit even then. We cannot suppose that there was an overlooked son of ahbc; useless to guess a posterity of Moses Dow ahbb

A NDOVER rec fail to show any children to Elizabeth (Moody) Dow by her 2nd m.

Ebenezer Dow ahbg lived with his stepfather until he enlisted at 15, and thereafter made his home in Andover until, in old age, he joined a son in Concord, N H. He m June 12, 1760, Elizabeth Wilson, wid of John Danforth of Andover. She had 2 children,—Elizabeth b 1755 and Hannah b 1757. Ebenezer was away fighting as much as he could be, and probably his wife was often put to it to care for her total of 11 children. A dau-in-law compiled many years later some account of the family and speaks rather vaguely of a 2nd m. Ebenezer d Concord Nov 1817 and his wife Elizabeth June 27, 1824. So, if a 2nd wife, her name was also Elizabeth. Hist Concord, Boughten's, gives quite a sketch of Ebenezer but knew little about his married life and went wrong on his children, putting in Timothy Dow, who is bcbebb. All the children were b Andover. In 1918 the Author received from Chas Asher Dow a ms of Phoebe Wells Dow ahbgi tracing Ebenezer's posterity as best she could, with additional notes by her son Isaac Wilson Dow to 1820. This ms, faded almost to illegibility, does not give the children in right order,— John, Edmund, Sally, Eb, Moody, Joseph, Isaac, Jacob. From this, Andover and Concord, we collate a list:

a Ebenezer b Feb 21, 1761 (Andover and Concord agreeing)
b John b Jan 27, 1763. Hist Concord says d young; Andover says a son d in army 1776. This is complete error
c Sarah b Feb 19, 1765
d Moody b (Hist Concord), or bap (Andover) Sept 28, 1766
e Joseph b or bap (rec differing as before) June 19, 1768
f Edmund bap June 24, 1770. Not mentioned in Concord
g Rhoda b Apr 30, 1772; both agreeing
h Isaac b Sept 12, 1773. Not found in Andover rec
i Jacob b Apr 5, 1775; bap Apr 14, 1776

Hist Concord gives very imperfectly two more generations, then ends abruptly. In 1917 the Author caused to be published on the front page of the Patriot, Concord's leading newspaper, a recital of Ebenezer Dow's career, with fresh incidents and proofs, requesting data of his descendants, promising in return the full ancestry of the Concord Dows to 1544. Not one reply was ever received.

For many years Ebenezer lived with his son Moody in west parish. He had his pension and was thoroughly comfortable. Thus he was able to sit by his doorway, shoulder his crutches and tell many tales how battles were won. There were grandchildren aplenty to listen, lots of other children and not a few grown-ups. Some of the latter thought from time to time that Ebenezer's stories grew bolder and a little exaggerated as time went on and with endless repetitions. Maybe, maybe; but the official records always bear him out. If his tales were collected they would make a good history of two wars. He told of being a ranger and scout at 16. Newbury rec back him up, showing he enlisted 1755 under Capt James Smith. At 17 he was serving as a ranger in the French war. In old age his hands were curiously disfigured, one mass of scar tissue with almost no nails. This, he explained, dated back to the French war about 1759. He had gotten information of an Indian camp in the forest about 3 days journey distant and guided a company to take it by surprise. Lamentably, they counted on re-provisioning by capture from the Indians. On arrival they found that the foe had suddenly decamped, doubtless warned, the only eatable left being a freshly killed deer hide found hanging on a tent. This they boiled for soup after cutting it into equal strips. On this they started back but the privations were such that only four survived. While crossing a lake, Ebenezer's show shoe became untied; taking off his mittens to fix it, they blew away and he made 20 miles bare handed. At the first house encountered, he found a goodwife boiling a pot of bean porridge. Frantic with frost bite and pain, he thrust both hands into the boiling mess. He was present at the capture of Ticonderoga, the battles of Crown Point and Ft William Henry; at the capture of Louisburg and next year at Quebec. At Quebec, he said, the fighting was the worst, hand to hand with knives. At the massacre of Ft William Henry he heard "the groans of the dying,— praying and cursing,—and yells of savages, all mixed together." He was in the service in 1760, apparently quitting at the time of his marriage.

Of course, he was too much of a war horse to stay at home in 1775. He left a newborn baby to be at Lexington and there he saw the dead patriots laid out. He was a minute man at Concord when the redcoats came to destroy the stores there. Again, he was at Bunker Hill, saw the whites of the British eyes and joined in the volleys, one, two, three, but this was easy, he remarked, nothing like the fighting of earlier days. He appears as sgt on the payroll for Lexington, 1 1-2 days, Capt Samuel Johnson, Col Wigglesworth. He next volunteered in the ill-fated expedition against Canada, headed by Benedict Arnold, suffering almost incredibly from cold, hunger and fatigue. At Quebec he was taken prisoner but was among those exchanged. So, he promptly re-enlisted and was present at the battles of Bennington and Saratoga. There are four rec in Rev rolls not clearly to be distinguished between adadh and ahbg. One or the other receipted Sept 12, 1777, for £6-13-3 in Col Gilman's reg. He was probably the sgt Ebenezer paid for 3 mos, 27 days Saratoga expedition Sept 1777, Capt Porter Kimball, Col Stephen Evans.

Ebenezer Dow ahbga appears but little outside the meager Concord rec. His 1st wife, Elizabeth (Wilson?) d Concord June 27, 1804; m 2nd July 21, 1805, Susannah Bailey of Concord bap Mch 22, 1763, dau of John and Susanna (Tenney). Children:

   a Molly (Mary) b Oct 5, 1806   b Ebenezer b Aug 23, 1810

Mary Dow ahbgaa. Hist Francestown does a little guessing, calling her dau of Ebenezer b Meriden, Conn, by 2nd wife Susannah Bailey. This is ahcf b Voluntown, Conn. Mary d May 15, 1892; m Dec 1, 1830, Charles Fred Bailey of Francestown, son of Phineas and Esther (Cluff) of Salem, Mass. Children, all b Dunbarton:

a   Elizabeth Ryder b July 30, 1833; m Nov 3, 1853, Ira C Brown of Dunbarton
b   True Morse b May 4, 1836; d Manitowac, Wis, Dec 26, 1860
c   Amos Cluff b Aug 3, 1838; corporal in 14th N H, wounded Cedar Creek; never fully recovered; d May 11, 1892
d   Susan Esther b Sept 2, 1840; m Dec 1865 William Hasilton of Dunbarton
e   Charles Fred b Aug 5, 1843; unm
f   Edward Buxton b Nov 21, 1845; lived Loudon
g   Myry Dane (twin) m Dec 14, 1893, Edward F Roper of Francestown

Ebenezer Dow ahbgab. Altho 1850 census gives Eben Dow b 1802, of Dunbarton, assessed at $200, the identity is highly probable. Census gives wife Rhoda, borne out by Dunbarton rec: Rhoda J (Kelly) Dow d Jan 30, 1888, ae 72, dau of Richard and Eunice (Kelly). A dau of Eben is found:

a   Florence Augusta b Dunbarton Apr 17, 1861; m Feb 25, 1893, Strowbridge Flanders of Dunbarton

John Dow ahbgb enlisted Gilmanton, ae 16, Capt Worthen, Col Mooney. One presumes he traveled to Gilmanton on account of some especial bounty offered by that martial town. The practice of going to enlist where bounties were attractive was rather general. A favorite tale in later years was his experience in riding Gen Benedict Arnold's horse. John certainly never lived in Concord, hence unknown to Hist Concord. After the war he went to Portland, Me, where he failed as a manufacturer. He then moved to Durham and taught school to save money for a fresh start. He opened a potash factory in Durham and succeeded. He was recalled by a grandniece as a tall, spare man with dark complexion and thin face. He was a genuine Dow, for one of his many habits was to hold lengthy conversations with himself, avoiding any talk whatever with others. When a neighbor asked why he did it, he replied that he liked to talk occasionally with a sensible man and this was the only way he could do it. He m Mch 1, 1791, Betsey Strout b Durham Feb 6, 1775, d Wilton 1847 (or Avon 1851, both in rec), dau of Capt Joshua and Betsey (Cobb). All John's posterity have at least 3 Revolutionary ancestors. In rec of 9th child her name is given, in error, Betsey Dingley. List of children from ms of Phoebe Wells Dow ahbgi:

a   Edmund b Mch 28, 1793; 7 sons, 3 dau
b   John b Apr 23, 1796; 5 children
c   Sally b Mch 24, 1798; m Moses Sanborn; 7 children
d   Betsey b May 24, 1800; d young
e   Socrates b July 16, 1802   f   Joshua b Aug 30, 1804
g   Mary b Mch 20, 1807; m Isaac Clark; 9 children
h   William b Oct 2, 1811; 7 children
i   Patience b May 10, 1814; living 1885
j   James; had 3 or 8 children (ms illegible). He was b June 26 1817

Edmund Dow ahbgba, pensioner of War of 1812, d Nov 25, 1879; bought a farm near his father's home; m Aug 20, 1820, Jane Robinson b Durham 1800, d 1856, dau of Samuel of Durham and Cape Elizabeth; 2nd 1856 Sarah Mace; 3rd 1864 Sarah Eames. Mrs Mellen Tryon has cleared up his whole line, left fragmentary by earlier Dow searchers. There remains in his family a farm bought by him in Brookline, Mass. Ten children:

  a   Betsey b Jan 7, 1821; d Wilton Aug 1, 1860; m Feb 24, 1848, Luther Ingalls; their children all d young
  b   Samuel R b Apr 26, 1823; d Sept 9, 1848; m 1846 probably no children
  c   John D b May 24, 1825   d   Charles Robinson b July 25, 1827
  e   Edmund b Sept 26, 1829   f   Mary Jane b Apr 6, 1832
  g   James Hilman b Apr 15. 1834   h   Joshua R b May 24, 1836
  i   Angelia M b Oct 26, 1839
  j   Lorenzo b Jan 20, 1844; d June 1, 1875, unm

John D Dow ahbgbac, carpenter of Lowell, Mass, wrote briefly genealogically in 1881 to Edgar R Dow; he d Lowell Dec 9, 1902; m July 14, 1850, Hannah Elizabeth Anderson b Fryeburg Sept 22, 1826. Children:

  a   Frank Bacon b Billerica June 21, 1851
  b   Lydia Jane b Lowell Feb 21, 1854

Frank B Dow ahbgbaca d Aug 14, 1916; m and left two children:

  a   Oscar Caswell b Oct 6, 1888
  b   John Anderson b May 12, 1891; both untraced. Oscar C appears in recent Lowell directory

Lydia J Dow ahbgbacb m Oct 11, 1886, Paul T Connell of Lowell. Child:

  a   Elizabeth Rebecca b Mch 30, 1892

Charles R Dow ahbgbad, farmer of Brookline, Mass, m Mch 30, 1852 Lucy Ellen Skillings b No Yarmouth, Me, Oct 5, 1832; both living Brookline, 1889. He d Mch 10, 1911. Eight children:

  a   Mary Jane b Jan 1853; d Sept 1887, unm
  b   Frank Albertine b Sept 13, 1855; unm   c   Nellie b 1857; d in infancy
  d   Charles Herbert b Nov 10, 1859; d Dec 5, 1920
  e   Edmund Scott b Yarmouth Sept 14, 1861
  f   and g   Abraham Lincoln and Hannibal Hamlin b 1863; d in infancy
  h   Grace Eaton b Oct 6, 1873; unm of Brookline 1923, a brilliant concert pianist

Charles H Dow ahbgbadd m Cora Shailer of Brookline. Two children:

  a   Margaret b Nov 10, 1890; m Samuel Breck of Brookline; 2 children
  b   H Shailer; in 1923 of N Y City

Edmund S Dow ahbgbade, physician of Allston Sta, Boston, m Nov 27, 1898, Mary Ellen Griggs b Brookline May 5, 1866, d 1895; 2nd Apr 24, 1905, Gertrude Mae Coburn. His land in Brookline was bought in 1820 by Edmund Dow ahbgba. Children:

  a   William G b Dec 6, 1891   b   Edmund Charles b Boston Dec 23, 1895
  c   Barbara Elizabeth b Sept 6, 1915

William G Dow ahbgbadea enlisted in the navy at the beginning of the War, in active service conducting transports; retained after the war; commissioned Lieut; in 1923 stationed in Honolulu; m Vera M Purdy of Newton. One child:

a ——son b Feb 1916

Edmund C Dow ahbgbadeb, grad Harvard Dental School; enlisted and commissioned 1st Lieut. Now practicing dentistry in Boston; living Brookline; m Hope Bryant; is Dept Commander of Boy Scouts. One child:

a Bryant Scott

Edmund Dow ahbgbae m Wilton Nov 13, 1857, Amanda Robinson; d Concord Jc Feb 1916; was veteran of Civil War; in 1889 living Carlisle, Mass. Five children:

a Cora Ellen m George Smith   b Elmer LeForest m Carrie Robbins
c Mabel Elizabeth m George Conant   d Charles Edmund
e Grace Maud m Charles Hunter

Charles Edmund Dow ahbgbaed m Acton, Mass (ae 37) Sept 22, 1909, Anna Augusta Davis, ae 45, dau of Alvin A and Mary T (Wetherbee).

Mary J Dow ahbgbaf m Scott Howe of Wilton. Children:

a George Delma b Aug 16, 1852; d Dec 27, 1917
b Charles Lee b Oct 1, 1865

James H Dow ahbgbag, veteran of Civil War, d Mch 18, 1869; m Anson, Me, Nov 5, 1866. Only child:

a Lizzie b Mch 20, 1868; grew up and m

Joshua R Dow ahbgbah, veteran of Civil War, served 6 mos 16th Me inf; wounded at Fredericksburg, d June 28, 1873; m Wilton Feb 24, 1868, Eldora R Cheney. Two children:

a Lizzie d Apr 26, 1872, ae 7 mos   b Nellie Emma d Dec 18, 1891, ae 22

Angelia M Dow ahbgbai d Jan 25, 1890; m Wilton Nov 29, 1866, Mellen Tryon of No Yarmouth, son of Andrew Jackson b Pownal and Lucinda N (Corliss) b No Yarmouth; one dau.

John Dow ahbgbb, lifelong resident of Avon, m wid Mary Love (Salley) Smith of Avon. He d Nov 19, 1864. Five children:

a Elizabeth, generally called Betsey, b Dec 20, 1825
b Anne m James Worthley; 1 child,—James Jr
c Caroline m —— Langley; only child,—Jessie
d Jane m —— Orbeton; children,—Frank, Joseph, Jane
e William Salley b before 1832

Elizabeth Dow ahbgbba d July 1, 1898; m about 1845 William R Billington. Children:

a Orlando Bradford b 1846; d young
b Zachary Taylor b 1848; d young

c Enoch Melvin b Nov 16, 1850; d Dec 29, 1907
d Mary Love b Apr 27, 1852; d Mch 9, 1911; m George R James
e Ida Anna b May 8, 1854; m 1869 George W Ranger of East Wilton; 2nd Dec 1881 Wesley A Heal; she d Feb 11, 1915. A dau Alice May Heal.m and lives Fla
f John Franklin b Apr 29, 1856   g Charles b Aug 1858, d ae 8 mos
h Caroline Dow b Nov 4, 1862; m June 18, 1894, John Calvin Norcross; 7 children
i Alice Lena b Nov 20, 1864; m June 15, 1892, Arthur S Atwood of Haverhill, Mass; 2 children

William S Dow ahbgbbe, of Avon, apparently living 1911, appears in m rec as William; m Permelia Sanborn b Avon, d Avon Jan 9, 1911, ae 78-5-9, dau of Moses and Sally (Dow) ahbgbc.   Children:

a George Lenville   b Elva; m —— Warren of Lynn, Mass
c Charles Moses   d Frank; unm

George L Dow ahbgbbea m Lenora (duplicate gives L Nora) Kennedy b Avon. One son found by own rec (there was also a dau):

a George Lenville b Phillips 1879

George L Dow ahbgbbeaa, master builder of Rangeley, m Portsmouth, N H, May 23, 1899. Portsmouth and Avon agree upon children, but differ hopelessly on wife. Portsmouth: Anna W Clark, ae 20, dau of Edward C and Ella M (Harrington). Avon: Anna Woodman Church b May 3, 1878, dau of Daniel Edward and Mary Ella (Brodie). Children:

a William Clark b Aug 4, 1899
b Margaret Lenora (Margaret Rebecca, Avon) b Dec 14, 1900

Charles M Dow ahbgbbec b Avon Feb 2, 1856; farmer of Avon; div, d May 7, 1911, further untraced.

C C Dow ahbgbjx seems of this family, but no proof; living 1900, m Caroline Ellsworth b Avon, d Avon Feb 4, 1900, dau of Levi and Lucy (McManus). No further rec. Three men in Maine found only by initials C C.

Socrates Dow ahbgbe, farmer of Foxcroft, d June 12, 1872, of strangulated hernia from a fall from an apple tree; m Apr 17, 1830, Julia Ann Dingley b July 16, 1807, d Auburn Oct 13, 1893, dau of Jeremiah and Lucy (Garcelon). Census 1850 calls her Betsey, farmers of Parkman, realty assessed $900. Children, list by their mother:

a Jeremiah Dingley b June 25, 1832; d Apr 2, 1897, unm
b John b Auburn Nov 13, 1833
c Lucy Dingley b Mch 24, 1838; d before 1887; unm
d Frances Ellen b Dec 15, 1842; d before 1887, unm
e Mary Leonora b Nov 14, 1851; worker in shoe factory, d Auburn Feb 20, 1907, unm

John Dow ahbgbeb served 14 mos from 1862 in 15th Me inf; in 1887 a shoemaker of Lynn; d Auburn, retired farmer, Mch 27, 1902; m Feb 12, 1865, Celia A Pillsbury of Sebec b June 28, 1841, dau of Joseph and Sarah A (Lowell); 2nd June 29, 1896, Adella C Elsmore, ae 54, div, dau of John and Abigail (Averill). She d June 12, 1900. Children, by his own letter:

a Nellie May b Nov 8, 1865   b Harry J b Mch 28, 1867
c Charlie Wilbur b Sebec Mch 8, 1871; d Nov 3, 1872
d Hattie Belle b Lynn June 11, 1881

Hattie B Dow ahbgbebd b Lynn m Fred M Cloon. Child:

a Cecil May b Lynn Nov 23, 1901

Joshua Dow ahbgbf, farmer of Avon, d May 6, 1883; m Nov 20, 1828, Eliza Haines b Avon Apr 27, 1810, d Phillips Dec 21, 1894, dau of Benjamin and Eliza (Ridlon) both b Limerick, Me. One son, 9 dau:

a Joshua b Avon Mch 9, 1830
b Jemima b May 21, 1832; m James Kinney, farmer of Madrid, Me
c Mary V b Jan 20, 1835; m W W Chaplin, carpenter of Lowell, Mass
d Fanny S b June 5, 1837; d Apr 30, 1859
e Sophronia H b July 28, 1840; living 1918; m Capt A Walton of Lowell
f Lucretia b Mch 12, 1843; m William Harnden, farmer of Phillips
g Tryphena b May 25, 1845; m Timothy Vining, farmer of Avon
h Diana b July 11, 1847; m George W Dickey, farmer of Avon; living 1918; did not answer letter of genealogical inquiry
i Ellen E b Dec 6, 1851; d Claremont, N H, 1919; m Hiram Ross of Lowell
j Clara E b Jan 12, 1855; d Mch 24, 1865

Joshua Dow ahbgbfa served 9 mos in 6th Mass vols; opened a restaurant in Lowell; d Lowell Mch 21, 1868; m Dec 31, 1850, Martha E Webster b Hooksett, N H, Mch 27, 1831, m 2nd Calvin Wyman of East Chelmsford, Mass. Two sons:

a Lenoir A b Lowell Nov 28, 1852
b Fernando A b about 1860; perhaps Avon

Lenoir A Dow ahbgbfaa, machinist with Waltham Watch Co, m Lowell Oct 28, 1875, Flora A Farrar b Bad Axe, Wis. Children:

a Euletta Flora b Boston Aug 21, 1878
b William Bryce b Boston May 9, 1880
c Carrie Farrar b Leominster May 9, 1882

Electa Flora Dow ahbgbfaaa (sic in m rec) m Newton June 12, 1901, Willard Elliott Higgins, ae 27, son of Willard S and H Maria (James).

William Bryce Dow ahbgbfaab m Waltham, Mass, Dec 4, 1907, Harriet E Wildman, ae 26, dau of Frank C and Ella (Miskell). Child:

a Eleanor Milborough b Waltham, d Boston May 11, 1909

Carrie F Dow ahbgbfaac m Waltham Nov 4, 1903, Charles Herbert David, ae 24, son of Charles A and Emma W (Larrabee).

Fernando A Dow ahbgbfab, farmer of Strong, m Mary Ella Grover b Avon; div; 2nd May 17, 1902, Ella M Fairbanks, ae 24, dau of Charles and —— (Harvey). Two children found:

a Merla d Avon Aug 27, 1895, ae 12, 5 mos
b Lewis (also Louis) E b Avon 1889

Lewis E Dow ahbgbfabb, mail carrier of Skowhegan, m Nov 4, 1903, Alice M Dutton, ae 21, dau of John W and Julia A (Towles). Children:

a Wayne Burchard b Feb 8, 1913   b ── dau b Jan 2, 1915

Mrs Eliza (Haines) Dow wrote in 1887 that three brothers, John, Rev veteran, Edmund and Moody, came from Concord, N H, and settled in Me; that Moody was a physician of Bowdoinham, that he had a son David. This is by all means too circumstantial to be dismissed. Unfortunately, the career of Moody Dow ahbgd is well known throughout. Also, every son of ahbg is accounted for, unless we have erred about Ebenezer ahbga.

Can Eliza H Dow be wholly mistaken about her own uncle? Let us consider the family here.

The earliest known Dow of Bowdoinham is David b probably by 1800. David Dow ahbgbx b Bowdoinham, shipbuilder of Bath m Nancy Cassidy b Bath. Children, by own rec:

a Reuben b Bowdoinham 1825   b David b 1829 (d rec says at Bath)
c Abby C d Lisbon Mch 2, 1880; m Nov 1860 James Horace Woodard d Soldiers' Home

Bowdoin 1850 census had **Eleanor C Dow** b Me 1782, apparently wid with dau Mary b 1821. This probably has no connection.

Bath 1850 census has a David Dow b Me 1806, carpenter; realty $300; wife Sarah b Me 1824. Barely possible this is identical with 2nd wife. Six children by census, untraced:

d Peter b 1841   e Abba b 1843   f Sophia b 1845
g George b 1846   h William b 1848   i Frances b 1849

Reuben Dow ahbgbxa carpenter m Emeline Webber b Richmond, d Gardiner Nov 28, 1903, ae 74, dau of William and Jane (Jack). Reuben d Bowdoin, unattended by physician, Apr 12, 1912. 1st born proved, others guessed:

a Stephen H b Richmond 1851
b Eliza. An old directory gives Eliza b Richmond, possibly error for Emeline Webber
c William K b Richmond about 1860

Stephen H Dow ahbgbxaa carpenter of Gardiner, d Jan 26, 1894; m July 21, 1879, Carrie L Carter b Richmond. One child found:

a George Lee b Gardiner 1881

George L Dow ahbgbxaaa publisher of Augusta failed to reply to letter of genealogical inquiry; m Apr 25, 1916, Mary Ella Fortier, wid ae 40, dau of George and Rose (Poulin) Butler of Waterville. No children. By 1st husband she had son Bernard in aviation 1918.

William K Dow ahbgbxac shoeworker of Keene, N H. m Fannie J Sibley b Richmond. A child:

a William K b Keene Apr 21, 1887; untraced

David Dow ahbgxb, joiner of Bath, d July 27, 1897; m Hannah J Moss b New Sharon 1828, d Bowdoin June 10, 1901, dau of Moses and Nancy (Dow) (unplaced). In son's rec she is Morse of Old Town, probably correct. There is a strong suggestion of bcdgd line. Child:

    a Sylvester E, painter, m, d Portland Sept 3, 1902, ae 36-7-25; otherwise unt.

John F Dow of Bath m Dec 8, 1874, Ellen R Lincoln of Bowdoin; untraced, perhaps not of same family.

William Dow ahbgbh was in 1850 farmer of Vienna assessed $500; wife Sally b Me 1817. Census gives 4 children. 3 b later:

    a Deborah b 1844   b Rosanna b 1845   c Sarah b 1848
    d Francis b Feb 1850, untraced

Patience Dow ahbgbi d Dec 4, 1892; m Oct 31, 1833, John Darling Towle b Aug 25, 1809, d Mch 17, 1894, son of Jonathan and Polly (Darling) of Avon; moved 1851 to Wis; 1861 to Pleasant Grove, Minn Children:

    a Joseph b Oct 4, 1834; d Jan 24, 1852
    b Arthur C b Jan 4, d Feb 14, 1836   c Mary b Oct 21, 1838
    d Martha Melissa b Nov 3, 1839-40
    e John Nelson b Aug 28, 1843; d May 13, 1863
    f Martin Richardson b May 28, 1848
    g Eva Lewella b Wis Sept 24, 1858

Sally Dow ahbgc m Sept 17, 1786 (family rec, Warner gives Nov 9), Nathaniel Merrill of Hopkinton. Children:

    a Hannah   b Nathaniel   c Ebenezer   d Sally   e Nancy
    f Roxa   g Betsey   h Manly V   i Raleigh   j Phebe

Moody Dow ahbgd d Canterbury Sept 25, 1838. His father lived with him for many years in West Concord. He m Oct 18, 1794 (Jan 1, 1795 also in rec), Margaret White of Bow b Oct 1, 1766, d Jan 1802; 2nd, June 25, 1802, Johanna Hoyt (Anna Hoit, Hoyt Gen) b Oct 3, 1770, dau of Oliver and Rebecca. Feb 24, 1830, he left his home in Concord and joined the Shakers of Canterbury. He did not desert his family in the usual sense of the word. He invited them to come with him; his piety and well meaning are not doubted; his fairness and wisdom wholly questionable. Shakers had a community of property and it is not easy to see how a divided family should be financed. Happily, the children were by this time self-supporting:

    a Betsey b Dec 7, 1795; m Mch 20, 1823, Jedediah Hoit, Jr
    b Clarissa b Mch 26, 1797   c Isaac White b Aug 4, 1801
    d Ira b Feb 16, 1803; d Concord 1830. A family account says some other Ira
        d 1830. Our Ira moved to Walden, Vt. See supplement.
    e Peggy b Mch 24, 1804   f Enoch Hoit b Feb 19, 1805
    g Moody b June 11, 1808   h Rebecca b May 10, 1810
    i Rhoda b May 12, 1811   j Ezra b Aug 14, 1813; untraced

Isaac W Dow ahbgdc m Lucy A Stevens; located Springfield,

Mass; returned about 1840 to Manchester; m 2nd Dec 3, 1843, Climena Maloon, both of Manchester. Children:

a   Albert W b Springfield about 1835
b   Abby M m July 22, 1865, Edward P Farnum, both of Concord
c   Climena A (dau of Isaac) of Fishersville m Nov 4, 1869, Henry F Pearson of Concord

Albert W Dow ahbgdca, killed in battle of the Wilderness, m Jan 4, 1864, Sarah Augusta Hinds b Hubbardston, Mass, Jan 27, 1836, dau of Cornelius and Augusta (Witt). Posthumous child b Templeton, Mass:

a   Albertine Musa b Nov 13, 1864

Enoch Hoit Dow ahbgdf d Feb 22, 1853; elected hog constable 1834, selectman of Concord 1837 and 1840, militia captain, prominent in civic affairs; discovered in 1833 the last wolf ever seen in Concord; tracked it for a week and shot it. He m Mch 30, 1837, Judith W Chandler b Boscawen 1807, d Webster May 9, 1887, dau of Nathan and Jane (Rolph). Children:

a   Nathan Moody b Nov 27, 1838; d Concord 1863 from disabilities received in 16th N H
b   Abiel Rolfe b Apr 14, 1842; d 1861 in Ill vol reg
c   Ellen Maria b Apr 22, 1844; m Sept 26, 1865, William Wirt Burbank of Webster
d   Luther b July 27, 1846; m July 9, 1873, Clarissa Alvina Lord of Newton, Mass; miller of Boston; at least 1 child,—Sarah Walker b Webster, Mch 13, 1878
e   Ezra Wilson b July 9, 1849; m Jan 4, 1874, Florence Barrett of Salina, Kan, b May 8, 1855, dau of Oliver P and Hannah M (Bassett) of Bennington, Vt. Untraced

Moody Dow ahbgdg seems to have lived some time in Me; in 1850 inn holder of Lynn, Mass, assessed $400; m Jan 8, 1835, Clarissa Leach b Me 1808. Children:

a   Charles L b Mass 1836; untraced   b   Anna R b 1838
c   Clara b and d York, Me, Mch 9, 1838
d   Franklin Henry b Lynn Feb 5, 1846; d May 4, 1847
e   Emily Frances b Concord 1848

Emily F Dow ahbgdge m Nantucket June 1871 James C Hammond, veteran, son of William and Susan B (King). A child:

a   Sadie H b and d Jan 6, 1873

Joseph Dow ahbge d 1817. Hist Concord gives list of children without further mention. He m Dec 9, 1793, Hannah Farnum of Concord, d Jan 1817. Capt Joseph Farnum m Ruth Walker and had:—Betsey m Joseph Cleasby, son of Joseph; 15 children; Hannah m Joseph Dow; Hebzibah m Isaac Dow; Susan m Reuben Goodwin, son of Samuel; 5 children. Joseph's children:

a   Joseph Farnum b Dec 9, 1794   b   Ruth Walker b Sept 6, 1797
c   George Washington b Dec 31, 1799   d   Jacob b Sept 24, 1801
e   Thomas Jefferson   f   Hannah
g   Hepzibah m June 15, 1842, Asaph Abbot of Concord
h   Phoebe Wells b 1812; d Concord May 1, 1833, unm
i   Emeline A

Joseph F Dow ahbgea m Eliza Parsons and is then dismissed by Hist Concord. Was in Capt Fuller's company 1814; constable 1834; on a prohibition committee 1843. Census 1850 gives him builder of Concord, realty assessed $1,200; wife Sarah M b Vt 1795. This either contradicts Hist Concord or is a 2nd m. Children:

    a Amelia B b 1824; school teacher, unm
    b James C b 1831; teacher in Concord about 1853; untraced
    c Abby F (not in census) d Concord Dec 29, 1869, ae 27

George W Dow ahbgec m Mary E Judkins d wid Port Jervis, N Y, May 23, 1894, ae 75. Children:

    a Emily A b 1843; d 1850
    b George W b 1846 (West Concord); railroad conductor of Pt Jervis, m June 5, 1873, Rosa E Jones, ae 25, b Merrimack, dau of Davis and Rosanna (Tewksbury)

Jacob Dow ahbged m Sarah T Judkins d wid Concord Sept 2, 1892, ae 75, 1 day. They seem to have moved to Franklin. At least 1 child:

    a Edwin H b West Concord 1844; m Franklin Apr 8, 1865, Abbie A Cass of Bridgewater, ae 19

Thomas J Dow ahbgee m Rhoda —— b Hopkinton 1797; moved to Hopkinton. At least 1 child:

    a Martin V B b May 1, 1836; farmer of Hopkinton, d tuberculosis Dec 9, 1863, unm

Edmund Dow ahbgf probably came to Concord and left too early to be recalled by its historian. His d rec in 1834 gives ae 73. He studied medicine and practiced successfully in Litchfield, Me, for 45 years; m Eleanor Clark, dau of Samuel and Elizabeth (Baker). A deed gives Edward Dow of Concord sold land in Rumford, Me, to David Abbot, originally allotted to Ebenezer Eastman. All five are Concord names. Children:

    a Diadema b Apr 11, 1802; m Timothy Lydston
    b Clark b Feb 22, 1804; d Feb 16, 1822
    c Moody b Feb 13, 1806; d ae 9   d Isaac b Sept 22, 1808; d ae 5
    e Eleanor m James Alexander   f Robert b 1813; drowned in river, unm
    g Lucinda b 1815; m Nathaniel Alexander
    h Mary b Aug 10, 1821; m (his 2nd) Timothy Lydston   i Edmund b 1826

Eleanor Dow ahbgfe m James Alexander; went west. Children:

    a Nathaniel b Nov 28, 1844; lived Calif
    b Eugene C b Oct 7, 1846; lived Wis
    c Samuel b Nov 1, 1848; lived Wis
    d Hannah b Oct 21, 1850; lived Bowdoin, Me
    e Nancy E b May 22, 1852   f Elizabeth b Nov 1, 1854

Edmund Dow ahbgfi bought a farm in Litchfield; m Sarah Tarr; d Dec 17, 1902. Children:

    a Edmund F b June 1, 1855; lived Sou America
    b Frank G b Aug 23, 1858

Frank G Dow ahbgfib, farmer of Litchfield, moved to Richmond·

m Lettie A Stinson b 1864, d Apr 27, 1908, dau of Bradley V and Abigail (Odiorne). Children:

    a Ernest Stinson b Nov 3, 1896   b Wallace B b Apr 3, 1900
    c Henry C b Sept 15, 1903

Ernest S Dow ahbgfiba, farmer of Richmond, m Nov 11, 1920, Pearl Lillian Berry, ac 19, dau of Charles E and Ada (Bates) of Bowdoinham.

Isaac Dow ahbgh, often called Squire Dow, continued to live West Concord, tanner and currier. His portrait is in Hist Concord; selectman 1822-3, always prominent in town affairs. At 50 he joined the Congregational church; d Feb 17, 1851; m Sept 21, 1796, Hepzibah Farnum b 1777, d Feb 3, 1855. Children:

    a Isaac Wilson b Dec 26, 1797; d 1815
    b Susan b July 14, 1799; d May 14, 1852
    c Judith b June 7, 1801; d Dec 29, 1835
    d Ebenezer b May 4, 1803; d Dec 2, 1825
    e Lucinda b May 9, 1805; d Jan 5, 1828
    f Maria b Feb 27, 1808; d July 22, 1831
    g Albert Gallatin b Nov 12, 1809
    h Mary Ann b Oct 2, 1811; d June 16, 1873; m June 6, 1842, Ralph Wells b Sept 11, 1804, son of William and Prudence (May) of Deerfield, Mass
    i John Rogers b Sept 13, 1813; d Aug 7, 1892, unm
    j Benjamin Franklin b Nov 9, 1815
    k James Monroe b Sept 13, 1817; d Feb 2, 1840
    l Elizabeth Wilson b Oct 10, 1919; d Oct 5, 1851

Albert G Dow ahbghg moved to Ohio; m Mch 6, 1833, Mary Hamilton b Northampton, Mass, Apr 1, 1807, d McKeen, Ill, Nov 8, 1875. Children:

    a Isaac Wilson b Feb 9, 1834; d May 7, 1876. Untraced
    b Adah Salisbury b Jan 17, 1836   c Mary Ann b Feb 14, 1838
    d Maria Hepzebah b Feb 27, 1840
    e John Rogers b Aug 14, 1843, untraced
    f Albert Gallatin b July 15, 1845; untraced

For many additions to the ahbg line from here forward, consult the supplement

Benjamin F Dow ahbghj inherited the homestead; member Board of Engineers 1845; member of Legislature 1853; d June 25, 1871; m Dec 14, 1841, Martha Jane Hall of Northfield, N H, b Oct 28, 1818. Children:

    a Benjamin Franklin b Oct 3, d Oct 24, 1842
    b James Monroe, twin, d Oct 24, 1842
    c Maria Elizabeth b Jan 30, 1845; m May 19, 1870 (his 2nd), Charles Henry Bacon b Boscawen Nov 17, 1835, veteran of 12th Vt, son of Henry and Dorcas (Carter)
    d Helen Hall b Jan 5, 1847   e Ella Forest b Sept 30, 1850
    f Isaac Walker b Sept 1853; d Aug 27, 1854
    g Hattie A b Mch 4, 1857; m Mch 28, 1876, Hazen R Little of Concord

Jacob Dow ahbgi, Lieut in war of 1812, d Canaan, N H, May 4, 1831; m Sept 15, 1802, Phoebe Wells b Apr 5, 1782, d Feb 19, 1867, dau of Capt Ezekiel and Phoebe (Meacham) of Colchester, Conn. The Wells family were original settlers of Canaan (ahbaad family in same party). One branch of the Meacham family went west and became

prominent in the Mormon church.   Jacob's farm was in West Canaan.
but no Dow left there in 1918.   Children:

  a Phoebe b June 2, 1803; d May 29, 1893; m May 29, 1824, David March; lived
      Nashua; Children,—Jacob, George
  b Izyphena (Isevina, Syphena, Isyphoner, etc) b Oct 2, 1804, d Jan 6, 1892, unm
  c Rosetta b Apr 21, 1806; d Sept 4, 1807
  d Jacob Trussell b Jan 1, 1808
  e Elvira b Nov 3, 1809; d Sept 6, 1863; m Mch 31, 1832, Edward B Chapman;
      no children
  f Armena b July 12, 1811; d Aug 3, 1831
  g Sarah b Apr 10, 1813; d May 15, 1891; m Aug 4, 1837, Ivory Hall, jeweler of
      Concord; children,—Minnie, Jennie, Frank, William
  h Mary b Mch 10, 1815; d July 7, 1817
  i William Wallace (rec errs twice, giving William Wales b Jan 17, 1816)
  j Mary b June 24, 1818; d Dec 8, 1852, unm
  k Isaac Wilson b Mch 9, 1820   l   Joseph b Dec 2, 1822
  m Caleb Wells b Aug 28, 1824

Jacob T Dow ahbgid, farm assessed $1,000 in 1850; m Mch 5,
1835, Ann Frances Blaisdell b Dorchester 1816, d wid Canaan June 22,
1894, ae 77-5-22, dau of Jacob and Mary (Jewett).   Children:

  a Edwin B b July 6, 1836; d Mch 4, 1841
  b Sylvanus b Dec 3, 1837; 3 years in 12th Mass vols; house painter and farmer
      of West Canaan; m Sept 6, 1877, Emily J Whaley of Richford, Vt, dau of
      Ephraim and Sarah. His brother Everett W lived with them. Probably no
      children
  c Emma S b Feb 5, 1840; d June 25, 1863
  d Everett W b Mch 30, 1842; d Oct 13, 1900; in 15th vols, re-enlisted in heavy
      artillery; presumably unm

William W Dow ahbgii d Dec 9, 1880; m Apr 15, 1840, Sally
Metcalf b Apr 17, 1820, d Apr 17, 1855; lived Irasburg, Vt; m 2nd, June
10, 1857, Jerusha S Waterman.   Children:

  a Elvira Rosetta b Jan 27, 1841; d Mch 27, 1843
  b Jane Wilson b Sept 26, 1842; d Sept 1, 1858
  c Lydia Metcalf b May 1, 1845   d   Frank Wells b Apr 17, 1852, untraced
  e ——   f   Ira Benton b Nov 18, 1854
  g Mary Eunice b Mch 17, 1858
  h Arthur W b Feb 13, 1860; d Aug 23, 1910

Ira B Dow ahbgiif of Van Buren Co, Iowa, m Feb 14, 1877, Phoebe
Lillian Rice b Denmark, Iowa, July 27, 1855.   Children:

  a Jonas Edward b Jan 12, 1878   b   Harry Edward b Feb 11, 1882

Jonas E Dow ahbgiifa continues the farm near Ft Madison, Iowa;
m Jan 7, 1900, Mary Eva Wilder b May 5, 1881.   Children:

  a Hartwell Guy b Nov 9, 1900   b   Fannie Evaline b July 18, 1908

Harry E Dow ahbgiifb, supt of schools, Hamburg, Iowa, m Aug 15,
1906, Nellie G Judy.   Children:

  a Mildred Lillian b Sept 8, 1909   b   Margaret b Mch 24, 1915

Isaac W Dow ahbgik m May 15, 1843, Abigal J Farrington; 2nd
Nov 10, 1853, Nancy Jane Waterman of Coolville, Ohio; d Jan 27,
1892.   Children:

  a Phoebe Jane Wilson b Hockingport, Ohio, Nov 20, 1844

b   Carrol Wells b Feb 23, 1846; d Nov 28, 1873
c   Charles Asher b Van Buren Co, Iowa, Jan 25, 1855
d   Clara Augusta b Oct 22, 1856; d Sept 6, 1858
e   Nancy Waterman b Sept 17, 1858; d May 24, 1906

Charles A Dow ahbgikc has a drug store and other business in Pond Creek, Okla, keenly interested in his family genealogy; m Oct 27, 1880, Alice Howard, dau of John and Margaret.   Children:

a   Lulu Juanita b Nov 12, 1890; m Nov 10, 1910, William Gumerson; has,—
     William Dow b Oct 1, 1911
b   Howard Wilson b Oct 1, 1900

Joseph Dow ahbgil shared the adventuresome spirit of his ancestors; d at his son's home, No Dak 1902.   Ae 12 he went to sea; returning, m Dec 25, 1843, Lydia J Keach of Waterford.   After 1850 they sold out and joined the gold rush to Calif.   Some years later they came back and bought a farm in Waterford.   Census 1850 shows them there, farm assessed $3,000.   Lydia d East Barnet, at home of son, Jan 4, 1889, ae 69.   Children:

a   John K b Sept 8, 1844; enlisted for 9 mos; d of illness in service; his mother
     brought him home to Waterford cemetery, Passumpsic, Vt.   Unm.   Some
     unidentified John K Dow was a farmer of Fittsville 1885, prob not of ahbg
     line
b   Beverly S b Dec 21, 1845; farmer of East Barnet; no children
c   Edward B b Sept 10, 1847; living 1923 Bakersville, So Dak; no children
d   William A b Feb 1, 1850; left no children
e   Lilla J b Feb 5, 1852; d Jaylet, Ill, 1898; m —— Schultz; a dau Mabel B m
     Lawrence E Grover of Southern Pines, Nor Car; 3 children
f   Frank S b Jan 4, 1856; left no children
g   Dexter D b Aug 12, 1857; went to Calif.   His family did not hear from him
     for over 20 years; d without children
h   Minnie L b July 3, 1859   i   Jose K b May 28, 1861

Beverly S Dow ahbgilb, farmer of Waterford and East Barnet, m Lillie Newman.   She survives (1923) in Passumpsic, Vt.

William A Dow ahbgild d St Johnsbury, Vt, Nov 8, 1915; his wife d Jan 6, 1908.

Frank S Dow ahbgilf d Spokane, Wash, June 4, 1921; his wid lives (1923) Berkeley, Calif.

Minnie L Dow ahbgilh, living 1923, m Almon O Page of Kirby, Vt; 3 children; 2nd, John A Bacon, farmer of Danville, Vt.   Children:

a   Blanche D d 1918   b   Harrison B, m and has a dau
c   Asa H d 1909   d   Elsie M, unm at home   e   Olia M, unm
f   Alice M d 1908, ae 10   g   Beverly J, at home

Jose K Dow ahbgili d So Dak 1902, leaving wid and 3 children, now of Bakersfield:

a   Walter E   b   Loverna L   c   Carl J

Caleb W Dow ahbgim moved to Iowa in 1846; m Jan 3, 1855, Sarah Glendora Whitham d Iowa June 1, 1905. Children:

a —— dau b and d Nov 25, 1855   b Walter Talbott b Jan 3, 1858
c Ida Santha b Oct 21, 1862; d Aug 23, 1885
d Frank Bryant b Oct 4, 1872

Frank B Dow ahbgimd, stock raiser of Stockport, Iowa; m Jan 3, 1899, Nina Shelman. Children:

a Caleb Miles b Sept 3, 1901   b Dove Glendora b Oct 29, 1906

A MORE complete account of the so-called "Connecticut Dow" has been the work of many years of Joy Wheeler Dow ahgchhc. This account is as complete as our ability has permitted. The Connecticut Dow are our lines of ahc, ahd, and ahg.

Ebenezer Dow ahc arrived and took his lot, with 29 others, in the unorganized district known as Volunteers' Settlement in 1715. He proceeded at once to build himself a house and clear land for planting. This done, he bent his efforts toward organizing a town, getting a church, and entering the body politic. Being diplomatic, he readily abandoned his Ipswich Congregationalism, which his brothers refused to do, and was elected deacon and was all his life presiding elder. In 1721 he was the first selectman chosen, was tax collector for the church, and on committee to locate the burying ground. The church organized in 1723, Ebenezer being on the committee to call a pastor. He was town clerk for 40 years. He d Oct 2, 1775; m Dec 29, 1720, Martha Harris b Oct 27 (Nov 26, Plainfield rec), 1696, d Voluntown Feb 4, 1791, dau of Ebenezer and Rebecca (Clark). Children:

a   Hannah b Voluntown Oct 23, 1721; d Apr 19, 1741
b   Daniel b May 13, 1723   c   Nathan b Feb 4, 1725; d young
d   Mary b Dec 8, 1726   e   Rebecca b Feb 3, 1729
f   Ebenezer b Mch 17, 1731   g   Aaron b Mch 12, 1733
h   Benjamin b Nov 6, 1735   i   Nathan b Mch 1, 1738

Daniel Dow ahcb, farmer, settled in Ashford, Windham Co, the family home ever since; m July 4, 1751, Elizabeth Marsh of Ashford, who survived him many years. Children:

a   Cyrus b 1753   b   Abel b 1758   c   Hendrick b 1761
d   Elizabeth m Nov 12, 1786, David Bolles Jr, both of Ashford
e   Thomas b 1769   f   Daniel b Feb 19, 1772

It is doubtful whether there were sons Joseph and James, the latter leaving 2 sons. Both seem mistaken identities.

Cyrus Dow ahcba m Nabby Rogers. By reliable family rec, they had but 2 children. The 1790 census gives him 4a, 1b, 2c. This must be doubling up with some other family. They moved to Sherburn, N J, where a son was living 1885. Children:

a   Cyrus Marsh   b   Almira

Abel Dow ahcbb m Sept 30, 1784, Olive Rogers. Ashford 1790 census gives him 1a, 1b, 2c and repeats the entry, presumably an error by the original census taker. Children:

a   Sally m Joseph Austin; children,—Marsh and Sally
b   William, teacher in Ashford; d unm
c   Lois H m 1818 Samuel H Carpenter, farmer of Ashford, son of Comfort. He b 1788, d 1850
d   Laura b Ashford 1796

Lois H Dow ahcbbc and Samuel H Carpenter had:

a William Dow, merchant of Ashford
b George W became farmer of San Francisco

Laura Dow ahcbbd m (his 2nd) Amos Trowbridge b Oct 16, 1790, son of James; 2 children; m 2nd Asher Hicks of Ashford; she d Aug 27, 1875. Children:

a Laura b Mch 1, 1820; d Oct 8, 1839   b Amos b Nov 8, 1822
c (Hicks) Amos   d Henry   e Gilbert   f Helen
g Mary Jane   h Henry Laurens; all lived Ashford

Hendrick Dow ahcbc was fitted for college by his pastor, Rev Enoch Pond; grad Yale 1784; preached in Sunderland and Shelburne, Mass; declined a call to latter; supplied for two years in the Fair Haven church of New Haven; m New Haven Apr 4, 1792, by Rev James Dana, Hannah Gilbert b Feb 12, 1765, d Nov 27, 1850, dau of Dea James and Eunice (Nichols); abandoned the ministry; tutored in Yale; studied law under Hon David Dagget of New Haven; practiced in Ashford until he d Jan 4, 1814. Three sons:

a Virgil b Ashford; grad Yale; d, a physician, July 4, 1851
b James Gilbert b May 3, 1798; grad Yale 1820; d New Haven, while taking
     post graduate work, Mch 28, 1821, unm
c Lucius Kalapon b May 3, 1803

Lucius K Dow ahcbcc, publisher of New Haven Advertiser, abandoned that to enter a drug business; d Apr 21, 1858; m May 4, 1830, Julia Ann Townsend b Apr 28, 1808, d Apr 28, 1895. Children:

a Virgil Mare b Apr 4, 1833; crippled by an accident; for many years physician
     and druggist of New Haven, unm
b Julia b Mch 5, 1837; m Dec 7, 1857, Pinckney Webster Ellsworth, M D, whose
     1st wife Julia Sterling of Bridgeport d Mch 18, 1854

Thomas Dow ahcbe, agriculturist and justice of the peace, m Lydia Clark of Woodstock d Jan 4, 1814, ae 53. He always lived Ashford; d Nov 7, 1850. Children:

a Henry Laurens   b Catherine   c Joseph Clark b July 7, 1805
d Elizabeth   e Marietta   f Thomas Kalapon d Oct 14, 1846, unm

Henry L Dow ahcbea d Apr 9, 1864; m Mary Sumner. Children:

a Mary Ann   b Kate   c Sarah   d Harriet   e Maria

Catherine Dow ahcbeb d Jan 26, 1880; m Zelda Butler. Children:

a Marian   b Charles   c Herbert

Joseph Clark Dow ahcbec practiced medicine in Ellington, Conn; moved to Milwaukee; d Aug 21, 1857; m Sept 23, 1829, Julia Elizabeth Grant b Stafford, Conn. Children:

a Joseph Edgar b Stafford; d Jan 1831
b Joseph Edgar   c Isabella Grant b Aug 10, 18—

Isabella G Dow ahcbecc m Apr 3, 1861, Joseph Henderson Meredith

of N Y City, b Eng Dec 8, 1838, d N Y Mch 29, 1886.   He was brevet
Col of 13th Conn vols; later deputy collector of customs.

Elizabeth Dow ahcbed d Oct 3, 1845; m Joseph Butler.   Children:

a   Marian   b   Charles   c   Herbert

Marietta Dow ahcbee d Apr 23, 1872; m Smith Jencks C Bartlett
of Smithfield, R I.   Children:

a   Susan   b   Imogene   c   George
d   Ella Jencks m May 5, 1899, Frank Wilson Green; no children
e   Kate

Daniel Dow ahcbf, as well known for fifty years as a clergyman can
be, figures in a remarkable aggregate of baptisms, marriages and funerals
in Rhode Island, Mass and Conn; grad Yale 1793, supported himself for
two years by teaching psalmody while studying for the ministry under
Rev Elizur Goodrich of Durham and his own pastor, Rev Enoch Pond,
grad Brown 1777.   He became pastor Apr 20, 1796, of the Thompson
Congregational church; had already m (Aug 20, 1795) Hannah Bolles,
dau of Dea Jesse of Woodstock.   Salaries were small; he began at $300,
soon increased to $400.   There was a great increase in cost of living after
the 1812 war and this drove him into debt about $500.   He asked dis-
mission from his church that he might go to work, but instead they raised
his salary to $500.   On this he got debt free in 1848.   He was elected a
fellow of Yale 1824; one of the principal founders of the Theological
Institute of Conn, East Windsor Hill, 1833; received honorary D D from
Williams 1840.   He was a vigorous preacher, always speaking without
written notes, his style unostentatious and earnest.   His theology was
of the old style, seeming ultra-conservative even in his own day.   He
deplored deeply the liberality of the Yale Divinity School and felt compelled to combat many of its doctrines.   He was active in the ministry
and with clear mind when he d suddenly July 19, 1849.   His wife survived
until Sept 8, 1853.   His portrait is in Larned, Hist Windham Co, and
many other places.   Of nine children, only 3 survived him:

a   Nancy b Thompson; m Feb 22, 1827, Hiram Ketchum of N Y
b   Daniel   c   Udolphus   d   Marcus   e   Jesse Erskine
f   Clarissa   g   Eliza   h   Sarah   i   —— unnamed

Jesse E Dow ahcbfe of Thompson became widely known for many
years as a journalist and general writer; author of many works now
hardly ever seen.   His poems were printed country-wide but have never
been collected; his witticisms widely quoted.   He m Eliza Stetson.   At
least 3 children:

a   Mary S
b   ——, son b Thompson 1835; went to sea with Commodore Elliott as professor
     of mathematics; later in the patent office, Washington
c   Julia Augusta b Thompson Dec 21, 1837; d Nov 10, 1886; m Oct 25, 1866,
     James Franklin Allen b Aug 13, 1841, son of Jonathan Leach and Caroline
     Brown (Allison); no children

Mary S Dow ahcbfea suffers from a garbled duplication of rec: m Feb 11, 1850, Aaron Thompson b Nov 2, 1826, son of Aaron and Betsey (Johnson); moved to San Antonio, Tex; child b Jan 1, 1861. The duplicate seems more accurate: m Feb 11, 1856, Aaron Johnson Corbin b Nov 25, 1826; child,—E —— b Jan 16, 1861.

Ebenezer Dow ahcf of Voluntown is in 1790 census 1a, 1b, 3c; m July 31, 1761, by Samuel Coit, J P, Susannah Hutchinson. He d of Sterling Apr 28, 1810. Children:

a Stephen b Voluntown Apr 26, 1762; d June 17, 1762
b Mary b Apr 18, 1764; d May 21, 1785
c Martha b Apr 18, 1766
d Hannah b Apr 1, 1768; m Mch 26, 1789, Jesse Matteson of Greenwich
e Ebenezer b Apr 13, 1770; m Voluntown Nov 30, 1794, Anna Stewart; beyond this untraced
f Aaron b June 19, 1772
g Stephen b July 30, 1774; raised a family in Columbia, Herkimer Co, N Y; untraced
h Susannah b Oct 6, 1776   i Ruth b Oct 6, 1778; d infancy
j Asa b Nov 22, 1780

Aaron Dow ahcff moved to Richfield Springs, N Y; m Elizabeth ——, d Mch 2, 1843. In Richfield both were prominent Episcopalians; he was ensign of Columbia Co militia in 1806, colonel in 1821. Both buried with son in Richfield churchyard, all stones still standing. Apparently an only child:

a Loren d Feb 24, 1864, ae 64; tombstone does not mention if m

Asa Dow ahcfj, farmer of Sterling, marched 1812 to defense of New London, but there does not seem to have been a fight. He was locally famous as a musician, singer in church, could play a great variety of instruments; could write any music on hearing it once; had the gift of "absolute pitch." He m Margaret Frink b Voluntown 1780, d Sterling May, 1863. Children:

a Uzziel m Mary Allen; no children
b Charles b Sterling 1816
c Susan m Henry Kennedy of Oneida, N Y; children,—John, Alfred
d Mary d in childhood   e Margaret m Tileston Thayer; no children
f Eliza m Thomas Gordon; a son Henry D

Charles Dow ahcfjb, farmer, inherited the homestead in Sterling; m Sept 14, 1842, Harriet W Allen b July 16, 1823. Children:

a Henry   b Edward; both d in childhood
c Charles H b Sterling Nov 6, 1851

Charles H Dow ahcfjbc d Brooklyn, N Y, about 1900; m Apr 9, 1881, Lucy M Russell b No Branford, Conn, Mch 22, 1846; she survived many years in the Brooklyn home. No children.

He left the farm to become a news reporter on the Springfield Republican, even then a famous paper. In a few years he took a wider position with the Providence, R I, Star; then abandoned newspaper work to become manager of a mine in Leadville, Colo. Not liking this he formulated plans to enter the news field in N Y City with Edward D Jones, with whom he had been associated on the Star. They took a third partner, Charles M Bergstresser of N Y, who supplied much needed capital. The essential idea was to improve upon existing methods of disseminating news, chiefly of financial interest, from moment to moment, with better facilities for gathering it. This had been done for some years by the late senator John J Kiernan with a few reporters and with slips printed slowly and distributed by boys from office to office, each boy visiting 10 to 15 offices. The service later developed into the sporting ticker. The method was crude, much time wasted in printing. Dow, Jones & Co began by systematizing the delivery, then by building up its collecting service, getting their own correspondents in all large cities and in Europe and maintaining a large staff of reporters in the financial district. They made reciprocal alliances with the press associations. Already the payroll had become fifty times greater than its predecessors. The service was at first sold at $20 a month, raised to $25, then to $30, later $75. Almost every bank and Stock Exchange house found the service a necessity.

The telephone service was greatly augmented. Often at some important dividend meeting a wire was especially strung, ending in the hand of a reporter in front of the meeting door. A small rotary press was invented inside the firm, by which about 200 words could be printed on slips at 500 or more per minute. This was used for "rush" news; longer articles were as before printed on slower flat bed presses.

The invention of the page printing electrical ticker, first seen in 1896, revolutionized the industry and Dow, Jones & Co quickly secured rights to it. A paper tape about 4 inches wide carries the news. The parent keyboard, like a typewriter, can transmit easily 30 or more words a minute and without any relaying delivers simultaneously and instantly in several thousand offices. Already leased telegraph wires were maintained to other cities. The page printing ticker now prints simultaneously in Boston, Chicago, Montreal, Washington and way points. Similar service to London consumes not over 50 seconds in transmission. The announcement of any important act is now made throughout the land in less than 10 seconds.

At the close of the day, all the news was summarized into a newspaper, with much editorial matter, financial analyses, etc, added. This is the Wall St Journal, now on the scale of a metropolitan daily paper. Until 1886 it was the whole endeavor of Charles H Dow to build up the news service. Then, for five years, he was the Stock Exchange member of Goodbody, Glyn & Dow, in which office the Author received his early financial training. In 1891 he returned to give his entire time to the Wall St Journal, his partners, of whom several were added, handling the news service. A building was bought to accommodate the enlarged business.

He enjoyed the confidence of all the captains of industry and was personally known to every financier in the country. He was known to be discreet and unbribable, his integrity tried again and again, when a piece of doctored news, a colored statement, would have brought him a fortune. On the other hand, his way of telling truth about a mismanaged corporation made him many enemies in high places. The firm was never sued for libel.

In later years he took some interest in his genealogy, feeling keenly that with his death a historic line would become extinct.

Aaron Dow ahcg disappears from Voluntown. He might fit an Aaron Dow of N Y City "out ward" of the 1790 census 3a, 3c, i e, with 2 sons of over 16 and 2 dau. Aaron Dow m (int pub N Y Mch 15, 1783) Margaret Kerby. If identical she must be a 2nd wife. There is no evidence of identity, no chance to connect with a posterity. There were a half dozen distinct families of Dow in N Y by this time.

Benjamin Dow ahch d 1794; enlisted on news of Lexington, but served but 20 days; was made sgt. In 1788 he was delegate to the Conn constitutional convention. He was on committee to establish the Voluntown-Sterling line, when the latter became a separate municipality. His service was recognized as proven by the D A R, Ill chapter, in 1894. He m May 17, 1758, Mary Hutchinson d May 20, 1766; m 2nd, Sept 27, 1768, Mercy Killam d Oct 2, 1805. Children:

a   Asa b Feb 11, 1759; d Aug 9, 1778
b   Nathan b Mch 20, 1761
c   Rebecca b June 20, 1763; m Henry Dow ahdaa
d   Elisha b May 27, 1763; d Aug 11, 1869
e   John b Aug 13, 1769   f   Daniel b Apr 22, 1771
g   Lucy b Apr 1, 1773   h   Benjamin b Feb 11, 1775
i   Moses b May 25, 1777; d Dec 22, 1778
j   Sarah b Jan 26, 1779; m Asahel Cole; left a son

Nathan Dow ahchb enlisted at 16 and was in service most of the rest of the war; was with Col Ethan Allen at Ticonderoga. In 1832 he lived Richfield Springs, N Y, applied for and received a pension. His service was proved for the D A R, Ill chapter, 1894.

The Voluntown 1790 census gives Nathan Dow 2a, 2c. Unless an adult is included, not his son, this cannot be our Nathan, who had been m only 3 years. Possibly it refers to Nathan ahci. Our Nathan m Sept 16, 1787, Agnes Gordon b Mch 6, 1766, dau of John Jr and Miriam (Dixson). Children:

a   Clarissa b Voluntown May 27, 1789; m Robert Benedict
b   Nancy b Jan 12, 1794; m John W Turnenlifft   c   Mary Ann

Mary Ann Dow ahchbc of Richfield, N Y, m Jan 6, 1820, Lucius Gould b Dec 12, 1787, d Aug 4, 1832, son of Isaac; moved to Eden, N Y. Children:

a   Nancy Amelia b Mch 30, 1821; d Aug 25, 1822
b   Lucius Dow b July 14, 1829
c   Mary A b July 29, 1832; m June 12, 1867, Lafayette Blue

John Dow ahchc settled about 1790 in Reading, Steuben Co, N Y; county judge and representative to Legislature. He wrote a pamphlet autobiography; m 1791 Mary Barnum, wid of —— Mallory. Her cousin was father of Phineas T Barnum, the show man. He m 2nd, ——. Three dau by 1st wife:

   a Lucy b 1792; d 1869; m 1812 Greeley Davis; at least one child,—**Ephraim**
      Lemuel
   c Polly m —— Dunham; has posterity in Pa

Daniel Dow ahchf moved from Richfield to College Springs, Iowa, farmer, d Feb 7, 1860; m Mch 28, 1799, Susanna Douglass b Voluntown Nov 23, 1777, d Richfield May 3, 1837, 6th in descent from William Douglass of New Haven 1679. Daniel lived to be a militant abolitionist and free soiler. Children:

   a Narcissa b Sterling Jan 15, 1800; d Richfield Jan 10, 1824
   b Olive b Feb 20, 1802; d Richfield Feb 20, 1827
   c Isabelle b June 4, 1804; m June 14, 1837, Cyrus Ladd of East Otto, N Y. He
      d Feb 20, 1870, ae 71
   d Daniel b Jan 12, 1807   e John b Feb 11, 1809
   f Benjamin b July 9, 1811
   g Rachel b Sept 10, 1813; d Erie, Pa, May 25, 1885; m Jan 1840 Elijah Owens;
      left a dau,—Mrs Mary O Mack of Erie
   h James b Armenia, N Y, Nov 16, 1816   i Aaron b May 9, 1819

Daniel Dow ahchfd d College Springs, Iowa, Sept 12, 1859; for many years at Richfield deacon of Presbyterian church, ardent abolitionist of the Garrett Smith School. In Iowa his activity was increased becoming a link in the underground railroad by which runaway slaves found freedom in Canada. He m Sept 30, 1830, Sarah Weber b Herkimer Co, N Y, June 27, 1808, d Lewis Co, Wash, Mch 13, 1891. Children:

   a Narcissa b Aug 17, 1836; d 1862
   b Henry Elisha b May 3, 1839; d 1857
   c Harlan Page b Richfield Springs Feb 20, 1840
   d Marion J b Oct 17, 1849   e Daniel Weber b Apr 7, 1852; d 1866

Harlan Page Dow ahchfdc d Chehalis, Wash, Nov 1, 1902, from an injury to spine. Real estate operator of Manhattan, Kan, living 1857-69 on the Mo-Iowa border, active with his father in all abolitionist acts. At the outbreak of war he enlisted at the call of provisional Gov Hamilton R Gamble, Lieut of Kimball's cav, State militia, commissioned Oct 31, 1861, for 6 mos. At expiration he enlisted as private in 4th cav; promoted Sept 25, 1862, to 2nd Lieut; mustered out 1865, but commissioned Capt for one year for special service; again mustered out July 25, 1865; in 1874 state senator for Riley, Davis and Dickinson counties; re-elected 1876, but resigned to become deputy revenue collector; resigned Nov 1, 1885; in 1888 member of school board of Manhattan, Kan. He m July 25, 1860, Nancy M Brown b Galesburg, Ill, July 25, 1840. Children:

   a **George Harlan** b College Springs Aug 9, **1861**
   b **Minnie Weber** b Dec 3, **1866**   c **Albert Henry** b Aug 11, **1868**
   d **Edna Elsa** b Sept **1870**   e **Helen Pearl** b Riley Co, Kan, Oct 15, **1871**

George Harlan Dow ahchfdca, physician, moved from Manhattan to Chehalis in 1887; m Mch 19, 1885, Clara E Lofinck b Nov 17, 1865 Children:

a Minnie Clara b Manhattan Nov 21, 1886   b Edna b Sept 1890
c Harlan Albert b Vance, Wash, Mch 6, 1895

Marion J Dow ahchfdd d Aug 20, 1887; m Dec 25, 1869, **Burton J** Ames of Riley, Kan, b Jan 28, 1844. Children:

a Frank Weber b Feb 23, 1871; of Pittsburgh, Pa
b Norman Burton b July 28, 1872
c Ernest Harlan b Jan 17, 1874; of Tacoma, Wash
d Orlo Wilder b Sept 3, 1878; of Homestead, Okla
e Irvin Garfield b July 28, 1880   f Henry Dow b Dec 8, 1882

John Dow ahchfe, farmer of East Otto, N Y, deacon of 1st Congregational church, several years overseer of poor, commissioned capt of militia by Gov Marcy Mch 10, 1835; capt, later major, 1837, 248th N Y vols; m 1st Apr 18, 1833, Eliza Weber b Herkimer Co Mch 10, 1810, d East Otto June 23, 1855, sister of ahchfd; m 2nd Sept 11, 1855, Maria A McDougal b Bennington, Vt, Sept 2, 1817, d East Otto Jan 15, 1886, dau of John Dudley. Children:

a Orinda Frances b Ashford, Conn, June 11, 1834; d Oct 30, 1835
b Daniel Mitchell b East Otto Sept 23, 1835
c William Chester b Ashford Dec 2, 1836
d Mary Eliza b Springville, N Y, Apr 16, 1838; m Nov 18, 1859, W N Wood of Clarinda, Iowa
e Susan b Ashford Oct 28, 1839; d Aug 18, 1845
f James Henry b June 3, 1841
g Gertrude Melvina b Jan 9, 1844: m Dec 24, 1867, Emory N Tefft of East Otto
h Isabelle Maria b East Otto Aug 24, 1862; m Sept 11, 1877, C W Flickenstine of East Otto

Daniel M Dow ahchfeb, farmer of Dustin, Neb, m Dec 11, 1859, Emily Louisa Bentley b East Otto Apr 10, 1840. Children:

a Weber Beach b Lenox, Ohio, Mch 12, 1861; d Aug 14, 1863
b Frederick Northrup b July 17, 1864; d Oct 5, 1864
c Allan Bentley b May 2, 1870; untraced

William Chester Dow ahchfec lived College Springs; m Mch 24, 1865, Luenda M Lafferty b Ashtabula, Ohio, Mch 17, 1841. Children:

a W Newton b Mercer Co, Ill, July 4, 1866; of St Joseph, Mo
b Nettie L b Page Co, Iowa, Aug 2, 1868; m May 2, 1887, Edwin S King; 1 child
c Gertrude L b Aug 4, 1870   d L Oella b Oct 8, 1872
e John Chester b Aug 20, 1874
f Walter Earl b Jan 11, 1880; of St Joseph 1918

James Henry Dow ahchfef, banker of Randolph, Kan, m Oct 30, 1877, Lauretta M King b Lenox, Ohio, Feb 9, 1844. No children.

Benjamin Dow ahchff m 1st Oct 18, 1833, Martha Doolittle; m 2nd Mary Doolittle. Our information on the ahch line comes from members who had little recollection of the junior branches and were unaware of whereabouts.

James Dow ahchfh, physician, d Longmont, Colo, Apr 3 1873; m Clarista Moore. Just prior to the Civil War he was a member of the faculty of William and Mary College. He made no concealment of his abolitionist views and a mob gave him 24 hours in which to leave. Realizing that a live abolitionist was more useful than a dead one, he left for the west. He left a dau, possibly other children.

Aaron Dow ahchfi d College Springs, Iowa, Sept 4, 1864. Like his brothers, cousins and all of his family who went west, he was an outspoken free soiler and abolitionist and, like them, was always suspected of participating in the "underground railway" by which runaway slaves were aided into Canada.

Aaron inherited the strong religious tendencies of the ahc line. His ambition was to become a foreign missionary and toward this end he entered Oberlin College. By this time the family had started west. He was unable to graduate on account of ill health, but acquired a knowledge of Latin, Greek, some Hebrew, and mathematics through calculus, which enabled him to become a college president years later. After leaving college, he taught "subscription schools," these becoming the usual method of education in the west at the time. In southeast Iowa he m Feb 10, 1842, Amy Hampton, a Quaker whose parents were among the Quaker migrants from the east through Indiana to Kansas and Iowa, where many of the original monthly meetings are still maintained.

Aaron readily gave up his membership in the Presbyterian church and joined the Society of Friends and the children by his 1st wife were brought up as strict Quakers. They located in a small village of Iowa very favorably situated in regard to a number of fine springs. He started a Quaker college and the name of the town was changed to College Springs. Aaron helped set out the extensions of the town and presided several years over the college. His wife d Jan 25, 1857, and Aaron m 2nd Apr 3, 1859, Mary J Wolf, returning at her request to the Presbyterian fold. Other men had taken over the college and Aaron staked out a homestead claim, farming for the rest of his life. In old days, once a Quaker, always a Quaker. About this time the custom began, especially in the middle west, of regarding the sect as merely a denomination of the evangelical churches and transferring memberships with freedom and as much frequency as desired.

The Hampton family Bible gives her m date as Mch 2, 1842. This is probably correct and Feb 10 would date the publication of the intention. Children:

a   Gershom b Wayne Co, Ind, Feb 22, 1843; enlisted; d Louisville, Ky, in the service July 27, 1865

b   Daniel b Jan 19, 1845   c   Elizabeth H b Iowa Dec 8, 1846
d   Elisha b Mch 20, 1849   e   John Gordon b Oct 11, 1851
f   Louisa M b Sept 21, 1853   g   Milton b Sept 18, 1855
h   Narcissa Chalista b Nov 19, 1857

By 2nd wife:
i   James M b Feb 13, 1860; d Oct 5, 1861

j   Peter Wolf b Dec 31, 1861; now of Vista, San Diego Co, Calif
k   Margaret Ann b Mch 10, 1865; came west with her brother

Daniel Dow ahchfib lived New Mexico; d Aug 4, 1881; m a Mexican girl and left some family.

Elizabeth H Dow ahchfic m July 30, 1863, William Le Roy Bagley d Apr 25, 1895; she now lives Parma, Idaho, with a dau.   Children:

a   George L b Aug 3, 1866, now of Tex   b   Amy Lucinda b Dec 10, 1868
c   David Daniel b Dec 17, 1870
d   Milton Aaron b Aug 5, 1873; d Sept 21, 1874
e   Laura J b Aug 29, 1874, of Parma   f   John D b Jan 23, 1876
g   Henry Elisha b Feb 20, d Sept 13, 1877
h   William Eugene b Mch 31, d June 17, 1878
i   Walter E b May 14, 1880   j   Charles Clarence b Jan 9, 1882
k   Alice Edith b May 4, 1885; d Jan 13, 1886
l   Vivian Adelbert b Jan 18, 1887

This family lived in several places Mo and Neb.

Elisha Dow ahchfid lived and d in New Mexico; m and left a family.   One was:

a   Elisha A now of Willard, N M

John G Dow ahchfie d Jan 1910; m near Albuquerque, N M, 1887, Addie Cora Bennett b Beaver Falls, Pa; now wid of San Diego, Calif. Children:

a   Grace; now Mrs L Ferrell of Calexico
b   Rex b May 2, 1900; now marine engineer of San Pedro; unm

Louisa M Dow ahchfif, now of Marshalltown, Iowa, is the family genealogist.   She joined the Friends when 14; m Mch 29, 1883, Lindley H Maddock d Aug 15, 1888.   That name occurs many years earlier among the Friends of Maine.   She m 2nd May 7, 1890, William Richardson d Mch 10, 1899. Only child:

a   Amy b Jan 20, 1884; grad Penn College; unm

Milton Dow ahchfig went to New Mex; d there; wife still living (1924).   A very considerable family; among them:

a   Bessie; now Mrs M A McGraw of Albuquerque
b   William D; in 1915 postmaster at Tajique
c, d, e   Milton, Millie, Mabel, in recent Albuquerque directory

Milton Dow does not seem old enough to be the Milton who m (no date) Sophia McLean, dau of Maj Nathaniel, a veteran of 1812, of Minneapolis.   This couple moved to Ft Snelling, Neb; further untraced.

N Chalista Dow ahchfih m Nov 20, 1877, Clayton Seamons now dead.   She d Oct 22, 1921, having lived Neb and Colo. Considerable family, one being:

a   Nora, now Mrs Denton of Nampa, Idaho

Peter Wolf Dow ahchfij.   His mother m 2nd —— Eggleston. Peter was kept to farm work but finally succeeded in attending Amity

College. He then taught school, drifting with others of the family to New Mexico. For years he was a wheat raiser of Riverside, Calif. Retiring, he built a home at Laguna Beach, Calif. He m 1885 Eunice Mary Weber, dau of a German patriot of 1848; 2nd 1896 Mollie O Coltharp. Her grandfather had been an abolitionist in Tenn. Her mother's father aided the cause differently. He bought as many slaves as he could afford and set each free at age of 40, giving to each 5 acres. One child by Mollie:

a Raymond Aaron b Mch 8, 1877; m Alma Winnifred Pettitt
b Neal b 1891; m Ella Monahan. Both sons now ranchers
c Edna May b 1893; d Nov 1923; m John P Barrett; 1 dau,—Ruth Elizabeth
d Ruth b Nov 18, 1898; d about 1917, unm

Margaret A Dow ahchfik m —— Hower of a German family coming in 1848. Both now dead. Children:

a Charles, now of Inglewood, Calif   b Emma   c John

Lucy Dow ahchg d Richfield Mch 30, 1854; m Jan 15, 1795, Asa Brown of Stonington b July 13, 1768, d Richfield Jan 22, 1860. Three sons, 8 dau, of whom:

a Asa b Brookfield, N Y, Feb 14, 1803; m Mch 5, 1829, Louisa Wilbur; lived Warren, N Y
b Benjamin Dow
c Emeline Marilla b Otsego Co Apr 8, 1816; d Lake Geneva, Wis, Feb 7, 1904; m Jonathan Wheeler; 7 children

Benjamin Dow ahchh of Windham m Oct 31, 1799, Merriam Dean; settled in Sterling. Children:

a Orra m Isaac Gallup of Plainfield   b Electa
c Samuel T had a family in Sterling, all dau; moved to Willimantic; untraced
d Nathan

Nathan Henry Dow ahchhd of Sterling grad Brown Univ 1840; subsequently unt.

Nathan Dow ahci is untraced; may be the Nathan of Voluntown 1790 census. He is in all probability the Nathan Dow enlisted Apr 18, 1760, ae 22, from Suffolk Co, N Y, Capt Jacob Smith. In this company there enlisted 1758 a Joseph Dow of Huntington, L I, and he is identical with Joseph who enlisted again, ae 48, in the Revolution. A considerable family of Dow were in Huntington before this time, but they cannot possibly be of ahc line; either of c line or an entirely distinct family. Of a posterity for ahci we get no trace.

There is left unplaced a member of ahcb: Horatio Dow b Ashford Jan 30, 1793; began medical practice Vernon 1818; m Vernon Nov 15, 1821, Mary Skinner; went to Ellington 1832, to N Y 1848; soon came back, d Ellington Sept 28, 1859. No children in rec.

L ONG headed Thomas Dow ah never let an opportunity to secure new land slip by; so, when he learned that bona fide settlers were wanted for the Volunteers' Land, east of Plainfield and north of Voluntown, Conn, he sent at least three of his sons thither. There is some evidence that he went himself. At all events three sons arrived there in 1715 and took lots, there being 30 original lot holders. The new settlers applied at once for annexation to Plainfield but this was refused and the place annexed to Voluntown in 1719. The homestead of Thomas was near the Plainfield line, so that all his rec are there.

Thomas Dow ahd became the Squire of Plainfield; d May 20, 1760, his will dated May 17, probated **Oct 17**, mentions wife Mary, which is the only rec we have of her. Thomas felt strongly, as no doubt did others, that his community should have a church and worked hard for one. It was accomplished in 1723 and Thomas was deputed to build it himself. A minister's tax was levied and a pastor called. But, the community was Presbyterian. Ebenezer Dow signed the Westminster confession of Faith, but Thomas and Ephraim refused. Nevertheless, Thomas went regularly to the church of his own handiwork. He was, of course, a farmer; every one was then. The early vital statistics of the place are wholly absent. They begin just in time to show that Thomas lost 5 children by a dysentery epidemic. For a century and a half it was the custom to build a well just by and below the cesspool. The children, except the 5 unfortunates, are arrived at from family rec:

a John b probably about 1730; perhaps his father m later than usual in that early time
b Lydia b about 1732; m Jan 1, 1761, Ezra Whipple?
c Hannah b about 1734; probably not the Hannah m Coventry Oct 22, 1778, Samuel Babcock
d Sarah b about 1736; m Canterbury June 3, 1762, Daniel Long Bottom?
e Abigail b about 1738
f Samuel b about 1741: 1790 census gives a Samuel Dow 2a, 1b, 1c, and this is the only evidence at hand that he ever existed; identity, of course, a guess
g Thomas b about 1744; bap Apr 12, 1752; d Nov 1, 1754. It may be that a son b after 1754 was also named Thomas. It is certain that some Thomas Dow shared the homestead of John Dow ahda, m a Miss Holmes of Salisbury, Mass, and d ae 44
h Daniel b, say, 1746; d Oct 15, 1754. The epidemic evidently took the young children
i Jeremiah b about 1748; d Oct 15, 1754
j Mary b about 1750; d Nov 1, 1754
k Edward b about 1752; d (Ede) Nov 8, 1754
l Olive bap Sept 25, 1748; probably d in infancy
m Olive bap Apr 21, 1750

The order of children is somewhat arbitrary; possibly early rec from ahc or even ahg line have crept in. No other Dow family were of Plainfield. It is quite possible that ahd had two wives.

John Dow ahda succeeded his father as village Squire, living to great age, tilling the inherited farm, having the full measure of yankee shrewdness looking toward his material prosperity. He d Dec 5, 1825; m Mch 8, 1764, Elizabeth Burton of Preston. Two of her brothers were pioneers into Ohio. The 1790 census gives John 4a, 1b, 6c, indicating 9 children. Reliable family rec says there were but six. Perhaps the discrepancy is from the inclusion of Thomas Dow. Children, apparently from a family Bible:

a   Henry b June 1, 1766; m Rebecca Dow, his cousin
b   John b May 6, 1768; a physician; m Dec 12, 1802, his cousin Elizabeth Burton
c   Elizabeth b May 23, 1770; m Jan 3, 1788, Jonathan Gallup
d   Thomas b Sept 19, 1772; m Dec 11, 1795, Anna S Kinney (Kinne in rec)
e   Mary b Nov 18, 1776; m Feb 9, 1797, Ephraim Prentice, farmer
f   Lydia b June 9, 1784; m Dec 15, 1806, Aaron Preston, farmer

A narrative coming from Dr G L Dow ahdadada in 1887 mentions an Elizabeth Dow and a Lorenzo Dow, farmer, as members of this family but does not indicate the relationship.

Henry Dow ahdaa abandoned the position of village Squire, going after 1815 to New Providence, Ind. He m Dec 6, 1787, Rebecca Dow ahchc. She d of typhoid, the juxtaposition of well and cesspool continuing popular in the west. They were farmers. Children:

a   Polly b Sept 8, 1788; m John Frawlee, an Englishman
b   Elisha b Feb 25, 1790; m Thankful Davis; 9 children. A Plainfield rec surely his: Mr Elisher Dow Child d Feb 13, 1812
c   Asa b Jan 27, 1792; d young   d   Henry b Plainfield May 13, 1794
e   Benjamin b Feb 16, 1797
f   John b Apr 15, 1799; m (by family rec) Harty Hart. Plainfield rec seems better,—m Mch 1, 1818, Harty Ellis; known to have had 9 children, all sons
g   Nathan b June 24, 1801
h   Asa b May 8, 1803; rec belongs to him: Mr Henary Dow Son d Nov 12, 1815
i   Rebecca b Aug 19, 1805; m John D (onins?; writing illegible); had 2 sons, 2 dau

Henry Dow ahdaad d New Providence Nov 3, 1873; m Oct 2, 1814, Mercy Kinney b Plainfield June 24, 1791, d New Providence, dau of Levi. They had 8 dau and 1 son:

d   Henry Daniel b New Providence Apr 19, 1824

Henry D Dow ahdaadd, farmer of New Providence, wrote in 1887 that he had a cousin Olive Custer, then ae about 75; that another cousin was John F Dow, son of ahdaaf, of Neoga, Ill; that he, Henry D, was the 4th child; his sisters included Mrs E H Phelps of Attica, Iowa; Mrs William Burns of New Providence; Mrs J D Baker of New Providence; Mrs Lydia B Peck of Fayetteville, Ark.

Henry D m Oct 8, 1844, Elizabeth Ann Baggerly b Clark Co, Ind, Sept 26, 1823. Children, all b New Providence:

a   Sally Ann b Aug 11, 1845; d May 30, 1849
b   Lydia Adeline b Jan 10, 1848; d May 30, 1849
c   Laura A b Jan 22, 1850; m Nov 14, 1867, John B Goss; 5 children
d   Henry E b June 2, 1852; d Mch 29, 1853
e   Daniel Milburn b Mch 1, 1854; m Nov 9, 1878, Philene Walker; untraced; but had 3 children by 1887
f   George W b July 17, 1856; m Nov 9, 1878, Anna Hurst; had 5 children; untraced

g Alice J b Sept 28, 1858; m Dec 2, 1886, James Piers; 2 children
h Mary A b May 5, 1862; unm
i Elizabeth C b Feb 11, 1864; m Apr 13, 1884, Ninian Martin; 2 children

Nathan Dow ahdaag m June 10, 1824, Martilda Robertson, no place being mentioned. They evidently went west. Children:

a Nancy J b Apr 21, 1825   b Margaret Ann b Oct 1826
c Charles Henry b Feb 27, 1828; of Martinsville, Ind, in 1887
d Rebecca Elizabeth b Feb 17, 1830
e David Benjamin b Feb 7, 1834; untraced
f Alexander R b Feb 7, 1834; in 1887 of Paragon, Ill
g Martha E b Sept 9, 1835   h Mary A b Dec 12, 1837

John Dow ahdab, physician, and Elizabeth Burton, his cousin and wife, were playmates from infancy brought up in the same house; lived and died in the old homestead, he Mch 20, 1851; she Dec 6, 1856, ae 96. Two children:

a Thomas d Sept 13, 1844, ae 40; he also m his cousin, Prudence Burton d June 23, 1866, ae 67; no children; they lived always in the homestead
b Susan m Dayton Kimball of Preston where both d without children. Apparently the repeated marriage of cousins extinguished this line

Elizabeth Dow ahdac m Jonathan Gallup, both living and dying in Plainfield. Three sons:

a David Dow   b Simon; both lived and d in Plainfield

Thomas Dow ahdad moved from the homestead to Franklin; he and his wife are buried there. He d Dec 4, 1814; she d Aug 12, 1817. Seven children:

a Jeremiah K   b Burton   c Martha m Jabin Armstrong
d Elizabeth m Hial Armstrong
e Phebe A m Henry Leonard; 2nd John Sanderson
f Rebecca b Nov 27, 1804; m (his 2nd) Jabin Armstrong
g Thomas Jefferson b Nov 10, 1812

Jeremiah K Dow ahdada, farmer, m Dec 11, 1818, Laura Hazen, both of Franklin. Children:

a Royal b Sept 6, 1819; a physician
b Eunice b Apr 27, 1821; d June 11, 1821
c John b Apr 1, 1822; a farmer
d Curtis L b Mch 12, 1825; a physician; a son George L Dow also a physician
e Philetus b Oct 3, 1828; a farmer
f Erastus b Aug 10, 1830; a farmer   g Mary E b Aug 20, 1832; d Nov 6, 1834

Mary Dow ahdae m Ephraim Prentice; son of Manassah and Asenath; moved late in life to Pigno, Ohio. Children:

a John   b David

Lydia Dow ahdaf m Aaron Preston; both lived and d at Moosup, Conn. Children:

a Joseph   b Elizabeth   c Rebecca
d Mary m —— Medbury; living 1887

IF **Jeremiah Dow** ahf went with father and brothers to consider taking up land in Connecticut in 1715, he was soon back. Little is known of his personality; he d Dec 20, 1731, seven years after marriage. The next generation was inclined to follow the sea. He m Nov 10 1724 (int pub Sept 5), Hephzebah Hobson b July 13, 1700; m 2nd Thomas Treadwell of Ipswich (Cf sub aia). She in most books of reference is called dau of John and Dorcas. N E Gen Reg gives dau of John and Elizabeth (Story). John Hobson was long a justice and was speaker of the House 1741. Children, list surely accurate:

a William b Aug 15, 1725   b Daniel b July 23, 1727
c Jeremiah b June 22, 1729
d Hepzibah b June 9, 1732. Two rec may apply, not absolutely necessarily
    inconsistent: Hepzibah m June 6, 1754, John Frazer of Rowley; Hepzibah
    Dow m —— Smith, had a dau bap Sept 12, 1756

William Dow ahfa int pub Lynn Aug 20, 1748, Elizabeth Blaney, both of Salem. One son is sure. Either to William or Daniel must belong a considerable posterity whose origin has never been found.

a Billey d N Y (Manchester rec) Aug 1776, ae 18 or 19
The others are from rec of maturity:

b Michael Dow of Manchester 1a, 2c in 1790 census; otherwise unknown
c Stephen Dow, Marblehead 1790 census 1a, 1b, 5c
d John Dow, Marblehead, 6 feet, dark, ship carpenter and officer of marines, brig
    Prospect, Capt John Vesey, June 20, 1781
e Moses Dow, Morristown or Manchester, private 3 mos, 14 days, Dec 1, 1776,
    and 26 days at later period, Capt Joseph Hooker, Col Williams

It may be noted that the 5th generation of ahf was ever fond of a good scrap.

Jeremiah Dow ahfc always lived Manchester; d Mch 28, 1807; m Aug 1750 Lois Thompson b 1730, d Jan 27, 1805. Knowledge of him is confined to vital statistics:

a Jeremiah b June 27, bap July 7, 1751
b Lois b Jan 1, 1753; m Nov 7, 1773, John Badcock
c Williams bap Jan 1, 1753; d (Billey) Aug 9, 1759, ae 6
d Sally bap Dec 1758; d Aug 7, 1759
e Hcphzibah d Aug 1759, ae 5 or 6
f William b May 28, 1760   g Seward b May 12, 1762
h John b July 17, 1764   i Jacob Hilton b Feb 9, 1766
j Hepzibah b Nov 11, 1767
k Patty b May 26, 1769; d unm, a domestic, Manchester May 1, 1849, cause old
    age

Jeremiah Dow ahfca, height 5 feet, 6, served 6 mos, from Sept 19, 1775, Capt John Whipple; re-enlisted for period of the war; serving 1779 in Worcester Co. Int to m Anna Eastkoot pub May 18, 1777, but the bans were forbidden by her mother, Mrs Anna Christian. She subsequently m his brother, showing that Mrs Christian's objections were personal and not family. He waited two years until matrimony was

made easy by a widow without a mother; m May 14, 1779, Mrs Lydia
Badcock (Manchester and Rowley rec) b 1756, d July 16, 1807.   Children:

    a David b Mch 3, 1787   b Samuel b July 1, 1789; untraced
    c Lois b 1793
    d Betsey b 1795. Of two Manchester rec neither may apply, but we know no
       other Betsey of Manchester: A son of Betsey Dow, illegitimate, a pauper, d
       May 12, 1825. Betsey Dow m June 16, 1841, Samuel Youlin of Gloucester.
       Perhaps both apply.   In Gloucester rec there are a number of similar
       instances in the Youlin family

David Dow ahfcaa of Manchester d Ipswich Aug 12, 1843; m Nov
1, 1815, Eunice Martin b July 28, 1790, d Apr 16, 1878. Children:

    a John Edward b June 14, 1818   b David Francis b Apr 3, 1820
    c Eunice Ann b 1822; d July 8, 1830   d Susan Hammond b May 11, 1824

John E Dow ahfcaaa, shoemaker, moved to Chester, N H; d Jan
31, 1899; m 1st Caroline ——, by whom 1 child; m 2nd Chester Mch
15, 1850, Mary S Bean b Fremont, dau of James and Sarah (Sanborn).
She d Chester May 12, 1900, ae 73-8-4, buried at her son's home Fremont.
Children:

    a John b May, 1845; d tuberculosis June 30, 1846
    b Charles Henry; minute man in 1861 in 1st N H; never returned; fate never
       known
    c John Albert b Fremont Jan 6, 1852
    d Elden Leslie b Jan 10, 1856; unm in 1921
    e Austin Herbert; in 1915 directory laborer of Chester, unm
    f Mary Ida   g Flora Inez

John A Dow ahfcaaac able, progressive man, sawyer of Deerfield,
Canterbury and Fremont, in 1921 lumber dealer of Pittsfield; m 1st,
July 3, 1874, Cora A Yeaton, ae 18, d Canterbury June 22, 1890, dau of
Alvin S and Martha of Deerfield; m 2nd Oct 4, 1893, Arianna (Orianna
and Annie in rec) Fletcher b Canterbury Nov 20, 1865, dau of Charles
Horace and Lucy Jane (Peverley). Only child:

    a Marion b Canterbury Sept 29, 1901; now of Pittsfield, unm

Mary Ida Dow ahfcaaaf m Dec 14, 1875, Austin J Lane of Chester.
Children:

    a Anna m James A Edwards of Chester
    b Lilla Jane m Charles D Rand of Chester

Flora Inez Dow ahfcaaag m Feb 10, 1883, Frank Barnard of
Chester. Children:

    a Ella m Leon P Midges   b Fred, grew up and m

David Francis Dow ahfcaab m (int pub Dec 24, 1849) Mary P
Annable b Hamilton July 9, 1820, d Ipswich Feb 14, 1881, dau of
Solomon. In 1850 census they appear weavers of Methuen. Children:

    a Arthur Wesley b Apr 6, 1857   b Dana Francis b about 1860

Arthur W Dow ahfcaaba and his brother were brought up by an artistic, well-to-do family of Glen Cove, L I, who do not appear to be related. He studied extensively abroad and was for many years head of the art dept of Columbia University; living Bronxville. He d 1922; m 1893 Elizabeth Pearson of Lowell, Mass.

Dana F Dow ahfcaabb is a well known landscape architect of Reading and Boston; m but no children.

William Dow ahfcf of Manchester, private May 1 to June, 1776, Capt Richard Dodge, Col Loammi Baldwin; m July 17, 1783, Margaret Hilton b 1761, d Beverly May 25, 1838, dau of Stilson and Margaret (Allen). Stilson was a veteran. Children:

    a   William b Jan 27, 1785; pauper, d fits Oct 19, 1832
    b   Margaret Hilton b Oct 2, 1787; m twice; left 1 child
    c   Thomas b Jan 29, 1791   d   Jacob Hilton b Dec 28, 1793
    e   John b Aug 23, 1796; d Sept 4, 1809
    f   Sally (in rec dau of wid Hannah) d Apr 12, 1802, ae 5
    g   Stilson Hilton b Sept 14, 1799; grew up, but no children

Thomas Dow ahfcfc of Manchester followed the sea, but retired to become a cabinet maker, realty assessed in 1850 at $1,200; m Sept 10, 1816, Abigail (Nabbie) Carter b Manchester Feb 14, 1797. Children:

    a   Abigail Carter b Sept 7, 1818; m Dec 14, 1840, William McCartney Jr of Salem
    b   Thomas b July 4, 1820   c   Albert Smith b Nov 21, 1822
    d   Jacob Hilton b Oct 18, 1826   e   Edward b Oct 13, 1829
    f   ——, dau d scarlet fever Feb 14, 1836, ae 4
    g   Mary Frances b Jan 9, 1834; m Charles Boardman of Gloucester; 1 child

Thomas Dow ahfcfcb, fisherman of Manchester, m July 22, 1846, Ina Arbuckle b 1828, dau of John, cabinet maker, and Margaret of Edinburg, Scotland. All six children were living 1884, but only two by name:

    a   George Edward b Nov 17, 1846   b   Charles b Sept 22, 1849

Albert Smith Dow ahfcfcc, cabinet maker of Manchester in 1850; m Nashua, N H, Oct 26, 1849, Susan Mink of Waterloo, Me. He enlisted and d in army in North Carolina. Children:

    a   John W   b   Andrew S   c   Susan; all untraced; living 1884

Jacob Hilton Dow ahfcfcd lost a leg in the army; returned to Manchester; m and had 3 children, all living in 1884. He d Feb 3, 1901.

Edward Dow ahfcfce, box maker of Lynn, m 1st, Gloucester June 1852, Caroline Mason b Nov 26, 1833, d Lynn Nov 16, 1865; m 2nd Hannah Perah of Lynn. Children:

    a   Caddie L b Manchester Sept 18, 1852; m Oct 11, 1876, Augustus A Giles of Beverly; children,—Nolan E, Walter M
    b   Joseph E b July 8, 1857; d June 25, 1865
    c   Lyman M b Manchester Apr 26, 1859; of Lynn m Apr 7, 1880
    d   Charles L b Beverly Aug 4, 1861; of East Boston 1884
    e   Melinda J b Manchester Apr 18, 1863; of Peabody, Mass
    f   John E b Lynn Sept 18, 1865; d June 26, 1866
    g   John Edward b Dec 6, 1871
    h   Albert Smith b Apr 27, 1874; both living 1884

Lyman M Dow ahfcfcec. His wife is Nellie L McGullion. Children, Lynn rec:

a   Helen L b 1883; m Lynn June 26, 1907, Henry J Nolan, ae 23, son of Robert and Mary (Tulon)
b   Marion Frances b Aug 25, 1902

John E Dow ahfcfceg of Lynn m Cora F Cronk. Children, youngest b Marblehead:

a   John Francis b Lynn June 2, 1902; d July 30, 1903
b   Frances May b Dec 9 1905   c   Ellen Margaret b Aug 23, 1908

Three John E Dow are somewhat confused, one being ahbaacfb. Some John E of Boston m Albertine M Stevens. Children:

a   Albert Edmund b Methuen Jan 30, 1901
b   Mildred Stevens b Lawrence May 17, 1902

Albert S Dow ahfcfceh m Lynn May 30, 1902, Jeanie Lang McKechnie, ae 34, b Scotland, dau of William and Jessie (Robertson). This rec gives his mother as Hannah N Mahan, probably correct and Hannah Perah given above is some error in transcription   A child:

a   Hannah Nora b Lynn Dec 19, 1905

Jacob Hilton Dow ahfcfd m Jan 19, 1819, Sarah (Sally) Hassam b Manchester Aug 18, 1791, d Manchester May 4, 1881, dau of Josiah and Sally (May). He became a master mariner at early age; in 1812 was returning with a cargo from France and off the Grand Banks bespoke the U S S Constitution, was informed that war had broken out and that he had successfully run the blockade. Unwilling to risk his luck again, he bought a farm, but returned to sea 1817 and was master mariner over 40 years. In 1850 of Beverly, realty assessed $600. Children:

a   Josiah H b Manchester May 12, 1829
b   Stilson H b 1832, both were chair makers of Beverly 1850

Josiah H Dow ahfcfda was for most of his life a mariner; m Apr 7, 1857, Marie Simpson b Charlestown Aug 18, 1839, d Manchester Sept 2, 1869. Children:

a   Josiah N b Manchester Mch 29, 1858; untraced; living 1884
b   Alma M b Dec 13, 1862; m May 14, 1881; of Salem; 1 child
c   Oren J b Dec 2, 1867; d Nov 15, 1869

Josiah N Dow ahfcfdaa of Manchester d widower Aug 10, 1902, ae 45, 5 mos. No rec of wife or children.

Stilson H Dow ahfcfdb d Reading July 23, 1903, ae 71-6-10. Wife was Hannah Merrill. A child:

a   Abbie b 1876; of Reading m Milford Dec 31, 1902, Frank Elmer Edwards, ae 21, son of George H and Mabel Rose (Carpenter)

Seward Dow ahfcg, private at Cambridge and Winter Hill from Apr

1778, does not reappear. There is every reason to think that he m and had 2 sons:

    a Seward d (Ipswich rec) Aug 14, 1793, ae about 9
    b Seward b Salem Oct 24, 1790. Census of 1790 does not show this family

Seward Dow ahfcgb was a cooper of New Chester, N H; m Apr 15, 1818, Elizabeth Tucker of Andover. Census of 1850 gives them of Andover, he b Mass, with wife Eliza b N H 1789; no children. His d rec Andover Dec 1, 1871, calls him single, error for widower.

John Dow ahfch m Dec 29, 1785, Jennie Badcock b Manchester June 7, 1757. Census of 1790 gives them 1a, 2c, probably accounted for:

    a Jane d Manchester Sept 28, 1813; parents not stated

Jacob Hilton Dow ahfci of Manchester m May 19, 1788, Anna Eastkoot d tuberculosis Oct 1821, ae 74. Children:

    a Beulah Bradford b Oct 10, 1790; m Sept 29, 1809, Nathan Lee, Jr
    b James b Feb 21, 1792 (Hist Manchester gives Jacob, clearly error)
    c Willard b Oct 24, 1795; d May 3, 1823, insane suicide
    d Sally b Sept 14, 1797

James Dow ahfcib m Jan 20, 1819, Eliza Roberts of Beverly b 1791; in 1850 farmer, realty assessed $1,800. Children:

    a James b Oct 10, 1820
    b Eliza Ann b 1829; m Beverly Apr 13, 1848, Franklin W Burchstead, cordwainer, ae 21, son of Allen and Eliza; a son James b 1849

James Dow ahfciba m Beverly Sept 22, 1842, Susan Larcom d tuberculosis Sept 29, 1843, ae 24-1-29, dau of Michael and Anna. Dau:

    a Susan Larcom b Feb 20, 1843

Census of 1850 shows John E Dow b 1832, shoemaker, living with them.

Susan L Dow ahfcibaa (Susie L, dau of —— and Susan W, in rec) of Salem, Mass, m Nov 17, 1869, Joseph Hemphill of Derry.

OVENTRY, Conn, has been the home of a very large number of
Dows, all of whom originate from a large farm situated close to
Coventry Pond. This family has been especially rich in men
of talent, even of genius, often coupled with impracticabilities. It has
been strong in musicians, writers, preachers, marked men. Imperturba-
bility has been a characteristic,—comparative indifference to the fluctuations of fortune, whereby one man was village squire, his son an inmate
of the poorhouse without loss of interest in life or his own self-complacency.
It has included many millionaires; its best known representative for
many years seldom knew whence was to come his next meal. Its members
who have been of mechanical turn of mind have been good inventors.

Ephraim Dow ahg was the financier of his family, went with his
brothers to Voluntown, Conn, and established a home. He m Nov 8,
1726, Elizabeth Clark of Rowley b 1704, d Mch 26, 1790, dau of Rev
Humphrey and Elizabeth. The death of his father required his presence
in Ipswich, for he was executor and residuary legatee. In 1735 he got
possession of some unexpected land,—the Narragansett grant to his late
father, situated in Buxton, Me. Whatever it realized, it was part of the
residuary estate, for all legacies to the other children had been met. It
was almost 1740 before he was able to settle down, and he then bought
the Coventry farm. Its price then was thrice as great as its present
value, but it came at a time of depreciated currency. This did not
worry Ephraim, whose assets were land, rather than cash. He lived
about ten years to enjoy his new home, dying 1750. His estate (will
probated Mch 12, 1750) inventories £3,588-7-6. Children:

a Lucy bap Nov 5, 1727   b Juliana bap May 28, 1732
c Ephraim bap May 28, 1732   d Levi bap Aug 11, 1734
e —— dau bap June or July 1736; d young
f Lemuel bap May 29, 1737   g Pelatiah bap May 30, 1739
h Humphrey Bean b Coventry July 3, 1742 i Calvin b Jan 10, 1747

Lucy Dow ahga m Joshua Coggleshall, Jr; joined the Shaker
community and are seen no more in Coventry. Children:

a Daniel b Mch 1, 1749   b Rufus b Feb 6, 1750
c Luther b July 25, 1754   d Serloma b Apr 17, 1767   e Mary, her twin

Juliana Dow ahgb m Thomas Judd, farmer of Coventry. Their
posterity still farms in Coventry. Children:

a Juliana b June 8, 1752; m Benjamin Babcock; 2 dau
b Elizabeth b Aug 7, 1754; d Feb 18, 1835
c Thomas b Oct 8, 1756; m Mary Young; 2nd Esther Carpenter; d Aug 18,
   1833
d Solomon b Sept 21, 1758; d Apr 12, 1851; m Anna Carpenter; 6 children
e Elias b Dec 15, 1760; d 1838; m Beulah Laribee of Coventry; 8 children
f Hannah b Apr 20, 1764; d 1848; m Asa Parker of Coventry
g Lois b May 20, 1766; d Mch 26, 1836
h John b May 25, 1768; d Sept 19, 1824

Ephraim Dow ahgc inherited part of the ample Coventry farm and headship of the family. Census 1790 gives Ephraim Dow 1a, 4b, 1c and Ephraim Dow 2nd 1a, 3b, 3c; this we do not understand (see ahgce). While Ephraim was no reckless spender and probably his family cost him not much more than families usually, he was able to leave little estate except his land. He d May 2, 1796; m 1st, Aug 15, 1752, Hepzibah Hawkins d Apr 7, 1775; 2nd, Aug 24, 1775, Mary (Ladd) Badger. Children:

a Daniel b Nov 27, 1752   b Jesse b May 1, 1754; d young
c Hannah b Nov 3, 1755; d Sept 6, 1784
d Jesse b Sept 8, 1758; father in will speaks of him with affection but states Jesse had already had his full share. No further rec
e Ephraim b Apr 9, 1762; d Oct 12, 1803. No rec of m; could not accumulate a family to fit 1790 census
f Livinia or Lavina m —— Palmer
g Hepzibah b Mch 6, 1767; d July 24, 1815; m Billdad Curtis; son,—Marvin
h Joseph b July 5, 1777   i Solomon b Dec 30, 1778
j Daniel Clark b Apr 8, 1783   k Betsey b Aug 26, 1786

Daniel Dow ahgca d Coventry May 1777 of small pox; buried in a solitary grave near Black Swamp, far from the village; m Mch 11, 1773, Mehitable Palmer b July 3 (or Aug 16, latter may be bap), 1753, d Nov 1794, dau of John and Abigail. She m 2nd, July 15, 1781, Ebenezer Crossman of Coventry, by him a dau,—Cynthia b July 22, 1783, m Ira Trowbridge. Daniel's children:

a Asenath b Sept 20, 1773   b Amasa b Mch 9, 1775
c Tirza b Jan 20, 1777; m Solomon Dow ahgci

Amasa Dow ahgcab, blacksmith and tool maker, d Black River, N Y, Sept 14, 1808; m Nov 27, 1800, Anna Marsh b Sutton, Mass, Aug 15, 1780, d Auburn, Mass, Dec 13, 1814. Children:

a Daniel b about 1801; d Nov 5, 1865
b Emeline d Apr 18, 1830; m Dec 25, 1825, James Patterson of Southbridge
c Amasa b near Utica, N Y, Oct 26, 1808 (posthumous)

Daniel Dow ahgcaba m Maria Brown m 2nd —— Boughton. His posterity are the Dow family of Carlisle, N Y. Children:

a Harriet Matilda b May 13, 1825
b Nancy m —— Becker of N Y State; lived to very advanced age
c Daniel J b 1830
d De Witt Clinton; disappeared in young manhood; never found
e —— dau d N Y State ae 92

Harriet M Dow ahgcabaa, living 1917 in Syracuse, wid, m Sept 18, 1844, Henry Hyde Huntington of Albany b Coventry Dec 25, 1816. Children:

a Louisa Clinton b Nov 2, 1845   b Florence Williams b June 5, 1852
c Henry Roswell b May 28, 1863   d Herbert Fitch b Sept 28, 1866

Daniel J Dow ahgcabac of Carlisle d 1905. A few facts given by his son:

a John L   b Daniel   c George L   d Matilda, all d young

 e George Edwards m but no children; in 1918 store keeper of Midland Beach,
  N Y
 f Nancy   g De Witt Clinton; untraced; unseen by brother many years

Amasa Dowe ahgcabc changed the spelling of his own name, as did the cousins in many lines, regarding it as the older, more correct form. This does not cause genealogical confusion, except in case of a Doe who adopted the spelling Dowe without altering its pronunciation. In this Book effort is made to spell a name as its owner elected, occasional errors being easily pardonable.

Amasa was member of Legislature 1859; m May 14, 1834, Harriet Sophronia Adams b Sturbridge, Mass, Mch 30, 1812, d Apr 17, 1879. Children:

 a Marshall Prouty b Providence June 20, 1835
 b Charlotte Emeline b Leicester Nov 12, 1840; d 1845
 c Harriet Anna bap Apr 28, 1843; m E C Carpenter; dau, Ann Amelia

Marshall P Dowe ahgcabca, merchant, town clerk, treasurer of Danielsonville, Conn, m June 30, 1856, Emily Adelia Davis b Plainfield Sept 15, 1834. Children:

 a John Marshall b Plainfield Apr 15, 1858. D A R list has Mrs John Dow nee
  Helen Safford of Danielson
 b Charles Amasa b Danielsonville Sept 30, 1859; lived Stillwater, Wis; recent
  directory has Charles A Dowe of Danielsonville. None of this family answered
  letters of genealogical inquiry

Joseph Dow ahgch d Dec 24, 1854; farmer and militia captain of Coventry. He issued his orders "as one in authority, and not as the Scribes."

A famous order was: "No drill today, boys, it's raining." He m May 8, 1799, Hannah Richardson b So Coventry Oct 13, 1780, d Sept 24, 1866; did not favor race suicide:

 a Eunice b June 28, 1800; d Danville, Ill, July 22, 1840; m Nathaniel Kingsbury;
  1 son
 b Rebecca b Apr 11, 1802; d July 24, 1804
 c Hannah b May 2, 1803; m Joseph Dorman; son Richard of N Y
 d Maria b Dec 16, 1804; d Apr 19, 1844
 e Joseph Newton b Nov 11, 1807 f Hezekiah Richardson b Mch 16, 1810
 g Lucia H b Feb 29, 1812; d Nov 2, 1891; m Adonijah White M D
 h Augustus b Feb 2, 1814 i Chauncey b Dec 20, 1815; d Jan 9, 1816
 j Edward H b Jan 7, 1817 k Elizabeth b Jan 6, d Mch 1, 1819
 l James Richardson b Aug 9, 1820 m Mary B b Mch 7, 1827

Joseph N Dow ahgche, lieut of militia, builder of wool-carding machines, m Oct 4, 1837, Sally Trapp b Mansfield Mch 27, 1813, d So Coventry Apr 1, 1870; m 2nd Feb 28, 1878, Almira Snow of Ashford b July 7, 1828. Children:

 a Mary Antoinetta b Aug 1, 1838; d Middletown Mch 15, 1897
 b Riou Duane b Feb 9, 1840; d Hartford Apr 1, 1898
 c Irville Leslie b June 6, 1842; d Hartford Aug 9, 1887
 d Cartez Newton b Dec 25, 1844; machinist of Hartford, unm 1920
 e Helen Jane b Apr 27, 1849; dressmaker of Elizabeth, N J, d Jan 1913, unm
 f Edith Hortense b July 31, 1853

Mary A Dow ahgchea m June 12, 1867, Charles S Brigham of Hartland, Vt, b Coventry Nov 13, 1826. Children, now of Woodstock, Vt:

a Caroline Edith b Vernon, Conn, June 28, 1869
b Herbert Dow b Apr 20, 1871   c Frederick Newton b Nov 14, 1872

Riou D Dow ahgcheb, machinist, tool maker, Hartford, m Mch 25, 1863, Sarah Ann Grant b Mansfield Aug 26, 1843. Children:

a Everett Elton b Oct 10, 1864   b Riou Leslie b Hartford Apr 10, 1869

Everett E Dow ahgcheba, accountant of Hartford, member of Sons of Revolution, m Hartford Oct 26, 1887, Caroline Goodwin Adams b Bloomfield, Conn, Jan 6, 1865. He aided much in the recent generations of his own family and locating other Conn Dows. Children, b Hartford:

a Marion Leslie b Oct 19, 1888   b Edna Frances b Nov 19, 1890
c Everett Duane b May 11, 1899

Marion L Dow ahgchebaa m Hartford Sept 29, 1914, Henry Franklin Cone. Child:

a James Brewster b Hartford Jan 23, 1919

Edna F Dow ahgchebab m Hartford Feb 11, 1915, Allan Platt Northend. Child:

a Frances Caroline b Hartford Nov 23, 1915

Riou L Dow ahgchebb m Windsor, Conn, Oct 26, 1892, Bessie Nelson Blake b Hartford Nov 2, 1871. Children:

a Riou Nelson b Mch 6, 1894; d Hartford July 21, 1895
b Raymond Everett b Sept 27, 1896; 1921 of Manchester, N H, unm

Irville L Dow ahgchec m Apr 5, 1882, Alice Josephine Beckley, b Milford Aug 23, 1863, d June 21, 1904, dau of Edgar and Elizabeth (Goodwin). Children:

a Bertha Beckley b Dec 31, 1882; d Oct 19, 1883
b Sadie Marion b Jan 8, 1885; of Washington, D C, unm

Hezekiah R Dow ahgchf d Toledo, Ohio, Jan 10, 1882; merchant and farmer of Van Buren, N Y, m Sept 19, 1842, Nancy Elizabeth Farrington b Baldwinsville Oct 24, 1824. Children:

a Merrill Patch b Feb 9, 1837; enlisted 1862; in Battle of Wilderness; taken prisoner while on picket duty; d Andersonville Sept 20, 1864
b Hezekiah Richardson b Van Buren; d young
c Harriet Elizabeth b Oct 12, 1843   d Lucia Maria b Feb 14, 1847
e Hezekiah Farrington b Nov 30, 1850
f Anna b June 24, d Aug 10, 1853   g James Wallace b Mch 22, 1855
h Charles Richardson b May 22, 1859
i Edmund Leroy b Jan 22, 1870

Harriet E Dow ahgchfc m Oct 4, 1871, Schuyler G Schenck of Toledo, Ohio, b Fulton, N Y, Mch 9, 1842. Children:

a Daniel Dow b Dec 9, 1875   b Mary Elizabeth b July 7, 1878
c Lewis Richardson b July 29, 1880   d Margaret Lucia b Sept 30, 1882

Lucia M Dow ahgchfd m Jan 12, 1869, Samuel B Paddock of Toledo. Children:

a Elizabeth B m —— Stevens of Toledo; 1 son, 1 dau   b Emma Dow

Hezekiah F Dow ahgchfe, life insurance of Syracuse, N Y, m Nov 6, 1872, Mary Northrop; of Detroit by recent directory. Two sons, of whom:

a Charles Farrington, descendant of Gov William Bradford, m Syracuse June 11, 1902, Florence May Hickok b May 10, 1880, dau of Grove Lawrence and Helen Gertrude (Ayer); has not answered letter of genealogical inquiry. They had a child: Farrington Lawrence b Springfield, Mass, May 30, 1905

James Wallace Dow ahgchfg of Baldwinsville m Oct 25, 1882, Adelaide Sears; 1 son, 1 dau.

Charles R Dow ahgchfh of Van Buren m Oct 8, 1903, Harriet Almstead.

Edmund L Dow ahgchfi grad cum laude Syracuse University and Columbia College of Physicians and Surgeons; married, practicing in N Y City.

Augustus Dow ahgchh d Fayetteville, N Y, Sept 8, 1865; lived N Y City; adopted a middle name Francisco; was a leader in the Unitarian movement; m ——, by whom 1 dau; 2nd, Sarah Bender Wheeler of N Y City, who survived him many years. Children:

a ——, Mrs Matteson of Wyoming, N J; 2 children
b Augustus Francisco b N Y City   c Joy Wheeler b 1859
d Ada; of Wyoming, N J, unm

Augustus F Dow ahgchhb, not now living, was with the Merchants Nat Bank of Chicago; m June 14, 1880, Ella Celeste Park b Charleston, S C, July 1, 1856. Children:

a Celeste Emily b June 15, 1881   b Sarah Augustella b Mch 8, 1883

Joy Wheeler Dow ahgchhc was to have been named Joseph for his grandfather, but at 22 was bap otherwise; a secretary and accountant, he studied architecture, becoming widely known; author of American Renaissance in Architecture and smaller works. He m Elizabeth Goodchild, dau of John, for many years member of New York Stock Exchange; of Summit, N J, and vicinity of Boston. Two children:

a John Goodchild; in 1924 student Brown Univ

Edward H Dow ahgchj d New Haven, Conn, Sept 10, 1871; farmer, m Henrietta Lyman (Tuttle Gen gives Henrietta Cutter b Jan 28, 1821, d Sept 28, 1862). Children:

a Lyman; in 1915 laborer of New Haven   b Josephine Harper
c Theodore   d James; both untraced

James R Dow ahgchl, physician of Brooklyn, d Feb 27, 1871; m

Sept 25, 1861, Emilie Richmond b 1843, dau of Charles and Ruth (Williams) of Warren. R I. Child:

 a Emily Genevieve b Apr 1863; m May 1884 Charles F Starr of Brookline, Mass; 1 dau

Mary B Dow ahgchm m Jan 1, 1852, John M Comstock b New London June 4, 1832. Children:

 a Willie D b and d Nov 5, 1852
 b Minnie R b Oct 23, 1853; d Sept 2, 1854
 c Mamie E b Apr 5, 1856; m Feb 25, 1879, William H McFarren of New London; child,—Minnie Dow

Solomon Dow ahgci, farmer of Coventry, d Jan 6, 1823; m Tirzah Dow ahgcac, d Coventry May 12, 1863. Coventry rec are clear for all the children "of Solomon and Tirzah." Yet, Erwin P Dow writes 1920 that his grandparents were John and Hannah. We note also that by the account herein Tirzah was niece of Solomon. Children:

 a Simon b Aug 17, 1798   b Cyrus b Sept 20, 1800
 c Solomon George b Sept 19, 1803   d Emily b May 3, 1806
 e Lucy b Mch 26, 1808; d Aug 11, 1809
 f Beverley Abbott b Nov 26, 1811   g Ezra Abbott b Sept 4, 1814

Simon Dow ahgcia m and had children, of whom:

 c Johnson

Johnson Dow ahgciac m Hartford Jane Ann Slocum b Washington, N Y, Sept 19, 1828, dau of Hiram and Maria (Ferdone) of New Haven. At least one child:

 a William E b Feb 23, 1852

William E Dow ahgciaca in 1920 directory of Rockville, Conn. Two dau:

 a Grace E   b Rosamund M, bookkeeper of Hartford

Cyrus Dow ahgcib, hatter and farmer of So Coventry, d 1885; m Sept 20, 1838, Charity A Chapman b Aug 20, 1811, d Ellington Mch 12, 1905. Children:

 a Ellen L b July 3, 1839; d June 22, 1842   b Augustus b Oct 9, 1841
 c Erwin P b Oct 17, 1848   d Carlos b Nov 20, 1850

Augustus Dow ahgcibb m Jennie Winans; 2nd, Judith Morton; lived Pittsfield, Ill, and Chicago. Children:

 a Erwin Augustus b 1865; d ae 7 mos
 b Harry Augustus b about 1870; officer of Harris Trust Co, Chicago

Erwin P Dow ahgcibc, merchant of Pittsfield, living 1921, m Florence E Hicks. Children:

 a Edwin Carlos b 1875; m Ethel Butler; lives Baylis, Ill; no children
 b William H b 1879; m Lottie Graves; lived Beaumont, Tex

Carlos Dow ahgcibd m Oct 5, 1875, Mary Fay; lived Wethersfield. Recent directory gives Carlos E Dow, traveling salesman, Wethersfield and Hartford.

Solomon G Dow ahgcic m Shelburne, Vt, Nov 7, 1826, Marcia C
Mills b Conn.   Census 1850 gives Tirzah Dow, presumably mother, with
them.   No children by census; barely possibly a dau:

   a Kate b Vt 1845; m Shelburne Apr 15, 1866, John McGee, ae 23

Beverley A Dow ahgcif of So Coventry m Apr 19, 1849, Elizabeth
A Cole of Norwich.   No subsequent rec.

Ezra A Dow ahgcig lived Brooklyn, N Y; m Apr 5, 1849, Jane E
Belden b Middletown, Conn, Jan 17, 1827; both living 1885.   Children:

   a Nellie Augustine b Dec 20, 1850; m Jan 24, 1875, Charles F Moulton; lived
       Brooklyn; 4 sons
   b De Witt Canfield b Hartford July 29, 1855; m Aug 12, 1875, Ida May Lydden;
       lived Brooklyn; 1 son
   c Jennie Louise b N Y City Sept 26, 1862; m Apr 2, 1885, Frank E Driscole

Daniel C Dow ahgcj became estranged from the family on account
of money matters.   He moved away, married and had a family; untraced.
Perhaps his older brother Jesse went to the same place.

Levi Dow ahgd, born, lived, died in Coventry, was an institution
of the community, his wife Phoebe Taylor just as much an institution as
he, in later years known for miles around as Uncle Levi and Aunt Phoebe.
In many ways he was the typical Dow.   He had his own way of doing
things and that way was generally different from that of any one else.
There had been many heirs to his father's property, his own inheritance
small, little but his land.   It took very long hours of very hard work
to produce enough from it to pay taxes, feed a big family, clothe them,
afford some protection to an unthrifty brother, and leave time to help
a neighbor whose barn was being roofed or whose corn lay unshucked.
No wonder that Aunt Phoebe sometimes peddled her own applesass
through Coventry streets.   Levi was a philosopher, mused as he worked.
took his ups and downs as a matter of course, always with apt remark,
always with helping hand.   Mindful of the custom of regaling neighbors
at huskings and other meetings, he provided for those who helped extricate the body of his youngest son, drowned and caught under a log:
"Now, boys, heave hard for the cider."   To their children they left a
sterling pedigree:

   a Mary b Dec 26, 1760   b Esther b Sept 3, 1762; unm
   c Samuel b Oct 3, 1766   d Jeremiah b Dec 28, 1770; d ae 17
   e John b Mch 17, 1773; d unm   f Sarah b Feb 17, 1775
   g Paul b June 28, 1777   h William b June 28, 1777
   i Anson b June 17, 1780
   j Harvey b Aug 19, 1792 (1782?); drowned in childhood

Samuel Dow ahgdc m Plainfield May 19, 1789, Mary Phillips, dau
of John.   Mary rejoiced in a string of gold beads now owned by a great
granddau.   Census 1790 shows them in Smithfield, R I, with one child.

Mary b Oct 27, 1767, survived her husband, d Jan 28, 1847, at her son's home, Schenectady; buried there. Children:

  a Samuel Whittlesea b Dec 17, 1789   b Joseph W b Dec 17, 1794 (1793?)
  c Elisha Branch b May 5, 1795   d Isaac R b July 20, 1807

Samuel W Dow ahgdca, village blacksmith, left a memorial in the number of church spires which he built and are still standing. Census 1850 finds him farmer of Lanesboro, Mass, realty assessed $4,000. He d Sept 6, 1866; m Lucy Pettibone; and 1847 Rebecca Ingalls b Cheshire 1806, d Oct 26, 1891, dau of Stephen and Rebecca (Wood). She wished intently that she should have a son who should become a clergyman. Three years later half of her wish was gratified and she lived many years to realize it all, altho her son at first gave little such promise. Children:

  a Lucy Ann b Dec 4, 1825; d July 29, 1859
  b Laura b Apr 4, 1827; d Aug 3, 1830
  c Urbana b Aug 26, 1831; d Mch 6, 1856; m Charles Ager
  d Amy b June 26, 1836
  e Sophronia b Jan 26, 1832; d Jan 6, 1916; m Alexander Richards; children,— Samuel, Alexander, Fred, George, Hattie, —— infant d May 13, 1859
  f Samuel Whittlesea b Jan 22, 1837
  g Purcell b 1850 (middle name Lorenzo adopted much later)

Lucy A Dow ahgdcaa m Stephen Whipple. Children:

  a Kate   b Josephine   c Gertrude   d ——, son

Samuel W Dow ahgdcaf, farmer and fruit grower of Lanesboro, retired about 1900; living 1922 with dau in Pittsfield; m Jan 22, 1861, Mary Tyler d Mch 5, 1921. Children:

  a Fred W b June 4, 1863; d July 17, 1865
  b Samuel E b May 16, 1866; d June 13, 1893
  c Lucy J b Nov 23, 1868; m Dec 25, 1899, George Le Barnes; now of Pittsfield; well versed in her own genealogy
  d May E b June 24, 1876; d Sept 24, 1911; grad Syracuse Univ; m Apr 3, 1901, George Carrier
    In m rec she is Mary Eunice m Apr 3, 1901, George Irving Carrier, ae 33, son of Ira R and Lucille (Hart)

Purcell Lorenzo Dow ahgdcag began life as a farmer with a milk route; ae 23 was converted and 2 years later entered the Methodist ministry; d at his sister's home, Pittsfield, Apr 26, 1919, after 44 years in the active ministry. During that time he officiated at about 60 marriages a year; in 1880 attached to the Troy, N Y, conference; 3 years at Cheshire; 3 West Lebanon; 3 East Nassau; 5 Trinity Church, Troy; 3 Hoosac Falls; 7 as dist supt Burlington, Vt; 6 or more Bennington, Vt; m Oct 27, 1870, Floretta Potter of Lanesboro; she d; m 2nd, Mary E Gedding of Troy; by whom 1 child:

  a Carrie R m Charles H Demming of Lanesboro; 2 children
  b George Hudson   c William L   d Purcell L d in childhood
  e Harold E d in camp Ft Leavenworth, Kan, Oct 1916

Carrie R Dow ahgdcaga of Lanesboro m Troy Nov 25, 1902, by her father, Charles H Demming, ae 38, son of Francis D and Mary J (Young).

George H Dow ahgdcagb, 1919 Methodist pastor Fultonville, 1922 White Plains, N Y, m Flora Bardwell; 2nd, Alma Green.   Child:

a   Purcell

William L Dow ahgdcagc, business man of Troy, m Catherine Bertha Tate.   One son, 1 dau:

a   Leroy Edward b Pittsfield Aug 20, 1907

Joseph W Dow ahgdcb of Schenectady d Aug, 1847; left a dau,— Maria.

Elisha B Dow ahgdcc moved to Nassau, N Y; m there July 3, 1823, Catherine Hicks b Apr 12, 1801; d July 24, 1871.   Both his parents joined them here.   They moved to Schenectady, where he d Apr 1, 1865. Children:

a   Jerome B b Dec 30, 1824; d Mch 15, 1905
b   Mary E b Jan 13, 1828; d Mch 29, 1898
c   Joseph W b Apr 17, 1831; d June 29, 1832
d   Isaac K b Jan 9, 1834; d Elgin, Ill, Sept 15, 1856
e   Kate E b Ballston Lake Mch 15, 1840; d Aug 16, 1915

Jerome B Dow ahgdcca of Schenectady m Jan 28, 1843, Caroline M Truax b Nov 23, 1823, d Dec 21, 1897.   Children:

a   Maria C b Oct 31, 1844; d Dec 3, 1901
b   Kate D b Apr 28, 1846; d May 27, 1874; m Aug 1, 1872, Charles A Clark; no children
c   Edgar E b Nov 28, 1848; d July 9, 1867, unm
d   Emma C b Oct 30, 1850; d Mch 11, 1877

Maria C Dow ahgdccaa m June 2, 1863, Lewis H Skinner of Charlton, N Y, b Jan 26, 1837; living 1927.   Only child:

a   Carrie Dow b June 16, 1865; d Jan 17, 1868

Emma C Dow ahgdccad m May 21, 1868, Stephen Gates Van Vranken b Dec 14, 1845, d Mch 9, 1891.   Only child:

a   Emma Carrie b Oct 24, 1869.   She m Jan 27, 1887, Robert Hamilton Gibbes of Union, S C, later of Schenectady.   Their son Lewis Hamilton Gibbes is veteran of World War; m Elizabeth C McDermott and lives Albany.   Mrs Gibbes is active in the National body of the D A R

Mary E Dow ahgdccb m Apr 22, 1851, Harmon D Swits, M D, of Schenectady b June 29, 1819, d June 25, 1883.   Children:

a   Jennie b Nov 15, 1854; d Mch 19, 1858
b   William J b Mch 19, 1859; d Apr 20, 1886; m Sept 26, 1883, Mary Beecher of Cleveland, Ohio.   Only child,—Kate Dow m Eldon Calvin Charpie; their son Harmon D m Mary C Cassel

Isaac R Dow ahgdcd moved to N Y State; d Aug 22, 1831, doubtless unm.

Sarah Dow ahgdf d Westmoreland, N H, Mch 7, 1842; m Jan 1796 Ebenezer Root Fitch b Sept 26, 1772, d Westmoreland Aug 19, 1820 (Fitch Gen, p 73).   Children:

a   Phoebe b Aug 1798; d 184—; m Bradford Seymour
b   Abner b Dec 1, 1800; farmer of Westmoreland, d 1862, unm

c   Statira b May 1803; m 1832 Samuel W Johnson; children,—Samuel, Sarah, Amos F, Thomas F
d   Arsinoe b Feb 1807; m May 24, 1832, Albert P Seymour, son of Bradford; children,—Alfred R b Jan 14, 1837, Bradford b Oct 28, 1841, Abner F b Sept 10, 1843, Mary b July 19, 1845, Albert L b Nov 9, 1846
e   Marianne b Mch 7, 1813; d Manchester, Vt, Aug 30, 1866; m May 4, 1837, James S T Stranahan b Peterboro, N H, Apr 25, 1808. Children,—Mary b Newark, N J, July 14, 1840; Fitch James b Newark Sept 25, 1843. Mr Stranahan is regarded as the founder of Prospect Park, Brooklyn. After the death of his wife, to whom he was greatly attached, he published as a memorial a sketch of her ancestry
f   Diantha b Apr 14, 1818; d unm

Paul Dowe ahgdg d Ithaca, N Y, Sept 1849; m Dec 13, 1801, Betsey Matilda Carpenter b Foster, R I, Jan 19, 1782, d Dryden, N Y, 1842. Children:

a   Christopher S C b Foster Sept 2, 1802
b   Harvey Anson b Exeter, N Y, Dec 30, 1814

Christopher S C Dowe ahgdga of Ithaca; wife not stated, had:

a   De Witt C   b   Sarah m —— Jennison; children,—Homer, Ella
c   Paul b Dryden Sept 5, 1835
d   Lorenzo H d Ithaca Academy of Asiatic cholera

De Witt C Dowe ahgdgaa m Jennie McArthur of Dryden. Children:

a   Frank d ae 16 or 17
b   Flora m Theron Ward of Danby; children,—Florence,Roy, Dow, Mary Adeline. Dow Ward of Washington, D C, had only child,—Florence m Halsey Benster of Moline, Ill, 1 son

Paul Dowe ahgdgac m July 3, 1861, Mary A Davis of New Hudson; living 1920 Rushford, N Y. No children. Edgar R Dow ms gave children Charles, Christopher; if correct, both d young.

Harvey A Dowe ahgdgb d Ithaca July 16, 1885, lawyer; for 2 terms district attorney; entered militia 1852; Aug 24, 1863, Brig-Gen of 28th brigade, resigning Sept 1, 1866; m Feb 1, 1844, Adeline Carr d Buffalo Oct 14, 1897. Children:

a   Richard Henry b Apr 14, 1845   b   Florence Adele b Nov 7, 1847
c   Bertha Matilda b Sept 22, 1852

Richard H Dow ahgdgba m Sept 17, 1869, Cornelia Murray White. Children:

a   Harvey Murray b Nov 7, 1872   b   Adeline Cornelia b Mch 28, 1874
c   Paul Lionel b Sept 16, 1877; unm

Harvey M Dowe ahgdgbaa m July 25, 1901, Anna Josephine Hawken. Children:

a   Esther Frances b Apr 4, 1902   b   Richard Harvey b Jan 28, 1904

Adeline C Dowe ahgdgbab m Patrick Henry Perry of Birmingham, Ala. Children:

a   Helen   b   Henry

Florence A Dowe ahgdgbb m July 15, 1879, Henry Burling Morris, of Ithaca, who appears in Americans of Royal Descent as 20th in descent from Meredydd, King of Powis, Wales. He d 1910; lived Michigan City, Ind. Children:

  a Albert Dowe b May 7, 1880; d July 11, 1880
  b Hilda Bertha b Jan 29, 1888

Bertha M Dowe ahgdgbc m Apr 13, 1882, Samuel Wilberforce Powel; live Buffalo, N Y. Children:

  a Florence Dowe b Hartford, Conn, Nov 1, 1883; d Buffalo Apr 7, 1895
  b Edith Adaline b Oct 24, 1885; m Dec 29, 1910, John Edward Harrison of
     Cleburne, Tex. Children,—Bertha Dowe, Eleanor Bradford
  c Harvey Dowe b May 5, 1887; m Apr 27, 1912, Norma Augusta Scheuerman;
     lives Buffalo. Children,—Robert Harvey, Dorothy Alice
  d Katherine Lorenz b Hamilton, Ohio, Mch 25, 1889; instructor in Simmons
     College, Boston
  e Charles Pise Carr b Hamilton Jan 1, 1892; m Dole, France, Jan 15, 1916,
     Jean Glor; dau,—Florence

William Dowe ahgdh d Bridgewater, N Y, 1833; m 1800 Cynthia Eels b Coventry, d Bridgewater 1830. Children:

  a Cynthia m Uriah Chapin   b John Eels b June 15, 1803
  c Delia m Jeñiah Clark   d Chauncey Handel b July 30, 1811
  e Eliza m Eber Peet

John Eels Dowe (Rev) ahgdhb, farmer and Methodist clergyman, West Unity, Ohio, d Apr 15, 1872; m 1826, Belina Rice b Bridgewater, Feb 2, 1809. Children:

  a John M b June 1827; for 50 years with the Pacific Mail S S Co in N Y and
     Panama; never married
  b Oscar E b Pompey, N Y, Aug 8, 1830
  c Wesley Summerfield b Manlius, N Y, Feb 12, 1844

Oscar E Dowe ahgdhbb, watch maker of Springfield, Ill; Lieut 95th Ill vols; m Oct 5, 1854, Agnes M Smythe b Painesville, Ohio, July 6, 1835. Children:

  a Inez L b Clear Lake, Minn, Sept 11, 1855; d Marengo, Ill, Dec 11, 1855
  b Charles E b Marengo July 25, 1857; sgt of Governor's Guard, Ill militia 1874-9;
     untraced
  c Mary Isabelle b Nov 4, 1860; d Springfield June 29, 1882
  d Grace Waterbury b Springfield June 12, 1871; d Aug 31, 1872
  e George Agnes b Sept 9, 1874; d Aug 24, 1875
  f Paul Le Baron b July 1, 1877; mechanical engraver of Chicago; wrote 1920
     promising to send in his own and fill the gaps of the ahgdhb line

Wesley S Dowe ahgdhbc, 1873 bookkeeper, 1916 trustee of Peoria, m July 3, 1873, Lillian Wray b Petersburg May 27, 1855. Children:

  a Ellen May b Apr 23, 1874   b Caroline b Jan 28, 1876
  c Mabel Elizabeth b Dec 13, 1878   d Ada Irene b Dec 22, 1880
  e Paul Vincent b Feb 8, 1882   f Lillian Isabel b July 17, 1885

Chauncey H Dowe ahgdhd of Syracuse, N Y, d Feb 12, 1865, at one time heavy operator in grain, made and lost several fortunes; m

Apr 8, 1834, Mary E Blanden b Burlington, N Y, Feb 26, 1817, d Syracuse Oct 8, 1871. Children:

    a Harvey L b July 31, 1835   b Olivia H b Jan 1, 1838
    c Mary B b Apr 30, 1840; d Feb 13, 1865
    d Bertha M b May 16, 1846; of Belvidere, Ill, 1918, unm
    e Edward D b June 16, 1848; d Jan 30, 1862
    f William B b Jan 28, 1856; untraced

Harvey L Dowe ahgdhda, for many years of Belvidere, in 1920 treas of Champaign, m Jan 5, 1857, Maryette Woleben b Portland, N Y, June 18, 1834. Children:

    a Alvin W b Marengo July 26, 1859; 1920 of Belvidere
    b Mary Kate b Feb 1, 1863; d Oct 24, 1873

Anson Dow ahgdi enlisted Coventry Apr 3, 1813; became **sgt;** d Mch 3, 1814; unm.

D ARTMOUTH College, Hanover, N H, founded by Rev Eleazer Wheelock as an Indian school, drew to its neighborhood many associates of the founder, who drove up the river from Conn and took up land. Local history of many towns along the way mentions the original procession of ox teams and earnest pioneers. Before many years the Indians were no longer here, leaving the school to serve the whites and gradually develop into a college of countrywide service.

Among these early settlers were two Dows from Coventry, whose posterity were powerful for a century in Hanover life. They have long since disappeared, no Dow now in Hanover. Strange,—not a single Hanover Dow is an alumnus of Dartmouth.

Lemuel Dowe ahgf came from Coventry about 1760; bought a Hanover farm; d Jan 23, 1818; enlisted 1777 for Ticonderoga, Capt Jonathan Chase, all turning back after 7 days; m Apr 27, 1758, Anna Millarton of Coventry d Hanover Oct 17, 1793; 2nd Nov 19, 1795, Rebecca Everett. Children:

  a Susannah b Coventry Apr 10, 1759   b Salmon b Apr 28, 1762
  c Anne b July 24, 1765; m Samuel Peck of Wheeling (now W Va)
  d Lemuel b Apr 25, 1768
  e Lydia b Feb 6, 1771; d Dec 8, 1840, unm
  f Abigail b Aug 1, 1774; d Apr 9, 1846; m D Alexander Phelps, son of Alexander and Theodora (Wheelock), grandson of Rev Eleazer Wheelock. Children,— Lorenzo, Alonzo, Lydia, Polly d unm. Lydia Phelps m —— Stevens and had,—Mrs E C Drake of Lebanon, George B of Ashland, Melvin A killed in 3rd Vt, William N killed in 15th Vt

Susannah Dowe ahgfa d Nov 28, 1837; m Jan 20, 1793, Ebenezer Kendall of Hebron, N H, d Feb 15, 1837. Children:

  a Anna b Apr 12, 1794; d Aug 16, 1833; m Jonathan Powers of Hebron
  b Ebenezer b Dec 10, 1795; d Bristol May 4, 1867: m Dec 16, 1821, Susan Allen
  c Lydia b Oct 22, 1797; d Sept 22, 1800
  d Lemuel b Mch 3, 1799; d Sept 1800
  e Mary b Oct 4, 1800; m Dec 1, 1824, Isaac Morse
  f Lemuel b Mch 6, 1803; lived Groton, N H; m Philinda Hastings

Salmon Dow ahgfb enlisted twice, once in N H; is the only Dow in Vt Rev rolls; service 73 days; farmer of Hanover, d Sept 28, 1838; m Mch 3, 1785, Luna Benton b Nov 21, 1764, d Hanover Mch 28, 1817, dau of Stephen; 2nd wid Abigail Bond. Children:

  a —— dau b Feb 2, d Feb 17, 1786
  b Ethelinda b Mch 2, 1787; m Jan 4, 1814, Seth Hall of Hanover, b Feb 2, 1786; moved to southern Ill; children,—Laura m Herman Caldwell; George; Diana b Jan 4, 1824; d Feb 14, 1857, m Edmund Southworth
  c Welthy b Sept 30, 1790; d Sept 5, 1793
  d Agrippa b Jan 27, 1794   e —— son b and d June 26, 1796
  f Thomas Sargent b Mch 7, 1798; d Aug 2, 1800
  g Salmon b July 23, 1801
  h Luna b Aug 15, 1803; d Dec 13, 1882; m W Waterman d June 18, 1883

Agrippa Dow ahgfbd moved to Sycamore, Ill; d Apr 5, 1888; m Jan 7, 1823, Polly Storrs of Hanover b Oct 28, 1801, d Nov 6, 1885, dau of Augustus. This couple lived together 63 years and seven of their eight children survived them. Both were in full possession of their faculties until the day of their deaths, taking active interest in passing events. They came finally to Sycamore because their oldest son was located there. Children:

a Roswell b Hanover Jan 14, 1824   b Eliza B b July 30, 1825
c Augustus Storrs b Oct 14, 1827   d Julia Augusta b May 25, 1830
e Mary Frances b May 25, 1830; lived Sycamore
f Lewis b Feb 22, 1838   g Laura Ann b Apr 22, 1840
h Clara Benton b Jan 2, 1844

Roswell Dow ahgfbda d Sycamore Oct 2, 1901; m Sept 6, 1851, Theresa Emilia Richards b Hamilton, N Y, Jan 16, 1831, d Sycamore June 13, 1917, dau of Solomon Nash and Emily (Carrier). She had been his pupil and then teacher in Dow Academy. They celebrated their golden wedding. When the first Congregational church of Sycamore was organized Theresa sang in the choir. On its 70th anniversary she and another charter member sang.

Roswell began teaching at 17 to get money to go through college. In 1843 he entered Norwich University, from which his youngest son graduated 52 years later. Contracting a chronic asthma, he was compelled to leave and started west for his health, staging to Troy, by canal to Buffalo, then by boat to Racine, Wis. In 1847 his parents joined him and he pre-empted 160 acres in Mayfield, Wis. By next year he was called to teach in Sycamore at the first graded school in De Kalb Co. A year later he began his own select (subscription) school, holding it in the court house, then moving to Temperance Hall. The next year he built Dow Academy, and it was in the big study room that he was married. They lived several years at the Academy, which he finally gave up, his time needed in public life. In 1855 he opposed the re-enactment of the Missouri compromise on the ground that it would hasten the inevitable contest to end slavery. He was always charged, and probably rightly, with aiding the underground railroad. Of course, he was a charter member of the Republican party, altho he abandoned it in 1886 for the Prohibition party.

He was forced into politics. The tax assessor having failed utterly, he was nominated in 1852 and defeated; but his opponent refused to qualify and the selectmen appointed Mr Dow, taking no refusal. He was later re-elected and the basis of his assessments has been lasting ever since. He was then forced to reform the county finances and two re-elections were without opposition.

Having a desire to become a farmer, he took and cleared a tract of "cut over" land a mile north of the town. This was his home for the rest of his life. He was the war supervisor of the town. Children:

a Thirza Richards b Sept 1, 1582
b Flora Jeannette b Feb 6, 1855; d July 2, 1905
c Edmund Terry b May 5, 1857   d Elsie Storrs b Sept 30, 1858
e Ray Storrs b July 4, 1871

Thirza R Dowe ahgfbdaa m Mch 18, 1873, Manlius Rogers b Aug 9, 1849, son of Artemus. Children:

a Burton Stowell b Aug 11, 1882
b Nettie Dowe b Feb 13, 1885; d Mch 18, 1889
c Roswell Dowe b Oct 24, 1886; d Mch 18, 1889
d Robert West b Oct 24, 1886   e Elsie Lurancy b Dec 11, 1889
f Albert Nash b Oct 4, 1890   g George Ensign b Jan 17, 1895

Edmund T Dow ahgfbdac appears in recent directories as Ed T of Blanca, Colo, farmer; m Beloit, Wis, June 10, 1891, Christine Davidson of Sycamore b Mch 26, 1872, now of Blanca. Children:

a Roswell b Mch 24, d July 3, 1892   b Arthur b May 20, 1893
c Mary Helen b Apr 12, 1895; m C H W Smith; a son Wallace Edmund

Arthur Dow ahgfbdacb m Nov 15, 1920, Viola Webster. Child:

a Barbara b 1922

Elsie S Dow ahgfbdad has been for 35 years instructor in English literature in Wheaton College, Ill. Her widowed sister Thirza lives with her.

Ray S Dow ahgfbdae, 1915 in postal service Medford, Mass, m June 22, 1898, Eva Jennie Holt b Oct 19, 1867. Children:

a Donald Holt b Feb 21, 1——
b Neal Richards b Somerville Sept 8, 1904

Eliza B Dowe ahgfbdb d Dec 24, 1884; m Jan 1, 1848, Franklin Camp b Hanover Feb 20, 1824, son of David and Elvira (Bridgeman); lived Mayfield, Ill. Children:

a Laura Esther b June 14, 1850; m Dec 9, 1864, Orlando A Joiner b July 27, 1846
b Charles Franklin b Jan 7, 1853; m Dec 15, 1873, Florence A Lott b Aug 17, 1853
c Lucy Maria b Nov 4, 1854, d Oct 6, 1899; m June 28, 1877, Edward J Drake b Jan 13, 1846
d Lida Elvira b May 31, 1856; m May 8, 1879, Daniel Perry Owen ahgfdcba b Oct 11, 1853
e Cora Ella b June 2, 1862; m Sycamore Dec 12, 1882, Charles Ernest Willard b Mch 22, 1859, son of Charles and Helen (Ash)

Augustus S Dowe ahgfbdc lived Boone Co, Iowa; killed by lightning June 5, 1860, while prospecting about 12 miles west of Ft Kearney, Neb; m Feb 14, 1857, Welthy A Bettis b La Platte Co, Iowa, July 8, 1844, dau of Alonzo and Julia (Lykins). Children:

a Della Luella b Mch 10, 1858; m June 19, 1879, Curtis A Willard b May 10, 1840, son of Oliver and Lucy (Weedon)
b Evangeline Augusta b Dec 14, 1859

Evangeline A Dowe ahgfbdcb m Sept 16, 1879, Serigna Edgar Nance b Jan 2, 1860, son of Cary Franklin and Eliza (Houghton). Children:

a Clarence Leroy b June 1, 1880   b Rose Augustus b Mch 4, 1882
c Bessie Lenore b June 20, 1884   d Norma Alberta b July 14, 1886
e Fern Eulalia b Feb 26, 1889

f   Dow Willard b May 7, 1891; d Feb 26, 1893
g   —— son b Feb 3, d Feb 9, 1895   h   —— son b Jan 16, d Jan 21, 1898

Julia A Dowe ahgfbdd m Dec 23, 1849, Carlos Clark of Osage Co, Kan, b Nov 29, 1819, son of Aruna and Betsey (Robinson).   Children:

a   Fanny Robinson b Oct 26, 1850; m Dec 21, 1880, David Understock   b Feb 11, 1842; 2 dau
b   Mary Elizabeth b May 29, 1852; d May 7, 1864
c   Horace Ernest b Sept 17, 1855; m June 18, 1885, Lucy Jane Hurle b Feb 11, 1863; 2 sons
d   Carlton Leslie b Apr 18, 1858;· m Feb 13, 1884, Ida Martha Hill b May 10, 1862: 3 sons, 1 dau
e   —son b and d 1860
f   Bion Ellis b May 3, d Aug 18, 1863
g   Leon Lewis b May 3, d Aug 30, 1863
h   Willie Dowe b Nov 14, 1864: m Sept 22, 1886, Mary Adele Loomis b May 12, 18—; 2 children

Lewis Dowe ahgfbdf, artist of Petaluma and San Francisco, m Dec 25, 1866, Mattie Hall Morse b Sanbornton, N H, May 8, 1834, teacher of Concord, dau of Aaron and Eliza A (Hayes).   She d Concord Oct 6, 1914.

Laura Ann Dow ahgfbdg m Sept 12, 1860, Samuel T Durkee of Eugene City, Ore, b Mch 31, 1835, Civil War veteran, son of Elisha and Rebecca W (Thayer).   Children:

a   —— son b and d Jan 27, 1864
b   Eda Dowe b Feb 19, 1865; m Salem, Ore, Alfred Denton Cridge b Pa Dec 28, 1860, d June 30, 1892
c   Elton Silas b Oct 16, 1867
d   Ethel Hayes b May 31, 1870; d Mch 22, 1872
e   Benton Storrs b Feb 2, 1872; m June 26, 1895, Lillie Edwards b Apr 21, 1872

Clara B Dow ahgfbdh m Feb 4, 1863, Hiram Holcomb of Sycamore b Oct 30, 1838, son of George and Amelia (Hibbard).   Children:

a   George Dowe b Mch 20, 1865
b   Sanford Augustus b Apr 11, 1867; m Dec 2, 1891, Clara Varty b Mch 1870
c   Frank Terry b Nov 4, 1871; d June 20, 1895
d   Arthur b June 7, 1875; m Oct 24, 1900, Clara Boynton
e   Millie Florence b July 11, 1883

Salmon Dowe ahgfbg, shoemaker, d Newbury, Vt, Sept 1, 1859; m Dec 15, 1825, Elizabeth Bush of Norwich b Feb 10, 1803, d Hanover Aug 3, 1846, dau of Fairbanks d Feb 24, 1873, on his 100th birthday. Her mother was a Youmans, whose sister was grandmother of Admiral George Dewey. Salmon m 2nd June 22, 1847, Mary W Bruce of Sharon. She m 2nd of Newbury Dec 8, 1862, Rufus Camp of Hanover.   The garbled rec gives her dau of Harvey and Matilda Bruer.   Children:

a   Albert Hall b East Brookfield, Vt, Nov 2, 1826
b   Eveline Elizabeth b Oct 3, 1828   c   Salmon Azro Bush   b Oct 2, 1838

Albert H Dow ahgfbga, painter, moved to Haverhill, Mass; m Haverhill May 18, 1853, Cleora Tenney b Aug 25, 1829, d Jan 23, 1889, dau of Reuben and Rebecca (Hopson); served in navy through the War; m 2nd June 19, 1891, Helen M Pike b Waltham 1836, living 1919, dau of John and Caroline S (Lovejoy), wid of J Arthur Chick of Boston.   A large hearted man, with no children, he adopted those of his widowed sister and they took his name.

Eveline E Dow ahgfbgb m Mch 8, 1849, Charles P Thomas of Bath, N H, d Feb 16, 1855; then lived with her brother; m after 20 years widowhood John O Haskell of Concord, Mass; again wid, living Athol 1920.   Children:

a   Charles A b July 14, 1850; expert tool maker, Waltham Watch Co.   No children
b   Edward Emerson b Jan 17, 1852
c   Frank D b June 22, 1853; d Aug 6, 1855

Edward E Dow ahgfbgbb m Carrie Etta Quimby, who survived, lives with son.   Only child:

a   Edward Albert b Haverhill Apr 1, 1880

Edward A Dow ahgfbgbba, with Endicott, Johnson Co, N Y City, m Lynn May 4, 1906, Cora Belle Brown of Lynn, Mass, ae 26, dau of Henry J and Abbie C (Bachiller).   Children:

a   Geraldine b July 13, 1907   b   Evelyn b Feb 8, 1909

Salmon A B Dow ahgfbgc, organist, pianist, music teacher of Haverhill, m Mch 26, 1863, Mary A Piper b Quincy, Ill, Dec 15, 1839, wid in Haverhill 1923.   Children:

a   Frank H b Jan 5, 1865; d Aug 9, 1866
b   William C b Aug 6, 1866; d Pasadena, Fla, Mch 1901
c   Alice E b Feb 23, 1870; m J E Chase M D of Haverhill
d   Howard B b May 28, 1877; d 1917 unm

Luna Dow ahgfbh d Dec 13, 1882; m W Waterman d June 18, 1883. Children:

a   Ford m Matilda Needham; lived Woodward, Iowa; served in Army Oct, 1861 to Nov 12, 1864

Lemuel Dowe ahgfd from a sickly childhood developed into a man of strength and unusual ability; went to school in Coventry to prepare for Dartmouth but health compelled him to abandon this. He nevertheless became a thoroughly educated man.   In 1787 he bought 50 acres of wild land in Hanover, the clearing of which restored his physique.   He taught school and singing school, practiced surveying, was 5 years selectman.   In 1812 he organized a company and served as captain; d Sept 26, 1852; m Mch 18, 1790, Tryphena Dodge b Windham, Conn, Mch 15, 1769, d Hanover Jan 23, 1857, dau of Isaac and Sarah (Utley).   She was a woman of energetic character and many tales are preserved of her devotion to exact truth and the trouble she caused to those who departed from it in the slightest degree.   The couple joined the Baptist church, but many years later became Presbyterian.   Children:

a   Francis b Apr 11, 1791   b   Alphonso b July 6, 1795
c   Minerva b Feb 20, 1799   d   Tryphena b Feb 28, 1805
e   Ulysses b Mch 5, 1808   f   Sarah Ann b Dec 31, 1814; d Jan 6, 1816

Francis Dowe ahgfda d Bethel, Vt, Sept 14, 1839; bought a farm in Hancock, Vt; taught school and justice of the peace; m July 14, 1814, Mary L Church of Lebanon b July 23, 1793, d Aug 17, 1823, dau of Charles and Hannah; m 2nd, Aug 22, 1824, Sarah French b Dec 14, 1790, d New Haven, Conn, Jan 11, 1870, dau of Gen John and Hannah of Randolph. Children:

    a Mary Ann b May 7, 1815; went to N Y, developed a fine business at unusual salary for those times, traveling between N Y and London. She took upon herself the care of her orphan nephew and niece; m 1886 Charles M Clark, a business associate. He d May 22, 1889, she surviving only a few weeks
    b Harriet b Feb 18, 1817; m Feb 4, 1836, Isaac Wentworth Ricker of Randolph
    c Alphonso b June 28, 1818
    d Nancy W b July 9, 1820; d 1841; m May 21, 1838, Samuel Gilbert; moved to Muncie, Ind. Children,—Mary A and Francis Dowe returned to Hanover
    e Francis b May 1, 1825   f William W d in infancy
    g John French b Aug 18, 1826   h Hannah Wales b Dec 27, 1828
    i Sarah F b Dec 14, 1831; d Oct 13, 1842   j William W b Bethel 1834

Alphonso Dow ahgfdac in the account inherited by the Author is said to have deserted his family and gone to Colo. He m Sept 30, 1840, Olive Barnes b Royalton, Vt, 1813. Census 1850 finds him laborer of Nashua, N H. Children:

    a Ella b 1841; m Edgar Waxam   b Nancy b 1843; living 1850
    c Lewis b 1848; living Nashua 1850; untraced

Francis Dow ahgfdae d Colo; blacksmith of Lyndon, Vt, m May 3, 1846, Emilia Kingman, both of Orford. d Feb 14, 1847; m 2nd, Naomi Highland; 3rd, Oct 12, 1861, Julia A Tarlton b N B, ae 32, dau of Alfred W and Irene B (Wright). Surely a dau, possibly the son:

    a Lorenzo, laborer of Orford, m Lomira E Hall b Landaff; a son b Orford Nov 24, 1867
    b Hattie F (no date in census)

John F Dow ahgfdag d Mch 26, 1888; m Nov 28, 1850, Elizabeth Marshall Stearns. Children:

    a Eunice Stearns b June 26, 1852; d Feb 1919
    b Sarah Frances b July 27, 1854; d Jan 5, 1860
    c Ellen Wales b Sept 5, 1861; now of Meriden, Conn, member of D A R; contributed richly to ahgfd line

Eunice S Dow ahgfdaga m Aug 13, 1873, Florence William Shelley. Children:

    a Lena Alice b Aug 12, 1876
    b Bessie Istell b Dec 12, 1878; d Sept 5, 1881
    c ——, dau d ae 5 mos
    d William Stearns b Aug 12, 1884; has children
    e Burton Istell b Dec 22, 1886; has children
    f Helen Florence b Oct 18, 1888   g Percy Rickley b Aug 26, 1894
    h Marjorie French b May 19, 1897

Hannah Wales Dowe ahgfdah d Apr 8, 1896; m Dec 26, 1853, Ulysses Dowe Tenney adgfdda. Tenney Gen errs, calling her Hannah Wales b Dec 29, 1828, m Dec 9, 1853, d Feb 5, 1890. He was for nearly fifty years one of the most prominent portrait painters in the country;

of Manchester, N H, 1859, chosen to paint the portrait of Pres Franklin Pierce for the Senate House; painted the portraits of all the Governors of his time; moved to New Haven 1864 to execute many portraits for Yale College.   N H State House has 54 of his portraits, many in Dartmouth, Portsmouth, elsewhere.   Children:

    a   Julia Flynn b Nov 29, 1854
    b   Arthur John b Jan 26, 1856; of New Haven m Dec 19, 1888, Laura Hammer b Oct 7, 1864

William W Dow aghfdaj, trader of Concord, N H, d Feb 6, 1880; m June 16, 1860, wid Mary J Watson, ae 22, d Weare Jan 5, 1896, ae 67-7-25, dau of David and Sarah A (Hunter) Taylor.

Minerva Dowe ahgfdc d Oct 27, 1887; m May 29, 1821, Daniel Perry Owen of Hanover.   Children:

    a   Daniel P d, a sophomore in Dartmouth
    b   Lemuel Dowe b Sept 8, 1824; m Mary Frances Bridgeman; went to Chicago
    c   Franklin Dodge b Sept 27, 1832; d Jan 23, 1896; lived Concord

Tryphena Dowe ahgfdd d May 18, 1877; m Dec 31, 1823, Capt John Tenney b Hanover July 30, 1801; d Nov 23, 1888, son of Capt John and Lucinda (Eaton).   He was captain of artillery company 1823-6; justice of the peace 1848-68, selectman 3 years.   Children:

    a   Ulysses Dowe b Apr 8, 1826; m Hannah Wales Dow ahgfdah
    b   John Francis b June 6, 1830; m Nancy Folsom; 2nd Jennie Carter; for his highly interesting career see Tenney Gen
    c   Lemuel Dowe b Mch 28, 1836; m May 23, 1860, Cornelia W Everett; lived Hanover

Ulysses Dowe ahgfde, farmer of Hanover, raised a company for the Civil War; d Hanover July 16, 1874; served as justice of the peace, selectman, representative to Legislature; m Apr 8, 1828, Esther Owen b Hanover 1806, d May 11, 1836, dau of Timothy of Hanover.   Children:

    a   Charles Byron b Dec 4, 1828   b —— dau d in infancy
    c   Ellen Esther b Mch 15, 1832

Charles B Dowe ahgfdea m Oct 20, 1853, Vina Hall Ross b Hanover, dau of Hon Isaac; moved 1861 to Darbyville, Ohio, where she d Mch 1861; he enlisted 155th Ohio and at close of War returned to Hanover. He m 2nd (her 3rd) Ellen (Smith) Foster, ae 37, of Athol, Mass, dau of Moses and Mehitable.   A man of ability, culture and refinement, he maintained the family standing in Hanover; by the death of both sons the Hanover Dow family became extinct.   He prepared the Dow section of Hist Hanover and worked hard in his later years on Dow Genealogy. He lacked the material for correctness in the early generations but his account of the ahgf line was excellent.   Children:

    a   Edward Perry b July 27, 1854; d Jan 29, 1863
    b   Lemuel Algernon b Jan 23, 1856; bookkeeper N Y City; lost health; d Hanover May 11, 1912, unm

Ellen E Dow ahgfdec d Aug 14, 1856; m Hanover Sept 14, 1854, Orlando Cullen Blackmer of Barnard, Vt; moved to Oak Park, Ill. Son:

    a Norbourn H; grad Williams College; entered Episcopalian ministry; lives Alford, Neb

PELATIAH Dow ahgg, b Ipswich, Mass, May 30, 1739, came with his parents to Coventry; d there Feb 4, 1829. He did not serve in the Revolutionary army; m 1762 Catherine Rose b 1740; d Coventry Apr 17, 1826. They do not appear to have gone at any time to Hanover, N H, where one son located. Children:

    a Mabel b Sept 25, 1763; d Coventry; unm
    b Sanford b Sept 18, 1764   c John b Dec 16, 1766
    d Elizabeth b Sept 29, 1768; m Nov 12, 1786, David Bolles Jr
    e Jane b Dec 28, 1773   f Hannah b Sept 29, 1775
    g Margery b Nov 28, 1777; d Hanover Dec 21, 1852; unm
    h Clarinda b Feb 14, 1780; m Jan 11, 1810, Joel Morris; moved to Vt

Sanford Dow ahggb m Coventry 1790 Polly Manley b 1766; d Hanover Nov 19, 1816. Soon after marriage they moved to Hanover, where he d 1813. Chas B Dow, who prepared the family genealogy for Hist Hanover, covered his own family only and made no mention of his kinsman, altho Sanford was a prominent citizen and held quite a number of town offices. In addition, the vital statistics of Hanover are quite defective and have suffered from garbling. Children:

    a Chloe b Nov 25, 1791; d Hanover unm, date not in rec
    b John Manley b Nov 11, 1793
    c Betsey b Mch 20, 1796; d unm, undated
    d Sylvester b Dec 8, 1798
    e Paulina b Apr 4, 1801; m Capt Simeon Pye
    f Edson b 1803 (rec missing); d Hanover Feb 14, 1806
    g Fannie b Oct 19, 1806; unt

John Manley Dow ahggbb m Mary B Wade; moved to N Y City. Two children:

    a Sylvester Manley b about 1819   b William W b about 1821

Sylvester M Dow ahggbba m N Y Apr 22, 1841, Catherine Ann Servin b Jan 22, 1829 (sic rec, but date obviously wrong). They had children, but whole line unt.

William W Dow ahggbbb was lost at sea about 1857; wife not found; three children:

    a Sylvester b about 1848; d young
    b John Melmouth b abt 1850; unt
    c Robert b about 1852; lived Newark, N J; had large family; unt

Sylvester Dow ahggbd m Doris Zants. All data lacking; may have had more than 1 child:

    a Melmoth, when and where b not found

Melmoth Dow ahggbda must have m young as did his father. One child known:

    a John Melmoth b N Y City 1842

John M Dow ahggbdaa, Civil War captain, m Elizabeth K Allan. It seems to run in this family for the men to marry at 21. Children:

    a Lizzie Allan   b Mary Wade   c Allan Wade b Aug 24, 1866
    d Bertha McLane

THE BOOK OF DOW

Allan W Dow ahggbdaac; grad Columbia Univ; m Nov 10, 1892, Jessie Cecelia Frank.   Consulting chemist Barber Asphalt Co and one of the outstanding chemists of the country.   Children:

a   Florence Miriam   b   Allan Wade b Newark abt 1895

Paulina Dow ahggbe m Capt Simeon Pye; unt.   A Hanover rec: Polly Dow m Feb 11, 1799, John Flanders of Hanover, is to us inexplicable.

Fanny Dow ahggbh m Sherman J Parker of Coventry.   Children:

a   Maria d unm   b   Henry F   c   Sarah m —— Tibbets
d   Sanford d Andersonville 1863   e   Mary m H H Brainard

Henry F Parker ahggbhb, blacksmith of Coventry, d 1918; m Elizabeth Bradbury; 2nd Carrie H Howard; 3rd Elizabeth Risley. Children,—Frank S, Ralph H, Marion Elizabeth. His knowledge of the lore of Coventry was unlimited, his anecdotes about the Dow tribe inexhaustible.   Possibly at time he was willing to sacrifice accuracy for the sake of the story.   If his chance conversation had been collected into a volume, it would be by far the most valuable local history in America.

John Dow ahggc, farmer of Coventry; d ae 84; m Clarissa Guile, dau of Samuel and Hannah (Newcomb), sixth in descent from Gov William Bradford.   This male line will become extinct this generation. Children:

a   Diantha b Sept 7, 1800; m Augustus Woodward; div; 2nd Solomon P Loomis
      of So Coventry
b   Almira b Aug 4, 1802   c   John Nelson b Feb 5, 1805
d   Silas Newcomb b Apr 25, 1810; d Mch 23, 1876

Almira Dow ahggcb m Aug 5, 1827, Samuel Wilson of Coventry b 1799, son of Charles and Ruth (Herrick).   Children:

a   John m —— Smith   b   Jane m —— Brainard
c   Lorenzo m Roxanna Wilson

John Nelson Dow ahggcc d Jan 7, 1865; m Mary Porter.   Children:

a   Lorenzo F b May 26, 1841; d unm
b   Arthur Park b Feb 19, 1845

Arthur Park Dow ahggccb, ranch owner of Verona, Wyo, is a genial gentleman, fond of looking up Dows in any part of the world; m Julia Whitman, not now living.   Only child:

a   Lorenzo Park, rancher of Wyoming; unm

Jane Dow ahgge m June 7, 1795, Jesse Dewey b Springfield, Mass, Mch 30, 1774.   Children:

a   Laura b Mch 9, 1803; d May 27, 1816
b   Jesse Edson b July 7, 1806   c   John Nelson b Feb 3, 1814
d   Horace Pease b Oct 11, 1818; other children d young

HUMPHREY **Bean Dow** ahgh either inherited or bought a small farm in Coventry, but depended on his trade of shoe making, tanning and currying his own leather. A shoemaker is apt to be a philosopher and Humphrey surely was. From all accounts he was an amiable, highminded man, occupying through his attainments a higher position in Coventry than depended on the mere possession of money. He saw considerable service in the French and Indian war, a private in several hard battles. Upon discharge he returned home to Coventry. His son Lorenzo in his journal, Sept 25, 1815, notes: "I find that my father is entitled to some crown land,—but probably he will be cheated out of it." The fact is that Humphrey could have applied to the Provincial government for and received a land allotment, probably 640 acres, but he never did so, and when fifty years later, the matter was brought to his attention, the United States government had been set up and it would have required a special act of Congress to reward a veteran for British service.

Humphrey m Oct 8, 1767, Tabitha Parker, member of an original Coventry family, whose members are still prominent in the community, a good wife and mother, who lived to see all her six children grow up and marry. Lorenzo makes note of hearing of her death while he was in Ireland, Dec, 1804. Her gravestone, a marble slab, is beside that of her husband in the Nathan Hale cemetery of Coventry, a little difference in wording probably due to the fact that the inscriptions were many years apart:

"The ashes of Tabitha Parker, wife of Humphrey B Dow, are buried here"

"The dust of Humphrey B Dow is buried here."

Humphrey appears in the 1790 census, 2a, 2b, 5c, indicating some youth in his household, perhaps an overlooked son, more likely an apprentice, possibly a pupil. The cobbler had an intellect of high order, acquiring unaided an unusual education for the time, especially fond of Latin, which he was qualified to teach through college grades. His surplus income went wholly for books, his library finally being divided among his children. They all received an excellent education; all four daughters taught school before they were married. Lorenzo, the best known son, received the least education, but was a diligent reader in his boyhood. His old age may not have been lonely, for, altho his sons were far away, two daughters had homes in Coventry. Peggy Dow, Lorenzo's wife, devoted much time to him while Lorenzo was away on trips for many months at a time and was greatly endeared to him by her gentle

care.   Happy incidents are mentioned in the journals of both Peggy and
Lorenzo.   Children:

   a Ulysses b Aug 4, 1768, name recalling Humphrey's fondness for the Odyssey.
      It is a curious fact that no mention of him, even incidental, occurs in Lorenzo's
      journal
   b Ethelinda   c Mirza
   d Orelena m Elisha Fish; had 4 children; m 2nd ——
   e Lorenzo b Oct 16, 1777, name recalling his father's appreciation of the
      Florentine patron of literature.   Probably more than 20,000 children have
      been named for him
   f Tabitha

O NLY one school existed in the thriving old town of New London, Conn, prior to 1834. This was taught from 1801 by Ulysses Dow, a true scion of his ancestors, striking in originality and force of character, who d New London Dec 2, 1844. A pamphlet published 1907 by Richard B Wall contains much anecdote of his career.

Ulysses Dow ahgha was brought up in Coventry, but after coming to New London seldom found time to revisit it. A few times Lorenzo visited the school, received with much ceremony. There were no grades in those days. In a single room sat as many as 300 pupils with only one teacher. They were of all ages, some learning the alphabet, others men who shipped before the mast in summer and learned higher navigation in winter. When Lorenzo approached the teacher's desk, he was met with the stern admonition: "Lorenzo, you will make obeisance to this school." This done, Ulysses stepped down, embraced his brother and said: "Welcome, Lorenzo." In taking his departure Lorenzo failed to recall the required etiquette. "Lorenzo, I demand that you make obeisance to this school." Lorenzo complied and went back to his ox carts. There were a few years of Lorenzo's material prosperity during which he was accustomed to do his marketing in Norwich, coming from Montville, apparently in state, never with less than two ox carts driven by a huge negro, who had come with him from the south. Only a partial reason for this seemingly useless display was Lorenzo's inability to walk far or easily, a weakness inducing him to adopt a close fitting leather vest. He was thus equipped when he came to visit his brother in New London.

Ulysses had every educational advantage not precluded by comparative poverty. The library in his father's home was unusual and Coventry had unusual advantages in the presence of Rev Joseph Huntington, an original trustee of Dartmouth college, who prepared many boys for college, among them Ulysses. The young man went to Dartmouth but did not graduate. Like many others, he went to stay as long as his finances permitted; all his money gone, he returned home. He then studied medicine with Dr Cardie Parker, his mother's brother, who stood high in the profession. While studying he taught school to support himself. In due time he was licensed to practice and from the point of view of medical ability succeeded well enough. Practically, however, he was a failure through supersensitiveness. The shock from the death of a patient endangered his own life, and if a patient failed to get well as soon as expected, the doctor took to his own bed until the case was relieved. His brother-in-law was asked to nominate a teacher for the New London free grammar school and Ulysses gladly accepted the position. The salary was nominally high,—$1,000 a year, he to find his own firewood.

Ulysses was thrice married,—1st June 26, 1788, to Anna Tilden of Coventry, who d with her infant child, leaving him a widower at 22; 2nd to Ann Tappan, who lived but a short time; 3rd Phoebe Griswold became his wife and companion for 44 years, surviving him three. On his death she retired to a little farm in Salem which he had bought many years before from his brother Lorenzo, somewhat sterile and somewhat isolated. No children came to them, but they had an adopted dau Cynthia, who survived them. For more than 30 years he and his wife had a daily custom of exchanging notes during school hours. The duty of carrying was given to some boy as a sort of reward of merit. Mrs Dow met him at the head of the cellar stairs on which stood a stone crock containing doughnuts. In cold weather he was given a seat to warm himself beside the kitchen fire. But woe to that boy who came not well washed or who misbehaved in Mrs Dow's kitchen.

Ulysses never departed from his dignity, never appeared without his high, white starched stock. His friend Elder Swan was different, mounting his pulpit in summer, taking off hat, coat, stock and tie, before running his fingers through his hair and launching upon either prayer or sermon. True, the school room was not swept once a year. The noise of small boy's creaking shoes was annoying and the thick layer of old paper, discarded goose quills and other waste material tended to deaden the sound. He gave a prize to that boy who appeared barefoot first in the spring. "Creaking tanbark" was his own expression. Ulysses never used tobacco; when some youth from the shipyards came with quid in mouth, observant Ulysses soon made him roll the quid in wood ashes until the lye gave him a sore tongue for the rest of the day. There was a sort of school committee in New London, but they were all elderly men, friends of Dr Dow, who never interfered in any way with the school government. The salary was not big enough to leave him anything but poor in his old age, penniless at 76. He lived well, bought many books, subscribed to any public charity. But, the bulk of the money, after the firewood was provided, went to those "little Jimmy boys" at school whose winter shoes were mostly holes or whose other wants were pressing. He ran a steady and large account with a nearby cobbler. In forty years fully 5,000 boys must have eaten Mrs Dow's doughnuts, been cobbled at the doctor's expense, or otherwise fathered. No matter how severe, the good boys loved the stiff old doctor. The best boy was allowed to come to the house and get the school key. Three or more were permitted to ring the bell, fifteen minutes before each session sufficing for any part of the town. If the ringing was not three sharp strokes at a time, the doctor would angrily demand: "Who boggles the bell?" Upstairs in the attic a drill master came at intervals to exercise the boys with wooden guns, otherwise there was only one teacher. Classes were so large that all read aloud in unison to save time. A majority were in first or second reader stage. Older ones, who had been to sea since childhood, might be struggling with the alphabet.　On the other hand, there was a class in Latin and the doctor, if called upon, would teach Greek, Hebrew or calculus.　One course of study was taken by all with as much diligence as the daily Bible reading.　This was boxing the compass.　Astronomy and navigation were always in demand.　The greatest career New London offered was to be captain of one's own ship.

The doctor had nicknames for most of the boys and a large vocabulary of invented terms.　All winter long some boy looked anxiously into the stove at the question,—"doth it hoozle?"　If it burned well without smoke, it hoozled.　One of the boys was Findoodle, whose fondness for truancy made occasional trouble.　A delegation in search of the wayward once called at his mother's house and addressed the lady as Mrs Findoodle, she being adept with the broom as a weapon.　Truant boys were generally to be found by the shipyards and thither repaired the monitor boys armed with cord and a huge basket.　The truant was tied in the basket and carried back to school.　About 1834 a rival school was opened by a Dr Bull.　His boys were at once known as Bullfrogs, the others as Dowhogs.　A Saturday battle was the regular thing. Against the bullfrogs' wooden guns, Dr Dow armed his boys with brooms and charged them to "spud them well."

No reports to parents were made, no marks recorded.　That boy who seemed to do best was given his choice of seat, naturally near the stove in winter and the window in summer.　The methods of punishment were many and no one believed in spoiling a child by sparing a rod.　The doctor was slender, 5 feet, 10, but he was strong and needed his strength. There were pupils as big as he and stronger.　On one occasion a big fellow defied him and to prevent his removal to the seat of punishment locked his leg around the leg of his chair.　He was yanked out but was lamed for life, a circumstance which the doctor mourned deeply.　He had many a fight, but the big boy in the end was invariably thrown on his back and forced to turn over in the proper attitude for "spanchazling." This was performed with a large flat ruler.　The hole in the chimney was reserved for major offences.　The culprit had to crawl into it, only his head sticking out.　If unrepentant, he might get a pitcher of water down the back of his neck.　The gibbet, the stocks and the place for toeing the mark were mild, altho in the stocks one leg protruded above the bar, the other below.　Boys who stuck pins through flies were struck on the nose with a goose quill.

After thirty odd years of this system, New London elected a school board of political appointees.　Then began the doctor's troubles, for he was not a whig nor a democrat or any other partisan.　He did not vote at all until 1840, when there was a tie in the mayoralty election and he was persuaded to break it and put into office a lifelong friend.　In religion he also found troubles, steadfastly refusing to be Baptist, Congregationalist, Methodist or Presbyterian, avoiding consecutive attendance at any church, altho personal friendship might lead him to Elder Swan. When the Universalists organized, no one would sell them a site at any price. Doctor Dow let them have a building lot at the low price it had cost him years before. This heresy made him enemies in all the other denominations. In 1837 the democrats carried the city and Dr Dow's was the first head for political decapitation. He was removed and a new teacher, more up-to-date, appointed. Ulysses accepted the situation, rented quarters for a private school. This drew all the scholars, in spite of its cost, so after two years the new teacher was dismissed and Dr Dow reinstated. His years, however, had begun to tell upon him. Things became not wholly satisfactory. People began to whisper that he was not altogether right in his head. It was even rumored that he had spat on a boy in the stocks. Only the pupils seemed satisfied, they had no complaint. Early in 1844 the school board was able to dismiss him, a tie broken by the absence of a member who would accept a resignation but not vote for a dismissal. The committee called and broke the news. Dr Dow, then 76, showed great inward emotion but merely said: "I presume I shall have to abide by your decision, gentlemen."

It was then found that in forty years he had not saved a cent. His unsalable farm, several hundred books and the little necessary furniture were his only assets. Quickly his former pupils rallied to his support with house rent and money as needed. By this time he had taken to his bed, his illness lasting several months. But, to the cemetery, one bleak December day, followed more men than ever before had attended a funeral in New London.

Ethelinda Dow ahghb m Joseph Bridgman; moved to Hardwick, Vt. Lorenzo mentions a visit to her in 1804 and to her sister (Tabitha) who lived about a mile away.

Mirza Dow ahghc d Coventry Jan 30, 1855, ae 84; m 1788 Joseph Huntington, son of Rev Joseph, trustee of Dartmouth. One son became Governor of Ohio, another at about the same time Governor of Connecticut. Joseph was an editor of Charlestown, S C; forced into a duel and killed Aug 19, 1794. Children:

    a Flavius J b Coventry May 13, 1789; m Laura Beckwith of Dalton, Mass b Nov 6, 1801
    b Edward G b Washington, N C, Oct 22, 1792; m 1st Dec 18, 1814, Nancy Loomis d 1827; m 2nd Jan 27, 1831, Eliza Clark; lived Sou Coventry; d Sept 15, 1857

Lorenzo Dow ahghe, preacher, d Alexandria, Va, Feb 2, 1834; m 1st Peggy Holcombe d Hebron, Conn, Jan 6, 1820, ae 39; m 2nd, Lucy Dolbeare of Montreville, Conn, d Oct 26, 1863, ae 77, dau of George B. One child, by 1st wife:

    a Letitia d young

TO the genealogist the facts of life are three, birth, marriage, death, all between merely incidental. To the historian, the student of heredity the three facts are as nothing, the incidental betweens constituting the whole,—all the story of self advancement or debasement, of altruistic endeavor or its absence. Altruistic endeavor is the only thing which can delay the final engulfment into the River of Oblivion. Of all the men who bear the name of Dow three stand out as by far the most widely known:—Capt Henry Dow ab, Marshal of New Hampshire, Neal Dow adhccbb, legislator, and Lorenzo Dow, crazy preacher. Two of these experienced great material prosperity, altho such was not their first aim. To Lorenzo Dow, except for the few years before his death, came nothing but his own altruism. He lacked almost through life most of the ordinary human comforts, including health, sufficient clothing, sufficient food. For a hundred years any Dow traveling through the south has found his own name the best "open sesame" he could carry. From Virginia to Arkansas the first question has been: "Are you related to Lorenzo Dow?" During the year when LaFayette toured this country Lorenzo was preaching in Ohio. The census shows a close race in the naming of children,—La Fayette and Lorenzo not far apart, George Washington and Andrew Jackson well behind. LaFayette was in vogue only a year or two. Lorenzo's namesakes are still appearing. A few years ago an attorney had to go on a land title errand to a place in the Ozark region of Missouri, and found there, many miles from a railroad, the most primitive people he had ever encountered. The justice of the peace and judge of probate, registrar of deeds were one,—Lorenzo Dow Haskins, towering far above 6 feet, barefooted, with bearskin cap, rags for coat and trousers, dispensing justice with dignity and spotless integrity, interpreting the law to the best of his lights. In the community were many named Lorenzo Dow 4th or 3rd. On inquiry it was found that these mountaineers were descendants of a colony which had come about 1830 from eastern Tennessee, where Lorenzo had occasionally preached. Throughout the south memory is kept alive of Lorenzo's customary farewell announcement: "Brethren, by the grace of God I shall be with you to preach again this day, four years." He might say two or five years, but he never failed to appear on the day and hour.

It goes almost without saying, then, that this man who seemed to have no other thought for fifty years than of his religion and its promulgation should be carefully weighed in the scales of criticism without prejudice against or favorable predisposition. Altho much of the anecdote of his later life is apocryphal, the essential facts are provable and there is ample material in his own daily journal which he kept for over thirty years.

Lorenzo was an itinerant preacher never wholly in favor with the church authorities, seldom, if ever, accredited to any organization and never with salary or allowances. His only support was the gifts of his hearers. His method of preaching was his own, abounding in gesticulation, in picturesque phraseology, emphasis and abruptness. His abruptness often brought trouble. He might at any time point his finger at some young woman whom he had never seen five seconds previously, about whom he knew nothing, and tell her without preliminary that she was surely going to Hell, that eternal fire was her lot. This often made a hysterical victim and Lorenzo was often thrashed under similar circumstances by some angry brother or father. The spontaneousness of his speech, the squalor of his person, absence of what are generally termed good manners, fastened attention upon him wherever he went. His preaching was as free as he could make it. He seldom allowed a collection to be taken, as the devil was always lurking near to induce some enemy to charge Lorenzo with being mercenary.

The history of the first five years of his ministry is well summed up in a single paragraph of his own journal: "But now arose a difficulty from another quarter: I had lost my great coat on the road whilst traveling, and my coat was so worn out that I was forced to borrow one; my shoes were unfit for further service, and I had not a farthing of money to help myself with, and no particular friends to look to for assistance. Thus one day whilst I was riding along, facing a hard, cold, northeast storm, very much chilled, I came to a wood, and alighting from my horse and falling upon my knees on the wet grass, I lifted up my voice and wept, and besought God either to release me from traveling and preaching, or else to raise me up friends. My soul was refreshed, my confidence was strengthened, and I did believe that God would do one or the other, and true it was, people, a few days after this, of their own accord, supplied all my necessities, and gave me a few shillings to bear my expenses."

It is not easy to comprehend the intensity of religious feeling which almost amounts to mania. From his fourth year Lorenzo's thought and dreams were of heaven, hell, damnation, salvation, prayer, free will, election, calling, predestination, and many other points of doctrinal difference. At the age of 12 he dreamed of a man calling him to preach. Long afterwards he saw for the first time a picture of John Wesley and at once became certain that he was the man of his dream. A revivalist held the village of Coventry by the ears. For some reason, not clear even to himself, Lorenzo could not bring himself to the mercy seat. Confident that, steeped in unpardonable sin, he would die and be in hell that very night, he spent his hours in alternate prayer and shrieks. His cousin had a like experience; he wrestled with himself in his garden "and his shrieks could be heard for upward of a mile; but in the evening he found peace."

By the age of 12 he developed a chronic asthma which discomforted him always, often preventing his lying down at night.   His illnesses were frequent and a stomach trouble engendered by unintelligent eating never left him.   Very often he had to abandon a sermon because of fainting or nausea.

Lorenzo's journal covers his life to the end of 1816 and is an auto-biography of such completeness as he wished.   By a little reading between the lines it becomes a basis for character estimate than which there can be no better.   Jan 7, 1796, is the date of the beginning of his ministry, for then he received orders from the circuit preacher to join the brethren at Tolland.   After one week of constant traveling and preaching, Nicholas Snethen, head of the Methodist organization in Connecticut, spoke to him frankly:

"You are but 18 years of age; you are too important, and you must be more humble and hear, and not be heard so much; keep your own station, for by the time you arrive at the age of 21 years, you will see wherein you have missed it; you had better, as my advice, learn some easy trade, and be still for two or three years yet; for your bodily health will not admit of your becoming a traveling preacher at present; although considering your advantages, your gifts are better than mine were when I first set out to preach, but it is my opinion that you will not be received at our next conference."

The next day C Spry, circuit preacher, spoke a little more delicately: "There are many scruples in my mind with regard to your traveling, as many think your health *and behavior* not adequate to it."

There does not seem to be anything in these warnings that could be regarded as persecution or improper self-interest, yet Lorenzo felt a life-long resentment against both, although he had fainted more than once during a sermon that week and was ill most of the time.   He rejected their counsel and traveled through Rhode Island.   His experience with the Methodists of that State was precisely similar. At the end of three months Elder Jesse Lee wrote to the Methodists of Coventry: "In several places Lorenzo Dow was liked by a great many people; at other places he was not liked so well, and at a few places they were not willing he should preach at all; we have therefore thought it necessary to advise him to return home for a season, until a further recommendation can be obtained from the Society and preachers of that circuit."

Upon receipt of this, kind-hearted C Spry, circuit preacher, gave to the broken hearted Lorenzo what the latter describes as a written license and orders to come to the quarterly meeting in Enfield.   Somehow his plan failed, for at Hanover, N H, he met Elder Lee of Rhode Island, who had dismissed him and who questioned his present authority.   At the quarterly meeting he was examined and rejected.   He joined a preacher on the Orange circuit and preached as often as possible.   The following June he met in Vershire, Vt, N Snethen, who practically forbade his preaching, and Elder Lee did the same at the next quarterly meeting.

Lorenzo declared that it was not the right of any man to stop his preaching for that was between God and his own soul, and it only belonged to Methodists to say whether he should preach in their connection. After this he returned home for a short while, having traveled constantly and over 8,000 miles.

In an appendix to Lorenzo's journal appears a letter from Rev N Snethen to the Irish Methodists in 1805. We doubt its genuineness; possibly it was handed to Lorenzo, whose use of it may be as unjustified as was the writing of it. Mr Snethen writes that Mr Lorenzo Dow had again embarked for Europe, "better furnished perhaps for success than when he was with you last. His confidence of success must at least be very considerably increased having succeeded so well in deceiving or duping so many of the preachers in the American connexion. I hope that our brethren in Europe will resolve to have nothing to do with him,—the lines of distinction should always be kept very clear between the Methodist preacher and his *ape*. I am sorry, my dear friend, that we can give you no better specimen of the fruits of Methodism in this country. Alas! Alas! Shame! Shame! It shall be published in the streets of London and Dublin that Methodist preachers in America have so departed from Wesley, and their discipline, as to countenance and bid God speed to such a man as Mr Dow, the last person in the world who should have been suffered to trample Methodism under foot with impunity or countenance. His manners have been clownish in the extreme; his habit and appearance more filthy than a savage Indian; his public discourses a mere rhapsody, the substance often an insult upon the gospel; but all the insults he has offered to decency, cleanliness and good breeding; all the impious trifling in the holy ministry; all the contempt he has poured upon the sacred scriptures, by refusing to open them, and frequently choosing the most vulgar saying as a motto to his discourses, in preference to the word of God—all this is as nothing in comparison. He has affected a recognizance of the secrets of men's hearts and lives, and even assumed the awful prerogative of prescience, and this not occasionally, but as it were habitually, to pretend to foretell, in a great number of instances, the deaths or calamities of persons, etc. I have confidence that---disciples of the great Wesley will make a stand against this shameless intruder, this most daring imposter."

This document does not look genuine. It terms Lorenzo as a specimen of the fruits of Methodism; then disavows it. It would have been perfectly simple and straightforward to have written as presiding elder to the official Methodist bodies of the United Kingdom stating that Lorenzo Dow had no connection with Methodism. At all events, genuine or not, it is clear that Lorenzo was an irregular, unaccredited preacher. He had by this time traveled for years through New England, New York and Quebec, preaching, exhorting, generally in a barn or a school house, as churches were seldom open to him. At

Williston, Vt, his uncle (*) and family came out to hear him but "behaved very rudely" and strove to persuade him to leave the town.   In Orwell, Can, he met his uncle, Daniel Rust (†), formerly of Coventry.   At Danby, Can, he became ill; a Quaker by the name of Dow (‡) who by accident heard him preach, came to see him and brought a quart of wine, a pint of brandy, a pound of raisins, and half a pound of loaf sugar.   Another man walked fifteen miles to give him a dollar.   He mentions meeting in Hanover, N H, his two sisters and brother-in-law, Joseph Bridgman.

Oct 16, 1799, his 22nd birthday, saw him in Montreal; a ship captain told him he was about to embark for Dublin, and Lorenzo at once resolved to go.

"What shall you charge?"

"Sometimes people give fifteen guineas, but I will carry one for eight."

"I'll give you five guineas and find myself."

"I will; but you are a devilish fool for going from a plentiful country with peace to that disturbed island."

So Lorenzo gave him five guineas and bought some provisions, and had a few shillings left.   Nov 27, he landed at Larne, north of Ireland, and reached Dublin Dec 15.   He managed to travel throughout the island with experiences not unlike his American ones, occasionally raising firm friends, sometimes running afoul with the authorities and generally at odds with the church officials of all denominations.   In August he contracted smallpox, coming near death and being heavily marked for the rest of his life.   His trip ended as usual, he penniless with no clear course. Some Dublin Quakers (§) gave him passage money and he sailed for America Apr 2, 1800.   A Dublin physician had given him a quantity of books to sell and buy a horse with the proceeds.   He kept the books and went afoot.   Arriving in New York he sold the books for £115 to a dealer who took advantage of his ignorance of values, and sent all the money to the donor.

Returning to Connecticut, he sought at once to attach himself to some Methodist circuit, but his proposed colleagues generally objected strenuously on the ground that "Crazy Dow" would break up the meetings. So he toured the various circuits independently.   His nickname of Crazy Dow went ahead of him and tended to draw crowds.   Some of the meetings were "large and tender," others much less so.   Occasional gifts of money apparently sufficed for his needs.   At New Hartford he hired a ball room for $1.50, that being the only available meeting place.

---

*Lemuel Dow ahgf

†Daniel Rust m his mother's sister

‡This Quaker, member of adb, adf or adh, has never been identified.   Lorenzo was unaware of any relationship, however remote.   His own impression was that he descended from three brothers who came direct from England to Connecticut.

§It may be noted that the Quakers more than all others throughout his career helped him out of trouble.

Oct, 1800, he decided upon more travel, considering either Bermuda or Georgia. He spent four days with his parents and started out, leaving horse behind. The ship captain for Bermuda refused to let him embark on account of his religious persuasion, but the captain bound for Savannah reduced his fare 20 per cent for the same reason. His finances were fairly satisfactory to himself for, altho he had only $1.50, there was $18 owing to him in Connecticut. His trip lasted only four months, but he travelled through most of Georgia. The next season was spent in travel as far as the Maine border. On return he crossed the Hudson, thence to Philadelphia. Here he was disowned by the Methodist connection and found it almost impossible to preach, so he proceeded to Wilmington, Del. At Baltimore some one gave him $3 and at Culpepper a gift was $1.50. He always noted with care such gifts in his journal. At Stetsville he sold his watch for $8.50 and a supper, which was quite satisfactory, since it had cost only $19 the month before. The buyer, however, persuaded the community that Lorenzo was a horse thief.

At a camp meeting in Georgia upward of $100 was given to him, and the Governor gave him a pass through the Indian reservations. The money did not last long. He sold his lame horse on credit,—which means he never got anything for it, and bought another for $150. The second beast was such that Lorenzo rather bitterly remarks that the seller was a Methodist so-called. A half breed Indian mulcted him for $1.50 for a night's lodging, and he finally arrived at Natchez, an 800-mile trip, without a cent in his pocket. He refused to accept a collection, but took corn for his horse. Six towns distant he sold his saddle cloth for more corn. In seven months he traveled 4,000 miles. His horse fetched almost nothing. He got back to Georgia barefoot, coatless and without a seat to his trousers. It is true, however, that he had rejected many offers of money, wherewith he could have reclothed himself. As he says: "It was with seriousness and consideration that I took these journeys, from conviction of duty, that God required it at my hands. And knowing that impostors are fond of money, I was convinced that Satan would not be found wanting, to whisper in the minds of the people that my motives were sinister or impure."

In the last paragraph camp meeting is mentioned for the first time. Lorenzo was the originator of this idea. It arose from the difficulty or impossibility of getting a church in which to hold a meeting. In pleasant weather some grove was chosen, for thereby his hearers were saved the cost of a room or the inconvenience of a barn offered freely. If the service was successful, the preacher and hearers preferred to have it last two or more days. The first camp meeting on record was held by Lorenzo at Bolton, Mass. A huge glacial boulder, from the top of which he probably preached, is still known as Dow's rock. Throughout the south, camp meetings became the usual form of religious gathering and were often planned to last a week. The Methodists (who rejected Lorenzo) were the ones above all others to adopt this form of meeting.

It is also mentioned here that Lorenzo reached Natchez, Miss. At the time there was not a single church in the whole State. In later years Lorenzo and his wife gave land for the first church in the State. It is where Jefferson College now stands, and the deed, signed by Lorenzo and Peggy Dow, is preserved in the archives of that institution. In the Government compilation of land grants is an entry that Lorenzo Dow claimed July 1, 1778, 600 acres in Bear Creek, Miss, originally granted to Joseph Jackson. There is no other Lorenzo Dow. The date must be that of the original grant, and Lorenzo's claim, the grounds for which are not stated, must have been after 1805.

At Petersburg, Va, Maj John Oliver gave him vest, pantaloons, umbrella, stockings, handkerchief, watch, etc. Others gave him shoes, a coat, cloak, and a few shillings. Thus he was equipped for a new tour,—the Carolinas, and Tennessee. This was a great success, a series of camp meetings. A daughter of a President of the United States came out to hear him preach and the Governor of South Carolina gave him a certificate of recommendation with the State seal attached. His very name drew thousands anxious for a sight of him. He was at peace with the local Methodist connections and as much so with the whole body as he ever could be. Here Elder Jesse Lee of Rhode Island greeted him. As for Elder Nicholas Snethen,—"God had knocked him down at a camp meeting, and gave him such a baptism as he never felt before."

Next season Lorenzo started for Boston but, wishing some printing done, sold his horse to pay for it. This made his progress much slower. By this time he had resolved to publish his journal. How to pay for it he did not know. The unprinted book, however, was a delightful perpetual asset. He gave away many thousand copies, to be delivered when published, as endowments to chapels and the like. When back to New York, planning a new 6,000-mile journey, he had not a cent in his pocket but found an interested printer. The latter would proceed on $100 down and a bond for the rest, willing to put up his own money for the actual cost. Either money or bond could not be obtained. As a matter of fact, the first edition of the journal was printed in Ireland, less than half its subsequent length. The Author has never found a copy of this edition. The American editions are over 100 and by 1860 the book had circulated second only to the Bible. Clean copies are often found in second hand book shops at 50 cents.

At Danbury, Conn, he got enough money to release his watch from pawn. He started on foot for New York State but fell in with some Quakers who drove him by carriage as far as Litchfield. Here he prepared for a long walk, but at the last moment a man brought up a good horse to be his on unlimited credit. Lorenzo felt badly because he was unable to pay in full until nearly four months had passed.

THE BOOK OF DOW — 513

In Western, N Y, Lorenzo encountered Smith Miller, an inn keeper, who came to arrange for a service in that town, and accepted an invitation to his house. Miller's wife was an orphan and had taken a young sister to live with her. The first evening not a word passed between Lorenzo and the young girl. Next morning he asked Miller "if he would object if he should talk to his daughter concerning matrimony." The reply was that if the girl had any regard for her foster father she would not marry so as to leave his house. Thereupon, Lorenzo walked straight into the house and asked Peggy: "Do you think you could accept such an object as me?" Peggy left the room without a word. Subsequently her people advised her against the marriage on the ground that Lorenzo would probably fail to survive his already planned trip to Mississippi. Lorenzo took that trip and planned another to Ireland, but on second thought that letters from Ireland might be intercepted, and cause gossip, pressed for the marriage, and it was performed Sept 3, 1804, by the first preacher who came along. No couple was ever more devoted. If one's wife is the best judge of a man's inmost self, there can be nothing but praise for Lorenzo. All her life Peggy was constantly impressed by his tenderness and she felt for him the highest admiration. Another trip to North Carolina was taken, followed by a tour of New England. Dec. 1815, saw him once again in Dublin, with his wife. Peggy had been left behind on many trips, but this time Lorenzo contrasts his two Irish experiences, the first alone and discredited, now "with wife and daughter, and the way opening before me."

The journal is very brief after 1806. Only a few of his many trips are mentioned with detail. June 9, 1813, "leaving Peggy in Buckingham Co, Va, where she was confined with ——," Lorenzo went on to preach in North Carolina. The last entry in the journal which bears a date is Mch 22, 1816. Lorenzo had returned from the Bahamas and found Peggy the happy guest of his father in Coventry. Lorenzo was then approaching forty and spoke of a probable early death. As we know, however, eighteen more years were given to him for constant traveling, constant preaching in almost every State of the Union.

The journal of Peggy Dow is included in all late editions of Lorenzo's; it covers also to 1816; its narrative more simple, sweeter in tone, none of the complaints about business unfairness of men, of being cheated and persecuted, which became common in Lorenzo's later narratives. She mentions her birth in Granville, Mass, 1780, of Presbyterian parents, but does not mention their names. Her mother died when she was six; her father married again six months later, but became very poor. So, when her sister, nine years her senior, married, Peggy went to the new home. Here her chief delight "was in going to meeting and praising and singing praises to my God and Savior."

Her courtship is described with simplicity: "My brother-in-law invited Lorenzo Dow, then on his way to Canada, to preach at our meeting house, and sent on the appointment a day or two beforehand, so that the people might get notice. As he was a singular character, we were very anxious to see and hear him. The day arrived, and the house was crowded; and we had such a good time! I was very much afraid of him, as I had heard such strange things about him!

"He was invited to my brother-in-law's, but did not come for several days. He had appointments to preach twice and thrice in a day. However, at last he came, and tarried all night. The next morning he was to preach five or six miles from our house; and little did I think that he had any thought of marrying, in particular that he should make any proposition of the kind to me; but so it was; he returned that day to dinner, and in conversation with my sister, concerning me, he inquired of her how long I had professed religion. She told him the length of time. He requested to know whether I kept company? She told him I did not; and observed that I had often said, 'I had rather marry a Preacher than any other man, provided I was worthy; and that I would wish him to travel and be useful to souls.' By this time I had happened to come into the room, and he asked me if I had made such a remark. I told him I had. He then asked me if I would accept of such an object as him. I made no reply, but went directly out of the room—as it was the first time he had spoken to me, I was very much surprised. He gave me to understand that he should return to our house again in a few days, and would have more conversation with me on the subject. Next day he told me he would marry provided that he could find some one that would consent to his traveling and preaching the gospel; and if I thought I could be willing to marry him, and give him up to go, and do his duty, and not see him or have his company more than one month out of thirteen, he should feel free to give his hand to me. Although I felt myself inadequate to the task, without the Grace of God to support me! Yet, I felt willing to cast my lot with his, and be a help, and not a hindrance to him, if the Lord would give me grace, as I had no doubt but He would, if I stood as I ought—and I accepted of his proposal. My Lorenzo was gone about seven months before he returned to me."

Several years later she writes: "They carried my sweet little Letitia, and consigned her to the tomb, there to rest until the last trump shall sound, and the body and spirit be re-united again; and then we shall see how glorious is immortality. I wrote to Lorenzo the day that our child died; but he did not get it."(*)

Peggy Dow was never compelled to be alone twelve months of the thirteen. She made many long tours with him and became almost as well known through the south. Hers was a quiet simplicity, her universe

*Lorenzo was making a third tour of Ireland at this time.

divided into four parts, her God, her Lorenzo, her child and her neighbor. Lorenzo was mobbed many times by those who disagreed or resented his ways; he was imprisoned and fined for slander, was often treated with great severity as a vagrant, was robbed and assaulted; but Peggy was invariably treated with the utmost respect by all and with love by those who knew her.

Her death notice: Peggy, wife of Lorenzo Dow, near Hebron, Conn, Apr 4, 1822.

The manner of the second marriage of Lorenzo Dow was thus: At the conclusion of a sermon he asked in a matter-of-fact tone: "Is there any woman in this audience who would like to marry Lorenzo Dow? If so, will she kindly stand? One woman arose, approaching middle age and in rusty black. She was the daughter of a local farmer. Lorenzo gave her a short examination wholly in reference to her "Godliness," then demanded that they be married on the spot. It was with the utmost difficulty that his friends prevailed upon him to wait until the following day. The marriage on the whole turned out quite successfully. The bride inherited a piece of farm land, hardly sufficient to afford a living, but always a home with reasonable comfort. She outlived her husband many years, well maintained by the royalties accruing from the journal.

Lorenzo himself got in later years enough from the sales of the journal to keep himself in comparative luxury. That he made many enemies there can be no doubt, that he was not able to keep on good terms with his neighbors, that he always saw a wrong done to him but was less charitable about wrongs he himself did. After his second marriage, altho he was traveling much, he often stayed home months at a time. He dammed a small stream on the farm, intending to build a mill, but was sued by those below him on the stream, whose water he had impounded. Judgment being given against him, he tore down the dam to give them a flood, all the water to which they were entitled and much more than they liked. Thus he was liable for damages again. His ostentatious way of living was criticized, being in remarkable contrast to his half starved earlier life. No doubt, the huge negro who was his constant body servant after 1816 was virtually if not legally a free man, but his enemies called him a slave holder. He traveled in state at home with two or more ox carts, a luxury laughed at as much as criticized. He became anxious to acquire property, land in Mississippi or the grant which might have come to his father for military service.

From his journal he omitted most that was disagreeable to him. For example he passed over his ministry in Claremont, N H, as unfruitful owing "to the opposition of the better classes." He found in Claremont a Methodist colony already inclined to revert to the older Congregationalism. Under the intensity of his vituperation they all "backslid" and at last a crowd of his angry parishioners escorted him to the town line.

Here Lorenzo with much ceremony took off his shoes, shook the dust of the town from his feet, and went on never to return. In 1822 he was preaching in Maine. In one town a congregation gathered taxing the standing room of the place. Lorenzo offered the customary prayer and preached a long sermon. At its conclusion he gave out a long hymn. While it was being sung, he jumped out of the window, mounted his horse and was out of sight before many knew what had happened. He delighted more and more as time went on in abrupt lack of good manners.

In his talk of his own persecutions there is much that suggests self delusion. Some of this in his own language: "When Cosmopolite (thus he always termed himself after he had become traveled) was on his last tour through—(Ireland) orders were sent from the "Castle," somewhere, by somebody, that he must be taken into custody; which body returning, replied for answer that Cosmopolite could not be found (Cosmopolite was on the chase seventeen hundred miles in sixty-seven days and held two hundred meetings—such being the distance from the people, without intimacy—and the velocity of the journey, that they scarcely knew from whence he came or where he was gone?)—this, more then once or twice. Moreover the Threshers pursued him two nights and one day for a noted heretic; but he unwittingly escaped from them likewise. The *martial* law was now proclaimed in four counties, which made it dangerous travelling without a pass; but Cosmopolite was providentially kept in peace."

On board ship: "Cosmopolite was accused with 'hush money' clandestinely, by some who were on board—on getting wind of it he had the *agreement* stated, and then produced the receipt of the full amount, which answered to the articles. Then he was accused of having received a present of ten pounds from the Captain, which they said should have been divided among the passengers—Cosmopolite said why? Was there any such agreement? They acknowledged not. Nevertheless ungenerously did some persist to make the impression that Cosmopolite was a swindler."

Whilst in Europe Cosmopolite was attacked with spasms of a most extraordinary kind, which baffled the skill of the most celebrated of the faculty, and reduced his nervous strength, and shook his constitution to the center, more than all his labors and exposures heretofore, which had been from seven to ten thousand miles a year and attending meeting from six to seven hundred times; but now his sun appeared declining, and his career drawing to a close. But the idea of yielding and giving up the *itinerant sphere* was trying to Cosmopolite, seeing that it was his element and *paradise* to travel and *preach the gospel*. Hence he got a stiff leather jacket girted with buckles to serve as stays, to support the tottering frame, to enable him to ride on horseback, to which the doctors remonstrated against; when they would answer no further, he took the gig and a little wagon, but was obliged to sit or lie down some part of the meeting to be able to finish his discourse, mostly for seven years."

Almost invariably he considered himself (and probably often was) cheated in buying a horse. "Cosmopolite bought a pair of mules, which were to have been fitted to the carriage against his return; but in lieu thereof, were put to a wagon and so broke down they were unfit for service; and hence he had to part with them for about half value, to be able to prosecute his journey; and the horse he had was shortly starved so as to fail, and he was obliged to part with him for one of little worth."

A criminal proceeding against him for slander resulted in a nominal imprisonment and a substantial fine. About this he wrote a volume of protest and self-justification, but the impression it leaves is unpleasant. He had slandered a man most grossly in print, in a way which, if unrebuked, would be the man's ruin. It is evident that he took some idle hearsay without any knowledge on his own part. In fact, his attitude was almost throughout that he could do no wrong and his was a happy irresponsibility. He had a long series of law suits, all of which went against, as justice could go no other way. Most of these were as endorser of some one's note, and he never had any assets on which to levy. "Reputation attacked on all sides, and in remote parts through the States, that he was revelling in riches and luxury, with a fine brick house, sugar and cotton plantations, flour and saw mills, *slaves*, and money in the banks, etc, like a nabob in the east. Whilst others made use of everything they could that would be to his discredit, among which, some few who had subscribed for his journals and paid in advance, but not getting their books, no allowance was made for the books being lost, but all was construed, "a design to cheat, and has got the property, and gone to the Mississippi to feather his nest."

Almost all the editions of the journal contain portraits of both Lorenzo and Peggy. So far as the Author has been able to ascertain, there are but three original pictures of himself and only one of Peggy. These have been re-drawn many times, and indifferently. An oil painting of him was made in South Carolina, but the local artist was so carried away with admiration for Lorenzo's character, that he did not attempt to make a single feature true to life, merely adapted the conventional idea of the likeness of the Christ. A drawing made when he was about 25 to 30, is idealized beyond recognition. At 28 he was described in an application for a passport as about 5 feet, 10 inches, heavily pockmarked, with pale blue eyes, brown hair, darker eyebrows, with a scrophulous mark under his chin. At 50 a drawing was made, the only one worthy of consideration. He had then changed as age and health dictated, slender nose with sunken bridge, pockmarks very distinct, a long beard which had no acquaintance with a comb, matted hair hanging on his shoulders. Tradition states with unmistakable emphasis that he disliked to waste the time to wash himself. If given a new suit of clothes, he either gave it away to someone less fortunate than himself or reduced it to rags in a few weeks.

Peggy's portrait varies only with the skill or lack of it of the engraver. While heavy featured and not beautiful, it suggests charm from freedom from affectation and simplicity of manner.

Tabitha Dow ahghf m Samuel French b Hoosick, Mass, came to Hardwick, Vt, about 1800; d 1848, ae 69. He was very active in town affairs and an energetic orator. There was no church in town when he arrived, so he set apart the most accessible corner of his farm and built one, a substantial affair designed to last, at his own expense and mostly with his own hands. He himself refused to have anything to do with any denomination or organization. His church was to be free to all, and pulpit open to any applicant. All his neighbors were Congregationalists and had the church to themselves about fifty-one weeks per year, but if an itinerant preacher came along Samuel gravely told the usual incumbent that he must wait until Monday or next week. The people tried to buy his church but he held it as long as he lived.

Calvin Dow ahgi never married but lived at home until his mother died. She gave him what pocket money she could and perhaps babied him a little more than his best interests called for. His mother was greatly devoted to casting her own horoscope, and in this Calvin could help. The horoscope always predicted her death at some early date. Each time the day came and passed finding her alive, she seemed neither pleased nor disappointed. She began at once to cast a new horoscope. Calvin was a amiable youth who never did any harm, any good or any work, if he could avoid it. When at last his mother died and his brother Levi insisted he should work, Calvin drifted with genteel indifference into the poor house, living until about 80. For a long while he seemed quite contented, but at last grew rather bitter against Levi, who had, he considered, deprived him of his inheritance. However, the almshouse fare was better than Levi had, and Levi was working fourteen hours a day. Calvin d Feb 25, 1834.

FINALLY the line of Henry Dow, immigrant, through his youngest son disappears in two generations.

Jeremiah Dow ai was an infant when his mother and step-father took him to Ipswich, which was his home always. He probably followed some trade, but has appeared only as a farmer. He was a considerable speculator in land, sometimes jointly with his brother Thomas, and was well to do for the times. In 1710 seats together were assigned to the brothers in the new meeting house. Both were surveyors of highways in 1694, and Jeremiah again 1710-11. Both were tything men 1698 to 1708 and both appear very frequently as witnesses to wills or deeds. Jeremiah was half owner of the Bradstreet farm on which Thomas lived and farmed for eight years. His last home was a farm at Jeffreys's Neck, which Thomas deeded to him Mch 27, 1712. Apr 18, 1722, he sold land in Hampton to Jabez Dow abd,—"granted to me by my mother—Margaret Dow." He d soon after, his will proved June 11, 1723, naming his nephew Daniel Dow aha as executor. He m (int put Sept 30, 1706, says Elizabeth) Susannah Sutton, wid. Inventory of his estate taken June 10 amounted to £504-4-0, "Sett out by a commission from ye Honorable John Appleton, Judge of Probate of Wills & in sd County of Essex, to widow of Jeremiah Dow, as her thirds or right of dower, ye great Loor Room in the Mantion House, next the street & ye Lenten Chambre." Susannah receipted as follows: "Jan 4, 1783 (sic) Rec'd of Daniel Dow Excetr of the Last Will and Testament of my late Husband Jeremiah Dow, one third part according Inventory of ye Personal Estate for my own use and benefit and am therewith fully Satisfy'd and contented. Rec'd by me In Presence of Nathl Knowlton

her
Susannah S Dow
mark"

Susannah had a family of her own, for in her will 1749 she left legacies to sons Joseph and Richard; grandson Ebenezer; sister Maria Lakeman, wid; dau Mary Trumbull, Mercy Hovey; Anna Sutton. Her sixth child was only child of Jeremiah Dow:

a Margaret b Ipswich Oct 4, 1707

Margaret Dow aia exercised a woman's privilege of changing her mind, in days when marriage engagements were regarded more seriously than now. Her int to Nathaniel Treadwell Jr pub Apr 17, 1725; int to Abraham Tilton 3rd pub Apr 1, 1727. This was surely an April Fool joke on Abraham, for Margaret m Aug 24, 1727, Henry Greenleaf, much her senior. No children; on his death she m 2nd (int pub Dec 8, 1733) John Lull of Ipswich (Thomas 2, Thomas 1). One child:

a John bap Oct 20, 1734; d July 25, 1735

Margaret d Nov 27, 1754.   John Lull m 2nd 1757 wid Anna (Nichols) Lord.   A son Jeremiah d 1777 ae 19, unm, and thus this particular Lull line became extinct. Anna Nichols m 3rd Daniel Choate. What became of Abraham Tilton and Nathaniel Treadwell is of no consequence to us. The Treadwells often found marriage rather difficult. Nathaniel's brother Thomas had the banns published three times before he succeeded. One was to Elizabeth Smith who jilted him and was banned to John Dow ahb. It was wid Hephzibah Dow ahfd who finally made the path easy and corralled Thomas for keeps.

THE LINE OF JOHN NUDD

SINCE Henry Dow, immigrant of 1637, kept his promise to his first wife, Joan Nudd, and provided for her little Tommy as his Owne Sonne, it is but fair that he should not be genealogically forgotten in the Book of Dow. The History of Hampton, N H, treats of him fairly fully and gives without omission one line of descent—that which stayed in Hampton and is well represented there today. The original homestead of Thomas Nudd remained in the family about 250 years. But, as Hist Hampton is out of print and inaccessible to most owners of the Dow Book, this line is reproduced here with minor alterations and recent additions. The American Nudd family is relatively small. In the third generation it divided into two branches, one in Hampton, the other moving to North Hampton, thence to Greenland, from where the fourth and fifth generation divided into branches, one to Wolfboro, one to Canterbury, one to Kensington. A sixth generation went into Maine. While the Author has not worked as hard on this chapter as on the Dow lines, he has for many years preserved every accessible reference to Nudd. Hist Canterbury followed one line to date. The Author connected this easily with James 4 Nudd of Greenland. The census of 1790 and 1850, the war rosters and vital statistics failed to trace any one line consistently and for many years the Nudds of Greenland were left in more or less fragmentary state. No one of the name ever seemed to take the slightest interest in the family genealogy. At last two ladies were found, both born Nudd, who untangled much of the confusion, carried the Kensington lines to date and cleared up at least one complete line of the Nudds of Wolfboro.

The Nudd family is one of the oldest in England. The Cymric Lludd (Lhuth) was a sky god and is the original of the famous king Lot of Arthurian times. The Gaelic equivalent was Nudd, Nuada or many other variations in spelling. Apparently, a family assuming this name descended from Gaelic times and remained in its original home in Norfolk Co, near the coast and survived the many Danish raids from the seventh century onward. By 1600 the family was numerically strong but almost wholly confined to the two parishes of Ormsby. This small town was surely the father of Hampton, N H, for on the boat which carried Henry Dow to Boston came also Thomas Nudd, John, Thomas and William Moulton, Robert Page, Robert and William Marston, William Palmer, all intermarried many times with Nudd and Dow of Hampton and their descendants elsewhere. From Ormsby also, but at a later date, came Margaret Cole, 2nd wife of Henry Dow, with the Metcalfe family, settling in Dedham. One more Nudd came to these shores. A deposition was made in court in Suffolk Co, Mass, 1648, by one Richard Nud, ae about

32. No other mention of him has been found and it is possible that the name is garbled and not Nud.

The first known Nudd of our line was John, citizen of Ormsby, who had a son Roger; no other fact being found. The Nudds were numerous in St Margaret's parish, on the coast side of Ormsby, but there are extant no parish records prior to 1675. The St Michael parish registers go back to 1586, but this was neither a Nudd nor a Dow home. A rent roll of Ormsby manor for 1610 is extant and shows a score of Nudds, either with planting ground or cottages. There is nothing to show a seafaring branch of Nudds. A bare possibility for our line is one William Nudd, farmer, with sons Thomas and W——. There was the late Robert Nudd Junr, late Nicholas Nudd, Robert Nudd pedder, another William Nudd, Agnes W wid, James, late Walter Nudd, whose yearly rent was 5d.

Roger Nudd was bap St Michael's parish June 11, 1598, the isolated entry indicating that his parents were recently from St Margaret's. His marriage to Joan has not been found. He was bur: Ormsby churchyard Dec 24, 1630, leaving an only child. This was Thomas, surely born 1628, as his inheritance from Henry Dow came 1649, to celebrate the 21st birthday of the *quasi* adopted son. Eight months after Roger Nudd died Henry Dow married his widow, the two families having been neighbors and friends.

Thomas Nudd ak (this arbitrary key separating by one letter from the Dow family), at one time official keeper of the calves with a large salary, to wit £11 per year, later selectman and prominent citizen of Hampton,—inherited from his stepfather ten acres off the easterly side of the homestead (on the road from Hampton to Great Boar's Head, about 1 1-4 miles from the present village); one share of the cow common and a proportionate share of the fresh water meadow and the salt marsh, being the Hampton estate of **Henry Dow**, gent. Thomas Nudd built himself a house on his ten-acre lot and did there take unto himself a wife,—Sarah dau of Godfrey Dearborn, weaver, leading pioneer of Hampton, bap 1603 in Lincolnshire, Eng. Sarah was the fifth child, b Exeter about 1641 and about 13 years younger than her husband. Apparently Thomas Nudd never knew exactly how old he was, for in a deposition made May 8, 1695, he gave it as about 66. He then stated that he had lived many years a servant for Timothy Dalton. Apparently the job of keeper of the calves was no sinecure, as he had to collect all each day at sunrise, drive them to pasture, gather them at sundown and return each to its owner. The position with Dalton was easier and fully as responsible. As a matter of fact, he managed one of Dalton's estates, that gentleman being very rich in land.

The Nudds had seven children, but only two grew to maturity:

a   Samuel b Sept 13, 1670
g   Hannah b Oct 23, 1678; d 1751; m Francis Page

Samuel Nudd ake d Mch 26, 1748; m Feb 27, 1701, Sarah Maloon, dau of Luke and Hannah (Clifford) of Dover. She d Feb 14, 1756, ae 77. Samuel retained and cultivated his inherited land and was backed by his father-in-law in the ownership of a small vessel carrying and trading between Hampton and Boston. This was the beginning of the family fortune, which by the end of the Revolution was considerable. Three children:

a Mary b about July 1705   b James bap Aug 10, 1707
c Thomas b Oct 8, 1708 (progenitor of all the Hampton Nudds)

Mary Nudd akea d Oct 20, 1776; m (his 2nd) June 28, 1727, Capt Ephraim Marston, son of Ephraim and Abial (Sanborn). His oldest dau Phoebe m Simon Dow abccb. Mary's children:

a Sarah b Dec 10, 1728; m Joseph T Weare
b John b Sept 12, 1731; m Comfort Green; 2nd Abigail Brown
c Mary b Jan 12, 1734; m June 17, 1756, Benjamin Dow abdcc
d Anna b Dec 22, 1737; d Apr 25, 1771, unm
e —— d Dec 28, 1742   f Samuel b 1745; d Oct 7, 1748

James Nudd akeb was by far the most prolific of his line. He d May 27, 1753; m Aug 10, 1726, Abigail Thomas, dau of Capt Benjamin and Mary (Leavitt) of No Hampton. The Thomas homestead was in the present town of Greenland and was much better than the half of the Hampton property which would accrue to James Dow. Therefore James moved to Greenland and became lost to Hampton annals. Hist Hampton gives the list of his children and ends there. Abigail d Greenland Oct 13, 1749, her husband continued the home farm. Every one of their sons saw Revolutionary service. Their genealogy has been difficult to trace, for until 1923 the Author was unable to find any one of the name or blood interested in the subject. As a whole, the family has been inconspicuous. So far as the Author can learn, not one has been selectman and all have avoided the Legislature and all public offices. None has held high military rank, *per contra*, not one of them has ever been in jail and none in the county farm.

The children of James and Abigail:

a Mary bap 1727   b Samuel bap 1731   c Benjamin bap 1733
d James bap 1735   e John bap 1737 or 1736
f Thomas bap 1740. Another Thomas Nudd was in service 1775
g Abigail bap 1742. Hist Hampton gives d 1742, probably error
h William; actual rec not found
i Jonathan bap 1747; not in 1790 census; probably d young
j Martha bap 1747   k Hannah d young; not the youngest

Mary Nudd akeba m Jeremiah Dearborn b Dec 20, 1726, son of Jeremiah and Sarah (Taylor). The Dearborn homestead passed down through this line. Children:

a Olive   b Sarah   c Elizabeth
d Samuel m Hannah Philbrick; inherited the homestead
e Mary   f Sarah   g Jeremiah

Samuel Nudd akebb. Family rec says that Benjamin Nudd akebc moved about 1806 to Wolfboro with his brothers Samuel and William and that they bought adjoining farms in the north part of the town. This statement is our only actual record of the identity of William, altho his mature record is well known. Samuel m Hannah Tarlton, according to Hist Hampton, but this seems confused with his nephew. Kensington rec is clear: m by Rev Jeremiah Fogg Dec 15, 1750, Jemima Weare. Of their children, only a son Weare appears in actual rec. Census 1790 gives two Samuels, of Chester, N H, 1a, 1b, 5c, and of Greenland, 1a, 1b, 3c. Presumably the Chester rec is akebb, coming to Wolfboro at age of about 75. There is no proof which enlistment is of akebb and which of akebba.

One enlisted June 26, 1775, and receipted for $4 for an overcoat. The other was under Capt Richard Shortridge June 27, 1775, rec of Col Enoch Poor. One or the other was under Capt Thomas Berry Nov 5, 1775, and one was at Pierce Island Nov 25, 1775, Capt Henry Elkins. Children, all but one conjectured:

a Samuel. Probably he m Hannah Tarlton. His enlistment June 27, 1780, gives him of Greenland, ae 25, 5 feet, 7, dark. In July 1780 he was at West Point, receipting for a pound of sugar and a pint of rum. His position is certain in the 1790 census,—of Greenland 1a, 1b, 3c. Beyond these data, he is untraced

b David. Rev rolls lists four men as deserting, David having enlisted Aug 29, 1782, to fill vacancy in company of Capt Titus Salter. The odd thing is that there is no record elsewhere of any such company. Such desertions are usual and mean little, especially from Greenland and thereabouts. Men enlisted for some fixed term, at the conclusion of which they went home without formality. David surely existed, for he m June 9, 1793, Sarah Smith, both of No Hampton

c Weare b 1758   d William b 1762

e Abigail. An Epping rec gives some Abigail d Aug 26, 1766, with no other data

f Mary b 1756; d Sept 8, 1831; m by Rev Sam Perley Oct 22, 1772, Abraham Gove

Weare Nudd akebbc, farmer of Kensington, d Feb 19, 1835, ae 77-3-9; not found in 1790 census; m Kensington Apr 11, 1781, by Rev Jeremiah Fogg, Hannah Sherburne d Kensington Aug 17, 1782, ae 22; 2nd Kensington Dec 15, 1785, by Rev Jeremiah Fogg, Jemima Blake d wid Kensington Dec 2, 1838, ae 74-6-24. Children:

a John S d July 25, 1782, in infancy

b John b May 12, 1787   c Sarah b July 5, 1789

d Hannah b Oct 27, 1791   e Jemima b Apr 11, 1796

John Nudd akebbcb, farmer of Kensington, d Jan 9, 1867, ae 79; m Chester, N H, July 31, 1814, Betsey Pilsbury of Candia d Kensington Nov 19, 1815, ae 27; 2nd Hampton Falls Jan 22, 1817, Mary Worthen d Kensington Mch 13, 1852, ae 64-9-11, dau of Enoch and Jemima (Quimby) (adkddc). He made a 3rd m to a lady still remembered by kinsfolk as "Aunt Sallie" and had no children of their own.

We are sorry to record that at his 3rd m John Nudd fibbed about his age, as men almost invariably do at 2nd and 3rd m. He stated he was

born 1809; farmer, widower, m 3rd, Kensington Apr 6, 1853, Sarah Page
Kimball b 1811, dau of Stephen and Clarissa (Hilliard). This statement
of age put the genealogist off the track for a long time. Children:

a William b Dec 14, 1817   b Betsey B b Mch 23, 1819
c Amos b Sept 6, 1820

William Nudd akebbcba d Exeter Aug 20, 1863, b erroneous in d
rec as 1815; farmer of Kensington, moved to Exeter soon after 1850. He
appears in census 1850, assessed $2,000; m June 27, 1843, Sarah Stevens
of East Kingston b 1823. Her middle initial appears in rec as P, T and
A. Children:

a Ella F b Feb 5, 1844
b Frank Herman b Mch 25, 1845; d Jan 8, 1848
c Eugenia Minerva b Aug 24, 1847   d Francelia b 1849
e —— dau b Dec 20, 1851   f Ida L b June 12, 1853
g —— son b Apr 4, 1855   h —— son b Dec 21, 1857
i —— son b Nov 9, 1860; 5 youngest b in Exeter

Ella F Nudd akebbcbaa m 1874 Edward F Gove, farmer of Portsmouth, N H, son of William N and Louisa J (Whitacar). No children.

Betsey B Nudd akebbcbb m Daniel York; her descendants still
live in the homestead built by Weare Nudd, her grandfather. Children:

a Augusta   b John. He d about 1922, leaving considerable family

Amos Nudd akebbcbc, farmer of Kensington, assessed 1850 at
$2,000; m Dec 22, 1840, July A James. Sometime after 1850, after a
quarrel with his father, he went to Seattle, Wash. Coming back to
make peace, he arrived in Kensington the day after his father's funeral.
Two youngest children b Exeter, older Kensington. Presumably he
returned to Seattle and had no later children:

a George b Aug 29, 1841; d Kensington Aug 15, 1846
b Georgianna L b Mch 24, 1847
c —— dau b Mch 27, 1852   d —— dau b May 29, 1855

Hannah Nudd akebbcd m a Mr Tilton, who d before 1845

Jemima Nudd akebbce m James Dearborn, both bur in Kensington
churchyard. Children:

a Sarah Nudd b about 1822; m George Sherburne Pendergast of Charlestown,
   Mass; she d Feb 15, 1870; 3 children
b George Elvin b Apr 16, 1825; m Kittery Navy Yard July 25, 1845, Catherine
   Stephenson b Norfolk, Va. Four children. A dau Ella Frances m 1870
   George W Smith U S N and still lives in Philadelphia. Much interested in
   genealogy, she completed the line of Kensington Nudds, which was left
   sadly defective in the vital records
c John Blake b Oct 23, 1828; m Hattie Eaton; no children

William Nudd akebbd has been more or less confused with his
uncle William akebh. It was certainly he who was in 1st militia June
27, 1780, ae 18, dark, 5 feet, 5, of Greenland. It is not certain which of
the two enlisted Hampton Falls July 19, 1779, receiving £30 bounty.

THE BOOK OF DOW

Only one William Nudd appears in 1790 census,—of Pittsfield 1a, 2b, 3c. We take this to be the uncle and have attributed the other records to him also. This may be error, altho Wolfboro annals give nothing safely attributable to a younger William.

Mary Nudd akebbf m Abraham Gove b Oct 28, 1750, d Sept 18, 1827, son of Capt Nathaniel and Susanna (Stickney); moved to Deering, where he was selectman. Children:

  a   Sarah b Nov 16, 1773; m Nathaniel Chase; 2 children
  b   Nancy b Mch 13, 1777; m Ephraim Jones; 3 children
  c   Jonathan b July 23, 1778; m Mary Goodale; 6 children
  d   Abraham b June 30, 1780; m Nancy Jones; 12 children
  e   Samuel b Nov 16, 1782; m Abigail Newman; 9 children
  f   Mary b July 5, 1784; m Jesse Patten; 6 children
  g   Betsey b Feb 17, 1785; m Moody Lakin; 4 children
  h   Ebenezer b Apr 17, 1787; m Anna Rowell; 2nd Miranda French; 4 children
  i   Lydia b Sept 26, 1791; d about 1861, unm
  j   Jemima b Sept 29, 1794; m Gardner T Brooks; 9 children
  k   Benjamin Franklin b Jan 16, 1797; m Mary Wallace; 9 children

Benjamin Nudd akebc enlisted as private for the Stillwater campaign Sept 8, 1777, Capt Nicholas Rawlings, Col Abraham Drake; entered as deserter Oct 10, 1777. We have already pointed out a large number of technical desertions and need not try to explain this particular case. He was back in Greenland in good odor 1781. He m Hampton Falls by Rev Sam Perley Nov 14, 1771, Mary Davison, she of Hampton Falls, he of Greenland. There is no proof of children by this marriage. The 1790 census gives a Benjamin Nudd of Pittsfield 1a, 3c. Possibly he is the 1st born of akebc, with wife and baby. Our Benjamin m 2nd, Greenland June 14, 1781, Rachel Leavitt. She was a cousin of Dudley Leavitt, author of the Farmers' Almanac and thus akin to the Dow adaaai line of So Hampton.

They settled in the north part of Wolfboro about 1806 and it seems improbable from Wolfboro annals that any children by 1st m came with them. By 2nd m eight children:

  a   Lucretia b 1783; d 1855, unm
  b   Henry b 1785; surely the child of Benjamin Nudd who d Greenland 1796.
       The 1790 census gives Benjamin 1a, 1b, 5c
  c   Daniel b 1787   d   Sally b 1789   e   Nancy b 1791
  f   George Emory b Jan 27, 1793
  g   Eliza b 1795; m Nathaniel Frost of Dover. Children: Mary Elizabeth m
       Luther West, Rachel Ann m John Stackpole, all of Dover
  h   Mary Ann b 1797; d 1854; m Paul Nute; no children; lived always in the
       Nudd homestead

Daniel Nudd akebcc, farmer, m Lucy Merrifield and moved soon to Maine.

Family rec name their children, leaving no room in this line for a Nudd family of Gardiner, Me, left with the disconnected Nudds at the end of this chapter. Children:

  a   Lucy   b   Katherine   c   Daniel; untraced

THE BOOK OF DOW

Nancy Nudd akebce m James Young and both always lived Wolfboro. Children:

a Rachel, teacher, later business woman of Boston
b Sarah Elnora, teacher, m Jan 1, 1835, George W Libby of Tuftonboro. They moved to Newark and for years kept a hotel in N Y City; 4 children
c James m Lucy Weeks; farmer of Gardiner, Me
d Lucretia, teacher, d ae 24
e Charles Woodbury, inherited the Young homestead; 1 dau

George E Nudd akebcf d July 26, 1849; long a capt of militia, he was always known by his military title; m Wolfboro Dec 13, 1827, Mrs Abigail (Jenkins) Rendall. The 1850 census gives her wid b 1794, 3 children, taxed on $1,500 realty. She m 3rd (int pub Mch 8, 1852) Daniel Martin. George E Nudd was an able man. Inheriting the homestead, he bought also the Hyde farm; the Libby homestead (which he occupied 1844-8); the No. 11 wood lot jointly with his cousin Samuel Nudd; and the Remick house (the family residence until 1861). He also bought about 1846 the farm of his uncle William Nudd akebh. This he willed to his oldest son. His children:

a Benjamin Leavitt b July 18, 1828; d Nov 24, 1903
b Sarah Abbie b June 23, 1832; d Nov 24, 1864; brilliant student, teacher, m May 1861 John Wingate Jr, lawyer, grad Bowdoin. A son d in infancy
c Mary Melissa b Feb 24, 1834
d George Van Buren b Dec 14, 1835; d Dover Mch 28, 1855, unm

Benjamin L Nudd akebcfa m Durham Apr 20, 1851, Mary Abbie Griffin of Lee, his cousin (2nd cousin?). She b June 23, 1827, d July 1900. After two years on his inherited farm he sold it and became baggage master at Dover. He had been capt of militia and was all his life an active temperance advocate. For 25 years he was a grocery clerk in Dover. Children:

a Mary Abby b 1853; living 1923 in Dover
b Celia Augusta b June 19, 1864; m John S Fuller of Dover; living 1923 Whitman, Mass
c John Leavitt b Dover Feb 24, 1867; m Florence Copeland; now engraver of Auburn, N Y. An only child, Bertha, m 1910 George Hopkins, draughtsman of Bath, Me

Mary M Nudd akebcfc grad Salem Normal School 1860 and has had a brilliant career as a teacher, notably as principal of female dept of Kimball Union Academy. She m May 22, 1872, Prof Thomas Robinson of Howard Univ, Washington, D C. A dau Louise is 1923 Mrs C H Gleason of Grand Rapids, Mich, much interested in Nudd genealogy and straightening out the detached records of Wolfboro. Mrs Robinson in 1870 erected in Wolfboro cemetery a monument for her kin.

James Nudd akebd. The scattered rec, the 1790 census and Hist Canterbury, N H, are easily pieced together, proving this line throughout. He was of No Hampton 1790, 3a, 2b, 2c. This agrees with Hist Canterbury, except latter does not mention the dau. He m Jan 6, 1765, Mary Warren b Exeter Feb 13, 1734. They lived in Exeter and No Hampton, but no rec to show at what times. The 4 sons are named by Hist Canterbury:

a Levi   b James   c Warren   d Joseph

Levi Nudd akebda of Goffstown m July 8, 1802, Mary Kennedy of Goffstown. D rec of son gives wife as Pollia, both b Northfield. Children:

a Levi C. A d rec of Laconia gives him d Oct 26, 1891, ae 7 days, parents as
    above. This is obviously garbled
b Enos H b Center Harbor 1823

Levi C Nudd akebdaa d Manchester, N H, Oct 26, 1891, ae 74. Census of 1850 proves him,—mason of Holderness, b 1818; realty $400; wife Mary A b Vt 1824. Only child in census:

a Helen M b Mass 1845

Enos H Nudd akebdab, married, mason and brick layer, of Plymouth and Campton, d Center Harbor year ended Mch 31, 1883, ae 60. Not found in 1850 census. Two rec give him as father:

a —— b Plymouth June 12, 1858   b —— b Holderness May 19, 1859

James Nudd akebdb, b about 1768, m —— Pinkham; 2nd, Canterbury Aug 21, 1796, Lois Flynn; they moved to Northfield. Children:

a William
b Joseph Warren (Hist Canterbury errs giving b 1769, date applies to uncle)
c Robert   d Isaac P   e Thomas
f Mary m Isaac Foss   g Finette   h Sarah   i Jonathan

Joseph W Nudd akebdbb of Northfield d 1831; m Dec 3, 1811, Judith Arlen of Northfield m 2nd, Hiram Kimball. Children, no attempt at proper order:

a Erastus b (by d rec) 1823   b Joseph Warren
c May (twin) m True Hill
d Almira m Luther Rogers of Northfield. A dau Abbie, wid of —— Dow, d
    July 9, 1884, ae 42
f Andrew J b 1825   g Benjamin B
h Clarissa d N Y City, unm   i David Kimball

Erastus O Nudd akebdbba d Lancaster May 29, 1897; for many years a charcoal burner on the shore of Forest Pond; m Catherine Reardon b Ireland 1823, d Concord Apr 20, 1892, ae 58-10-15, dau of Dennis; m 2nd, Laconia Nov 1893 Annie Jane Dearden (sic in rec; Reardon?) b Canada, d Concord Oct 14, 1896, ae 52, dau of James and Kate (Shea). Erastus' realty assessed $700. Children:

a Otis W b 1852; carpenter, d Concord Sept 19, 1904, unm
b Mary m —— Sargent of Laconia; a child b Canterbury Aug 8, 1858
c Martha m —— Willey, who d Lancaster June 24, 1904
d Clara d Concord June 20, 1904; m —— McIntire

Joseph W Nudd akebdbbb moved to Hingham, Mass; d June 11, 1854; m Apr 18, 1839, Hannah C Loring b Hingham Apr 19, 1814, dau of Enoch and Hannah C (Taylor). Children:

a Joseph Warren b 1840; d Boston Oct 26, 1883, unm
b Hosea L b 1841; d Sept 4, 1843

c   Oliver F b Dec 1842; d Sept 2, 1843
d   Mary Jane Loring b Sept 1844; d Boston Dec 16, 1879, unm
e   Hannah T b 1846; m Dec 25, 1869, Joseph E Parker of Boston
f   Oliver F b Boston 1848; untraced
g   and h Elizabeth and Margaret b Apr 1850; d in infancy
i   Ann Bowers b Sept 5, 1851

Andrew J Nudd akebdbbf, farmer of Northfield, m (int pub Sept 18, 1850) Sarah Elizabeth Glines b Aug 1, 1837. He d May 5, 1873; she m 2nd, Leroy M Brown. Children:

a   Isabelle b May 6, 1854; m Mch 18, 1871, John Lakin; 2nd Fred Longley
b   Elizabeth b 1856; d 1864
c   Erastus b 1857; d Belmont Feb 10, 1899
d   Josephine b July 11, 1859; m Henry Glines of Franklin; 2nd Wilbur Rollins of New Hampton
e   Warren b Nov 19, 1862   f   Orren Clark b 1864; untraced
g   Florette b Nov 25, 1868; m Apr 24, 1884, Nathan E Sanborn of Belmont

Warren Nudd akebdbbfe m Jan 16, 1890, Mabel P Downing b Apr 29, 1872; both living Tilton 1919. Children:

a   Abbie Emma b Apr 20, 1892   b   George Warren b Dec 29, 1894
c   Elmer Russell b Dec 19, 1896; d Sept 5, 1897

George Warren Nudd akebdbbfeb m Northfield Oct 2, 1912, Pearl Ruby Cole, div wife of —— Moulton, ae 24, dau of Henry and Louisa; both employes of hosiery mill; div; m 2nd Northfield Oct 6, 1918, Florence Louise Hill of Sunapee, ae 21, dau of Joseph A and M Louisa (Jones). Children:

a   Katherine Louisa b Auburn Oct 10, 1918
b   Raymond George b Franklin Feb 8, 1920

Benjamin B Nudd (Capt) akebdbbg, farmer and lumberman, d Canterbury Mch 13, 1900; m Canterbury Nov 14, 1843, Rebecca C Perkins of Loudon; 2nd (*fide* Hist Canterbury), Melinda Whitcher; 3rd, June 14, 1859, Martha Jane Currier. Children:

a   Warren Benjamin b 1843   b   Joseph H b Sept 15, 1846
c   Andrew T b 1849
d   Horace G (order of children surely not accurate)
e   Otis W m Concord Oct 25, 1888, Annie E ——. Untraced
f   Hiram b 1850; laborer married, d Canterbury Oct 1, 1896; untraced
g   John K b Canterbury Nov 15, 1853
h   Flora Belle b Canterbury Jan 25, 1862; m —— Rogers

Warren B Nudd akebdbbga, mechanic of Concord, d Nov 20, 1917, ae 75-3-13; m (farmer of Canterbury) Mch 19, 1865, Nancy Marsh, dressmaker, b 1847, dau of Stephen D and Sarah; d with 1 child; m 2nd (int pub Mch 19, 1865), Mary Marsh; 3rd, Dec 7, 1885, Addie S Emerson; 4th, Concord Nov 10, 1914, Mary Ann Tilton, nurse, ae 51, b Charlestown, Me, dau of John D and Ann E (Patten). Child:

a   Fred W d Concord Jan 8, 1900, ae 36-2-2

Fred W Nudd akebdbbgaa, salesman of Concord, m Alice H Sanborn of Manchester. Child:

a   Herbert W d Concord July 12, 1895, ae 2-9-14

Joseph H Nudd akebdbbgb, farmer of Warner, d Aug 19, 1916, ae 69-11-6; married.

Andrew T Nudd akebdbbgc d Bristol Jan 9, 1882; m Abra A Drake of Bristol, d Laconia Sept 4, 1892, ae 41, dau of Philippe and Harriet (Lock).

Horace G Nudd akebdbbgd m Warner Sept 18, 1870, Alice B Brown, ae 17, dau of Mark and Esther Melissa (Chase).   Children:

a   John B b Warner 1870   b   Charles H b 1882
c   —— dau b and d Apr 28, 1885   d   Archie H b 1888
e   (a guess) Alice M b 1888, more likely akebdbbgb

John B Nudd akebdbbgda, boatman of Webster, later in strawboard mill, later farmer of Hopkinton, m Contoocook May 30, 1909, Emma J Clark, ae 19, dau of Frank and Georgianna (McDole).   Children:

a   Frank Horace b Hopkinton May 29, 1910
b   Dau b Sept 12, 1912   c   —— dau b Jan 25, 1914
d   Helen Louise b Aug 31, 1918   e   Hattie Marie b May 23, 1920

Charles H Nudd akebdbbgdb, sawmill employe of Warner, m Hopkinton July 4, 1914, Charlotte M Martel, ae 17, bookkeeper, dau of Zeno and Eugena (Singney).   Children: b Concord:

a   Charles Grover b Mch 1, 1915   b   Raleigh Martel b July 16, 1916
c   Robert Louis b July 5, 1919

Archie H Nudd akebdbbgdd, machinist in Warner straw mills, m Warner Mch 31, 1910, Clara Clermont, div, ae 22, dau of Joe and Jeanne (Bucor) Blanchette.   Child:

a   —— dau b Hopkinton Aug 7, 1911

Alice M Nudd akebdbbgde of Warner m John T Robertson.   Child:

a   Bessie Viola b Webster July 27, 1905; d Hopkinton Aug 10, 1911

David K Nudd akebdbbi, b Northfield Feb 3, 1831; Civil War veteran, moved to Exeter, stone mason; m Canterbury July 11, 1852, Lavina Jane Chaplain b Canterbury Apr 25, 1834, dau of Marquis D and Martha (Willey); 2nd, Nancy M Pickard b Canterbury 1862, d Exeter Nov 29, 1911, dau of Elias and —— (Glines).   Children:

a   Elbridge Chaplain b Apr 26, 1853; d ae 15
b   Orianna J b Nov 25, 1854; m John Gilman of Tilton; 7 children
c   Mary Ella b June 15, 1856; m July 19, 1873, James Clark of Northfield; 3
     children
d   Olive Annette b May 24, 1859; d young
e   Ellen Amanda b Oct 2, 1862; m Aug 17, 1878, Frank F Fellows; a dau Mary
     m Albert Clifford of Concord
f   Manson Harlan b Feb 7, 1865; d May 15, 1880
g   Walter Elbridge b Mch 26, 1869; all above b Canterbury
h   Elgie Scott b Exeter 1886   i   Charles F, twin

Walter E Nudd akebdbbig, machinist of Concord, m Victoria M Wallace; div; m 2nd, Apr 21, 1900, Annie Laura Varner b New Germany, N S, July 18, 1880, dau of Joseph and Sarah L (Varner).   Children:

a   Wallace b Sandwich June 19, 1895   b   Ethel Mary b Oct 26, 1902

c Arthur Edward b Oct 26, 1902   d Clarence William b Jan 21, 1907
e Harold Douglas b Dec 15, 1912

Wallace Nudd akebdbbiga, painter of Sandwich, m Boscawen Nov 24, 1913, Blanche Le Clair, ae 19, b Northfield, dau of Dennis and Josephine (Merchant). Children:

a Walter b Apr 10, 1916   b Caroline Tappan b Apr 17, 1918
c Edna May b Dec 12, 1919

Elgie S Nudd akebdbbih, shoe packer of Bradford, Mass, laborer, box fitter, teamster of Exeter, m Salem, N H, Dec 16, 1907, Florence Pendleton b Lincolnville, Me, 1888, dau of Frank and Mary (Poland). Children:

a —— dau b Exeter July 8, 1908   b —— son b Brentwood July 1, 1909
c Marion Philbrook b Dec 16, 1910; d Mch 1, 1911
d —— dau b Exeter Mch 8, 1912
e Eleanor F d Mch 23, 1914, ae 33 days
f —— son b Dec 17, 1914   g Carleton H d Aug 6, 1919, ae 2-7-19
h Virginia b Mch 2, 1918   i Gladys b Apr 15, 1920

Charles F Nudd akebdbbii, shoemaker of Exeter, m July 29, 1907, Mary Riley b Portsmouth 1883, dau of Michael and Annie of Ireland. Son:

a —— b Exeter Nov 16, 1907

Isaac P Nudd akebdbd, said by Hist Canterbury b Aug 13, 1812; lived Franklin Falls; m Nov 17, 1836, Abigail P Sanborn, b Sanbornton, dau of Hiram and Sarah C (Burleigh). Children:

a Carlos d suddenly Cambridge, Mass, where he was arranging for a tombstone
    for his parents
b Arthur b 1841; d in infancy

John Nudd akebe is surely he who enlisted from Hampton Falls 1759 in the same company as Ebenezer Dow adgf and Gideon Dow adgg for the Canadian campaign. Presumably he was the John Nudd of No Hampton corporal from Nov 5, 1775. Census 1790 mentions but one John Nudd,—1a, 5c. This probably indicates wife and four unm dau. If he had sons, which is not improbable, they were married and gone by 1790.

Thomas Nudd akebf was a veteran, as was every Nudd. Two Thomas Nudds are on the rolls,—enlisted Apr 4, 1780, disch Dec 30, 1780, Lieut Col Dearborn; and enlisted No Hampton July 29, 1780, ae 19. The latter is presumably the son 1st born. Census 1790 gives Thomas Nudd of Wakefield 3a, 4c. This grown-up family can only come from one b by 1740. Thomas Nudd of Greenland by census 1a, 1b, 4c must be the junior. The inference is that Thomas Nudd settled in Wakefield, leaving some older members of his family in Greenland and that the

Wakefield Nudds are his posterity. Possibly some of the akebe line are of Greenland disconnected. We find (index letters for convenience):

John Nudd akebfb m Greenland May 9, 1792, Martha Blaze.

Thomas Nudd akebfc m Greenland Mch 15, 1784, Susannah Simpson.

Thomas Nudd Jr m Mch 13, 1794, Betsey Wiggin, both of Wakefield. This last makes it not improbable that Thomas Nudd of Greenland 1790 census is son of John akebe.

Stephen Nudd akebfd m Newmarket Sept 20, 1817,—both of Durham. Name of wife overlooked, but she or her mother was Wiggin. Probably identical is Stephen Nudd d Stratham Aug 21, 1833. Presumably the next is his son:

Stephen W Nudd akebfda m Sept 9, 1846, Hannah D Piper, both of Stratham.   One child sure:

a ——— son of Stephen S d July 27, 1847, ae 5 mos

Abigail Nudd akebg. Hist Hampton says d 1742 seems error. New Eng Gen Reg 1901 inquires for parents of Abigail Nudd b Hampton m Feb 29, 1764, Samuel Robie b No Hampton Mch 25, 1743. Author replied to this query but got no answer.

William Nudd akebh. We have already noted the confusion between him and William akebbd. Our William moved about 1806 to Wolfboro and we have seen that his homestead farm was bought about 1846 by his nephew George E Nudd. Census gives him children and apparently at least one son was of Wolfboro in 1846. We cannot understand then why the homestead should be sold. Of his earlier career, we attribute to him, rather than to his nephew, a number of data. Enlisted in 3rd militia July 5, 1779, for 6 months, Capt Samuel Runnels, Col Hercules Mooney.   Married July 5, 1784, Polly Bean, both of Greenland. The William Nudd of Pittsfield by 1790 census had 2 sons, 2 dau, rather rapid progress for 6 years. William Nudd m Wolfboro Dec 6, 1798, Polly Moore.   Children, attributed with some uncertainty:

a   Richard b 1784
b   Samuel.   One Samuel b 1785, another 1791, still another 1802
c   Abigail   d   Martha; two youngest guessed

Richard Nudd akebha m Oct 22, 1807, Eleanor Hanes, both of Wolfboro. Census 1850 gives her b 1788; he farmer with children:

a   Richard T b 1824   b   Charles H b 1832, both unm farmers

Samuel Nudd akebhb. We suppose him to be the Samuel d married Wolfboro Feb 26, 1875, ae 84; m May 9, 1816, Nancy Perkins, both of Wolfboro. Census 1850 gives Nancy b 1795 and only 1 child:

a   Ira P b 1828-9 (census duplicates him), in 1850 merchant of Wolfboro, unm

An elderly resident of Wolfboro recalls 1923 that Samuel Nudd had 1 son, and 1 dau, but cannot differentiate between the various Samuels:

  a Charles H, grew to maturity
  b Ruth P m (int pub Sept 4, 1848) Nathaniel Huggins; they were cousins, but perhaps not 1st cousins

Abigail Nudd akebhc int pub Mch 18, 1818, to Silas Tibbetts of Rochester.

Martha Nudd akebhd int pub June 4, 1806, to John Hames. We presume right name Haynes and a brother of Eleanor Hanes akebha.

There are left unattached many Nudds of the akeb line and this is especially so in Wolfboro. Vital statistics here included a church register containing a great number of marriage intentions, unaccompanied by any other data. We index all here for convenience, hoping to attach many as times goes on.

Benjamin Nudd akebi int pub Oct 13, 1817, Wolfboro, to Hannah Nudd. Perhaps he soon d, for Mrs Hannah Nudd int pub Nov 24, 1819, James Smith.

Samuel Nudd akebia b Wolfboro 1802; d Milton Feb 23, 1853; moved to Milton prior to 1850, for census gives him of Milton, wife Nancy b N H 1803, and 3 children, all shoemakers, all b N H:

  a Charles W b 1834   b Mary M b 1836   c Josephine C b 1839

Mary Nudd akebib int pub May 29, 1827, to James Nute, Jr.

Sophronia Nudd int pub Sept 25, 1827, to Hale Young.

Henry Nudd akebic m Nov 21, 1828, Jemima Babcock, both of Wolfboro.

Thomas L Nudd of Wolfboro m Jan 19, 1837, Fanny Lord of Dover.

Eliza A Chamberlain, wid of —— **Nudd,** b Brookfield, dau of Dudley and Abigail (Goldsmith), d Wolfboro July 15, 1883, ae 61, 1 mo.

Peabody Nudd akebie b Wolfboro 1827; d Wolfboro Oct 28, 1851.

Elizabeth M Nudd akebif int pub Feb 19, 1828, to Nathaniel Frost.

Capt Samuel Nudd akebig m Middleton Aug 14, 1828, Nancy Frances Whitten, both of Wolfboro.

Adeline Nudd akebih int pub July 23, 1838, to Thomas Nute.

Three Maine items cannot well be of akebc line.
Ivory Nudd akebii of West Gardiner was capt of riflemen 1831.

Wife was a dau of John Savels, who built the Gardiner paper mill 1812-13. This family came from N H. Presumably they had a son,—for

a Simon Nudd citizen of West Gardiner in 1851, local directory. **Probably he had a sister, for,-**
b Louisa Nudd b Nov 21, 1824; m Nov 21, 1844, Joseph Whitney b Apr 10, 1823, son of Henry and Nabby (Fuller) of Wiscasset and East Cambridge, Mass. They had 2 children,—Frederick b Mch 26, 1853, unm; Kate b July 2, 1855, m —— Roaf (Rolfe?)

David Nudd akebij m Dec 18, 1814, by Rev Jonathan French (abbeebc), Sarah Godfree, both of No Hampton. This may be 2nd m of akebbb.

For the rest the detached rec seem to be of akebd line.

David Nudd akebik m Northfield Mch 10, 1847, by Peter Wadleigh justice of the peace, Malinda Whitcher (garbled for akebdbbg?).

Sarah P Nudd akebil, wid, d Nashua June 16, 1889, ae 74.

David Nudd akebim is possibly garbled identity with David akebik. By son's rec he m Melinda Hanson, both b Campton. A son found:

a John b Canterbury Apr 18, 1859; d farmer of Canterbury married, May 18, 1912. Hist Canterbury does not place him genealogically

William H Nudd akebina of Rumney had a brother Joseph; m Plymouth Apr 15, 1838, Abigail Chamberlain of Northfield, Vt. In 1886 he a stage driver. One child found by own rec:

a Charles H b Rumney; d Andover May 7, 1886, ae 44-1-7

Joseph Nudd akebinb, surely brother of above, b 1819, farmer of Rumney, m Manchester Nov 18, 1841, Lucinda Matthews. Census gives her b 1805. Children, by census:

a Clifton W b Benton 1843; d Rumney Jan 9, 1850
b Alvin F b 1845; untraced   c Ruth M b 1846

William H Nudd Jr akebio, b Cambridgeport, Mass, 1880, barber of Francestown, m Gertrude Skidmore b Eng. At least 4 children, 2 found:

a Frank Everett b Sept 21, 1908   b Albert Willis b May 24, 1911

Clara G Nudd akebip, wid, d Center Harbor Jan 29, 1886, ae 50, dau of Richard M and Rachel R (Wilkinson) Hadley.

David P Nudd akebiq m Calista E Burnside. At least 1 child:

a David P d Salem, N H, Aug 20, 1889, ae 6 mos, 5 days

John B Nudd akebir m Sarah Stickney. Two children found by own rec:

a John H b N H 1839; only Nudd in Salem, N H, 1850 census
b George I b Dracut, Mass; painter, married, d Salem June 1, 1892, ae 49-9-28

Addie Adeline Nudd akebis, married, b Surry, Me; d Concord Feb 7, 1914, ae 64-6-16, dau of Nathan and Jane (Carter) Mann.

Benjamin F Nudd akebit, b Rumney (perhaps brother of William H and Joseph, above), m Susan E—— b Lee.   Child found by own rec:

a   Susan b Lawrence, Mass; d Epping Apr 20, 1875, ae 23

Georgiette S Nudd akebiu, married, b East Boston, dau of William C and Mary A Smith, d Manchester, N H, Sept 9, 1888, ae 36-11-9.

Elizabeth Nudd akebiv, wid b Loudon, dau of David S and Martha O (Smith) Fogg, d Canterbury Jan 16, 1899, ae 46, 4 mos.

Charles H Nudd akebiw, married, d Auburn, Me, Aug 23, 1911, ae 57-5-23; bur Manchester, N H.

William E Nudd akebix had a son A E b Canterbury, d Concord May 14, 1870, ae 3.

Fred J Nudd akebiy b Worcester 1873; painter of Wilmot, N H; m Hattie M Peaslee b Wilmot 1874.   Children:

a   Guy Leon b 1895
b   Leon Peaslee b Wilmot; d July 6, 1895, ae 1 mo, 21 days

Forest L Nudd akebiz d Lowell Mch 19, 1895, ae 5 mos, 14 days; probably from Dover, N H.

Benjamin Nudd akebj, b N H 1789; farmer of Wentworth, realty assessed $100 in 1850; wife Deziah b N H 1798.   Possibly is akebcx with 2nd wife.   Children, by census:

a   John A b 1833   b   Martha A b 1836   c   Charles b 1839

John B Nudd akebjd, b Warner, N H, 1880-1, laborer of Warner and Hopkinton; m Gertrude Chase b 1886.   A child:

a   Warren Alfred b Hopkinton Feb 18, 1904; d Warner Aug 20, 1905

Howard M Nudd akebje, prominent 1910-23 in educational work N Y City; has 2 unm aunts in Philadelphia; promised 1918 to send what he knew or could ascertain from them of his ancestry.

O NLY two grandsons of Thomas Nudd, immigrant, left posterity. As we have seen, the senior branch, spreading northward from No Hampton, is poorly traced, only two lines developed through to the present. The junior branch, like the senior branch of the Dow family, remained closely identified with Hampton, the resemblance being all the closer in that few are left, the male lines dying out. The homestead remained in the family for a little over 200 years.

Thomas Nudd akcc can be fairly said to have occupied a rather more prominent place than his father, who, in turn, had improved the family position over the status of the immigrant grandfather. As justice of the peace, he got the title of Esquire, by which he was known over half his life. He also served as coroner and selectman; continued to farm the homestead; m May 23, 1733, Deborah Marston, dau of Simon (abbefe). Children:

    a Simon b Feb 6, 1735; d Oct 30, 1818
    b Hannah b Oct 19, 1737; d Nov 9, 1819
    c Samuel b Feb 5, 1739; d Aug 26, 1739
    d Sarah b Jan 10, 1741; d Nov 12, 1820
    e Molly b Dec 5, 1746; d Apr 28, 1838

Simon Nudd akeca arrived at the highest point of prosperity to which the name has developed. His business interests were many and as he made money, he invested it constantly in additional lands contiguous as far as possible to the homestead. In this way he was able to leave a substantial farm to each of his sons. He was known throughout his adult years by his military title of Cornet and was active in preparations for the Revolution. He himself found a wife out of town, but his children married without exception into pioneer families of Hampton. He m Elizabeth Hook of Salisbury, who d Oct 14, 1799, ae 59. Children:

    a Thomas b Nov 28, 1763; d Apr 1806
    b Simon b Sept 29, 1765; d Sept 18, 1766
    c Mary b Sept 30, 1767; d May 25, 1847   d Betty b Feb 28, 1770; d 1857
    e Simon b Nov 1, 1773   f Moses b Dec 29, 1775; d Jan 4, 1859
    g Samuel b Dec 4, 1777; d Nov 4, 1846
    h David b Apr 20, 1780; d Nov 20, 1858   i Jacob b 1782; d Nov 24, 1782

Thomas Nudd akecaa took for his inheritance a place on the mill road; m Oct 28, 1784, Abigail Marston, dau of Jonathan; 2nd, Susey Brown, dau of Samuel. Children:

    a Josiah b Mch 28, 1786; d May 1, 1859; unm
    b Thomas b Nov 13, 1788; d Feb 11, 1850
    c James b Nov 13, 1790; farmer, 1850 census; d July 23, 1879, unm
    d Samuel d young   e Moses d young
    f Daniel drowned Dec 30, 1822, unm
    g John; left a dau Mary m Josiah Roby
    h Eliza m Joseph Coburn, stone mason of Boston; children,—Edward; Adeline
         m William Gile of Boston; Adelaide m Alfred Lewis of N Y City; John;
         Gridley

Thomas Nudd akecaab m Abigail Towle, dau of Amos; she living 1850; lived with his father until 1826, then took a share of the former Ox Common at South Beach.   Children:

  a   Oliver b Apr 19, 1814
  b   Julia b Aug 15, 1815; m Frederick Frederickson
  c   Abigail M b July 2, 1818; d Mch 9, 1875, unm
  d   Louisa b Nov 21, 1824   e   Nancy b July 21, 1827; d Nov 7, 1848

Oliver Nudd akecaaba continued on the Ox Common homestead, taxed 1850 on $2,000; m Jan 5, 1843, Sarah Elizabeth Redman, dau of John.   Children:

  a   John Philip b Jan 26, 1843; d Oct 17, 1849
  b   Thomas Hale b Jan 3, 1845   c   Clara Maria b Oct 4, 1846
  d   Ednah; lived home unm
  e   Julia Ann b Apr 25, 1856; m Charles W Ross of Newcastle, who came to live
        with her father.   Children,—Bessie Marston b Sept 25, 1883;——son b May
        21, 1892
  f   Oliver W b Nov 8, 1859; d Jan 6, 1860

Thomas H Nudd akecaabab lived on the lot next south of his father; m Nov 28, 1871, Sarah M Young, dau of Enoch P; 2nd, June 30, 1884, Nellie Sullivan.   Children:

  a   Mabel Josephine b Aug 18, 1874   b   Dora W b Aug 10, d Aug 31, 1878
  c   Florence Lucy b Nov 6, 1884

Clara M Nudd akecaabac m Jan 1, 1867, David J Lamprey of No Hampton, son of Hezekiah B and Mary Ann (Jenness).   Children:

  a   Austin b Nov 25, 1867   b   Marion Ardelle b Apr 20, 1874
  c   Warren Carleton b Dec 19, 1875

Mary Nudd akecac m Mch 16, 1786, Joseph F Dearborn, son of Maj Josiah and Sarah (Freese); lived on part of the homestead.   Children:

  a   Simon Nudd b Aug 6, 1786; m Hannah Towle
  b   Sarah b Feb 16, 1790; m Samuel Batchelder
  c   Betsey b Sept 27, 1796; m James Johnson
  d   Mary Ann b Dec 15, 1800; m Josiah Marston

Betty Nudd akecad m Aug 16, 1792, Philip Towle, son of Ensign Philip and Anna (Page); lived on the homestead.   Children:

  a   Sally Bartlett b Nov 30, 1792; m Dr George Odell of Greenland
  b   David b Oct 12, 1794; unm
  c   Nancy b Feb 13, 1796; d Jan 1, 1876, unm; traveled over 3 continents
        preaching, advocating prohibition and anti-Mormonism
  d   Philip b Sept 29, 1798; a physician; m wid Sarah Leavitt
  e   Eliza Hook b Mch 31, 1800; m George Berry; 2nd Col Jonathan Marston
  f   Simon b May 24, 1803; m Sarah Berry
  g   Mary b Nov 23, 1805; m Moses Collins
  h   Patience Jane b Feb 28, 1807; m Willard E Nudd akecahb
  i   Lydia Hale b June 1, 1811; m Hiram Wood of Newburyport

Simon Nudd akecae took the place where Jacob T Godfrey lived a century later; d Sept 21, 1806; m Sally Johnson, dau of Nathaniel abbcce.   Children:

  a   Ruth b May 7, 1798; d Apr 23, 1885; m Jonathan Leavitt, son of Moses; no
        children

b Betsey bap Sept 6, 1801; d Hampton May 23, 1875; m William Taylor of
   Exeter; 3 children; m 2nd Rev Tobias Miller of Portsmouth
c Sarah bap Nov 21, 1802; d Nov 19, 1881
d Mary bap Nov 10, 1803; d Jan 6, 1858, unm

Sarah Nudd akecaec m Oliver Lamprey, son of Dudley and Miriam
(Locke); lived on the homestead.   Children:

a Charles Thatcher b Sept 17, 1828; m Mary J Palmer
b William T b Feb 9, 1830; m Sarah A Leavitt; lived Somerville, Mass
c Sarah Maria b Oct 24, 1832; m James N Brown
d Jonathan L (twin) d in infancy
e Jonathan L b June 30, 1834; m Lucy A Lufkin; went to Calif
f Simon Nudd b Dec 22, 1837; killed in battle 1864
g Oliver Freeman b Dec 20, 1840; unm
h Frank b Sept 21, 1843; m Mary E Nute of Wolfboro; lived Charlestown,
   Mass

Moses Nudd (Lieut) akecaf took the place across the road from the
homestead; m Apr 22, 1802, Sarah Marston, dau of Capt Jonathan.
Children:

a Louisa b 1802; d in infancy
b Jeremiah Smith b Apr 10, 1804; d May 25, 1847, unm
c Lydia b Feb 27, 1806; d Oct 23, 1837; had a son Haley, preacher and ranch
   owner in Oregon
d Almira b Dec 27, 1808; m Col Josiah Dow abbeebb
e Simon b Nov 29, 1810; left home while young; never heard of again
f Jonathan b Dec 1, 1812; drowned near Mobile, Ala, Apr 2, 1832
g Mary D b Nov 29, 1814; d Sept 25, 1879, unm
h Sarah Ann b Nov 1816   i Clarissa Ann b Aug 1, 1820
j Ann Clarissa b Aug 1, d Oct 1820
k Emeline b Aug 10, 1822; m Apr 2, 1843, Bradley Drake of Effingham; d Jan
   12, 1850. Children,—Sarah Emeline and Almira became 1st and 2nd wives
   of Hon John M Woods of Somerville, Mass

Sarah A Nudd akecafh m Capt Nathaniel Batchelder, son of
Sanborn and Mary (Elkins).   Children:

a Warren Woodbury b June 3, 1840; d Jan 15, 1856
b Edwin Bradley b Feb 8, 1842; unm
c George Nathaniel b Oct 11, 1844, unm
d Mary Emeline b Mch 25, 1848; m Henry L Dodge
e Warren M b Jan 8, 1857; m Abbie S Marston

Clarissa A Nudd akecafi m 1842 Jonathan Philbrick, son of John
and Hannah (Godfrey); lived No Hampton.   Children:

a Mary Abby   b Martha Ann   c John Leonard
d Anna Sarah   e John Warren m Jennie S Berry
f Carrie Nudd

Samuel Nudd akecag occupied the original homestead; m Mch 25,
1801, Elizabeth Lamprey, dau of Reuben.   Children:

a Abraham b Oct 1801; d May 10, 1860
b Sarah b Aug 27, 1804; had a son,—George F Nudd, carpenter, m Sarah Rundlett
   of Bangor, Me, d July 7, 1881. George F inherited the homestead on the
   death of his uncle Abraham, but d childless Jan 10, 1888, ae about 68. His
   mother m Benjamin Shaw, became a wid, returned to the homestead, lived
   to inherit it. This was the homestead received on his 21st birthday by
   Thomas Nudd, the immigrant of 1637

Abraham Nudd akecaga m Sarah Ann Sleeper, dau of William of

Rye; lived Rye for a few years; returned to the homestead. She d Mch 8, 1859; he then lived with dau in Exeter; d Exeter May 10, 1860. Children:

a Harriet Ann b Mch 8, 1835; m Dec 1856 Charles Lane, blacksmith of Exeter
b Charles William; reported missing in Union army; supposed to have been killed in battle

David Nudd akecah took another part of the estate; m Abigail Emery, dau of Lieut Willard. Children:

a Stacy Leavitt b Aug 5, 1803; d Jan 10, 1866; m July 15, 1839, Mary Ann Dow adhcdad. No children. He built and conducted the Ocean House at Hampton Beach; living winters in Hampton Falls
b Willard Emery b June 7, 1806; d Feb 18, 1869
c Caroline b Apr 9, 1808; d Jan 22, 1881; m Dudley S Locke of Seabrook. Children: John D m Aug 23, 1854, Martha M Brown of Seabrook; Abbot A m Helen S Chase of Seabrook, dau of David
d Sarah Ann b Oct 13, 1810; d Feb 21, 1847
e Elizabeth Frances b July 30, 1815; m May 10, 1841, Franklin Williams of Boston; moved to Calif; left a dau
f Martha T b Dec 18, 1818
g Joseph Ward b Jan 13, 1820; kept the Boar's Head Hotel; drowned with Thomas Hale Leavitt on Hampton River Oct 11, 1847; unm
h John Adams b Mch 13, 1825
i Martha E b Feb 15, 1828; d May 19, 1832
j Marcia A b Nov 24, 1830; d Jan 29, 18-9, unm

Willard E Nudd akecahb, landlord of Eagle House, Great Boar's Head, m Patience Jane Towle akecadh. Children:

a Lewis Philip b Feb 6, 1833   b David Franklin b Apr 9, 1835

Lewis P Nudd akecahba inherited the Eagle House; m Nov 7, 1855, Caroline E Leavitt, dau of Moses. Children:

a Joseph L b Mch 28, 1857   b Addie Jane b Jan 5, 1859; d Sept 3, 1864
c Gracie Leavitt b Feb 4, 1866; d Oct 31, 1867
d Caroline Belle b Mch 13, 1871

Joseph L Nudd akecahbaa lived on the homestead; m Mary Ida Perkins, dau of Albert S. Children:

a Ethel Mae b June 20, 1887   b Everett Lewis b Oct 14, 1889

David F Nudd akecahbb lived on part of the homestead; m Nov 6, 1867, Rosina E Philbrick, dau of Josiah of Danville. He kept a boat for fishing, and boarders. Children:

a Eugene Frank b Nov 1, 1871; m June 21, 1892, Minerva A Perkins, dau of Henry J
b Harry E b Sept 30, 1874; d Feb 13, 1875
c Maude b May 14, d July 27, 1877   d Benjamin b June 3, d Aug 25, 1879

Sarah A Nudd akecahd m Amos Tuck, son of John and Betsey (Towle), teacher, judge, member of Congress, banker. He engaged his lifelong friend Joseph Dow, historian of Hampton, to prepare the Tuck Genealogy. Children:

a Abby Elizabeth b Nov 4, 1835; m William Rufus Nelson of Peekskill, N Y; 2nd Orrin F Frye of Boston
b Charles b Dec 26, 1836; d Apr 19, 1842

    c   Ellen b Apr 4, 1838; m Francis Ormond French
    d   Edward b June 6, 1841; m Julia Stell
    e   Isabella b Apr 25, d Sept 10, 1844
    f   Charles b July 10, 1845; d Dec 10, 1849
    g   Amos Otis b Aug 26, 1846; d Nov 3, 1848

Martha T Nudd akecahf m Alfred Johnson Batchelder, son of Josiah and Molly (Towle). He had hotels at Boar's Head and elsewhere. Children:

    a   George L b May 7, 1841; m Cornelia Seavey
    b   Marcia A b Apr 3, 1843; m George D Whitney of Boston
    c   Amy H b Aug 4, 1846; m Charles F Barker of Salem, Mass
    d   Mary A b June 23, 1854; m J J Leavitt of Stratham; 2nd J A Bowman of
        Sou Dak

John A Nudd akecahh inherited the homestead established by Cornet Nudd; m Dec 16, 1852, Elizabeth Olive Knowles, dau of Dea Jesse. Children:

    a   Marietta F b Oct 12, 1855
    b   Electa Wilder b May 15, d Aug 30, 1859
    c   Stacy L b June 8, d Oct 13, 1861
    d   Moses Paul b Dec 4, 1863   e   Stacy Leavitt b Mch 31, 1866

Stacy L Nudd akecahhe lived on the homestead; m Nov 23, 1887, Ada Flagg Emery, dau of Samuel T. Children:

    a   Olive Etta b Sept 20, 1890   b —— dau b Aug 3, 1892
    c   Moses Paul b 1895

Moses P Nudd akecahhec of Portsmouth, N H, m Feb 2, 1918, Isabella Gentleman, ae 23, b Scotland, dau of Robert and Isabella (Sanderman). Child:

    a   Ada Isabella b Portsmouth Nov 15, 1919

Hannah Nudd akecb m Jan 31, 1759, Cotton Ward, son of Noah and Sarah (Shaw); lived on the homestead; a Lieut in Revolution. Children:

    a   Simon (Capt) b May 1, 1760; m Abigail Fullenton; 2nd Polly Edmunds of
        Candia; moved to Candia
    b   Sarah b Feb 12, 1762; m Jonathan Drake
    c   Hannah b Oct 31, 1763; m Maj James Drake of Chichester
    d   Rachel b Nov 24, 1765; m William Berry of Greenland; 12 children
    e   Deborah b Jan 11, 1768; m Levi Batchelder
    f   Thomas b Jan 2, 1770; m Lydia Garland

Sarah Nudd akecd m June 30, 1763, Amos Towle, son of Joseph and Sarah (Dalton); always lived Hampton. Children:

    a   Betty b July 15, 1764; d Aug 6, 1776
    b   Daniel b Oct 29, 1767; m Lydia Towle
    c   Sally bap Apr 24, 1774; m John Redman
    d   Betsey b Aug 5, 1783; m John Tuck akecahd

Molly Nudd akece m Isaac Marston, son of Cornet David and Abigail (Garland); lived on the homestead. Children:

    a   Daniel b Mch 22, 1764; m Mary Smith; moved to Parsonsfield, Me
    b   Isaac bap Mch 1, 1767; m Mary Mace

c Cotton Ward bap Aug 6, 1769; m Comfort Marston
d Simon bap Mch 14, 1773   e Deborah b 1778; m Abraham Marston
f David b 1780; m Comfort Towle

Abigail Nudd akex of Hampton is named in Gove Gen, error probably only in her christian name; m (his 2nd) June 14, 1815, Abner Gove b Seabrook May 4, 1775, son of William and Mehitable (Philbrick). He had 2 dau by 1st wife Abigail Hastings. A dau by Abigail Nudd; they having moved to Weare:

a Mehitable P m Edward Gove Clark of Henniker b Nov 29, 1799. They had 7 or 8 children. He m 2nd wid Martha G (Hoyt) Dow, wid of bcbebbca. He was son of Benjamin and Hannah (Gove) of Henniker; d July 19, 1875

Hannah Nudd akg m Jan 27, 1698, Francis Page, son of Dea Francis and Meribah (Smith); they bought a place at Little River, Hampton, from David Marston. Their posterity has frequently inter-married with Dow. Children:

a Sarah b Oct 18, 1698; m Josiah Batchelder
b Anna b Nov 17, 1700; d young
c Meribah bap Feb 2, 1707; m William Locke of Rye
d Elisha b Mch 3, 1708; m Meribah Batchelder
e Josiah b July 22, 1709   f Anna b July 26, 1711; m Reuben Dearborn
g Charity b Oct 13, 1713; d June 30, 1715
h Hannah b Feb 17, 1716   i Mary bap Feb 9, 1718

www.ingramcontent.com/pod-product-compliance
Lightning Source LLC
Chambersburg PA
CBHW050328270326
41926CB00016B/3353